Art

Engagement

Economy

The Working Practice of
Caroline Woolard

Readers will notice words on the edges of
each page of the book. This is a navigation
system that Woolard has created with designer
Angela Lorenzo that aims to take readers
through Woolard's working process (on the
right and left edges of the book's pages)
and to note whether the endeavor is collectively-initiated or is an institutional
invitation (on the bottom of the page).

Reflect

Idea in Public

Experiment

Timeframe

Inquiry

Commitment

Study

Experience

Institutional
Invitation

Collectively-
Initiated

Making

Managing

Making Mediating

Title of Project /
Platform / Practice

Contents

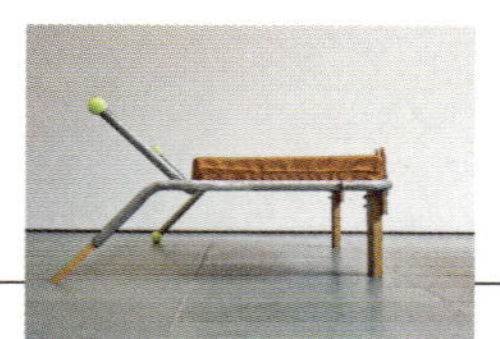

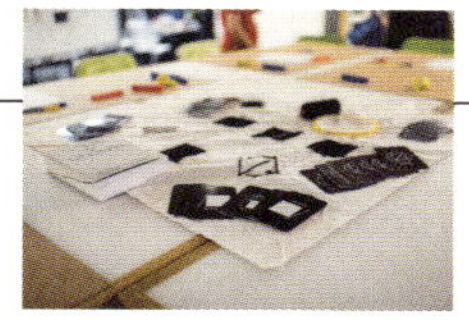

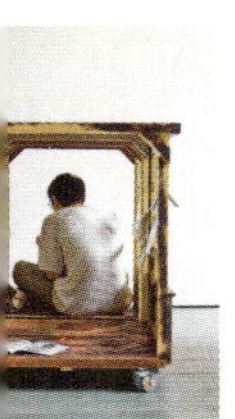

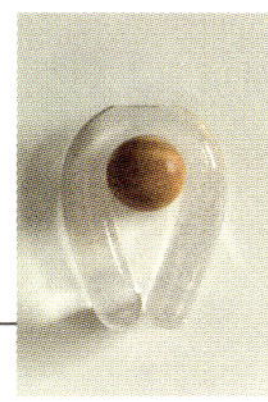

Foreword

Patricia C. Phillips, Chief Academic Officer and Academic Dean of Moore College of Art & Design, May 2020.

Patricia C. Phillips is Chief Academic Officer at Moore College of Art & Design and an independent writer and curator. Phillips is the author of *City Speculations*, *It is Difficult: Alfredo Jaar*, and *Ursula von Rydingsvard: Working*. Phillips's curatorial projects include a one-person exhibition on the artist Mierle Laderman Ukeles at the Queens Museum in Flushing, Queens and *Making Sense: Five Artists' Installations on Sensation* at the Katonah Museum of Art, Katonah, New York.

My work celebrates collective capacities for care and critique. —Caroline Woolard, 2018

In spring 2018, Moore College of Art & Design launched the Jane and David Walentas Endowed Fellowship to bring a significant artist, designer, or scholar to engage with the Moore community and Philadelphia organizations on special projects and initiatives during a two-year appointment. The expectation for the Fellowship is open exploration through high-impact initiatives. Embedded in a historic art and design college founded in 1848 by Sarah Worthington Peter to educate, empower, and prepare women to work in new nineteenth century industries, there is an intrinsic (or inevitable) engagement of contemporary art and design pedagogy, yet it is not a teaching fellowship. Instead, the Walentas Fellow was conceived by the donors, with leadership at Moore, as a creative and generative participant, collaborator, and lively "interventionist" in Moore and the expanded urban and cultural environment.

Following a panel review of many nominees, artist Caroline Woolard was selected as the inaugural Walentas Fellow. She nimbly navigates different sites and conditions of contemporary art and design. She has created striking forms in glass and in 3D-printed ceramic and metal that act as objects for facilitation. She is active and facile with networks and open source environments around the world, as well as studios and sites of design, fabrication, and production that bring global reach, organizational theory, and tactile immersion to work that is authentically interdisciplinary, economically based, and centered on justice and equity, including OurGoods.org [see chapter 3] (non-monetary artist exchange); TradeSchool.coop [see chapter 3] (an alternative peer-learning site); BFAMFAPhD.com [see chapter 5] (that focuses on cultural access and equity); and The NYC Real Estate Cooperative (that organizes and incentivizes artists to share resources to create stable and shareable work spaces).

It is often exciting and occasionally daunting to be "the first," yet she embraced the elasticity and novelty of the fellowship at Moore and applied dynamic vision to develop a two-year prospectus of initiatives, including workshops with students and Moore faculty on inclusive critique practices, participation in programming at The Free Library of Philadelphia's new Robert and Eileen Kennedy Heim Center for Civic and Cultural Engagement, and work with Esteban Kelly, Director of the United States Federation of Worker Cooperatives on conflict transformation tactics and strategies.

As a self-determined artist and indefatigable organizer (and analyst) of established and emergent forms of cooperation and collaboration within creative communities, Woolard is a striking example of the evolving priorities, passions, and critical practices of contemporary artists. Art and justice, work and life, critical introspection and organizational theory are consistently (re)formed through speculative research and inquisitive future-mindedness. She notates and performs a continuing and scalable choreography animated by questions of work, purpose, and values of community and critique.

a vivid example of artists' practice that transcends boundaries of creative work and social justice, independent art and organizations, work and life — based and formed by both historic research and future speculations

Caroline asks:
   "What does a culture of reflection and listening look like?"

This is a question that motivates Caroline's work, especially at this time. As organizer and collaborator, she has witnessed how creative coalitions dynamically advance or slowly fail. She is committed to bring art process and art objects into spaces and situations where they are often unexpected. The exhibition we invited Woolard to install in The Galleries at Moore in the summer of 2019 is now a traveling exhibition and publication. The book includes ephemera and eclectic evidence of creative and collaborative processes. In the exhibition format, Woolard's participatory installation, *The Meeting* see chapter 1, is central, presenting a large conference table and discursive space to convene, examine, and critique meetings as the unexamined anatomy of organizational (and educational) cultures. She created a series of facilitating and listening objects—artifacts and interventions to reveal the dynamics, power inequities, and challenges of communication and (as she writes) the "unavoidable antagonisms of working together" frequently in numbingly unimaginative spaces.

She is committed to bring art process and art objects into spaces and situations where they are often unexpected.

Caroline asks:
> "What if the tables and objects in our spaces
> were as imaginative as the conversations we
> are having?"

Based on work she has developed over the past two years, she will launch a new and ambitious chapter of this work to insert compelling sculptural objects into spaces, circumstances, meetings, and other quotidian events and encounters. These intervening objects are beautiful objects for facilitation settings, meetings, and other group settings. Some of these once migrated throughout Moore and now (with other new additions) become a visceral part of The Free Library of Philadelphia's extraordinary loanable collection of resources. While animating the Free Library as a center for contemporary art and collaborative cross-sector initiatives, Caroline's objects will be checked out, like books and videos, to support community organizations and artist-led workshops that create and sustain Philadelphia's dynamic cultural and collaborative communities.

This book is a vivid, summative representation of her dynamic engagements as the first Walentas Fellow at Moore.

A Way of Working*

Gabrielle Lavin Suzenski began her career in the Fabric Workshop and Museum's post-college apprenticeship program, which led to a full-time position working with the founder/artistic director in coordinating the museums's relocation in 2006. She has an MBA in Entrepreneurship & Innovation and a BFA in Sculpture and Printmaking, both from Penn State University.

*

Adapted from the exhibition wall text at The Galleries at Moore, September 2019.

1
Marcos Arruda, "Solidarity Economy and the Rebirth of a Matristic Human Society," (Towards People's Economy: Realities and Strategies from Local to Global, World Social Forum, Mumbai, India, January 2004), available, http://base.socioeco.org/docs/doc-7390_en.pdf, 2.

Gabrielle Lavin Suzenski, Rochelle F. Levy Director of The Galleries at Moore College of Art & Design.

This book presents a selection of imagery, critical essays, commentary, and ephemera from socially engaged and collective projects by New York-based artist Caroline Woolard (b. 1984, Rhode Island) produced over the past decade. While Woolard's multi-year, immersive installations are meant to be experienced in person and in site-sensitive contexts, the artist wanted to share her working process here so readers could get a sense of the skills that are required to make socially engaged projects. The photographs in this book act as visual reference points for an artistic practice that resists a single image or encounter. The documentation, correspondence, technical drawings, budgets, and writing included here reveal the ways in which Woolard balances making, managing, and mediating her projects. For Woolard, the process—a way of working—is as important as the result.

In running the online barter networks OurGoods.org and TradeSchool.coop [see chapter 3], creating a café at MoMA that circulated the desires of visitors as currency [see chapter 4], and studying collective practices in the visual arts in The Study Center for Group Work [see chapter 2], Woolard asks viewers and participants alike to reconsider daily activities of exchange. The Community Economies Collective, which informs Woolard's practice, writes, "How we imagine, frame and talk about our economy influences how we act. Contemporary economic politics confronts the economy as a bounded object separated from other social processes. In order to remake the economy we need different representations and framings that enable new modes of calculation and materialization." If the economy is not a "bounded object," what role do artists play in representing and remaking economies? Woolard's practice encourages open-ended conversation around that question.

Woolard writes that she "employs sculpture, installation, and online networks to imagine and enact the solidarity economy in the arts." The term "solidarity economy" emerged in the Global South (as "economia solidária") in the 1990s and spread globally as an interdependent movement after the first annual World Social Forum in Brazil in 2001, which popularized the slogan "another world is possible."[1] The solidarity economy is recognized as a way to value people and the planet over profits and to unite grassroots practices like lending circles, credit unions, worker cooperatives, and community land trusts to form a base of political power.

What is unusual about Woolard's approach to art and design is that she makes objects as well as multi-year, public initiatives using both online networks and sculptural environments. Woolard co-creates open-source Web 2.0 technology while hand-building objects that compose larger, immersive installations. From a real estate investment cooperative to tables shaped like a pack of she-wolves, Woolard offers unconventional spaces for reflection about exchange and collective agency. Woolard's aesthetic infrastructure — textual, digital, and physical — asks art audiences to consider that "the economy" is not separate from their daily actions.

Woolard's daily actions are made visible in this book, as heated email negotiations and mundane budgets are presented alongside documentation of finished gallery installations. Readers are invited to follow the behind-the-scenes work that is required to produce interdisciplinary art projects, from a commission at MoMA to a self-organized, international barter network with over 20,000 participants. The book in your hands proposes a politics of transparent production in the arts. It suggests that artists can bring studio-based sculptural techniques to interdisciplinary collaboration and dialogue.

The first two chapters of this book present Woolard's most recent endeavors: a short-term project called *The Meeting* see chapter 1 and a multi-year initiative called The Study Center for Group Work see chapter 2. From there, the chapters are organized chronologically and demonstrate Woolard's persistence as she develops multi-year, collectively initiated platforms alongside short-term projects produced at the invitation of institutions like Moore College of Art & Design. Readers will notice that Woolard's research and practice centers upon the following practices within the solidarity economy: barter and mutual aid see chapter 3, community currencies see chapter 4, collectives see chapter 5, worker cooperatives see chapter 6 and chapter 2, and a deepened emphasis on group communication and collective governance see chapters 1, 2, 7, 8.

The solidarity economy framework is explained at length by
Woolard in the next section. On those pages, and the pages
that follow, readers will notice words on the edges of each
page of the book. This is a navigation system that Woolard has
created with designer Angela Lorenzo that aims to take readers
through her working process (on the right and left edges of
the book's pages) and to note whether the endeavor is collectively-initiated or is an institutional invitation (on the bottom
of the page).

The correspondence, grants, applications, budgets, and
ephemera shown in this book have been reproduced with the
consent of Woolard's collaborators and the partner organizations and institutions she has worked with. The photographs
in this book have been carefully chosen by Woolard in order to
emphasize the sculptures, objects, and installations that she
has created that invite collective dialogue. Woolard insisted
that the book would not document and circulate images of
people that she does not know personally. The pages in each
chapter that read simply "imagine a group gathering" were
placed there by Woolard to remind readers of the limitations of
photographic documentation of socially engaged and collective practices, as these images are often indistinct from gallery
openings or images of everyday life. The ephemera presented
in this book will continue to be annotated and adapted in
future exhibitions, as they were in the exhibition from which
this book emerged.

Welcome

Caroline Woolard, Artist, Walentas Fellow 2018–2020

When Patti Phillips, Chief Academic Officer, Academic Dean at Moore College of Art & Design, asked me what I wanted to do most as the inaugural Jane and David Walentas Endowed Fellow at Moore College of Art and Design from 2018–2020, I said I needed to think about it. This Fellowship is a huge privilege, and it came without an application, giving me two years to "bring my vision for the future of cultural production to the Moore community and the larger artistic community of Philadelphia." This was an opportunity that few artists ever get.

After thinking it over, I decided that I wanted to create a public art project (*The Meeting* see chapter 1), but also to openly share my working process with students at Moore. This book—made for anyone who might be interested in learning about the ways that I have navigated institutional invitations as well as self-organized, multi-year projects in the arts—is my best attempt to share my working process. The materials in this book can also be accessed online at CarolineWoolard.com, and in a traveling exhibition. When I was in school, getting my BFA from 2002–2007 at Cooper Union in New York City, I always wondered about the realities of working as an artist. How do artists survive? How do artists negotiate and manage research-based, socially engaged, and large-scale projects? How do artists build organizations, collectives, and the art worlds they want to see? Who gets to be an artist, and why?

I have written about communal property in *The Social Life of Artistic Property*, co-authored with Pablo Helguera, William Powhida, and Amy Whitaker in 2014, about co-organizing barter-based education in *TRADE SCHOOL: 2009–2019*, a volume that I also edited, and about a holistic model for arts pedagogy in *Making and Being*, co-authored with Susan Jahoda in 2019, but I have never reflected deeply upon my own practice. This is an attempt to share the material conditions of the way I work, alongside imagery of finished projects. This book, and the corresponding open-access exhibition, accessible online at CarolineWoolard.com, aims to provide information about the specific ways that I move from a BIG VISION of the solidarity arts economy to the EVERYDAY PRACTICES AND STRUCTURES that are required when working on inter-disciplinary projects. Of course, this book is based upon my experiences and opinions, which are only one perspective of many, and the projects have all emerged from the particular conditions, limitations, and opportunities available to me, and to arts collectives based in New York City and in arts institutions in the United States, from the financial crisis of 2007/2008 to the COVID-19 pandemic of 2020.

In trying to explain my working process to students, I wrote up eight steps that go like this:

```
1. Notice daily EXPERIENCES and ask: "Why is
this the case?"

2. Begin a process of collective STUDY to
understand these experiences.

3. Make a COMMITMENT to something that will
shape your decisions and actions.

4. Focus the INQUIRY on an area that
feels particularly exciting and troubling
and possible.

5. Determine what TIMEFRAME the work will
take. Will it be a short-term project or
a multi-year platform? What practices are
necessary to sustain this?

6. Begin to EXPERIMENT with ways of
gathering, materials, forms, resources,
and ways of representing your inquiry as
a project or platform.

7. Share the idea in PUBLIC for feedback,
debate, and learning.

8. REFLECT upon this process, and return
to #1.
```

I made a diagram to visualize the process of moving from unconstrained exploration to focused circling around a decision. It charts the movement from wide-ranging research and associations, saying yes to all ideas and following as

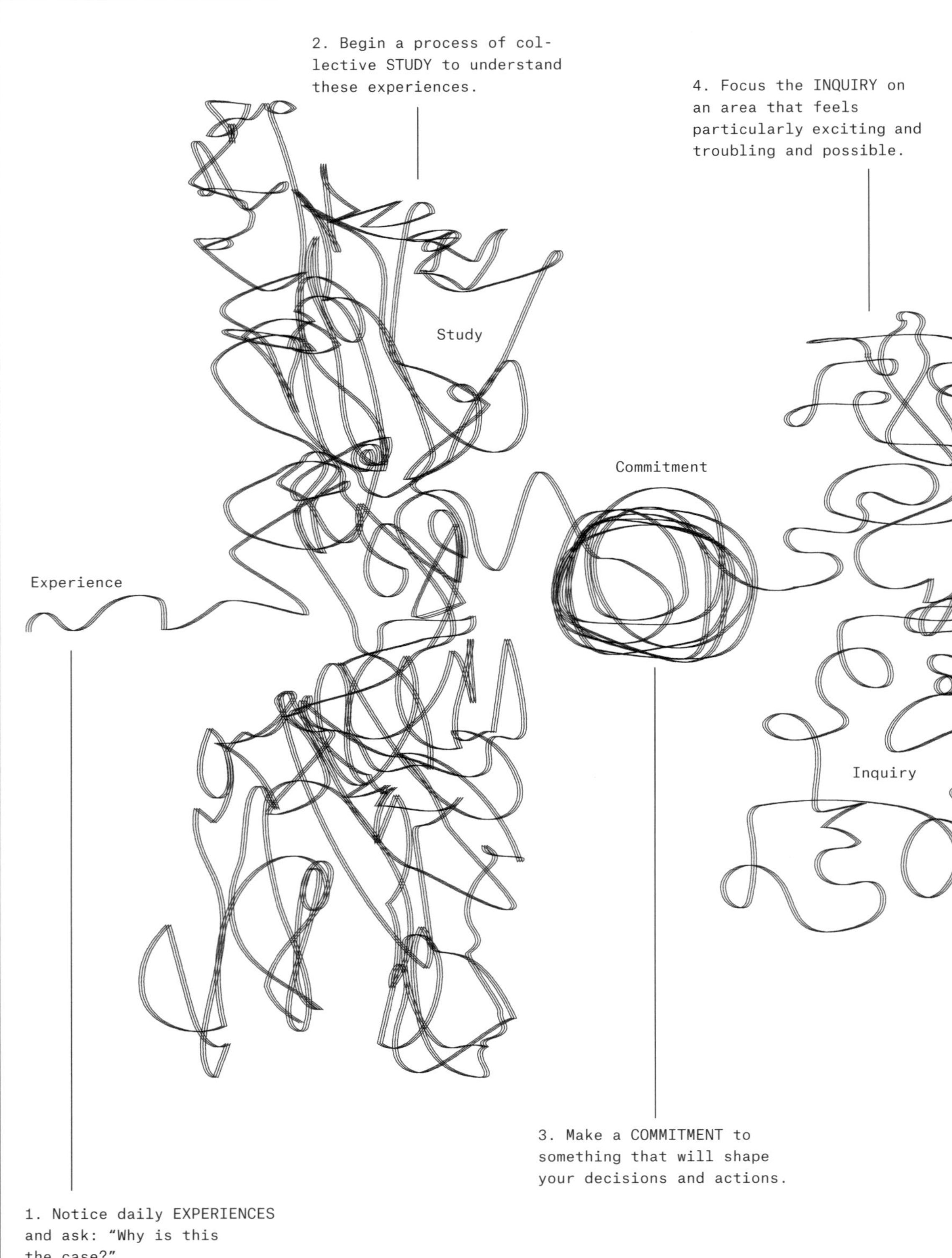
Reflect
Idea in Public
Experiment
Timeframe
Inquiry
Commitment
Study
Experience
2. Begin a process of col- lective STUDY to understand these experiences.
4. Focus the INQUIRY on an area that feels particularly exciting and troubling and possible.
Study
Commitment
Experience
Inquiry
3. Make a COMMITMENT to something that will shape your decisions and actions.
1. Notice daily EXPERIENCES and ask: "Why is this the case?"

many as possible to see where they lead, to narrowing and focusing and making decisions so that you can see where a specific idea leads when it is materialized and made public.

I made this Process Diagram to explain how I work and to see if it might apply to other artists, as a visualization of a research-based, interdisciplinary arts practice. The teacher in me made it into a numbered list, but of course, no path is linear.

5. Determine what TIMEFRAME the work will take. Will it be a short-term project or a multi-year platform? What practices are necessary to sustain this?

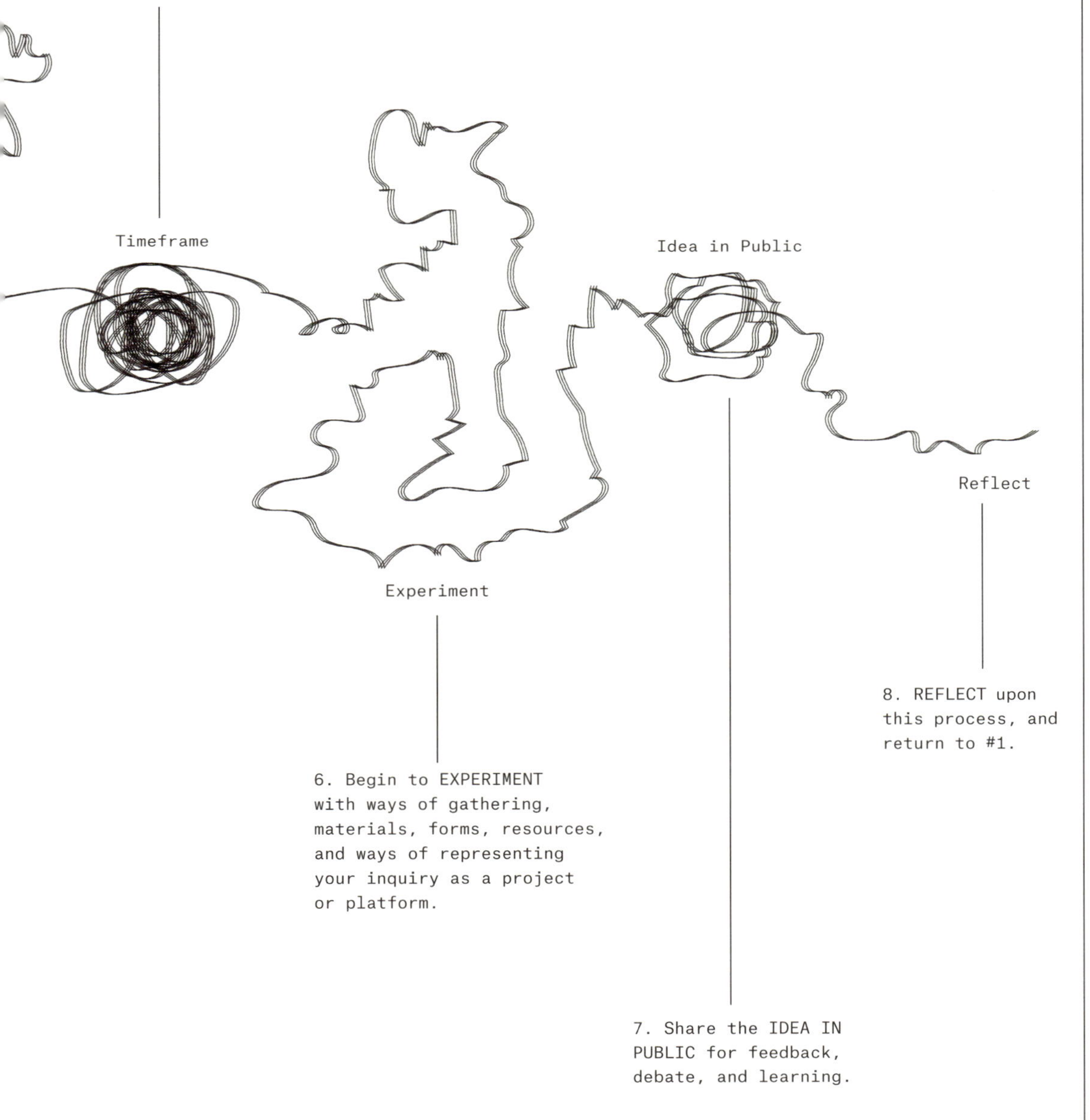

6. Begin to EXPERIMENT with ways of gathering, materials, forms, resources, and ways of representing your inquiry as a project or platform.

7. Share the IDEA IN PUBLIC for feedback, debate, and learning.

8. REFLECT upon this process, and return to #1.

1. Pay attention. Notice daily EXPERIENCES and ask: "Why is this the case?"

For example, if art is so important, why is it so hard to survive in the arts? If women and men are equal, why are women expected to clean up after men in so many settings? If Black, Indigenous, and people of color are equal to white people, why do white people have unequal access to cash, property, police protection, high quality public education, and media that affirms their dignity?

2. Begin a process of collective STUDY to understand these experiences. Who can you learn with and from?

The idea that each person in the United States, artist or otherwise, can "pull themselves up by their bootstraps" and survive alone, with success based upon merit, is both ridiculous and lonely. It is my life's project to heal the trauma of alienation that I sense around me by embodying a living commitment to the pleasures and pains of interdependence. My parents both taught me to distrust my neighbors at a young age. They said they had survived this far by "only relying on one another." While I knew that this logic made sense to them, I knew it could not be true. I felt the pain of their isolation daily and decided to seek ways to begin to heal the intergenerational wounds that deepen with distrust and fear. When I was 23, working a night shift from 10p.m.–6a.m. as a studio monitor at Cooper Union, from which I had just graduated, I found a website called The Community Economies Collective. The knowledge and connections I found there changed my life. I read everything on the website, and contacted the info@ email address. They put me in touch with people living and working for the community economy, or solidarity economy, in my neighborhood. Eventually, I was welcomed into a community of visual artists, as an artist myself, and into the solidarity economy movement, as an activist. I found "home" with people making conceptual art and with people organizing for economic justice, and for the solidarity economy, in New York City.

I often ask, "What is the economy that art wants?" I believe that the economy art wants is one of the commons. I define the commons as shared resources that are managed by and for the people who use those resources. The commons involve shared ownership, cooperation, and solidarity—in other words, economic justice. Rather than believing that the economy is a monolithic entity which cannot be altered, I aim to co-create equitable systems that privilege communal well-being over personal gain. I try to make discrete art projects within systems, or collectively initiated platforms, that are aligned with my values. This is no easy task.

3. Make a COMMITMENT to something that will shape your decisions and actions. Circle around it. How do you want to show up?

In Generative Somatics, a commitment refers to an ability for individuals and groups to "return to a positive vision and act from their values under pressure; to identify what they care about and make it known to others." Working with Alta Starr of Generative Somatics, I know that my current commitment is to slowing down and staying with the pleasures and the pains of interdependence. Since 2007/2008, I have made a commitment to creating artworks within the solidarity economy. What does this mean? Each project I make is informed by, and aims to contribute to, a sector of the solidarity economy. For example, barter networks, community currencies, collectives, and community land trusts are all part of the solidarity economy. Here is a text I wrote, together with Michael Johnson, Cheyenna Layne Weber, and members of the collective

SolidarityNYC, in 2011, during the spring and summer before Occupy Wall Street began.

WHAT IS SOLIDARITY?
Solidarity is a collective process of taking active responsibility for our inter-relationships on both a local and global level. This is how we empower ourselves and take control of our lives.

WHEN WE PRACTICE SOLIDARITY, WE RECOGNIZE:
- that our fates are bound up with the fates of others, both human and non-human.
- that our interconnections—sometimes profoundly unequal and oppressive—demand conscious action and transformation.

THROUGH SOLIDARITY:
- we recognize the diversity, autonomy, power, and dignity of others.
- we come to understand that our struggles to be free and joyful are interdependent, not separate or distant from one another as we may have thought.
- we begin to develop an ethical practice of shared struggle that crosses race and ethnic lines, class lines, sex and gender lines.

PEOPLE MAY SHARE SUCH VALUES AS:
- Unity-in-diversity
- Shared power (as opposed to power-over)
- Autonomy (always both individual and collective)
- Communication (horizontal, not top-down)
- Cooperation and mutual-aid (shared struggle)
- Local rootedness, global interconnection

Alternatives to economic and social exploitation are growing strong across the globe, especially in places like Brazil, Quebec, Northern Italy, and the Basque region of Spain. They call it Solidarity Economics, a grassroots form of cooperative economics. It is working throughout the world, connecting thousands of local alternatives together to create large-scale, viable, and creative networks for both economic and social change.

ECONOMY: The many different ways in which we human beings collectively generate livelihoods to meet our needs in relation with each other and with the rest of the earth.

SOLIDARITY: The process of taking active responsibility for our relationships in ways that foster diversity, autonomy, cooperation, communication, and shared-power.

SOLIDARITY ECONOMY: Interconnected and diverse ways of generating our livelihoods that encourage and embody practices of solidarity. An "economy of economies" that resists individualistic, competitive, and exploitative economics.

The Solidarity Economy's values-based, big tent organizing approach enables groups to build real economic relationships between producers, solidarity-committed investors, retailers, and consumers; and then link to other grassroots social movements in networks of mutual support and exchange.

We believe that it is not enough to be "against," nor is it enough to create. We must build social movements that encompass and connect many forms of action:

defensive action
- to protect ourselves and our communities from immediate harm;
offensive action
- to challenge the current structures of oppression and exploitation in all of their racist, sexist, classist, homophobic, and otherwise exclusionary forms;
healing action
- to work through and recover from the pain and brokenness that we have imposed on ourselves and others have imposed on us in so many ways;

creative action
- to build alternative structures that meet
  our daily needs and help us secede from the
  oppressions of the dominant society
  and economy; and

transformative action
- personally and collectively becoming the
  change we want to bring to the world.

Understanding economies of solidarity and artmaking as always already intertwined matters to me because the arts are not valued in the United States in the way that they are in other countries, and I cannot separate the value of artistic labor and production from the value of land, health, or education, all of which are integral to human dignity, self-determination, and survival. Without affordable space, healthcare, or education, how can culture thrive?

4. Focus your study. Create an INQUIRY in an area that feels particularly exciting and troubling and possible.

Once I am grounded in my deep commitment to the solidarity economy in the arts, I begin to ask myself what my role can be as an artist in this larger movement of cooperatives, credit unions, land trusts, and barter networks. I continuously work to understand my social identity and the histories that shape my beliefs.

For example, my father was the first person in his family to go to college; he raised me with an awareness of the rights and responsibilities that come with educational privilege. As a member of the LGBTQIA community, I am acutely aware of my positionality as a creative practitioner, cultural equity advocate, and teacher. My ability to be in trusting, vulnerable, and transformative relationships across race, class, ability, age, citizenship status, nationality, gender, sexual orientation, and other aspects of identity is contingent upon an evolving awareness of my social position. I am committed to ongoing study and struggle in relationship to the histories and present-day conditions that give people minority status, produce bias, and structure everyday, interpersonal dynamics, because this work makes life and learning possible.

I then try to notice patterns—social, technological, and political—that are emerging in real time, and consider ways to adapt ideas from non-arts fields or sectors to the arts, or from the arts to non-arts sectors. For example, what is possible as blockchain emerges, the Jumpstart Our Business Startups (JOBS) passes, and thousands of people advocate for community land trusts across sectors, in New York City, all around 2012?

5. Sustain the effort. Determine what TIMEFRAME the work will take. Circle around it. Will it be a short-term project or a multi-year platform? What practices are necessary to sustain this?

I believe that every artist has a core question or idea that only a few other artists in the world share, and that they need to find the other artists who want to refine that idea or core question, together. What is the point of making a new approach to art if other artists do not recognize it? I have been inspired by Thomas Kuhn's notion of a "paradigm shift" in the structure of scientific revolutions which states that in order to recognize innovation, there needs to be consensus. Of course Kuhn's scale is entirely different; he discusses historical periods. But what motivates me is that, ironically, standardization and innovation go together. Without agreement about a theory or model, it is impossible to know when a new knowledge has been created.

For this reason, I try to connect my specific interests to broader groups of artists and non-artists. Often this requires making more than a project. It requires long term collective dialogue, online networks, and gatherings to debate and refine key ideas with one another.

I believe that artists need to learn to think organizationally in order to imagine how artwork and ideas might circulate in the world, and that we can work together to create opportunities for ourselves and for one another. I have created a diagram to describe my approach using a tree as an analogy.

PROJECTS. The fruit and leaves: shiny and short-lived. You might also call projects artworks, objects, or events. A project is an object or experience which is produced with an imagined audience that is larger than the artist or group involved in the effort of creation.

PLATFORMS. The tree trunk and branches: strong and enduring. You might also call platforms organizations, initiatives, or collectives. A platform is a multi-year initiative that aims to reproduce itself in order to reliably provide support for projects.

PRACTICES. The roots or mycelium: underground and life-giving. A practice is a way of doing things intentionally on a regular basis to develop an ability or awareness. Practices nurture platforms.

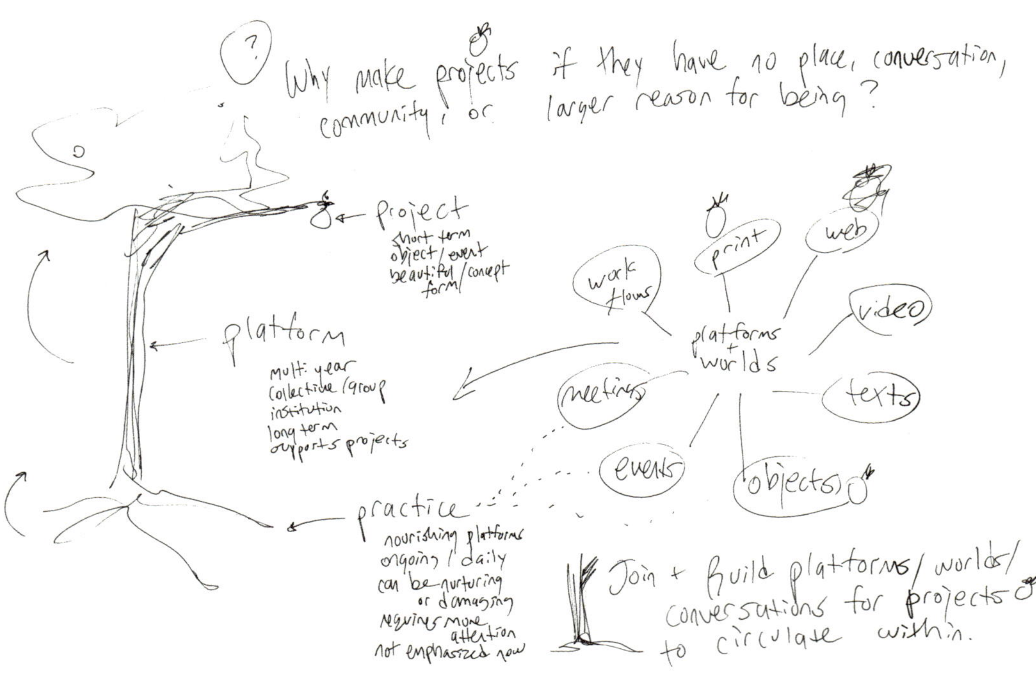

Sharon Louden reminds us that we can be as creative in making opportunities for ourselves as we are in making our artwork. I hope this framework helps artists to connect the ideas in their artwork, or "projects," to the organizations, or "platforms," and practices that they engage with on a daily basis.

I am part of a generation of artists who talk about arts advocacy and cultural organizing (platforms) alongside their studio practice (projects). I believe that the future of art includes a critical attention to multi-year initiatives or platforms alongside discrete projects. Think of all the artists who made major cultural institutions like El Museo del Barrio or Fourth Arts Block possible, but who didn't feel the need (or have the ability) to present this work alongside their artistic practice. Their institutions and their art practices remained separate. I hope to bridge this divide with my work, and I hope to encourage other artists to do the same. I think this future of art will only be possible if artists in the academy reconcile the practiced ignorance—or epistemo- logical violence—that has excluded community arts and cultural organizing from the art academy for so long. Luckily, my generation has been raised in Occupy Wall Street and in Black Lives Matter, so the transformation of the academy and of the arts ecosystem is already underway.

6. Begin to EXPERIMENT with materials, forms, resources, ways of gathering, and ways of repre- senting your inquiry as a project or platform.

I try out different ideas and notice which skill sets and personalities might work well together to pursue an idea in a collaborative team. In most groups, I am looking for people who are more detail-oriented than I am, who have expertise with computer engineering and design, and who are relational and intuitive, as I can be very task-oriented and focused on work rather than on building deep relationships by hanging out. I bring an awareness of material and form to the objects we make, analytical skills as a researcher, an intense passion for work I believe in, a desire to meet lots of people, charisma, project management, writing, public speaking, and media-making skills. I continue to listen to group feedback and to see group work as a space for transformation. We make material tests and loop back to the beginning of this process, changing ideas, collaborators, and our sense of emergent patterns, in a dynamic and non-linear process, until the idea feels solid.

7. Share the idea in PUBLIC for feedback, debate, and learning. Circle around it.

When the idea is solid, it goes live and we share it with participants, peers, the public, and the press. Some projects cannot be described in arts spaces, or in books like this one, because to do so would be to limit their political power. For example, the NYC Real Estate Investment Cooperative and SolidarityNYC, both of which I helped to create, need to exist outside of any individual artist's narrative. It is important that in these cases, I am a contributor and member, but I am more aware today than I was previously of the ways that writing about them in a book like this, which will circulate in arts spaces, will enclose the public understanding of these long-term platforms (initiatives, para-institutions, autonomous institutions, etc.) as an "artwork" with a singular author and will give them a limited capacity to transform.

8. REFLECT upon this process, and return to #1.

For example: What did we/I do well? What can we/I improve? What capacities did we/I embody? How did the contradictions of upholding our/my commitment show up in this work?

Throughout this entire process, I think about the knowledge that I must learn from mentors and collaborators. I use *The Braid* as a diagram to help think through a constant movement between making, managing, and mediating—between subjectivity, material, form, and poetics (making); structure, governance, and policy (managing); and public presentation, text, and media making (mediating). This image, and the idea that some of this knowledge is tacit, and should become more explicit, comes from Adelheid Mers. Mers is an artist, theorist, and a member of The Study Center for Group Work, a collectively initiated project that I describe in this book see chapter 2.

Mers' practice centers around what she calls Performative Diagrammatics, which "range from verbal prompts to pre-printed diagrams on whiteboards, fabricated objects, and live-streaming, custom-coded 360° video. This work develops by carefully observing how lay and professional cultural producers animate the systems through which they operate; and by creating tools collaboratively, with volunteers and other contributors, who share experiences and ways of knowing." She has developed *The Braid* in dialogue with performing and visual artists over many years, and has made open access diagrams that artists can download online and adapt to their own practices. I have done this, with the support of Mers. Following the practice of braiding, as Mers' would call it, you will notice that making, mediating, and managing run throughout the entire production process, and throughout this book.

Adelheid Mers, *The Braid*, V3, 2016, dimensions variable. Image courtesy of the artist.

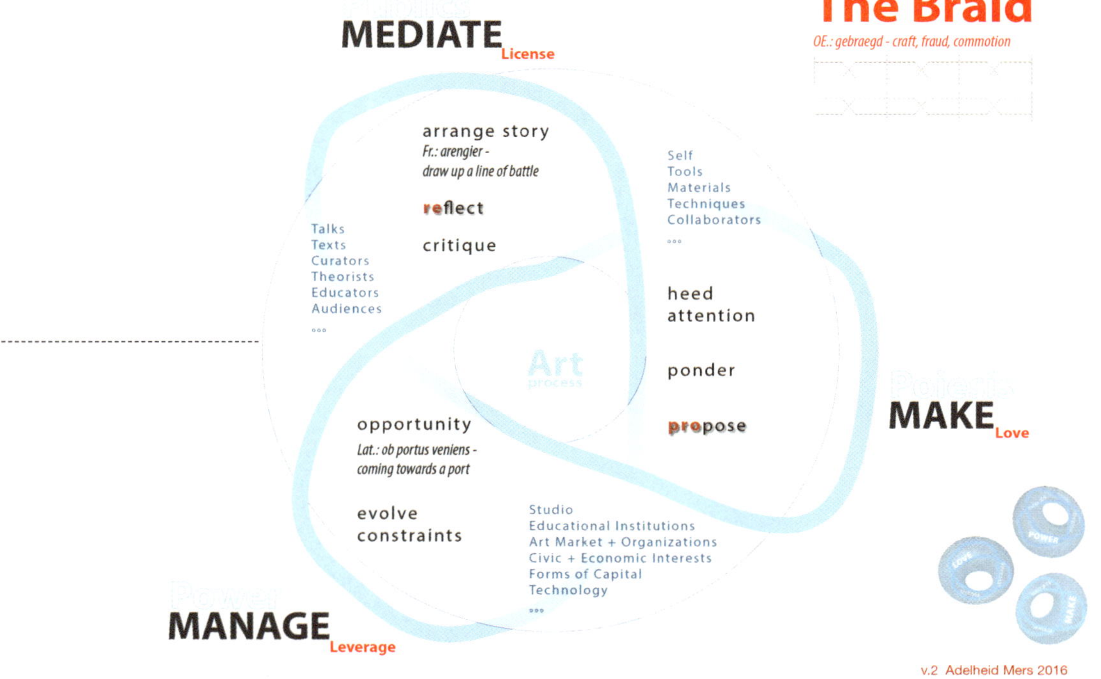

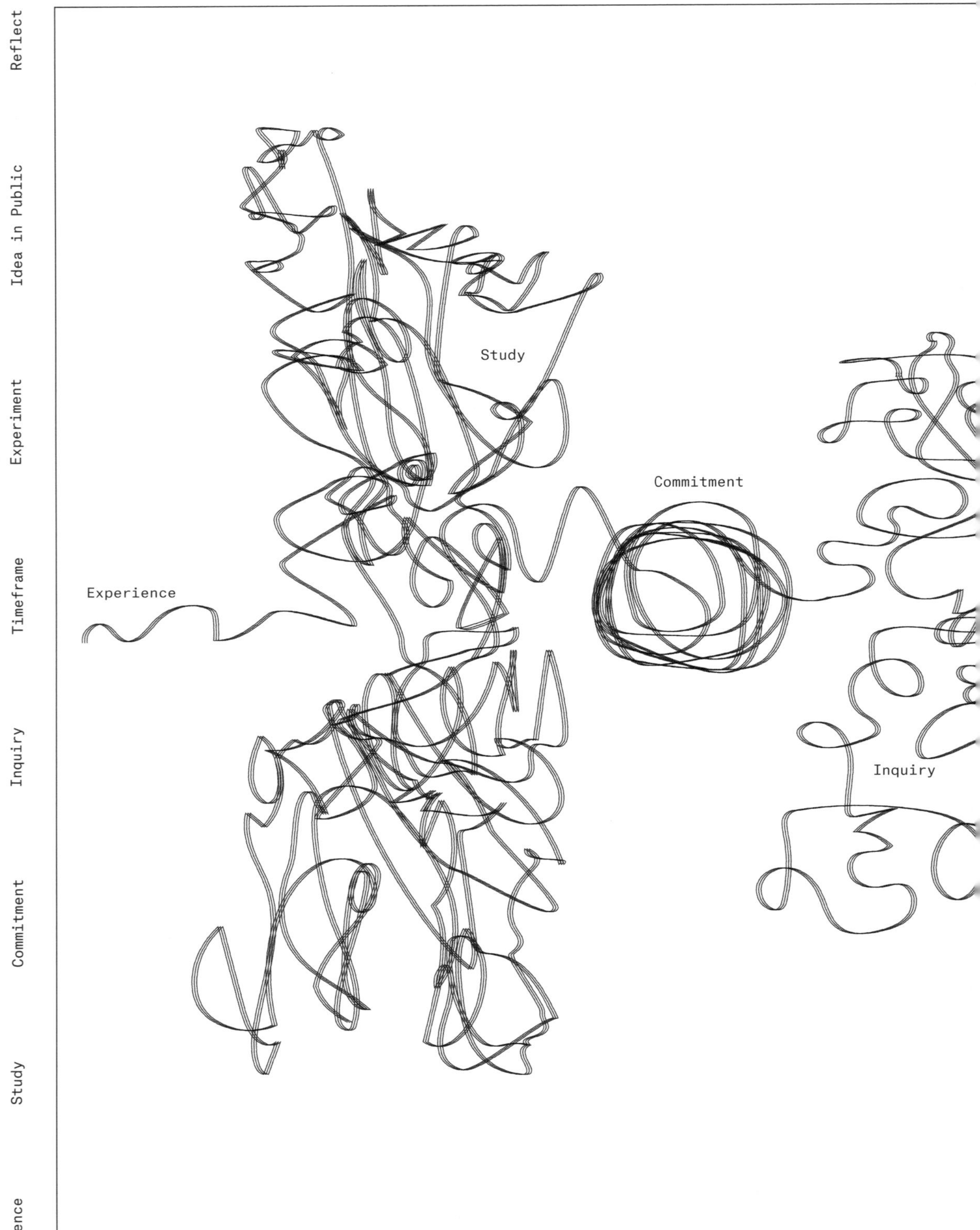

Experience
Study
Commitment
Inquiry
Timeframe
Experiment
Idea in Public
Reflect
Study
Commitment
Experience
Inquiry

If you love diagrams, as I do, look at this Process Diagram that I made to visualize the experience of moving from unrestrained EXPLORATION to CIRCLING and focus. Imagine that it is a three-dimensional braid, with three strands that represent Making, Mediating, and Managing, woven together to form a fluid and dynamic practice ^{see chapter 2}.

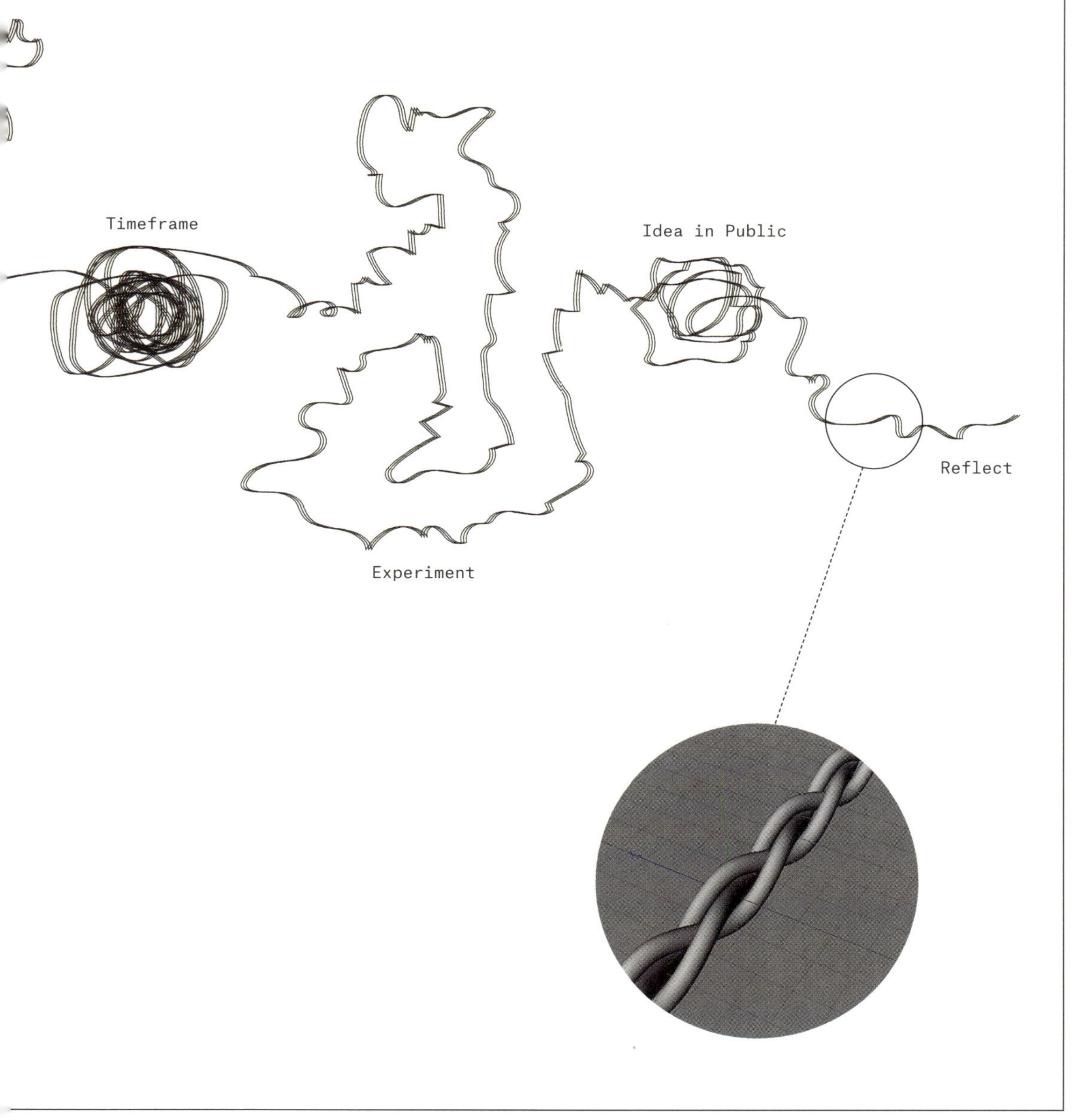

The work collected in this volume—and indeed my last ten years of work—is shaped by twin capitalist crises: the first, the 2007 global credit crises and subsequent "great recession" that hollowed out the budgets of arts organizations nationally; the second, the recent (and ongoing, as I write) global pandemic, a consequence of capitalist development. It's too soon to say what this second crisis will cause, even though (another) legacy of austerity seems all but certain. Regardless of the unknown, our economic system has bequeathed a legacy of pain, racism, austerity, and scarcity. I have taken these effects as sites to produce art within and, I hope, to offer some sense of community as a response to a critique of the economy.

If ever there were a time to dream up art worlds that work for artists, this is it. What are the art worlds that you want? Who do you want to be in community with? Where do you want your artwork to go, after you make it?

My art seeks to undo some of the most pernicious doings of capitalism on an interpersonal level: that system of private property, individual rights, class and race-based inequality out of which it generates its profits. How should an artist work in such a system? How can she work and to what end? The need for any truly progressive economic transition to be both a way of thinking and a way of doing animates my practice of making artistic objects that operate symbolically and making alter-institutions that require artists to work with one another cooperatively.

Likewise, my desire to keep the material conditions (budgets, emails, chore lists, the very labor of production) alongside the traditional curatorial essay and installation imagery hopes to enact this very dialectical possibility: our material conditions are not understood through our artwork, they become our artwork, they make our artwork possible and provide the lens through which it will be critiqued. If we actually do believe—as so many theorists and artists profess to—that art is not simply an object but a long process of negotiation, production and circulation, shouldn't that belief enter into how we display, envision, and critique art? As Shannon Jackson says, describing Mierle Laderman Ukeles practice, this is a "move from a discrete notion of an art "work" to a process-based notion of the work it takes to make art." [2]

2
Shannon Jackson, *Social Works: Performing Art, Supporting Publics* (New York and London: Routledge, 2011).

During the COVID-19 pandemic, more and more people agree that the dominant "art world"—a term that signifies all of the people and networks and organizations that enable the learning, discussion, making, presenting, and circulation of art—is not functioning as so many of us artists would like it to. As art critic Jerry Saltz wrote in April of 2020:

> The mighty Met estimates it could lose $100 million and has announced widespread layoffs; the Hammer Museum laid off 150 part-time workers; L.A. MoCA laid off its entire part-time staff; S.F. MoMA expects to lay off 135 on-call staff members; Mass. MoCA is laying off 120 employees. Meanwhile, many maintain restoration labs, care for vast collections, pay insurance premiums, electric bills, and thousands of other unseen costs. Other than the Getty, Kimble, the Met, and MoMA, most museums don't have vast endowments that can allow them to get through [a pandemic] like this.[3]

Beyond prioritizing insurance premiums over employees, the art world is too white, too colonial, too extractive, too hierarchical, too male, too straight, and too market-driven. And yet this realization—of the dominant art-world's limitations—occurs during every capitalist crisis, every decade or so now, it seems. New art worlds were dreamt into existence by artists in 2007/2008 as well as in the long down-turn of the 1970s fiscal crisis. New art worlds are dreamt into existence in every crisis.

New art worlds are dreamt into existence in every crisis.

In response to COVID-19:

- the US Federation of Worker Cooperatives has just launched a national worker-owned freelancer cooperative;
- artists Vallejo Gantner, Alex Reeves, Erica Schnitzer, Chet Kerr, and James Dennin started the online marketplace hireartists.org to give work to "accomplished, dedicated practitioners from across the arts [who can] share their knowledge or to help with creative and everyday needs";

The ideal arts space is simple: it's one in which art and culture are not sequestered from the lived experience of artists and their communities.

—Carolyn Lazard, 2019 *

* Carolyn Lazard, "Accessibility in the Arts: A Promise and a Practice," 2019, promiseandpractice.art.

3
Jerry Saltz, "The Last Days of the Art World … and Perhaps the First Days of a New One," *Vulture*, April 2, 2020, https://www.vulture.com/2020/04/how-the-coronavirus-will-transform-the-art-world.html.

– artist Linda Goode Bryant and cultural worker Sarah Workneh opened a free and expanded food pantry to "help supply and supplement the already at-risk communities of Brownsville and East New York";
– and President Sanjit Sethi of Minneapolis College of Art and Design has announced that the school "will offer immediate, temporary space to be used by organizations and nonprofits that have been displaced." [4]

And initiatives of mutual aid, solidarity, and cooperation need not be unique to a crisis. In fact, these art worlds are dreamt into existence every week by artists and people who survive the daily "crisis" of being told that we are not valuable, that we should not exist, that we need to continually justify our own existence.

Take a moment to sense the spaces, networks, and communities created by artists around you. Sense the art worlds led by Black artists, Indigenous artists, and artists of color, by disabled artists, by trans artists, by queer artists, by nonbinary artists, by neurodivergent artists, by undocumented artists, by immigrant artists, by poor artists, and by so many people who are not only surviving, but flourishing, in art worlds of cooperation and mutual aid. Artist-centric networks, organizations, and initiatives — in short, solidarity art worlds — are not only possible, they already exist.

Allow yourself to sense the power of these art worlds around you, and allow yourself to dream into the art worlds that you want. Just as last decade's global crisis transformed the art world, so now producers and critics are beginning to imagine what a post-Covid-19 art world will look like. How do "social distance" and "social practice" go together? What is the temporality of exhibits, installations, and biennials with little global travel, reduced capacity in all indoor spaces, and fear of contagion? One imagines, at the very least, we will be witnessing a re-localization of the arts, one combined with a new scale of intimacy of the kind only predicted by globalizations boosters in the 1990s — now a conversation with a collaborator in Seoul truly is the same as with one around the corner — they both take place on Zoom.

Whatever else this terrible pandemic produces, it may in fact lead artists and arts organizations to ask and answer the

4
Sarah Workneh, personal email, May 6, 2020, and MCAD newsletter June 2, 2020.

most basic questions anew: what are we doing and why are we doing it? The opportunity to consider such fundamental propositions are also the moments in which institutions like MoMA—whose only desire is to reproduce themselves—may not adapt, while local initiatives, those with collective power and the ability to transform nimbly, may emerge and perhaps harness the productive capacity of new groups and coalitions of artists.

I have long had an interest in community-generated currencies and other ways to imagine and visualize the flow of resources outside of our existing, capital-driven economy. I believe that the only way in which we will have a new economy and an economy that works for many artists is for artists themselves to begin the project of imagining, representing, and instantiating new organizations of labor, currency, and infrastructure.

Solidarity Art Economy Manifesto/ From Artist to Solidarity Arts Economy Organizer*

*
Adapted from Caroline Woolard,
"Solidarity Art Worlds,"
Brooklyn Rail, February 2013.

Rather than waiting to "go back to normal," to an art world and system of production and distribution that works for very few people, now is the time to dream.

Allow yourself to dream.

Allow yourself to dream with friends.

I am going to invite you to dream with me.

1.

Remember a moment when you chose to be in the arts, or the arts chose you.

Despite a dominant culture that values reading, writing, and speaking, you made a commitment to drawing, moving, or singing—to visual and embodied ways of knowing.

You are told you that are stupid, passionate, stubborn, or crazy because you live in your imagination.

This lack of respect for the arts continues to make you feel alone, but you have survived, and your persistence is part of your strength, your internal power that no one can take away from you.

How do you feel?

2.

You are told that you will never get a job, that you will be a "starving artist" in the United States, and you understand this to mean that artists are not paid well, that the arts are not well funded in the United States.

You want to be an artist anyway. You are told you are stupid, passionate, stubborn, or crazy.

The impossibility of making a living in the arts makes you feel alone, but you survive, and your persistence becomes part of your strength, your internal power that no one can take away from you.

3.

You come to realize that the arts are devalued like all work that sustains life, all work that allows people to rest, dream, and return to work the next day (what is called social reproduction).

You come to understand that the arts are aligned with service work, domestic work, sex work, agricultural work, healing work, educational work, spiritual work, social work, and all racialized and gendered labor in the United States that is not compensated adequately.

You realize that the people who do all of these kinds of labor have been told that they too, are stupid, passionate, stubborn, or crazy.

You now know that you share this internal power, together.

4.

You begin to wonder: If the artistic work required in order to collectively celebrate, to communicate without words, to draw, to dance, to sing, to build shared symbols and imagined futures, to raise children, to clean homes, to collect the garbage, to grow food, to heal, to learn, and to connect is not compensated or supported, how does it continue?

How is life sustained? You are transfixed by this question.

And here you begin a process of studying the political economy, of analyzing your material conditions, and the conditions that you share with others.

5.

Through study, you become aware that life is sustained by gift giving, by mutual aid, by lending, and by informal exchanges.

But you also are told—by the people who call you stupid, passionate, stubborn, or crazy—that the work of sustaining life is not really labor. You think: Perhaps this work will always be devalued, existing only to support the dominant economy of waged labor so that some people can make a lot of money, while those of us that sustain life continue to be un- or undercompensated.

But, because you have survived, and you have this internal strength, this persistence, you think: Perhaps, there is another way.

What if the work that sustains life can be valued, connected, and strengthened?

You think: What if the work that sustains life is the economy we need, the economy of peace, of community, of cooperation?

You know, as you know of your own survival, that this work has power.

6.

You seek to learn more about the power of this work.

The knowledge you seek has been hidden and devalued, like the knowledge that is embodied and visual, but you find it.

You sense it in the arts, and around you, in the healers, the guides, and the caregivers.

You learn that this idea—giving power and compensation to the labor that sustains life—is called the solidarity economy, and that it emerged from the global South in the 1990s, as economia solidária to describe economic practices and models which advance values of democracy, mutualism, cooperation, ecological sustainability, justice, and reciprocity. You learn that these economic practices can be visualized as follows:

CREATION: IDEAS AND RESOURCES
    the commons: ecological and intellectual
    free and open-source software and technology
    community land trusts
    skill shares
    free schools

PRODUCTION: HOW THINGS ARE MADE
    worker cooperatives
    producer cooperatives
    non-profit artisan collectives
    self-employment
    labor unions
    democratic employee stock ownership programs
    local self-reliance

TRANSFER AND EXCHANGE: THE WAY WE SHARE GOODS AND SERVICES
    barter networks
    freeganism
    sliding scale pricing
    time banks
    gifts
    clothing swaps
    tool shares

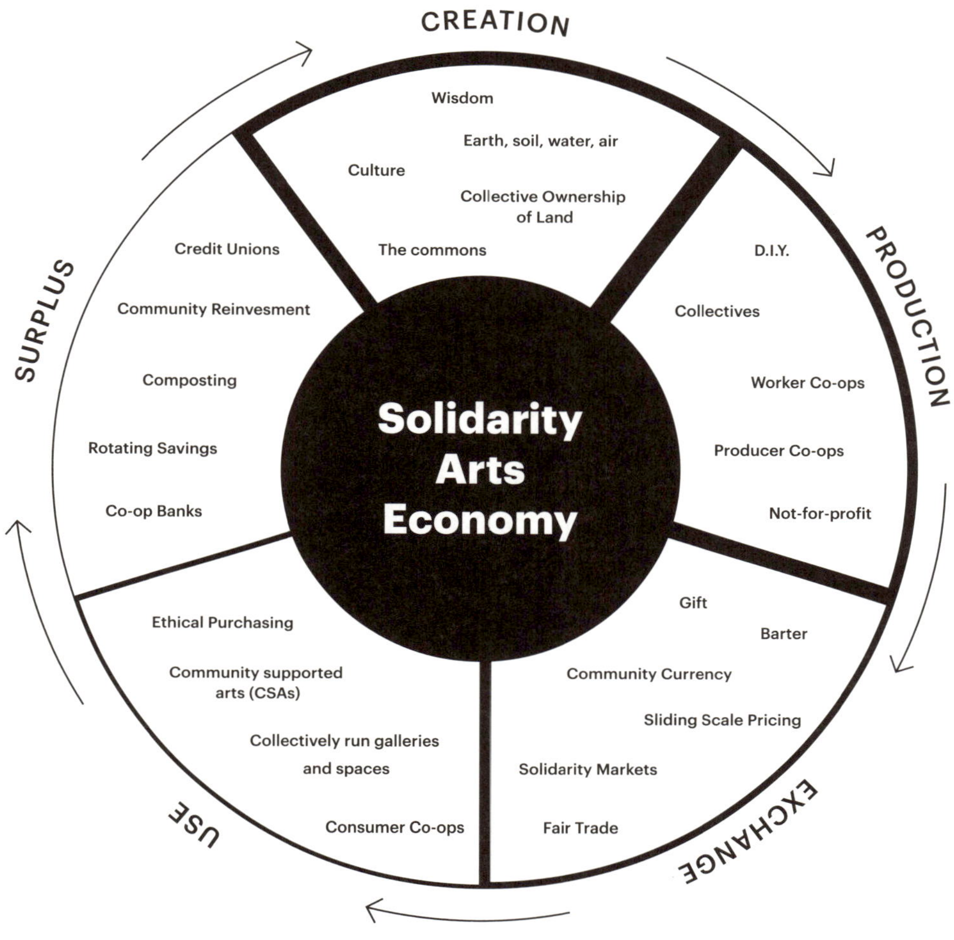

community currencies
fair trade
community supported agriculture
community supported kitchens
consumer (usually food) cooperatives
housing cooperatives and collectives
intentional communities
self-provisioning
non-profit buying clubs

SURPLUS ALLOCATION: THE WAY WE CREATE ECONOMIC SECURITY

credit unions and community development credit unions
cooperative loan funds
rotating savings and credit associations

Solidarity Economy. This Solidarity Economy diagram has been adapted from Ethan Miller's diagram and was designed by Topos Graphics for the book *Making and Being* by Susan Jahoda and Caroline Woolard (Pioneer Works Press / DAP, 2019).

mutual aid societies
cooperative banks
community development banks

7.

You realize that the economy that art needs is one of the commons — of the solidarity economy — and that in order to sustain shared imagery, culture, communication without words, and embodied knowledge, the solidarity economy is critical.

You begin to connect artmaking to this economy of care, knowing that your power, your survival, is connected to the survival of these other practices and people, well beyond the arts.

You find community with these practices, and feel slightly less alone.

8.

You feel a tension between what you know are collective ways of meeting collective needs and what you are told is the horizon of possibility, that there is no alternative to being a starving artist, to doing household work without pay, to capital-ism, in short.

You learn that the tension between art and life, between a wage and a livelihood is as old as capitalism; it is capitalism. And you realize that you have been feeling, bodily, what so many people have felt for over 400 years.

Only in that economic system — capitalism — does art confront the world as separate, as symbolic and non-reproductive; only with the rise of capitalism was art cast out of the world of daily life and rendered newly "useless."

You understand that the tension you feel arises from a 400-year old historical contradiction that must be held collectively and used to inform collective work; it is not a tension that can be resolved on a personal level.

9.

As you join in some collective work, you continue to learn about the history of organizing against profit for the few, against the exploitation of work that sustains life, against capitalism, and against the kind of art world capitalism bequeaths.

You feel, with collective strength and experience, that another economy is possible in the arts, and beyond, because it already exists. Just as you have survived, this economy has survived, and is surviving.

This economy of care, of cooperation, and of mutual aid is thriving, despite being marginalized and devalued.

You continue to connect, grow, and strengthen solidarity economy practices and networks, and to learn about the ways that political power for the solidarity economy is growing internationally, in countries where cooperative economies are given more support than in the United States.

You witness the wisdom in the collective work around you, the shared persistence, and shared strength.

You begin to move through the world with awareness of this collective power, and begin to know that you are not alone.

This awareness of collective power becomes part of your internal power that no one can take away from you.

10.

You continue to transform, in community.

You understand that the solidarity economy has always been led by Black, Indigenous, and people of color, especially women, nonbinary people, and trans people. You explore the parts of you that are held up by dominant culture, and the parts that are not.

You explore how you show up in groups, and you see how this ongoing work makes deep connections across differences possible.

When you can, you take resources from the dominant economy and put them into alternative and post-capitalist economies so that they can continue to grow.

You divest from exploitation and invest in the work that sustains life.

You join the worker cooperatives, credit unions, land trusts, community gardens, and initiatives that extend well beyond the arts.

You address and move through the interpersonal difficulties of collective work, of the pain of trying to be less alone, and you strengthen the collective capacity within you.

How do you feel?

11.

When the economy collapses, as it has and will, again and again, under capitalism, you know how to survive.

You might lose your job, but you cannot lose your identity, as no one can take this—your creativity, your collective strength, your gift economies—away from you.

You know that the solidarity economy, with your deep relationships of care, your mutual aid networks, your community currencies, your barter networks, and your community gardens, land trusts, and cooperatives will sustain themselves, as they always have.

You know that, despite being told that you are stupid, passionate, stubborn, or crazy, you have collective strength with you. You are practicing a powerful economy of care, together. You have all survived, are all working together. This is your internal power that no one can take away from any of you. And you continue to thrive. How do you feel?

page 39
I Don't Have A Boss,
Caroline Woolard for
SolidarityNYC, typeset by
Andrew Persoff, 2010.

Sometimes New York seems like the center of cut-throat competition.
But there are many New Yorkers thriving in mutual benefit.

They say:

I DON'T HAVE A BOSS.

I'M A WORKER-OWNER IN A COOPERATIVE BUSINESS.

I DON'T HAVE A LANDLORD.

I'M A MEMBER OF A LAND TRUST, CO-OP, OR INTENTIONAL COMMUNITY.

I DON'T PAY FOR SCHOOL.

I PARTICIPATE IN SELF-ORGANIZED SCHOOLS AND DEMAND FREE EDUCATION.

I DON'T HOARD MY STUFF.

I TAKE PART IN TOOL-SHARES, BARTER CLUBS, AND CLOTHING SWAPS.

I DON'T BUY FOOD THAT KILLS.

I'M A MEMBER OF A FOOD CO-OP, CSA, AND COMMUNITY GARDEN.

I DON'T LET MY BANK PROFIT OFF ME.

I JOINED A CREDIT UNION, SO MY MONEY STAYS IN THE COMMUNITY.

There are so many ways to be part of an economy that supports people and the planet over profit.

We're mapping the ones in New York City at SolidarityNYC.org.

SOLIDARITY NYC

WWW.SOLIDARITYNYC.ORG

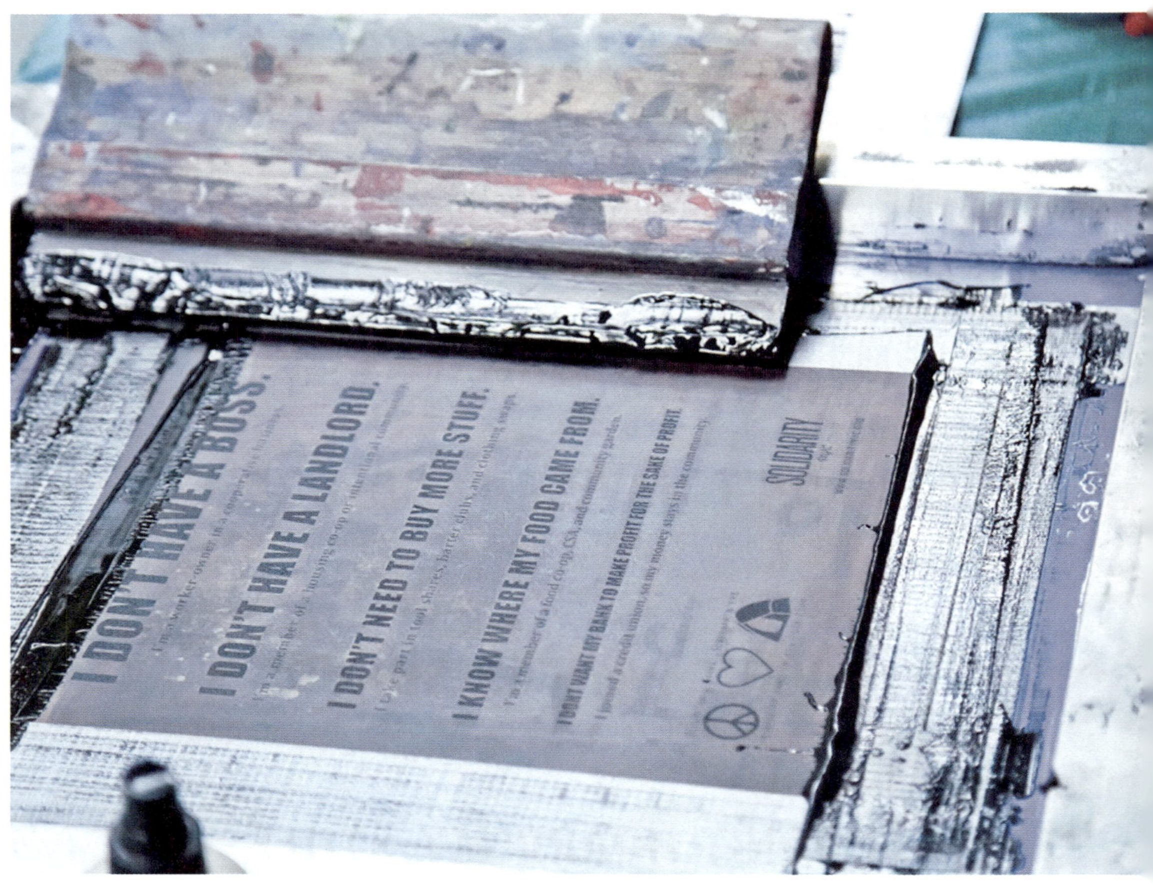

pages 40-41
I Don't Have A Boss, Caroline Woolard for SolidarityNYC, typeset by Andrew Persoff, printed by Patrick Rowe at Exchange Café, 2013.

12.

One day, someone acknowledges your strength, and you smile, and say something like: I know, in the depths of my being, that I help sustain life, and that, as an artist, I am able to let myself feel, and to be present with those feelings.

I am in control of my labor.

I structure desire and imagination. I create space for emotionally open responses. I make memorable symbols. I help to solidify memories and histories. I speak truth to power. I can communicate without words. I use the powers of fiction and play to question norms and reveal possibility. I connect communities—geographic, identity-based, and professional.

How do you feel?

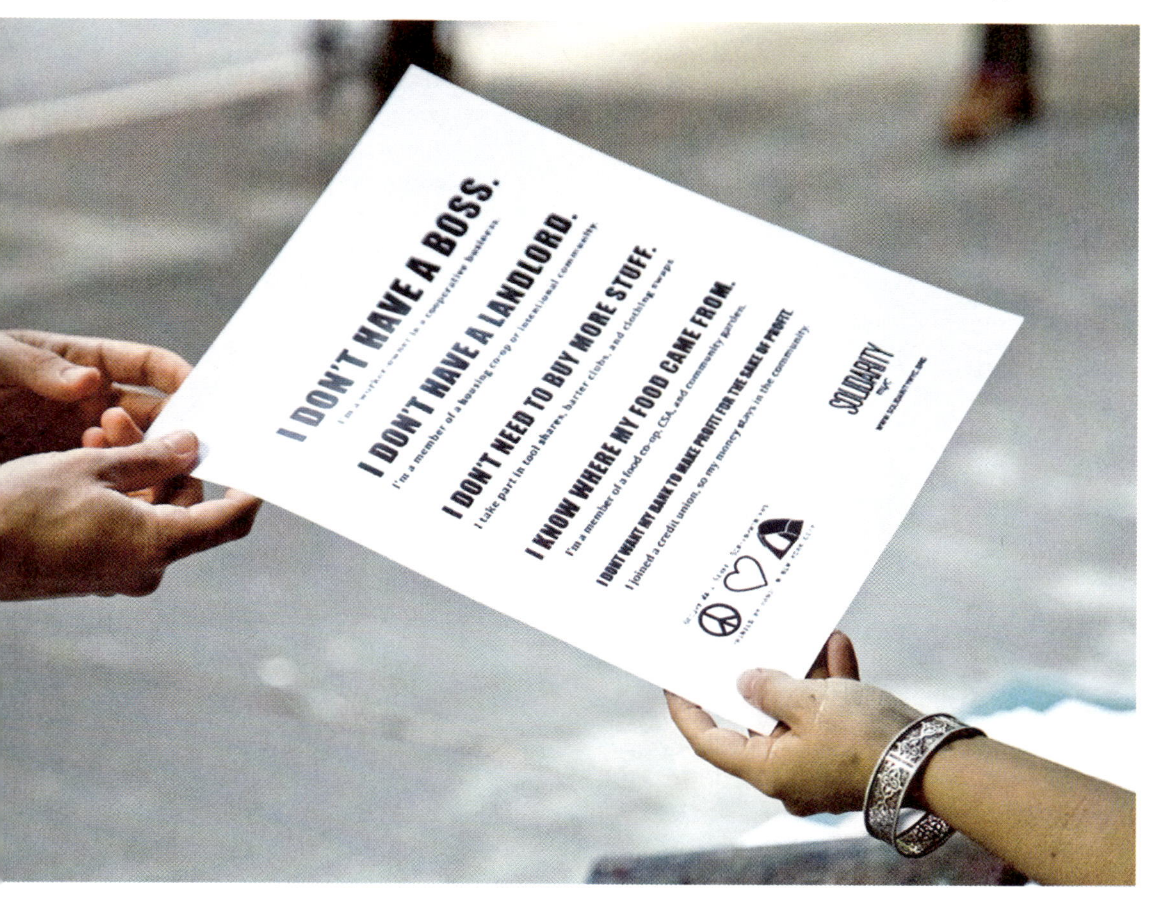

13.

What is here? Dream into it.

Take in the feelings, smells, tastes.

How do you feel?

I invite you to keep dreaming.

In Conversation:
Mierle Laderman Ukeles
and Caroline Woolard

Since 1977, when Mierle Laderman Ukeles became
the official, unsalaried Artist-in-Residence
at the New York City Department of Sanitation—
a position she still holds—she has created art
that deals with the endless maintenance and
service work that "keeps the city alive," urban
waste flows, recycling, ecology, urban sustainability and our power to transform degraded
land and water into healthy inhabitable public
places. Ukeles asks whether we can design modes
of survival—for a thriving planet, not an entropic
one—that don't crush our personal and civic
freedom and silence the individual's voice.

Caroline Woolard (CW):

I remember meeting you at Carol Padberg's
house with Sherry Buckberrough in 2018
when you visited for the 55th anniversary of
your work at the Wadsworth in Connecticut.
You said that you already knew my work,
and you thanked me for it. I want to thank
you for making work like mine possible,
and to acknowledge the path that you have
made for artists by doing what you know is
important work, regardless of what the "art
world" around you says is possible. You
showed us all that long-term projects and
long-term collaborations are possible in the
arts, that the line between "art" and "work"
must continuously be challenged, and that
all art is political. Can we talk about the
similarities and differences between 1969,
when you wrote the *MANIFESTO FOR
MAINTENANCE ART* and now, the pandemic
of COVID-19 in 2020? What has stayed the
same, and what work does the next generation need to make possible?

Mierle Laderman Ukeles (MLU):

In my generation, those feminist
artists who gathered for discussions and meetings at Lucy
Lippard's house didn't talk about
their children. I don't think
they ever mentioned a child in any
of our conversations. And they
also didn't talk about money.
Wow. Imagine the constraints of
that structure.

CW: Wow.

MLU: We didn't talk about these
things then as feminist artists.
So I'm just absolutely so grateful that you have taken on this
subject of economy, just like I
took on maintenance. I'm saying:
Listen, it's not behind the
scenes anymore. It's not just at
night. Behind or below, out of
sight. Here we are! Deal! And
you're saying the same thing about
cultural workers, about getting
paychecks, about exchange.

CW: Yes. Here we are!

MLU: One reason I feel so connected
to you, Caroline, and so grateful, is that in the Sanitation
Department, every two weeks,
people got a paycheck and they
left the office. They said, "I
have to go to the bank now." And
I thought, "Oh, OK." But I didn't
get a paycheck as an artist. And
every single time that happened,
I felt bad. I felt jealous and
really bad. And now I think, well,

there's Caroline. She's going to take care of it. She's got to go talk about it.

you have taken on this subject of economy, just like I took on maintenance.

CW: It is a task for all of us, over generations. And we should note that some artists in other countries—Denmark, Norway, Sweden, and Germany—do get paychecks, as artists, from the government, to make their art. They don't rely on the market or philanthropy like we do in the United States. And it is awful that you do not have the support you deserve. And also: you keep going. Can you say something about your persistence?

MLU: I think this is very important. My persistence. Well, I understood in the depths of my soul then in 1969, with the *MANIFESTO FOR MAINTENANCE ART, 1969!* that I had realized something profound, and that gave me a sense of calm. It enabled me to keep going. It was about hope, seeing life whole. You know, it could be very discouraging and scary and all that, I have to tell you. I mean, the ongoing challenge of my work at Fresh Kills in Staten Island. I got this commission in 1989—Were you alive then?

CW: I was five years old.

MLU: OK. You were five years old. I got a commission to be the Percent for Art Artist of the Fresh Kills Landfill that was the only operating municipal landfill in NYC at that time, the largest in the world, but many were already planning and dreaming for it to become a park. I had worked to develop around 18 proposals. And eventually it came down to one called *LANDING*. I conceptualized it and got it dedicated to a particular site in 2008. *LANDING* is an environmental public artwork, a daring cantilevered overlook soaring over a tidal inlet, with two earthworks on each side. That was twelve years ago and it's still not complete!

CW: Persistence, for sure. Whenever you're doing something that seems impossible or rude or not in the norm, it takes a lot of organizing and persistence and time. How do you keep going?

MLU: People like you make me feel supported. Jack, my life partner, makes me feel supported. I think Leigh Claire, your partner, makes you feel supported. Yeah, you're doing something together. Many workers and public officials have also stuck their own necks out for me along the way. That's very necessary. I think without that support—oh, no—that would be maybe too hard.

CW: Yes, and that is also where the collective work comes in: shared projects, friendships, chosen family.

MLU: Yes. But art also has to have room for the destabilizing individual voice. Where's the room for that voice, which can be raw and disruptive, even to the community and the peaceable contracts that are required to make these communities work? You know, breaking a sense of respect because you're exploding with the original insight that comes from artists. Humans have a capability of human creativity that is so powerful that it has no limits. We can create. We can also just destroy: destroy ourselves, destroy the whole world, which we've just about done. We're on our way. So I see the tension between the free individual and sustaining an effort as often in a kind of conflict.

Where's the room for that voice, which can be raw and disruptive, even to the community and the peaceable contracts that are required to make these communities work?

CW: Between community and this raw and disruptive individual voice? Yes. You also have to balance or hold or consider this tension in your work.

MLU: I've been thinking about solidarity. Solidarity. Art. Economy. Your Manifesto. What is the genesis of this "solidarity economy"?

CW: People trace it back to the '90s and organizing efforts internationally that led to The World Social Forum in Brazil—created in response to the conservative World Economic Forum in Davos, Switzerland, among many other things. The first World Social Forum met in 2001 and connected people working under the umbrella term "solidarity economy," or economic justice. This term is used in many places—Brazil, Italy, Mexico—and also in Montreal and also in the Basque region in Spain, where there's the Mondragon University, a cooperative university. Some people in the United States would say "cooperative economy" or "people's economy" because that's easier to understand here, where we think solidarity is connected only with labor unions, or only with socialism.

MLU: Can you give an example of the solidarity economy in the arts?

CW: I tried to get into MoMA once without paying. You know, it was twenty dollars to get in, in 2009, but I had no cash. So I tried to barter with them. I told the cashier all the things I could give them, like artwork, you know, or singing, or jam. And the cashier was like, "No, sorry, I'm not in charge."

MLU: [Laughs] Hysterical.

CW: And that's when I realized, oh, this is the problem with this structure, because one on one we can make a decision together; in collectives we can make a decision together; in worker-owned businesses we can make a decision together. We can exchange with each other. We can recognize our resources. But with an institution with a hierarchy like MoMA, it's impossible. And that's how I began to understand the power and the limits of one-to-one action, of barter networks and mutual aid. We need the resources to flow regardless of these structures! And it might seem that barter only works at a very small and grassroots scale, but we can look to other countries where these efforts are connected — barter networks, credit unions, land trusts, co-ops—and have political power. So it seems hard to connect these efforts, but actually, we can learn how to do it.

> MLU: When I sent my Manifesto, whose full title is *MANIFESTO FOR MAINTENANCE ART 1969!* Proposal for an exhibition "CARE," to the Whitney in 1969—as a proposal for a full exhibition—I wanted the whole building. I needed that whole entire building for my exhibition. Imagine if you would have seen "CARE" in the early 1970s! The whole entire building would be care for the earth, care for the people, care for the society. We could have gotten much further along as a culture if they took it and let me do it. Instead, I got a response back on one-half of a piece of paper, not even a whole piece of paper. They said: "Try your ideas on or in a gallery first before approaching a museum." I understand that much of the "art world," as it functions, does not function for you and me and that we are going to have to make our way through.

CW: Yes, we must acknowledge that this system of art support is not functioning for the majority of really interesting and powerful artists. And so it is our job to remake these systems because they're collapsing all around us. It's a historical moment to do that, you know.

> MLU: Now, there's the conflict that Ed Ruscha, an artist whose work I admire, is getting

fifty-two million dollars. He's my age. And I am in so much trouble financially. He's getting fifty-two million dollars for one painting.

CW: Well he is not getting that money. A collector is. Someone else in the secondary market is going to see that money. But yeah. Continue. You're not getting fifty-two million.

> MLU: Thank God I still have my project, archives, and office as an Artist In Residence at the New York City Department of Sanitation. But I have to give up my private studio, because I can't pay the rent. People might feel this is a little negative. Like, you know, it's rude. Impolite. To talk about money, like it was to talk about children, before. But that's where I'm at. So I'm saying. Caroline, go do it!

CW: [Laughs] We are up against a lot, but we can talk about money, and about making the art worlds we want to see. Let's hope this book helps.

> MLU: I mean, I know that you have 561 pages here.

In Conversation:
Tina Rivers Ryan and
Caroline Woolard

Tina Rivers Ryan, PhD, is a curator, historian, critic, and educator specializing in art since the 1960s. Her work focuses on the uses of new media technologies. She holds five degrees in art history, including a BA from Harvard and PhD from Columbia.

Tina Rivers Ryan (TRR):

While you've produced many projects focusing on social practices and relations, on a fundamental level, you're a sculptor, so I want to begin this conversation by looking closely at your use of materials. *The Meeting*, for example, is an installation-cum-performance site comprising a boardroom table and chairs; sculptures of walnut, nylon, and rubber; and a single-channel video. I'd like to talk about how the objects relate to your understanding of social space.

Caroline Woolard (CW):

The Meeting see chapter 1 started when I realized that I had spent a decade of my life in meetings. In order to be in interdisciplinary collective projects, I had to spend so many nights and days in awful office spaces and community gathering spaces with fluorescent lighting and Formica tables. And it suddenly occurred to me that, rather than thinking of those spaces as a way to get to a final project or long-term initiative, I could take the meeting itself on as a site to intervene in, both symbolically and structurally. I like thinking about the existing structures that influence behavior, maybe without people noticing or thinking critically about those physical structures and the spatial politics that they imbue in our interactions. I then create objects that recommend entirely different behaviors, thinking about what could happen differently in a boardroom, for example.

TRR: That's clearly a throughline in your practice: your work understands architectural or physical space as fundamentally social. Your sculptures poetically capture—in a visceral, material way—the way that we feel in these spaces. For example, at the table, participants can use wood, acrylic, and paper spheres to transfer the ability to speak and to determine what kinds of communication are going to transpire; their tactility and weight helps us understand that our verbal communication is very much embodied and informed by its physical and discursive contexts.

The Meeting see chapter 1 also includes a bust made of mycelium, the mushroom material that eats agricultural waste, which underscores your almost ecological concern with interdependence in group dynamics. It's suspended in a net that hangs on the wall, which really gives us a sense of gravity acting on the body. I look at these objects and I see echoes of post-minimalism: you're building on the legacy of an artist like Eva Hesse, who similarly used netting to suspend objects from a wall, haunting abstract sculpture with reminders of the body.

your work understands architectural or physical space as fundamentally social.

CW: I appreciate what you're saying about materiality and the corporeal experience so much. It's important to me that these sculptures, for example, could be carried by a facilitator to a meeting—so they have a functional purpose—but that they also can hang on the wall and refer to Eva Hesse's work as art objects.

TRR: In terms of the way that you build on the legacy of post-minimalism, it seems to me that you're connecting the concerns of sculpture to our supposedly dematerialized information economy (which of course is tied to meetings that happen around boardroom tables just like yours). What would it mean to think about this installation, and the components that comprise it, as being new media art? For example, I wonder if your use of netting here refers not only to Hesse, but also to the internet, which itself is a network of social relations?

CW: For me, yes, the netting is about the internet, or a network, but it's also about trapping, about containment, about capture. It's about the expansive potential of a material to suggest such a disparate range of concepts, like a network, but it's also about a colonial net. It was important to me—even if very few people would understand this—that the net itself would materially speak to a core tension in the socially engaged art world. When an artist represents a collective practice in an art context, the artist instrumentalizes something that is deeply contextual. This has a colonial legacy, taking something that is so contextual, like a practice of facilitation within a specific community, and appropriating it for the artist's own purposes, making it autonomous from its original context. This was my internal realization about what it means to present facilitation practices. Working with Esteban Kelly, the director of the US Federation of Worker Co-ops, outside of art spaces but also in The Galleries at Moore and at the Rose Art Museum, how could I maturely speak to that core conflict and allow the object to symbolically hold that tension? It was a lot about that. This led me to thinking about colonial net making: the net here is actually a kind of landing net that was used in Philadelphia that I morphed into a square. The person who wove the net is part of a colonial reenactment group that makes landing nets as a hobby. In terms of extended practice, it's important to me that the laborers identify with something conceptually that I am interested in.

netting is about the internet, or a network, but it's also about trapping, about containment, about capture.

TRR: I love the way that your thinking engages the ideas that are central to "net" art, but from within a sculptural practice. For example, you point out the fundamental paradox of trying to instrumentalize social practices that happen within a particular context as sculptural installations that inevitably are divorced from that context. This relates to one of the essential aspects of how information and ideas circulate on the internet, right? The internet is basically a machine for generating content that then becomes divorced from its source.

I wonder how this connects with the way that a single project of yours can exist in different media. It reminds me of hypertext, which allows for a nonlinear, non-hierarchical relationship between ideas. There's something about the way that you are dealing with performance and social practice, and translating these into installations or sculptures—these all become hyper-texted to each other, in a kind of horizontal way (for example, the objects don't become secondary to the performances, like relics). They all point to each other and refer to each other, in a constellation of practices and objects.

I was also thinking about hypertext in relationship to your work to the degree that your work is about protocols. A lot of net artists focus on the protocols that govern how we navigate the web, and how information is distributed (e.g., through hyperlinks). Your work is also, in its own way, about the protocols that structure our communication. You're not dealing with uniform resource locators, but you are dealing with the ways we "address" each other, and the protocols that we use to determine our interactions. Your work

can help us understand how these protocols function, and how they shape our social space in the same way as, for example, the boardroom table that is at the center of this work. It's one of those objects that seems completely innocuous and designed to not draw attention to itself, much like the protocols of the modern information economy. And yet its form actually encodes values. The table identifies a community of people who are allowed to participate in this dialogue; it separates actors from bystanders. Even the rectangularity of it, with two "heads," implies that this is a space that may not be as egalitarian as it seems. And then the specificity of the chairs that you use—they look like Aeron knock-offs—points to a particular kind of white-collar (and racially white) space.

Speaking of communities: even the way that you work, which is through collaborations between networks of people that unfold over time, reminds me of early net art, which often was explicitly opposed to the individualism of the art world and/or credited to anonymous collectives.

A lot of net artists focus on the protocols that govern how we navigate the web

CW: It excited me when you said that the work can speak to protocols and the idea that you can always link to something else. I cannot imagine a sculptural object without a long-term platform, like a multi-year collective, or a long-term initiative. Often these have online networks that I collaborate on with developers, computer engineers, and graphic designers. I never imagine that the first encounter with the object will be in a gallery space, which is still often the norm in sculptural practice. So I love this idea that it is always already mediated in multiple ways. That's what I've been trying to tease out in this crazy process diagram about the flow of my mind from studying, for example, the solidarity economy, to making a commitment, moving into a space of inquiry, choosing whether to be a short-term project or a long-term platform, experimenting, and then studying again. What I'm trying to show is that every aspect of the mediation or life of the object needs to be considered from the outside.

It feels important also to say that mycelium relates to the metaphor of the rhizome, which is also very present in the net itself. I think about every sculpture as a kind of fruit within a tree. It's the shiny and short lived thing, but then the tree is the long-term platform that really shapes discourse. The practices are like mycelial roots that connect all these other initiatives to one another, which is absolutely a net art kind of image.

This book itself holds that problem. I think in the worst case—the most boring case—it could be seen as a monograph. A monograph focuses on products rather than the process; in my mind, a book about an artist's practice is most interesting when it reveals behind-the-scenes labor, so there's a lot of budgets and correspondences here. At the same time, this book examines my own working method, and it's the first time I've ever done something like this. While I want to share how I work, to do

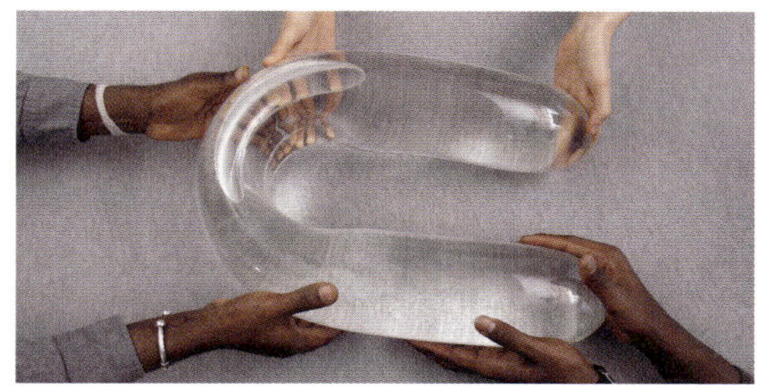

so required checking in with collaborators to see if I could share our process. This points to a core tension in collaborative work: who gets to name their collaborators, and who is the collaborator who doesn't have a book like this? It's been an ongoing challenge for me to figure out when to work collectively, which I always do for long-term projects because I think that shifting discourse requires that, and when to work individually, which for now I do when I'm making sculptural objects that are more symbolic and that can allow me to be with the quirks and whims of my own aesthetic desires for a short-term project.

This points to a core tension in collaborative work: who gets to name their collaborators, and who is the collaborator who doesn't have a book like this?

TRR: Maybe it helps to think about that core tension as being essentially a question of perspective. Especially with interdisciplinary practices like yours, the designation of the main protagonist—or the person who "gets to name their collaborators"—depends on who's telling the story. In the case of *Carried on Both Sides*, which looks at the history and future of the @ symbol [see chapter 8] I would say, as a curator, that you and Helen Lee are the primary protagonists. But if I was a glass blower instead of a curator, then Jason Christian and Daryl Smith, the master crafts-people at Pilchuck Glass School who fabricated some of your works, might be the main protagonists and you and Helen would be secondary.

As long as I brought up your work at Pilchuck, I want to talk about *Countermeasures* [see chapter 8]. You have included this description of the work in this book: "made of glass and filled with mineral oil, each object may reach a level state through the process of being shared, held, and manipulated. In gatherings facilitated by the artist, visitors are asked to remove these objects from the wall and reach a level with others in the space, whether friends or strangers."

Glass is this incredibly evocative material with a very long history that you have explored elsewhere in your work. In the twentieth century, glass gained a powerful association with modernism and with the values of modernism, such as transparency and universality. There have been a lot of artists who have gone back to that legacy and tried to understand it and complicate it; I am thinking of everybody from Dan Graham to Josiah McElheny. But in the context of your practice, and your interest in networks, I'm also thinking about how glass in fiber optic cables and silica in silicon chips have become literally the medium of electronic communications and computing. The world we live in now depends on the transmission of information through transparent mediums, which is ironic, as communication is not transparent, or disembodied, or universal—as this work points out. The intention is for the group to put their hands on the glass object and work together to make it level—but it's an impossible task. So instead of a flattening of difference—a "leveling" of subjects—it enacts the constant recalibration of group dynamics.

This idea of leveling for me ties back to the work of Lygia Clark, specifically her stone and air sculpture from 1966, which was this plastic bag filled with air with a stone balanced on it. You would compress the bag with your hands and then release it, causing the stone to rise and fall into and out of the bag. She intended this to have a kind of therapeutic effect on the person using it (the work was inspired by the bag that protected the cast around her fractured hand). In your work, the healing is a kind of group healing, or group therapy.

CW: I love the work of Lygia Clark. What's exciting to me about someone who leaves the arts, as she did, is that they say "yes, I want to be the protagonist of another story," as you were saying. I appreciate that about her practice and her object making. I think if you're truly interdisciplinary, you're up against that tension all the time. When is your work so far into another discipline that it might grow more in dialogue with that discipline? In terms of the idea of leveling, I called this work *Countermeasures* see chapter 8 because it can't really be level. It's not flat, it's this sort of sensual clear blob, and it droops in this shape that wants to be like a Martin Puryear sculpture, but it can be held and touched.

It's important to me to preserve the formal sensuality that I see in the artists whom I love who come from this legacy of modernism that resists social and political context, but also to activate my objects as hypertexts and countermeasures. Hopefully it can hold those contradictions of wanting to bring a group together while knowing the impossibility of doing that in any fully horizontal or fair way.

When is your work so far into another discipline that it might grow more in dialogue with that discipline?

TRR: The way you describe *Countermeasures* see chapter 8 also reminds me of the legacy parallel to modernism of avant-garde artists like Marcel Duchamp, who also worked with glass, but who consistently resisted the rhetoric of transparency and emphasized embodiment, and even produced what we could call "countermeasures," like the *3 Standard Stoppages* or *50 cc of Paris Air*. Thinking of Duchamp and the conceptualism that emerged in his wake, your work is also

about understanding that the point is the process, right? That there is no end to it: it's a constantly unfolding act of engagement.

CW: Yes, you know what I love! While Duchamp took credit for the famous urinal, *Fountain*, when in fact it was made by Elsa von Freytag-Loringhoven, I am obsessed with *3 Standard Stoppages*. The first project I proposed at MoMA was not Exchange Café see chapter 4, it was a project all about unconventional measures, including *Stoppages* and Robert Watts' and George Maciunas' *10-Hour Flux Clock*. Anyway, one reason I'm drawn to glass is that it can constantly be reused and recycled, especially if you use clear glass instead of colored glass. You can literally throw this back in the furnace. So that's exciting to me as a material reality. But at the same time, there's a political economy here: it costs thousands of dollars to run a glass shop.

TRR: Speaking of economies: We have this fantasy that the exchange of information is frictionless, that our entire economy is frictionless. In reality, of course none of this is frictionless. Bitcoin mining, for example, generates heat and requires incredible energy resources. I wonder if a lot of your work is about exploring friction. Looking at *Countermeasures* see chapter 8 in particular, it looks vaguely like a sex toy, which perhaps signals the idea of finding the pleasure in friction, as opposed to in the frictionless. I wanted to talk about the shape of this because it has this strange, bodily connotation (perhaps another reference to Hesse): it's weirdly bulbous

and could be read as phallic, but
also could be read as sort of like
pendulous breasts—an ambiguity
that seems to demand an analysis
of the work in terms of your own
identity as a queer woman.

That said, I'm wary of a politics
of representation that calls upon
artists to represent themselves
and their identities in their
art. There's a tension between
the demand for visibility, which
for some people is the premise of
political action, and the refusal
to be visible, which for other
people is the premise of safety.
In terms of queer aethetics, I
think about the work of David
Getsy on the minimalism of Scott
Burton, and the way that Burton's
sculptures—even his totally
abstract minimal ones—can be read
as being queer.

CW: I just taught a whole class about that kind of queer minimalism, I love that writing and that work! I would be honored for my work to be read in relationship to the queer aesthetics outlined by Getsy. But, I agree, I question evoking my minoritized identities in the reading of my, or really anyone's work, as we do not see that happening with straight, white, men. I feel torn in exactly the ways you outlined, between visibility as a trap that limits the reading of any work and visibility as a way of forming solidarity for artists who feel invisible and want a shared platform. I often talk at art schools to very young people who don't feel supported or loved, who might want to hear that I am alive, and even thriving at times, as a queer person.

But on the other hand, I think of Audre Lorde saying, "There's always someone asking you to underline one piece of yourself—whether it's Black, woman, mother, dyke, teacher, etc.— because that's the piece that they need to key in to. They want to dismiss everything else." I go back and forth, because I'd say it's more important to think of myself as one person in the vast sea of history. You know, in the C. L. R. James and historical materialist way? As individuals, history shapes each of us far more than we can shape history. What I mean is that I just happened to be alive during the rise of web 2.0 and the financial crisis and because I was in New York City and went to Cooper Union, among so many things, including my identity, I was able to work with friends and make projects that were taken seriously and given opportunities to explore ideas in ways that other people absolutely do not get—and I wouldn't have had these opportunities, I think, if I'd been born even ten years earlier or later. I happened to ride a wave of history, to flow like a wave among my fellow waves.

TRR: Do we want to be meta for a
second again and talk about the
way in which the structure of the
book that people are holding in
their hands is itself informed by
your identity, and your practice?

CW: There is a navigation structure that I worked on with the designer, Angela Lorenzo, that reflects my working process, so as you're moving through the book you can see where you are. There's also a kind of associational cartographic index at the end that's organized by collaborator or material or tension (maybe we should call it friction now). The idea is that you can move through the book in multiple ways, like you would online, while allowing it to still flow from cover to cover if you wish.

TRR: It seems like in the designing of the book you captured so many of the themes that run throughout your practice: the importance of context; the question of labor and the material conditions of labor; and what I call hypertext (although maybe there's a better word for it), or the notion of the interdependence or interrelation of ideas and people, which manifests in your index. I wonder if the design will help people see that there is a tension in your work between being very tight and internally consistent, and being very open and pointing to all these different associations, thanks to the amount of research into different bodies of knowledge and historical periods that you have done for a lot of your projects. (For example, this manifests in your use of netting to refer to the internet and networks of people and traps and colonial histories.) I think of your work as being almost like a supernova, something incredibly dense but that explodes and goes in many directions.

CW: My friend Susan Jahoda, who I collaborate and work on pedagogical projects with, says I'm like the air. I'm zooming around like a balloon because I'm so interested in making associations and connections, in bringing in new people and doing wide-ranging research. I'm also, in that way, incredibly messy. So it's interesting to juxtapose that apparent aesthetic neatness with the lived material reality of constantly making associations. For example, my desk is a mess. I put everything in different bags—it's like my net sculpture—because I see everything as possibly connected; I see patterns and potential all around. While it might not seem this way, it's very, very hard for me to get to a place of polish. Maybe your metaphor of a supernova makes sense in that way, with every object connected to infinite associations, events, long term initiatives, and websites.

Another thing your supernova reminded me of is this part in Robert Musil's unfinished novel *The Man Without Qualities*, where he writes something like "believing in kings is like believing in stars that one sees even though they ceased to exist thousands of years ago." Maybe there's something about the supernova that I can relate to in that the moment this book is out it will already be … past. Sure, we can believe in these practices, but the conditions that allowed them to be possible are already like a star that you might admire but is long gone. So you have to invent your own narrative, ride your own wave in the sea of history—in other words, envision and work within your own material conditions—to be able to really make use of this book.

1

The Meeting

Many artists have a sense that art and life should be fused. We know that art does not belong exclusively in galleries, museums, or in institutional spaces, as creativity is everywhere and cannot be contained or made scarce. Even if we show our work in galleries and museums, we know that the majority of things we make will come back home to live with us. Every art object we make cannot be collected or sold; there are too many.

And so, for most of us, the question arises: How can I fuse art and life?

> Should my art live in the streets, to support political protest?
>
> Should my art live in a garden, to support regenerative life?
>
> Should my art live in a home, to support maintenance and social reproduction?
>
> Should my art live in a learning space, to support skill sharing and growth?

In 2013, I decided: my art should live in meetings, to support discussion and debate about the solidarity economy. This began a long exploration of ways to fuse my love of group processes with my love of object-making.

I am devoted to meetings where everyone attends voluntarily, where people are not obligated by a boss to be present. I spend the majority of my time in meetings with two to twenty people that take place in community groups, cooperatives, artist-run spaces, and collectives; I prefer these spaces to meetings that happen in workplaces where workers do not get to weigh in on the conditions that they work within. In the best moments, in voluntary meetings, there is a sense among participants that the process is spontaneous, collaborative, and transformative.

Meetings are what make my projects possible. I love to plan meetings, to participate in them, and to think about them. I define a meeting as a scheduled gathering of people where participants are able to speak extemporaneously about a shared topic. At their best, meetings are a form of mediation. They ask participants to reconsider practices and habits and potentially allow something new to emerge, both relationally and conceptually.

I define a meeting as a scheduled gathering of people where participants are able to speak extemporaneously about a shared topic.

For me, meetings of this form are a space for lifelong learning. Where else can you go to think with other people, to move from study to action, to build friendships, and to transform your understanding of the world, in community?

At a SolidarityNYC meeting in 2009, I remember finding out about the emergent cooperative movement in New York City, and being invited to bring my media-making skills to the work ahead. It was exciting to be sitting at a table with people who talked about how to connect worker-owned businesses to credit unions and community gardens across the city, and then to help as we did this by making videos, a website, and graphics with the group. It was here that I learned about transformative organizing, as the SolidarityNYC collective invited members to gather every weekend to talk about the challenges we each faced in "becoming the change" we wanted to see in the world. Each person would have 30 minutes, or an hour, to share the ways that they lived and worked through the contradictions of desiring a cooperative world and living in an extractive and exploitative one.

As an artist, I wondered: What might strange objects (sculptures) do to the conventions of meetings? Can objects open up space for reflection and the wild unknown? I wanted to do more than to make posters, websites, murals, and traditional media for groups of activists and organizers.

I have always been interested in objects that can guide a space. I thought: There must be something more powerful than a sticky note or a circle of chairs for a meeting. As a white, European-American person, raised agnostic yet celebrating a market-driven version of Christmas, I grew up with an impoverished cultural imaginary about aesthetically compelling, emotionally open, or directly democratic gatherings. My parents, their parents, and their parents all passed down to me a false legacy of "whiteness" as our general racial identity and heritage. Rather than being told about my German and Swedish heritage, for example, I was told that I was simply "white" with no connection to any particular ancestral lineage; without culturally specific rituals or objects that I might take pride in beyond assimilation into a dominant culture of white, settler-colonial America. In this way, and many others, my parents participated in an unspoken project of assimilation into whiteness as a monolithic category.

> What rituals for gatherings can I bring to gatherings? Again, I want to make objects for secular meeting spaces, but my family passed down no ritual objects or awareness of the specificity of my heritage that I could draw from. I started thinking about contemporary artists who have reimagined ritual spaces and objects from their own social positions and heritage.
>
> For example:
>
> The sculptor and performance artist Allison Smith writes that she is "motivated by a sense of accountability for harms caused by my

ancestors," and has therefore "spent many years investigating the cultural phenomenon of historical reenactment as the ritualized performance of unresolved trauma."[5]

The project *Game Remains, (Guelph)* created by Postcommodity in 2013, uses, as the collective describes, a "ceremonial conceptual framework" to "transform participants into musicians engaged in a community instrument of self-determination."[6]

The mixed-media installation with video, *I prayed to the wrong god for you*, made by Tiona Nekkia McClodden in 2019, includes a ritual for the Santería/Lucumi god Shango as well as documentation of the creation of ritual objects.

The temporary shelter made for shared meals during the Jewish festival of harvest during Succoth, *Gardening Sukkah*, from 2000 by Allan Wexler.

Most facilitators — people who guide meetings — do not assume specific religious or shared cultural heritage in the majority of the community meetings I have attended. What objects already exist in these secular community meeting spaces? Sticky notes, clocks, fluorescent bulbs, ceiling tiles, formica tables, old plastic chairs. What excites me is the possibility that an object can produce a shared meaning within the context of a gathering; that it can guide meeting participants to some genuinely new space or thought or make the travel of reaching such a destination that much easier. I have also had to check my own assumptions in this process.

As an artist who spends hours each day looking at and making art, the references that shape the way I "read" any object, including the ones that I make, are far different from

---

5
Artist's website:
allisonsmithstudio.com/
s-t-a-t-e-m-e-n-t

6
Artist's website:
postcommodity.com/GameRemains

many of the people I find myself in meetings with, who are not artists. For example, the giant mycelium head that I made was only used by facilitators and groups that already include theatricality and role playing as part of their meeting culture. In many of the meetings I attended, and offered objects for gathering, the mycelium head simply sat there, unused, as it seemed too strange or too much like an expensive art-object.

I grew up with an impoverished cultural imaginary about aesthetically compelling, emotionally open, or directly democratic gatherings

I finally accepted that my glass water clocks, my mycelium head, and my nets took too long to explain for the majority of meeting scenarios; they required a facilitator who would introduce them, and move the group from a culture of verbal discussion to a culture of movement, haptic awareness, and embodied leadership. Not wanting my objects to seem elite, ritual-like, or untouchable, I began to develop *The Meeting Game*. This game asks participants to roll spheres across the table. I found that this game was approachable because the spheres live easily on a meeting table, imply movement, cannot break, and come in multiples so they do not seem precious.

What excites me is the possibility that an object can produce a shared meaning within the context of a gathering; that it can guide meeting participants to some genuinely new space or thought

The game visualizes the flow of dialogue, as each person starts out with the same number of spheres, and a person must roll a sphere to another person, or "spend it," in order to speak. In this way, the spheres act as a kind of currency. People can redistribute spheres without speaking, if they wish. When played in a meeting, the game has the effect of both slowing down the flow of conversation and exchange as well as making visible who is speaking, how often, and to whom. In this intersection of artistic relation and social relation, I see an opening toward a new work culture and perhaps a new economic formation as well.

The game visualizes the flow of dialogue, as each person starts out with the same number of spheres, and a person must roll a sphere to another person, or "spend it," in order to speak. In this way, the spheres act as a kind of currency.

I have long had an interest in community-generating currencies and other ways to imagine and visualize the flow of resources outside of our existing, capital-driven economy. For example, I did so at both Exchange Café see chapter 4 as well as the barter networks TradeSchool.coop and OurGoods.org see chapter 3. I believe that the only way in which we will have a new economy and an economy that works for many artists is for artists themselves to begin the project of imagining, representing, and instantiating new organizations of labor, currency, and infrastructure. It is my lifelong ambition to make art that enables people to imagine and enact practices of solidarity economies.

Imagine that the next time you walk into a meeting room and sit down, rather than getting out your laptop, iPad or notebook, you pick up a group of ceramic spheres and start rolling them across the table to signal who is speaking, who is not, and for how long. Imagine that addressing items on an agenda involves a collective somatic experience — the picking up and putting down of tactile things, the exchange of objects that invite a different kind of relationship with your peers. This is the work of Caroline Woolard.

—Curators Anna Harsanyi and Macushla Robinson, 2019

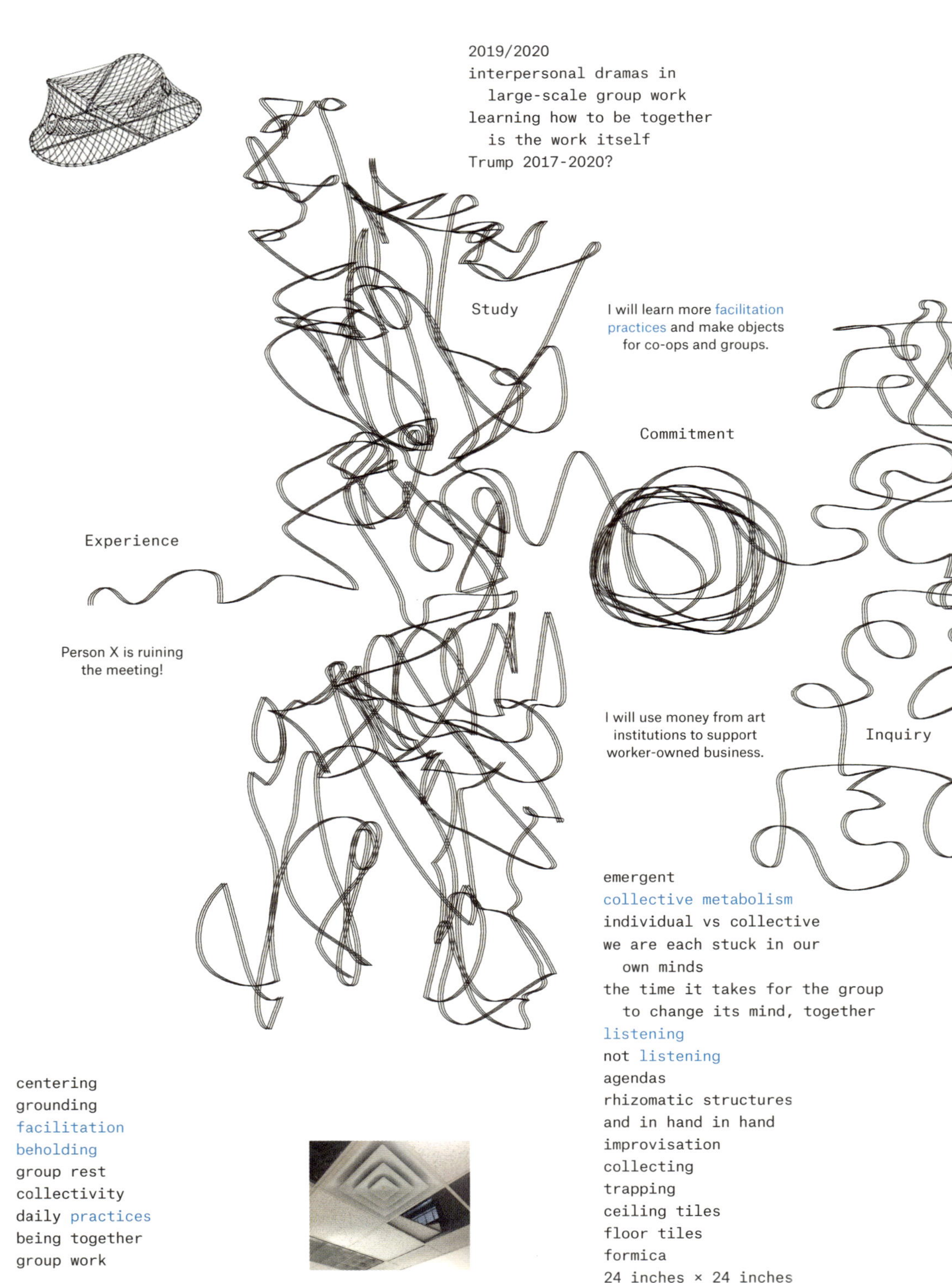
Reflect
Idea in Public
Experiment
Timeframe
Inquiry
Commitment
Study
Experience

2019/2020
interpersonal dramas in
   large-scale group work
learning how to be together
   is the work itself
Trump 2017-2020?

Study

I will learn more facilitation
practices and make objects
for co-ops and groups.

Commitment

Experience

Person X is ruining
the meeting!

I will use money from art
institutions to support
worker-owned business.

Inquiry

emergent
collective metabolism
individual vs collective
we are each stuck in our
   own minds
the time it takes for the group
   to change its mind, together
listening
not listening
agendas
rhizomatic structures
and in hand in hand
improvisation
collecting
trapping
ceiling tiles
floor tiles
formica
24 inches × 24 inches

centering
grounding
facilitation
beholding
group rest
collectivity
daily practices
being together
group work

Institutional
Invitation

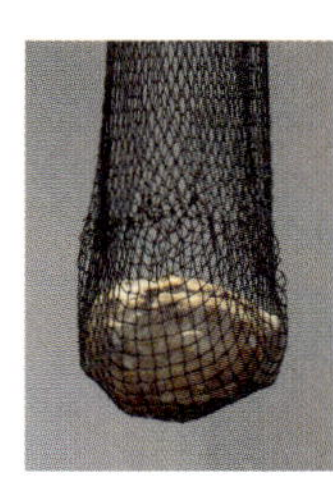

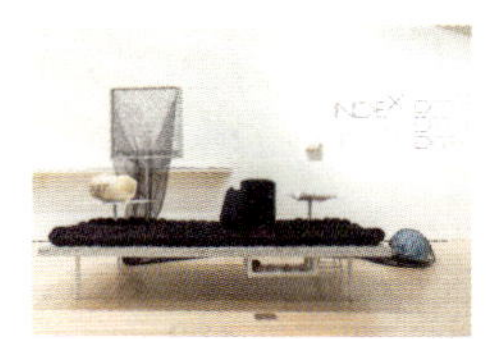

objects for meetings
like Clue
ritual
the artist with the candle
  in the ballroom
continuous study
facilitation : sculpture
local facilitators using
  objects I make
U.S. Federation of Worker
  Cooperatives
Ombuds
DePaul Labor Education Center

rolling
balls
spheres
mycelium bust
Zeus
video
nets
ceiling tiles
daybed
website
events

Timeframe

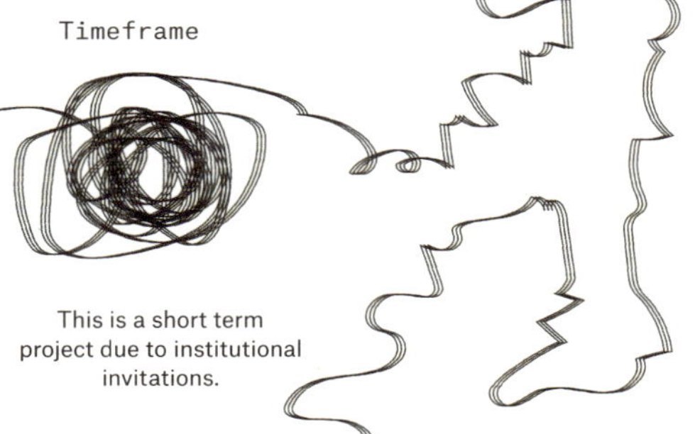

This is a short term
project due to institutional
invitations.

Idea in Public

Objects for groups that a
library patron can check out.

Reflect

Experiment

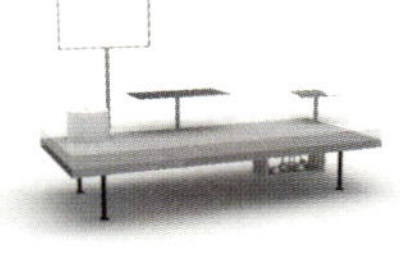

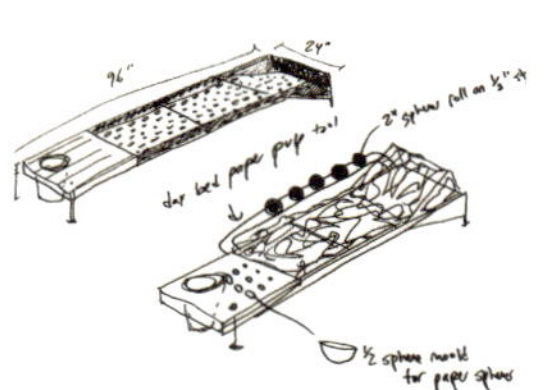

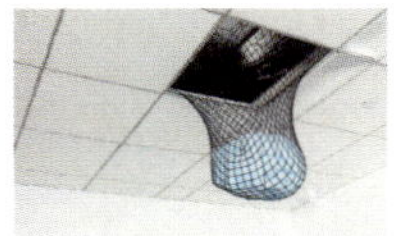

Study Center for Group Work
can contextual, local collective
  practices be shared?
cultural appropriation
talking sticks
indigenous and colonial net
  making
minimalist artists' nets
Eva Hesse
Jiro Takamatsu
history of ceiling tiles
"dropped" ceiling

"false" ceiling
air diffusers, smoke detectors,
  sprinklers, CCTV cameras, and
  neon lights
"debt ceiling"
"glass" ceiling"
a limit
mycelial networks
transformative organizing
U.S.Federation of Worker
  Cooperatives
disability justice

conflict transformation
Generative Somatics
Judith Leemann and
  Kenneth Bailey
UltraRed
Center for Artistic Activism
SOVRN state Scott Benaglio
Process Work Institute

The Meeting

Gabrielle Lavin Suzenski, Rochelle F. Levy
Director of The Galleries at Moore College of
Art & Design

Gabrielle Lavin Suzenski, Rochelle F. Levy
Director of the Galleries at Moore, began her
career in the Fabric Workshop and Museum's
post-college apprenticeship program, which
led to a full time position working with the
founder/artistic director in coordinating the
museums's relocation in 2006. She has an MBA
in Entrepreneurship & Innovation and a BFA
in Sculpture and Printmaking, both from Penn
State University.

*Think of the last meeting you were in. What did
it feel like?*

The Meeting presents a selection of recent
work by New York-based artist Caroline
Woolard (b. 1984, Rhode Island) that takes
"the meeting" itself—the gathering of people
for a formal purpose—as a site for artistic
and social intervention. Themes of collectivity
and political economy recur in Woolard's work,
and after a decade of working in arts collectives and creating socially engaged projects,
she recognized that she had spent at least half
of her artistic life in meetings.

Most people will spend over a quarter of their
lives at work. For office workers, a large
portion of this time will occur in meetings. In
The Meeting, Woolard evokes the human body
through its absence in the banal physicality of
offices. Electrical outlets, ceiling tiles, and
meeting tables intimate the power dynamics
of meetings. A tongue hangs from the ceiling.
This array of sculptural objects, as well as a
series of videos and a game placed on a
boardroom table, reflect upon the unavoidable
antagonisms of working together.

As the first recipient of the Jane & David
Walentas Endowed Fellowship, Woolard asks:
Can a job be pleasurable? Does pleasure in
work require self-determination? How do
workers without bosses (i.e. worker-owners in
cooperative businesses) transform workplace
conflict? Woolard has taken the past year to
learn facilitation practices from the United
States Federation of Worker Cooperatives

Study

(USFWC), the national grassroots membership organization for worker-owned businesses.

In cooperatives, unlike other businesses, workers share profits and participate in oversight, and often in the management of the enterprise, using democratic practices. Facilitation—the skillful guiding of the meeting process—is a key part of running a cooperative or self-organized group, because people in horizontal groups such as a cooperative share power and must attend meetings in order to make decisions together. Woolard has learned conflict transformation techniques from facilitators at USFWC while developing sculptural objects that are used to facilitate meetings. Sculptural objects like these will be available at the Free Library of Philadelphia in the spring of 2020 for library patrons to check out and use.

Can a job be pleasurable? Does pleasure in work require self-determination?

One set of objects is presented in framed nets. Cascading from the ceiling and hung on the wall, these nets "catch" and "trap" facilitation objects and make reference to both the fishing nets of colonial Philadelphia and to the minimalist, conceptual works of the artists Eva Hesse and Jiro Takamatsu. Here, square walnut frames mirror the shape and scale of ubiquitous ceiling tiles, suspended overhead in meeting spaces as "dropped" or "false" ceilings. By definition, the false ceiling is a surface that hides the infrastructure installed above it—air diffusers, smoke detectors, sprinklers, CCTV cameras, and neon lights—from the room below. In everyday speech, the ceiling acts as a metaphor for a limit which cannot be trusted. Think of a "glass ceiling" or a "debt ceiling." The net sculptures fit perfectly in everyday office ceilings and have been installed in the gallery as well as in an unnamed office in the area.

This exhibition suggests that artists can bring studio-based sculptural techniques to an approach to art-making that emphasizes participation and dialogue.

The artist writes:

> My approach arises from three desires I have: (1) to make objects that resonate in the field of art and that acknowledge the cultural specificity of the field itself; (2) to make objects that are used by facilitators in co-op and self-organized settings; (3) to allow myself to participate in a non-extractive way in facilitation settings and meetings with groups that are not concerned with the field of art. I want to offer my skills as an artist and honor existing, slowly developed, community-generated facilitation skills in the context of organizing for economic justice. For example, rather than putting co-op members on display for a museum performance, I will attempt to display objects that reflect upon co-op practices.

Woolard has determined to present sculptural objects as surrogates for the social practices of cooperative meetings.

I want to offer my skills as an artist and honor existing, slowly developed, community-generated facilitation skills in the context of organizing for economic justice.

While some objects are exhibited for contemplation on the wall, or trapped in the ceiling in a net, *The Meeting Game* invites interaction and rewrites the meeting script. Participation here occurs as visitors wait in the lobby at Moore, or as art classes gather around the table, rather than in a spectacular event in public space with the artist. At the boardroom table in the gallery, facilitation objects are available for use, to encourage new forms of interpersonal exchange. Viewers are invited to watch the video, learn how to play the game, and roll a ball that corresponds to a way of speaking. In doing so, viewers may become more aware of the flow of dialogue in any conversation. This game, developed in collaboration with USFWC's Executive Director, Esteban Kelly, will continue to be refined by the USFWC in nonart settings and also throughout the semester in workshops and public programs with the artist. In *The Meeting*, viewers are encouraged to be present with their concerns or curiosity about work, and about working together.

Study

Institutional
Invitation

INDEX: The Meeting

Caitlin Julia Rubin, Assistant Curator, Rose Art Museum, 2020.

Caitlin Julia Rubin is a curator at the Rose Art Museum at Brandeis University. Since joining the Rose, she has organized exhibitions and projects by Mark Dion, Rosalyn Drexler, Jennie C. Jones, and Tuesday Smillie, among others, and collaborated with visiting artists to foster new, site-responsive initiatives, including Caroline Woolard's *INDEX: The Meeting* (2019–20).

In the Fall of 2019, the Rose Art Museum debuted a new initiative, INDEX at the Lee Gallery. INDEX seeks to experiment with new formats for engagement in the museum's galleries; within its ongoing program, two artists per year are invited to create site-responsive and participatory projects. Though centered in the museum's Lee gallery, the influence of these projects radiates across the whole of the Rose Art Museum's spaces and processes. Each artist engagement is, at its base, an invitation to disrupt and make room to rethink what the museum does, and by what means it might build community and space for collective action. It was very early in our brainstorming about INDEX that I realized I knew the perfect person to lead the charge of its first installment: Caroline Woolard.

As the Rose Art Musuem's inaugural INDEX artist and the museum's 2019–20 Ruth Ann and Nathan Perlmutter Artist-in-Residence, Woolard chose the meeting as a site for artistic and social intervention. Her INDEX entry, *The Meeting*, invited participants to explore more open, aware, and intentional exchanges, designating the Lee Gallery as a space for generative dialogue. Combining the formal language of her sculptural practice with tools and techniques used for group facilitation, her central work *The Meeting Game* (2019–ongoing) built off of the conventional meeting format to open an investigation into different systems for collaboration and cooperation.

Spurred by Woolard's proposition, museum visitors, organized groups, and university classes collectively contributed to *The Meeting Game*'s evolving platform, using it to think through ideas and to foster discussion. Members of the Brandeis University community hosted open conversations centered on specific, challenging topics: how to talk about politics at the dinner table, cultures of bullying on campus, and even the occasionally intimidating nature of contemporary art itself. Over the course of Woolard's residency, *The Meeting Game* continued to be refined in workshops, public programs, and the addition of sculptural facilitation tools constructed in collaboration with students, faculty, and staff at Brandeis.

These tools—new balls, nets, experimental mats for game organization, and sculptural busts for directed conversation—were shown in various stages of development, displayed on and adjacent to *The Meeting Game*'s playing surface. Their inclusion allowed visitors to engage not only with the means and methods for collaboration, but also the fabrication of objects that structure these engagements.

Woolard began to create sculptures using mycelium, the vegetative root structure of fungi. Activated and tended over time, this living material can expand into shaped form. At the Rose Art Museum, partnership with the Brandeis MakerLab and the support of their Impact Maker Program enabled Woolard to expand the processes of her studio within the gallery. In a mold rendered from the digital scan of a carved bust of Zeus—an object found by Woolard in the museum's permanent collection—Brandeis sculpture and biology undergraduates packed and then cultivated a mycelium mixture. In the Rose Art Museum's Lee Gallery, they grew a sculpture. The use of this mycelium might be read as a material metaphor for Woolard's

approach to a socially engaged artistic practice—a practice in which she seeks, through meaningful collaboration, to activate and ally latent and often disparate energies into generative form. In her work, and through her INDEX project, Woolard asks: what potential exists within our own community, and how can we connect through conversations that will allow us to work, in better ways, together?

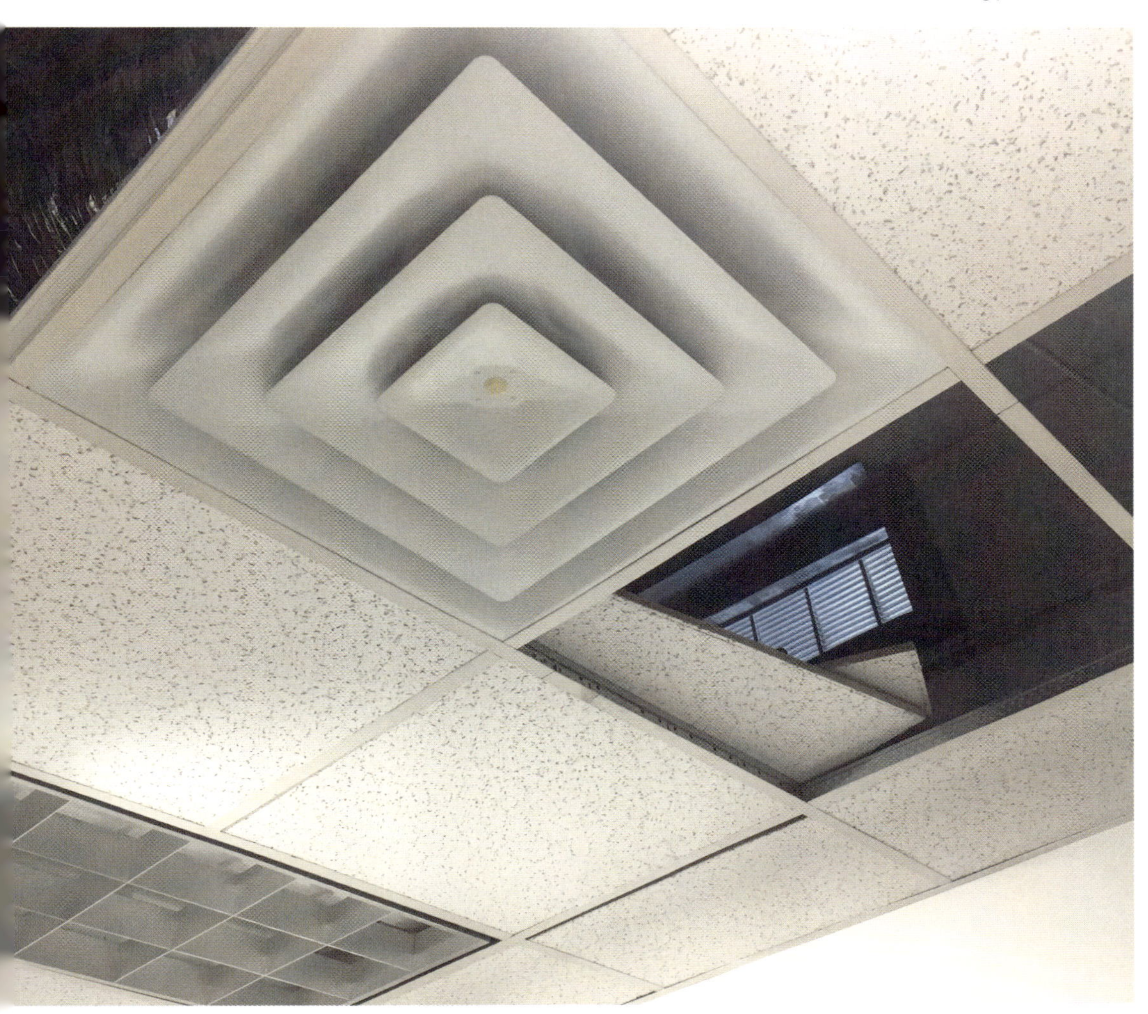

        fig. 1-1
Research image of ceiling
tile taken by Caroline Woolard
in 2017.

IMAGINE A GROUP GATHERING

IMAGINE A GROUP GATHERING

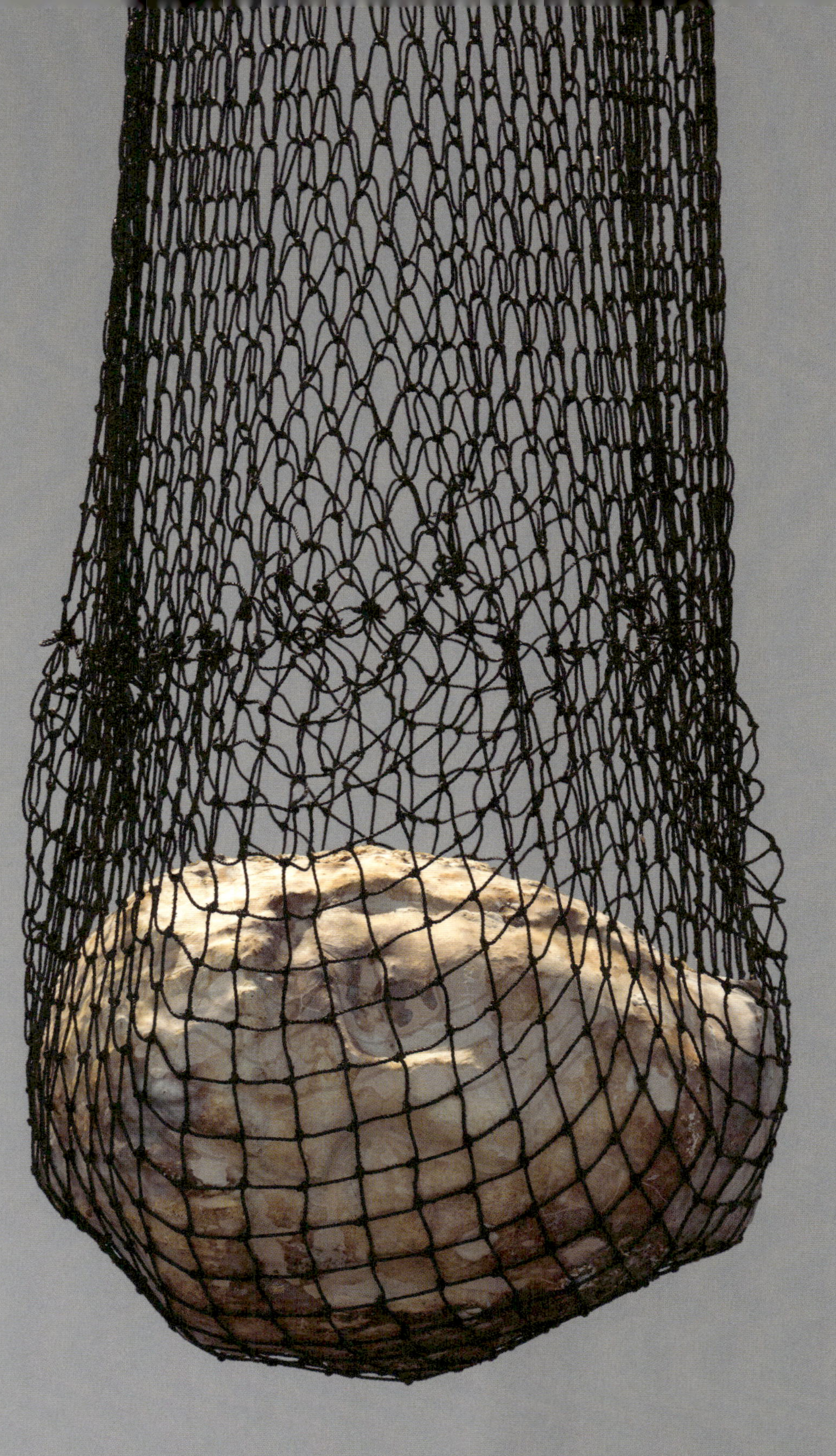

This project would not be possible without the labors of Ecovative Design, Firefly Finishes, Susan Jahoda of BFAMFAPhD, Esteban Kelly, Zaq Landsberg, Maine Thread Company, Alex Mallis, Meerkat Media Collective, Daniel Ramos, Hannah Rawe, and Corinne Spencer. Additional project support comes from Brandeis University, Bennington College, the New School, the School of the Art Institute of Chicago, and Tenthaus in Oslo.

```
     fig. 1-2
The Meeting (detail), 2018-2020,
mycelium, boardroom office table
and chairs, walnut, nylon, pop-
lar, acrylic, hardware, per-
formance, dimensions variable.
Installation at The Galleries At
Moore. Photo by Joseph Hu.
```

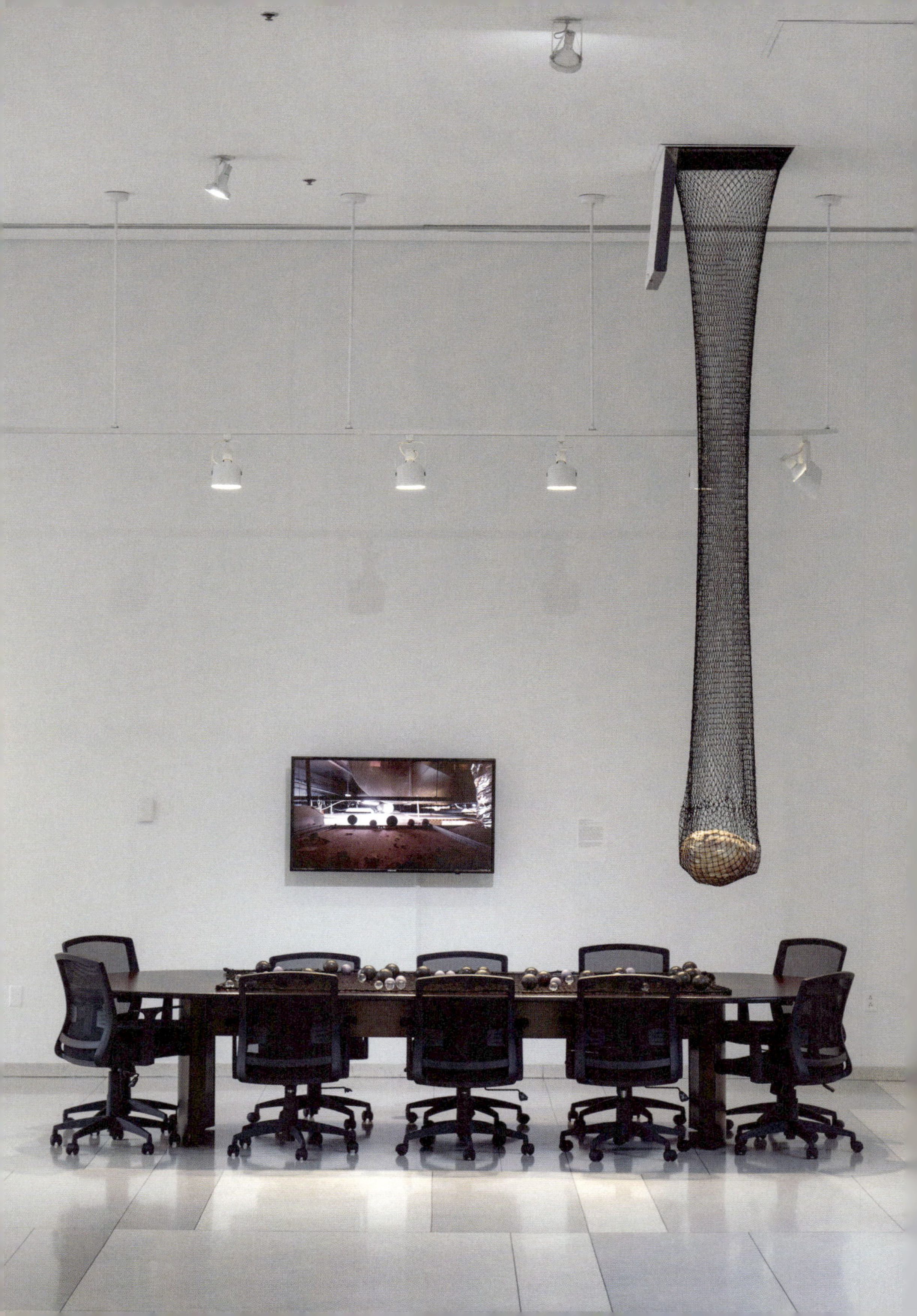

The Meeting Game (in progress) invites interaction and rewrites the meeting script. At the boardroom table, facilitation objects are available for use, to encourage new forms of interpersonal exchange. Visitors are invited to watch the video, learn how to play the game, and roll a ball that corresponds to a way of speaking. In doing so, viewers may become more aware of the flow of dialogue in any conversation. This game, developed in collaboration with the US Federation of Worker Cooperatives' (USFWC) Executive Director, Esteban Kelly, will continue to be refined by the USFWC in nonart settings and also throughout the semester in workshops and public programs with the artist.

The single-channel video was made possible by Alex Mallis, director of photography and editor, and Meerkat Media. Meerkat is a production company cooperative and arts collective committed to making films through a non-hierarchical collaborative process.

fig. 1-3
The Meeting, 2018-2020, mycelium, boardroom office table and chairs, walnut, nylon, poplar, acrylic, hardware, performance, dimensions variable. Installation at The Galleries At Moore. Photo by Joseph Hu.

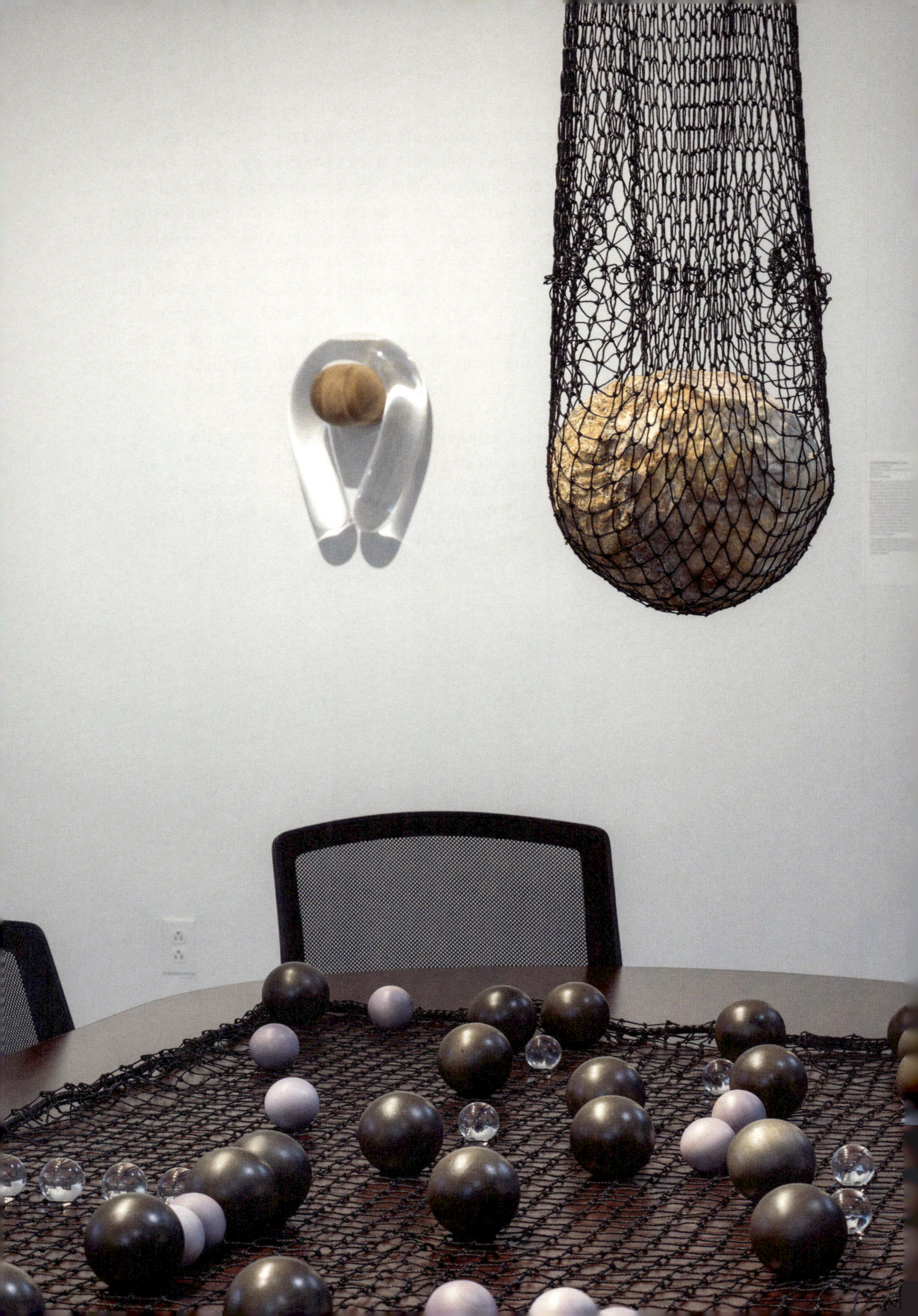

A marble is significant both in its physicality and in common sayings in the English language.

Physically, any sphere implies motion; it has no single base. A marble is a wonderful example of what we do as sculptors: consider material in space, responding to gravity. Within art disciplines, Sculpture is the place where gravity is considered most.

In common sayings, a marble holds so much. Think about common English-language figures of speech that have to do with marbles. For example, marbles have to do with sanity, "losing your marbles;" or betting for everything, "for all the marbles;" or with speech, having a "mouthful of marbles."

Who is said to be sane, who has "lost their marbles"? Who has "all the marbles" to risk playing with and losing? Who is understandable or does not have a "mouthful of marbles"?

Larger spheres and balls hint at these common sayings, without being so direct.

    fig. 1-4
The Meeting (detail), 2018-2020, mycelium, boardroom office table and chairs, walnut, nylon, poplar, acrylic, hardware, performance, dimensions variable. Installation at The Galleries At Moore. Photo by Joseph Hu.

    fig. 1-5 (overleaf)
The Meeting (detail).

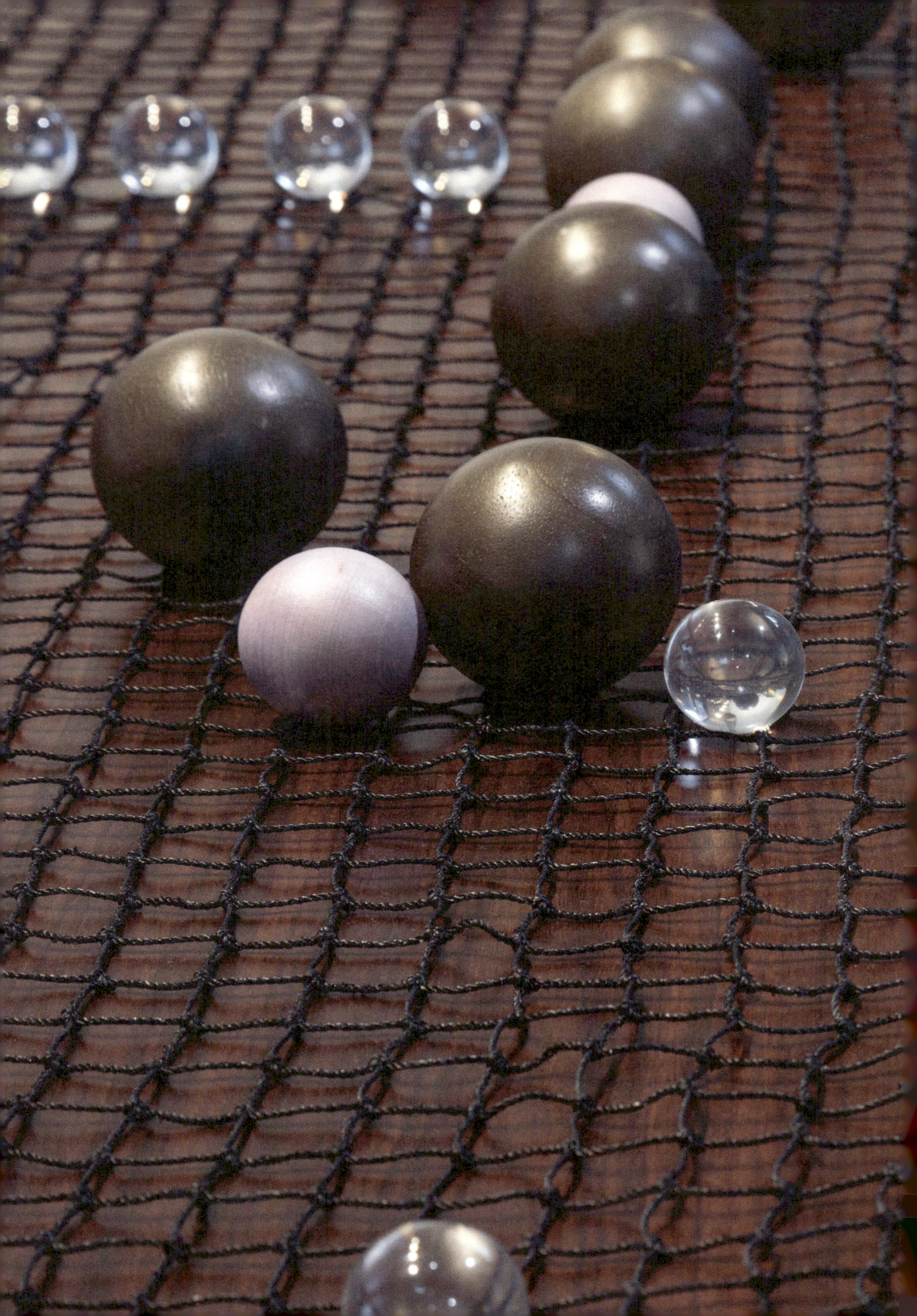

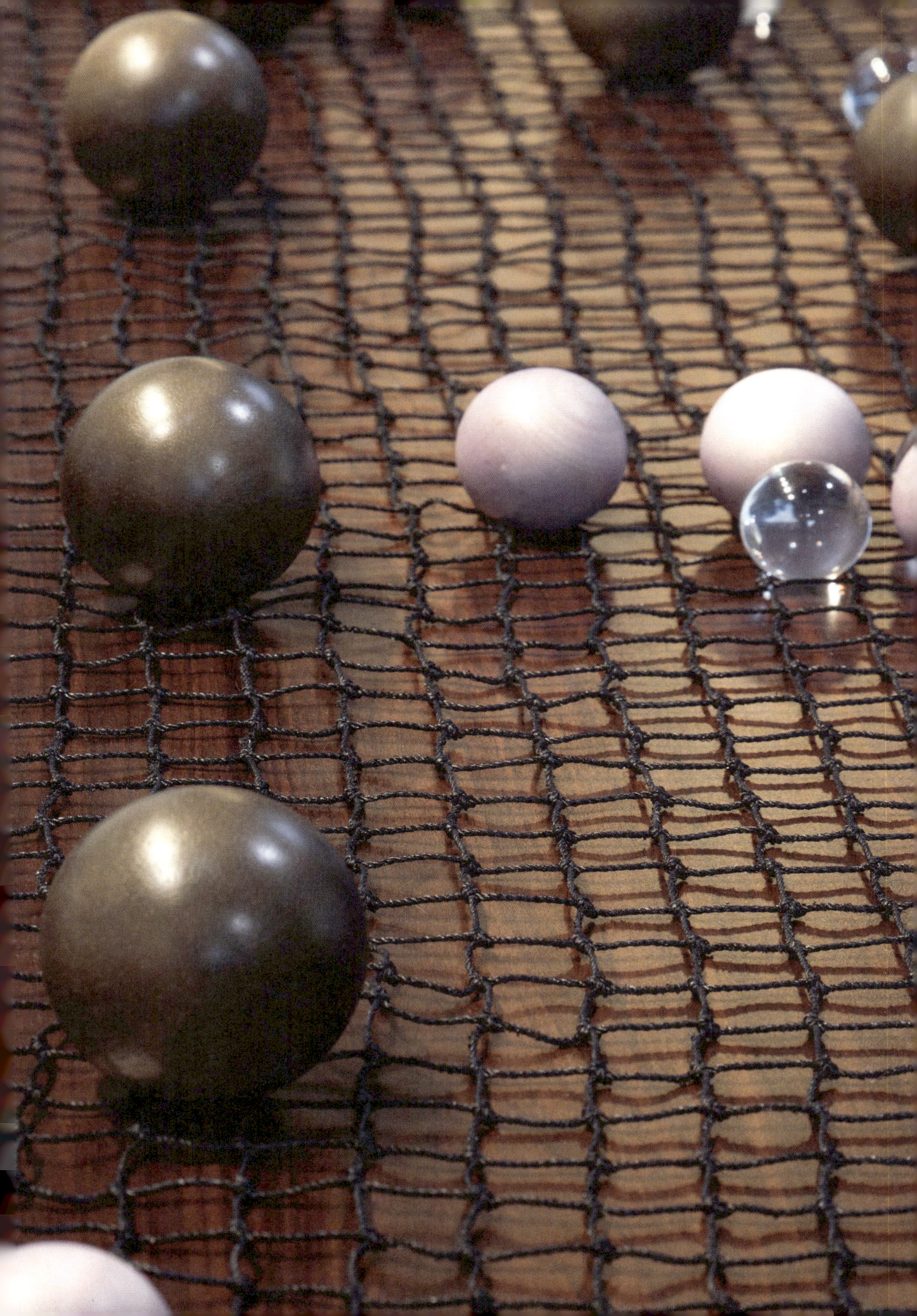

Idea in Public

fig. 1-6
The Meeting, 2018-2020, mycelium,
boardroom office table and
chairs, walnut, nylon, poplar,
acrylic, hardware, performance,
dimensions variable. Installation at The Galleries At Moore
College of Art & Design. Photo
by Joseph Hu.

fig. 1-7 (pages 80-81)
The Meeting (office view), 2019,
mycelium, boardroom office table
and chairs, walnut, nylon, poplar,
acrylic, hardware, performance,
dimensions variable. Installation
in The Vera List Center for Art
and Politics at the New School.
Photo by Levi Mandel.

fig. 1-8 (pages 82-83)
Modular Daybed for Touching Art,
2020, steel, aluminum, walnut,
popular, acrylic, newspaper
pulp, mycelium, organic cotton,
kapock, hardware, 80 × 15 × 38
inches, dimensions variable with
adjustable components. Installation at Rose Art Museum. Special
thanks to the University Ombuds,
Ecovative, DIY Natural Bedding,
Juju and Jake, and Ian Whittemore
for help creating this project.
Images: Courtesy of the artist.
Photo by Mel Taing.

fig. 1-9 (pages 84-85)
Still from *The Meeting Game*,
single-channel video loop,
produced in collaboration
with Alex Mallis and Meerkat
Media, 2019.

fig. 1-10 (pages 86-87)
Still from *The Meeting Game*,
single-channel video loop,
produced in collaboration
with Alex Mallis and Meerkat
Media, 2019.

Institutional
Invitation

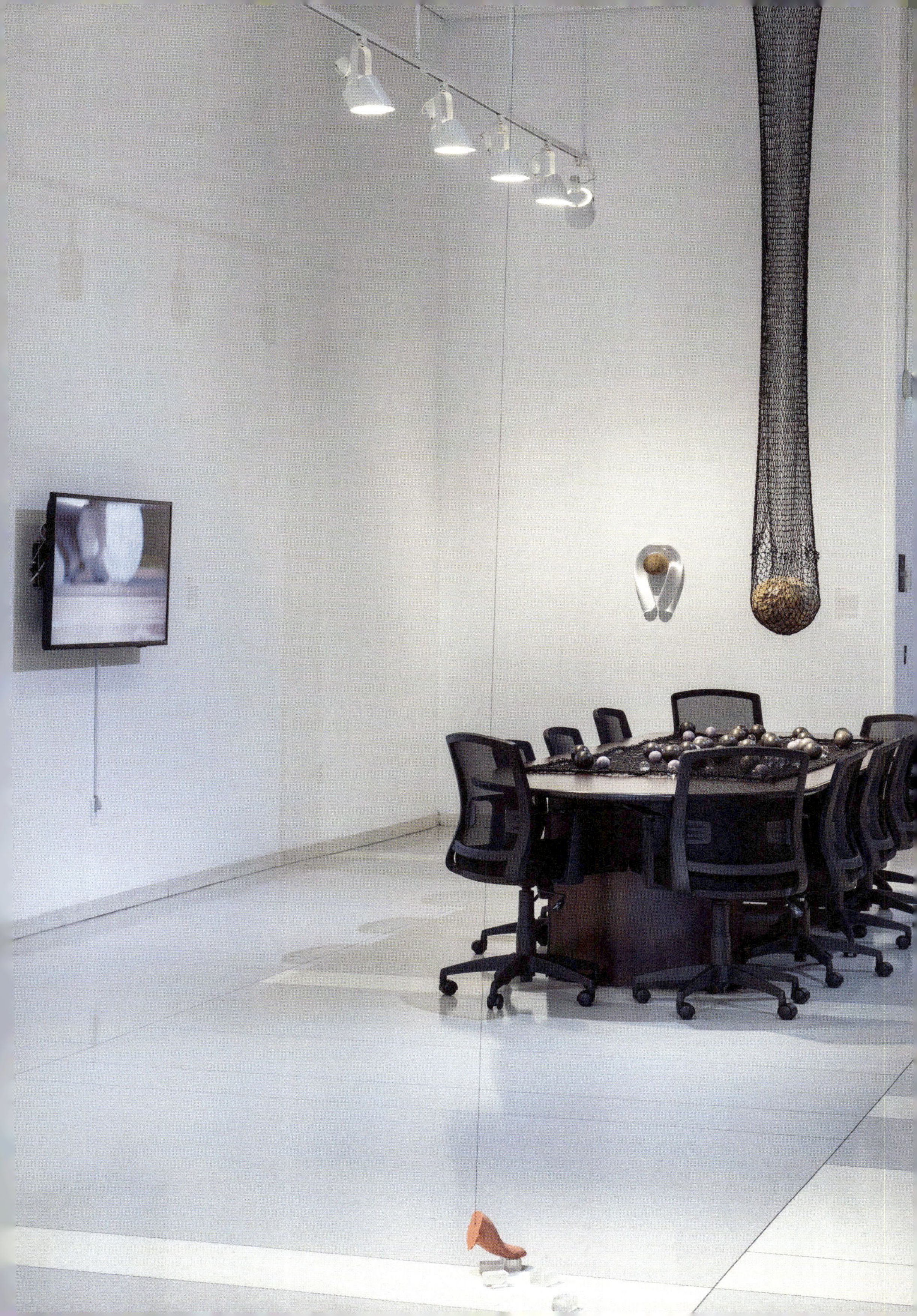

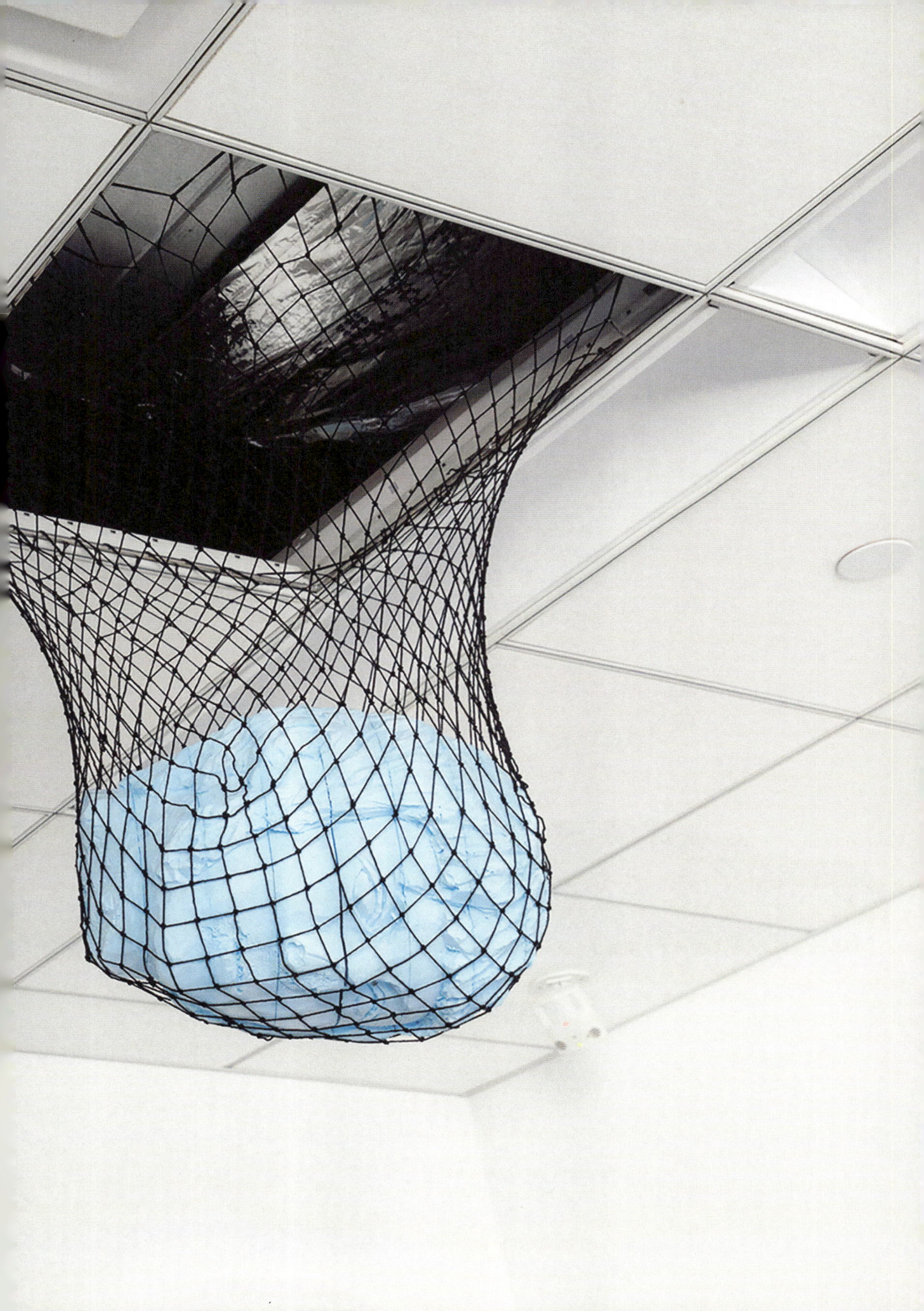

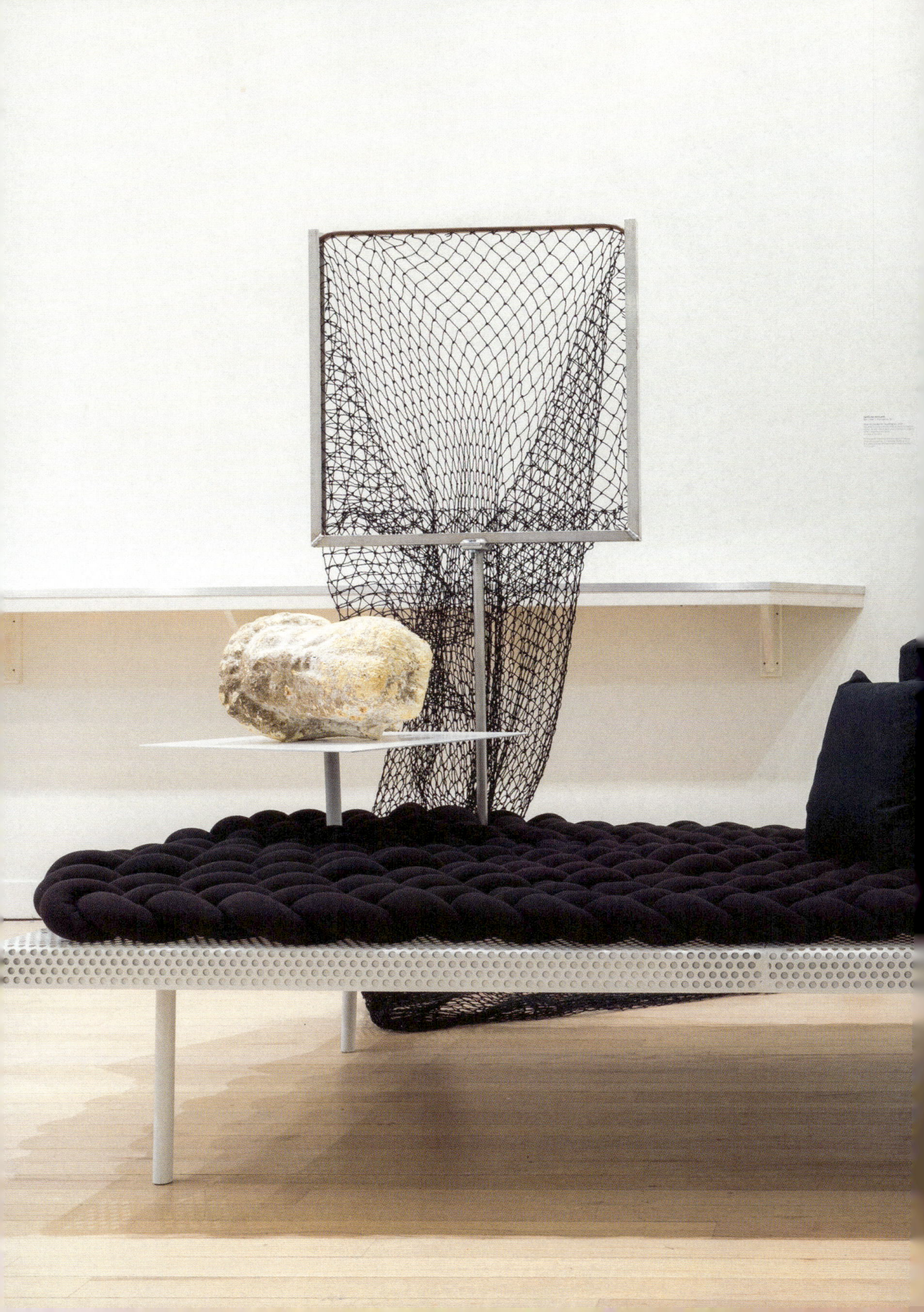

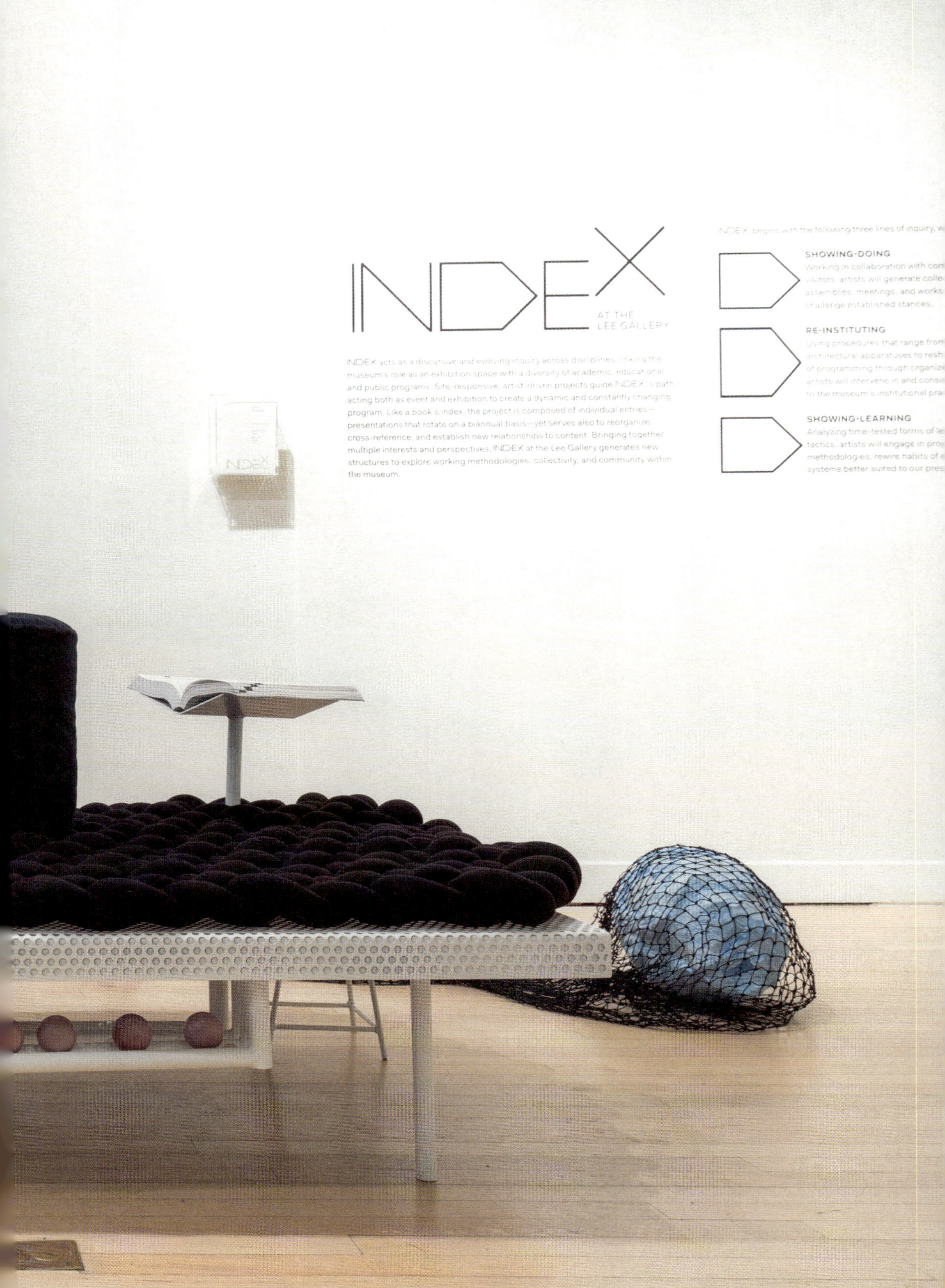

INDEX
AT THE
LEE GALLERY

INDEX acts as a discursive and evolving inquiry across disciplines, linking the museum's role as an exhibition space with a diversity of academic, educational and public programs. Site-responsive, artist-driven projects guide INDEX's path, acting both as event and exhibition to create a dynamic and constantly changing program. Like a book's index, the project is composed of individual entries—presentations that rotate on a biannual basis—yet serves also to reorganize, cross-reference, and establish new relationships to content. Bringing together multiple interests and perspectives, INDEX at the Lee Gallery generates new structures to explore working methodologies, collectivity, and community within the museum.

INDEX begins with the following three lines of inquiry, w

SHOWING-DOING
Working in collaboration with com
visitors, artists will generate colle
assemblies, meetings, and works
challenge established stances.

RE-INSTITUTING
Using procedures that range from
architectural apparatuses to resh
of programming through organize
artists will intervene in and consi
to the museum's institutional pra

SHOWING-LEARNING
Analyzing time-tested forms of le
tactics, artists will engage in proj
methodologies, rewire habits of e
systems better suited to our pres

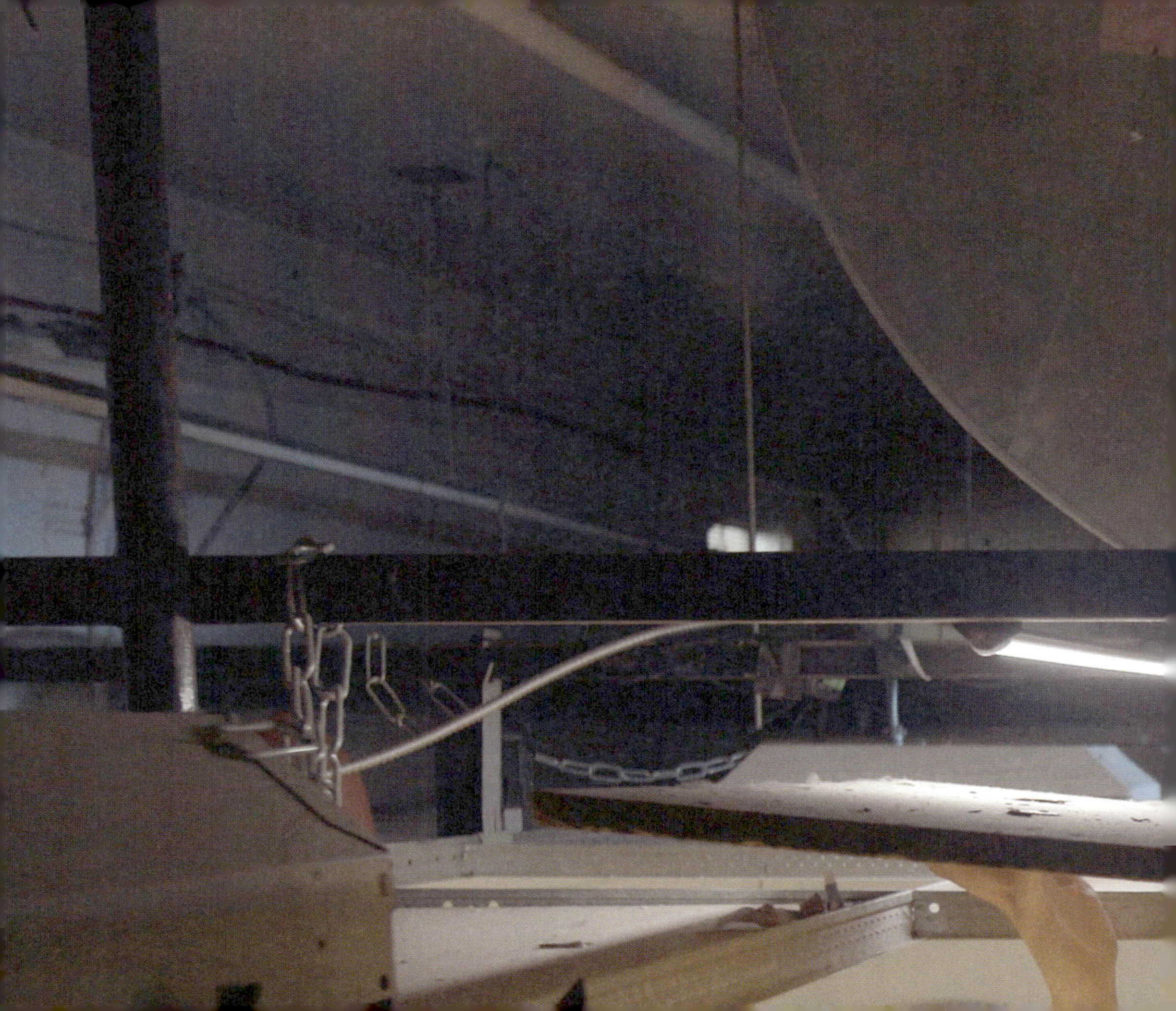

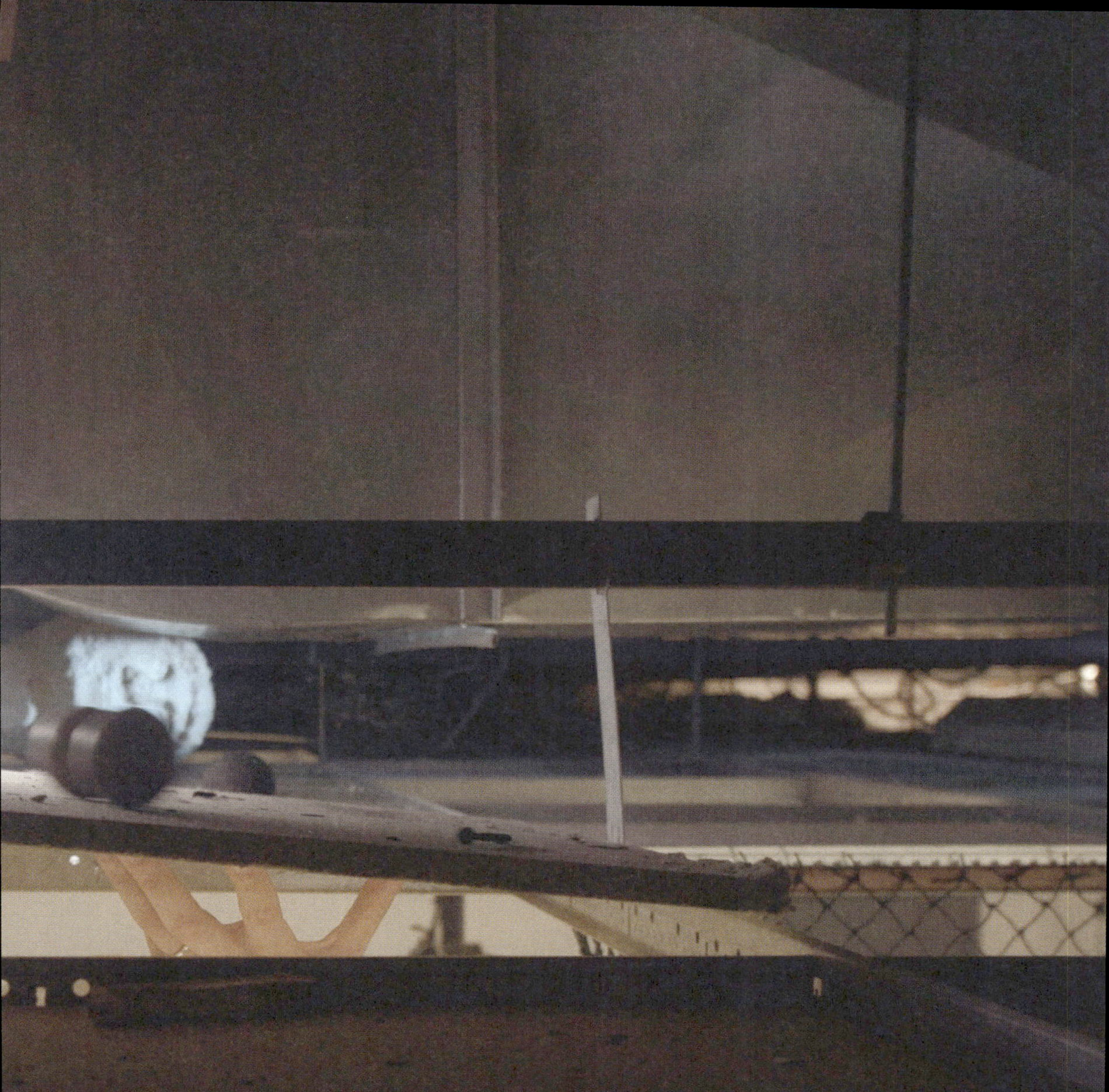

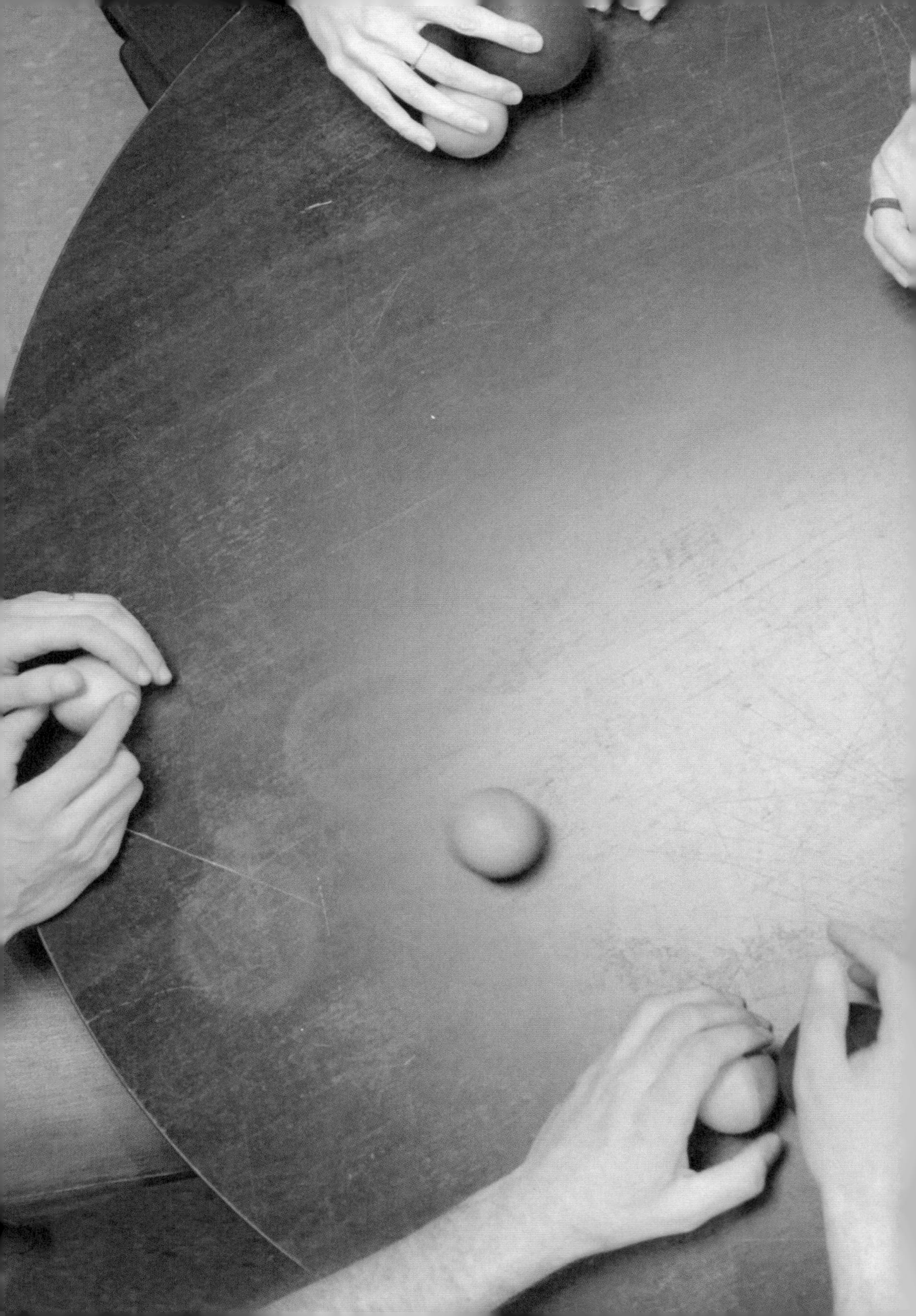

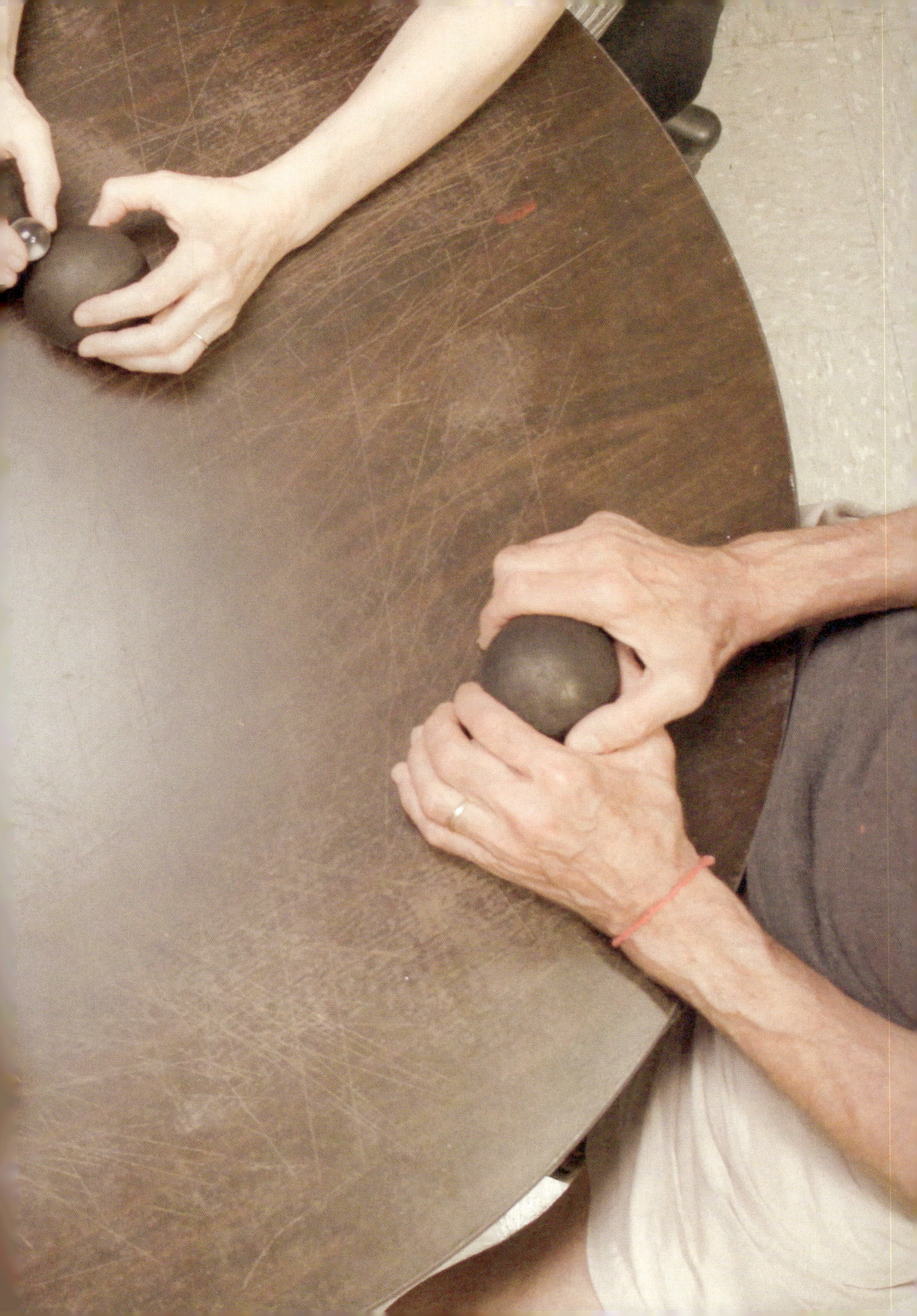

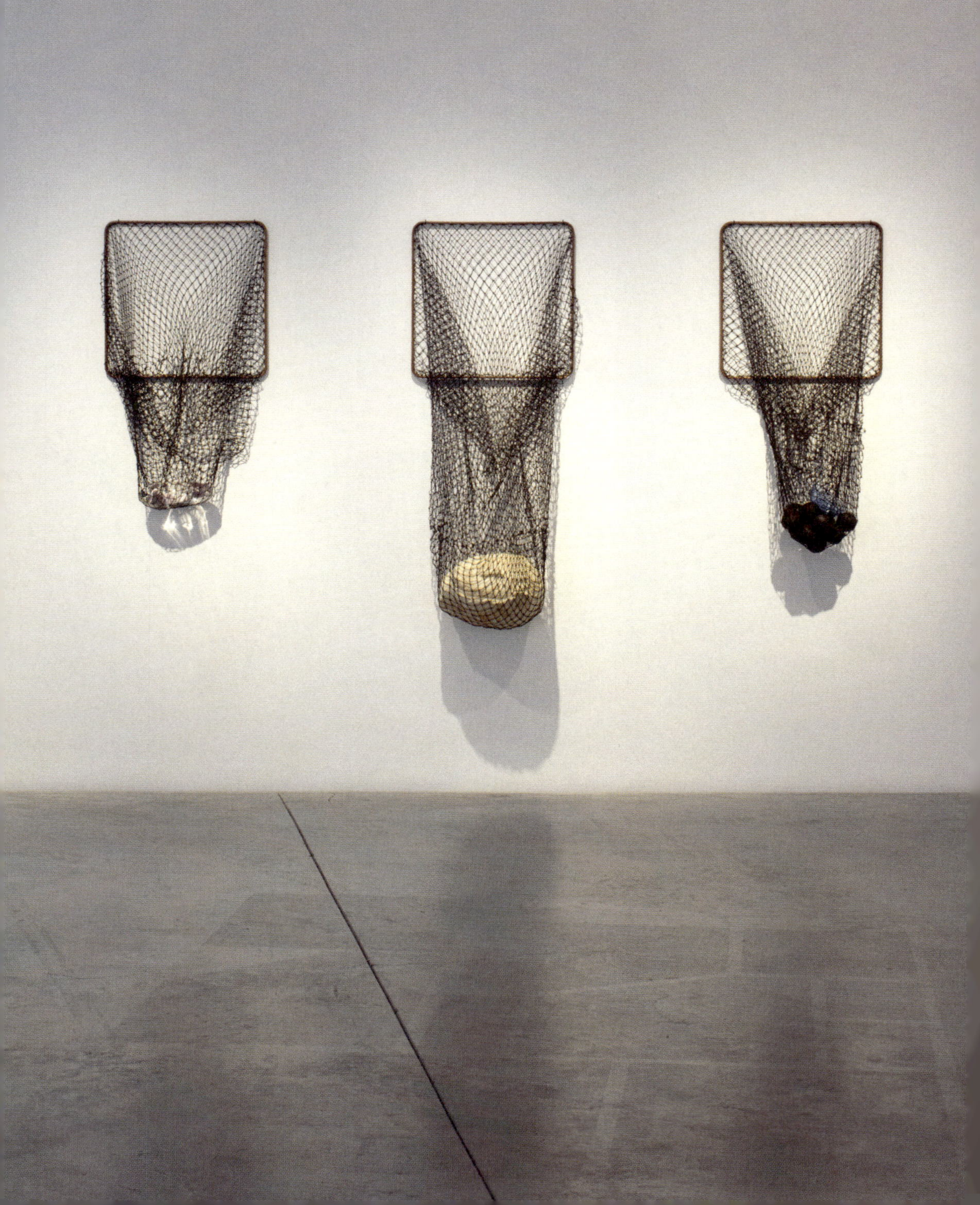

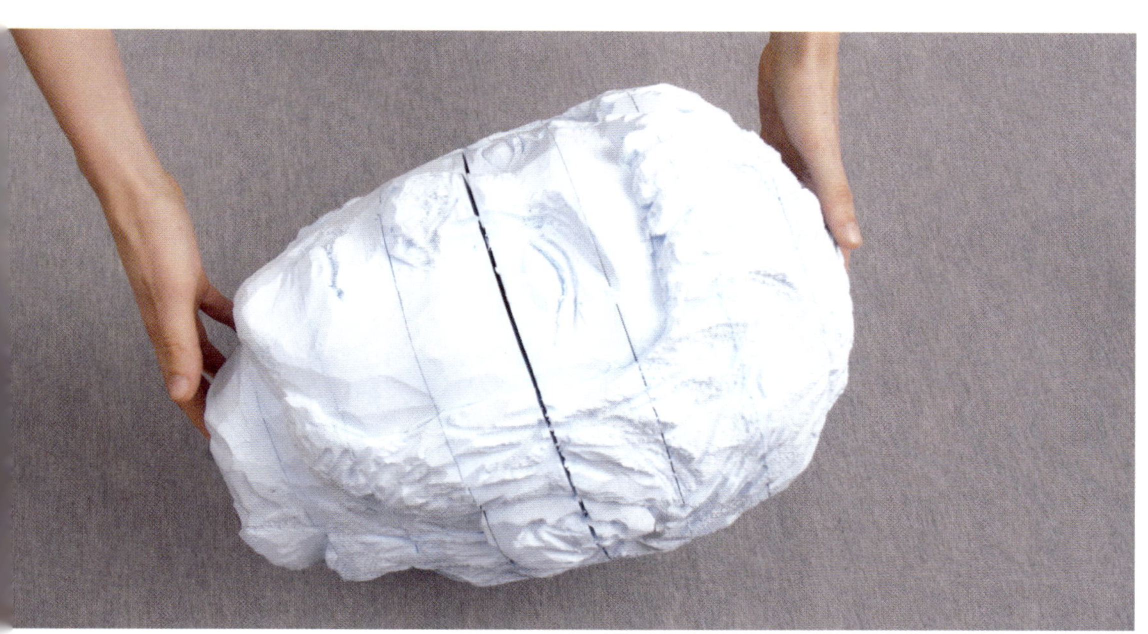

fig. 1-11
The Meeting (gallery view),
2018-2019, mycelium, walnut,
nylon, glass, hardware, performance, dimensions variable.
Photo by Daniel Chou.

fig. 1-12
Caroline Woolard, *Untitled
(Objects for Facilitation)*,
2018. Video still by Herman
Jean-Noel.

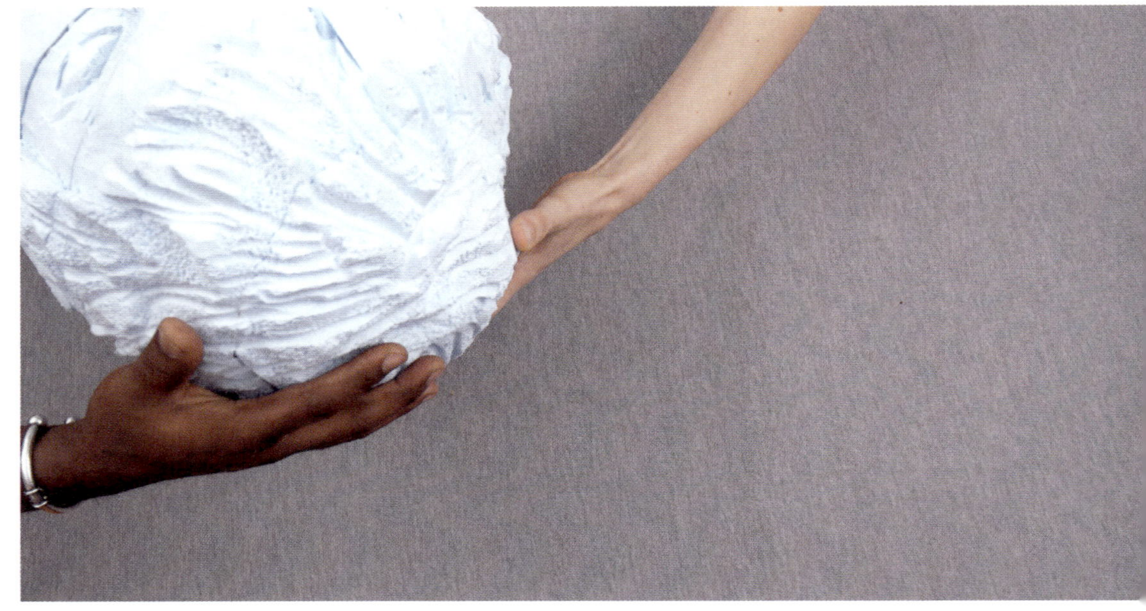

fig. 1-13
Caroline Woolard, *Untitled
(Objects for Facilitation)*,
2018. Video still by Herman
Jean-Noel.

Ephemera

Woolard has selected ephemera that serves as visual reference points for *The Meeting*.

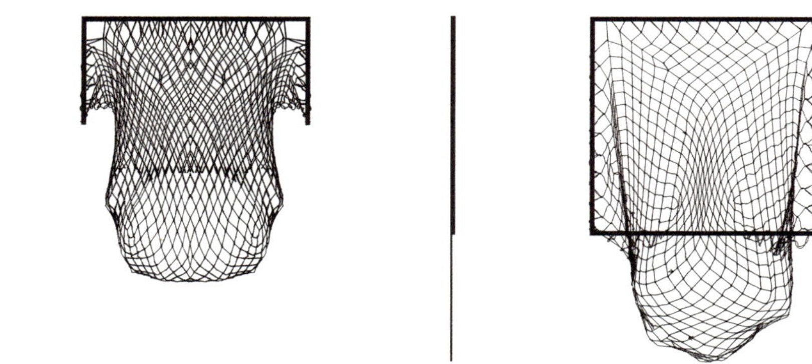

        fig. 1-14
Technical drawing with key
for scale, made to produce the
framed net for *The Meeting*.

10

SPORE GERMINATION
SPORULATION
FUSION OF
COMPATIBLE HYPHAE
HYPHAL KNOT
PINHEAD
PRIMORDIUM
FRUITBODY
FIG. 15 - GAUGING MESH SIZE
funnel (opera house) trap
funnel trap
FIG. 25 - HALF-MESH KNOT
L TO R WEAVING

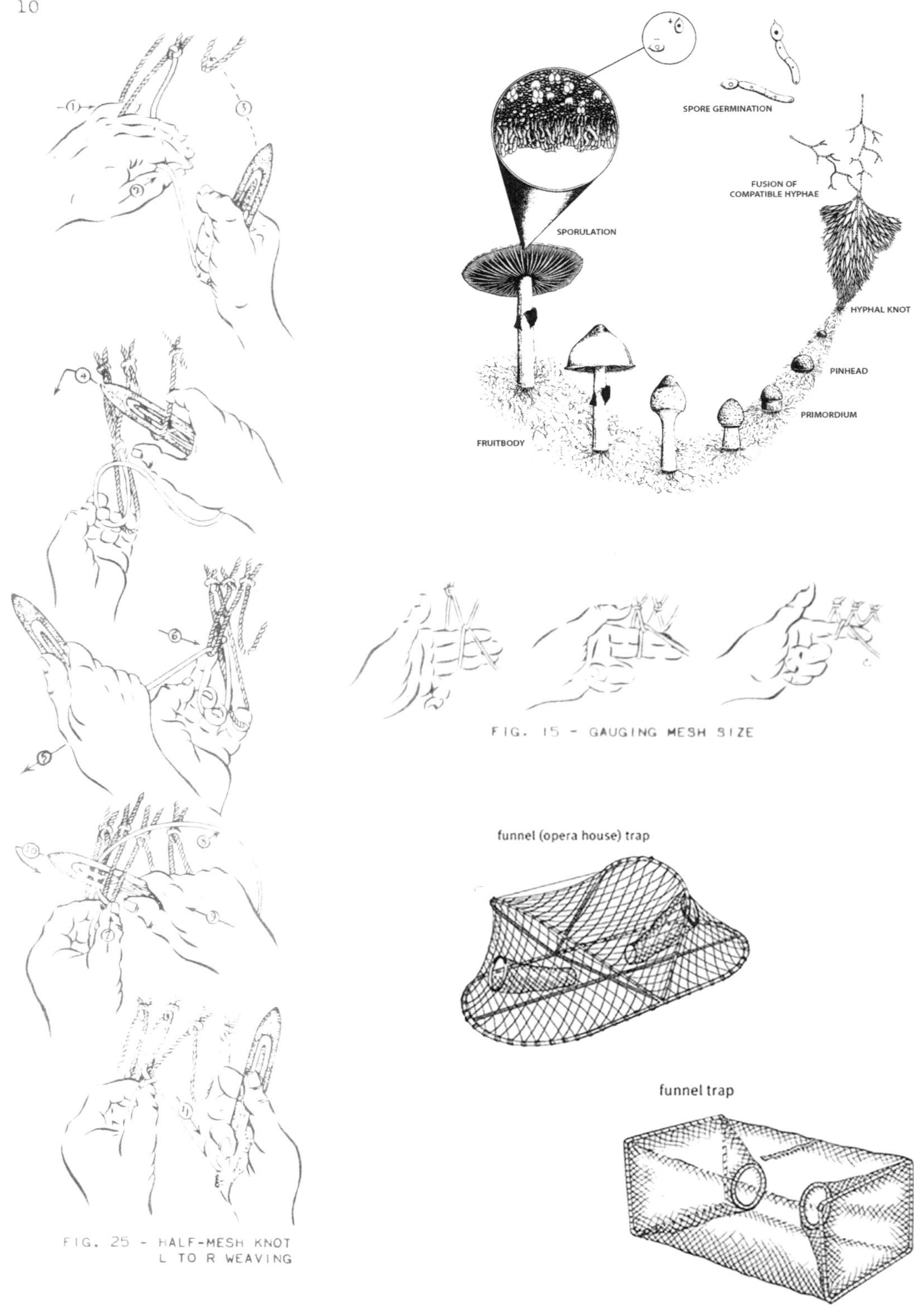

Making

I learned from *LISTEN*^{see chapter 6} that I wanted to continue my work on the role of objects in facilitation, but this time, I wanted to be in charge of the quirky weirdness of form, and to find a project partner who would be open to trying out unexpected objects for meetings, rather than determining the form of the objects together with non-arts partners. I knew Esteban Kelly, a founding member of Anti-Oppression Resource and Training Alliance (AORTA), a worker-owned cooperative devoted to "strengthening movements for social justice and a solidarity economy." Members of TradeSchool.coop^{see chapter 3} New York had hired AORTA to lead a training for our collective in 2011, and I remembered that Esteban used a lot of visual analogies and theater games, and was open to unconventional facilitation techniques. He is based in Philadelphia, and is now the Director of the US Federation of Worker Cooperatives. I was excited about the potential for a collaborative project, and by the idea that he was already sharing conflict transformation techniques with worker-owners nationally.

```
Subject: Conflict transformation in Philly

July 29, 2018
Esteban,

I just found out that I got a fellowship to
be in Philly a few times over the next year
to make a project at Moore, and I'm wondering
if you know a great intensive or coach for
conflict transformation. I'm also interested
in thinking/talking with you about how we
might work together on something—I have been
really into making objects that reflect groups'
existing facilitation and listening practices.

Let me know if anything comes to mind for
conflict transformation.

In cooperation,
Caroline
```

I want these objects to be
created soup-to-nuts, by you,
the artist. I don't want to
take over the process by
saying: "more of this, more
of that." The purpose of art
is for you all [artists] to
do your thing without us
mucking things up. This is
not our area of expertise.

—Esteban Kelly, 2018

fig. 1-15
Collage of mushroom mycelium and nets found while doing research to determine the form that objects might take in *The Meeting*, and thinking about knots, capture, mending, and trapping. Images from P. Stamets, *Mycelium Running: How Mushrooms Can Help Save the World* (Berkeley: Ten Speed Press, 2005), and J. A. Krug, *Fishery Leaflet 241: Methods of Mending—New England* (Washington D.C.: United States Department of the Interior, Fish and Wildlife Service), 6, 10.

July 30, 2018
Caroline,

Sure, I'd be happy to chat. Let me know more about what sort of coaching training you envision. I may have capacity to do that while you're around, or I might have ideas for referrals if I'm not a good fit.

I'm cc'ing Kevin to help us find a time to chat. I'm pretty available as of next week.

September 27, 2018
Hi Caroline,

Thanks for circling back! I'm just getting back to the office after a few weeks away. The back of the envelope budget range is:

at $200/hr it would be:
$1,600 for 4 or $3,200 for 8 sessions

at $250/hr it would be:
2,000 for 4 or $4,000 for 8 sessions

I believe I mentioned our sliding scale in our previous call. It's similar to how AORTA's rates work. I'll defer to you to figure out what works best for your budget and appropriate scale-fit.

September 27, 2018
Esteban,

This is great news, and yes to going with your role at the US Federation of Worker Co-ops. As for sliding scale, I don't see the sliding scale for individuals. That said, my salary at the University

What I envision is imagination and critical speculation going together with a material process of transformation of the institutional art field: a process where both autonomy — as the subjective power of the encounter with an artwork — and heteronomy — as the process of erosion of art disciplinary borders into non-art and into the social dimension — are mobilized.

—Marco Baravalle, 2020

Institutional
Invitation

of Hartford is \$62k a year and the
budget for labor to make these objects,
materials, travel, food, contractors,
marketing, and stipends like this
is \$50k.

This makes me think that 8 sessions
for \$4000 makes sense, but perhaps each
"session" refers to one-on-one training
and the fly on the wall time is unpaid,
or that it's \$150/hour for one-on-one
training and \$50/hour to be a fly on
the wall, which works out to the same.
Does that make sense?

When do we start?

Looking forward to it,
Caroline

With Esteban on board, I knew I could begin researching
and developing ideas for meeting spaces.

I began searching for a space to work with. Daniel Tucker, an
artist and faculty member at Moore, suggested a number of
possible partners. Patti also introduced me to a number of
people with exhibition spaces and unconventional spaces,
including Andrew Nurkin at the Free Library. When I spoke
to Andrew, everything seemed to align.

October 29, 2018
Hi Caroline,

I'm also excited about collaborating on this.
As I have shared our conversation with my
colleagues, they have affirmed what an engaging opportunity this will be!

I keep returning to the idea of a kind of
lending library for objects and practices that
facilitate deep group work, with the "check

out" point in our new Heim Center for Cultural
and Civic Engagement. This could extend to an
installation that functions as a kind of intentional space for this work, open to groups
already in process (from community groups to
groups of coworkers). I'm sure more ideas will
spark as we continue to talk, but I like the
link between your work and new ideas about the
traditional "lending" role of the library.
Specifically, how to see others in a group as
experts/knowledge bearers and then enter a
process that draws out that knowledge toward
a shared goal.

Are we still on for you to visit the library on
Nov. 16?

Thanks,
Andrew

I then began thinking about the meeting space itself,
developing furniture for the space, with support from the
Rose Art Museum.

fig. 1-16
Research image of ceiling
tile taken by Caroline Woolard
in 2017.

fig. 1-17
Renderings for *INDEX* at the
Rose Art Museum playing with the
idea of a thicket, of rolling
spheres, and of paper pulp. The
idea for the furniture is connected to paper waste. It looks
like a typical day bed but it
is a "tool" which is capable of
making large paper pulp lounge
objects (making itself).

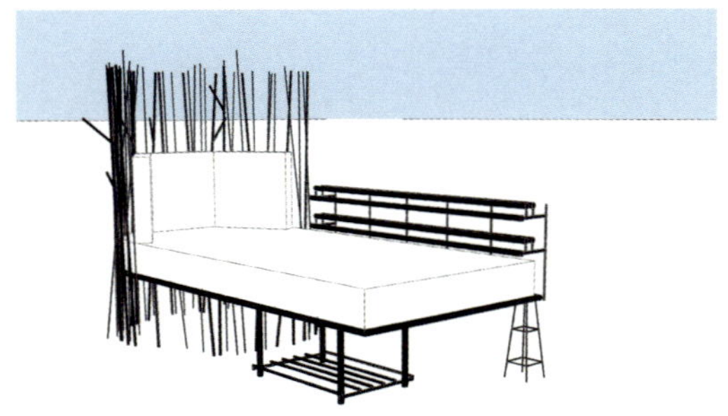

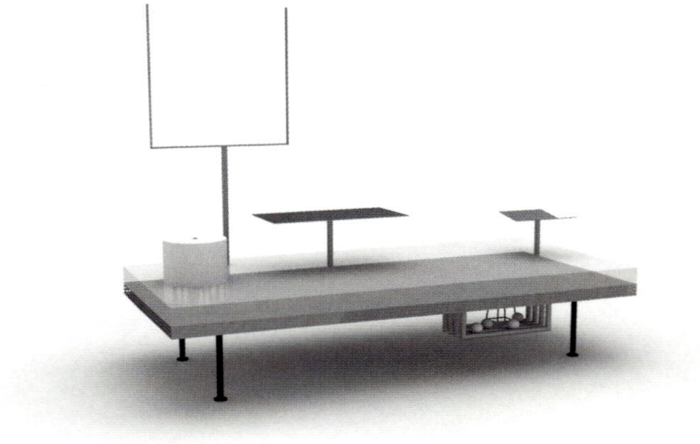

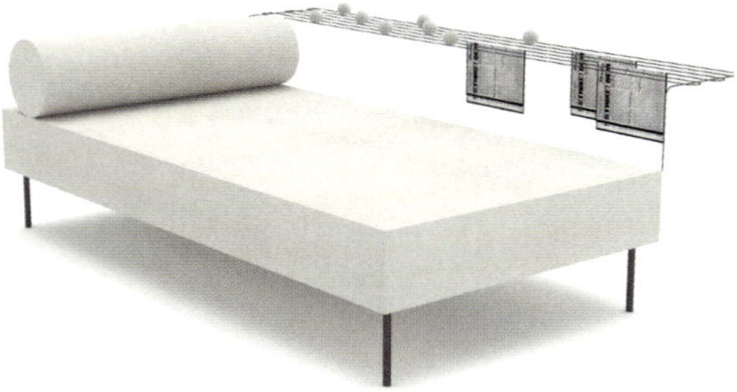

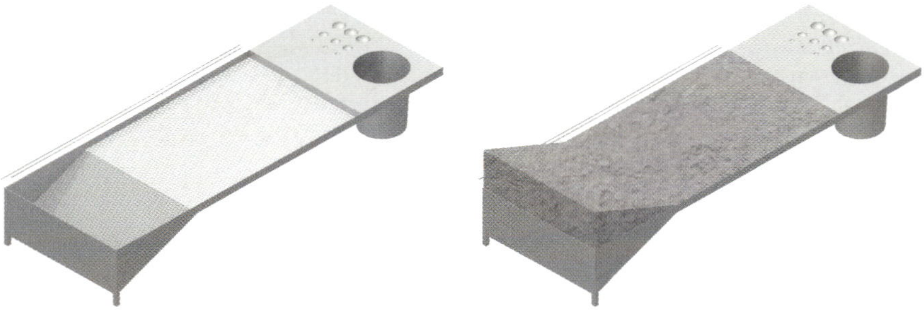

Institutional
Invitation

fig. 1-18
Technical drawings for the
Modular Daybed as well as the
idea of the daybed as thicket,
made in preparation to build
the object.

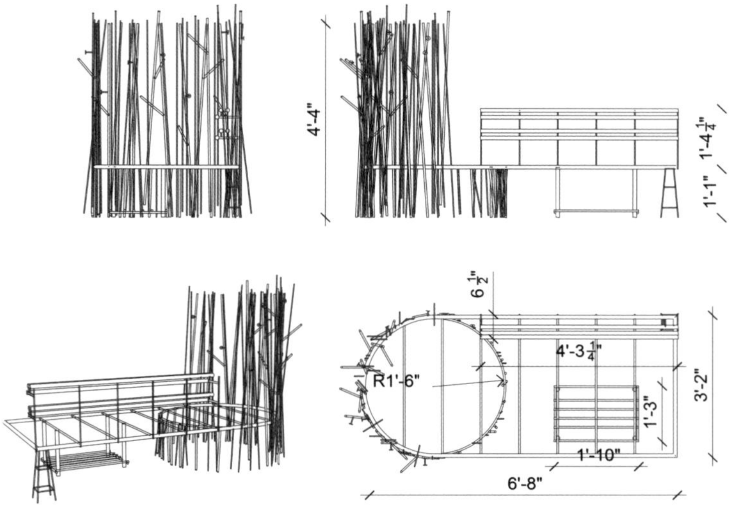

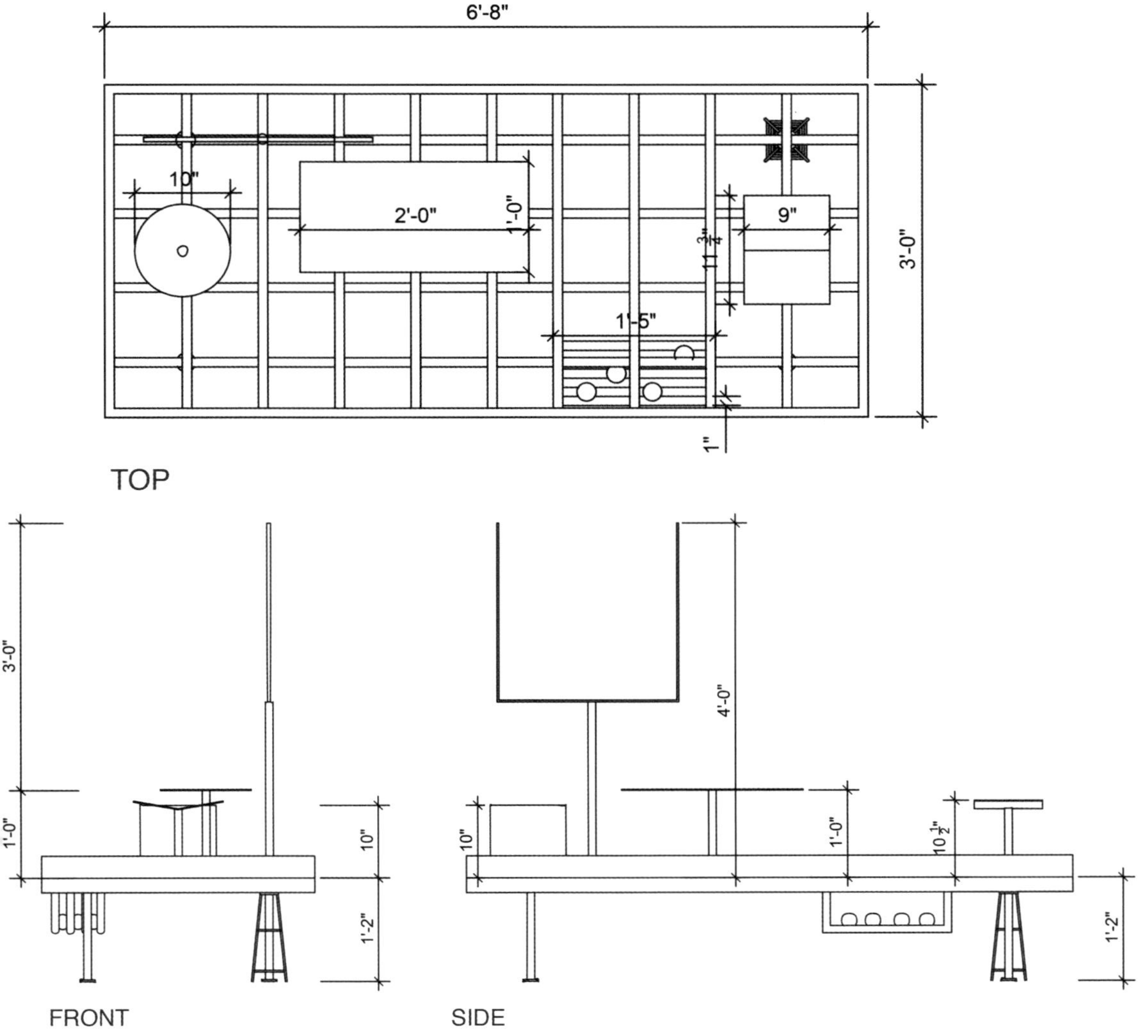

TOP

FRONT

SIDE

fig. 1-19
Every project begins with
quick sketches, which turn
into technical drawings, then
renderings, then built tests
and prototypes, and finally,
the finished object.

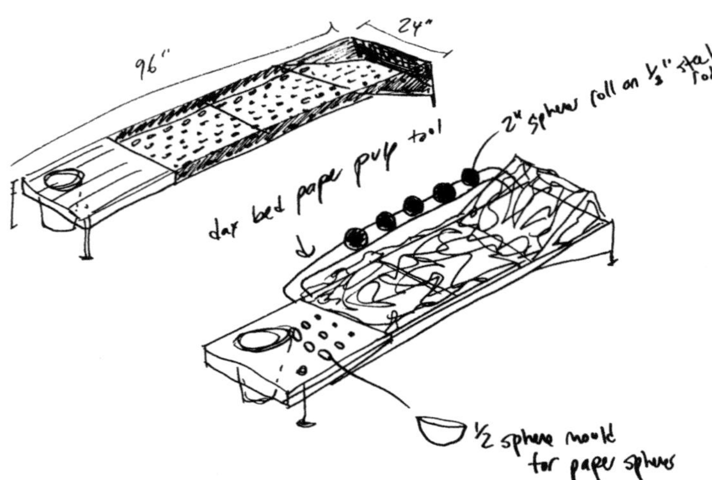

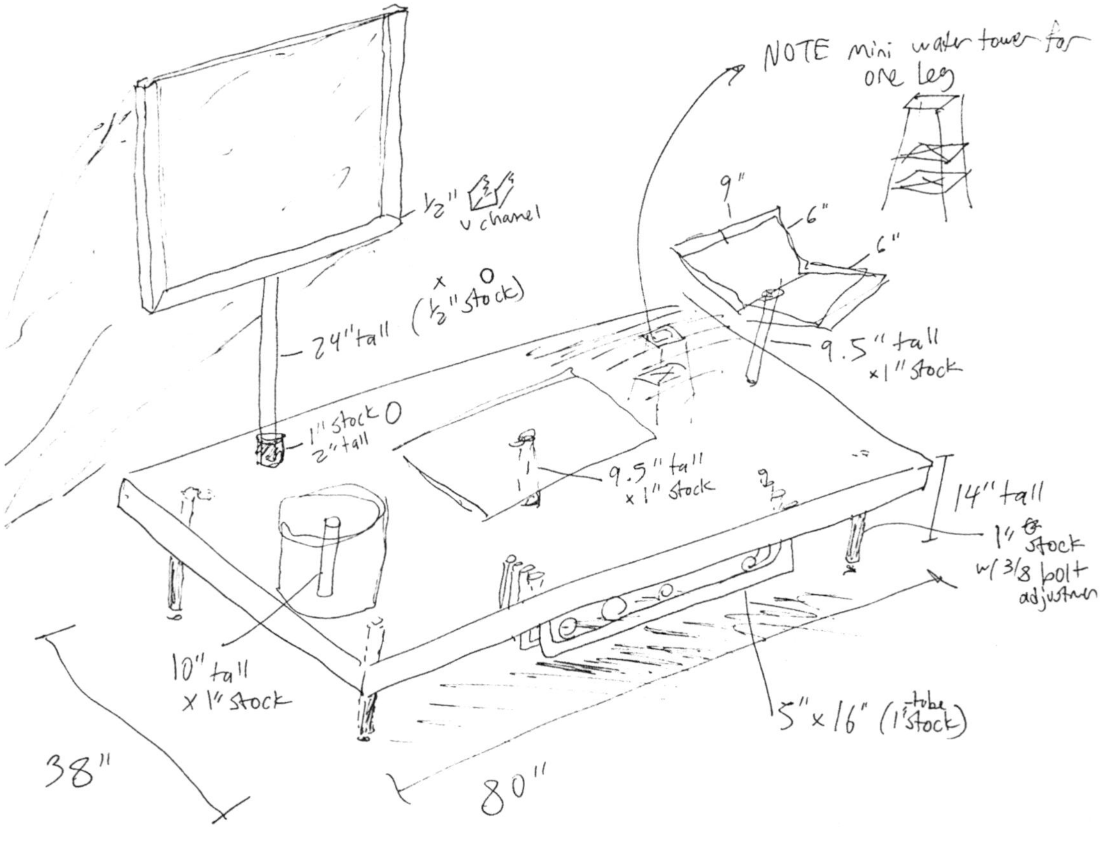

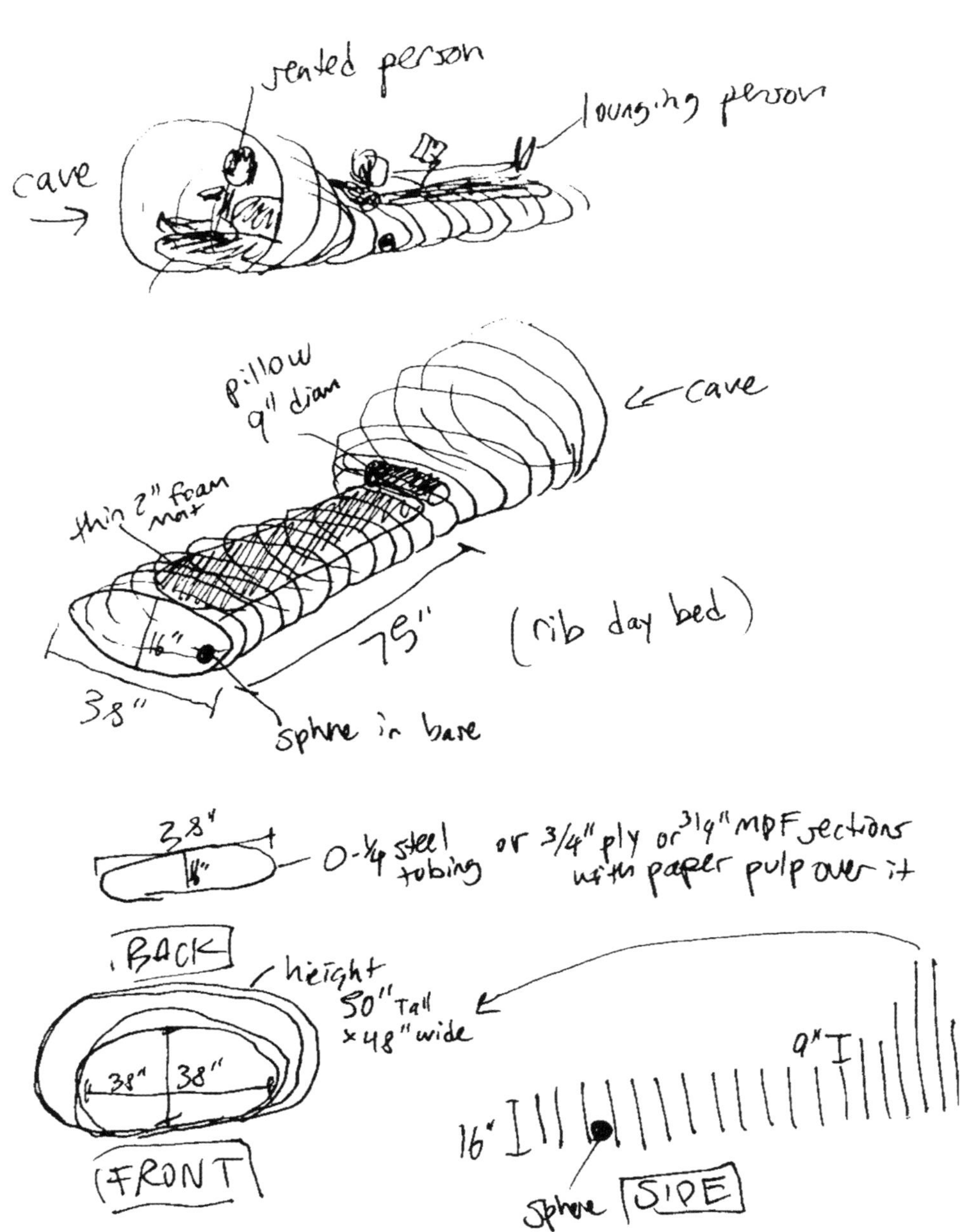
seated person
lounging person
cave
pillow
9" diam
thin 2" foam mat
cave
75"
(rib day bed)
16"
38"
sphere in base
38"
16"
0-¼ steel tubing or 3/4" ply or ¾" MDF sections with paper pulp over it
BACK
height
50" tall
x 48" wide
38"   38"
FRONT
9" I
16" I
sphere   SIDE

Managing

This project began in an unconventional way. I was in the grocery store when I saw an email from Patti Phillips on my phone. It was the middle of the summer, and the message seemed to be that I was in the running for a huge a fellowship that I had not applied for. It was too good to be true. I showed it to my partner, asking her if it was spam.

```
Subject: Letter for Caroline Woolard
July 11, 2018

Dear Caroline,

Kindly see the attached letter from Moore
College of Art & Design. We look forward to
your response.

Sincerely,

Patricia C. Phillips
Academic Dean
```

Experience

Institutional
Invitation

June 11, 2018
Dear Caroline Woolard,

Moore College of Art & Design has announced a fellowship to support and advance its historical mission and 21st century vision to educate women to be creative leaders, agents, and entrepreneurs. The College is delighted to inaugurate a new and unique fellowship that adds value to the academic experience and research community by making significant connections within the College, as well as the creative and civic life of Philadelphia. Jane Zimmerman Walentas graduated from Moore in 1966 and, with her husband David, has endowed this fellowship. The Jane & David Walentas Endowed Distinguished Fellowship supports an ongoing commitment to confirm and perpetuate the highest values of Moore College of Art & Design and represent the remarkable vision and generosity of the donors.

The Walentas Endowed Distinguished Fellowship is a term appointment of distinction for an artist, designer, scholar, curator, thinker, and/or innovator who embodies creative and visionary leadership, seeks to inspire Moore students, and create opportunities for collaboration between academic programs, the Galleries, and other areas of the College. The Walentas Fellow will participate in a "customized" residency at Moore for one-to two-years and is expected to be a passionate contributor to the creative and intellectual life of the College and city. The Fellowship is both responsive to Moore's priorities, new alliances, emerging opportunities, and other cultural developments, while being highly flexible to meet the expectations and schedule of a Fellow. The distinguished appointment may include a combination of teaching and workshops, interdisciplinary or discipline-based research, creative projects and programs, and other special projects and initiatives developed through collaborations with Moore faculty, students, and external partners. As part of the appointment, the Fellow will give a major presentation—the Walentas Distinguished Public Lecture.

Recently, a panel including Moore President Cecelia Fitzgibbon, the donor Jane Walentas, two faculty members, and the Academic Dean convened to review prospective Walentas Fellows. The list of potential Fellows was developed through nominations from the Moore community, as well as the College's extended community of cultural leaders and supporters. The panel reviewed all nominations and developed a prioritized short list. We

Managing

are delighted to let you know that
you are one of the leading nominees
to be the first Walentas Endowed
Distinguished Fellow.

At this time, we invite you to
confirm your interest to explore
this opportunity with us — and your
potential engagement in a process
that includes submission of materials
on your work, participation in a
remote or on-campus interview to
explore ways you may choose to focus
and shape the Fellowship, and an
openness and excitement to help launch
the first successful and generative
chapter of the Walentas Endowed
Distinguished Fellowship at Moore —
and in Philadelphia. The Walentas
Fellowship will provide remuneration
for whatever form the residency may
take, as well as support for related
expenses for travel, materials, and
other requirements of the Fellowship.

Kindly contact Patricia Phillips
(see information below) indicating your interest and willingness
to explore and participate in this
review process at Moore.

Sincerely,

Cecelia Fitzgibbon, President
Patricia C. Phillips, Chief Academic
Officer/Academic Dean

I immediately wrote back, sending Patti questions, ideas, and suggestions.

> June 11, 2018
> Dear Patricia Phillips,
>
> What an honor. I would love to submit my materials for review. One important note: I now have a full time, tenure-track job at the University of Hartford, so to participate in this opportunity during the academic year, I would need my Dean's approval and I would need to be bought out of full time teaching commitment ($62,000 a year). Alternatively, we could schedule the residency in the summer, if possible, though I doubt that is ideal for the mission of the program.
>
> Please let me know if you'd like to speak on the phone. I'm available in PST as I'm at a residency in Seattle.
>
> Best wishes,
> Caroline Woolard

Patti explained that I did not need to be in Philadelphia full time for this Fellowship. We scheduled a call, and I sent her this email after we spoke in person about her vision for the inaugural Fellowship.

> June 19, 2018
> Patti,
>
> I am so excited by the possibility of this Fellowship at Moore. As I mentioned, I teach Mondays-Wednesdays in Hartford, so I could do something once a month on a Thursday-Friday, or a long weekend (Friday-Sunday), and/or I could do a week-long intensive. I am certain we can make it work.

As I said, I started making objects for meetings because I want the physical environment of the meeting itself to be as wildly imaginative as the conversations that occur in those spaces. Recently, I have focused on furniture-clocks-objects for an intimate and alternative time. I have found that by bringing gatherings, like my *Capitoline Wolf* tables and my *Water Clock* timekeeping devices see chapter 7, I make tangible the slow temporality of community-building; people sense the care that has gone into the facilitation practices I bring to group work.

For more information about my recent work, please see: https://brooklynrail.org/2018/02/art/The-Art-of-Institutional-Possibility-CAROLINE-WOOLARD-with-Thyrza-Nichols-Goodeve

and

https://art21.org/artist/caroline-woolard/

Best wishes,
Caroline

PS: Here are some ideas to begin a dialogue:

(1) Study Center for Group Work see chapter 2

The Study Center for Group Work is an open access library of collaborative methods. The Center focuses on collaborative methods that have been recommended by artists. These methods often embrace the unknown, encouraging people to listen deeply enough to be transformed.

More info: http://studycollaboration.com/
Also this short video: https://vimeo.com/223191451
And also: https://vimeo.com/198242353
(this was the day after the election, so the tone is a bit somber)

The first iteration of the Center was run at Cooper Union in 2016-2017. It then moved to the Cincinnati Contemporary Arts Center (2018) and is now being piloted at the Glasgow School of Art (2018-2019). It would be a great thrill to bring this to Moore.

(2) Countermeasures: Water Clocks

Water clocks (or clepsydrae) work like this: one large vessel is made, and filled with water. On the water's surface, a smaller vessel is placed. The smaller vessel is made with a small hole at the bottom that allows the water to flow in. One interval has passed when the bowl sinks to the bottom of the larger bowl.

Time-keeping devices are always time-producing devices. Rather than understanding time as neatly divisible, linear, and disciplinary—the project of modernization—this project begins with the premise that certain practices and sculptural objects can offer an experience of an alternative and intimate time, a time which is specifically marked by our social engagement with one another.

More info: http://carolinewoolard.com/project/amulet/

(3) Website as Exhibition

What is unusual about my approach to cultural production is that I create multi-year initiatives with open-source Web 2.0 technology while also hand-building objects in immersive installations. In the past decade, I have created discrete sculptural objects while also building four service organizations with digital technology: (1) OurGoods.org, software that facilitates non-monetary exchanges between artists, (2) TradeSchool.coop, a program for peer learning in thirty cities globally, (3) BFAMFAPhD.com, an advocacy platform for cultural equity, (4) and the New York City Real Estate Investment Cooperative, to democratically finance affordable space.

I would love to create a website for peer-to-peer review of student work, across institutions, and ideally, across counties, so that Moore supports a kind of technology for the commons, to cultural exchange for artists and emerging artists. We could determine the shape this would take, at Moore.

More info: creativecommons.org/2016/08/23/caroline-woolard/

After a few emails and two phone calls, I got this email from Patti, announcing that I had received the Fellowship. I was overjoyed. It seemed unreal.

July 9, 2018
Hi Caroline,

Please accept my apologies for not getting back to you sooner. President Fitzgibbon has been away and we finally have been able to discuss "next steps." We would be delighted to have you as the inaugural Walentas Endowed Fellow. (We have been in conversation with one other person, but we think the timing/potential content is better for the next iteration of this initiative.)

The next step is for you and I to begin to bring some shape—with respect to focus/content and temporal frame/availability/commitment—to what this fellowship can become. As you know there is no precedent for this at Moore (but certainly good examples at other schools and organizations), so we will imagine this into existence. Caroline, let's begin with some phone calls, and I also am happy to visit with you in New York—and/or invite you to Moore to meet with

Cecelia (president), faculty, etc. I know that
you have had significant experience creating
programs, so I am wildly enthusiastic to begin
the conversation, hear your ideas, and also
answer your questions and provide relevant
background and context.

I am flying to California on Wednesday and
return Tuesday morning, July 17. It is possible that I may have some time to talk on
Thursday, July 12. Or we can wait until I am
back in Philadelphia. Where are you and what
is your availability?

Best wishes,
Patti

I had learned from my *Capitoline Wolves* [see chapter 7] project at
Cornell to be careful about the budget, so I explained to Patti
that I wanted a very clear separation between the artist fee,
the partner fee, and the production budget for making objects.
I asked for this almost immediately, but it was not until after
I had visited Moore and met with the faculty and staff that I
wrote again to find out about the scope of the project.

August 23, 2018
Patti,

I am inspired to dream after this first visit
to Moore. This week is busy, as I am about to
open https://www.pratt.edu/events/event/13873/
on Tuesday and https://knockdown.center/event/
carried-on-both-sides-encounter-three/ on
Thursday. Would you, Jane, and Cecelia be able
to join me for a private tour of my show at
the Knockdown Center on Saturday, October 27th
from 2-4 p.m.? See the invitation attached,
and please share it with them as well. Send my
thanks! After this week, I move to CT and will
take a week or two to settle in, and can begin
to make a plan for this big project, and have
regular phone calls with you, starting in late
September, I imagine.

Managing

To get the ball rolling on this Fellowship, I
keep wondering: What is the scale of this project? I'd really like to get clear about labor/
materials/stipend/in-kind budget soon, so that
I can be realistic in my dreaming, and also
think strategically about partners who can
also bring some funding and in-kind gifts like
spaces/venues for this endeavor.

(1) Is it possible to work with an undergraduate
or graduate assistant? Could this be an internship or other work-study position? I would love
to do this, starting in the spring, and continuing into the fall and spring of 2019/2020,
to have assistance with research, follow up
with faculty/staff/partners, and on-the-ground
connections to groups.

(2) Can you give me a budget break down, so
I know when and how I will be paid a stipend,
how you will disburse funds (do I give you
receipts?), and whether travel/hotel/hospital-
ity/marketing are covered, or in a separate
budget? In my experiences with MoMA, Cooper
Union, Cornell, and the CAC in Ohio, 1/3 of the
budget went to hotel/travel/marketing, so this
makes a big difference. I would prefer to be
reimbursed by you for materials and labor, or
for you to purchase them directly.

(3) Can you tell me which departments/areas of
Moore might be able to supplement the budget/
assistantships, so I can know whether they are
covering things like fees, partner stipends,
communications design work, video, photography,
meals, travel, etc, or if this is coming out of
the $50k?

Once I know this, I can think about an appropriate and equitable scale for my dreams.

Sending thanks and gratitude,
Caroline

September 7, 2018
Hi Caroline,

Thank you for your patience. The conclusion of the summer and opening of the new
school year has been labor intensive but
good (four staff and faculty searches to
complete, opening of the renovated library,
etc.) I will respond to your questions
below as fully as I can. This will get us
started and then, as you suggest, we should
schedule phone calls and/or other meetings. And we also should think about when
you might want to make another trip to
Moore and Philadelphia — and what would be
your priorities regarding an itinerary of
conversations, meetings, etc.

What is the scale of this project?

Caroline, you are the first so we will be
dreaming and precedent-setting together.
We imagine this as a two-year experience/
fellowship. The unfolding, timing, length
and frequency of visits is something that
will be developed based on your proposed
project/work, ideas, thoughts on cadence
and timing and, of course, your availability. The Walentas Endowment provides
$25,000 annually — a total of $50,000. I do
believe that a significant part of this has
to be secured for your artist fee/honorar-
ium with the remaining resources dedicated
to expenses (project-related, your travel,
housing and other costs while in Philadelphia,
etc.) Once we get a little further into
this process, I would be happy (with your
guidance) to draft a working and revisable
budget that we can work with … I also
believe that what you may propose to do may
interest or attract other resources/partners
(Mural Arts? Jacque's Liu's office? Free
Library? Barnes?)

(1) Is it possible to work with an under-graduate or graduate assistant?

I think it will be wonderful to engage student interns or assistants. I am confident that we can identify 1-2 students for spring 2019. And all BFA students are required to do a summer internship between the junior and senior year. I am sure there would be students who would be thrilled to do their summer 2019 internship with you. And for our next admission cycle for the MFA/MA—and as we are doing financial aid offers—we can build 1-2 graduate assistantships into your project for 2019-2020. And I am currently working with a second year MFA student who will have some available hours on her annual assistantship to work with you.

(2) Can you give me a budget break down, so I know when and how I will be paid a stipend, how you will disburse funds (do I give you receipts?)

Caroline, I expect that I will need to check in with our Business Office to develop some scenarios for how we will release money to you. But I did imagine that your fees/ compensation should be a significant part of the overall budget of $50,000. And then we should begin to get a sense of what other expenses would be (# of trips to Philadelphia for the duration of the Fellowship, materials and other project expenses, etc.) I think that if I can begin to draft a budget with you, this will be illuminating and also begin to bring both a temporal and physical shape and realistic scope to your proposed project—or whatever it becomes.

(3) Can you tell me which departments/areas of Moore might be able to supplement the

budget/assistantships, so I can know whether they are covering things like fees, partner stipends, communications design work, video, photography, meals, travel, etc, or if this is coming out of the $50k?

Any student interns or assistants will be covered by the college through financial aid, graduate assistantships, etc. All students will be compensated and be given clear "contracts" regarding their scope of work, estimated hours to be worked, hourly wages, etc. We have a great new Executive Director of Marketing and Communication (Nicole Steinberg) who will be delighted (and I am sure) to support communications, etc. We will seek to be imaginative and resourceful in our use of existing budgets and available funds at the college.

Once I know this, I can think about an appropriate and equitable scale for my dreams.

Shall we schedule a phone call in the next few weeks? I generally am around and happy to work with your availability.

I am excited about working with you, Caroline—and doing all that I can to support your ideas and vision. By the way, I recently had dinner with Mierle Laderman Ukeles in New York. She said that you had wondered if she had nominated you for the Walentas Fellow. She did not. Actually, I did. In our "call" we invited Moore faculty and staff to make nominations/recommenda- tions—and I exercised my opportunity to participate. Of course, I was delighted by the outcome of the panel's deliberations and decision.

Not sure why my computer inexplicably keeps
changing the font. Sorry for this.

All best,
Patti

Soon after this, I created a Google spreadsheet of the budget and Patti's assistant helped to add expenses to keep track of what was being spent on production versus my artists fee. Because the Fellowship was new, and because we needed to confirm the various partnerships were in place, including with the U.S. Federation of Worker Cooperatives and the Free Library of Philadelphia, it took awhile for the Fellowship to be official. Although I worked intensively from August 2018 on, it wasn't until seven months later, in February 2019, that the Fellowship was announced to the public, and it took until March 2019 for my consulting agreement to be finalized. It is important to note that the scope of work described here was supported fully by Patti Philips, who helped translate my proposals and ideas into a form that the Business Office at Moore would accept.

CONSULTING SERVICES AGREEMENT
This consulting services agreement
("Agreement") is made and entered
into on March 1, 2019 between Moore
College of Art & Design, "College"
and Caroline Woolard, "Consultant,"
and is effective retroactive to
March 1, 2019.

Background/Scope:
The College is engaging the
Consultant to serve as the inaugural
Jane & David Walentas Fellow. During
this engagement, the Consultant
will collaborate with members of the
College community and selected
artists, cultural and other community
organizations in the Philadelphia
area. During this collaboration, the
Consultant will work with members
of the Moore community to bring art
process and art objects into spaces,
circumstances, meetings, and other
quotidian settings and passages. The
Consultant will make, with support
of Moore studio technicians, who
shall perform such work during their
regular work time for the College,
beautiful objects for facilitation
settings, meetings, and other
group settings.

These objects will be displayed
first at Moore, and then shall be
loaned to and become a central part
of the Free Library of Philadelphia's
new Public Engagement space where
they can be used on site and/or
borrowed for use by community organizations and artist-led workshops

to enhance collaboration among
community and art institutions while
animating the library and its new
community engagement space as a
center for contemporary art.

Other key collaborators include the
United States Federation of Worker
Cooperatives; Maya Pindyck,
Director of the Margaret Minik
Writers Studio; Joanna Jenkins,
Associate Dean of Graduate,
Professional, and Continuing
Education; Ashley York, Head Studio
Technician; and Nicole Steinberg,
Chief Marketing & Communications
Officer, as well as a number of
College faculty members.

Timeline:
March 2019—Launch of public pro-
graming and events

Summer 2019—Planning of objects,
engagement, and additional public
programs

Fall 2019—Project development, fabrication of art objects, publicity
of programs

Spring 2020—Exhibition opening and
ongoing events

Term:
This consulting agreement will begin
on March 1, 2019 and end on April
30, 2020.

Termination:
This agreement can be terminated by the College at any time, in its sole discretion, with 30 days notice to the Consultant.

Compensation:
Consultant will receive a total of $22,512 paid in 14 monthly installments of $1,608 beginning on March 1, 2019 through April 1, 2020.

Independent Contractor Status:
The Consultant is an independent contractor and the College will not withhold taxes from fees paid. Consultant is responsible for payment of all federal, state, and local taxes, including any withholding taxes.

Intellectual Property:
The Consultant will own all artwork created by Consultant in connection with this Agreement, and at the expiration of the term of the Agreement she may take or retain physical possession of such artwork, or donate it to the College or to such other person or organization, including the Free Library of Philadelphia, as she deems appropriate.

By signing this Agreement, Consultant agrees that the College may, both during and after the term of the Agreement, take photographs of any artwork, and may reproduce images of any artwork or written materials created in connection with this Agreement, including but not limited to:
- in publicity and/or publications in conjunction with this Agreement;
- in promoting the College in any media (including but not limited to, print, catalogs, websites, and social media)
- for educational use.

The College, in its sole discretion, may choose at any time not to display a particular art object on College property, or may remove any art object from display on College property, and such action shall not constitute a breach of the Agreement.

Miscellaneous:
No changes or additions to this agreement shall be effective unless approved in writing by both parties.

Applicable Law:
This agreement shall be governed by, and construed in accordance with, the laws of the Commonwealth of Pennsylvania.

This Agreement may be executed in counterparts, each of which shall be binding upon the party signing, and all of which together shall constitute a single Agreement.

In consideration of the foregoing,
and intending to be legally
bound, the parties have executed
this agreement on the date set
forth above.

Signed by
Caroline Woolard

Within a few months of accepting this Fellowship, five big commissions came my way from other institutions. In October, 2018, I had an invitation from curator Alison Burstein to do a project at Tenthaus in Oslo. At the same time, an invitation came from Daniel Eisenberg and Ellen Rothenberg to do a project for a group show about labor which included Mierle Laderman Ukeles, at the School of the Art Institute of Chicago. In December 2018, after a few months of conversation and proposals, a formal invitation came from Macushla Catherine Robinson and Anna Harsanyi to do a project that would coincide with a centennial exhibition at the New School. Six months after these first round of invitations came in, in March 2019, I got an invitation from Caitlin Rubin at the Rose Art Museum to be a Perlmutter Resident artist and the inaugural INDEX artist for "a new initiative at the museum, housed in the Lee Gallery, bi-annual projects by INDEX artists will produce site-responsive and participatory platforms and programs." I was excited, but overwhelmed.

One reason I was overwhelmed is that I had decided to enroll in an unusual, low-residency, free MFA program, and I knew that I would be traveling to Bennington, VT once a week. I was one of two MFA candidates in the first cohort of the MFA in Public Action program, created and directed by Robert Ransick, which is "specifically geared to professionals working in the arts, including visual and performing artists and leaders, who are making significant contributions to the field of socially and civically engaged creative practice." I was starting my second year in a tenure-track job, teaching three courses per semester at the University of Hartford, and one course per quarter at Bennington, as part of the work required for the MFA program. In addition to this, I was working to finish *Making and Being*, a book for arts educators, co-authored by Susan Jahoda. See Chapter 5 on BFAMFAPhD for more about this book, which was a priority. A lot was going on.

I knew that I could not make five different projects in one summer; I had learned from at Exchange Café see chapter 4 at MoMA and from *LISTEN* see chapter 6 at the Contemporary Art Center in Cincinnati that working this way would overwhelm me and result in projects that were not fully developed. I had also been learning from my partner, Leigh Claire La Berge,

Around this time, I began training for a 120 mile circumnavigation of Mont-Blanc, the highest mountain in Europe.

who works daily toward one book that is finished every three–seven years. Without taking on other big projects, she showed me the daily patience of sitting with one idea, and letting it build and deepen, over years. In one of our discussions at Bennington, I asked my friend Aaron Landsman, a playwright who I recruited to join the MFA cohort with me, what to do. Should I cancel the other projects or could I combine them, somehow? Aaron told me that in the performing arts, singular plays and dance works would be shown multiple times, with something called a "rolling premiere," which would be produced by all of the theaters that supported the showings of the work in progress. I loved this idea. This thrilled me. Why couldn't I do this in the visual arts?

I decided to make a rolling premiere for the project I was developing at Moore. I would show it as it evolved, and adapt it to each location: at The Galleries at Moore, at Tenthaus in Oslo, at the Sullivan Galleries at the School of the Art Institute of Chicago, at the Anna Maria and Stephen Kellen Gallery at the New School, and at the Rose Art Museum. I would make one video, and bring objects for facilitation to local groups to adapt and improve, based upon their contexts, groups, and conditions. With each site, I would work with a local facilitator. For example, in Chicago, I knew Jessica Cook-Qurayshi, the Director of the Labor Education Center at DePaul University was interested in working with objects to facilitate dialogue. She used the objects I made in workshops about labor negotiations for union members. At the Rose Art Museum, curator Caitlin Rubin put me in touch with Don Greenstein of the University Ombuds. Don continues to use the objects I have made, both in workshops at the Rose Art Museum, and in his office, outside of an art setting.

Mediating

To ensure that the concept of the rolling premiere was understood, I created text that I sent to the curators at each site, for the wall labels, and I included it in the video that I directed for the project.

> This project would not be possible without the labors of Jessica Cook-Qurayshi, Director of the DePaul University Labor Education Center; Esteban Kelly, Director of the U.S. Federation of Worker Cooperatives; Zaq Landsberg; Alex Mallis and Cori Spencer of Meerkat Media film cooperative; Susan Jahoda and members of BFAMFAPhD; Ecovative; and Firefly Finishes. This project is part of a rolling premiere with commissions from Moore College of Art & Design, Brandeis University, Tenthaus, Bennington College, the School of the Art Institute of Chicago, and the New School.

In addition to this, for the exhibition in Oslo, I brought in The Study Center for Group Work [see chapter 2], and used part of that budget to create a booklet that showcased my work as simply one of many objects for groups.

I also made 3D-printed versions of *The Meeting Game*, and a facilitation guide, in dialogue with curator Caitlin Rubin, to share *The Meeting Game* widely in arts and non-arts contexts. Working with The Free Library of Philadelphia, I will continue this work.

> RULES OF *THE MEETING GAME*
>
> Two or more people can play at a time. To start, each player needs at least one of each kind of ball. For example: 1 small ball, 2-5 big balls, and 2-5 medium balls. Each person starts with one of each kind of ball, and these instructions.
>
> - Only one person can speak at a time.
> - In order to speak, you must roll a ball to someone else at the table.

- Roll a small ball to introduce a new topic,
  a big ball to respond, and a medium ball to
  make connections.
- The person receiving a rolling ball does not
  need to respond.
- You may redistribute your balls at any time,
  without speaking.
- The game is over when the group says it is.

This game is inspired by *Threeing*, a collaborative practice that was developed by the video-artist Paul Ryan between 1971 and the end of his life, in 2013. *Threeing* is "a voluntary practice in which three people take turns playing three different roles: initiator, respondent, and mediator." See chapter 2

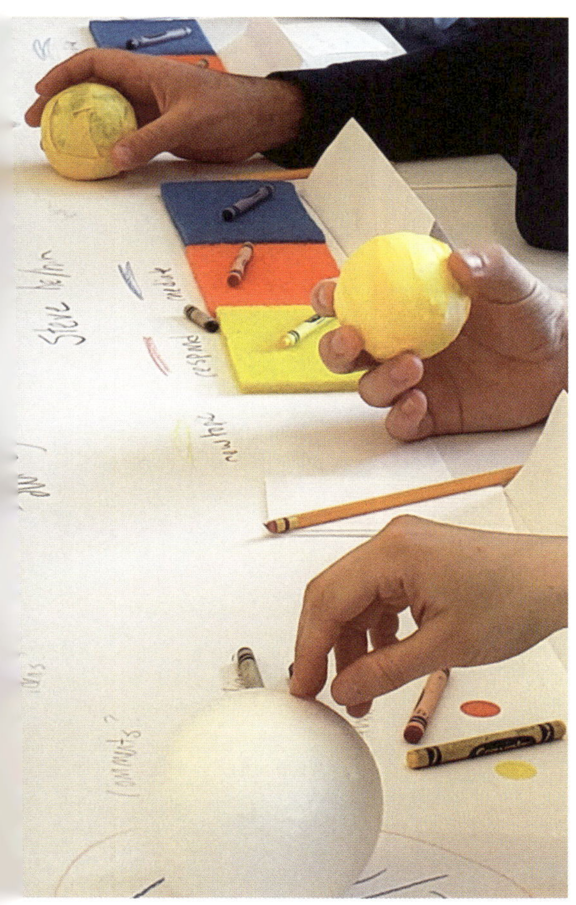

fig. 1-20
The Meeting Game in progress,
tested in 2018 at The Free Library
by the MFA Studio Art and MFA
Community Practice students at
Moore, thanks to Graduate
Director, Daniel Tucker. Photo
by Nicole Steinberg.

The Meeting

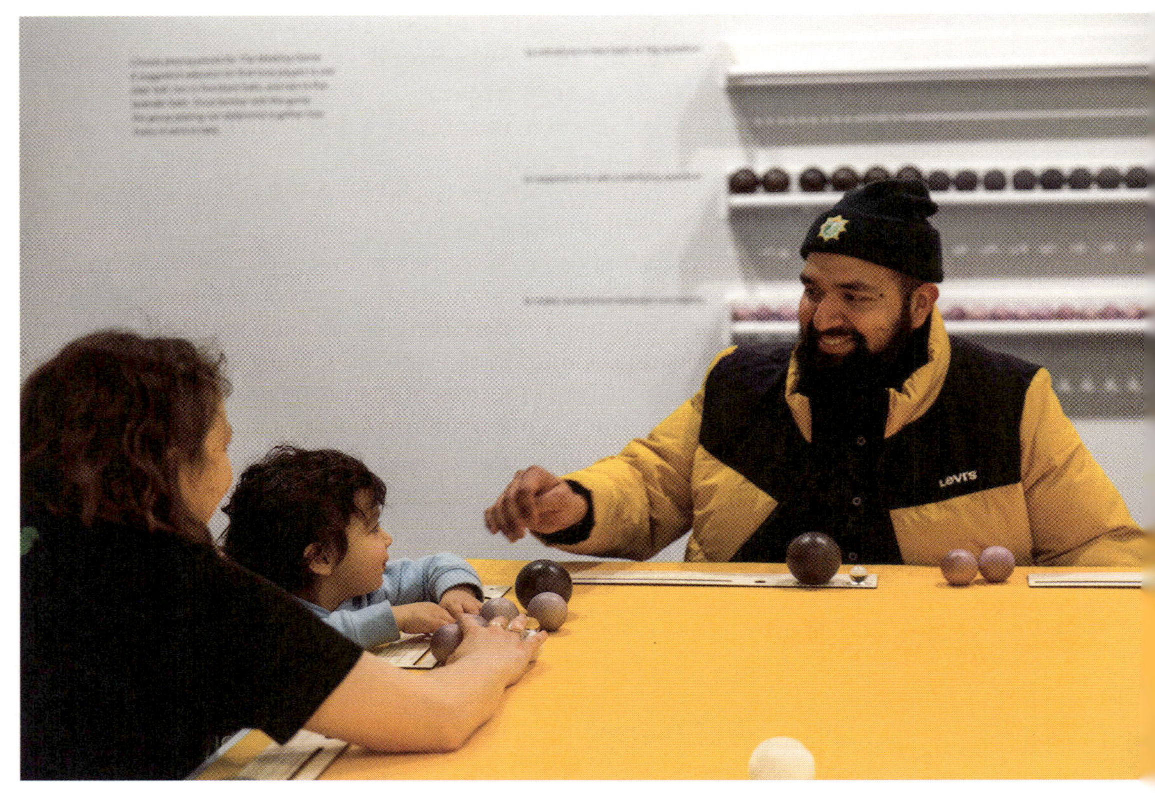

fig. 1-21
The Meeting Game in progress,
tested in 2019 at the Rose Art
Museum by Abigail Satinsky
Curator, Tufts University Art
Galleries, artist Anthony
Romero, and their child, Kahlo.
Photo by Mel Taing as part of
INDEX, curated by Caitlin Rubin.

Institutional
Invitation

In addition to a video artwork I created with Alex Mallis, that explains *The Meeting Game* in an obscure manner, I made an informational video with Don Greenstein, an "Ombuds" person at Brandeis University who I worked with at the Rose Art Museum. According to the Brandeis website, the Ombuds are "a confidential, independent, impartial, and informal resource for all members of the Brandeis community including undergraduates and graduate students, faculty, staff, and alumni." Don worked with me as a facilitator, using the objects I created, from October through April, and he asked me if he could present our work together at a conference for meditators and Ombuds people. I am always excited when a project in the arts finds advocates who take initiative to share the work in non-arts contexts. In preparation for his presentation, he wrote about his experiences with *The Meeting Game*.

> Strange Objects on the Table
> Don Greenstein, 2020
>
> As a mediator, conflict resolver, facilitator, trainer, and person who cares about people, I'm always seeking ways to engage with participants, empowering them to find options and outcomes that work for them. Recently, I spent some time experiencing Caroline Woolard's *Meeting Game*, with various sized spheres on a felt covered ping pong table. I have always had flowers, things (stones, feathers, shells, etc.) on my round mediation table in my office. When I was asked to participate in her recent presentation at the Rose Art Museum, I was happy to participate, and look at what value unique objects bring to difficult conversations.
>
> I facilitated 4 different conversations with the objects she made and participated in another 3. What I personally experienced and observed was that people enjoy holding something in their hands when having difficult conversations. I listen more intently while moving a sphere (or other object) through my hand, while listening or speaking. I did ask a

few people about their experiences of picking something up off the Ombuds table, that are placed there for people to hold or play with during any given session. Sometimes people even ask to take something with them when they leave the process. I was told that it is a distraction that helps with positive or a relaxed mindful communicative process.

I have a sense that some people feel they can put the negative or positive energy into an object and remove it from their own psyche. I have never had anyone complain about these objects or use them in an inappropriate manner. I do find at times some people ask why I have them on the table. No one asked while sitting at Caroline's *Meeting Game* table. There may be a difference in facilitating in an art museum as opposed to an Ombuds or Mediators office! Whatever the case, I have personally observed and experienced that having unique objects in a CR process adds value.

I look forward to collaborating more with Caroline as I believe her interest in how art and conflict resolution interact has great value to the work I care deeply about. I find that even having a pen and paper on the table, people frequently doodle on paper. I see this as another manner of helping an individual focus and listen at a deeper level. I think Caroline's work is useful to conflict resolvers and people who are in conflict. I can see many ways to use her artistic work in conflict resolution processes, facilitated meetings, and even in one-on-one coaching situations. I too as a facilitator, mediator or ombuds frequently hold or touch something with my hands, feet, or arms. It's a manner of helping me listen attentively to a difficult discussion being presented to me and others.

As with every project, I wanted a public program to be associated with objects for groups, to shift discourse about what is possible in the arts, and to tie in artists from The Study Center for Group Work ^{see chapter 2}. I proposed that the Free Library of Philadelphia run a conference about the role of objects in groups. The Free Library was excited about this, but unsure about funding. I decided to apply for a Guggenheim for this, and asked Stephanie Bursese at Haverford if she would support the project, as she had been enthusiastic about my work at Moore, and had invited me to propose a project for the Philadelphia Area Creative Collaboratives Program that she Directs at Haverford College. I found out that I did not get the Guggenheim in early April, a few weeks after the COVID-19 pandemic spread and nearly every school and art space had closed and turned to online forms of gathering.

Now, in May 2020, I am adapting both the *The Meeting Game* and the day-long convening of artists and facilitators, which I am calling *The Gathering*, to online contexts for groups, as COVID-19 has upended two assumptions that I had made: (1) that participants would be able to gather in an enclosed space, and (2) that participants would be comfortable touching objects. I am now experimenting with objects for homes and public spaces as well as online platforms for gathering, including virtual reality platforms.

At the Free Library, for example, patrons will now be able to receive objects by mail, or to pick up *The Meeting Game* with curbside pick up, as no one can enter the library at this time. In addition to this game, which can be used by patrons at home and then cleaned by library staff, I am developing a new series of objects that can be 3D-printed at local maker spaces and taken home to keep, and an audio guide for public gatherings in parks about ways to transform conflict in groups. The audio guide will be produced at a high level to allow people to learn at their own pace.

In addition to this, Don Greenstein, the "Ombuds" person at Brandeis University is now training facilitators nationally to bring *The Meeting Game* to Zoom and other online communication platforms as part of the International Ombudsman conference. Esteban Kelly and I are adapting our facilitation process to Zoom by mailing materials to participants in advance (when budgets allow) or inviting workshop participants to work with the materials and objects that already exist around them.

September 16, 2019

A Guggenheim Fellowship will support the development and completion
of *The Gathering*, a research-based
sculptural installation and a two-
day conference about conflict transformation in self-organized groups.
This project will be presented in
Philadelphia, PA (fall 2021) in
partnership with Haverford College
and the Center for Peace and Global
Citizenship, in Bennington, VT
(winter 2021) at the Center for the
Advancement of Public Action, and in
Santa Ana, CA at Grand Central Arts
Center (spring 2022). *The Gathering*
will be the subject of the documentary
series New York Close Up, a digital
film series produced by Art21.

The Gathering is an immersive
installation of sculpture and a
two-day conference in an abandoned
office building. Visitors will
approach sculptures, placed in the
banal physicality of everyday
offices, that evoke the human body
through its absence. In the past, I
have worked with electrical outlets,
clocks, and meeting tables because
they intimate the power dynamics of
meetings. In a recent installation,
a tongue hangs from the ceiling.
Enormous glass levels are pulled by
gravity over wooden knobs. A deflated
object is plugged into a box the
size of a ceiling tile, always
charging. An hourglass never runs
out of time. This array of

sculptural objects, as well as a
series of videos and a game placed
on a boardroom table, reflect upon
the unavoidable antagonisms of
working together.

The Gathering will deepen my practice through a large-scale installation and two-day conference with
members of worker-owned businesses,
artists, and people interested in
economic justice and the arts who
activate the installation. This
project takes "the meeting" itself—
the gathering of people for a formal
purpose—as a site for artistic and
social intervention. Most people
will spend over a quarter of their
lives at work. For office workers,
a large portion of this time will
occur in meetings. Facilitation—
the skillful guiding of the meeting
process—is a key part of running
self-organized groups and worker-
owned businesses, because these
are horizontal organizations that
share power and require that members
attend meetings in order to make
decisions together.

Rather than trying to "solve" conflict
in groups, I have been learning to
see interpersonal conflict as an
opportunity to transform relationships, groups, and to consider the
systems that make antagonism inevitable. This approach to conflict is
called conflict transformation,
rather than conflict resolution,
and is often used by members of

worker-owned businesses. I have been learning from these groups and making objects in response to them, and am now ready to bring these groups together in a public conference.

A central component of *The Gathering* is an installation of handmade nets that hang from square ceiling grids. My interest in nets comes from a formal experiment with the metaphor of the colonial net, a tool that traps, and holds, in my use of it, a mushroom bust of a head. Cascading from the ceiling and hung on the wall, these nets I have been developing "catch" sculptures and make reference to both the fishing nets of colonial Philadelphia and to the minimalist, conceptual works of the artists Eva Hesse and Jiro Takamatsu. I want the project to hold this tension.

I have started making square walnut frames that mirror the shape and scale of ubiquitous ceiling tiles, suspended overhead in meeting spaces as "dropped" or "false" ceilings. The false ceiling is a surface that hides the infrastructure installed above it—air diffusers, smoke detectors, sprinklers, CCTV cameras, and neon lights—from the room below. In everyday speech, the ceiling acts as a metaphor for a limit which cannot be trusted. Think of a "glass ceiling" or a "debt ceiling." The square frames hold net sculptures that fit perfectly in everyday office ceilings and can be installed in a gallery, an office, or

transported by meeting facilitators. The work reaches beyond this apparent limit.

The Gathering follows on the heels of two years of material experimentation with glass-blowing, net-making, mycelium-growing, and research about worker-owned businesses with members of the United States Federation of Worker Cooperatives (USFWC). As the inaugural Walentas Endowed Fellow at Moore College of Art & Design (2018-2020), and as the Ruth Ann and Nathan Perlmutter Artist-in-Residence at the Rose Art Museum (2019-2020), I have had time to develop ideas that have taken me to *The Gathering*. I am ready to create a project on a large scale.

With a Guggenheim Fellowship, I will be able to continue this work with Esteban Kelly, Director of the USFWC, learning conflict transformation techniques that inform the sculptures and videos that I will make. At Haverford College, I will work with confirmed partners Craig Borowiak, Associate Professor of Political Science, and the Center for Peace and Global Citizenship to develop public programs around unconventional meeting practices with sculptural objects and to convene artists, organizers, and activists, as well as campus communities. I will also work with Stephanie Bursese, Philadelphia Area Creative Collaboratives Program Manager, to premiere *The Gathering*, a public project, in 2020-2021. Stephanie and Craig have been following my work at Moore College, and have invited me to create this project at Haverford.

The Fellowship will also allow me to travel to the Center for the Advancement of Public Action in Bennington, VT (2021), where Director Susan Sgorbati will support a convening focused on conflict transformation in the arts, and then to Grand Central Arts Center, and in Santa Ana, CA at Grand Central Arts Center, where Director John Spiak will support a residency to work in glass at California State University at Fullerton and an exhibition and premiere of *The Gathering* (2022). I will also continue my work with mycelium, a mushroom material, and my work with colonial landing nets and net-making. Rose Art Museum curator Caitlin Rubin writes that my use of mycelium "might be read as a material metaphor for Woolard's approach to public practice—a practice in which she seeks, through meaningful collaboration, to acti-vate and ally latent and often disparate energies into generative form." It is my hope that I can continue to deepen my studio-based sculptural techniques in an approach to art-making that emphasizes par-ticipation and dialogue.

I sent a draft of my Guggenheim application to Stephanie Bursese, Program Manager of the Philadelphia Area Creative Collaboratives (PACC) at Haverford, as she had attended my lecture at Moore and expressed interest in working together. Stephanie moved quickly to support a version of *The Gathering* at Haverford, bringing together two faculty members (Shannan Hayes and Craig Borowiak), Esteban Kelly, and me, to run a series of workshops both at Haverford and in a community space in Philadelphia. The Philadelphia Area Creative Collaboratives seed grant provides $500 for each faculty member, $3,000 for the artist, and $3,000 for the partner organization (Esteban), and $3,000 for food, transportation, space rentals, and materials. Stephanie invited us all to edit the description of the project in a shared Google document. Here is the way we decided to describe the initiative and the first of three workshops:

Through Conflict

What skills — emotional and organizational — help us work together to achieve progressive social change? How might we create bonds of trust amidst interpersonal conflict, while still allowing space for difference and autonomy? How might the pressures generated by austerity and economic crisis generate either new openness to change or greater rigidity and closure? How can interpersonal conflict in groups be transformed into an opportunity for greater communication, new perspectives, and enhanced collective capacity? What does it actually take to create the kinds of spaces that allow people to make mistakes and come back again? And how might aesthetic objects aid us through such difficult dynamics, interrupting pre-given scripts and opening new, collaborative visions? 'Through Conflict: Collective Capacity amidst Capitalist Crisis' brings together the work of artist Caroline Woolard, leading community-oriented transformative justice educator Esteban Kelly from the United States Federation of Worker Cooperatives, and faculty members Shannan Hayes and Craig Borowiak, teaching Haverford

College courses on political economy and affect
theory, in a semester-long investigation into
the above questions.

Workshop, Saturday, March 7th, 1-4 p.m.

In recent years, communities have garnered
breathtaking momentum in building a movement
for new frameworks of justice. Transformative
Justice builds on the intentions of restorative
justice and seeks a more fundamental change in
mitigating alarming trends of the prison
industrial complex and adequately addressing
perpetrators and survivors of sexual assault,
intimate partner abuse, and other forms of
violence. Esteban Kelly of the US Federation of
Worker Cooperatives (USFWC) and AORTA Co-op
(Anti Oppression Resource & Training Alliance)
will guide a workshop where we will explore why
we use transformative justice practice,
stories of how these practices have been used in
the past, and concrete tools we can use in our
own communities.

I also sent a draft of my Guggenheim application to my
partner's friend, Lara Cohen, who is an Associate Professor of
English Literature at Swarthmore. I asked Lara if she would
want to bring this event to Swarthmore, as the location is
relatively close to Esteban Kelly's home, the Free Library of
Philadelphia, and to Haverford College. Lara said yes, and went
ahead and applied for funding from William J. Cooper
Foundation and Promise Fund Grant at Swarthmore without
even telling me. This grant earmarked $4000 for my honorar-
ium, $2500 for Esteban Kelly, budgeted $1000 for travel,
lodging, and meals, and allocated $2000 for materials. To
write the grant on her own, Lara looked through texts that I
sent her, and wrote:

Organized by New York-based sculptor and installation artist Caroline Woolard, *The Gathering*
is a series of workshops that explores how
material objects can interrupt the unavoidable

antagonisms of working together. In the first
workshop, Woolard will lead participants in a
discussion about the role that object-making can
play in collaboration, interpersonal conflict,
and collective capacity. In the next workshop,
participants will respond in material form to
the methods they discussed by creating sculptural objects for use in group communication.
Finally, Woolard, in collaboration with Esteban
Kelly, Director of the US Federation of Worker
Co-ops, will train all interested members of
the community on how to use the objects created
in the workshop in order to enable embodied,
somatic, and haptic knowledge that does not
emerge in purely verbal facilitation methods.

I think that both of these opportunities for support—at
Haverford and at Swarthmore—arose because I wrote to
people to see if they could adapt *The Gathering* to their
contexts and because my idea was articulated clearly in
the text that I wrote for my Guggenheim application. The
Philadelphia Area Creative Collaboratives group decided to
write a text that emphasized the skills required for progressive social change because we were offering free workshops
about transformative justice to activists and organizers in
Philadelphia who we knew personally, and who might not
be able to attend these workshops elsewhere. Lara Cohen
at Swarthmore opted to focus on haptic knowledge in group
work, as the William J. Cooper Foundation and Promise Fund
Grant is intended for students at Haverford who might be
new to organizing or activism. Both grants enabled me to take
funding from elite academic institutions and to channel them
into the solidarity economy, supporting the work of The United
States Federation of Worker Cooperatives and the training
of Philadelphia-based activists and organizers, in addition to
students at those colleges.

2

The Study Center for Group Work

The Study Center for Group Work is both an online resource and an informal network of artists who gather to study practices of collaboration. The Center exists to cultivate behaviors that allow groups to gather together and has been directed by founder Caroline Woolard since 2015.

Listening and looking are forms of artistic attention. Collaboration requires both. What kinds of listening and looking are provoked by contemporary artworks? How can we develop capacities of listening and looking that enable us to become more nuanced critics and practitioners of collaborative work? The Study Center for Group Work starts with the premise that certain practices and tools can offer an experience of collaborative time, a time which is specifically marked by our engagement with one another.

At the invitation of curator Stamatina Gregory, Woolard created a social space called *WOUND: The Study Center for Group Work* at Cooper Union. At Cooper Union, the Center offered trainings in practices of listening, attention, and collaboration using sculptural tools for communication that have been developed by artists who work in groups. The exhibition presented a library of collaborative tools that visitors could check out and use, including "*Threeing* sticks" made by artists Jean Gardner and Paul Ryan. The group Project 404 taught visitors how to sustain attention with imagery by focusing on a single image on their smartphones, and the Design Studio for

Social Intervention offered workshops with the artist Judith Leemann on the power of unconventional analogy in speech and in drawing. The collective Ultra-red offered workshops on modes of listening.

The Study Center for Group Work starts with the premise that certain practices and tools can offer an experience of collaborative time, a time which is specifically marked by our engagement with one another.

Since 2015, members of the Center have convened to share their methods and to make them freely available online. Portions of the Center have travelled to the Glasgow School of Art, Tenthaus in Oslo, and the Free Library of Philadelphia. See *The Meeting* see chapter 1 for objects that Woolard has developed to facilitate dialogue, in collaboration with the US Federation of Worker Cooperatives, Ombudspeople at Brandeis University, and labor union organizers in Chicago.

More information is online at: http://studycollaboration.com

2013/2014
Occupy Wall Street 2011
New York City Community Land
Initiative officially
forms 2013

New York City creates $1.2
million Worker Cooperative
Business Development
Initiative 2014
NYC Real Estate Investment
Cooperative (NYCREIC)
forms 2015
350 members, huge interpersonal
conflict in NYCREIC
Obama 2009-2017
Trump 2017-2020?

Study

I will connect people
who are making objects
for groups.

Commitment

Experience

Person X is destroying the
group's ability to work together.

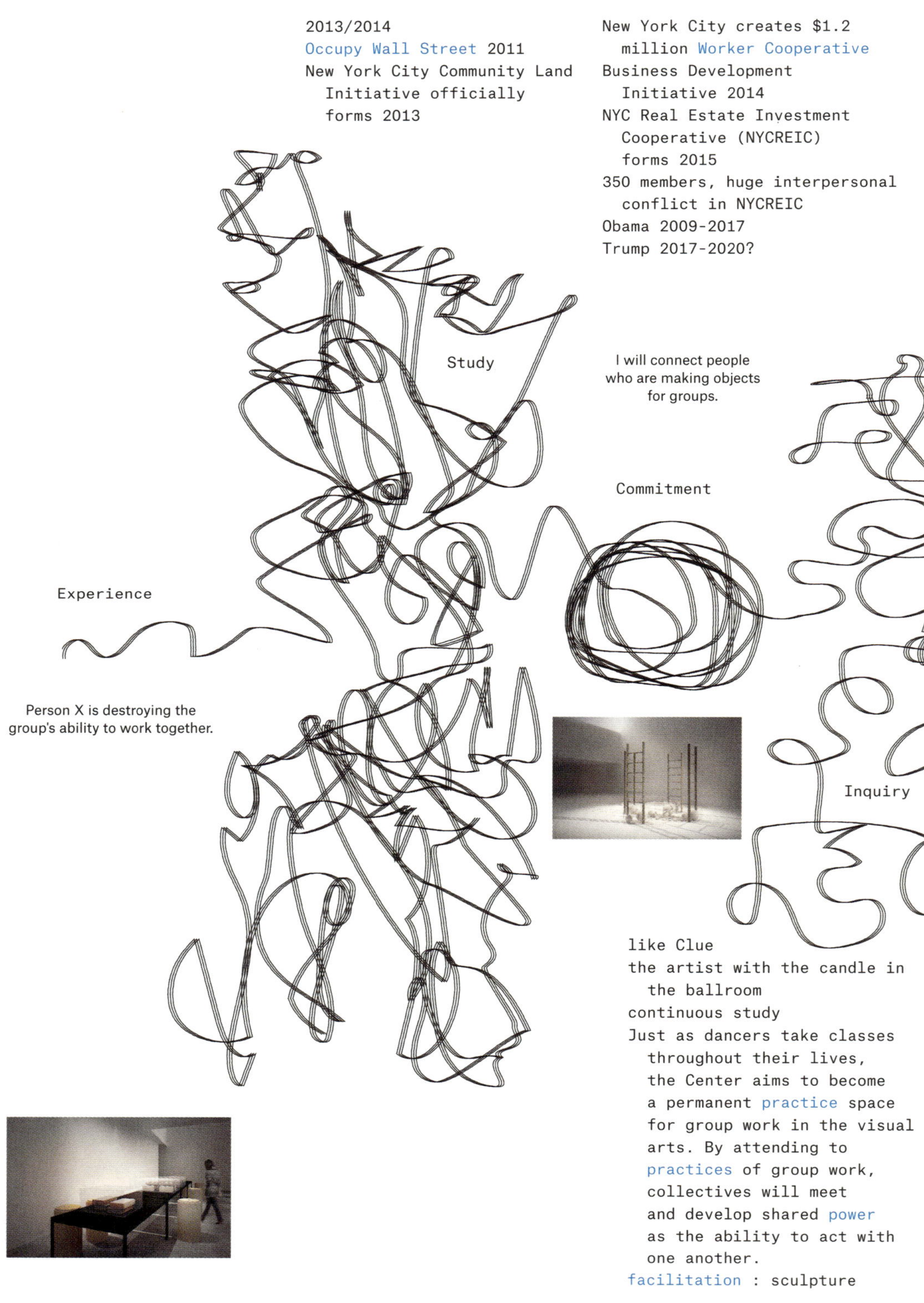

Inquiry

like Clue
the artist with the candle in
   the ballroom
continuous study
Just as dancers take classes
   throughout their lives,
   the Center aims to become
   a permanent practice space
   for group work in the visual
   arts. By attending to
   practices of group work,
   collectives will meet
   and develop shared power
   as the ability to act with
   one another.
facilitation : sculpture

consensus
voting
facilitation
collaboration
collectivity
mutual aid
temperature checks

transformative organizing
US Federation of
  Worker Cooperatives
disability justice
conflict transformation
Generative Somatics
Judith Leemann and
  Kenneth Bailey
UltraRed
Center for Artistic Activism
SOVRN state Scott Benaglio
Process Work Institute

I spend my life in meetings.
Can they be transformative?

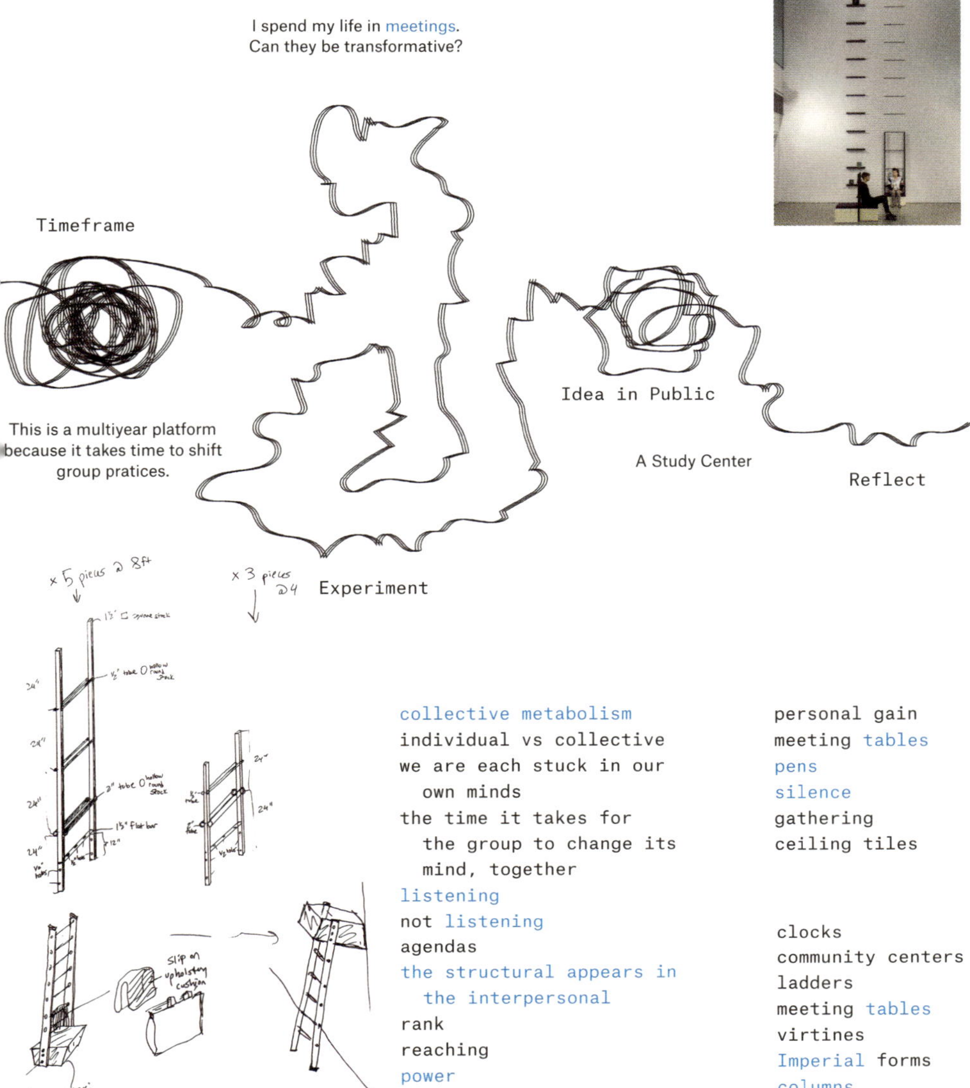

collective metabolism
individual vs collective
we are each stuck in our
  own minds
the time it takes for
  the group to change its
  mind, together
listening
not listening
agendas
the structural appears in
  the interpersonal
rank
reaching
power
privilege

personal gain
meeting tables
pens
silence
gathering
ceiling tiles

clocks
community centers
ladders
meeting tables
virtines
Imperial forms
columns

The Study Center
for Group Work

Institutional Possibility

Alison Burstein is the Curator of Media and Engagement at The Kitchen in New York. As an independent curator, she has curated exhibitions or programs for institutions including Tenthaus (Oslo), Mana Contemporary (Jersey City), The Luminary (St. Louis), Knockdown Center (Queens), Museum of Jurassic Technology (Los Angeles), and NURTUREart (Brooklyn).

Alison Burstein, Curator of Media and Engagement at The Kitchen, 2019

Two tactics have been dominant in the field of artist–institution relationships over the past five decades. While some artists have chosen to create works of institutional critique that put pressure on an institution's structures and ideologies from within, others have stepped outside existing frameworks to build institutions that correct perceived shortcomings in traditional institutional protocols. Caroline Woolard's work is in dialogue with both of these traditions. However Woolard expands upon the practices of institutional critique and alternative institution building by mapping a unique third course—one that is guided by an investment in what she calls "institutional possibility." What distinguishes her strategy is the deliberateness with which she creates new institutions that have the potential to operate both independently and in partnership with other parties: Woolard's institutional projects are designed to be embedded, scaled, and/or reproduced.

Take The Study Center for Group Work. According to a timeline on the institution's webpage, Woolard developed the idea for the project in 2013 and immediately began conversations to find a "partner" organization to support its realization in New York City. Three years later, Woolard collaborated with curator Stamatina Gregory to bring the institution to life at Cooper Union's 41 Cooper Gallery in the form of an exhibition called *WOUND: The Study Center for Group Work*. Since 2016, Woolard and a number of collaborators have continued to run this institution in several different forms and contexts, including through short-term installations and activations of The Study Center's collections within

Collectively-Initiated

institutional spaces and via the continuous maintenance of the institution's website as a resource-sharing platform.

While some artists have chosen to create works of institutional critique that put pressure on an institution's structures and ideologies from within, others have stepped outside existing frameworks

In steering The Study Center's trajectory from its conception through to its functional forms, Woolard has located spaces of institutional possibility within and outside of established institutions. The original iteration of The Study Center as a temporary institutional presence embedded within the larger institution of Cooper Union demonstrated the feasibility of using an existing entity as a launchpad for an independent initiative. Here Woolard utilized the resources available for the exhibition to facilitate the development of The Study Center's collection of artistic practices and associated objects, and she harnessed the visibility associated with staging an exhibition within a prestigious school's gallery in order to bring a broad public into contact with these offerings.

Building on the momentum gained during the exhibition's run—the involvement of artists who contributed objects and led public workshops outlining their practices, the critical praise voiced in exhibition reviews, and the interest of audiences who visited

WOUND—Woolard was then able to secure additional streams of support for the institution. The subsequent iterations of The Study Center reveal the institution's ability to function on varying scales within different physical spaces and organizational infrastructures. Whether a viewer encounters The Study Center's collection of objects (in full or in part) in a physical space or they download PDFs outlining individual artistic practices from www.studycollaboration.org, the institution continues to serve its aim of calling attention to and encouraging experimentation with tools that foster collaborative working methods. And across all of its forms, The Study Center's focus on artistic practices—exercises that are meant to be enacted time and time again with the aim of refining a particular skill or set of skills—defines the institution's commitment to reproducibility: to engage with The Study Center is to learn tools that are by their very nature intended for application across contexts.

Woolard's institutional projects are designed to be embedded, scaled, and/or reproduced.

With The Study Center, as with her other institutional initiatives, Woolard productively collapses the distance between institution-critical strategies and the efforts of institutional formation. The result is an extensive field of possibility in which artists can test new modes of interacting with institutions.

More recent iterations of The Study Center reveal the institution's ability to function on varying scales within different physical spaces and organizational infrastructures.

fig. 2-1
Project 404 teaches practices of attention using the very devices that threaten to distract us. Image courtesy of Project 404 from a practice in 2014. Photo by Filip Wolak.

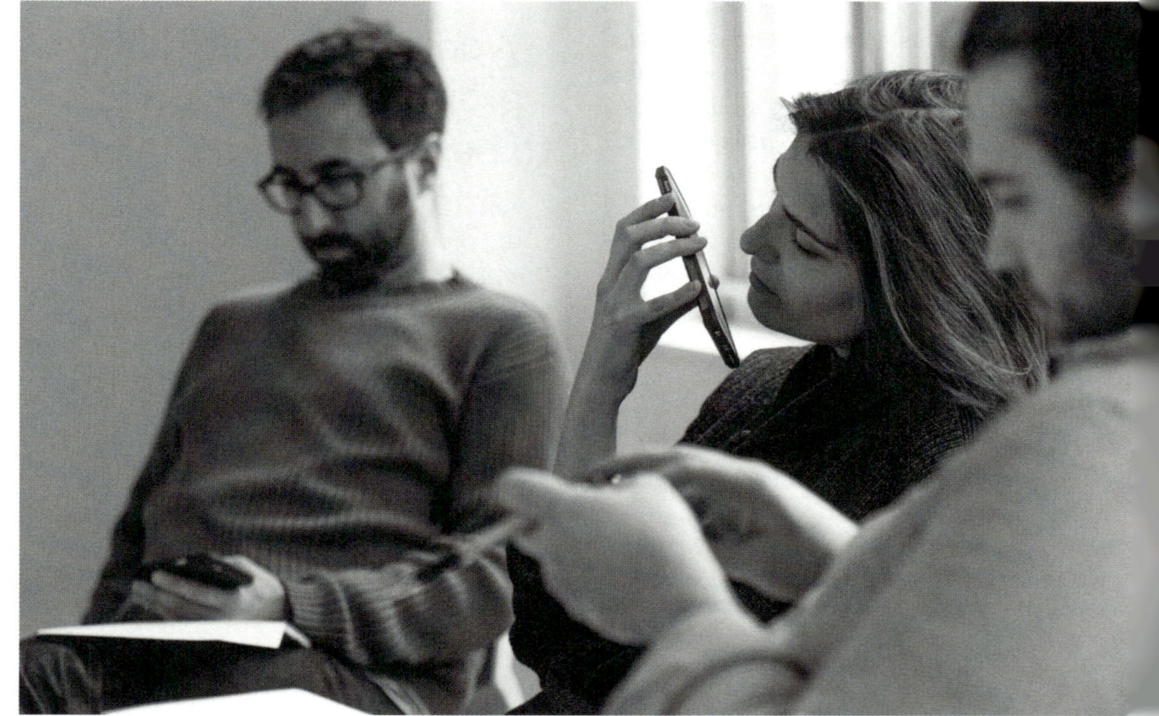

Collectively-
Initiated

A Musculature
of Attention

Stamatina Gregory is the Director of Curatorial
Programs at the Leslie-Lohman Museum of Art.
She has organized exhibitions for institutions
including The Cooper Union, FLAG Art Foundation,
Austrian Cultural Forum, the Institute of
Contemporary Art, Philadelphia, and the Santa
Monica Museum of Art, and was the Deputy Curator
of the inaugural pavilion of The Bahamas at the
55th Venice Biennale.

Stamatina Gregory, Director of Curatorial Programs, Leslie-Lohman Museum of Art, 2020

Can simply being present together be a form of learning, a way of transforming one another? There is something dubiously utopic—or perhaps merely banal—about this question. Yet, it has prodded my thinking as a writer and curator for some time now, even making it into a recent exhibition wall text (as one of several questions on forms of learning and unlearning in contemporary feminisms). In a real economy driven by shares, clicks, and likes, movements toward social justice have had their vision all but replaced by the politics of visibility, in which momentary and disembodied acknowledgment can too easily stand in for solidarity. In a time of escalating and far-reaching humanitarian crisis, what might be the potential for a practice in collectivity that is haptic, that we can touch and feel?

artistic practice ... is continually made and remade through its participants

Artists have considered some of these questions for years, even decades. Caroline Woolard's Study Center for Group Work is an online, iterative resource for listening and communication methods and protocols developed by artists and arts collective. When we collaborated on a physical iteration of the Study Center, which opened to the public as an exhibition and meeting space in the fall of 2016, individual persons and groups were able to develop and exercise what Woolard calls a "musculature of attention" through textual directives (printed on handheld panels), sculptures

The Study Center
for Group Work

our need to negotiate new ways of being together in aural and digital space is more urgent than ever

meant to be held and manipulated, and workshops ranging from restructuring group work practices to understanding phenomenologies of pain. We included no lens-based media among the objects available, to emphasize forms of seeing, hearing, and touching that exceed our relationship to screens. After the 2016 election, the Study Center became a place to collectively process grief, a place to express and imagine past and impending violence through directed physical touch, a place to express and empathize with chronic pain, a place to speak and to learn to listen. Woolard's vision of artistic practice as something that is continually made and remade through its participants, as an ethical force to penetrate our unconscious ways of being with one another, has since only become more urgent. Four years later, as meetings and gatherings are placed on hold by the COVID-19 pandemic, our need to negotiate new ways of being together in aural and digital space is more urgent than ever, with our collective agency, creative practices, and activism at stake—along with our lives. Woolard's practice remains an ethical force to shift and redirect our unconscious ways of being.

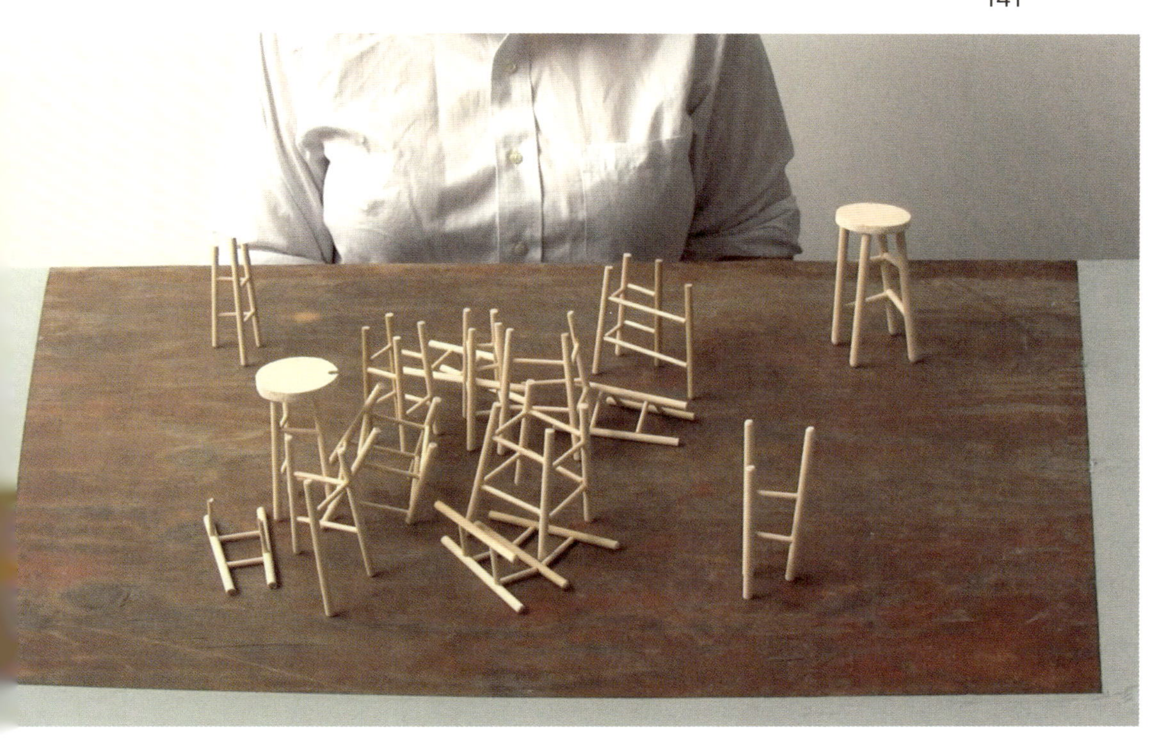

fig. 2-2
Judith Leemann, *preposition and prosthesis*, 2013, found and made objects, dimensions variable. Courtesy of the artist.

These found and made objects were first used to choreograph wordless didactics for *Resonating Bodies*, an examination of the participatory in large-scale sculpture (curated by Shannon Stratton, Soap Factory, 2013) and have been activated as part of The Study Center since 2015.

IMAGINE A GROUP GATHERING

Collectively-
Initiated

IMAGINE A GROUP GATHERING

fig 2-3
Cooper WOUND Furniture (Ladder Chairs), Installation view of Wound: the Study Center for Group Work, 2016, plywood, steel, paint, three-ing rug on loan from Jean Gardener and the Estate of Paul Ryan, dimensions variable. Courtesy of the artist. Photo by João Enxuto.

Sitting there, the chair provides choreography of absent presence, comfortable with the body's void. The chairs that stand and sit and lounge about the Watermill Center are happier than any traditional museum chair. Residents work on and with these chairs. Fluctuating between chair-for-use and chair-as-autonomous-object, these chairs flirt with users/viewers in ways that most museum objects cannot touch. It is this in betweenness that we seek to cultivate, for all objects wish at once to be left alone (to suggest without acting), and to be held, used, and fused with a body.

—Caroline Woolard, excerpt from successful Watermill Residency application, 2009

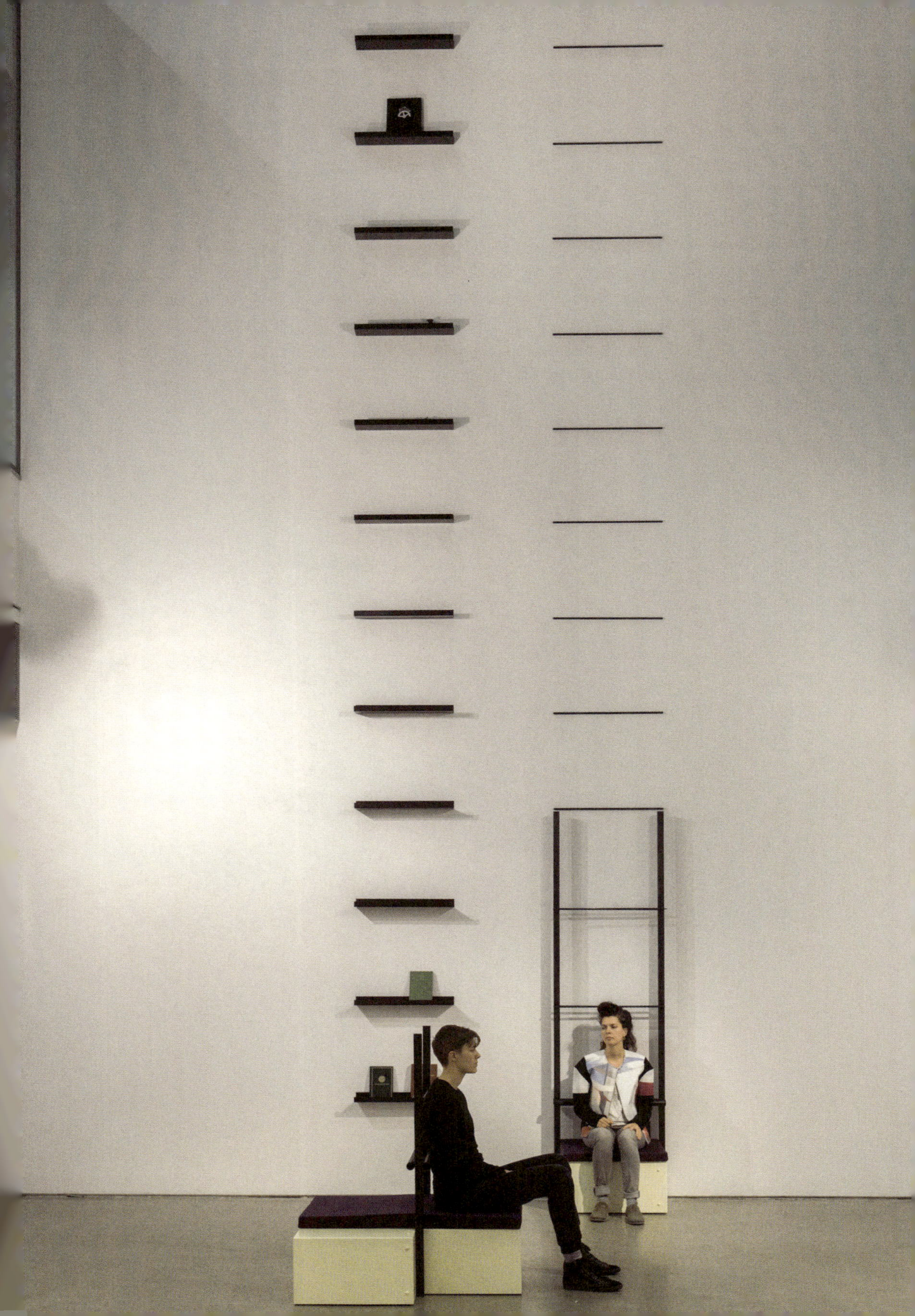

fig. 2-4
*Cooper WOUND Furniture
(Ladder Chairs)*, Installation
view of Wound: the Study
Center for Group Work, 2016,
plywood, steel, paint,
Threeing rug on loan from
Jean Gardener and the Estate
of Paul Ryan, dimensions
variable. Courtesy of the
artist. Photo by João Enxuto.

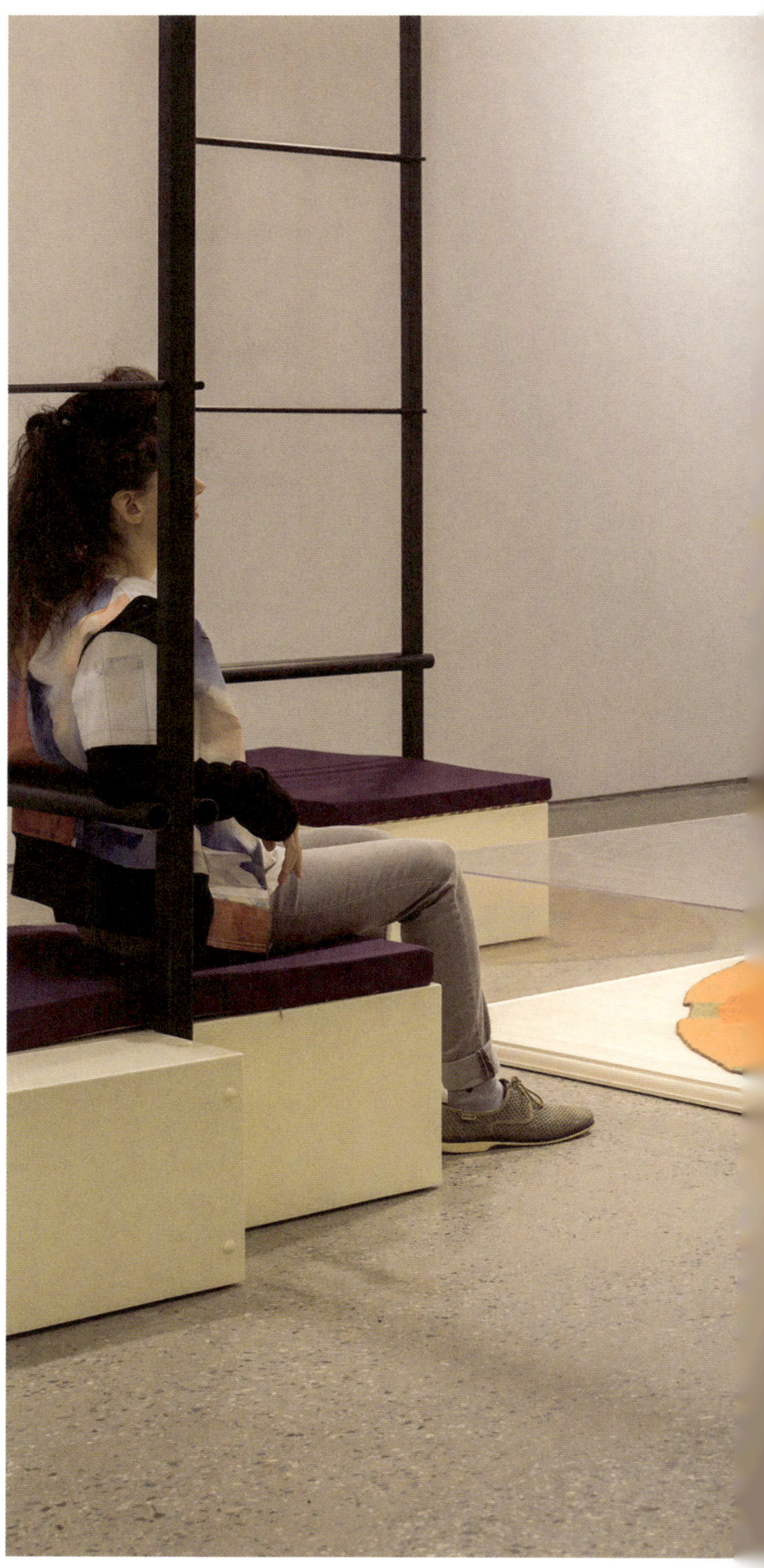

Collectively-
Initiated

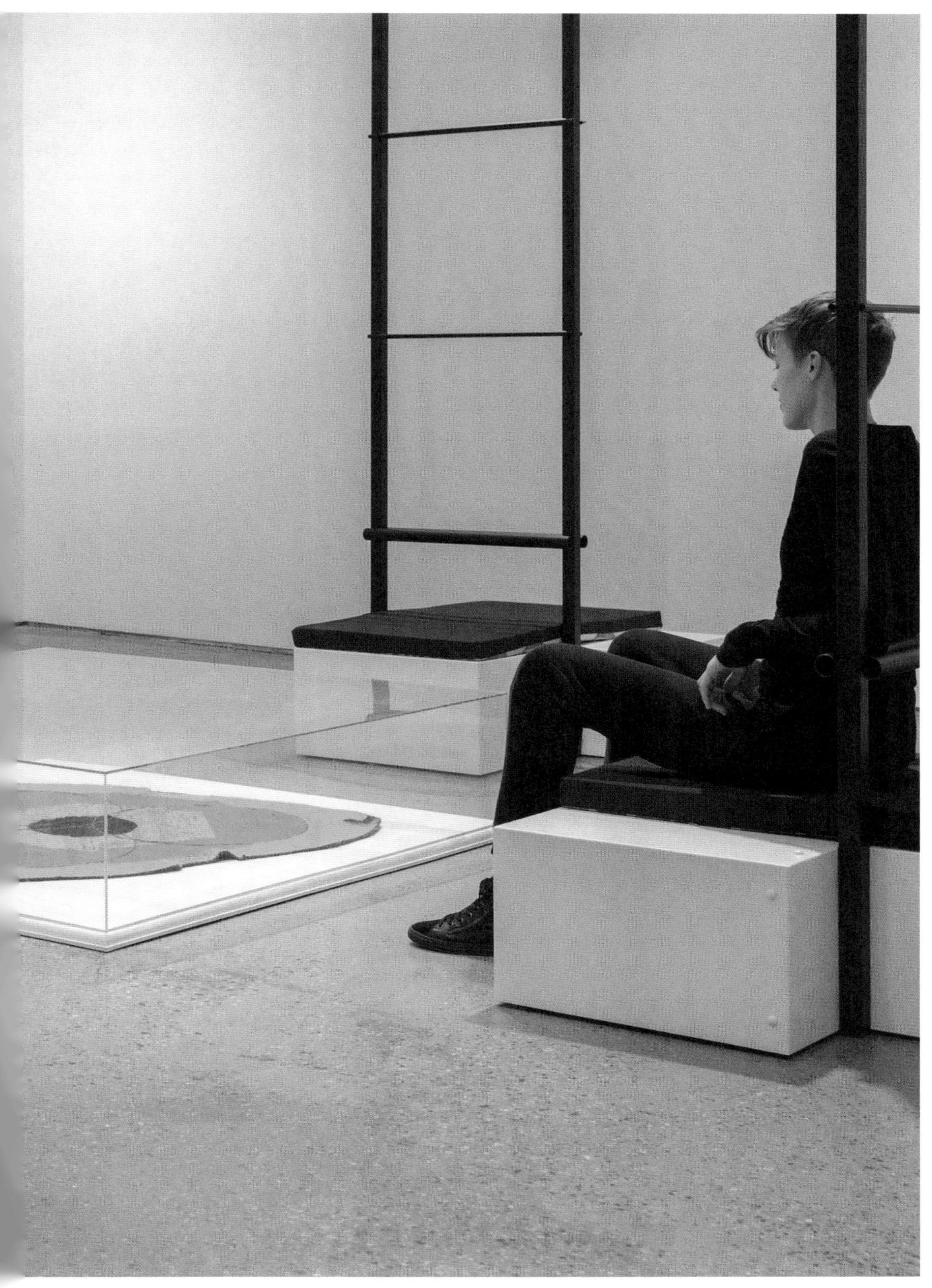

The Study Center
for Group Work

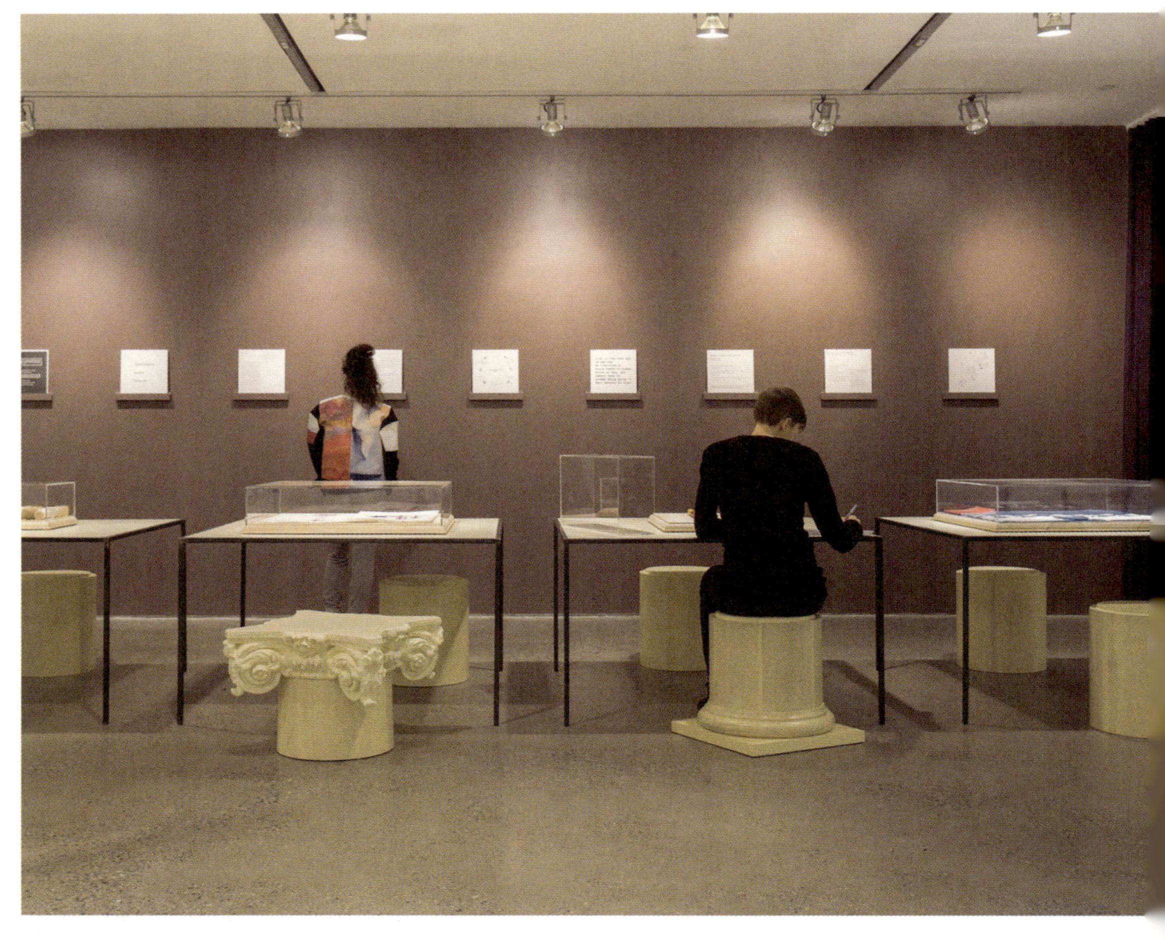

fig. 2-5
DIY Ruin Columns, 2016-2018,
turned poplar, oil paint pickling,
felt, 18 × 16 × 16 inches each.
Courtesy of the artist.

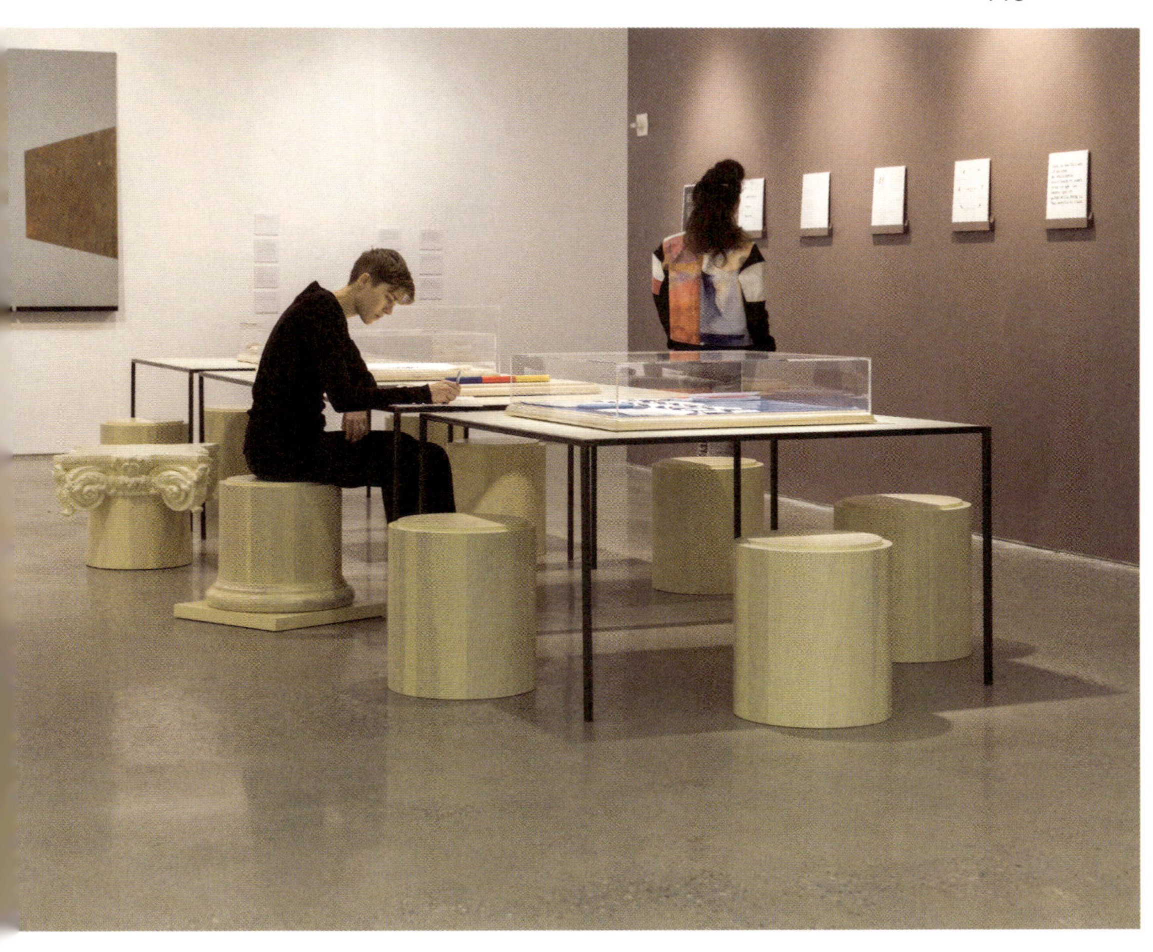

fig. 2-6
DIY Ruin Columns, 2016-2018,
turned poplar, oil paint pickling, felt, 18 × 16 × 16 inches
each. Courtesy of the artist.

fig. 2-7 (overleaf)
DIY Ruin Columns, 2016-2018,
turned poplar, oil paint pickling, felt, 18 × 16 × 16 inches
each. Courtesy of the artist.

The Study Center
for Group Work

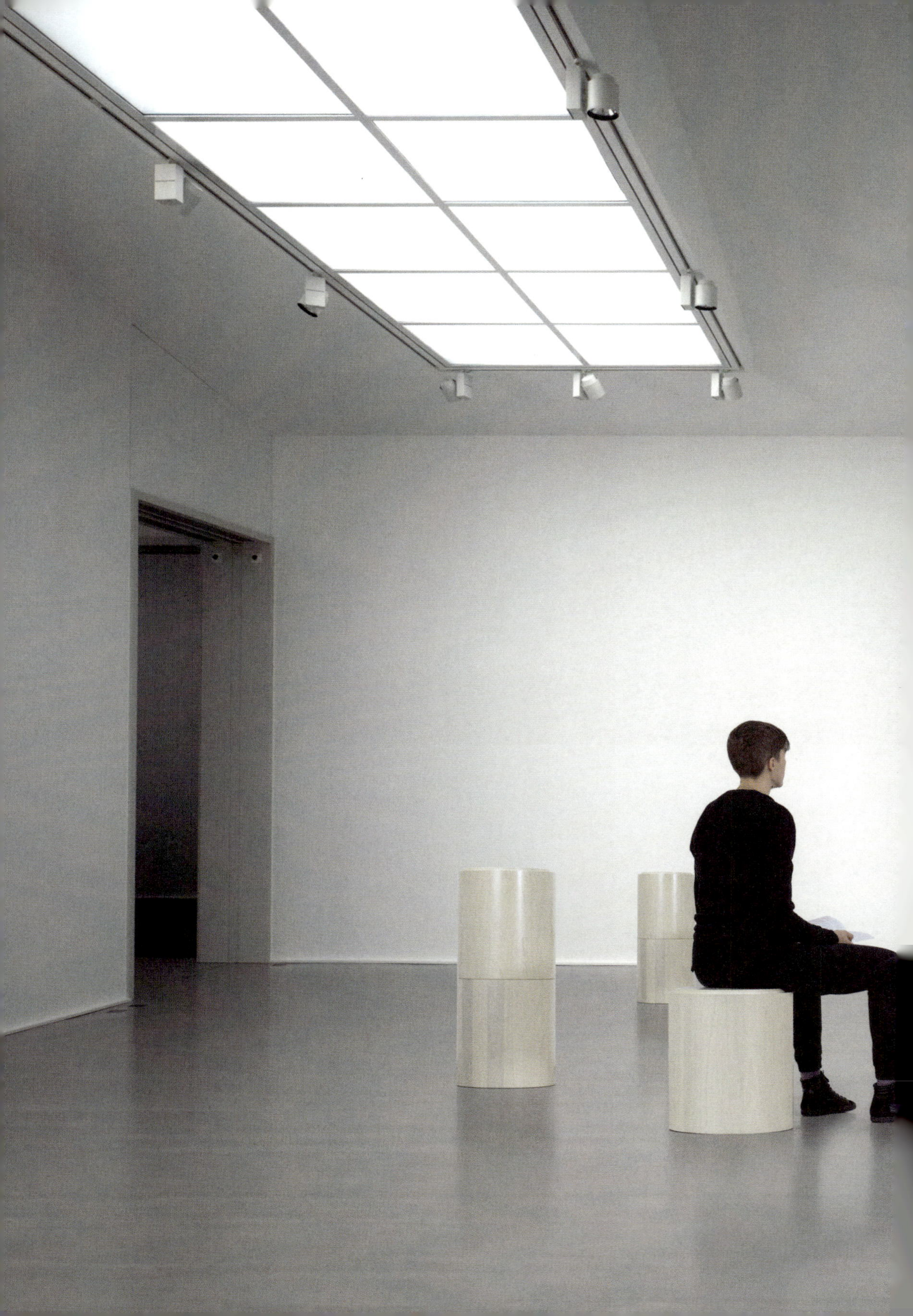

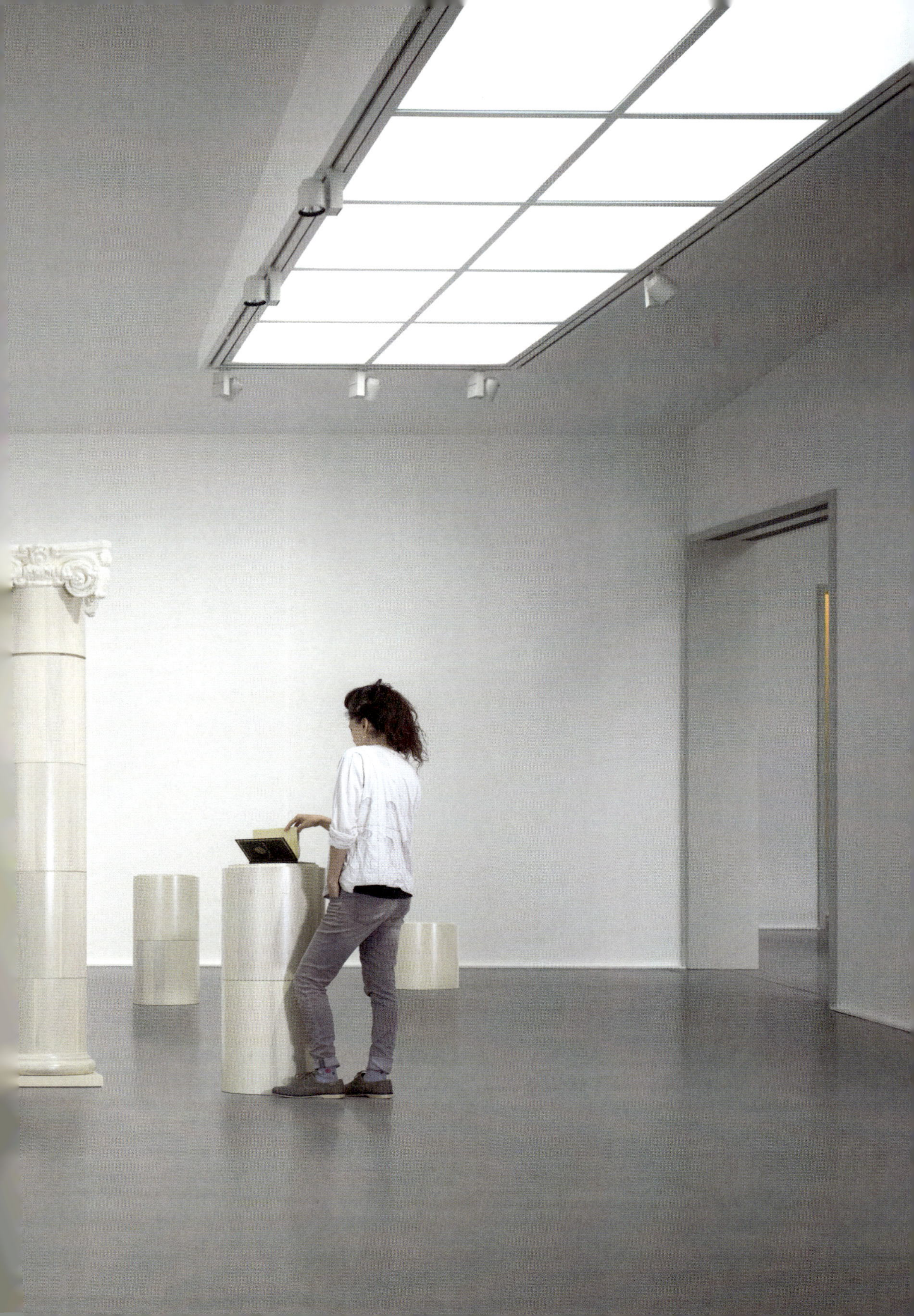

Ephemera

In the pages that follow, you will find correspondence, budgets, grants, technical drawings, and renderings required to create and run the exhibition, online platform, and network of artists in The Study Center for Group Work.

A short documentary video about The Study Center for Group Work was commissioned by the Glasgow School of Art and filmed and edited by Herman Jean-Noel, founder of NEGLAKAY PRODUCTIONS, a grassroots video production house. Artists from the Center who are included in the video are: Chloë Bass, Melanie Crean, Jean Gardener, Judith Leemann, Shaun Leonardo, Adelheid Mers, Leonard Nalencz, Project 404, Paul Ryan, Sable Elyse Smith, Sal Randolph of ESTAR(SER), and Anna Riley.

Woolard has selected ephemera that serves as visual reference points for The Study Center for Group Work. All materials here are reproduced with the consent of collaborators.

Making

In the exhibition at 21 Cooper Gallery, at Cooper Union, it was very important to me that The Study Center balanced the tropes of a white-walled gallery exhibition with my interest in interaction and study. This meant providing lots of space around objects, while also creating furniture that encouraged people to transition from viewer to participant or library patron. I designed a system of tables and plinths and vitrines to hold the objects that could be touched, upon request. I also designed the exhibition to offer both small, intimate spaces and large, gathering spaces, which were activated in public programs.

The Study Center balanced the tropes of a white-walled gallery exhibition with my interest in interaction and study.

Surrounding the tables in the Study Center were stools which can be stacked together to form a life-size Roman column. This sculptural furniture, called *DIY Ruin*, takes its shape from smugglers who took ancient columns away in sections. *DIY Ruin* draws on the North American adoption of classical motifs in the organization of social life and of social space on campus. The columns mimic the Ionic columns used in buildings for education, justice, and government in the United States, particularly the columns of the White House, and invite people to dismantle the column. The *Ladder Chairs* were stationed around low objects, standing in for a desire to climb, both socially and physically.

I'm really interested in how collectives are able to communicate with each other, how they can heal each other, and often how they learn to listen to one another, rather than focusing mainly on speaking, or taking action. I think of art as a space for reflection and celebration, so not always for productivity.

—Caroline Woolard, 2016

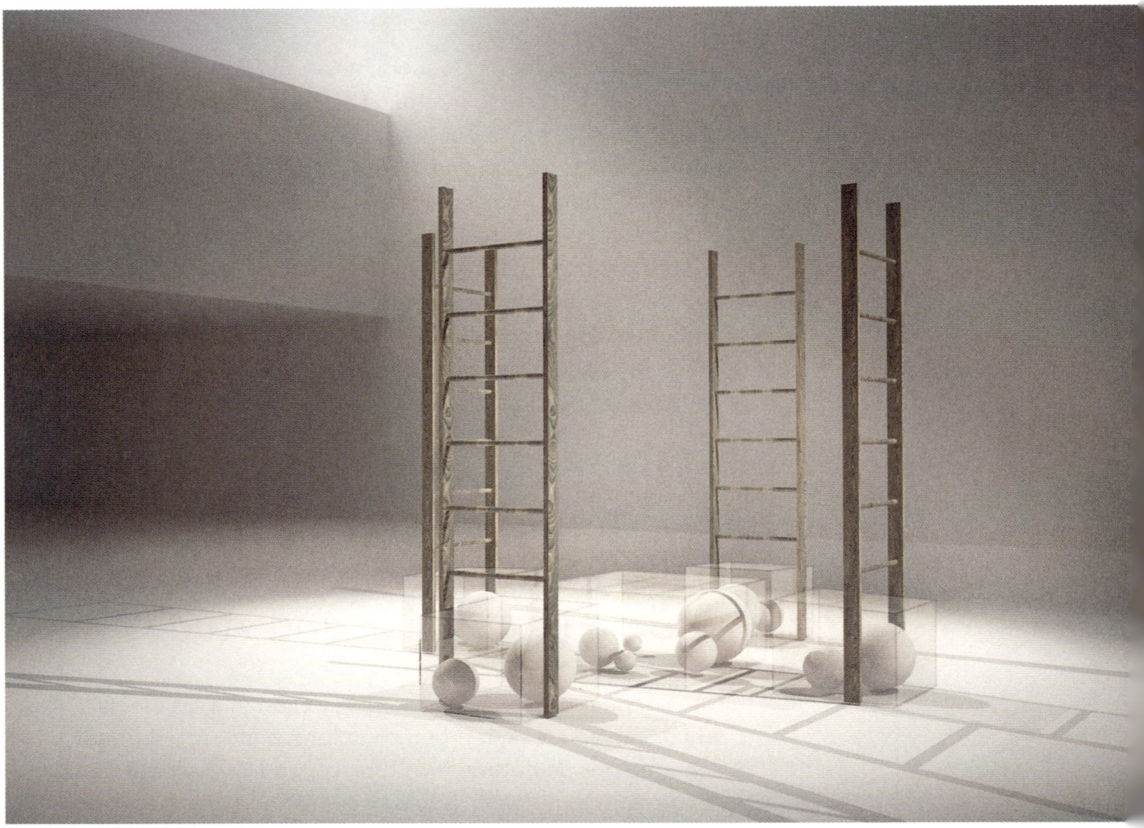

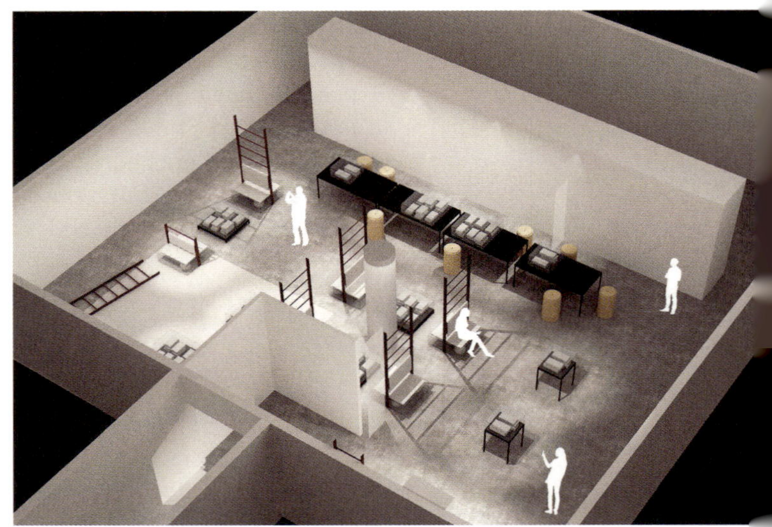

Collectively-
Initiated

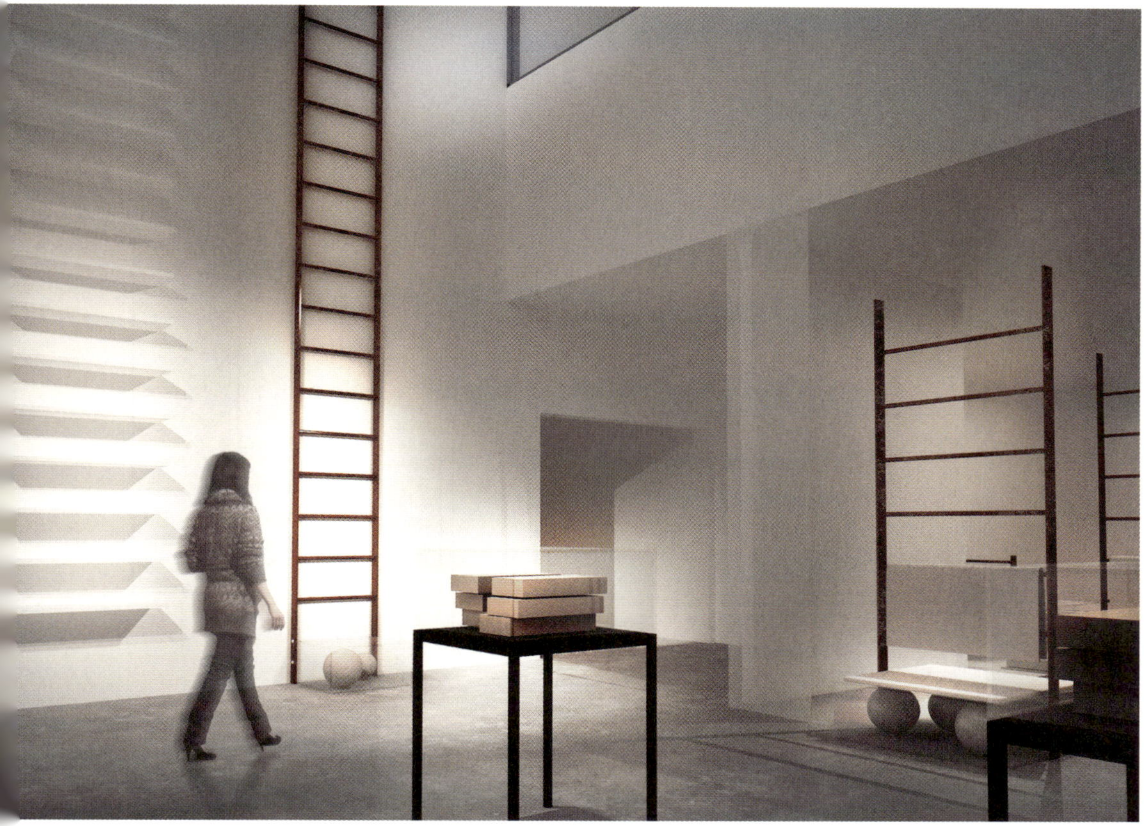

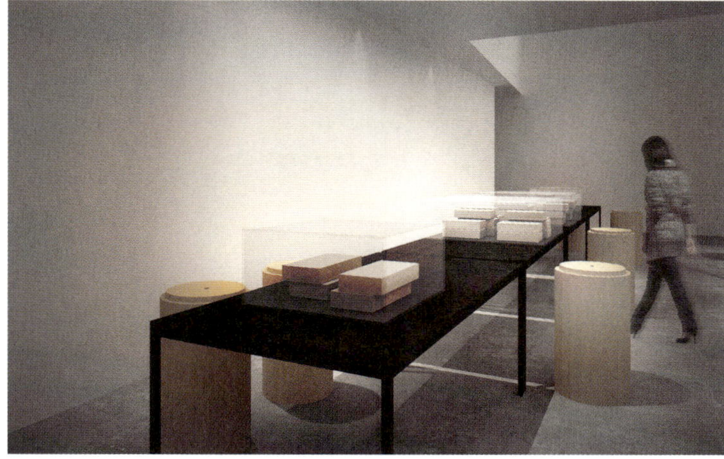

fig. 2-8
Renderings for The Study Center
for Group Work, 2015, dimensions
variable. Courtesy of the artist.

fig. 2-9
Technical drawings for *DIY Ruin*
and *Ladder Chairs* for The Study
Center for Group Work, 2015,
dimensions variable. Courtesy
of the artist.

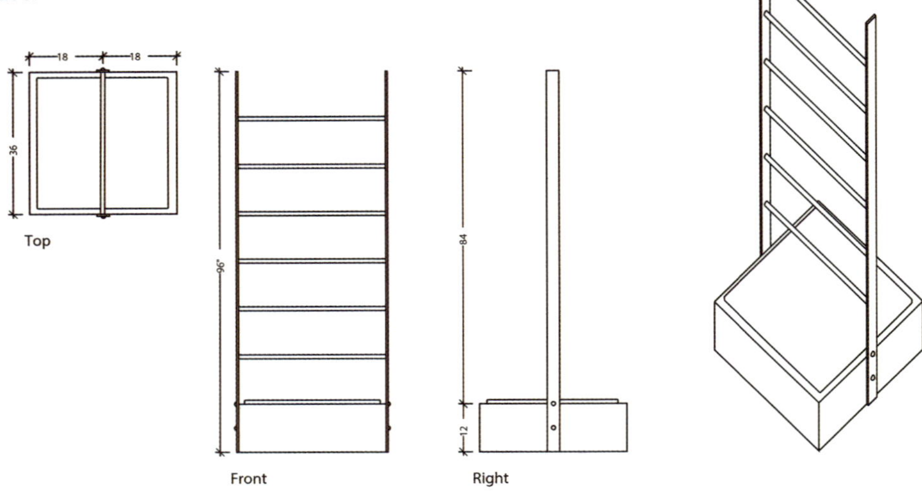

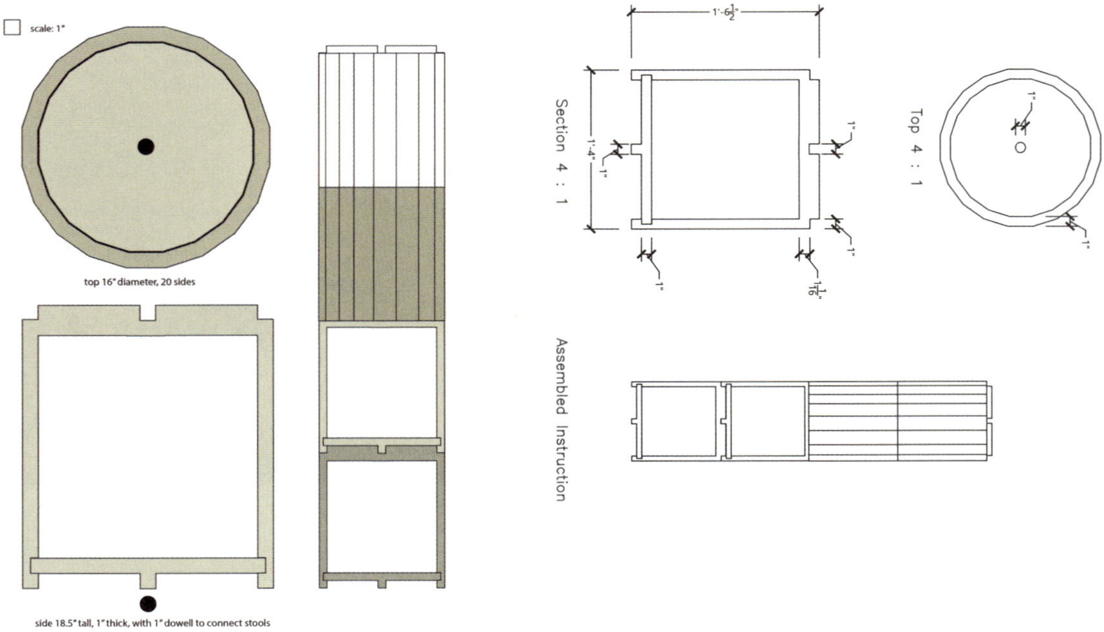

fig. 2-10
Sketches for Ladder Chairs and
exhibition design for The Study
Center for Group Work, 2015,
dimensions variable. Courtesy
of the artist.

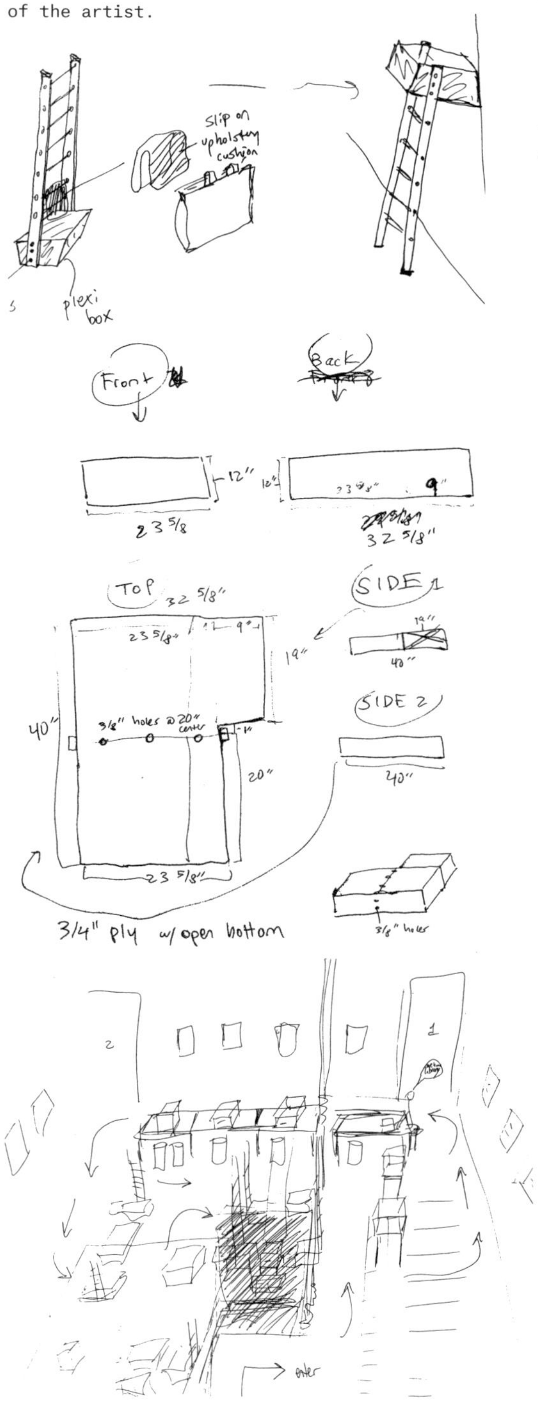

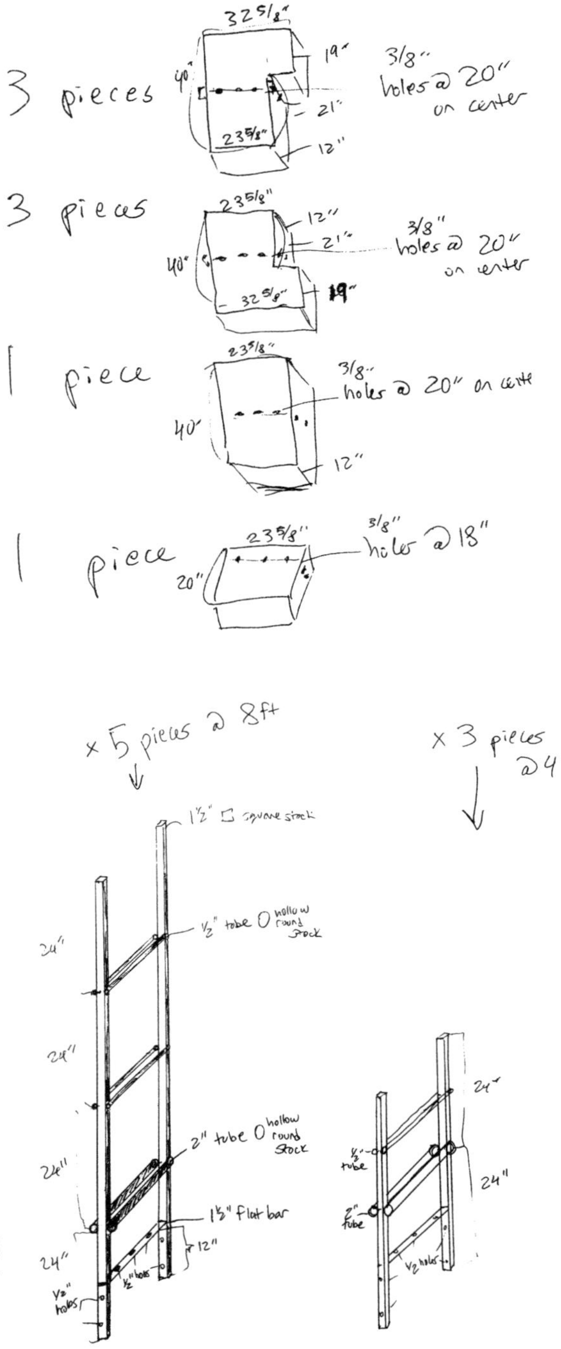

The artists in the Study Center were selected based upon the following criteria that Stamatina Gregory and I created:

Groups under consideration, 2015

At least 3 of these qualities are present:
- is a practice that has been taught to other groups and that they now use (practice over author)
- is a practice that has been refined for years (rigor/commitment)
- is a practice that is used for conflict resolution, anti-racism, feminism, or queer activism

fig. 2-11
Reference collage (clockwise from left): Lucia Moholy, Alma Buscher's *Ladder Chair for Children's Room*, 1923; Aleksandr Mikhaïlovich Rodchenko, *Fire Escape*, 1925; Trisha Brown. *Woman Walking Down a Ladder*, 1973; Lawrence Shustak, *Lette Eisenhauer Ascending Ladder in "The Courtyard,"* a Happening by Allan Kaprow, New York City, 1962; Yoko Ono, *CEILING PAINTING*, 1966; Mel Bochner, *Measurement: Shadow*, 1969.

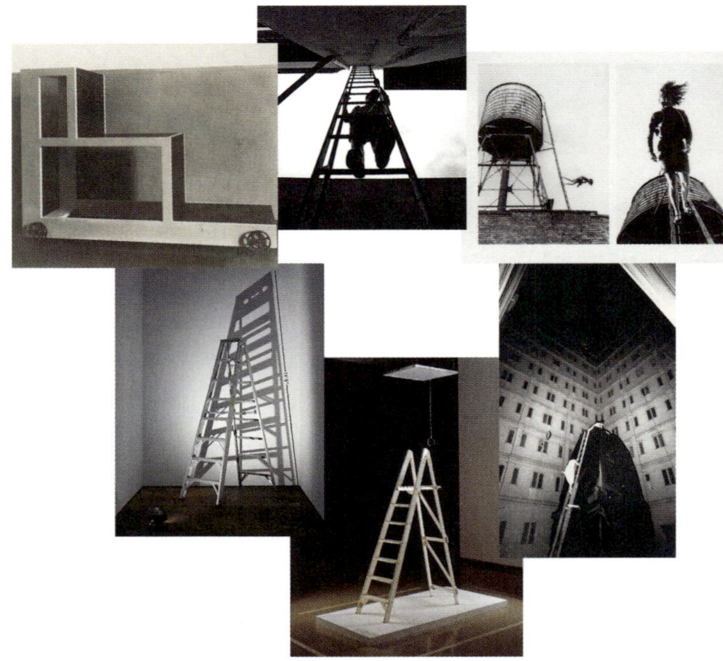

```
- is a practice with a beautiful sculptural tool
- is a practice with facilitators locally (in
  NYC in our case)
- is a practice that could occur over a year
- is a practice that might be "disruptive,"
  that has perhaps-untested potential for
  progressive or "radical" social change
- what else?
```

I continue to work with many of the artists from the show at 21 Cooper Gallery. In the years following the exhibition that Stamatina curated, the artists Adelheid Mers, Judith Leemann, and Project 404 have continued to participate in The Study Center by sharing practices with one another. Recently, we were invited to be part of an exhibition that Alison Burstein curated at Tenthaus in Oslo about artist-run institutions, including The Study Center for Group Work.

– is a practice that has been taught to other groups and that they now use (practice over author)
– is a practice that has been refined for years (rigor/ commitment)
– is a practice that is used for conflict resolution, anti-racism, feminism, or queer activism

The interviews and information that follows comes from the publication that was created for the exhibition in Oslo in 2019.

The Braid /
Performative Diagramatics

Adelheid Mers (b. 1960, Düsseldorf, Germany; lives in Chicago, Illinois) has developed a generative, topological method for talking about arts production and collaboration. Mers creates diagrams for workshops with artists, arts managers, and theorists that include fractals, matrices, and braids to guide conversations about art works and art practice. Mers writes that she "draws on the performative tools of studio critique. Formally, diagrams are defined by their operativity, engendering action and reflection. Mers' diagrams are presented as manipulable whiteboards, with occasions for use and response. In addition, they are often distributed freely, online and in poster and flyer format." As visual arts pedagogy shifts to embrace collaboration and social action, the "tools" of Adelheid Mers are helpful models for dialogue.

Online: http://studycollaboration.com/practice/
performative-diagrammatics-braid

Caroline:
Adelheid, why do you make objects for groups? What got you into this? What is possible with an object in a group, that would not be possible if the object were not there?

Adelheid:
The Diagrammatic templates and conversation facilitation objects I have developed serve to promote ways of thinking and perceiving flexibly, reshaping regimes of making sense by admitting unnoticed or undervalued perceptions, and loosening petrified knowledge. These facilitation objects are animated by prompts that a facilitator delivers, or that an accompanying text provides. Facilitated conversations are embedded in a performance that is structured by the object. Think jumping rope while telling a story. In this way, users open themselves to interactions between propositional knowledge (what is readily stated) and embodied knowing (what is readily enacted).

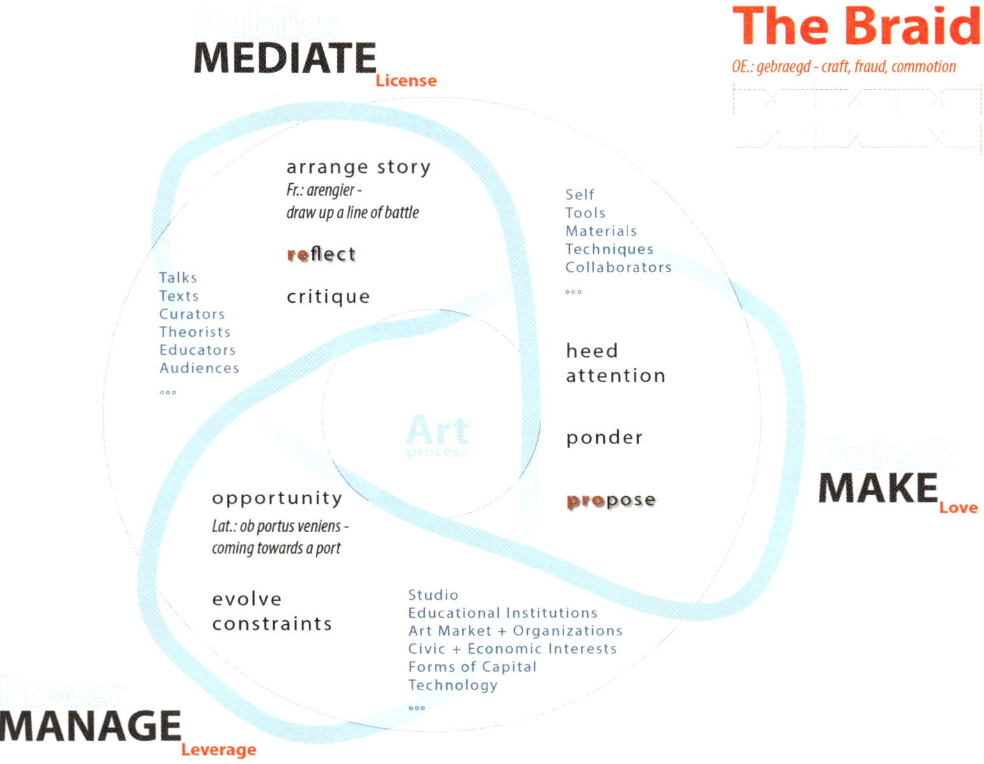

fig. 2-12
Adelheid Mers, *The Braid*, V3, 2019, dimensions variable. Image courtesy of the artist.

The Braid diagram is a tool that is designed to aid users in discussing and comparing how they recognize and work within the forcefields they inhabit. It is aimed at artists and other cultural producers. The diagram contains verbal prompts that emerged from individual conversations with artists, who derive agency from more or less intentionally integrating epistemic, critical and administrative needs and capacities into an idiosyncratic practice. Prompts are associated with a path wound around a continuum. The path is represented by a trefoil, the continuum by a torus. These mathematical shapes evoke topology as a metaphor through which to inclusively model and by that also brace the practices of cultural practitioners.

The key prompts are marked by an alliteration:

MAKING includes forms of attention, epistemic and material work processes, in the studio or equivalent.

MEDIATING contains forms of reflection on all aspect of cultural practice, and verbal articulation of narratives among stakeholders.

MANAGING broadly frames generative and normative institutional exposures. These areas may expand or contract at different times of practice. There is no specified point of entry.

The Study Center
for Group Work

These facilitation objects are animated by prompts that a facilitator delivers, or that an accompanying text provides.

Seemingly simple conversation/performances of this kind can bring embodied knowing into play, or alternatively dislodge hardened ideas. Performative actions promoted by *The Braid* template, for example, may consist of walking across and placing oneself within areas outlined by a rope designated as "artist studio," "public discourse zone," or "exhibition opportunity"; shifting the gaze to the ground and lowering one's center of gravity while feeling a site's presence anew; or refashioning the rope into an expanded shape to accommodate a story. Similarly, observing others perform can reframe perceptions.

This yoking of conversation to physical situation resonates with recent research in cognitive science that addresses the connection of space- and text-based practices. John O'Keefe, May-Britt Moser, and Edvard I. Moser received a Nobel prize in 2014 for showing that "grid cells" in the brain are used both for mapping space and for the processing of abstract thought. Facilitating user experiences through diagram-based objects also interlinks with theory that presents diagrams as inherently implying an invitation to act. The invitation to act, also known as operativity, further confirms the character of diagrams as performative objects.

By presenting facilitation situations as art, I claim an ethico-aesthetic surplus that emerges from the public performance of diverse, cognitive ecologies. A focus on users shows my approach to thinking and being with others. It is

Study

centered on the recognition of cognitive diversity, or cognitive preference, which I understand as situated on a continuum, similar to how gender and sexual preference are now understood. This perception was shaped in large part through the formal and informal studio conversations that are part of arts pedagogy, leading me to intentionally map artists ways of knowing or making sense: artistic epistemic engines, accessed in conversations about art making. To mobilize such resources as diagrammatic tools puts me in line with Félix Guattari's project of metamodeling. Metamodeling draws on existing frameworks across multiple areas of life to develop a personal mode of sensemaking and acting that works. Beautifully, Guattari embodies an ethics of a "New Gentleness" in this conception. My diagrammatic templates and facilitation objects function in that spirit. I believe that the cognitive and affective implications of play within a formalized game can, gently, promote skills towards discourse that is needed to keep peace.

By presenting facilitation situations as art, I claim an ethico-aesthetic surplus that emerges from the public performance of diverse, cognitive ecologies.

Object Lessons

Judith Leemann (b. 1971, Walnut Creek, California; lives in Boston, Massachusetts) is an artist, educator, and writer, whose hybrid practice plays the boundaries between distinct areas of professional practice. Her performative and collaborative work includes what she calls object lessons: attempts to develop form languages for rendering relation. In her words, "since 2007 I've been experimenting with crafting wordless explanations, in which hands manipulating objects on a small stage are asked to take on the work of explanation that usually rests with language. Over time, I've come to be most curious about the way in which language permits certain kinds of sense to come forward while actively preventing other kinds of sense from being made. Can this play of hands and objects do the work of foregrounding relations such that the relation itself becomes the subject?"

Online: http://studycollaboration.com/practice/object-lessons

Caroline:
Judith, why do you make objects for groups? What got you into this? What is possible with an object in a group, that would not be possible if the object were not there?

Judith:

    Initially the objects were simply tools for me,
    extensions or externalizations of objects of
    thought. The fact that they were located in the
    realm of the physical and not in the realm of
    the imaginary meant that their constraints and
    affordances (a brick can't roll, an object with
    an axis can and must point) led to new insights
    into things already fairly well thought through.

    I invited others to model something that occu-
    pied their thoughts, asking them to explain that
    thing to me using only hands moving objects,
    without any words. I began to see how productive
    it was to block the grooves cut by repeated
    verbal telling. Watching the objects being moved,
    without knowing what they stood for, I could see
    spatial and temporal patterns inside the telling
    that the use of words would have masked.

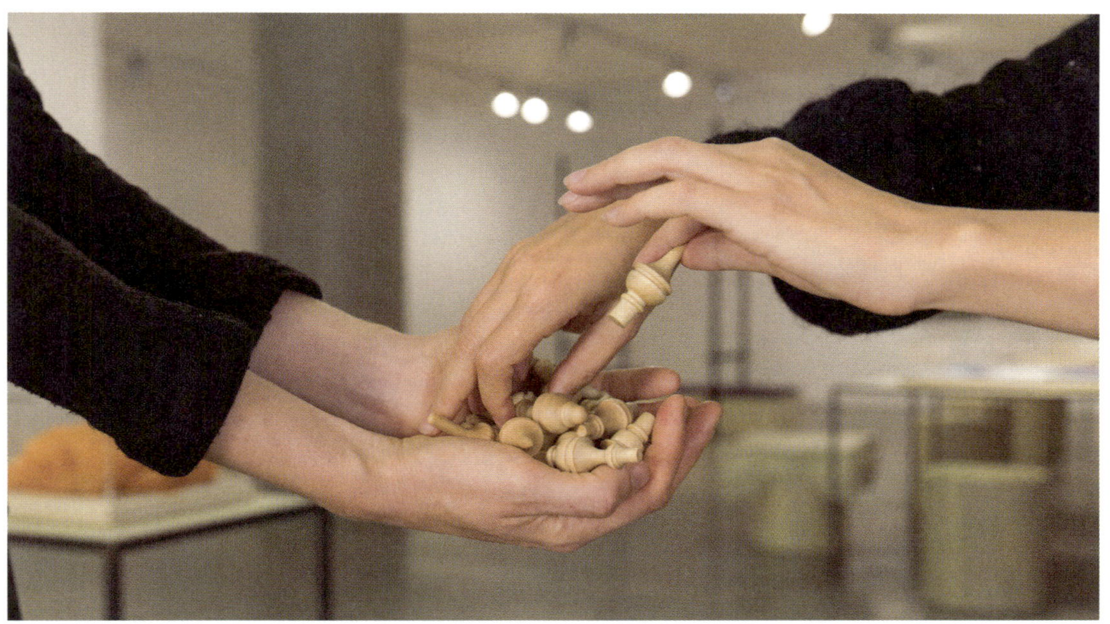

fig. 2-13
Judith Leemann, object lessons,
2013-present, found and made
objects, dimensions variable.
Courtesy the artist. Leemann's
performative and collaborative
work includes what she calls
object lessons, or "attempts
to develop form languages
for behaviors."

I wanted a way to thicken the
possibilities for encounter with
something new inside the well
rehearsed telling of knowing.

—Judith Leemann

Nouns and proper names disappeared from the
telling, I couldn't see who or what, just that
a something approached another something with
a pace that caused a sudden retreat. And the
role of pace, which had no place in the verbal
telling, now becomes legible as a potential
point of shift. Analog aspects of communica-
tional interaction lifted into ready recognition, while digital aspects necessarily
took a back seat. Organizing metaphors became
apparent, shareable, testable, in other words,
workable. (I recently made myself a personal
reminder: choose workable metaphors. In other
words, let the image you use to describe a
condition to yourself be one that has articu-
lations, perforations, ways in and out. Don't
accidentally describe corners that you then
find cornering you. Or do. But know that
you are).

In some ways this is utterly ordinary, continuous with reaching for the salt shaker to move
it around the water glass to show a dinner
companion just how the thing happened. By
making sets of objects for particular telling
contexts (turned wooden forms to talk about

artists' conceptions of time, found and manipulated objects to work through experiences of the
liminal) I wanted a way to thicken the possibilities for encounter with something new inside
the well rehearsed telling of knowing. I root my
embodied understanding of the challenge of
meeting habit and cultivating space for 'the
new' in years of somatic learning via Alexander
Technique and Contact Improvisation, as well
as in the pedagogies of the Goat Island performance group.

I could see spatial and temporal patterns inside the telling that the use of words would have masked.

Summoning a habitual response and running it into
an obstacle breaks open space for the emergent
in ways that no amount of deciding to do something new will ever allow. The anthropologist
Gregory Bateson famously proposed that noise was
the only source of the new—noise introduced or
arriving in a system around which that system
would now need to reorganize itself. Bateson's
frequent co-conspirator Paul Watzlawick suggested
that if you wanted to understand what was keeping
a problem in place, look at what is being done
to solve the problem, that solution very likely
being where the cycle turns and begins again.

Watzlawick's pithy "description embeds prescrip-
tion" is a touchstone for me. How we describe,
and with what languages we describe, prescribes
what is seeable, touchable, actionable. The
play of these object based choreographies is my
contribution to multiplying the languages we
have at hand for casting relation anew.

Project 404

Project 404 (founded 2014, New York) teaches practices
of attention using the very devices that threaten to distract
us. This protocol asks participants to focus on one image
for twelve minutes of silence with the phone or device in
airplane mode. The ambition of the project, as the name
indicates, is to reverse the "not found" message often seen
when looking for a website, and to send it back—briefly—to
who or whatever else wants attention.

Protocol of Attention and Adaptation
15 minute silent phase,
60–75 minute colloquy.
↓
Download the image to your smart phone.
Turn your phone on airplane mode.
Look in silence at the image provided, following
these prompts.
↓
1. What do you notice? What do you notice now?
5 minutes: bell

2. Use your phone to modify or change the image
(do whatever you like, while staying in airplane mode).
What do you see?
5 minutes: bell

3. What is your relationship to this image?
Have you become crucial to what you see?
5 minutes: bell
↓
(Take a few minutes to jot down some notes about
your experience of each of the three phases of the
protocol. When we are finished we will begin colloquy.)

Online:
http://studycollaboration.com/practice/protocol-of-
attention-and-adaptation

The [404] practice empowers
you to be imaginative in your
relationship with your technology. The phone demands certain types of attention: texts
pop up, we scroll through
images, but with 404 you permit
yourself to spend time with a
single image.

—Anna Riley, Project 404
facilitator, 2019

The [404] practice isn't academic—we are not looking at an image to be right and know things about it; the practice is creative. We use attention as a creative medium, and the tenet of generosity extends to the image itself, of course; to the other people participating, whom we are going to listen to with generosity; and to the practice itself, which we want to treat with a certain amount of generosity.

—Len Nalencz, Project 404 facilitator, 2019

fig. 2-14
Image of Seph Rodney facilitating a practice of Project 404 in 2015. Photo by Filip Wolak.

Caroline:

Project 404, why do you make protocols for groups? What got you into this? What is possible with a protocol in a group, that would not be possible if the protocol were not there?

Project404:

Project 404 began as a practice of sustained looking at works of art with the kinds of students I teach: digital natives, mostly first generation college students from immigrant families. The *Protocol of Attention and Adaptation* asks participants to use attention as a medium for creativity; the objects we look at are digital images, either made by the participants or found online. Doing practices of attention in a group requires generosity, both toward the image that is the object of the practice and toward each other as participants. Doing practices of attention together, and using the devices that usually divide us from others, enables us to connect through our powers of creativity, and offers us unexpected glimpses of ourselves.

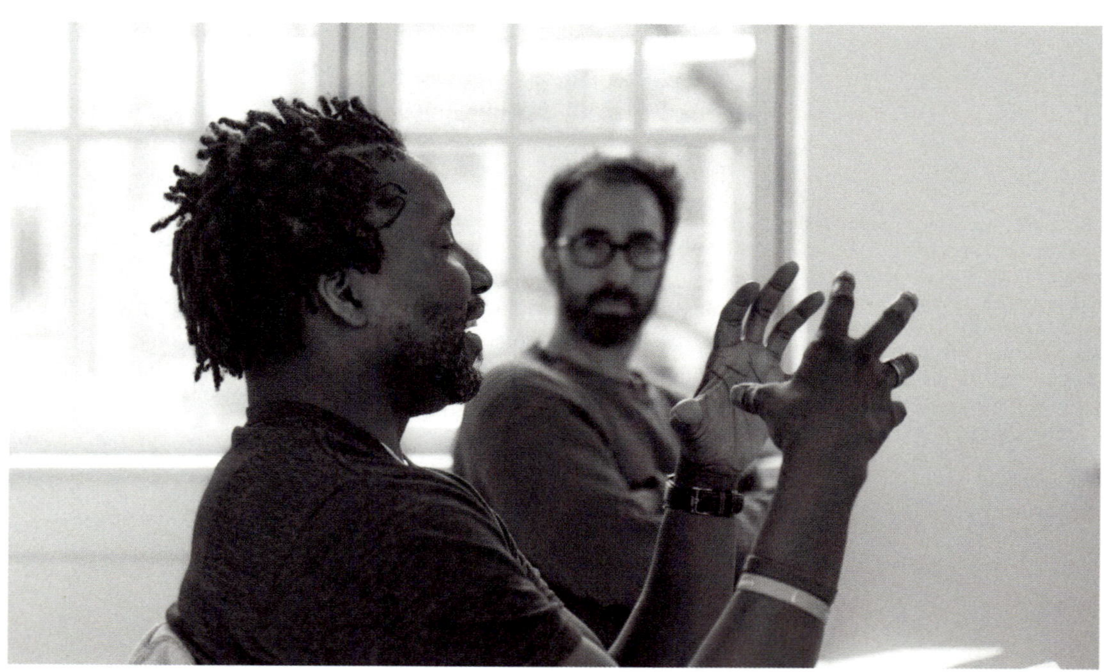

Collectively-
Initiated

Mediating

From the outset, I wanted the exhibition to "read" as a long-term project. I knew that a website would be central to this, so I made sure that the budget for the exhibition made room for an independent website, to launch in tandem with the physical exhibition. I used the following language on the website, to help visitors imagine a long-term project:

```
WOUND, adj.
/waʊnd/ mending time and attention

WOUND is a study center for practices of
listening and collaboration. The study center
offers free trainings in listening, attention,
and collaboration, all of which foreground
the relationship between capitalism and time,
practice and temporality. Trainings are led
by UltraRed, Shaun Leonardo, the Order of the
Third Bird, Project 404, the Canaries, the
Design Studio for Social Intervention,
Generative Somatics (Alta Starr and RJ Maccani),
and the Extrapolation Factory. WOUND displays
a collection of sculptural tools which can be
used by visitors who have been trained. Outside
of training hours, the study center is a quiet
place to sit, read, and contemplate conceptions
of time as articulated by Yoko Ono, taisha
paggett and Ashley Hunt, Dave McKenzie, Judith
Leeman, Adelheid Mers, Chloe Bass, Linda
Montano, Danica Phelps, the New York Horological
Society, and the National Watch and Clock Museum.

STAFF
Interim Director: Caroline Woolard
Art Historian: Stamatina Gregory
Assistants: to be announced soon
Facilitators: (link to facilitators)
Trainings: (link to trainings)
Tools: (link to tools)
```


The Study Center
for Group Work

MEMBERSHIP
To support WOUND, please become a member.
Membership is offered at sliding scale, from
$20-$200, based on what you can afford. Members
are notified of trainings before the general
public, and enable us to continue our work.

THANKS
Special thanks to Stamatina Gregory and Cooper
Union for making this project possible. Thanks
also to Jennifer Monson, Aaron Landsman, Risa
Shoup, Abigail Statinksy, Alicia Boone Jean-
Noel, Robert Sember, and Athena Kokoronis for
introducing Stamatina Gregory and Caroline
Woolard to artists, designers, dancers, and
facilitators. This project would not be possi-
ble without ongoing conversations with Leigh
Claire La Berge, Louise Ma, Or Zubalsky, Susan
Jahoda, Emilio Martínez Poppe, and Pedagogy
Group members. WOUND is supported by a gener-
ous grant from the Rubin Foundation and from
Cooper Union.

HOURS: Wednesday through Sunday from 1-8 p.m.
from October 12-November 11
GRAND OPENING PARTY: October 13, 6-8 p.m.
LOCATION: 41 Cooper Gallery, 41 Cooper Square,
on Third Avenue between 6th and 7th Streets

If you would like to host WOUND, please contact
<email>. WOUND is currently seeking spaces
that can host facilitation and training.

Curator Stamatina Gregory allowed me to add the following
text to the curatorial statement that a viewer would read
when entering the gallery, as a wall text in vinyl:

WOUND is a study center for practices of
listening, attention, and collaboration. In
its month-long installment at The Cooper
Union, WOUND director Caroline Woolard worked

with curator Stamatina Gregory to select
tools from artists and collectives whose
multi-year practices register in the visual
arts. In its online archive, WOUND will present
a full spectrum of tools, facilitators, and
practices from the performing arts, speculative design, community organizing, geography,
and engineering. Director Caroline Woolard
calls WOUND, "a study center for the mending
of time and attention"…

By writing a "month-long installment at The Cooper Union,"
and "director Caroline Woolard," rather than "this exhibition,"
and "artist Caroline Woolard," I convinced more than a few
people that the center had been open for years, and was on
its way to other locations. By writing this on the wall, and
online, in many ways, it became true. I was approached by
Malick Kane, a curator from Dakar, about bringing the center
there, at the opening. The center traveled to Glasgow, to
Oslo, and to the Free Library of Philadelphia.

In addition to the wall text, I wanted to make sure that I hired
people to engage visitors in the space in ways that created
an atmosphere of "study" and welcome. For the first installment of The Study Center, in the gallery space at Cooper
Union, I knew that I needed to train facilitators. I hired
people who had been students of mine at the New School
and at Cooper Union, and recent graduates that Stamatina
Gregory recommended, to work in the space: Emilio
Martínez Poppe, Jordan Delzell, Anna Vila, Anna Zinovieff
Papadimitriou, and Samantha Rosner. I held a training for
them, and I also created a printed PDF for the facilitators to
review, at work, so that they would be prepared to answer
questions that visitors might ask.

As someone who has spent the
last decade in a lot of
meetings with groups, I have
realised that to organize new
projects you essentially spend
your life either sitting at a
table in a meeting or typing
on a computer. I'm hoping that
we can move from sitting in
spaces that feel very allergic
to imagination, the formica
table and fluorescent lights
that you imagine at most
organising spaces — to spaces
that are exciting that are
developed with artists and
organisers so that the furniture itself reminds us of the
vision of the world we want
to see.

— Caroline Woolard, 2016

The Study Center
for Group Work

WELCOME!
Welcome to The Study Center. We call the objects here "tools," because they are used to facilitate listening, attention, or collaboration. The Study Center is dedicated to mending time and attention, which means that we aim to offer experiences of collaborative time: time which is specifically marked by our engagement with one another.

You can use a few of the "tools" right now, if you like. If you are interested in trying out any of the "text tools" over here, you are welcome to check one out and work with it anywhere in The Study Center. We have two practice spaces in the back and many places to sit. Or, if you would like to practice using Judith Leemann's tools for non-verbal communication, taisha paggett and Ashley Hunt's par course mirror, or the Extrapolation Factory's speculative design tools, I can show you how to use any of these.

Many of the "tools" are activated in events—which we call "trainings" —where the artists who have created certain tools will demonstrate their use. If you are interested in coming to a training, please see the flyer and be sure to RSVP online. I can RSVP for you, right now, if you prefer.

You can use a few of the "tools" right now, if you like. If you are interested in trying out any of the "text tools" over here, you are welcome to check one out and work with it anywhere in The Study Center.

Some of the tools in The Study Center are on view only. These tools cannot be used either because there are no trainings scheduled at this time or because the tools are too precious to be used by the general public. For example, we have one of the only prototypes of Paul Ryan's *Threeing* rugs, called *Rose Window*. This was created by Paul Ryan (1943-2013) and Luis Berríos-Negrón (b. 1971) as a 1:3 scale-model for dOCUMENTA 13 (2010-12) in hand-spun alpaca which was hand-dyed and woven in Peru. This work comes to us from the collection of Jean Gardner, Paul Ryan's widow, who teaches at the New School.

Q&A
HOW DO YOU "MEND TIME AND ATTENTION"?

WOUND aims to mend time and attention by providing:
(1) Practice Spaces for groups
(2) A study center for practice-related readings and sculptural tools
(3) Trainings in practices of listening, attention, and collaboration.

WHY DO VISUAL ARTISTS NEED PRACTICE SPACES?

Just as dancers take classes throughout their lives, WOUND aims to become a permanent practice space for group work in the visual arts. Practice requires duration. Art departments and art institutions have increased funding for social practice since the early 2000s, but the communities that are rewarded within academic and non-profit spaces tend to be short-lived and outcome-oriented. Transformative practices cannot be developed or contained in a month-long exhibition, a four-year or two-year degree, or a year-long grant. To move toward an aesthetic of practice, further study is required.

WOUND aims to become a permanent practice space for group work in the visual arts.

WHAT "TOOLS" DOES THE STUDY CENTER COLLECT AND STUDY?

The Study Center holds a collection of small objects, writing, and ephemera used in group work. This Study Center makes impossible the fantasy of an autonomous object, one removed from collective practice and historical context. Every object in The Study Center is called a "tool" and is either "on view" or "in use" in trainings by collectives and politically engaged artists. WOUND links a wide range of collaborative and participatory practices, from the so-called 1960s dematerialization of the art object (tool on view: Yoko Ono), to 1970s cybernetic systems (tool on view: Paul Ryan), to 1980s feminist durational performances (Linda Montano). The Study Center places practices of the 1960s, 1970s, and 1980s in conversation with artists and collectives of the 2000s who continue to emphasize collective practice by distributing texts, prototypes, and tools.

WHY DO WE NEED TO BE TRAINED?

If most New Yorkers have no experiences of democracy at work, at home, in school, or online, how will we learn to work together? This Study Center provides a practice space for joint work and joint decision-making.

The Study Center
for Group Work

Every object in The Study Center is called a "tool" and is either "on view" or "in use" in trainings by collectives and politically engaged artists.

If democracy is "an endless meeting" and socialism "requires too many evenings," then WOUND cultivates behaviors that might allow groups to gather together more carefully. WOUND director Caroline Woolard says, "I see this study center as a demonstration of the future of art school. Art departments will be the places where interdisciplinary teams are formed, utilizing practices of listening, attention, and collaboration that this study center honors."

IS IT WOOOND OR WAAAAUND?

You decide. We say waaaund, to remind ourselves that time-keeping devices are always time-producing devices. As the past participle of the verb to wind, "wound" reaches back to a past that has seemingly been set in motion. And yet, as a present participle of the same verb, as seen, for example, in the phrase "the clock is wound," the verb

indicates a potentiality that can be altered, it indexes a conclusion that is not foregone. Nonetheless, when most visitors first see the word W-O-U-N-D, they will make an association to the much more common noun form: a wound, as in a harm or an injury.

Perhaps the current injury on view at WOUND is in thinking that time has been wound against our desires: there is "too little time," time moves "too quickly," our time has been attenuated. WOUND asks: How, through collaboration, can we unwind time in order to render it open, unspecified, and inviting? How can we recognize the nature of our seemingly dwindling attention not as the result of being "wound up," but as the result of being hurt or injured, an emotional claim which, necessarily, implies the ability to be healed? Can these practices render time a qualitative not quantitative phenomenon, something that is marked and construed for groups through mutuality rather than received through authority?

WHO MADE THIS SPACE?

WOUND director Caroline Woolard worked with curator Stamatina Gregory to select tools from artists and collectives whose multi-year practices register in the visual arts. Caroline Woolard is the creative director and exhibition designer for the space, and the "tools" in use and on view come from 19 artists and collectives: Ultra-red, Shaun Leonardo, the Order of the Third Bird, Project 404, Sick Time with Canaries, the Design Studio for Social Intervention, the Extrapolation Factory, Yoko Ono, taisha paggett and Ashley Hunt, Paul Ryan, Dave McKenzie, Judith Leemann, Adelheid Mers, Chloe Bass, Linda Montano, Danica Phelps, Matthew Buckingham, Nightwood, the New York Horological Society, and the National Watch and Clock Museum. Caroline Woolard makes art and institutions for the solidarity economy. Her method enjoins objects to their contexts of circulation. Woolard builds sculptures for barter only as she also co-creates international barter networks; she fabricates model Shaker housing as she also co-convenes organizers of community land trusts. WOUND, the study center launched here at 41 Cooper Gallery, is a continuation of Woolard's dedication to art and also to the institutions which enable these objects to circulate.

Can these practices render time a qualitative not quantitative phenomenon?

In its online archive, WOUND will present a full spectrum of tools, facilitators, and practices from the performing arts, speculative design, community organizing, geography, and engineering.

WHERE WILL THE STUDY CENTER GO NEXT?

We are looking for a permanent location. For inquiries regarding travelling The Study Center's collection, or to offer a space to WOUND, please email Caroline Woolard at caroline@woundstudycenter.com.

WHERE CAN I GET MORE INFORMATION?

Go to http://woundstudycenter.com and read more about the artists and collectives in the show from this binder here.

HOW CAN I SUPPORT WOUND?

Please become a member. Yearly membership is offered at a sliding scale, from $20-$200, based on what you can afford. Members are notified of trainings before the general public, have access to tools on member-only days, and enable us to continue to provide trainings to the public. Please write to info@woundstudycenter.com if you would like to become a member.

The Study Center
for Group Work

When the Glasgow School of Art invited me to give a lecture in Glasgow, I convinced them to commission a video so that I would not need to travel, and the video would honor the practices of a wide range of people in The Study Center. This way, the $1000 could be used to pay filmmakers and go online, visible to thousands of people. I wrote an email, asking members of The Study Center to participate, and explaining the overall budget. Many people agreed to be involved, so I went ahead and hired Herman Jean-Noel, a filmmaker who I met at TradeSchool.coop see chapter 3, and who made a film about my work at Cornell.

I wrote Herman an email to see if he would be able to do this job.

> SUBJECT: job? … study center video update for $1k by March 10th (shooting video Feb 16th)
>
> February 3, 2019
> Good morning dear Herman,
>
> I hope you are loving CA! I just got an invitation to make an updated video of The Study Center to be shown at the Glasgow School of Art (in place of me going there, as this way other groups can use it). I want it to be like the beautiful one you made two whole years ago, but updated as I will describe below.
>
> Questions:
> - Do you have time/interest to do this? (see below for project scope)
> - Are you free on Saturday Feb 16th to shoot video for it (location TBA, but someplace with good light/sound that isn't too far from us)
> - Can you do this for $1k? That's what they are giving me, so I would have them send it to you directly, or I can Venmo you if that's better for tax reasons.
>
> Scope:
> You would be doing the audio, titles, a bit more video shooting, and editing. I would use

the intro audio in your video (https://vimeo.
com/198242353 starting at 00:11 and going to
00:42 … possibly until 01:18 or even 01:47)
From there, it could move into more of a tutorial where I teach people how to do *THREEING*
(I can explain) while these objects are in the
background, on a meeting table, to hint at all
the things we could get help with in groups:

- a ruler and a ribbon from Chloe Bass
  http://studycollaboration.com/practice/
  field-guide-spatial-intimacy

- an orange scarf from the *Order of
  the Third Bird* http://www.mildred-
  slane.com/upcoming/2018/8/6/
  attention-lab-order-of-the-third-bird

- the water clock, keeping time
  http://carolinewoolard.com/project/amulet/

- a marker board, from http://studycollabora-
  tion.com/practice/three-line-matrix

- an object TBA from https://cargocollective.
  com/mirrorechotilt

It needs to be done by March 10th.

Let me know what's possible, and if you can
do it, or not. No hard feelings if the budget
is too small, or if you are too busy. I wish
it were a bigger budget, but here we go. I'm
giving the whole budget to you (or to another
person, if you can't do it). Just let me
know, when you can, or perhaps we can talk
later today.

Sending light and appreciation,
Caroline

The Study Center
for Group Work

Herman said yes, so I coordinated with the artists from the Study Center who were open to doing this shoot and sharing their existing footage with us. To orient Herman as the filmmaker and editor, I created a document that outlined the plan for the day of shooting and that outlined the clips to use from existing footage artists had sent me.

```
THIS Sunday: 567 Carlton Ave Brooklyn NY
(not the best light)

10-11:00  Set up 45 mins — Herman

11-11:30  Chloe

11:30-12:00  Caroline misc objects video shoot
(see below)

12 or 12:30  Sal around noon

1:00-1:30  Caroline Threeing / misc objects video
shoot (see below)

1:30-2:00  Pack up / leave

Here is the link to the videos.
http://www.mediafire.com/file/gvhw5eciuyqhf0t/
Archive.zip/file
```

VIDEO SCRIPT / CUTS / SHOT LIST:
Use old Intro https://vimeo.com/198242353
(00:12 – 00:42 … possibly until 01:18 or
even 01:47)

Record new audio:
Hello, my name is Caroline Woolard. I am the
interim Director of the Study Center for Group
Work. Today I want to introduce you to some of
the practices that you might want to try out in
your own self-organized groups. Self-organized
means that you are doing this without a boss.

I started this center because I spend half of
my time thinking about art, and the other half
of my time thinking about how people can work
together to effect social change. I love making
objects, and yet, I am often in ugly meeting
spaces with formica and horrible lighting.

I wondered: what if the objects in our meetings were as beautiful as the conversations we
were having?

I realized that a lot of artists have been
working on this—creating ways for groups to
gather together and often using objects to do
so—so I started this Study Center to share
what I was learning about all of the artists
who want to facilitate group work, dialogue,
and transformation.

———

I like to say: What if the tables and objects
in our spaces were as imaginative as the conversations we were having? I have found that
by bringing sculptural objects to community
gatherings, I make tangible the slow temporality of community-building; people sense the care
that has gone into the facilitation practices
I bring to group work.

The reason I am so excited about making objects
for facilitation is that it solves two deep
desires I have: (1) to make beautiful objects
and also (2) remain in facilitation settings,
meetings, and group settings where I can offer
my skills as an artist and honor existing,
slowly-developed, community-generated facilitation skills without trying to author them.

———

(1) to make beautiful objects and also (2) remain in facilitation settings, meetings, and group settings where I can offer my skills as an artist and honor exist-ing, slowly-developed, community-generated facilitation skills without trying to author them.

Think of the last time you were trying to get
people together to do something… maybe you
wanted to ask for a pay raise, for better working conditions, or to create a project together.

What is so difficult about people coming together, on their own terms, without a boss?

Have you ever tried to get together with a
group of people, outside of work, and had a
horrible time getting things done?

Most people have very little experience with
group work. They might come together and wonder: Who is going to send out invitations to
gather together? How can we make decisions once
we are together? Can we trust one another to do
what we say we are going to do, without a boss?

It turns out that visual artists have been
thinking about how to collaborate, and developing collaborative methods that they want to
share. Today, I want to describe a few of the
collaborative methods that artists have developed to help us work on:
- group roles (*Threeing*),
- the politics of the space between us (field

The Study Center
for Group Work

Idea in Public

guide to spatial intimacy),
- non-verbal communication (*Preposition
  and Prosthesis*)
- attention as a medium (the *Protocol* of
  Attention and Adaptation, the Birds)
- theater games to explore structural violence/
  social identity (mirror/echo/tilt)

Threeing: Starting in the 1970s, the video
artist (not politician) Paul Ryan developed a
method for collaboration called *Threeing*. Ryan
described *Threeing* in this way: "Just as training wheels help one learn to ride a bicycle, so
the [*Threeing* method] helps people to learn
Threeing. Once people learn to change roles
without confusion, the training wheels come off,
the [facilitation objects can be] discarded."

- Smithsonian Video to use

Here is how to practice *Threeing*:
EXERCISE # 1 DRAWING
Give each participant a drawing pad and a drawing pencil or marker. Each person is asked to
draw one spontaneous line on the paper, all at
the same time (First Skill Set).

Team rotates the pad to the other members of
the team. Now each member of the team reacts to
the line in front of them with another single
line that indicates their reaction (Second
Skill Set). Rotate pads again.

Each team member takes their time and adds another line to the drawing that seeks to balance
or mediate between the two lines in front of
them (Third Skill Set).

Show each other the final compositions.
Repeat procedure for as much time as you have.

The Field Guide to Spatial Intimacy is…
(Chloe audio recording on Sunday)
Chloe Bass video

Propositions and Prosthesis is…
(audio from Judith???)
- http://www.judithleemann.com/object-lessons/

The Braid is…(audio coming from Adelheid by
Monday) Olivia Junell and Asha Iman Veal video
to use

I condensed *The Braid* template from a large
number of conversations with artists whom I
asked: How do you work? It became very clear
that nothing can be considered external to
doing cultural work. Because of that, *The Braid*
is visualized as a continuum that is traversed
by a path. I think of it as a topology. It can
stretch, but not tear.

The Braid template was made as an invitation.
You are invited to unfold it into the present
moment, your present moment, to inscribe your
own practice as a unique path within a continuum that is both personal and shared. This works
really well in pairs, with each person appre-
ciatively inquiring about how the conversation
partner works.

We made videos of artists and other cultural workers using the template to share how we
inhabit these spaces differently, and to give
examples how *The Braid* template can be used.

The Birds are…(video with Sal on Sunday)
- attention as a medium (the *Protocol* of
  Attention and Adaptation, the Birds)

Mirror/Echo Tilt is…
(video coming from Melanie/Shaun)
- waiting…

Project 404 is…(audio coming from Len
by Monday)
- the theater of social identity
  (mirror/echo/tilt)

Water Clocks…to record Sunday
- to think about time in groups, to mark it
  unconventionally
- include the video of the hour glass that
  never runs out
- include video of the net and the ceiling?
- include video of the aqueous event object?

This project continues today, as it is core to my interest in making objects for groups, and in continuing to learn how to transform myself in relationship to other people, through collaboration. See *The Meeting* [see chapter 1] for more.

The Study Center
for Group Work

Managing

Ideas take a long time to form, and even longer to find financial support, if that is what they require. I want to share an unsuccessful grant with you, to demonstrate the patience and persistence that I believe are required to bring a big project to life. For example, I wrote this Creative Capital grant for what would become The Study Center in 2013, but I did not get it.

Collectively-
Initiated

If democracy is an endless meeting, why not make meetings beautiful? *A Beautiful Meeting* honors process over product, connecting groups who want better meetings to a collective of artist-facilitators who use sculptural tools and installation environments to create beautiful meetings.

A Beautiful Meeting honors group work by creating a living collection of sculptural tools and a system for booking artist-facilitators in installation environments. Members of the public will browse sculptures made for dialog and request artist-facilitators for unconventional meetings in installation environments. The collective will be comprised of artists from The Exchange Archive (from the Exchange Café at MoMA) as well as artists who emerge from a call for participants that will be made with the launch of this project. This project will shift the context for socially engaged art, cultivating primary publics for these works. Looking back to Lygia Clark and Paul Ryan, a growing group of artists are interested in sculptures made by and for small groups.

HISTORY: Last year at MoMA, working on Artists Experiment, I found many 20th century precedents for one-on-one relational practices. I found artworks, neither singular nor static, that revolve around voluntary, reciprocal commitments and sculptural tools. Rather than sitting alone on a pedestal, these artworks use tools to facilitate dialog. Meaning is made in action as two people gather, build, and distribute ideas. These artworks refuse to separate production from objecthood; political economy from the presentation of ideas. I want to honor this history, and make it contemporary by creating a nomadic collective, a distributed network of artist-facilitators who make and use sculptural objects and are dedicated to group process. *A Beautiful Meeting* is the Dematerialization of the Art Object in the 21st century—the facilitation context of the art object made manifest.

APPROACH: *A Beautiful Meeting* accepts the fusion of websites with interactions, social practices with social networks. Noticing that the cultural landscape of the 21st century is not a lake or a mountain, but a google search bar, *A Beautiful Meeting* demands that more publics be created for social engagement of shared decision-making. What if works circulated not for their uniqueness or autonomy, but for their beauty within a commitment to community struggle, for their ability to be replicated and altered? This work carries on the traditions

Managing

of fluxus, dada, situationists, and conceptual art: replicable objects made in and for groups.

IMPACT: When collaboration is understood as "working jointly to create something new," it often translates to "my whim is your labor." This project is an attempt to wrestle the term "collaboration" from ambiguous descriptions of contemporary cultural experience, making collaboration not simply shared labor, but shared decision-making power. While participation, which I define as informed engagement in a predetermined structure, is valuable and necessary in many contexts, understanding the drive for collaboration as an enthusiasm for shared decision-making power, not just joint work, has wide-ranging implications for direct democracy in art projects, businesses, and classrooms.

I had to convince NYFA that The Study Center was going to become a business.

I write over twenty grants for every grant I get. It was not until 2015, when Stamatina Gregory approached me, that this project was able to come to life. After that, I applied for a $25,000 grant from the New York Foundation for the Arts (NYFA), and I got it. I had to convince NYFA that The Study Center was going to become a business. To write this, I clarified aspects of the previous Creative Capital application that had been unclear, looked at the text I had written for the exhibition at Cooper Union, and used the start-up and computer engineering jargon that I learned through OurGoods.org and TradeSchool.coop [see chapter 3].

Managing

Additional thanks to:
Peter Cobb at NYFA (Producer),
Rudy Kanhye at the Glasgow
School of Art (Producer),
Or Zubalsky (UX Designer,
Developer), Leonard Nalencz
(Researcher), Anna Riley
(Researcher), Herman Jean-Noel
and Neglakay Productions
(Video), Danielle Jackson
(Event Facilitator and
Researcher), Anna Vila (Event
Facilitator), Emilio Martinez
Poppe (Event Facilitator),
Anna Papadimitriou (Event
Facilitator).

The Study Center
for Group Work

NYFA: What need does your enterprise fill for the public, or what problem do you solve?

If democracy is an endless meeting, how can we learn to gather together more beautifully? I believe that the future of arts education lies in the ability for artists to teach collaboration to interdisciplinary teams across sectors.

NYFA: What will your company make, or what service will you provide?

Caroline Woolard is the Director/CEO of a new Study Center for Group Work in New York City. The Center offers meeting-facilitation and collaboration trainings to corporate clients and community based organizations using sculptural tools in unconventional environments. For example, Project 404 teaches CEOs how to focus on a single image on their smart phone in a gallery in Chelsea; Extrapolation Factory provides futurist scenarios for activists in the basement of a museum.

NYFA: Describe the market (or potential market) for your enterprise's product or service.

According to informational interviews with Charlie O'Donnel of Brooklyn Ventures and Scott Benaglio of SOVRN State, corporate clients spend $5000 on similar half-day retreats and team-building events. Non-profits are able to spend $1000 for a similar experience, and wealthy individuals are willing to spend $100 each for workshops of this nature. I will provide scholarships and low-cost workshops to grassroots organizations and people who demonstrate need with philanthropic support and a sliding-scale pricing model.

NYFA: What kinds of sales has your company had thus far? If none, what other metrics might indicate traction or future success?

The Study Center received a grant of $30,000 from the Rubin Foundation as well as a matching grant of $20,000 from Cooper Union to open a pilot program from October 13-November 18th at the Cooper Union. In under a month, The Study Center held twelve workshops with over 150 participants, an opening party with 300 people in attendance, and reviews in the *New York Times*, *Artforum*, *Vice*, and *Art in America*. After launching a successful pilot at Cooper Union this year, Caroline Woolard is seeking support to move this Study Center from its current phase toward a sustainable business for artists, designers, and facilitators.

Study

NYFA: Who are your competitors? Who else is doing what you do?

No one is providing training in group work led by artists. The Center for Art and Activism and the Center for Story-based Strategy both provide trainings for artists who are interested in using creativity in activism, but no arts-based consultancies specialize in artist-led group work. SOVRN State offers unique arts-based experiences and artwork license agreements to corporate clients, but does not do experiences related to group work led by artists. While many artists attempt to work with clients on an individual basis, artists have yet to band together to create a visible platform for their services surrounding group work. The Study Center does exactly this.

NYFA: How is this enterprise involved in the arts?

During our pilot program, The Study Center revealed a shift in the arts toward group work.

"Wound" also shows how the art world's breakneck schedule of exhibitions, fairs and biennials undercuts the ability of socially engaged artists to develop long-term strategies and practices.
—The New York Times

"And yet "Mending Time and Attention," an exhibition and a series of workshops organized by WOUND, seeks to heal the pain inflicted by late capitalism's compartmentalization and commodification of time."
—Artforum

"When artists create opportunities for support and mutual aid rather than unquestioningly competing with one another for meager resources, they open a small space of resistance to the divisiveness that comes from an economically precarious existence."
—Art in America

NYFA: Please describe the roles of each team member.

Caroline Woolard is the founding Director, currently operating as a technical project manager, communications director, and HR support for The Study Center. Or Zubalsky is the lead computer engineer, responsible for development of the website. Staff assistants in The Study Center include Emilio Martínez Poppe, Jordan Delzell, Anna Vila, Anna Zinovieff Papadimitriou, and Samantha Rosner. Mentors include Robin Chase of ZipCar, Charlie O'Donnell of Brooklyn Ventures, and Tom Finkelpearl of the NYC Department of Cultural Affairs.

Managing

NYFA: Has anyone on the team started a company before? If so, what?

Caroline Woolard ran an 8,000 square foot studio space for 40 artists for eight years: from 2008-2016. The space led to Woolard convening the NYC Real Estate Investment Cooperative.

More information is here: http://www.art21.org/newyorkcloseup/films/caroline-woolard-flips-the-real-estate-script/

NYFA: What other significant accomplishments have team members had that we should know about?

Woolard's practice produces objects and develops new contexts in which those objects may circulate. For Woolard, the enjoining of object and context is the sine qua non of artistic practice. Since 2007, she has created Exchange Café (MoMA, 2014), the barter networks OurGoods.org and TradeSchool.coop (2008-present), as well as cultural equity platform BFAMFAPhD (2013-present) and the NYC Real Estate Investment Cooperative (2015-present).

The budget for the project is here: https://docs.google.com/spreadsheets/d/1L9iqjkEPirBhu-znWeOXufa3GVthii_O5smX-pzkMrWs/edit?usp=sharing

NOTES:

2016 reflects the annual budget based upon what it would be, had we run our pilot for longer than one month.

*

New Foundation TBA refers to multiple Foundations I am in dialog with, many of whom I have cultivated relationships with over years.

**

Nonprofit Commissions/ Speaking refers to public speaking and commissions.

Currently, Caroline Woolard makes $20k a year on public speaking, with a public lecture every week Sept-Dec and Feb-May at $1000. As visibility for the Study Center increases, public speaking invitations will increase as well.

***

Workshop space was donated by Cooper Union during the pilot in October and November of 2016. In 2017, space will be donated by NYPL and RISD.

****

"Partner Shares for Outreach" is the grant funding the study center shares with outreach partner organizations. I find that these partnerships are more successful when the partner has a financial stake in the project.

INCOME	2016	2017	2018
Individual Support			
Individual donations	$0	$10,000 (pending)	$10,000 (pending)
Memberships (@$100 yearly)	$0	$1,000 (pending×10)	$10,000 (pending×100)
Total individual support	$0	$11,000	$20,000
Foundations			
Cooper Union	$15,000	$0	$0
Rubin Foundation	$20,000	$0	$0
New Foundation TBA*	$0	$5,000 (pending)	$10,000 (pending)
NYFA	$0	$15,000 (pending)	$0 (pending)
Total Foundations	$35,000	$20,000	$10,000
Sales			
Nonprofit Commisions/speaking	$750	$1,500 (pending)	$14,000 (pending)
Low-cost Workshops (@ $500)	$5,000 (secured x 10)	$5,000 (pending×10)	$7,500 (pending×15)
Corporate Workshops (@ $5k)	$0	$25,000 (pending×5)	$50,000 (pending ×10)
University Workshops (@ $1k)	$0	$5,000 (pending×5)	$10,000 (pending×10)
Total Sales	$5,750	$36,500	$81,500
In Kind			
Site Engineer	$5,500 (secured)	$0	$0
Site Coding	$12,700 (secured)	$0	$0
Graphic Design	$3,000 (secured)	$0	$0
Outreach	$10,050 (secured)	$0	$0
Fundraising	$11,800 (secured)	$25,000 (secured)	$0
Utilities	$2,400 (secured)	$2,400 (secured)	$2,400 (secured)
Workshop space ***	$50,000 (secured)	$50,000 (secured)	$50,000 (pending)
Home Office Expense	$9,000 (secured)	$9,000 (secured)	$0 (secured)
Total In Kind	$104,450	$86,400	$52,400
TOTAL INCOME	$145,200	$153,900	$163,900
EXPENSES	TOTAL/IN-KIND	TOTAL/IN-KIND	TOTAL/IN-KIND
Personnel			
Site Back End Engineer	$7,500/$5,500	$5,000/$0	$5,000/$0
Site Front End Coding	$15,000/$12,700	$2,000/$0	$2,000/$0
Graphic Designer	$3,000/$3,000	$3,000/$0	$3,000/$0
Outreach Staff	$12,250/$10,050	$30,000/$0	$30,000/$0
Fundraising Staff	$14,000/$11,800	$30,000/$25,000	$30,000/$0
Facilitators (@ $500 per event)	$5,000/$0	$10,000/$0	$17,500/$0
Event Assistants (@ $100 per event)	$1,000/$0	$2,000/$0	$3,500/$0
Total Personnel	$57,750/$43,050	$82,000/$25,000	$91,000/$0
General Administrative Expenses			
Printed Materials	$600/$0	$1,000/$0	$1,000/$0
Office Supplies	$300/$0	$500/$0	$500/$0
Utilities	$2,400/$2,400	$2,400/$2,400	$2,400/$2,400
Workshop space ***	$50,000/$50,000	$50,000/$50,000	$50,000/$50,000
Home office expense	$9,000/$9,000	$9,000/$9,000	$9,000/$0
Total Administrative	$62,300/$61,400	$62,900/$61,400	$62,900/$52,400
Other			
Partner shares for outreach ****	$0/$0	$5,000/$0	$5,000/$0
Total Other	$0/$0	$5,000/$0	$5,000/$0
TOTAL EXPENSES	$120,050/$104,450	$86,400/$86,400	$158,900/$52,400
Surplus/(Deficit)	*$25,150*	*$4,000*	*$5,000*

Managing

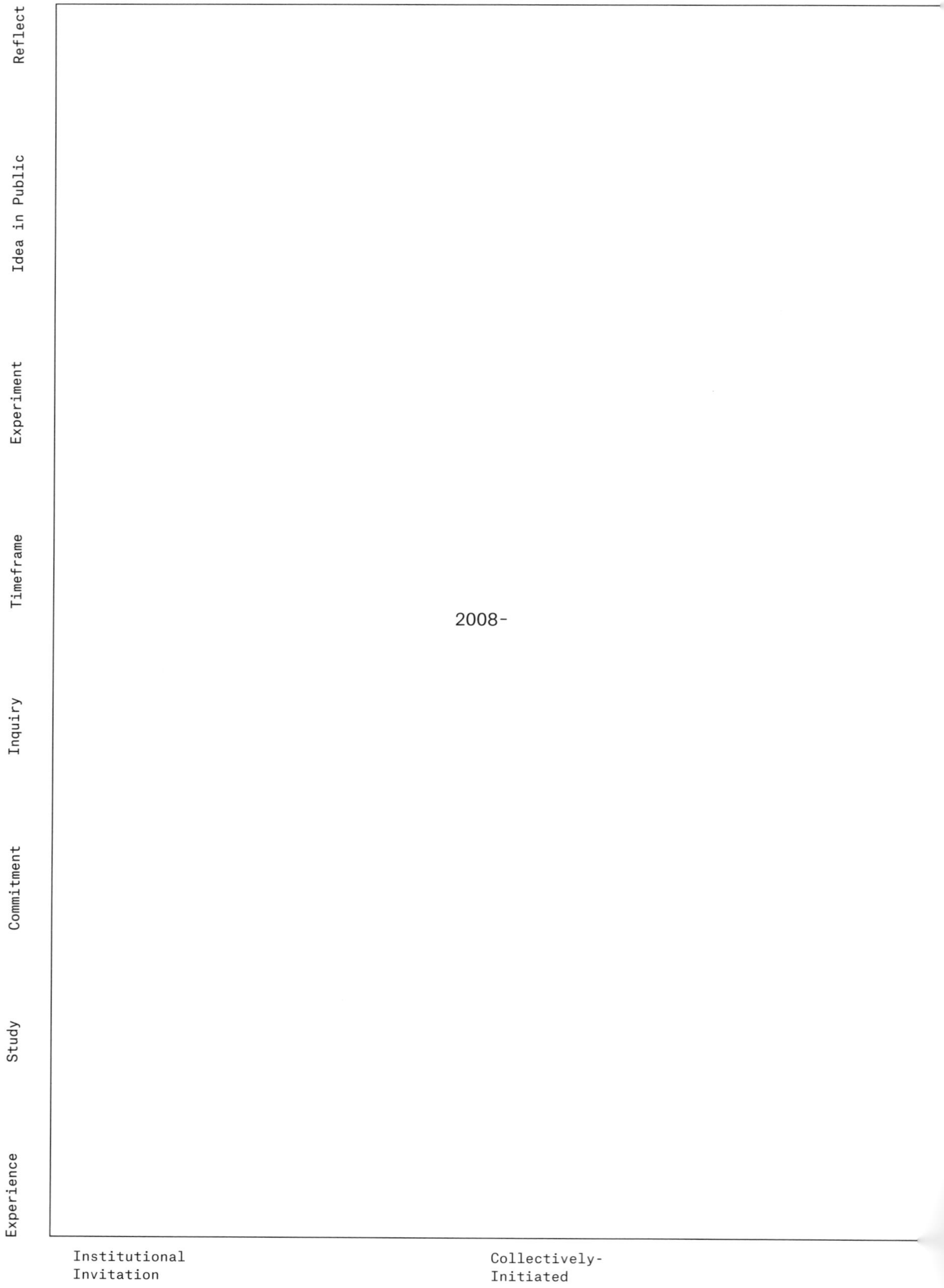

Reflect

Idea in Public

Experiment

Timeframe

Inquiry

Commitment

Study

Experience

2008-

Institutional
Invitation

Collectively-
Initiated

Making

Managing

Making Mediating

2018

Title of Project /
Platform / Practice

3

OurGoods.org & TradeSchool.coop

OurGoods.org was a resource sharing network for cultural producers that was co-founded by Jen Abrams, Louise Ma, Carl Tashian, Rich Watts, and Caroline Woolard in 2008 and run by the group as a collective until 2016. The website and public events connected over 7000 artists, craftspeople, and activists in New York City to share skills, spaces, and objects and to get independent projects done in a culture of mutual aid. More information is online at: http://ourgoods.org

TradeSchool.coop was a self-organized learning platform that ran on barter from 2009–2019. Students exchanged barter items rather than money with their teachers, making space for reciprocal and radical pedagogy. Co-founded by Louise Ma, Rich Watts, and Caroline Woolard in New York in 2009, and then run by Christhian Diaz, Aimée Lutkin, Louise Ma, Rachel Vera Steinberg, Caroline Woolard, and Or Zubalsky in New York until 2012, TradeSchool.coop expanded to become a global network of barter-based schools, with thirty local chapters and over 22,000 students and teachers. More information is online at: http://tradeschool.coop/story

While forced digital mediation
of the body is a political
tragedy, the coding of digital
space against global capitalist
platforms should be taken very
seriously. The digital infrastructure for radical permanence
should be a tool to break the
process of individualization of
people, to make them gather and
come together in the physical
space, it should aim to organize
political common encounters as
opposed to tear us apart into
the depoliticized isolations of
individual time.

—Marco Baravalle, 2020

When you barter with someone,
especially a creative person, the
labor is known. When you talk to
that person about the thing they
have made, they can even show
you the shop where it's made and
where they sourced the materials.
So barter is a way to think about
the economy in a very direct manner. You are meeting the person
whose labor is embodied in the
object you're trading.

—Caroline Woolard, 2010

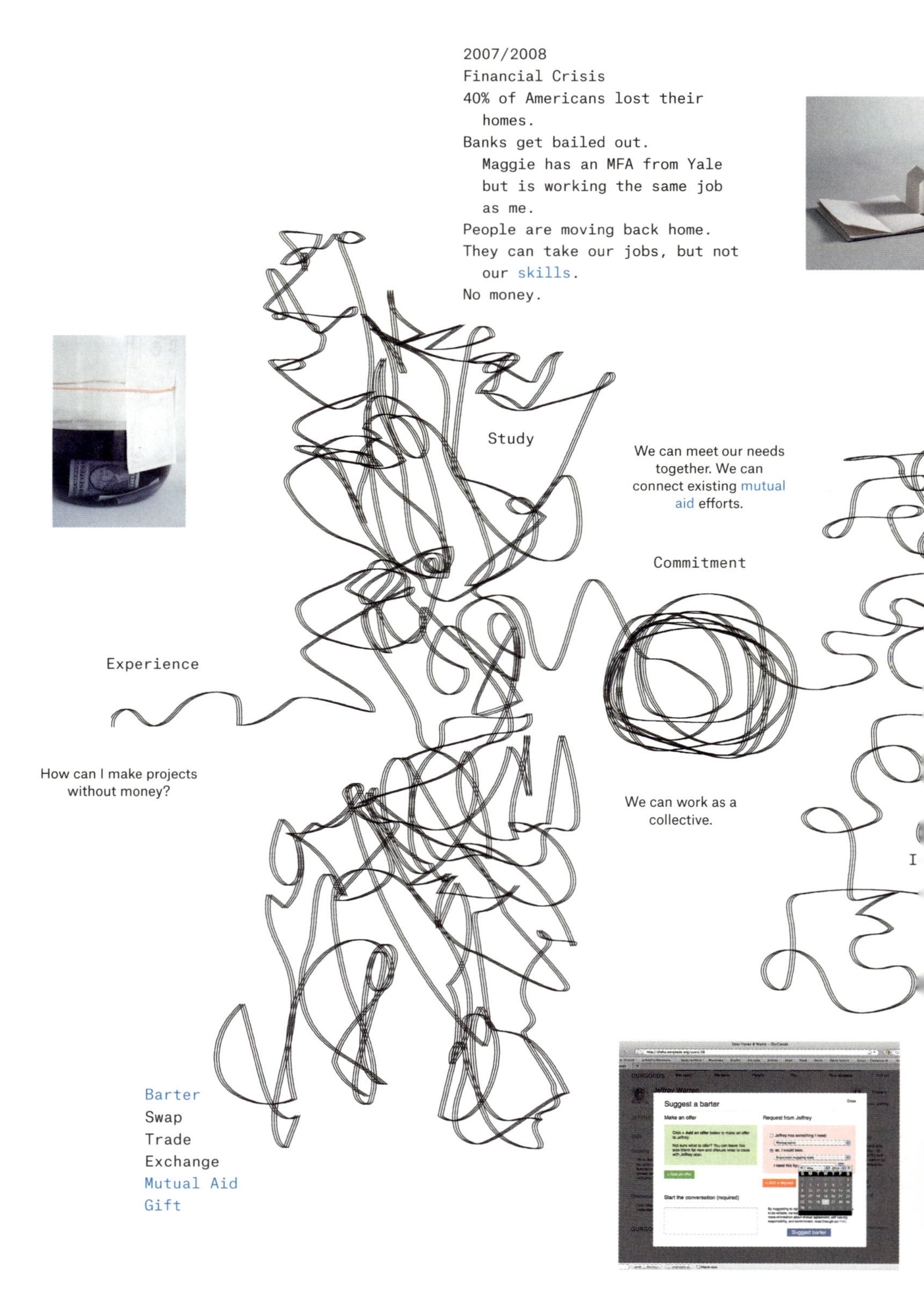

Collectively-
Initiated

Freecycle
Value
Rank
Capitalism
exchange value vs. use value
solidarity economy
Neoliberalism
power
Carolina Caycedo
art

domestic work
Farah Tannis
Black Women's Blueprint
"the coincidence of wants"
"the elegant negotiable"
Lewis Hyde
WOW Café Theater
Jesse Reiley's Time Bank
Craigslist
Germaine Koh

Logo constantly changes
    icons, a continuous barter
Newspaper becomes a hat
business cards break in half
Furniture has a U to connect,
    like barter
website
events

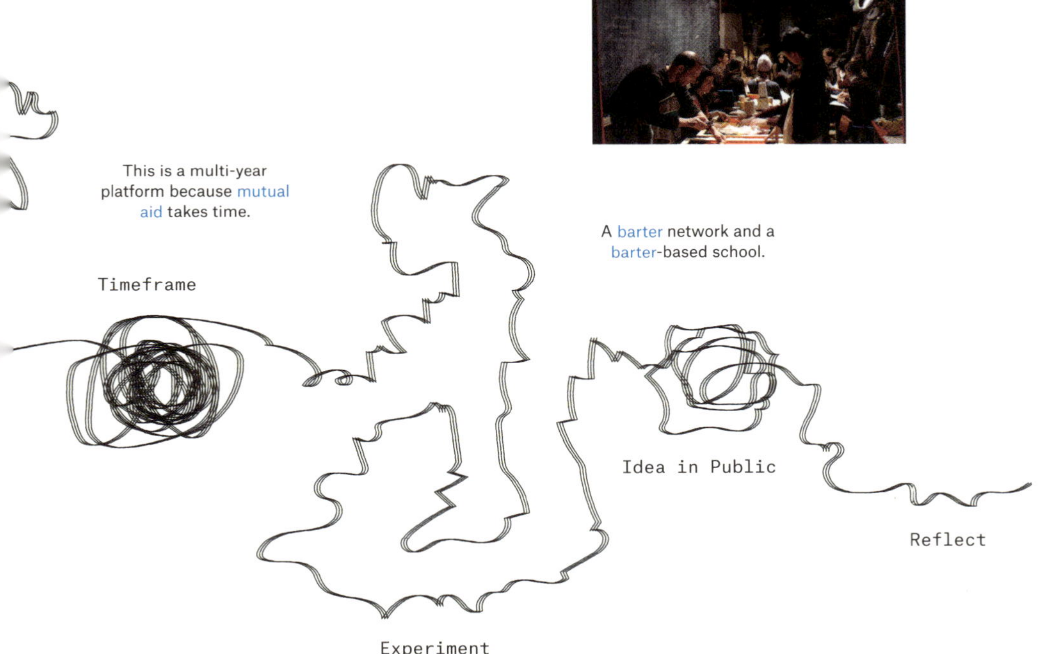

This is a multi-year
platform because mutual
aid takes time.

Timeframe

A barter network and a
barter-based school.

Idea in Public

Reflect

Experiment

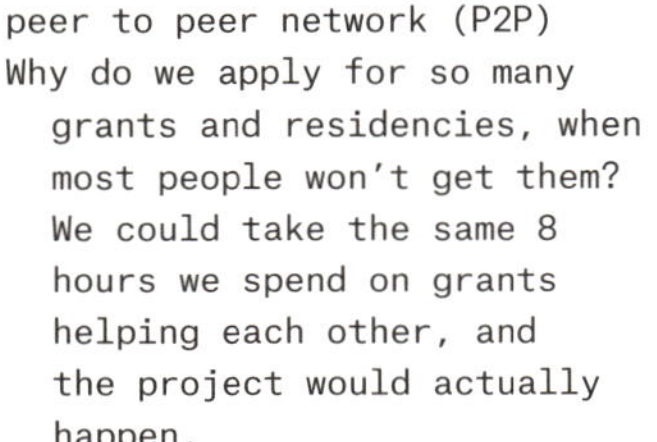

peer to peer network (P2P)
Why do we apply for so many
    grants and residencies, when
    most people won't get them?
    We could take the same 8
    hours we spend on grants
    helping each other, and
    the project would actually
    happen.
With mutual respect, anything
    is possible.

1:1
Nonlinear time
Two people
Eyes
Folded paper
Clamshell
Bilateral symmetry
Dyad

Decommodified Labor

Leigh Claire La Berge, PhD, professes at the intersection of arts, literature, *visual culture* and *political economy*. She is the author of *Scandals and Abstraction: Financial Fiction of the Long 1980s* (Oxford University Press) and *Wages Against Artwork: Decommodified Labor and the Claims of Socially Engaged Art* (Duke University Press, 2019). She is Associate Professor of English in the Department of English at BMCC CUNY.

Leigh Claire La Berge, critical theorist, adapted from *Wages Against Artwork: Decommodified Labor and the Claims of Socially Engaged Art*. [7]

An international network of schools in which anyone may take classes by bartering with teachers, in which any collective may start a branch in their own town or city; a barter network for artists to offer and receive skills, materials, and labor; a café installed at the Museum of Modern Art where visitors are invited to invent the value of their own currency on notes provided and to use this currency to purchase tea; an artist-run think tank centered upon the political economy of art education; a real estate investment cooperative that aims to remove land from market-based circulation and place it in a community land trust. Each of these works is a project started by the artist Caroline Woolard with a range of interdisciplinary collaborators, and in each we notice a particular orientation toward the construction of value: how we value, why we value, and for whom. The first, TradeSchool.coop, conflates the act of trading with the language of craft but also with the commodification of education; the second, OurGoods.org, makes a public claim to utility in the face of the more common assignation of value to the individual possession of talent; and the third, Exchange Café [see chapter 4], asks its visitors to reimagine the act of using money within the defining experience of a museum-based café, itself so often the place to find respite from whatever artwork-viewing

[7] Leigh Clare La Berge, *Wages Against Artwork: Decommodified Labor and the Claims of Socially Engaged Art* (Duke, 2019).

Collectively-
Initiated

opportunities the museum has on offer; the fourth, BFAMFAPhD see chapter 5, investigates the political economy of arts education; and, finally the NYC Real Estate Investment Cooperative aims to suspend the commodification of a piece of urban land. [8]

we notice a particular orientation toward the construction of value: how we value, why we value, and for whom.

Beginning with the 2007–8 credit crisis, which coincided with Woolard's graduation from the once-tuition-free art school Cooper Union, Woolard began constructing what she now understands specifically as "institutions," what I will call "institutions-as-art." Woolard's institutions comprise shifting coalitions of artists who devote themselves both to making art and to making it possible for other artists to make art. For Woolard, the institution concretizes and navigates a space more capacious than the individual—thus institutions-as-art mitigate against being reduced to the artist's ego, to the artist's oeuvre, or to some potential canonical assignment; rather, the institution remains open to change but also simply remains as a form of duration. Yet the institution-as-art must avoid the well-known temptation of focusing on its own duration over the ends it supposedly serves. According to Woolard, if an institution can maintain that

nuanced space, it may exist as both an art form and as a social form for artists.

Each of the above "institutions-as-art" might be seen as an answer to a question about how artists can sustain their practice in an age of decommodified labor. Where do artists go after school, if they want to continue their education? They go to TradeSchool.coop, that is, they learn to continue their own schooling through nonmonetary exchange. How do artists make artwork after being displaced from their studios, and if they don't have the resources that art school had afforded them? They use OurGoods.org to find a network of like-minded practitioners with whom to exchange skills and materials, time and space. Where should artists work and where should they practice? They might join the Real Estate Investment Cooperative in an attempt to create permanently affordable space or to find others with whom to share a space. What do they do when they realize that their art education has seemingly no better prepared them to be a working artist than had they not gone to art school, particularly if they are a woman or a person of color? They might join BFAMFAPhD, a group that investigates the political economy of arts education and arts professionalization.

Taken together, these questions continue an investigation into the transformation of artwork and artists' work under conditions

8

Images and descriptions are available at carolinewoolard.com; see also www.tradeschool.coop; ourgoods.org; and Exchange Café at "MoMA Studio: Exchange Café," http://www.moma.org/visit/calendar/exhibitions/1364. For an in-depth look at Woolard's work on the Real Estate Investment Cooperative, see Art21's documentary production, "Caroline Woolard Flips the Real Estate Script," Art21, July 31, 2015, at https://art21.org/watch/new-york-close-up/caroline-woolard-flips-the-real-estate-script/

Yet the institution-as-art must avoid the well-known temptation of focusing on its own duration over the ends it supposedly serves.

of the decommodification of their artistic labor. If decommodification allows for the removal of land, labor, or money from market-based circulation, then many artists, socially engaged or not, are already working within its historical ambit. Like deindustrialization, decommodification moves in a cyclical fashion, and for labor to be decommodified it must first have been commodified. Our current moment of the decommodification of artistic labor follows, as both Sharon Zukin and Donna M. Binkiwicz have detailed, a 1950–60s expansion of "artists' ability to claim their art as a career" through the proliferation of artist's agencies, granting bodies, foundations, universities' arts programs, and so on. This was an economic moment when, as Binkiwicz recounts, New York Senator Jacob Javits could suggest that "since the principle of government subsidy … [is] well established with many industries … why could this same principle not be applied to the arts?"[9] And yet, simultaneously with this flourishing of an artistic life as a possible professional life, a foreshortened labor market for artists appeared on the horizon. Zukin notes that by 1963 the US Labor Department was already producing "gloomy projections" about art-based employment. Furthermore, she qualifies the kind of workers sociologists and government officials believed artistic work would engender: "Expanding jobs in the arts could be expected to produce a fairly amorphous and relatively quiescent labor force."[10]

Woolard's practice, including her work on *Artists Report Back* with the collective she founded, BFAMFAPhD, might be understood as a contemporary, artistic response to the kind of social history of the professionalizing and commodifying art world that Zukin and Binkiwicz provide. In Zukin and Binkiwicz's respective histories, the Kennedy administration inaugurates the National Endowment for the Arts; in Woolard's public presentations of the barter network OurGoods.org, she notes the fiscal decimation of that agency. In Zukin's history, the federal government expands arts funding through universities in the form of student grants; in *Artists Report Back*, funding sources are understood to have been converted from grants to loans. After school, artistic careers are still possible in universities, but those careers will be restricted to a few, while the majority who attempt them will become part of the contingent academic labor force. Such facts must be read as a reminder that much as commodification famously delivers what Marx calls the "double freedom" of a waged life—you're free to sell

9
Donna M. Binkiwicz, *Federalizing the Muse: United States Arts Policy and the National Endowment for the Arts, 1965-1980* (Chapel Hill: University of North Carolina Press, 2004), 32.

10
Sharon Zukin, *Loft Living: Culture and Capital in Urban Change* (New Brunswick, NJ: Rutgers University Press, 1986), 98.

Collectively-
Initiated

your labor to whomever you choose; you have to sell your labor—so does decommodification: you're free not to sell your labor; you can't sell it. Woolard's works respond to this situation with nuance and pragmatism, and the tenor of their responses derives in part from their institutional forms. Indeed, they insist that artists will keep working, even without a wage, that artists refuse not to work, that even as they are deprofessionalized, they will remain professionals.

What I claim is the need for artists to secure their own forms of labor exchange outside of the strictures of the art institutions of the waged world, Woolard sees as "a need to make both artistic objects and an institutional context in which those objects can meaningfully circulate," because artists' lack of a wage will limit their ability to circulate in formal art spaces.[11] When Woolard graduated from the Cooper Union with her own Bachelor of Fine Arts degree, she emerged into the 2007–8 credit crisis and subsequent "Great Recession." She supported herself by continuing to work at Cooper Union and then by collecting unemployment, an allowance she lists on her cv under "grants and funding sources." It is fitting that being compensated by the government for not working provided the time, space, and the decommodified freedom to develop two institutions that both respond to and allow for a (partially) decommodified artistic practice. And it is more fitting still that Woolard made the decision not to pursue a Master of Fine Arts in her

11
In conversation with the artist.

twenties, but rather to develop her own artist-run institutions of education and resource sharing, which she conceived of as crucial parts of her practice.

If decommodification allows for the removal of land, labor, or money from market-based circulation, then many artists, socially engaged or not, are already working within its historical ambit.

OurGoods.org and TradeSchool.coop are two barter-based networks that Woolard organized with collaborators who included grant writers, computer programmers, graphic designers, and a range of visual and performing artists. OurGoods.org is a web-based network for individual barter, whereas TradeSchool.coop provides a similar web-based network for group barter; groups of students barter for classes with instructors. We might understand the second as an expanded application of the first. Founded in 2009, OurGoods.org had at its peak seven thousand members, most of whom were based in New York City. Members create a profile detailing what skills and materials they have to offer and what skills and materials they need for their own artistic projects. They communicate how any barter will be incorporated into their project or practice. "I need translation services for an art poster," one profile might say, for example, or "space for an event." The benefit of a single barter is that one agrees to trade what one has. The disadvantage is that forms of socially accepted measures of equivalence, time for money, still obtain here as members decide how or whether to trade a higher income-generating and often masculine skill, say web development, for a lower, often feminized one, say childcare. Yet unlike the similar, short-lived artist-run institution Time Bank by Anton Vidokle of eflux, OurGoods .org does not enforce such a form of equivalence, that is, you put in an hour, you get back an hour. Rather, members negotiate these exchanges on their own.

The site does not track the actual barter exchanges to which members agree. Rather, members engage in these exchanges in real time and space, trading messages through the OurGoods.org portal. This individual correspondence doubles as a limit on how barter is represented in a manner reminiscent of the challenges of performance art and its documentation. Much like a performance never happens the same way twice, barter has an improvisational quality. Unlike performance, however, there are no spectacles here: one doesn't get to watch others barter. To watch, you have to do. Woolard has compared barter acts to storytelling and oral traditions in which the same story produces different effects when told or enacted by different tellers and listeners. I want to follow the project's own literary language and think about how, when read as art, the barter-based transactions facilitated by OurGoods.org may be seen as a kind of metaphor in that word's historical sense of being a vehicle for conducting meaning. "Metaphor" etymologically breaks down to mean "to carry over"; it denotes a movement in which meaning is transported from one object to another in speech and writing. Barter structures a specific type of metaphor, perhaps akin to what David Halperin calls a practical allegory, in that it is instantiated through activity.[12] The barters performed through OurGoods.org metaphorize what an other, new economy would look like while simultaneously constituting that new economy. If I barter two hours of my editing skills for one hour of soundtrack-laying ability, our exchange represents a mode of economic transformation. It also constitutes that mode. The representation and its efficaciousness become one.

OurGoods.org follows the movement that Shannon Jackson describes as a transposition from a "discrete notion of the work of art to a process-based notion of the work it takes to make art."[13] Why do artists barter? They barter because they have potential artistic labor but no market in which to sell it. Why else do they barter? Because they need others' potential artistic labor but have no money with which to purchase it. Their labor and consequently their potential to earn a wage have

12
Richard Halperin, *Shakespeare Among the Moderns* (Ithaca, NY: Cornell University Press, 1997), 12.

13
Jackson here is discussing Mierle Laderman Ukeles's "maintenance artwork," which finds an easy aesthetic correlation in what it takes to maintain both an individual art practice (a wife) and an art institution and art world.

Collectively-
Initiated

been decommodified, and now each will find another in a scene of decommodification in which the definitional properties of commodification as such — "made by waged labor and sold on the market" — will not be brought to bear. OurGoods.org instead offers the chance to work for one's self, but not through a conception of the kind of neoliberal self-capitalization. Rather, one works through a different form of being "a partner in exchange" in which another is required for mutually enhancing but not profit-generating reciprocity.

being compensated by the government for not working provided the time, space, and the decommodified freedom to develop two institutions that both respond to and allow for a (partially) decommodified artistic practice

The potential trades facilitated by OurGoods.org may expand ad infinitum, even as each individual trade will never be represented to others and composes a niche economy scaled at two. It was the limitation of the one-to-one scale of OurGoods.org that laid the foundation for the next collective, similarly decommodifying

14
Caroline Woolard, "Dear Potential Trade School Organizer," *Social Text Online*, October 14, 2013, http://socialtextjournal.org/periscope_article/trade-school/ (accessed February 2016).

institution, TradeSchool.coop. This web-based platform may be downloaded by any individual or group, can be translated into multiple languages, and has spawned "schools" as local as New York and Indianapolis and as international as Quito and Glasgow. In narrating how the project came to be, Woolard herself makes frequent recourse to the availability of time and space that are one possible result of decommodified labor. Writing in *Social Text*, she explains: "On February 25th to March 1st, 2010, we ran [the first] TradeSchool. coop … Over the course of 35 days, more than 800 people participated in 76 single session classes … In exchange for instruction, teachers received everything from running shoes to mixed cds … We ran out of time slots for teachers to teach and classes filled up so quickly that we had to turn people away. [Thus we reopened] … in an empty school, paying rent with the support of charitable donations and running on donated time from 8–20 volunteers."[14]

OurGoods.org is a web-based network for individual barter, whereas TradeSchool.coop provides a similar web-based network for group barter; groups of students barter for classes with instructors.

The converse of "having time" to give, of course, is that such projects "take time" to run—Antonio Negri's "tautological time" seems apt.[15] Barters reclaim the tautological time of real subsumption; Negri asks, "When all life is work, who measures whom?" "We will introduce our own measures," Woolard seems to respond. Both OurGoods.org and TradeSchool.coop require time for planning, for engaging, and especially for communicating. Before any given TradeSchool.coop class, teachers agree with students on what their recompense will be. The institution operates through given time and given space, what we may understand as decommodified time and decommodified space. As of 2019, Woolard estimates that around twenty-three thousand students and teachers have participated in the project. Barter remains the currency. Anyone may propose a course (for barter) and anyone may take a course (for barter). Different schools will develop different local cultures; for example, TradeSchool.coop in Glasgow has a mental health and senior care focus, whereas TradeSchool.coop in New York is more arts-focused.

For Woolard, the representation and self-constitution of artistic labor should transpire on a plane of some mutually recognized equality. The institution, not reducible to any individual, should enable that equality by providing a platform in which artists can encounter each other through the exchange of their decommodified labor. In that temporal constitution of the barter, there must have been, however brief, a recognition of reciprocity. The point is not to assert that the commodification of labor is bad and its decommodification is good—a fundamentally facile claim—but rather to show the course that labor takes in its various forms in the aesthetic realm. The labors of Woolard's institutions do not assume reified status because they are continually called on to circulate intersubjectively, to be exchanged from one position to the other. Crucially, the focus of the barters remains the relationality of the artistic laborers to each other, not the relationality of the object produced by such labor to the viewer. Here we find ourselves quite close to the claim made by Nicholas Bourriaud in his foundational *Relational Aesthetics*—namely, that what distinguishes socially engaged artwork is that its "substrate is intersubjectivity."[16] Yet that intersubjectivity must itself have both a material and an affective form. We may say that the likely form of that intersubjectivity in socially engaged art derives from the content of its decommodified labor.

In the larger discussion of the divaricated theoretical trajectories of the real subsumption of labor and the neoliberalization of the economy that structures my argument, the necessary questions for Woolard's institutions remain: Do they produce value for others (real subsumption) and/or do they necessitate that the artist assume the subject position

15
Nicolas Bourriaud, *Relational Aesthetics* (Paris: Presses Du Reel, 2002), 21.

16
Nicholas Bourriaud, *Relational Aesthetics* (Paris: Presses Du Reel, 2002).

17
All citations to Marina Vishmidt, "'Mimesis of the Hardened and Alienated': Social Practice as a Business Model," *e-flux Journal*, no. 43 (March 2013), http://www.e-flux.com/journal/43/60197/mimesis-of-the-hardened-and-alienated-social-practice-as-business-model.

Collectively-
Initiated

of "entrepreneur of herself" (neoliberaliza-tion)? Which is the more appropriate framing of the decommodified labor that structures these artworks? Answering these questions will help us to explore another—namely, the fluid boundary that critics have suggested is the sometimes muddled difference between "socially engaged art" and "socially engaged business," a tension helpfully grouped under the rubric Marina Vishmidt has called "social practice [art] as business model."[17] Vishmidt is concerned that the most successful social practice artists engage in what she memo-rably calls "shovel-ready" art practices. She quite rightly asks, "Isn't it the case that the [art] practices viewed as most successful [have been] the overtly entrepreneurial ones … because they occupied both the commu-nity-facing and business-minded ends of the relational [aesthetics] spectrum?" Vishmidt continues to claim that such art illustrates "how entrepreneurialism and autonomy conjoin in a resolutely post-critical and results-oriented agenda," similar to an NGO or a nonprofit.

there are no spectacles here: one doesn't get to watch others barter. To watch, you have to do.

To support her claims, Vishmidt provides the example of one of the most well-known, certainly protocanonical, socially engaged artists working today, Theaster Gates. Gates refers to himself as a "hustler" and calls his art practice an "insurgent business"; the New York Times has desig-nated him "Chicago's opportunity artist."[18] Consider Gates's Dorchester Projects on Chicago's impoverished, mostly black, South Side. Partnering with his employer, the University of Chicago, Gates has built community centers, libraries, a cinema, and the like.[19] Vishmidt writes: "Gates's entrepreneurial outlook—promoting the virtues of labor in social change, preferably the labor of others, while he interfaces with real estate developers, art institutions, and ngos—is resolutely and unapologetically 'post-political.'"[20]

Some of Vishmidt's criticisms could be applied to OurGoods.org and TradeSchool.coop. Indeed, OurGoods.org and TradeSchool.coop have not been consis-tently legible as artworks, but as some-thing more like a community partnership. Woolard herself is more agnostic. During their making she didn't necessarily refer to them as art. Now she understands them as institutions for artists that double as art. One the one hand, Woolard herself explains

18
That the University of Chicago itself has been partly responsi-ble for the decimation of black areas of culture and business development is an omitted part of this narrative.

19
Ben Austen, "Chicago's Op-portunity Artist," *The New York Times Magazine*, December 20, 2013, http://www.nytimes.com/2013/12/22/magazine/chica-gos-opportunity-artist.html.

20
An example similar to Gates may be found in the work of the Houston-based artist Rick Lowe, whose residential development, Project Row Houses, is, by its self-de-scription, "founded on the principle that art—and the community it creates—can be the foundation for revital-izing depressed inner-city neighborhoods." Cited in Fin-kelpearl, What We Made, 132.

OurGoods.org &
TradeSchool.coop

of OurGoods.org, "We didn't want to call it a work of art because then people wouldn't use it. They would feel as if we were using them for our own performance."[21] Yet, these works have been presented at canonical institutions of art including the Whitney, MoMA, and the Brooklyn Museum, as well as less canonical but still important venues like Creative Time's summit, Living as Form. And many artists who make similar work do call them art, appealing, for example, to Joseph Beuys's notion of "social sculpture" to anchor these kinds of works in an art historical trajectory.

The barters performed through OurGoods.org metaphorize what an other, new economy would look like while simultaneously constituting that new economy.

Nonetheless, while Woolard herself has been identified as the artist, and the institutions she has helped create have been identified as artworks, OurGoods.org and TradeSchool.coop have — perhaps suspiciously — garnered attention from members of the world of so-called social entrepreneurship and the recently anointed "sharing economy." Such a sensibility was on display when Levi Strauss and Co. offered to purchase and franchise TradeSchool.coop (which Woolard declined), and when the real estate developer Ron Spurga sought to organize a monetization of OurGoods.org's database of members (also declined by Woolard). The intimacy of an opposition often creates opportunities for radical misidentification, and that was the case when OurGoods.org's and TradeSchool.coop's scene of almost totally decommodified labor was interpreted as a site for the possibility of their complete commodification.

So-called sharing economy companies such as Lyft or Airbnb truck in the fantasy of being able to commodify all personal time and space while simultaneously "not working." It's not really "work" to drive someone in your car via Lyft (after all, you're not a taxi driver) or have them sleep in your home via Airbnb (nor are you a hotel proprietor). You're just doing what you would be doing anyway — driving, sleeping, cooking, being in your home, and so on — but now you are "sharing" with others and you are making money while doing so. Here we note one example of how the neoliberal disappearance of the concept of labor takes daily, ideological form: Airbnb and Lyft eagerly suggest that their users' activities, those that make money for the company and the individual through the allotment of time, should not be understood as work.

Woolard's collective projects provide the precise refusal of this logic. While engaged in a barter-based transaction, you're doing what you'd be doing anyway and you're still not making money. OurGoods.org and TradeSchool.coop insist that such activities are serious, real, professional, even; they become a kind of work but without the wage. With Lyft you set your own schedule,

21
In conversation with the artist, 2013.

but not your own wage. With Woolard's institutions, you enter into a mutual time/space in which your artistic labor may be recognized and evaluated according to new, if nonwaged, metrics.

These aspects of Woolard's projects finally allow us to make a link to the neoliberal claim—articulated most clearly in Foucault's famous reading of the Neoliberals—that our contemporary economy has undergone "a breakdown of labor into capital and income."[22] What we can affirm here through a reading of Woolard's institutions-as-art, is that the neoliberal, post-labor declaration is essentially a descriptive claim. The activities remain the same only to be conceived of and narrated differently. Thus we can affirm Jason Read's crucial suggestion that "neoliberalism is the ideology of real subsumption," and we can demonstrate its truth in the field of cultural production.[23] This demonstration should help us to clarify the relation between a change in economic organization and a discourse about that change.

My contention in this essay—indeed in my book, *Wages Against Artwork*—is that a change in the value composition of capital will necessarily result in a change in how labor is valorized. In our contemporary moment of finance's ascendance and labor's degradation, "precarity" has been suggested as an appropriate descriptor. The problem with this suggestion is that "precarity" does not index a change at the level of the labor commodity; rather, it only indexes a change in the social reception of that labor. By using the term "decommodified labor," I hope to isolate a change in the composition of labor and how that changed labor takes an aesthetic form.

In the work I have discussed, the labor that renders the art is not a commodity, nor is the art object that emerges from it. There is no ethical claim to be made here. Nor do we need to turn to the imposition of finance or regimes of accumulation for our heuristics; here, those become too abstract. Rather, we should return the critical paradox set out in Stewart Martin's perspicacious work on art's commodity status. Martin suggests that "within a society in which commodification is dominant, everything that is external to this commodification becomes marginal, liable to be socially irrelevant or merely yet-to-be-commodified."[24] Art cannot be a commodity because if it were, it would forfeit its critical power. But art cannot not be a commodity because were it external to commodification, it would also forfeit its critical power. This paradox presents the balance of the socially engaged art that derives from decommodified labor: namely, that it may be worthless in more ways than one.

If a socially engaged artist like Theaster Gates avails himself of both gallery-based commodification and nonprofit-based infrastructural support, then Woolard's two institutional platforms, OurGoods.org and TradeSchool.coop, reached neither of these pivot points precisely. Remainders of OurGoods.org or TradeSchool.coop were not sold off in a gallery, nor were the

22
Michel Foucault, *Birth of Biopolitics: Lectures at the Collège de France, 1978-1979* (London: Palgrave, 2009), 224.

23
See Jason Read, "A Genealogy of Homo-Economicus: Neoliberalism and the Production of Subjectivity," Foucault Studies, no. 6 (2009): 25-36.

24
Stewart Martin, "The Absolute Artwork Meets the Absolute Commodity," *Radical Philosophy* 146 (November/December 2007), 18.

OurGoods.org &
TradeSchool.coop

institutions in their entirety given over to a nonprofit, as in the case of Gates's Dorchester Projects and its association with the University of Chicago. They did not offer themselves up to corporate "sponsors," as did socially engaged artist Rick Lowes's Project Row Houses through its association with the Houston-based oil services company, Chevron. Had Woolard and her collaborators accepted offers to franchise and monetize private concerns, money would have been exchanged for labor already done. The institutions in question would have ceased to be decommodifying and would have relied instead on a familiar organization whereby some labor would be done without wages — namely, the bartering relationships — but out of that lack, surplus value would be generated via the organization itself. Here we must remember Marx's point that "the secret of the self-expansion of capital resolves itself into having the disposal of a definite quantity of other people's unpaid labour."[25]

a change in the value composition of capital will necessarily result in a change in how labor is valorized

With both OurGoods.org and TradeSchool. coop, the offers out of decommodification were rejected. Woolard and her collaborators concluded that if someone gets paid, then everyone should get paid. And once everyone gets paid, not only do expenses increase exponentially, but increasing time

25
Marx, *Capital*, vol. 1, 377.

must be devoted to organizing, disbursing, accounting for, and tracking payment. Then the artist really does become an entrepreneur, and not the philosophical type memorialized by Foucault. Rather, she becomes a kind of payroll manager. Money has its own expenses and introduces its own scale. The old adage that it takes money to make money is certainly true, but so is its converse: it takes money to break even or operate at a loss. Money takes money. Woolard and her collaborators at TradeSchool.coop decided that no commodification was a better state of affairs than some commodification, because some money generated through commodification would have demonstrated that there really was a scarcity of money, that all members really could not be compensated for their labor.

Woolard and her institutions adhered to their decommodification. They believed that such a choice gave their institutions more freedom, more inclusivity, indeed, even an ability to be perceived as art. But then, decommodification cannot be hailed as a "solution" in any way beyond the boundaries of the aesthetic. When commodification is the regime, decommodification may offer a pause, a temporary respite, and it does so only in relation to prevailing social conditions of commodification. After running for six years, OurGoods.org came to a close; the New York City branch of TradeSchool. coop shut down, and Woolard and her collaborators passed the management and software development on to a new generation of artists and activists. The conclusion of these projects in some sense furthers their status as artworks. As Claire Bishop questions of a different socially engaged art project, also a school, run by the artist Tania Bruguera, "Why do you need to call it a work of art? Can't it just be something you do in Havana? For this to be a work of art, you have to finish it. It can't be ongoing." [26]

Without money or sale, without incorporation of some sort, parts of these institutions ended. And yet, other parts continued. This ending seems a likely consequence of decommodified labor. But it also reasserts a kind of singularity so important to the aesthetic. Woolard's work provides a decommodified aesthetics that is itself a decommodification of some of our most important commodities: labor and education. In Epsing-Andersen's original formulation, the welfare state decommodifies certain goods and services so that its citizens may socially reproduce outside of certain market constraints. In the post welfare state, however, this relationship is inverted, and enterprising citizens, in a Foucauldian gesture, structure their own decommodification to achieve a certain freedom. We are not yet prepared to qualify this freedom as misplaced or genuine; rather, in keeping with Foucault's less often examined language of neoliberalism, we can only say that in this moment it is understood as a certain freedom by those who practice it. Those momentary freedoms are aesthetic, par excellence.

26
Finkelpearl, What We Made, 205.

IMAGINE A GROUP GATHERING

IMAGINE A GROUP GATHERING

fig. 3-1
The Space Between Us, 2008,
paper, thread, book board,
4 × 6 × 15 inches. Courtesy
of the artist.

A barter brings up these
questions: What is possible,
between us, when we determine
what our work is worth?

Like so many artists in the
United States, where home
ownership is linked so
directly to race, class, and
access to education, I am
interested in the home as a
symbol and also the home as
an active site of struggle
politically, to ensure that
housing is a human right and
that we can see development
without displacement of long
term residents.

Think of Mel Chin's *Safehouse*,
the house as a giant vault,
his 2008 sculptural icon
of Operation Paydirt in New
Orleans, or David Hammons'
*House Of The Future & America
Street*, his 2007-2017 collaboration with a local build-
er, a 6' × 20'-foot teaching
model of Charleston, South
Carolina's signature style,
or think of Alan Wexler's
1990 *Crate House*, where all
tools slide in and out of the
house, or Gordon Matt-Clark's
interventions in the 1970s,
when his brother had committed suicide and his parents
got divorced, or think of J.
Morgan Puett's living-hous-
ing-workstyling at Mildred's
Lane since the 1990s.

—Caroline Woolard, interview
with Larissa Harris at the
Queens Museum, 2020

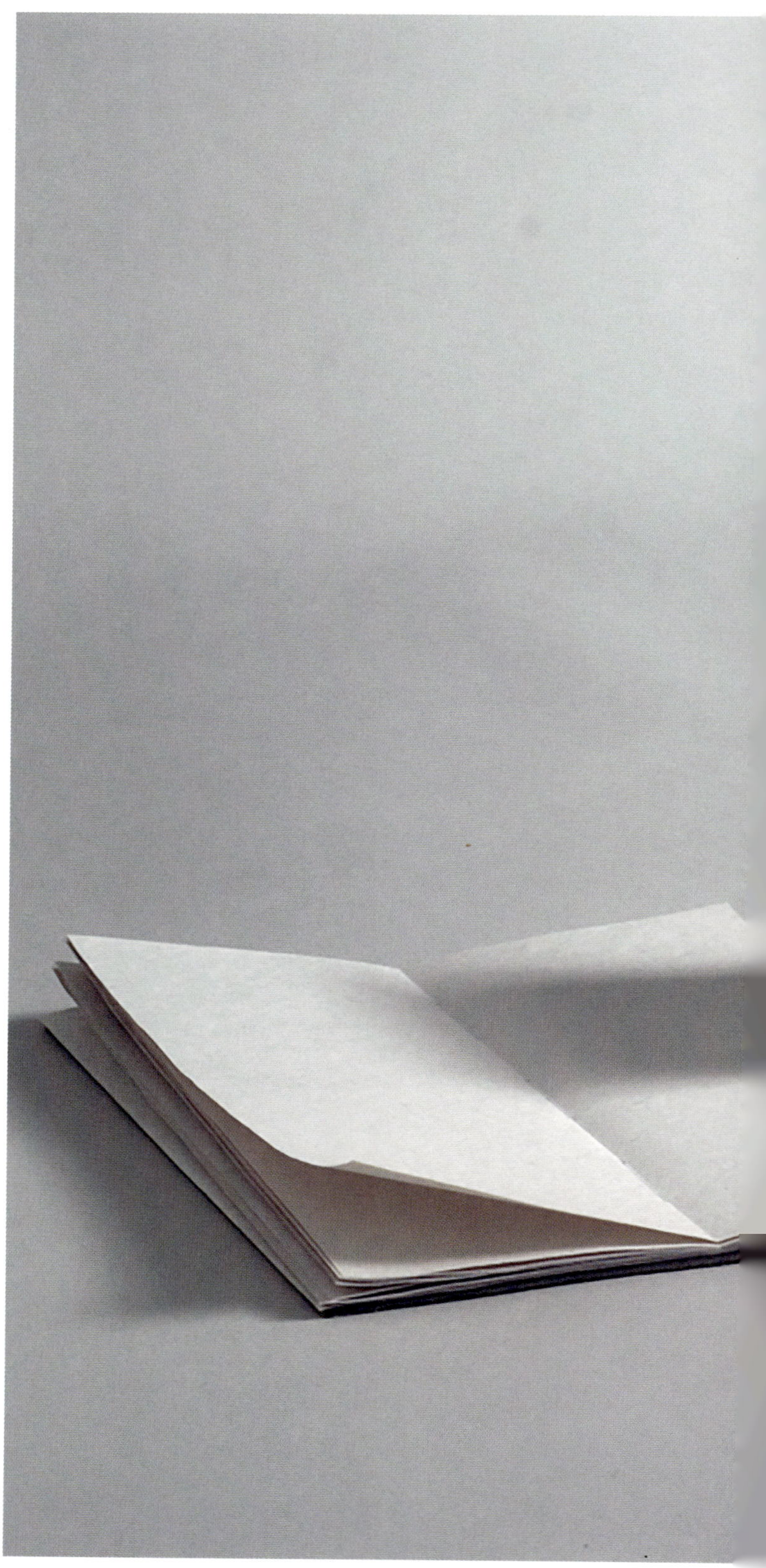

Collectively-
Initiated

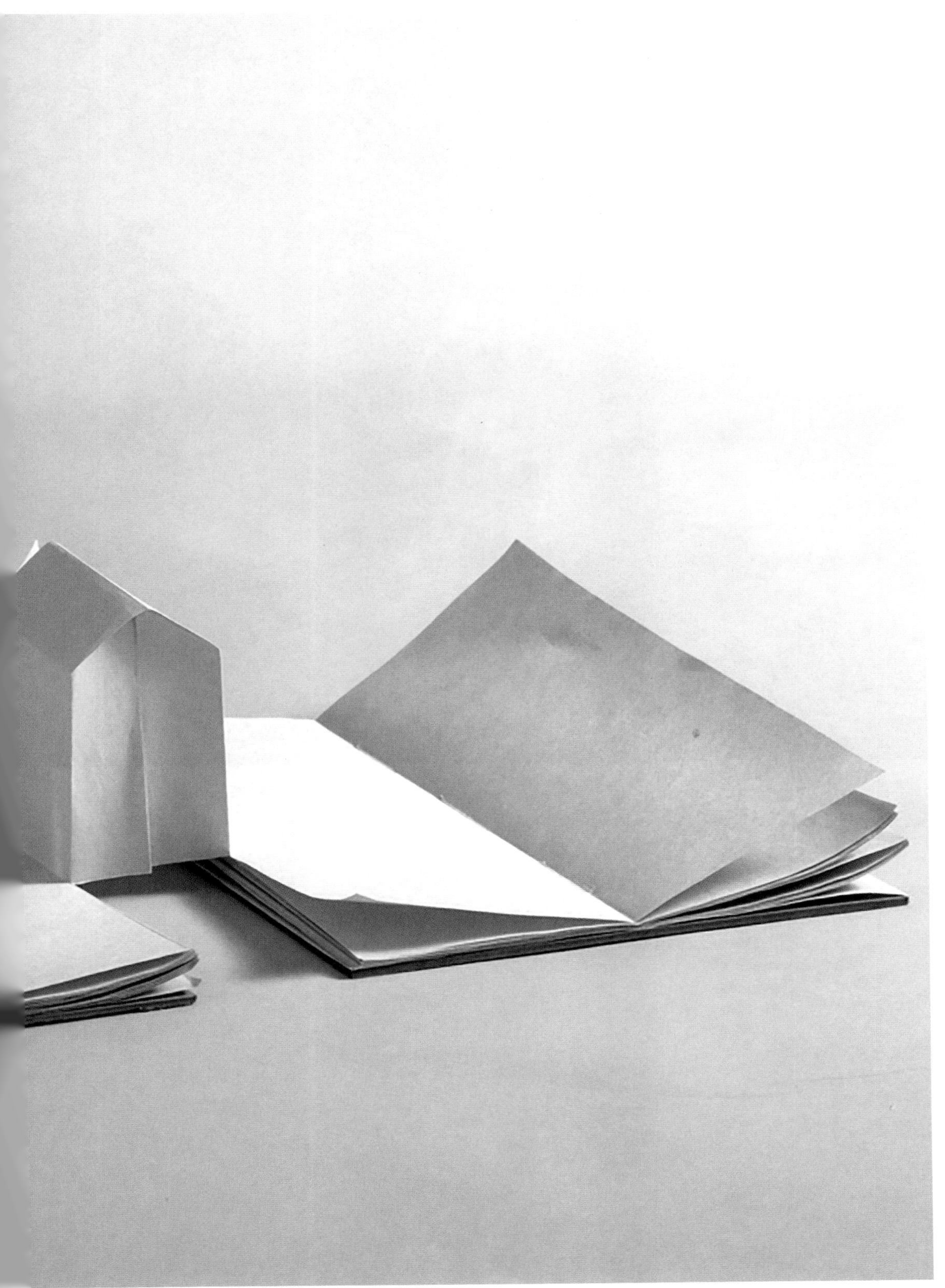

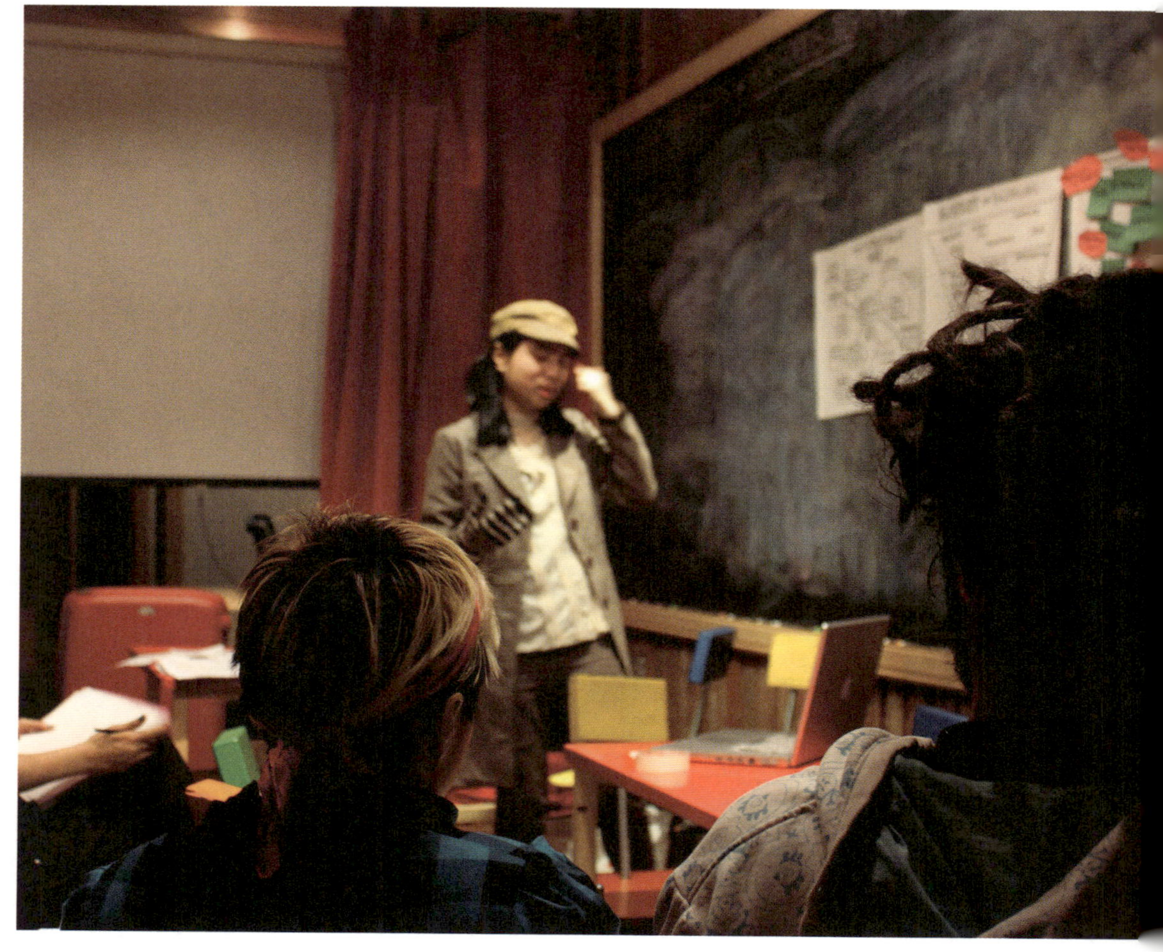

fig. 3-2
Artist Andrea Liu teaches a
class about Jean Baudrillard
at Trade School in 2009. Photo
courtesy of TradeSchool.coop.

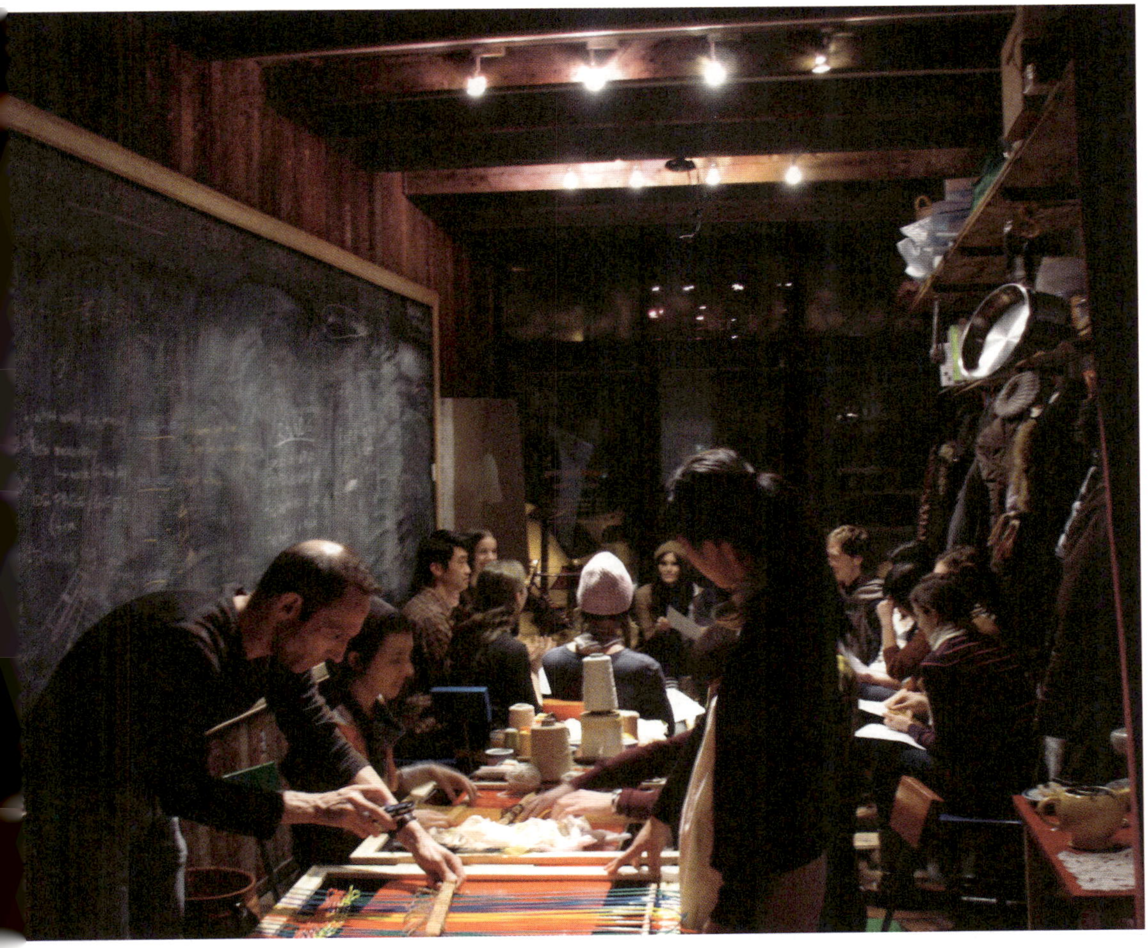

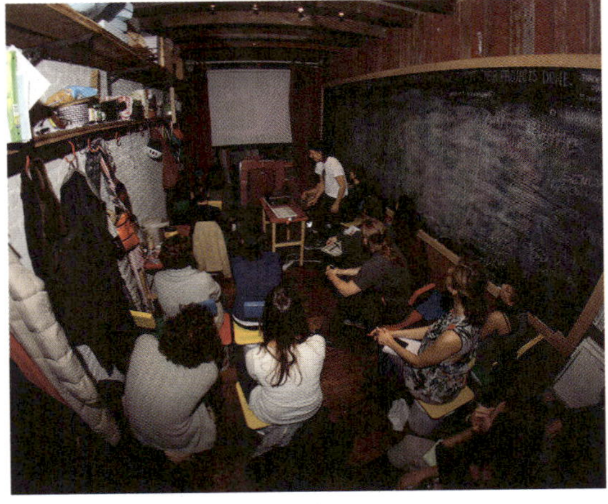

fig. 3-3
Artist Hương Ngô teaches a
weaving class at Trade School
in 2009. Photo courtesy of
TradeSchool.coop.

fig. 3-4
Artist and entrepreneur Perry
Chen teaches a class about
fundraising at Trade School
in 2009. Photo courtesy of
TradeSchool.coop.

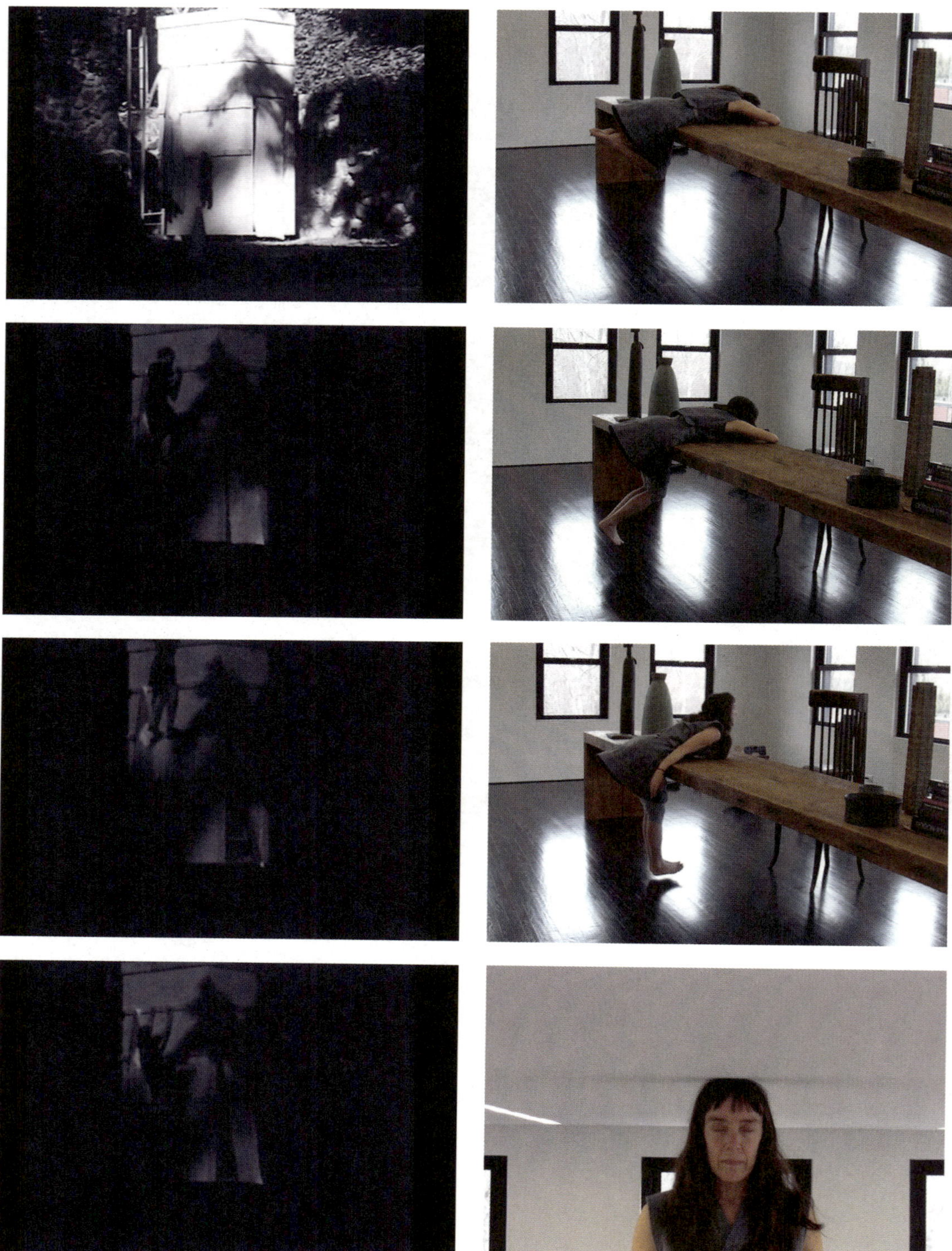

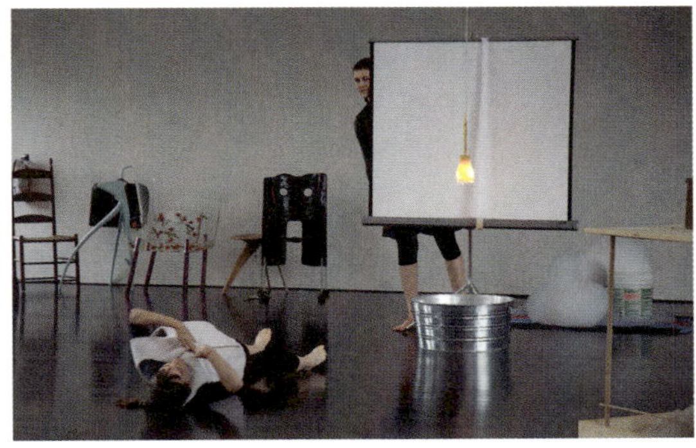
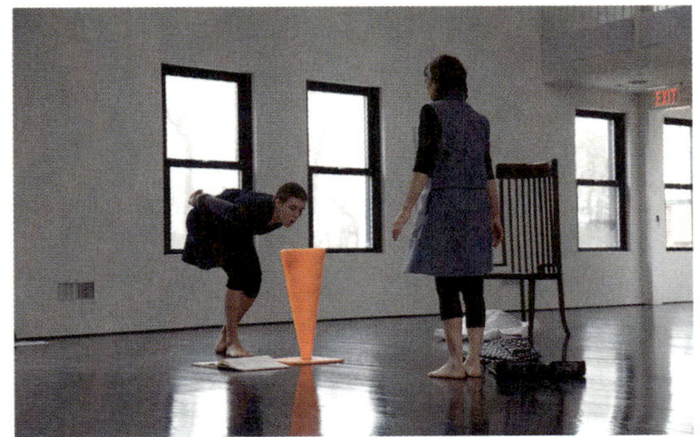
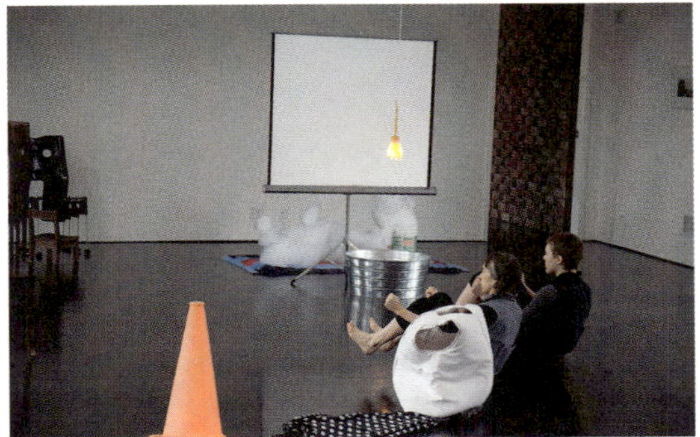
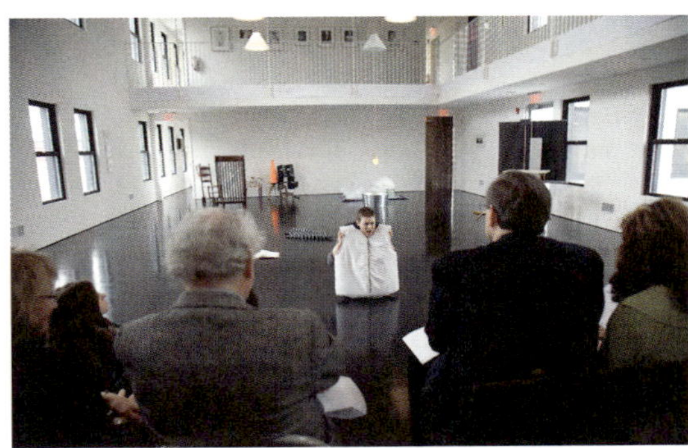
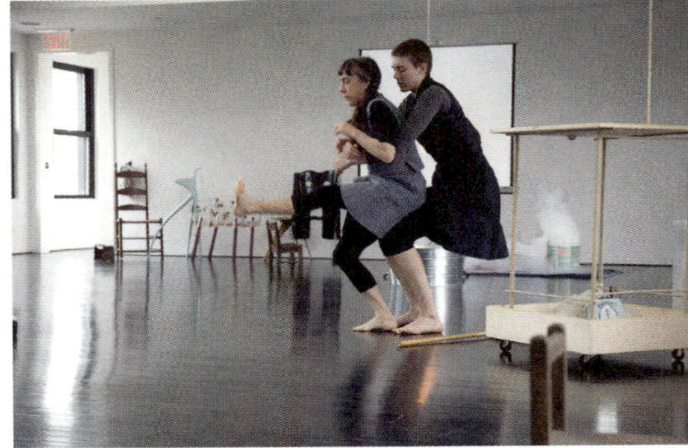
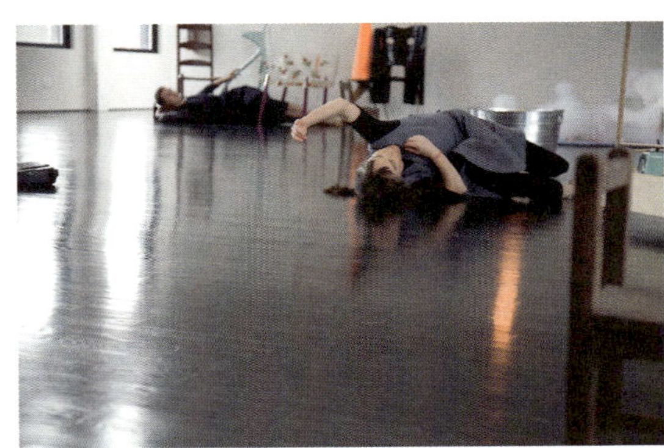
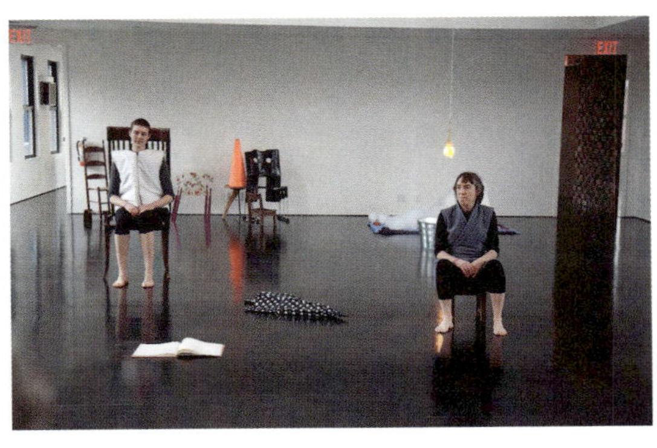
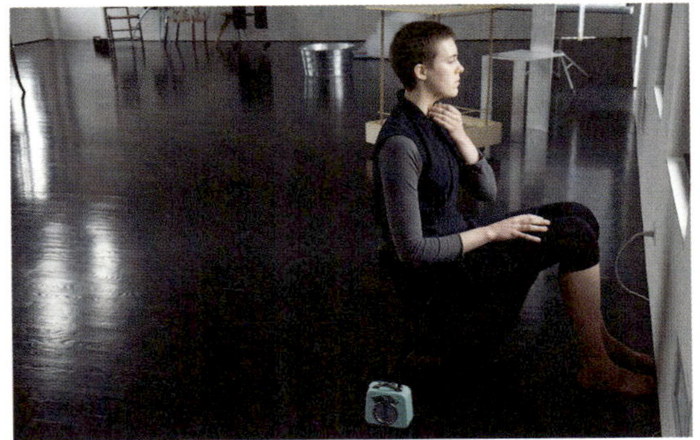

fig. 3-5 (overleaf)
Was That You or the House?,
2010, documentation video of
performance with Linda Austin
wearing *The Work Dress*.
Courtesy of the artist and
the Watermill Center.

fig. 3-6
The Work Dress, 2007-2013,
cordura, canvas, cotton-denim
blend, size Tall / Medium.
Courtesy of the artist. Photograph by Martyna Szczęsna.

Woolard's *Work Dress*, hanging
on a ladder, was available
for barter only from 2008-
2013 and led to the creation
of OurGoods.org. The photograph documenting the dress
was taken by Martyna Szczęsna
as a barter, in exchange for
a dress.

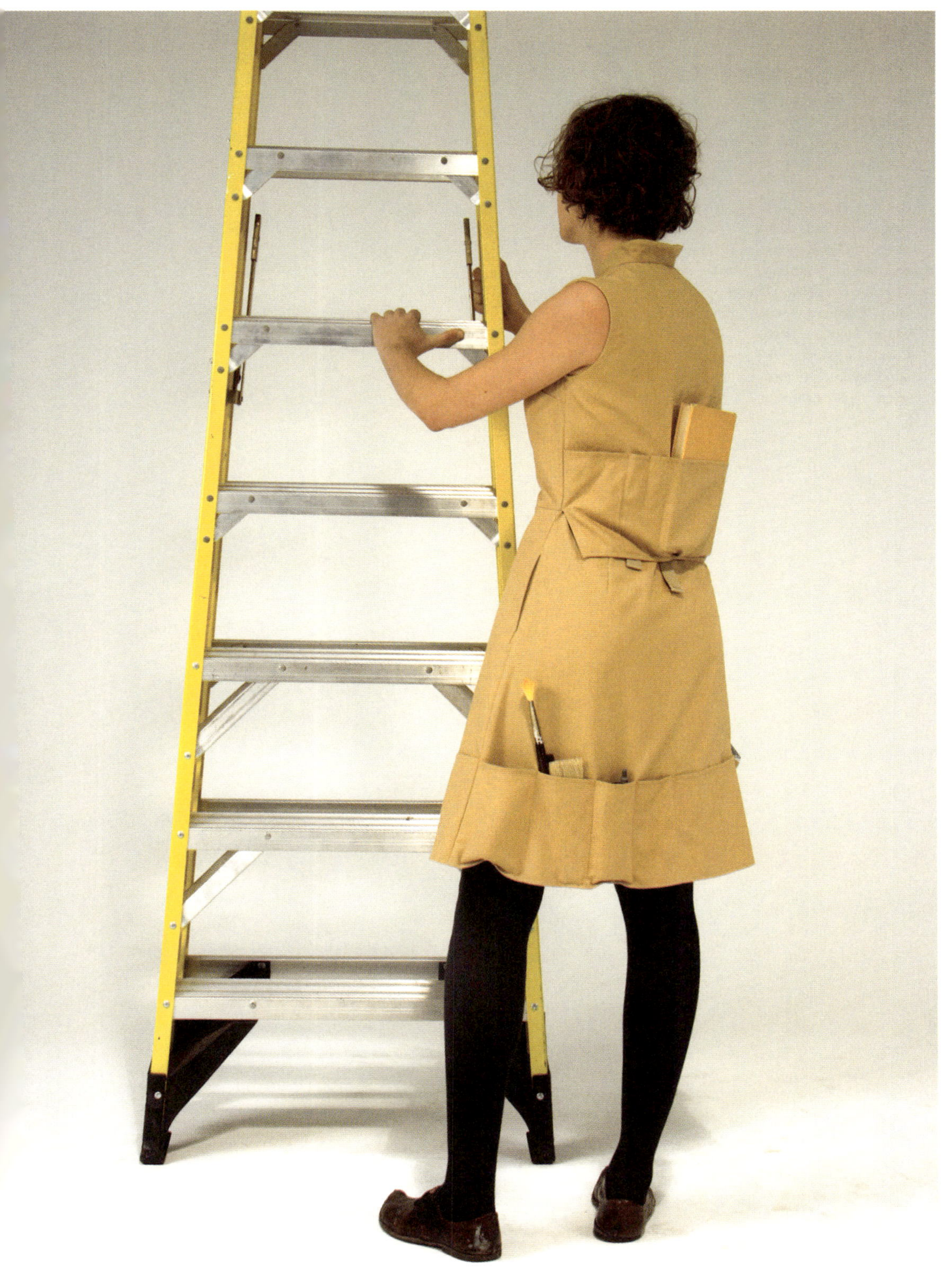

fig. 3-7
Erased Washington, 2008, legal
tender, Purple Power concentrated
industrial cleaning fluid,
rubber band, performance.
Courtesy of the artist.

Barter, time banking, and
community currency reveal that
national money is only one
medium of exchange; only one
store of value. There are so
many ways to encourage flows of
value to circulate in communities. Legal tender is simply ink
on cotton. It can be erased
with car cleaner.

Collectively-
Initiated

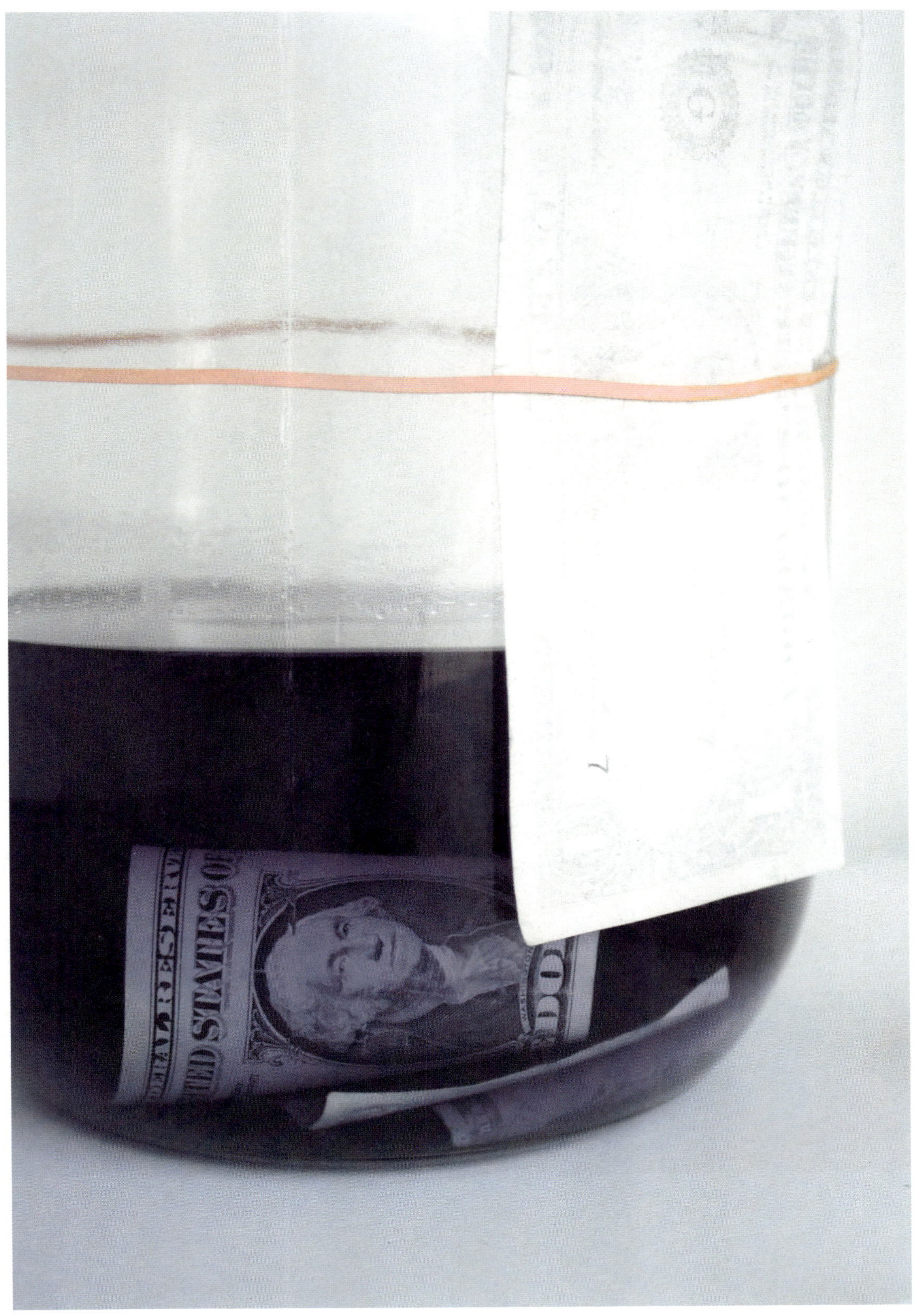

Idea in Public

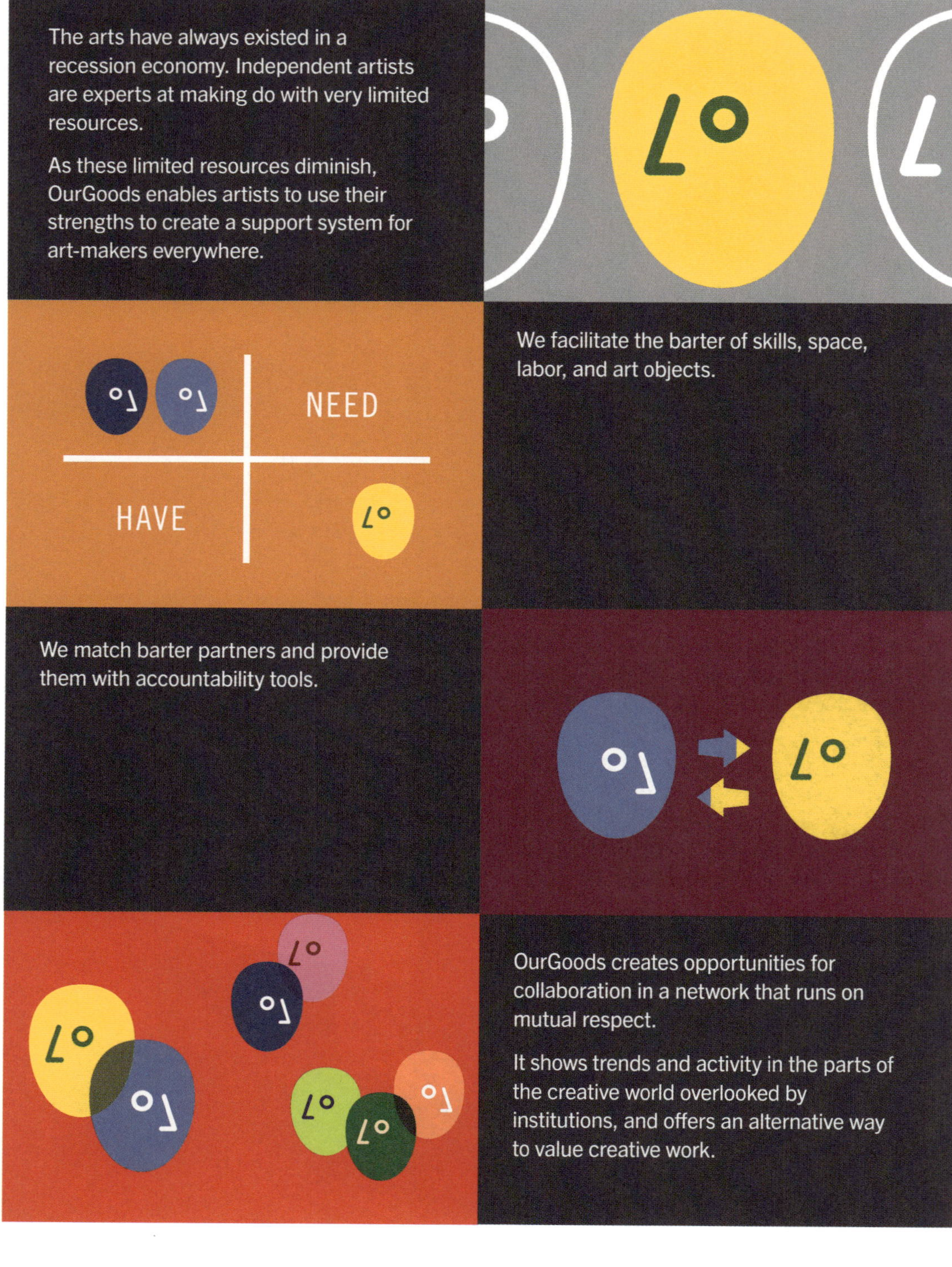

The arts have always existed in a recession economy. Independent artists are experts at making do with very limited resources.

As these limited resources diminish, OurGoods enables artists to use their strengths to create a support system for art-makers everywhere.

NEED
HAVE

We facilitate the barter of skills, space, labor, and art objects.

We match barter partners and provide them with accountability tools.

OurGoods creates opportunities for collaboration in a network that runs on mutual respect.

It shows trends and activity in the parts of the creative world overlooked by institutions, and offers an alternative way to value creative work.

Ephemera

In the pages that follow, you will find the correspondence, budgets, grants, readings, and design ideas required to create and collectively run the barter-based initiatives OurGoods.org and TradeSchool.coop from 2009–2019. You will also find excerpts from *TRADE SCHOOL: 2009–2019*, a book of teaching tools and stories written by TradeSchool.coop organizers in thirty barter-run learning spaces around the world. Woolard has selected ephemera that serves as visual reference points for OurGoods.org and TradeSchool.coop. All materials here are reproduced with the consent of collaborators.

fig. 3-8
How it Works, 2009, designed by Louise Ma, dimensions variable. Courtesy of OurGoods.org.

Managing

In American culture, especially if you are owning-
class and/or white, you're
told that success is
self-reliance. It means
making enough money so you
can buy help, you don't
have to ask anyone for
anything. And it makes two
kinds of people: we see
people who have a lot of
needs, and then people who
have succeeded, pulled
themselves up by their
bootstraps, and who might
be charitable towards these
other people. This image
of assumed need over here
and success and self
reliance over there is
something we want to do away
with altogether.

—Caroline Woolard, at
an event with Jen Abrams
in 2013

I graduated with a BFA from Cooper Union in the winter of 2007. At that time, I worked a lot of odd jobs, ranging from graphic design to service work gigs, to working part-time as a research and studio assistant for Natalie Jeremijenko. I also had a job working the night shift from 10 p.m. to 6 a.m. where I was required to stay awake all night and monitor a studio space by walking around every hour, on the hour, and making sure people were working safely. I had a computer in my office, so when I wasn't monitoring the studio, I spent a lot of time reading, listening to things, sewing, and thinking about what to do after school. One night in 2008, I read about a grant called Economic Revitalization for Performing Artists (or ERPA, for short), funded by a non-profit called The Field. They described the grant in the following ways:

> ERPA grows from the premise that the traditional non-profit model of fundraising does not support the majority of performing artists in New York City. This lack of financial solvency leads to early departures from New York, early departures from art-making, and ultimately, a diminishment of New York's vibrancy and vitality. ERPA aims to combat these challenges by asking artists to conceive dynamic solutions for financial stability, and giving them the tools, resources, and cash to help develop their ideas. As its name implies, ERPA aims to thus revitalize performing artists' and arts organizations' economic lives for long-term impact.

After listening to the "information sessions" that The Field made accessible online, I decided to try to apply for the grant, and to convince The Field that I was a performing artist, even though I went to school to study visual art. What follows is the first successful grant that I wrote, at age 23, right out of school. This got me $5,000, a mentorship from Jennifer Wright Cook, and meetings with a cohort of professional artists who supported me and believed in my idea. This also allowed me to convince four other people to join me in creating a multi-year project.

ARTISTIC STATEMENT —
CAROLINE WOOLARD
NOVEMBER 5, 2008

+ ABOUT ME: I endeavor to exist as
both a rigorous artist and decent
human being, moving daily with curiosity, generosity, and integrity.
I attempt to find a wide audience
for an ever-expanding notion of art,
pushing for creative dissatisfaction: plausible alternatives to the
monotonous routine.

+ CV IN PARAGRAPH FORM: Born on
an island in RI and based in
NY, Caroline Woolard received a
BFA from Cooper Union for the
Advancement of Science and Art in
2006. As a Research Scholar at
NYU's Environmental Health Clinic,
a Research Assistant at Mildred's
Lane, and an Artist in Residence
at the Brecht Forum, Woolard investigates the construction of subjectivity in architecture, art,
and design. Woolard's interventions are presented publicly in the
urban environment and have been
affiliated with psychogeographic
events like Conflux in NY, Cryptic
Providence in RI, and Unoccupied
Spaces in Montreal. These interventions enter the public imagination and have been investigated
by *TimeOut NY* and *Wallpaper**
Magazine. Caroline Woolard is the
recipient of a MacDowell Colony
Residency, a Watermill Residency,

a Pilchuck Scholarship, the Leon
Levy Foundation Grant, and The
Elliot Lash Award for Excellence in
Sculpture. Her work has been shown
at the Newport Art Museum in RI,
Jackson Gallery in GA, Oxbow Gallery
in MI, and The Bruce High Quality
Foundation in NY.

+ ABOUT MY WORK: In 2004, I moved
to the edge of a discipline (sculpture) and peered into the abyss of
another (dance). My interdisciplinary work combines sculptural tools
and bodies, pushing boundaries with
creative dissatisfaction, what Helen
Cixous describes as "the possibility of taking a mountain into one's
arms." I create platforms for experience in public space. I subvert
domestic objects like chairs and
lights to cultivate collective curiosity. I explore the space between
people and architecture: making a
place for the body amidst gigantic
buildings on the street of NY and
finding new ways to occupy pedes-
trian space. My sculptures are often
tools for action, implying protagonists in an unknown narrative.
Currently, I am developing a performance with Linda Austin inspired by
the absurd wonder of human factors
engineering: I witness and record
her as she uses my swings, mega-
phones, curtains, light bulbs, and
utility dresses as I choreograph a
new work for Watermill in March.

Managing

+ SUPPORT: I am employed by Cooper Union as a studio monitor, where I work the night shift. I am also "supported" by residencies like the MacDowell Colony and Watermill and by mentors that I met in school or introduced myself to. I also receive small payments for the pedagogical assistance I give to Morgan Puett at Mildred's Lane in PA, Richard Reiss at Artist As Citizen in NY, and Natalie Jeremijenko at the Environmental Health Clinic in NY.

+ IN 5 YEARS: I hope to have settled into one or two long term projects (2-5 years) with a community. I hope to find the best structure for public participation and financial self sufficiency: will it be public art projects with community invested stocks? Will it be a new kind of "house party" that enables community solidarity without the obligatory hierarchy of institutionalized artist heroes? Will it be a design firm or an alternative restaurant as a parallel revenue stream alongside my artistic practice?

+ INNOVATIVE SOLUTION: In June of this year, I started an LLC and studio space with a group of peers. We built out an 8,000 square foot warehouse and now rent it to 28 incredible people in order to stay in one place for eight years and partially subsidize our own studios.

Although studio renovations are commonplace, the large scale collaborative effort that enabled this endeavor seems unusual to me. Each day we learn something new and/or teach a skill to at least one other person. Each person exchanges individual resources for rent: one artist pays part of her rent in vegetables from the farmer's market where she works, another in web design assistance, and many others in construction labor. We pool many other resources and have group critiques. This peer group is responsible for my intellectual/ spiritual well being. I am excited to advise others about our process and will speak at RISD's professional practice class in 2009.

+ ERPA IDEA/PROJECT: Online Network for Peer-to-Peer Artistic Support (P2P-AS) An online network for peer-to-peer artistic support. Artists upload proposals that require more money, space, volunteers, or materials and any interested party can donate the necessary goods. Rather than the ubiquitous online portfolio site of self interested megalomania, which perpetuates a hierarchy with support from above, this website helps artists look to each other for recognition and fulfillment. Here, artists upload project proposals with requests for support (money, space, materials, volunteers, etc). AND make personal donations to other people's projects. This network will visualize contemporary trends, create artistic bonds, and foster communication between the public at large and individual artists.

Questions that will be made visible are: Which artist gets the most support from other artists? Do users have more time, money, space, or materials to donate? Do users end up helping the same person that helped them, essentially bartering resources? What longstanding bonds can be made through volunteering? How can peer-to-peer generosity adapt to other fields?

+ NEW FINANCIAL STREAMS: Modeling itself off of websites like kiva. org, craigslist.org, and couchsurfing.com, this website will state that it is also in need of monetary support. Hopefully, artists will donate to the "mothership" as their "satelite" projects are successfully supported.

+ CONNECTION TO ARTISTIC STATEMENT: My projects are often presented in public space because I want to introduce positive alternatives to the status quo in the public imagination. This project presents artists as generous people who are invested in more than egomania.

Instead of perpetuating the model of a successful career as a ruthlessly claimed top seat in a competitive pyramid of success, the website will help artists look to each other for recognition and fulfillment. Real world connections will also establish a more densely interconnected fabric of human relations in the creative community. Lastly, artists will learn how to manage volunteers and organize generosity more effectively.

+ FEASIBILITY AND MY GUARANTEE FOR COMPLETION: The minimum grant of $5,000 will easily support the server costs and web designer salary. I am in contact with many young web designers who I could hire to complete the project: from Jeffrey Warren at MIT's media lab to Roy Rub of toposgraphics.com and Louise Ma at the *New York Times'* design team. Stefan Sagmeister supported my subway swing project and could help me find an excellent designer as well. I outsource my projects when specialization is the most effective solution (as I did with the fabrication of my subway swings) and am quite familiar with these contracts from my work for Natalie Jeremijenko at the Environmental Health Clinic. Frankly, this project simply must happen and I am undeterred in finding a way to produce it.

+ IMPACT OF ERPA RESOURCES: I know that simply creating a framework for peer-to-peer generosity is not enough. For example: How effectively will individual artists manage volunteers? ERPA's human resources are invaluable, as individual experience in sustainable venture philanthropy will help guide the underlying methodology and structure the site with pragmatism and dignity. I suspect that ERPA has web design suggestions and contacts that could provide technical support as well.

+ REPLICABILITY/SUSTAINABILITY: This website has no foreseen end and could be replicated in any field.

+ EXCITEMENT FOR ERPA'S IDEAS AND RESOURCES: I am inspired by the incredible human resources at ERPA: the network of entrepreneurs (especially women) who are committed to conscious capitalism and social entrepreneurship. Many ideas I've had are being carried out by pioneers who spoke at ERPA workshops. Access to this level of self determination and collaborative genius is so exciting that I may have to track these people down individually no matter what.

Ideological note about venues: I am committed to performing in public space. I firmly believe in the importance of spontaneous interruptions in daily life because predictability stifles imagination. Unexpected encounters with high quality performance works in public space enrich the cultural experience of any place. I make certain that participation or viewership is organized respectfully, so that users self nominate and audiences self organize and no one feels obligated to experience the event. Further, my work involves constructing experiences with tools and props that choreograph actions, following a history of interventionist practice and performance art.

2008
Was That You or the House?,
Watermill March 28 (upcoming)

2007
Swinging on the Subway,
the L train

2006
For Mom

2005
Suspicious Packages,
Cooper Union, ongoing
director/choreographer

Making

I think OurGoods.org functioned as a multi-year project because I was able to gather a team of amazing people with skills and personalities that complimented each other. I knew that I needed at least three people to make the project: a grant-writer, a designer, and a computer engineer. When I got the $5,000 grant from The Field, I asked Louise Ma and Rich Watts if they wanted to work with me. While we were not friends, Louise, Rich, and I went to Cooper Union together, and I had seen how they worked in design classes. I knew that they were both generous, rigorous, and very talented.

```
November 21, 2008
Louise,

It is VERY late, but perhaps you still have
time to do this dress website? I will have a
window installation in Providence on Dec 6-
March 13 and will be bartering Utility Dresses
in it. I will have images of the dress soon,
but until then, can you make a single page
that says the following:

FINAL DAYS!!! IT IS THE END OF THE WORLD AS
WE KNOW IT!!! THANKS FOR YOUR LOYALTY.
GETTING OUT OF BUSINESS!!! BARTERS ACCEPTED!!!
BIG DISCOUNTS FOR LOCAL ARTISTS DESIGNERS
CRAFTSPEOPLE!!! MAKE ME AN OFFER—I trade NEW
UTILITY DRESS for ceramics, jewlery, painting,
web design, and other artwork. SLIDING SCALE!!!

I accept locally grown vegetables, old photo-
graphs of RI/NY, window space in Manhattan,
50s-80s design patterns, haircuts, massage,
dental work, shoe repair, yoga instruction,
health consultation, hydroponic/indoor vege-
table training, canning tutorials, secret
recipes, conversational spanish tutoring,
accounting help, liability law services, and
many other skills … If you cannot barter, you
can pay a penalty of $200 and take a dress.
LAST DAY MARCH 13, 2009.
```

Then I just need you to create a form they fill out to make me an offer, or a button they click to contact me … also a Buy Now option would be good for those people who want to fork over the money. And, if you have time to respond conceptually, maybe instead of my GETTING OUT OF BUSINESS vernacular (which is really a call for the end of capitalism) I should just offer another approach (bartering) triumphantly from the outset … then the text should read:

INTRODUCING COMMUNITY CURRENCY, a fashion line which can ONLY BE EXCHANGED FOR LOCAL GOODS AND SERVICES. Utility Dresses by Caroline Woolard can be exchanged for: ceramics, jewelry, painting, web design, fabric, furniture, photo/video documentation, locally grown vegetables, old photographs of RI / NY, 50s-80s design patterns, haircuts, massage, dental work, … etc.

What do you think?
Caroline

When Jennifer Wright Cook, the Director of The Field put me in touch with Jen Abrams, who she said "had a similar idea to mine," I was excited to collaborate with Jen, rather than thinking she was my competitor. I did not know Jen at all, but we seemed compatible. Plus, I was only 23 and Jen was 38, bringing over a decade of wisdom and experience from WOW Café Theater, the oldest all women and trans theater space in the United States, running on a gift system.

Before we started working together, Jen suggested that we write about a list of questions that she generated, based upon her experiences at WOW. Writing over email, we shared our strengths and weaknesses, to see if we would work well together.

So I'm at WOW, and I'm sitting in the circle, and I for the first time raise my hand, and I say, 'I need someone to design the lights for my show.' This was terrifying for me for a couple of reasons, first of all because I'm not totally sure they're going to do it right, and second of all because I'm not totally sure I'm a person who deserves that kind of help.

— Jen Abrams, 2013

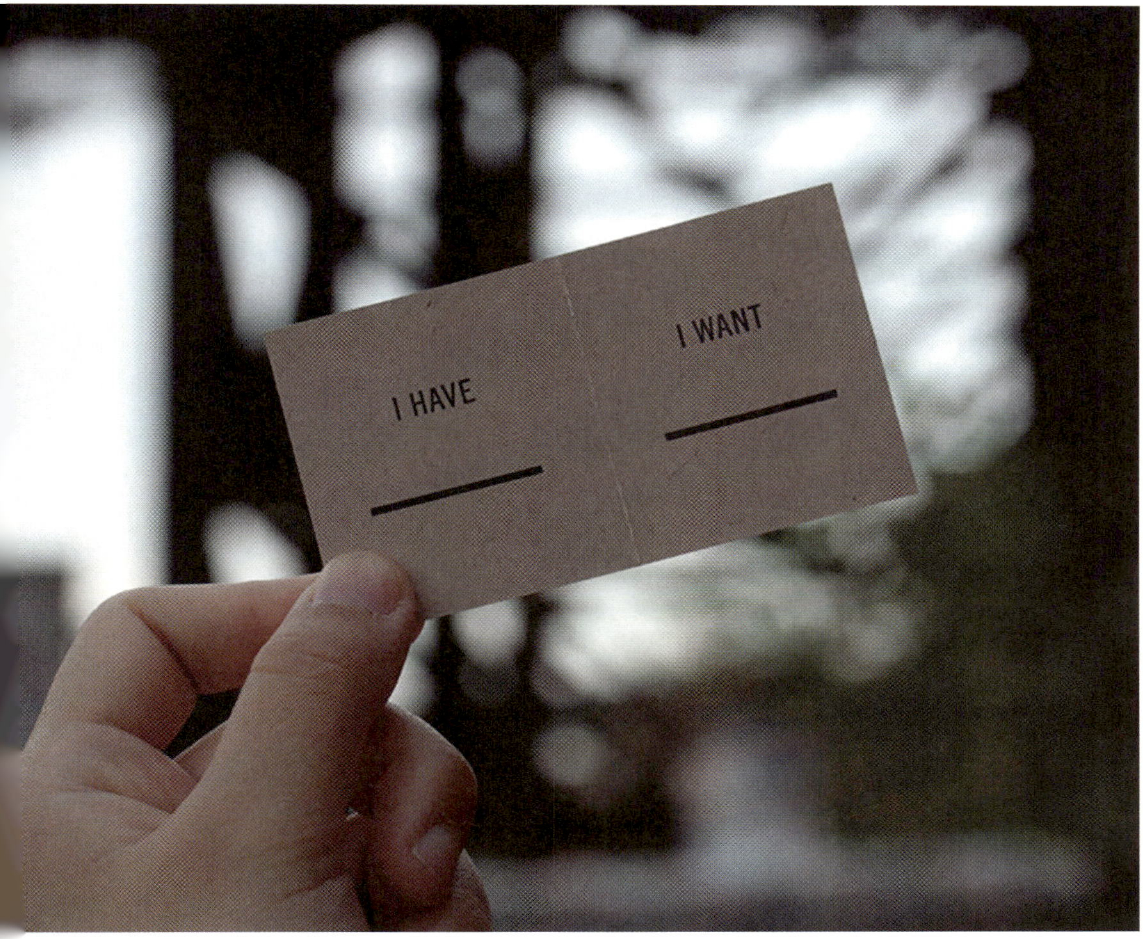

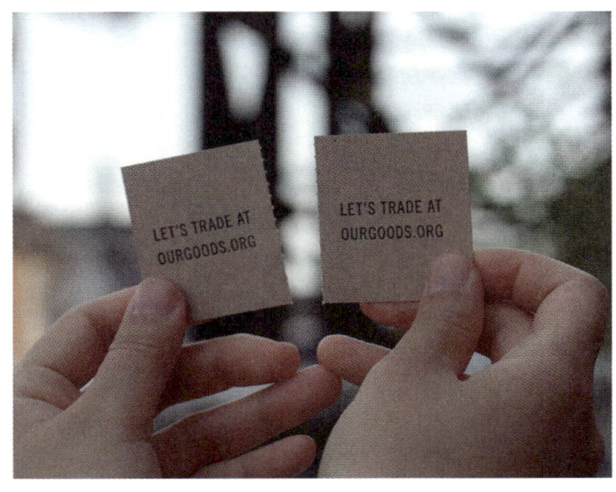

fig. 3-9
Business card for OurGoods.org,
2008, designed by Louise Ma and
Rich Watts.

OurGoods.org &
TradeSchool.coop

Experiment

CAROLINE'S STRENGTHS/WEAKNESSES

<u>Have no unenumerated expectations
of individuals</u>.
This is hard for me. I'm not sure
that I KNOW everything I expect. I
will keep thinking about it…this
is what I can think of:
- Be RELIABLE: Show up, honor your
  word, etc.
- Be loyal. Give me credit and
  respect my work.
- Work hard!
- Hold me accountable. Work through
  problems with me. Address problems
  as they arise (this will be hard
  if we have short meetings and then
  represent the project publicly…
  working through the mission will
  help this. Perhaps we will agree
  through writing grants and testing our ideas in presentations/
  interviews with friends).

<u>Voice your own project-related
strengths/interests/likes</u>
- Understanding personality types/
  needs—this facilitates project
  strategy/effect.
- One-on-One socializing/planning:
  I love meeting new people and have
  broad interests (weakness: I am
  TERRIBLE with names).
- Interests…Skills of my close
  friends: 5 Environmental
  Activists, 6 Public-Art/Project-
  Based Artists, 1 dancer/chef, 3
  Architects, 1 Social Worker, 2

new media/web people, 3 graphic
designers, 1 painter.
- I love exploring the city, sourc-
  ing materials, digging up information, finding a way IN…I go to
  too many lectures/workshops/tours
  and cannot stop myself.
- I'm pretty even-tempered and try
  to be nice to as many people
  as possible.
- I feel best when I sense that the
  community respects me, values my
  integrity (my priority is to be
  acknowledged for hard work and
  intelligence by the group).

<u>Voice your own sensitivities/
areas with a slow learning
curve/motivations</u>.
- I have a bad long-term memory and
  hate myself for forgetting what
  I've learned.
- I have a pride issue with being
  told how to do things unless I
  ask for it—I am working on this.
  Basically, I would rather volunteer than be told.
- I may take on more than I can
  actually manage—I hope to deal
  with this. I gave you my schedule,
  but we can go through this again
  to predict time crunches! For
  example, I'm about to go MIA from
  March 18-30.
- I need to learn how to delegate
  group tasks (perhaps less relevant here).
- I procrastinate and build things

last minute—I HAVE to change this: this is less of a problem with OurGoods.org because I am managing it rather than building it!
- I HATE public speaking/dealing with groups. I'm trying to get better at it.
- I have a complicated relationship to authority and access—I want power, but I distrust it. I have a hard time working with people who love hierarchy.

Know who you're dealing with:
my WORK
You can see my new work if I send it to you, but most of it is offline.

Know who you're dealing with:
my CONTACTS
These people can tell you a lot about me:
1. Christine Wang, my business partner in the studio space
2. Chris Kennedy, my friend/past co-worker
3. Natalie Jeremijenko, artist/past employer at NYU
4. Alexis Thompson, my current employer
5. Nancy Austin, my mom

Know what you need and when you need it.
- We need the code person now!
- But we need to fundraise to pay this code person first.
- I think our "tactics of deployment" need to be discussed.

JEN'S STRENGTHS/WEAKNESSES

I will strive to be:
- Reliable. When I say I'll do something, I'll do it.
- Competent. When I do something, I'll do it right.
- Clear. If I've said I'll do something and it turns out I can't, I'll tell you. If I have an expectation, I'll articulate it. If I have a problem, I'll talk about it.
- Honest. If I'm concerned about something, not sure of myself, or know I'm getting close to a discomfort area, I'll let you know. If I'm bad at something, I'll tell you. If I screw up, I'll admit it.
- Supportive. When I appreciate what you've done, I'll tell you so. If you are struggling with something, I'll do my best to help.
- Receptive. If you have feedback, I'll listen. My main expectation of a collaborative relationship is that both parties strive toward the above, value them, and work together to fulfill them.

Some strengths I think will help:
- When I make a commitment, I keep it. Period.
- I'm extremely organized, good with schedules and accountability.
- I'm good at public speaking, good at articulating ideas verbally and on paper.
- I do really well with groups.

- I'm really good at offering positive feedback.
- I handle conflict pretty well.
- I'm a really good manager, good at
working toward a deadline. I have
a good sense of my own time and
what I can and can't realistically
get done.

My weaknesses (that I know of):
- When I make a commitment, I keep
it. Period. This can make me
inflexible, and it sometimes means
I don't know when to quit.
- I'm a control freak. I've been
working hard on this for…ever,
actually. At this point I'm pretty
good at noticing when I'm control-
freaking, but I am definitely
capable of lapsing. This comes up
the most when there isn't trust.
I feel pretty good about our trust
level at this point.
- I can get impatient. I'll want to
do things in the most efficient
way, which sometimes causes me to
miss stuff I'd have seen if we'd
been more exploratory.
- I have an excellent long-term
memory, which sometimes translates
into holding onto stuff too long.
- I like to keep moving forward—
can be resistant to going back
over ground I feel we've covered
already.

Issues I/we should keep an eye on:
- I have many more obligations than
you do. My partner and I are about
to buy a place together that will
require a lot of fixing up. I'm
working 20 hours a week at a job
I can't do other stuff at. And
I'm trying to finish making an
evening-length work. I work hard,
smartly, and efficiently, but I
don't think I have as much time
to work as you do.
- I tend toward the very practical.
I'm more interested in the practical aspects of this than in the
philosophical aspects, whereas I
think you're more interested in
the philosophical aspects. That
can be a good pairing as long as
we both keep respecting both.
- I need this to generate income for
me and you don't. If that looks
like it's not going to happen,
I'll have to ratchet my investment
way down at some point (but I
won't abandon the project, and
I'll let you know in advance if/
when that time approaches).

Jennifer Wright Cook, Executive Director of The Field, 2020:

When I met you, I never imagined that you'd become one of those people that stick in my head and my heart. We meet so many people in our lives. Some folks say an "average" person meets 10,000 people. Someone else said it's more like 490. Whatever the number, how many people actually stick in you? I met you in 2008 when our work intersected. One day you said I was a "connector." It meant so much to me. I hadn't thought of myself that way. It felt like you saw me, the me beyond the me that worked with you. The me beyond the me that I thought made me me. That's something that you do. You see people. You see them beyond their borders and boundaries. You look at them. You slow down and listen. You ask. You laugh BIG. You taught me so much. You came in talking about barter and collaboration, public objects and facilitating actions, accountability and expectations. I felt lost. I was so drawn to your belief and optimism but it was unfamiliar to me. I needed to move faster, I needed to draw lines in the sand, I needed to be the boss, to make decisions quickly, to get it done. I was in the thick of the non-profit NYC arts sector, as a white, cisgendered, able-bodied woman with economic privilege. You showed me an inside-out, upside-down world. You didn't shove, or holler, you just lived and wondered. "We Are No Longer Strangers" is the title of the small book we wrote at the end of our official work time with you in 2010. That poetic title came from you, in an email you wrote to me about your work, our work together. It's beautiful because it declares our present state from inside our past. Dear you, you stick in my head and heart.

Experiment

Commitment

The Challenge: Since the 2008 market crash, cultural producers have struggled to come to terms with the new economic landscape.

—Caroline Woolard and Jen Abrams, from Rockefeller Foundation's New York City Cultural Innovation Fund Grant Application, 2011

In Jen Abrams' words:

> I came to this process, as Caroline mentioned, through Jennifer Wright Cook's matchmaking. That by itself had to do with Jennifer seeing an alignment of how Caroline and I moved in the world. I think you can't underestimate the power of relationships to catalyze something like OurGoods.org.
>
> In some ways I was a mismatch—fifteen years older than Rich, Caroline, and Louise and ten years older than Carl, in a very different phase of my life, and a performing artist rather than a visual artist. There were GenX/Millennial communication and cultural differences, and the social expectations in the visual art world are very different from those in the performing arts world. I had so much more experience, but the rest of the team had so much more time and energy, and they shared language and expectations that I didn't understand.
>
> Part of what made it work was true care for each other as people. If our only focus had been the project, we wouldn't have made it 6 months. I wanted to be around Caroline's profound optimism and vision of a different world, Rich's sense of humor and intense commitment, Louise's sense of hilarity and magic, Carl's ability to see every situation positively. It was a real leap of faith—I barely knew Caroline, and Rich, Louise, and Carl were total strangers. I think it's really important to listen closely to your body when choosing collaborators. The phrase is "trust your gut" for a reason, but it's not just your gut. Your whole body knows who you can work with and who you can't, and it will tell you if you listen.
>
> Because I was older and more experienced, I had to find a delicate balance between surrender

and insistence. Ninety percent of the time, I needed to yield to the group—even if we were going down a path I'd gone down before unsuccessfully. There are things a person can't know without doing them themselves, and linear progress wasn't our goal. OurGoods.org had to be about developing everyone on the team's capacity, and sometimes that meant winding up in a cul-de-sac I'd visited ten years ago. Learning to name that as a success was important for me.

Ten percent of the time, it was important for me to insist on something. I wish I had clear criteria for when to yield and when to insist, but I don't. I know I got it wrong sometimes. For instance, I insisted that we use the word "barter," and build one-to-one reciprocity into the system. At the time, I didn't think people would trust a gift economy. I felt they needed to know what was in it for them. I think I was wrong. Other times I think I got it right—for instance, when it came to structuring certain things so that they could be understood by funders, even if it wasn't the very best way for us to do it, and when it came to thinking about sustainability and burn-out.

When Rich, Louise, and Jen agreed to take on the project, at $1k each for a year, I was thrilled. Jen and I made a pretty amazing team, working 2–4 days a week for many years. I think we were self-aware enough to sense that this would be possible when we first met and talked over our strengths and weaknesses. Jen Abrams taught me how to do public speaking, budgeting, accounting, hiring, and hone my professionalism in the nonprofit and performing arts worlds. I think I brought research and storytelling skills, commitment to high-quality design, passion and charisma, and the endless energy of my twenties to the project. Jen became my main collaborator from 2008–2014.

If politics is something that helps people think about the way power is organized, and the way they live it in their lives, then OurGoods is a political project.

—Caroline Woolard, 2010

```
fig. 3-10
```
User experience wireframes and web sketches for Our-Goods.org made by Louise Ma and Rich Watts in 2009.

The difference between a simple website, for example, an art portfolio, and a peer-to-peer Web 2.0 website like OurGoods.org is that OurGoods.org enables peer-to-peer communication. This means that each person must have a unique account, be able to log in, and have conversations with other users. To make the user experience fluid, designers, developers, and user experience experts need to create user experience maps, wire frames, and front and back end designs such as these.

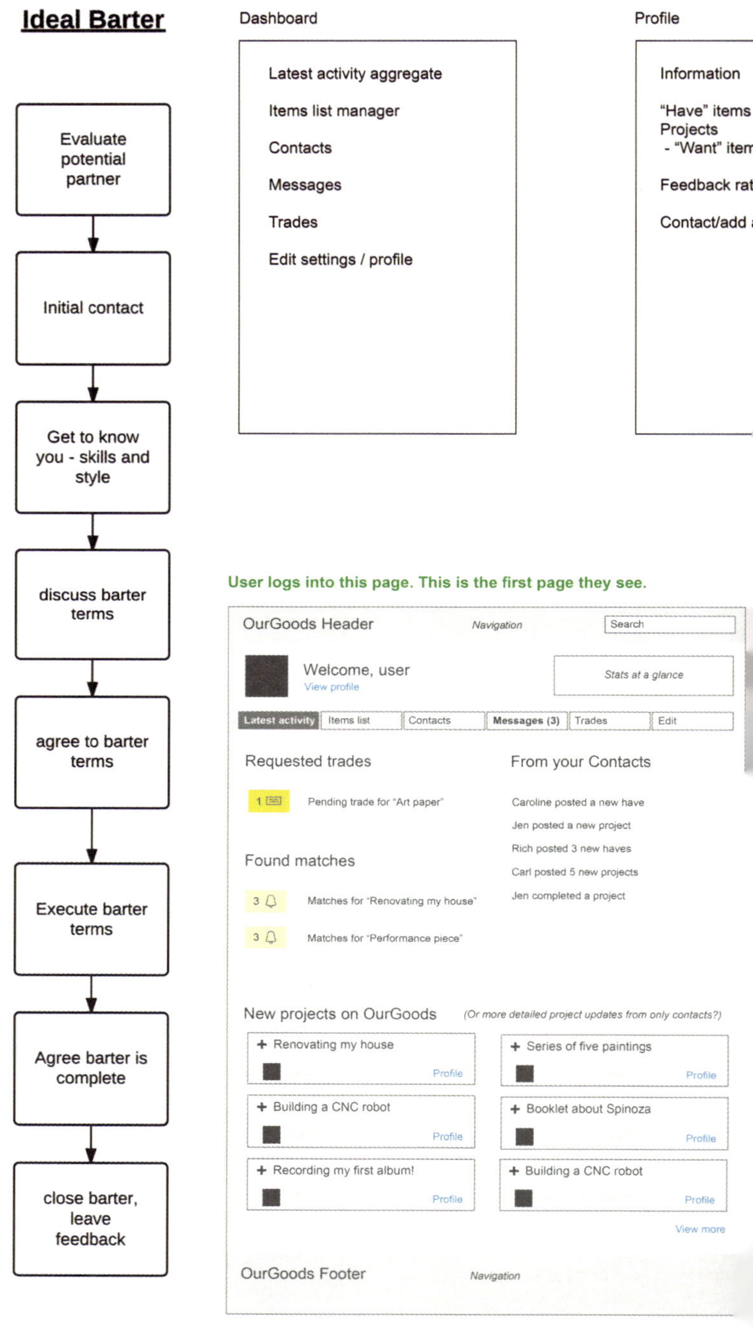

Find/Browse

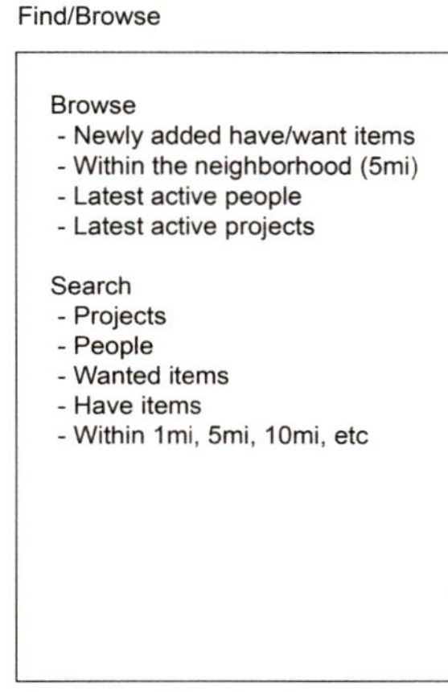

Ancillary pages

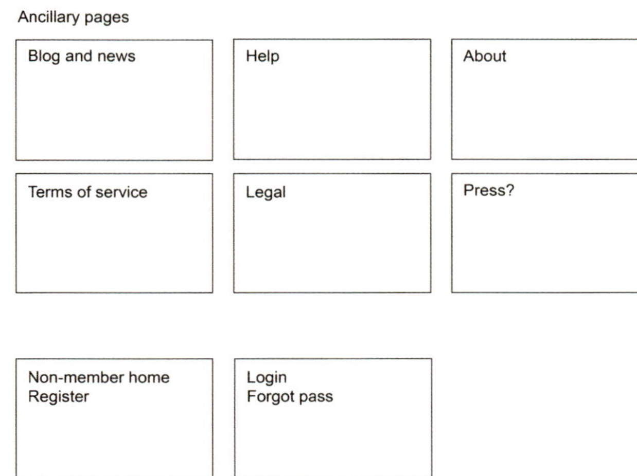

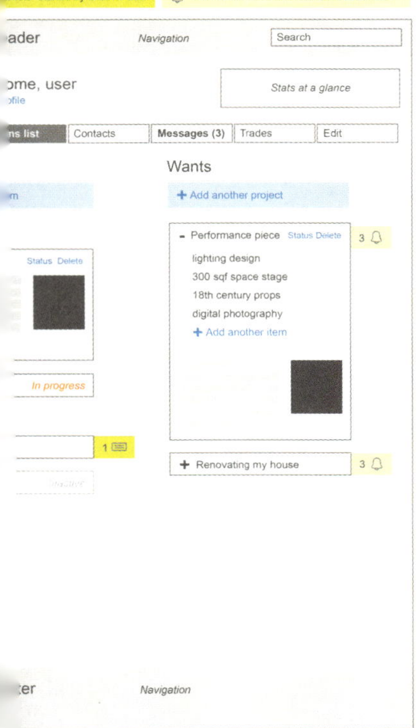

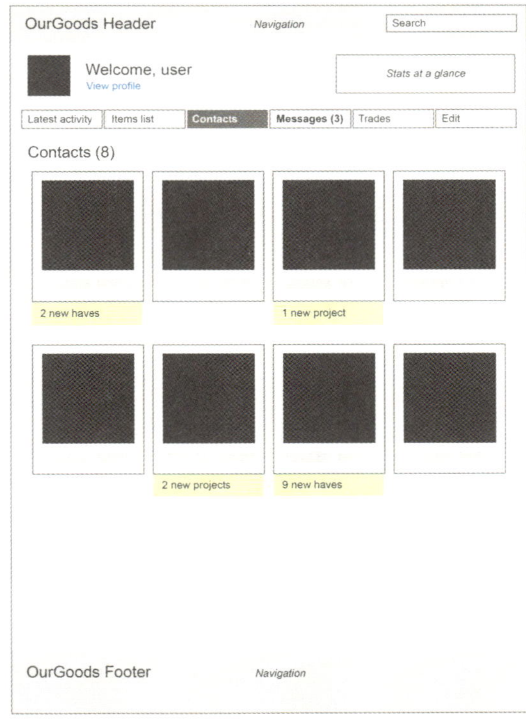

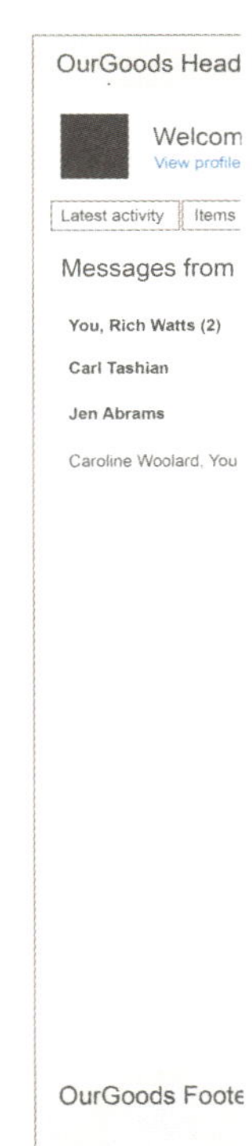

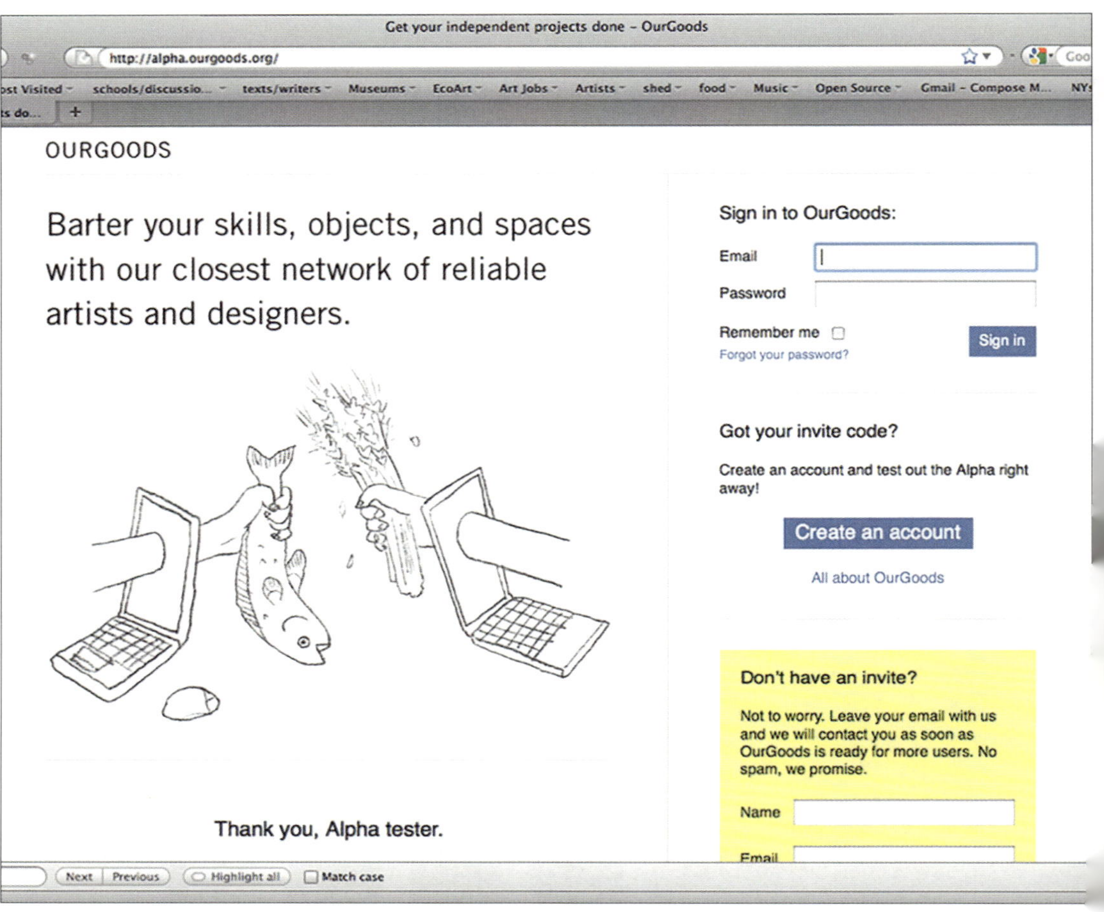

fig. 3-11
OurGoods.org alpha (original)
website, 2008, dimensions variable. Courtesy of the artists.

The dominant economy values
the outputs of our production
(completed artworks) far less
than it values the inputs to
our production (rehearsal
space, materials, skill, time,
energy). OurGoods sidesteps
this persistent imbalance by
helping cultural producers
exchange directly with each
other, creating an alternate
economy based on shared values.

—Caroline Woolard and Jen
Abrams, from Rockefeller
Foundation's New York City
Cultural Innovation Fund Grant
Application, 2011

fig. 3-12 (overleaf)
Wireframes, 2010, dimensions
variable, OurGoods.org.
Courtesy of the artists.

OurGoods.org &
TradeSchool.coop

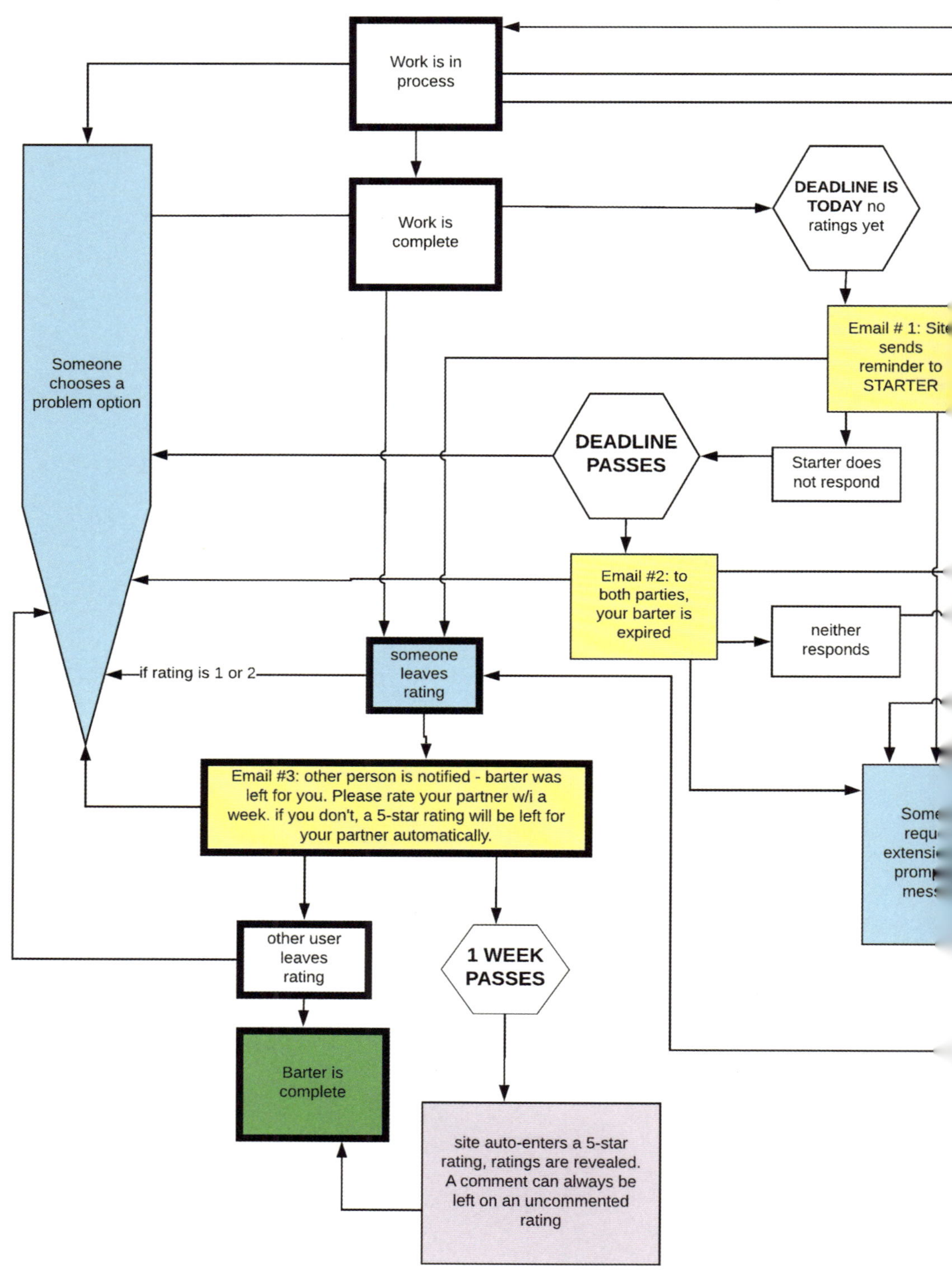

Idea in Public
Work is in process
Work is complete
DEADLINE IS TODAY no ratings yet
Email # 1: Site sends reminder to STARTER
Someone chooses a problem option
DEADLINE PASSES
Starter does not respond
Email #2: to both parties, your barter is expired
neither responds
if rating is 1 or 2
someone leaves rating
Some reque extensi promp mess
Email #3: other person is notified - barter was left for you. Please rate your partner w/i a week. if you don't, a 5-star rating will be left for your partner automatically.
other user leaves rating
1 WEEK PASSES
Barter is complete
site auto-enters a 5-star rating, ratings are revealed. A comment can always be left on an uncommented rating
Collectively-Initiated

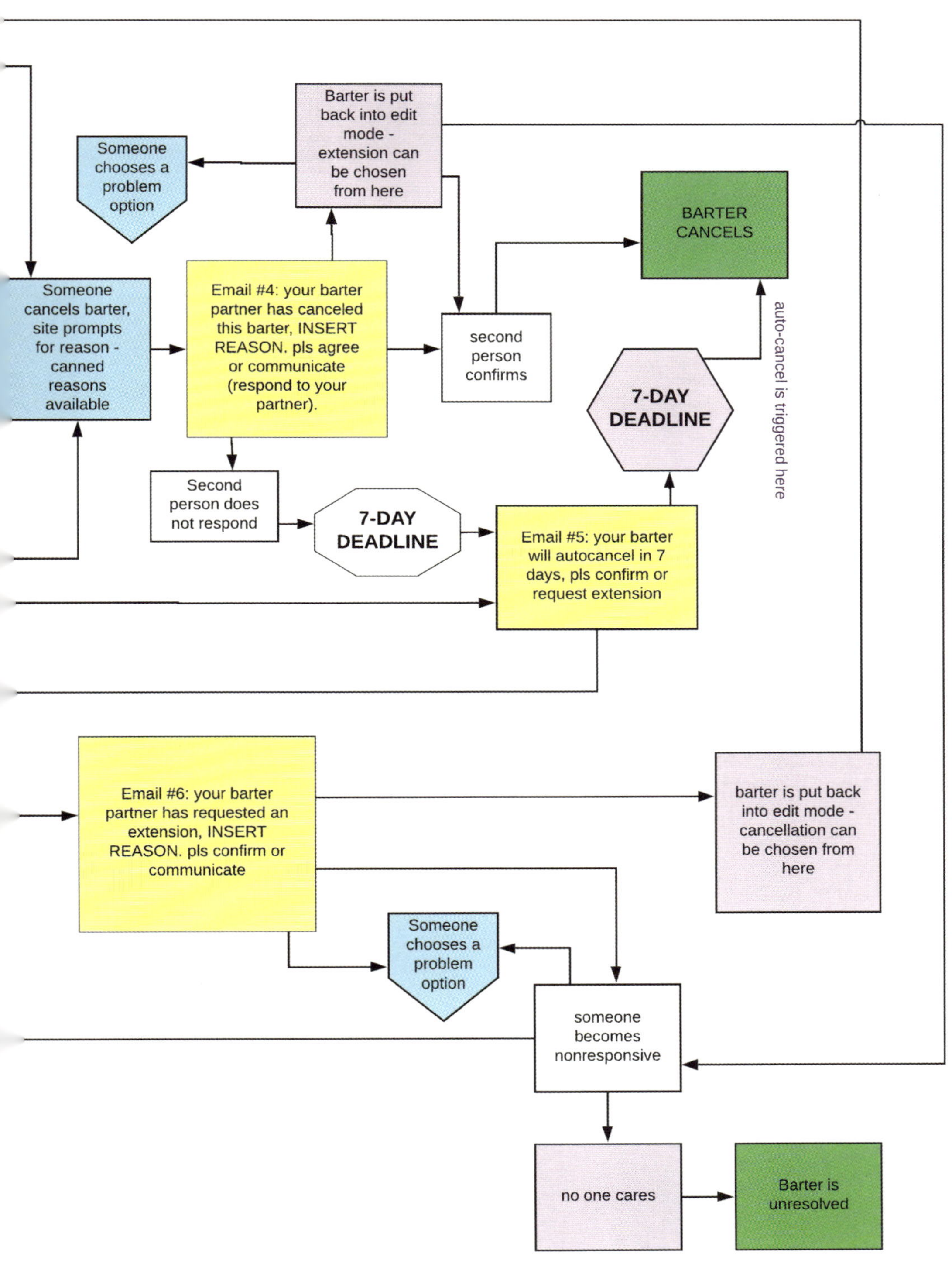
Someone chooses a problem option
Barter is put back into edit mode - extension can be chosen from here
BARTER CANCELS
Someone cancels barter, site prompts for reason - canned reasons available
Email #4: your barter partner has canceled this barter, INSERT REASON. pls agree or communicate (respond to your partner).
second person confirms
7-DAY DEADLINE
auto-cancel is triggered here
Second person does not respond
7-DAY DEADLINE
Email #5: your barter will autocancel in 7 days, pls confirm or request extension
Email #6: your barter partner has requested an extension, INSERT REASON. pls confirm or communicate
barter is put back into edit mode - cancellation can be chosen from here
Someone chooses a problem option
someone becomes nonresponsive
no one cares
Barter is unresolved

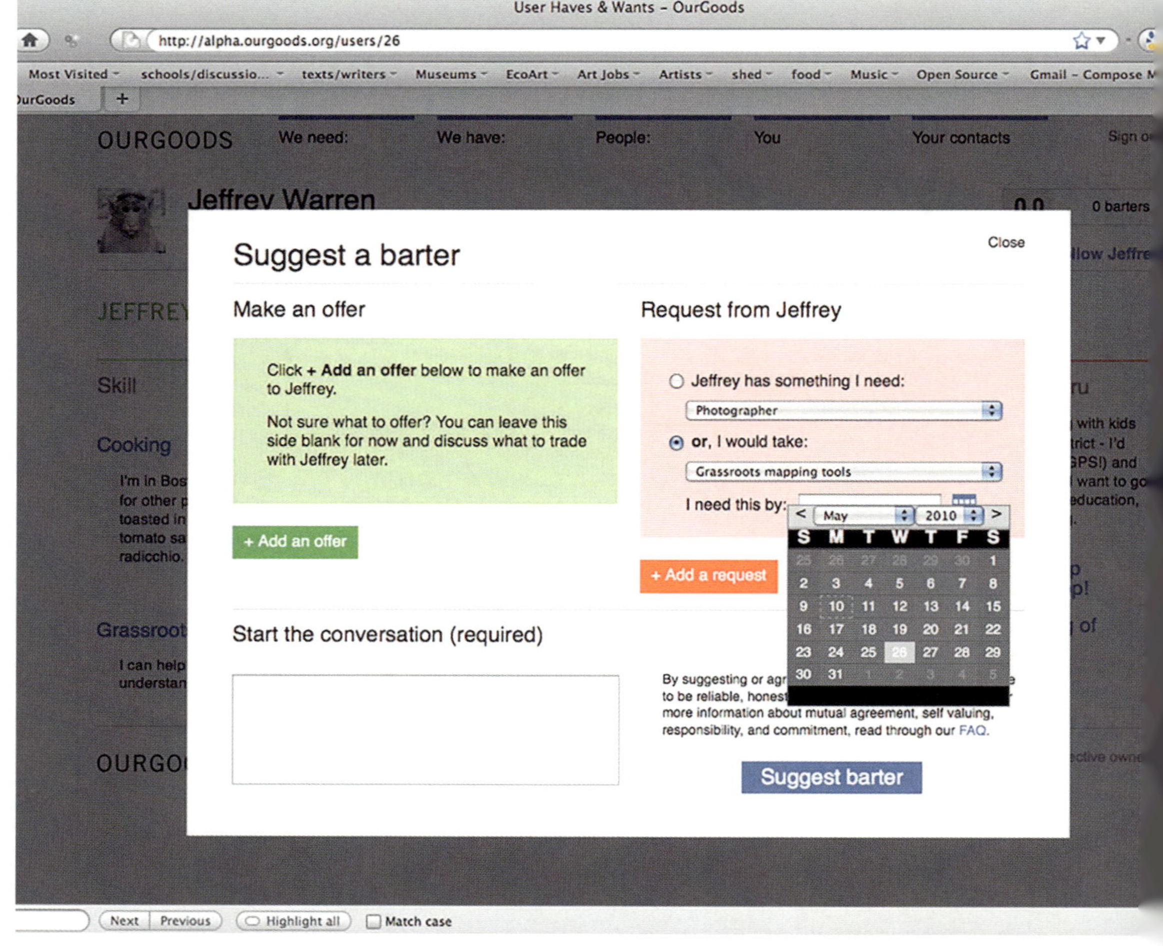

fig. 3-13
OurGoods.org alpha version of
the website, screenshot, 2009,
dimensions variable.

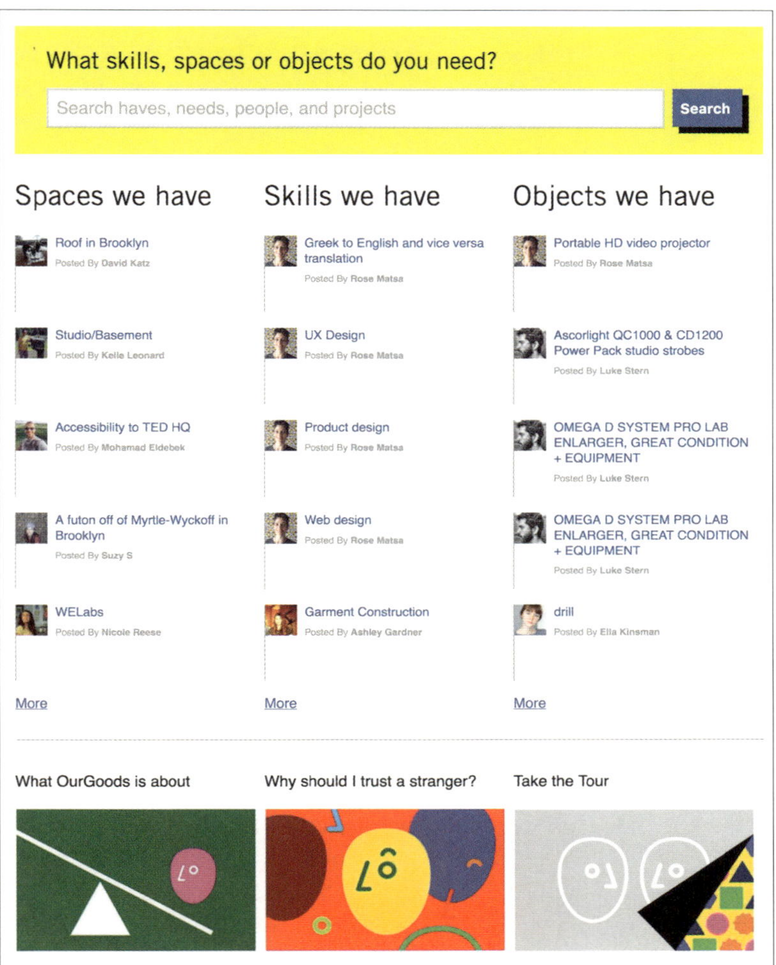

fig. 3-14
OurGoods.org front end home
page, beta version, 2011,
designed by Louise Ma
and Rich Watts, developed
by Carl Tashian.

It took a long time to find Carl Tashian, the computer engineer, but we did, and he was a perfect fit because he wanted to work on collaborative projects that mattered. In Carl Tashian's words:

> OurGoods.org was a special project for me because of the quality of the collaboration. I had moved to New York a year earlier, hardly knowing anyone, and I learned through working with Caroline, Jen, Rich, and Louise that this kind of collaboration was really what I had come to the city for: people who cared as much as I did about building something great.
>
> We gelled as a team really quickly. The five of us did not always agree on everything, so we learned to have productive conflicts. Our time together was very productive in general. There was a level of trust and commitment, mutual respect, and role clarity that made it possible for us to organize ourselves and get a lot done. OurGoods.org came to life quickly this way. We'd have these bursts of flowy productivity where we'd work late into the night at Rich's studio or Jen's apartment. We always ate well—whether it was good Chinese takeout, coffee and pie from around the corner, or something delicious that Jen cooked up. We laughed a lot, listened to music, and just jammed for hours. It's hard to ask for anything more than that in a creative endeavor.

The five of us did not always agree on everything, so we learned to have productive conflicts.

You can see, in our second application for $25,000 from The Field, in 2009, that Jen had already taught me to write in a more "professional" nonprofit grant-ese vernacular.*

Timeframe

More and more we're coming back to the importance of community building that's face to face. So in the same way that we meet around this table and we hold each other accountable based on mutual relationships of trust, we do a lot of in person events as a compliment to the software. It's not a replacement, it's an addition.

—Caroline Woolard, 2014

Commitment

*
see CarolineWooalrd.com for the rest of this document

ERPA - APPLICATION COVER SHEET

1. LEAD ARTIST CONTACT INFORMATION (please type)

Name _____________Caroline Woolard_________________________________

Company name (if applicable) ___________OurGoods.org___________________________

Alternate contact name and title ___________Jen Abrams, co-director___________________

2. PROJECT SUMMARY

OurGoods is an innovative response to the crisis in funding brought on by the recession. It is an online community of artists that facilitates barters of skills, space, labor, and art objects. The site matches barter partners, provides accountability tools, and offers technical assistance resources. It is an instigator for generosity, a locus of empowerment, and an innovative model for supporting the work of artists. We request $25,000 to complete the beta test and hard launch of the site in New York City, and to replicate the model in one medium-sized city by August 2010.

3. REQUEST AMOUNT $ 25,000   TOTAL PROJECT BUDGET $ 89,980

PHASE 2: PROGRESS REPORT · OurGoods.org Caroline Woolard

WHAT CHANGED: Initially, I proposed a website where artists with new projects would ask for help without expectations of direct reciprocity. I imagined artists proposing projects that require space, money, volunteers, or materials so that any interested artist could donate the necessary goods or skills. I saw artists as patrons and philanthropists. Quite quickly, however, I realized that direct exchange is necessary. Both written accounts of the problems of exchange and wise advice from experienced barter communities led me to understand that expectations need to be enumerated for successful trading. (see Phase 3: Project Description for more)

INFORMING MY WORK: The Field provided access to over nine hours of grant-writing advice from Audra Lang, an ERPA group discussion with Jonathan Bowles at The Center for an Urban Future about how to support the creative sector, time with Fran Kirsmer on the concept of "cause marketing," and an insightful conversation with Lara Galinsky of Echoing Green. Bi-weekly meetings with Jennifer Wright Cook emboldened my sense of purpose and created an ongoing dialog about the hours I spent ingesting podcasts and texts focused on complimentary currency, gift economies, and social entrepreneurship. I now have an OurGoods research library and bibliography to share, including: Creating and Understanding Alternatives to Legal Tender by Thomas Greco, The Gift by Lewis Hyde, Slow Money by Woody Tasch, The International Journal of Community Currency Research, Predictably Irrational by Dan Ariely, John Ruskin's Unto This Last, and Miwon Kown's new work on problems of exchange. I designed a WorkDress and traded it for goods and services with over 20 artists, living the experiment to better understand barter. I presented www.OurGoods.org/workdress at The President Street Forum, FEAST, Cooper Union, RISD, Pratt, Mildred's Lane, and Nil's Norman's Free Skool.

NEW COLLABORATORS: The Field has amplified the potential of OurGoods with more than advice and seed money. Two of the four collaborators I chose to work with came through The Field's network. Jen Abrams told Pele Bauch that she was planning a project similar to OurGoods and Pele put us in touch immediately. This connection has been crucial to our success because Jen and I have skills that compliment one another quite effectively. The last piece of the puzzle came from another ERPA participant. After over twenty interviews with computer engineers, Karl Cronin (representing Equus Projects) befriended me and recommended computer engineer Carl Tashian. Carl is both more qualified and more invested than any of the previous candidates for programming, a gifted engineer with enormously good intentions. Rich Watts and Louise Ma joined OurGoods even before I heard back from ERPA about Phase 2 funding, designing the initial website, suggesting readings, and initiating our bi-weekly team meetings in January. I am continually awestruck by the motivation, skill, and generosity I find myself surrounded by while working with this team on OurGoods. (see "Personnel" in Phase 3 for more)

MY WORK IN THE LARGER ARTS ECONOMY: The ERPA mentorship landed me in a community seeking to dispel taboos surrounding financial transparency in the arts. I learned how to value my labor, even as an in-kind donation, and to approach my practice as a business. Most of all, I disseminate my changed expectations for remuneration at every venue possible, using each speaking engagement to push artists to pair cultural agency with financial literacy.

ERPA FAILURES AND SUCCESSES: The hybrid funding-mentorship model is incredible. ERPA provided the perfect amount of time for planning and team organizing. While I thought I would gather a team and produce OurGoods by April, ERPA was wise to allocate nine months for the confluence of strategy AND personnel prepared for implementation. The biggest ERPA success for me was in learning from the other ERPA participants and The Field. The biggest failure of ERPA was in not getting all 7 ERPA participants in the same room more frequently. I think we missed an opportunity for sustained, candid conversation and peer advising.

ERPA, Page 2 of 7

PHASE 2: PROGRESS REPORT · OurGoods.org Caroline Woolard

WHAT CHANGED: Initially, I proposed a website where artists with new projects would ask for help without expectations of direct reciprocity. I imagined artists proposing projects that require space, money, volunteers, or materials so that any interested artist could donate the necessary goods or skills. I saw artists as patrons and philanthropists. Quite quickly, however, I realized that direct exchange is necessary. Both written accounts of the problems of exchange and wise advice from experienced barter communities led me to understand that expectations need to be enumerated for successful trading. (see Phase 3: Project Description for more)

INFORMING MY WORK: The Field provided access to over nine hours of grant-writing advice from Audra Lang, an ERPA group discussion with Jonathan Bowles at The Center for an Urban Future about how to support the creative sector, time with Fran Kirsmer on the concept of "cause marketing," and an insightful conversation with Lara Galinsky of Echoing Green. Bi-weekly meetings with Jennifer Wright Cook emboldened my sense of purpose and created an ongoing dialog about the hours I spent ingesting podcasts and texts focused on complimentary currency, gift economies, and social entrepreneurship. I now have an OurGoods research library and bibliography to share, including: Creating and Understanding Alternatives to Legal Tender by Thomas Greco, The Gift by Lewis Hyde, Slow Money by Woody Tasch, The International Journal of Community Currency Research, Predictably Irrational by Dan Ariely, John Ruskin's Unto This Last, and Miwon Kown's new work on problems of exchange. I designed a WorkDress and traded it for goods and services with over 20 artists, living the experiment to better understand barter. I presented www.OurGoods.org/workdress at The President Street Forum, FEAST, Cooper Union, RISD, Pratt, Mildred's Lane, and Nil's Norman's Free Skool.

NEW COLLABORATORS: The Field has amplified the potential of OurGoods with more than advice and seed money. Two of the four collaborators I chose to work with came through The Field's network. Jen Abrams told Pele Bauch that she was planning a project similar to OurGoods and Pele put us in touch immediately. This connection has been crucial to our success because Jen and I have skills that compliment one another quite effectively. The last piece of the puzzle came from another ERPA participant. After over twenty interviews with computer engineers, Karl Cronin (representing Equus Projects) befriended me and recommended computer engineer Carl Tashian. Carl is both more qualified and more invested than any of the previous candidates for programming, a gifted engineer with enormously good intentions. Rich Watts and Louise Ma joined OurGoods even before I heard back from ERPA about Phase 2 funding, designing the initial website, suggesting readings, and initiating our bi-weekly team meetings in January. I am continually awestruck by the motivation, skill, and generosity I find myself surrounded by while working with this team on OurGoods. (see "Personnel" in Phase 3 for more)

MY WORK IN THE LARGER ARTS ECONOMY: The ERPA mentorship landed me in a community seeking to dispel taboos surrounding financial transparency in the arts. I learned how to value my labor, even as an in-kind donation, and to approach my practice as a business. Most of all, I disseminate my changed expectations for remuneration at every venue possible, using each speaking engagement to push artists to pair cultural agency with financial literacy.

ERPA FAILURES AND SUCCESSES: The hybrid funding-mentorship model is incredible. ERPA provided the perfect amount of time for planning and team organizing. While I thought I would gather a team and produce OurGoods by April, ERPA was wise to allocate nine months for the confluence of strategy AND personnel prepared for implementation. The biggest ERPA success for me was in learning from the other ERPA participants and The Field. The biggest failure of ERPA was in not getting all 7 ERPA participants in the same room more frequently. I think we missed an opportunity for sustained, candid conversation and peer advising.

ERPA, Page 2 of 7

PHASE 3: PROJECT DESCRIPTION: OurGoods.org Caroline Woolard

What question/challenge are you addressing and how did you identify it?

The financial crisis is front-page news every day. The challenges this poses for artists are clear – the funding community will have significantly less money to give to artists in the coming years. Charitable giving is likely to recover more slowly than the larger economy. How can we maintain a vibrant creative workforce in this environment? How can artists emerge from this crisis stronger and supported by a more sustainable community?

How are you addressing the aforementioned challenge?

OurGoods is an online bartering system that addresses the serious shortage of available funding for creative projects while building community, facilitating dialogue, increasing exposure, and building the skill base of the creative workforce. At the heart of OurGoods is the person-to-person exchange: I write your press release; you design my postcard. Beyond that, the site offers a dynamic online environment in which artists can follow each other's creative development; visualize the "under the radar" artistic activity of their community; develop mutually supportive relationships offline; and learn new skills to enable their own work and the work of others. OurGoods makes the creative workforce's depth and breadth of skills accessible, so that an artist can complete an entire project without cash funding of any kind.

OurGoods starts online with a state-of-the-art website based on successful social networking and resource-sharing models. The site allows users to post "haves" and "wants," and provides a search engine that matches users with complimentary needs. Users are also able to post information about the projects the barters will support. Some sample barters are: grant writing for web design; costume design for an art object; video documentation for studio use; welding expertise for singing lessons. The site gives artists the agency to self-value their "haves" and agree to (or decline) the terms of each barter, ensuring that each partner derives value from the exchange. The site provides detailed personality and skill profiles to help users find good barter partners, and accountability tools to foster reliability (accountability is further discussed in the "Future" document). Members can track other members' responses to each potential barter partner's past transactions. OurGoods offers written resources to help users navigate barters, as well as resources like production timelines, model press releases, and basic production budgets to support good planning of projects. To the extent that such resources are already offered by organizations like NYFA, Dance/NYC and Fractured Atlas, the site links to and supports them.

Because there may not always be a direct barter available on the site, OurGoods will introduce a point system if the need is established. The point system allows users to offer something they have in exchange for points, which they then use to get what they want from any other user. As with direct barters, point transactions are self-valued. Numerous excellent models for community currencies exist on which we have based the OurGoods point system.

The OurGoods community offers more than cash funding offers artists. It helps us honor and value our work. It draws the creative community together into mutually supportive relationships. It is a locus of generosity and a hub of collaboration. OurGoods makes passion productive. It replaces the zero-sum funding game with a game of "the more you get, the more I get."

What ways do you foresee replicating this project? What resources do you need?

We envision a Craigslist model for replicating OurGoods. OurGoods' site architecture is scalable to any amount of traffic, and can be segmented by city. Once we have polished the model, we will roll it out in other cities.

The first step is to establish the model in New York City. We will begin with an alpha test of the site with about one hundred trusted users, many of whom have already been recruited. The alpha testers will provide us with feedback on the basic functionality of the site, the user experience, and the relevance and

ERPA, Page 3 of 7

---

usefulness of OurGoods to their needs. After completion of the alpha phase, we will integrate feedback and revamp the site for the beta test. We will gather and respond to feedback in real time. Concurrent with alpha testing, we will reach out to the organizations NYC artists already turn to – NYFA, Dance/NYC, ART/NY, Fractured Atlas, etc. – to let them know about the site and ask for their support in recruiting users. With their help, we will recruit an extended network of users to begin the beta test.

Concurrent with the beta phase, we will reach out to service organizations, community leaders and stakeholders in possible expansion cities. We began this process in June, when Jen Abrams attended the Dance/USA conference. There she spoke to community leaders and found tremendous support for the idea and interest in replication in Philadelphia. Philadelphia's Dance/USA office showed the strongest interest, and will likely be the first expansion city. The replication process is described in detail in the "future" document.

To successfully establish the program model and replicate it in Philadelphia within the year, we will need: access to community leaders in NYC and Philadelphia; help recruiting users to the site; help with media/marketing plan for site; legal advice to refer users to IRS barter stipulations; funding for the coding and graphic design of the site; printed materials for outreach and fundraising; server space to house the site; and to individual donors interested in creative solutions to the persistent problem of funding scarcity. We are also asking a low yearly membership fee of $10-$15. We expect post-beta member base to reach at least 1000 in the first year and 4000-5000 in future years. A membership fee would pay the site administrators a very modest fee for time spent planning the model and bringing it to both communities.

Tell us how your project will build new financial streams for your work long-term.

We believe OurGoods is an extremely fundable project. For every dollar spent on this project, we can clearly demonstrate the delivery of many hundreds of dollars in direct support to artists within the first year. OurGoods provides tremendous "bang for buck" to funders. Together with the urgency of the problem it addresses, and its innovative use of technology, we believe OurGoods will be attractive to established funders like the Ford Foundation and the Rockefeller Foundation, to Web 2.0 funders like the Mozilla Foundation, and to individual donors interested in creative solutions to the persistent problem of funding scarcity. We are also asking a low yearly membership fee of $10-$15. We expect post-beta member base to reach at least 1000 in the first year and 4000-5000 in future years. A membership fee would pay the site administrators a very modest fee while supporting the server costs.

What is the timeframe of your implementation project?

Sept 09: Alpha site completed, 100 alpha testers recruited. Print materials ready. Alpha testing begins. Begin to establish relationships with funders. Cultivate press contacts. http://www.ourgoods.org/lite/
Oct 09: NYC user outreach, NYC and Philly community leader outreach, alpha testing continues. Funder and press relationship-building continues. Some press coverage published.
Nov 09: Alpha test concludes. Solicit feedback from alpha testers, continue user and community leader outreach. NYC and Philly community leader outreach continues. NYC beta user recruitment continues. Funder relationship building continues. Press ramps up.
Dec 09: Prepare beta site, integrating alpha feedback. User recruitment continues. Core Philly stakeholders and leaders are on board. Continue progress with funders, press.
Jan 10: Beta site launch with 200 users. Continue to build usership. Serious Phase 3 and 4 funding from beta users. Planning sessions with core Philly team for site expansion. Gather feedback from beta users, ramp up to beta shape.
Feb 10: Hard launch of site with full press coverage, build to 500 users. Begin recruitment of Philly users. Continue working on funding. Introduce membership fee in NYC.
Mar-Apr 10: Continue building NYC usership to 1000 users. Recruit Philly users. Initial funding contacts begin to bear fruit. Continue relationship-building with funders. Cultivate Philly press.
May-Jun 10: Philly beta launch with 200 users, continue recruiting Philly users. NYC usership at 1500. Grant funding begins to come in.
Jul 10: Evaluate Philly beta test, adjust the model to accommodate local needs. Continue recruiting users in NYC and Philly.
Aug 10: Philly hard launch with 500 users. Introduce membership fee in Philly.

ERPA, Page 4 of 7

Sample outreach opportunities (confirmed):
Sept 09: NurtureArt, Conflux, ABC No Rio, Chez Bushwick, Capital B
Oct 09: Asian American Arts Alliance Town Hall, Cooper Union
Nov 09: Temporary Services' Art Labor and Economics publication launch, discussions

How will you/your organization   add this work to your current programming? Will other programs or projects be cut?

OurGoods is currently a volunteer effort, and a project of passion for each member of the core team. We support our work on OurGoods through paid "day job" work. Each of us has already declined shows and put opportunities on hold to focus on this project. We've each invested a significant amount of time in OurGoods, and are committed to seeing it through. We will continue to do so on a volunteer basis until a funding stream is established. Once funding becomes available, Caroline and Jen will leave other paid work to work for OurGoods.

Who will lead this project and why? Who else will work significantly on this project?

Caroline Woolard provides project management leadership, as well as a broad vision for the site. She connects a disparate network of interdisciplinary artists, garnering support and community for OurGoods. In her work, Woolard creates infrastructure for mutualism. Just as she made public seating from 2004-2006, OurGoods makes tangible Woolard's commitment to community. Caroline has organized numerous collaborative, interdisciplinary projects, supported by grants from The MacDowell Colony, iLAND, and Watermill in the past year. Caroline is a founding member of a 30-person, 8-year, 8,000 square foot studio space that runs on mutual respect and financial transparency. OurGoods will expand her network of rigorous, honest, interdisciplinary artists.

Jen Abrams provides leadership in fundraising, organizational management, and the conceptualization and troubleshooting of the barter environment. She brings fifteen years of arts administration experience to the project. She is a skilled institutional and individual fundraiser, with a background in strategic planning for and management of small and founder-led non-profits. As an artist, she brings fifteen years of self-production experience to the project. Ten of those years were spent making and producing her work at WOW Café Theater, a collectively-run theater in the East Village which has run on a barter system for thirty years. Jen sees OurGoods as a way to make the WOW model available to a much larger community.

The site is being built by Carl Tashian. He provides leadership in site architecture and prodigious coding experience. Carl was the senior site engineer at Zip Car for five years, bringing the business from a one-city, 50-car network to it's current market dominance. He brings a wealth of knowledge about how to create an online environment that elicits respect for shared resources. He is writing a book on incentives for sharing the virtual and environmental commons. In addition to his personal commitment to enabling resource-sharing, he is interested in OurGoods as a case study for the book. Carl sees OurGoods as Zip Car for the artistic community and has already donated $8,000 in coding time towards the alpha site.

Louise Ma and Rich Watts design the user-interface and printed matter for OurGoods. Companies like The New York Times Online, The Dart Center, and Grand Opening contract their design firm, The Last Studio on Earth. Louise and Rich took OurGoods on as a personal project because they believe it will revolutionize the way artists and designers work together. So far, they have contributed over $10,000 in design work.

ERPA, Page 5 of 7

PHASE 4: THE FUTURE – OurGoods.org Narrative and Finance Caroline Woolard

a) Narrative

OurGoods creates an alternative economic model in which the value of labor, expertise, and creative endeavor is set directly by the individual participants rather than by institutions or gatekeepers. OurGoods is a recession-proof support network for the creative workforce, insulating artists from shifting funder priorities and from the vagaries of the economy. As OurGoods expands to other cities, we envision it as a platform for inter-city touring and a hub for collaborative, interdisciplinary exchange.

By the end of August 2010, we expect to have replicated the project in Philadelphia. That process will give us invaluable information about where the needs of different communities overlap and differ. We will also understand the process of successfully replicating an OurGoods community. OurGoods will expand to the number of communities as can be productively served by our model. Depending on funding levels and interest, we could expand to as many as five or six new areas a year.

We see outreach, recruitment and cultivation of stakeholders as essential for building a robust community in each city. Caroline and Jen are committed to the long-term implementation of this project, and have already begun to build relationships with leaders and funders in possible expansion cities. Our current model for new OurGoods communities begins with building relationships in order to understand each community's existing resources and needs. Those relationships connect us to the organizations and informal networks we must engage with in order to reach the range of independent artists working there.

Through this outreach, we will establish a team of committed individual artists and community leaders to recruit members and guide the rollout of the site in that area. We will serve as consultants, sharing our experiences and responding to local needs by adjusting the site. We will visit each expansion community as needed to guide its growth and refine the model.

For Caroline and Jen, this project emerges from their individual needs to create support structures for their own work. Jen has supported her work in this way for ten years. Caroline's work has always been philosophically aligned with this approach. Rather than a diversion from their artistic work, this project represents an opening to a larger community. As OurGoods grows, the personal opportunities for Caroline and Jen grow. It is a deeply symbiotic relationship.

Site Evaluation: The site will self-evaluate through an integrated user feedback mechanism. We will also evaluate success by quantifiable measures such as level of activity, user evaluations of each barter, membership growth, and the amount of offers members make to the larger community. We will see which components of the site users find most important: project tracking, feedback mechanisms, navigation networks, or other unexpected behaviors. Perhaps users will use the site as a peer-to-peer portfolio and critique space. Perhaps users will find the project management and mutual contracts most helpful. Based on feedback and user navigation preferences, we will develop a robust model to take to other cities.

Both the dialog surrounding the site's refinement, and the site's user activity, will provide metrics for serving artists beyond OurGoods. Often, artistic work created outside institutional support structures is not visible to the wider community or to institutions that endeavor to serve artists. OurGoods is a way to visualize and track that artistic activity, both to better serve artists and to study culture as it gets produced.

Robust Community As the OurGoods community becomes more robust, we will encourage members to expand the skill set of the entire community by offering workshops in their area of expertise. These members will be motivated either by receiving points from participants, or by the stature in the community that making such an offering affords them. We will also include members who are not artists. By recruiting lawyers, dentists, farmers, plumbers, accountants, etc. to the site, we can provide artists with the services they need while orienting the larger community to the real value of the goods and services artists offer.

ERPA, Page 6 of 7

<u>Accountability</u>: The accountability tools and mediation techniques we have built into the site and the community will be tested in the first year and perfected in the second year. A structure for accountability is absolutely necessary to establish the trust required for successful barters. Without it, the site will fail. Anonymity is not allowed, nor is an individual allowed to have more than one identity. Once a member's identity is verified by another user, the site offers extensive information so that members can choose their barter partners carefully. Each barter will be guided by an online contract with agreed-on expectations and completion dates. Members must give feedback on each barter and sign off on its completion to close the contract. Members can see how long another member has been on the site, how many barters they have completed, whether they have expired incomplete contracts, and what feedback has been left by their past barter partners. The site's core team will offer mediation in cases of dispute, and in rare situations, reserve the right to remove a repeat offender from the site.

B) Long-Term Financial Sustainability

As we discussed in the Project Description, we believe this model is extremely fundable because of its enormous multiplier effect. Based on the expansion model described above, we anticipate it will cost an average of $30,000 per city to replicate the project (see attached supplementary budget). Conservative projections show **$800,000**[*] worth of goods and services supplied to artists as a direct result of funding. As funders seek to derive more and more value for each charitable dollar, OurGoods will provide an efficient and innovative solution. We also believe "the ask" to individual donors is very strong.

If fundraising efforts are unsuccessful, the site will still serve the community. Once the site is built, it is possible for it to run itself. Server space and coding updates to the site will cost less than $4000/year, and will be comfortably covered by a small membership fee of $10/year. The site will grow more slowly in that scenario, but we are confident it will grow.

Because the site requests ZIP code information from users, it can self-segment by area. If the need is great enough, new members could use the site to generate a network in their area spontaneously, without the assistance of the OurGoods team. We see this as a rockier path to replication, but a path nonetheless. It could yield interesting insights on how communities of need develop and organize themselves, and provide valuable lessons for the project as a whole.

Assuming modest funding, Jen Abrams and Caroline Woolard will become part-time employees of the organization in September 2010, and designers Louise Ma, Rich Watts, and Carl Tashian will become paid consultants. OurGoods will raise money locally and nationally to fund the $30k rollout in each new community. Once rollout is complete, OurGoods as an organization will require $10k-$15k/year per city to pay staff and consultants to continue to develop the model, expand server space, add new features to the site, troubleshoot as community-specific problems arise, and find new ways for the site to serve all OurGoods members. This could be supported by membership fees or by local and national fundraising. We are also open to exploring carefully curated advertising (for instance, by local organizations serving artists, and/or by individuals and institutions promoting performances and exhibitions). And we are open to exploring being subsumed by a larger arts service organization, if a good match can be found.

c) Supplementary: Please find the OurGoods Future Budget attached.

---

[*] Calculation as follows: 1000 participating members complete an average of four barters per year. Barter values range from $60 ($30 per partner) for an exchange of 3 hours of flyer distribution for 3 hours of data entry, to $2000 ($1000 per partner) for an exchange of a basic portfolio website for a 2-camera shoot of a performance. Assume a very conservative mean barter value of $200 for an exchange of massage therapy for a small pottery piece. In the first year, artists will receive **$800,000** worth of goods and services.

ERPA, Page 7 of 7

In 2011, we applied for even more money for OurGoods.org. We applied for $100,000 from the Rockefeller Foundation's New York City Cultural Innovation Fund, and we got it! It came at precisely the right moment, as the five of us had met the night before and had decided that, without funding, we could not continue to give 2–3 days a week to the project as volunteers. Here is what Jen and I wrote, and the actual budget that we used, going forward.*

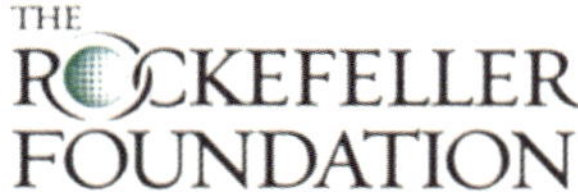

THE ROCKEFELLER FOUNDATION

Welcome, Jen Abrams   **Applications are due Monday, March 7th, 2011.**

Home | Change Password | FAQ | Guidelines | Logout

| Guidelines | Contact | Organization | Project | Lead Project Personnel | Budget | Cultural Data Project | Print | Submit |

Print

You may **Print** a copy of this application for your records.

When you are done, proceed to Submit.

Main Contact

Honorific	Ms.
First Name	Jen
Last Name	Abrams
Title	Co-Founder

*

see CarolineWoolard.com for the
rest of this document

Collectively-
Initiated

ORGANIZATIONAL BIO
OurGoods.org is an online barter network for artists. As the 2008 financial crisis hit, OurGoods.org's co-founders asked two questions:
1) How can we facilitate a stronger, more sustainable network of cultural producers?
2) How can we value cultural abundance in an economy driven by scarcity?
OurGoods was born in response to these questions.

…

MISSION STATEMENT
OurGoods is a barter network for creative people. Our barter community offers a sustainable model for cultural production by making it possible for artists to create an entire project outside of the cash economy. We address artists' immediate needs by connecting individuals who can help each other, and we address artists' long-term needs by helping them create a support network based on mutual respect.

…

OVERVIEW AND STORY
Please describe the proposed project/process. What challenge is this project addressing? What would be the impact of this project and who would benefit from this impact? How will this project contribute to New York City?:

The Challenge: Since the 2008 market crash, cultural producers have struggled to come to terms with the new economic landscape.

…

A wide range of foundation leaders, technical assistance peers, and other artists see OurGoods.org as an elegant and essential answer to a longstanding problem. The dominant economy values the outputs of our production (completed artworks) far less than it values than the inputs to our production (rehearsal space, materials, skill, time, energy). OurGoods.org sidesteps this persistent imbalance by helping cultural producers exchange directly with each other, creating an alternate economy based on shared values.

…

Because support for projects is based on relationships and common goals, rather than on scarcity or the aesthetics of gatekeepers, work that is difficult to fund traditionally can thrive.

…

As individual skills, spaces, and items for barter are aggregated on OurGoods, we will be able to see where we need to build capacity in our community, individually and as a network. We will research existing opportunities for users to build their skills, and seek out experts within and outside of our community to offer skill-building workshops to our users.

…

INNOVATION
The Resource Sharing Landscape: Resource sharing has exploded in recent years, driven by new technology and the growth of social media, and by the economic crisis. Though this trend is growing, it is not yet adequately serving independent artists. Existing barter and recycling sites (e.g. Freecycle, Craigslist, SwapTree, Scoodi) focus on manufactured objects and allow users to operate anonymously, without trust. Existing mutual aid systems like time banking (e.g. TINY, Time|Bank) are not widely used by our peers, in part because our peers do not consider all hours as equal for every task. Most sites ignore skill-sharing entirely, and no sites are built exclusively to connect the creative community in non-cash working relationships.

Our Organization: The five co-founders of OurGoods have formed a powerful R&D team, working towards this site for the past two years. Carl Tashian and Jen Abrams joined the group with years of experience in resource sharing communities,

and the other three co-founders (Caroline Woolard, Rich Watts, and Louise Ma) have spent the past two years implementing TradeSchool.coop, (a project of OurGoods.org, described in the "Communication" section).

…

When money mediates transactions, the value is finite. When we barter, we get the value of the object/ service and we form relationships while engaging with the creative landscape. These relationships connect artists to new professional opportunities, form the basis of friendships that support artists' lives as well as their art, and help us respond to changing conditions within our community. These relationships intertwine to create a network that allows artists to make their work regardless of the economic climate.

Barter creates value, but it also causes us to rethink our relationship to value in a market economy. The market sets prices/renumeration for cultural production that bear little resemblance to the value artists put on each others' work, or to the value derived by their audience. By allowing users to self-value skills and objects, we create a new model for valuing cultural production and for legitimizing the work of artists outside institutions and

art markets. Within this alternative
economy, we can increase cultural
dialogue and create an environment
of abundance and community.

…

RISKS
Describe any potential risks associated with this project and how you
would mitigate them:

The two main risks to this project
are not reaching a critical mass
of active users, and not being
able to sustain the project after
CIF funding.
…

BUDGET
If you receive a smaller amount
than requested, what would your
contingency plan be?:

OurGoods is a project of passion
for all five co-founders. We have
committed many thousands of volunteer hours to this project, and will
continue to volunteer our time to
make OurGoods successful. Our staff
is currently mostly unpaid.

The scale of the project we have
proposed assumes that we can begin
to pay ourselves modestly for our
work. If we are given less than we
have requested, we will adjust the
scale to reflect that reality. Our
usership will grow more slowly,

features will be added less frequently, and the overall output and
quality of the site will be reduced.

We believe our team has the skills
and experience required to make
OurGoods.org a successful stand-
alone organization. However, if
it serves our mission, we would
be open to being absorbed into a
larger organization.

…

Although this budget includes
part-time salaries for OurGoods.org
co-founders, it does so at a rate
significantly below what we would
earn for the same in another organization. $8k of the in-kind income
reflects home office expenses
donated by the co-founders to the
project. The remainder reflects
the difference between the market
value of the work of OurGoods.org
co-founders and what they will be
paid. Payment goes up in Year 2,
so in-kind goes down.

Timeframe

Column 1

Org. Type	501(c)3
Name of Applicant / Organization	OurGoods
Web site Address	http://ourgoods.org

Organizational Bio

OurGoods is an online barter network for artists. As the 2008 financial crisis hit, OurGoods' co-founders asked two questions:
1) How can we facilitate a stronger, more sustainable network of cultural producers?
2) How can we value cultural abundance in an economy driven by scarcity?
OurGoods was born in response to these questions.

The team consists of visual artist and cooperative artist space manager Caroline Woolard, choreographer and arts administrator Jen Abrams, graphic designers Rich Watts and Louise Ma, and former Senior Site Engineer for ZipCar, Carl Tashian. The co-founders share a commitment to resource-sharing as a model for cultural production and community-building.

We have found tremendous support in NY's non-profit community. The Queens Museum of Art, Eyebeam, the New Museum, Dance/NYC, the Lower Manhattan Cultural Council, Dance Theater Workshop, Dixon Place, Brooklyn Arts Exchange, Smack Mellon, Chez Bushwick, the Elizabeth Foundation for the Arts, and EFA's Arts Center are among the dozens of organizations who have committed to helping us succeed.

3-Year Highlights

Tested alpha site with 150 users in 2010, added functionality based on user feedback, launched beta site in October 2010, expanded to over 1200 members. Used open-source software and will make available under a GNU Public License. See the site at http://ourgoods.org by using login SplinterAndHog@gmail.com, password: Barter.

2009 Accepted into Rockefeller-funded Economic Revitalization for Performing Artists (ERPA) program with 15% startup funds. Granted 2nd round of $15k in 2010 and 3rd round of $20k in 2011. Also received $1900 from Brooklyn Arts Council. Initiated relationships with potential funders including Department of Cultural Affairs, ConEd, Open Meadows, Black Rock, Brooklyn Community Foundation, and City Councilmembers.

Appearances at F.E.A.S.T., Cooper Union, WNYC, the Armory Show, Walker Arts Center, MoMA, Prelude Festival, Dance/USA.

Feb 2010 Trade School (project of OurGoods, described below) offers over 100 classes in 35 days to over 800 students. Feb 2011 Trade School re-opens with 19% funding raised from 238 people through Kickstarter, runs through April 2011.

Featured in two books: What's Mine Is Yours: The Rise of Collaborative Consumption; Re-defining Community: Portraits of Emergent New Culture; and Life, Inc (by Douglas Rushkoff). Media coverage on WNYC, Good Magazine, NYTimes and Fox News, among others.

Mission Statement

OurGoods is a barter network for creative people. Our barter community offers a sustainable model for cultural production by making it possible for artists to create an entire project outside of the cash economy. We address artists' immediate needs by connecting individuals who can help each other, and we address artists' long-term needs by helping them create a support network based on mutual respect.

Our website fosters an online community of people who barter skills, space,

[column 1, middle band]

cycle and artists can respond more immediately to their world. Space is created for marginalized voices to come forward. The entire cultural landscape becomes richer.

But perhaps most importantly, we have found that our users derive satisfaction from helping other artists over and above what they get from the barter itself. The level of generosity we have observed is surprising and overwhelming, and is perhaps our community's greatest asset.

The Impact

The site will have its largest impact on independent artists and their projects. We estimate an average user will derive $1500 in value from the site per year. This assumes 3 transactions/year, at an average value of $250 (ie, you write my press release, I design your postcard, each side of the transaction is worth $250). We value a year of transactions between 1500 users at $2.25 million. Assuming the site costs $100k/yr to run (after initial site creation costs), the return on investment in the site on $1 is $22.50.

Beyond that, OurGoods.org reveals trends and opportunities in the NYC cultural community as they emerge. Browsing individual Needs and Project Needs provides a dynamic window into the creative process of a wide range of cultural producers at any given moment.

As individual skills, spaces, and items for barter are aggregated on OurGoods, we will be able to see where we need to build capacity in our community, individually and as a network. We will research existing opportunities for users to build their skills, and seek out experts within and outside of our community to offer skill-building workshops to our users.

We will be able to collect data on the under-the-radar activity of independent artists - how many there are, where they are, how active they are, and what kinds of projects they are working on. These metrics will be an important source of information for technical assistance organizations, funders, advocates and elected officials as they seek to serve individual artists better, and better advocate for support for the arts.

Over 1000 users of OurGoods are already connecting and incorporating unexpected skills to expand and innovate creatively right now.

Our Request

We request $100k from CIF to fund five part-time staff members. Staff time will focus on:

- User recruitment to increase ownership, including developing relationships with organizations that can connect us with their constituents, implementing recruitment plans in partnership with those organizations, and building live barter events to familiarize potential users with our model.

- Usability testing to determine when site improvements are required to help us meet our usership goals, and coding time to implement those improvements.

- Relationship-building with other funders to build future support for the site. Because we do not fit neatly into traditional funding categories, we need to cultivate these relationships carefully and over time. We will also research alternatives to advertising and site membership fees in the earned income area.

By the end of CIF funding, OurGoods will be a fully-functional site with a sustainable future funding base, providing an essential resource for over 1500 NYC artists, and a model for supporting cultural production in other

[column 1, lower band]

Barter creates value, but it also causes us to rethink our relationship to value in a market economy. The market sets prices/remuneration for cultural production that bear little resemblance to the value artists put on each others' work, or to the value derived by their audience. By attaching users to self-value skills and objects, we create a model for valuing cultural production and for legitimizing the work of artists outside institutions and art markets. Within this alternative economy, we can increase cultural dialogue and create an environment of abundance and creativity.

COMMUNICATIONS

Who is the audience for this project and how are you communicating with them about the project?

Audience

Visual artists, designers, architects, writers, musicians, and craftspeople are all included in our target audience. We are currently focused on the NYC area. Our users range from college age to retirement, but the majority of our users are in their 20's-40's.

Communicating via Partner Organizations

We will partner with organizations that our target audience trusts. We are in dialogue with the following potential partners (among others): The Queens Museum of Art, EFA/Project Space, Smack Mellon, Etsy, ART/NY, Theater Communications Group, Dance New Amsterdam, Asian American Arts Alliance, and MoCADA. We will work with each partner organization to determine how best to reach their constituencies. Ideas include: live barter events, info sessions at large gatherings, presence on their website, printed materials in their space, and inclusion in newsletters and emails. By working with partners like Dance/NY and DTW in this way in 2010 we increased traffic to the site by a factor of ten.

Communicating via Storefront Space

In 2010 Trade School held classes for 35 days and over 800 students bartered with teachers in exchange for instruction. The website received over 18,000 unique visits from NYC residents and press from Fox Business News, The Wall Street Journal, NPR, and The New York Times. 2011's Trade School is currently in session, and will run for three months. Many Trade School students and teachers are now actively bartering on OurGoods.

Funders

CIF funding will help us communicate with arts funders about the importance of resource-sharing technology for the creative community. We will build relationships through meetings, invitations to live events, website demonstrations, and regular updates about the site's progress. Wherever possible, we will get introductions to program officers through our existing allies. It will take funders some time to understand how OurGoods fits into their mission. By the end of CIF funding, we hope that these relationships will make our funding applications successful.

RISKS

Describe any potential risks associated with this project and how you would mitigate them.

The two main risks to this project are not reaching a critical mass of active users, and not being able to sustain the project after CIF funding.

There are currently two barriers to active users: 1) potential users don't know about the site, and/or are not yet comfortable with barter, and 2) interested users are not active on the site because the site needs improvements (ie, the workflow is not intuitive, they encounter bugs, or they forget to check their messages).

The main barrier to funding is time - forming the necessary relationships to implement a fundraising strategy is time-intensive.

[column 1 income table]

$30,000 ::	$60,000:	Income / Funding: Anticipated / Pending: Foundation Grants
$61,000 ::	$31,000:	Income / Funding: In-Kind: Personnel Expenses
$8,000 ::	$7,000:	Income / Funding: In-Kind: Office Expense
$50,000 ::	$50,000:	Income / Funding: NYC CIF Grant Request: Grant Request

Income Total Year 1: $152,000
Income Total Year 2: $152,000

Budget Narrative

Income:

We have already begun building relationships with the Department of Cultural Affairs and several City Councilmembers. We have also had preliminary conversations with program officers at New Life, the Fund for the City of New York, Doris Duke, the Brooklyn Community Foundation, and Lila Wallace. Everyone we've spoken to has been positive about our project, and has offered to help us make connections with other foundations in addition to offering us guidance on their foundation. On our list of funders to explore in the near future are Robert Sterling Clark, the Windgate Foundation, Warhol-Gilmore, Sheaffer, John B. and James L. Knight, the Margaret A. Cargill Foundation, Ford, Jerome and Harkness.

We may be able to make a case to certain funders (for instance, Creative Capital, Black Rock and Franklin Furnace) to fund OurGoods as an art project rather than as technical assistance. OurGoods and Trade School have been curated into time-based art festivals by the New Museum and the Whitney this year. We will further explore this option with CIF funding.

Although this budget includes partime salaries for OurGoods co-founders, it does so at a rate significantly below what we would ask for the same in another organization. 28% of the in-kind income reflects home office expenses donated by the co-founders to the project. The remainder reflects the difference between the market value of the work of OurGoods co-founders and what they will be paid. Payment goes up in Year 2, as in-kind goes down.

Expenses:

Personnel Expenses:

We have classified all personnel as direct because we have only charged time spent executing duties directly related to the project to this budget. We have not included any administrative overhead time.

Carl Tashian, Site Coding (writing the underlying code that powers the site). 230 hours/yr @ $125/hr = $29,000. Paid $16k in Year 1 ($13k in-kind) and $22k in Year 2 ($7k in-kind).

Rich Watts, User Interface (building on underlying code to power the actual user experience). 300 hours/yr @ $85/hr = $25k. Paid $16k in Year 1 ($9k in-kind) and $22k in Year 2 ($3k in-kind).

Louise Ma, Graphic Design and Art Direction. 300 hours/yr @ $85/hr = $25k. Paid $16k in Year 1 ($9k in-kind) and $22k in Year 2 ($3k in-kind).

Column 2

labor, and art objects. The site matches barter partners, provides accountability tools, and offers technical assistance resources. We also offer live barter events where potential barter partners can meet and form relationships.

OurGoods is an instigator for generosity, a locus of empowerment, and an innovative model for supporting the work of artists. OurGoods makes room for social, ethical, environmental, and aesthetic values to guide exchange behavior. We place ourselves within a growing societal movement towards resource-sharing and the inherent value of creative communities.

Trade School, a pop-up storefront for education, is a project of OurGoods. At Trade School, all classes are available for barter only. Trade School grounds OurGoods' dynamic virtual network in the context of real-world interactions, helping artists develop working relationships and expanding the barter community in person.

Earned	0.00
Contributed	11500.00
Expenses	11500.00

Budget Notes

We have considered a number of advertising and membership models that would generate an earned income stream for OurGoods, and have not yet found one that is consonant with the trust community we are building. We will continue to look for an earned income model that works for us, while we work to build contributed income streams.

Partnerships

Partner #1

Organization Name	The Field (fiscal sponsor)
Web site	www.thefield.org
Contact Name	Tanya
Contact Title	Calamoneri
Contact Phone	212-691-6969
Contact Email	tanya@thefield.org

Project Information

Project Title	OurGoods Capacity-Building
Project Grant Request Amount	100000.00

Project Summary

OurGoods is a barter network for the creative sector. A new model for cultural production, OurGoods connects members of the creative community to develop mutually-supportive working relationships. We seek Rockefeller funding to fulfill our site's potential as an essential resource for NYC's independent artists.

Our success depends upon 1) attracting enough users to match a diversity of barter requests, 2) building a well-organized, well-designed, fully-functional site, and 3) finding new charitable funding for the site beyond the CIF grant.

A CIF grant will support 1) user recruitment to grow our community, 2) significant user interface improvements based on rigorous usability testing, and 3) capacity-building to help OurGoods replace CIF support with

cities.

PROJECT TIMELINE

Please lay out a project timeline in list form continuing for two years. Please highlight the projected dates for the most important events leading up to your projected dates for deliverables.

FUNDRAISING DELIVERABLES:
Raise $33k by Jul 2012
Raise an additional $65k by Jul 2013

Jul 2011-Jun 2013: Network with colleagues to seek advice, identify 15 potential funders, set up meetings, apply for grants. See budget notes for potential funders already identified.

USERSHIP AND SITE UPDATE DELIVERABLES:
750 active users, 1500 completed barters by Jul 2012
1500 active users, 4500 completed barters by Jul 2013
Deliver six rounds of significant site upgrades at regular intervals

Because the site aims to actively serve artists, we set our goals in terms of active users and completed barters rather than overall site traffic. Active users have full profiles including Needs and Haves, respond to messages from other users, and complete at least one barter a year. Currently the site has over 1400 members, but only about 15% of them are active according to this definition.

We will achieve our goals in part by simply driving more traffic to the site (which requires more user recruitment), and in part by offering a more functional site that increases user activity once they arrive. For instance, we'd like the site to email users with unmet Needs as soon as a new user posts that item as a Have. Some users are having trouble understanding how to use the site. We'd like to offer them more pop-up instructions, FAQ's and tutorials. CIF funding will support recruitment efforts and site upgrades.

User Recruitment:
Jul 2011-Dec 2011: Build relationships with 15 new organizational partners, create user recruitment strategies (see Communications section).
Jan 2012-Jun 2012: Implement recruitment strategies
Jul 2012-Jun 2013: repeat cycle with 15 additional organizations

Site Improvement:
Jul 2011-Sep 2011: Conduct usability interviews with 50 users
Oct 2011: aggregate and analyze interview data, identify comprehensive list of necessary site upgrades, prioritize improvements
Nov 2011: deliver first set of upgrades
Dec 2011-Jan 2012: less intensive round of user interviews to determine success of upgrades
Feb 2012: revise and re-prioritize next round of upgrades
Mar 2012: deliver second set of upgrades
Apr 2012-Jul 2012: Interviews, evaluation, third set of upgrades
Aug 2012-Nov 2012: fourth upgrade cycle
Dec 2012- Mar 2013: fifth upgrade cycle
Apr 2013-Jul 2013: sixth upgrade cycle

Usability testing involves systematic observation of a user performing predetermined tasks, followed by questions about the experience. Testing will help us understand how different types of users interact with the site and where they have trouble.

INNOVATION

Please define what makes this project innovative. What or whose work has inspired or informed this project and strategy (this need not be limited to arts organizations)? How is this project different from other work being done in the field? How is this project different from your past work? Why is your organization appropriate to execute this project? How will this project increase your organization's relevance?

The Resource Sharing Landscape

Resource sharing has exploded in recent years, driven by new technology and

[column 2, lower band]

We need 1) more outreach, informing potential users about the site and getting them excited about barter, 2) design and code upgrades, and 3) time dedicated to fundraising. We have constructed this proposal in direct response to these needs.

Without CIF funding, we will continue to fit OurGoods in between our day jobs. In that scenario, user recruitment and site improvements might happen too slowly to keep up with changing technology and expectations on the internet, making it possible that critical mass may not ever be met.

Liability is a third risk factor. It is important that our users understand the IRS ramifications for barter. We will inform users of their IRS obligations, and make it clear that the site takes no further responsibility. eBay and others have implemented similar solutions with success.

All online interaction, be it Facebook or E-Harmony or Freecycle, carries some risk of an individual taking advantage of a trust community. These sites have modeled basic guidelines for staying safe. We will take these lessons, as well as offering tips on personal safety. We will make it easy for users to alert us to any questionable behavior, and respond quickly to complaints. We will offer mediation services when necessary, and rely on our accountability tools to help users make smart choices for barter partners. Both Carl Tashian's experience at Zip Car and Jen Abrams' tenure at WOW provide expertise and wisdom in shaping a positive community.

BUDGET

If you receive a smaller amount than requested, what would your contingency plan be?

OurGoods is a project of passion for all five co-founders. We have committed many thousands of volunteer hours to this project, and will continue to volunteer our time to make OurGoods successful. Our staff is currently mostly unpaid.

The scale of the project we have proposed assumes that we can begin to pay ourselves modestly for our work. If we are given less than we have requested, we will adjust the scale to reflect that reality. Our usership will grow more slowly, features will be added less frequently, and the overall output and quality of the site will be reduced.

We believe our team has the skills and experience required to make OurGoods a successful stand-alone organization. However, if it serves our mission, we would be open to being absorbed into a larger organization.

Personnel Bios / Co-founders & Partners

Personnel Bio #1

Jen Abrams has sixteen years of arts administration experience. She is a skilled institutional and individual fundraiser, with a background in strategic planning for and management of small and founder-led non-profits. Most recently she has served as Managing Director of Risa Jaroslow and Dancers, a modern dance company and Director of Development for CavanKerry Press, a small poetry press based in New Jersey. From 2000-2003 she was Poetry in The Branches Coordinator at Poets House, where she trained librarians to bring poetry to their patrons and helped develop the program into a replicable model. Prior to that she was Administrative Manager of Guild Complex, a literary-based multicultural multi-arts organization. There Jen was responsible for all administrative operations, including production of 100-120 events per year, for five years. Since 1995, Jen has also served as consultant to small arts organizations, working on strategic planning, fundraising, board development, and human resource issues. Since '99 Jen has been a member of WOW Café Theater, a collectively-run theater in the East Village which has functioned on a barter system for thirty years.

Personnel Bio #2

[column 2, bottom band]

Jen Abrams, Fundraising and User Recruitment. 20 hrs/wk, 52 weeks/yr @ $25/hr = $26k. Paid $16k in Year 1 ($10k in-kind) and $22k in Year 2 ($4k in-kind).

Non-Personnel Expenses:

Travel: Carl Tashian lives in San Francisco, and Rich will travel there to work with him for four days of intensive coding for each site upgrade cycle. This line covers only airfare and per diem. He will stay with Carl.

Supplies: basic office supplies and supplies to make business cards, buttons, etc.

Server space: $67/month in Year 1. $85/month in Year 2. As usership increases, we will increase server space.

Office Expense: Co-founders all work from home. This line is a rough estimate of the cost to operate a small office in Brooklyn for a year, and is included fully as in-kind in Year 1. In Year 2 we will offer co-founders a small reimbursement for in-home office expenses.

(continued)

Column 3

sustainable future funding streams.

OVERVIEW AND STORY

Please describe the proposed project/process. What challenge is this project addressing? What would be the impact of this project and who would benefit from this impact? How will this project contribute to New York City?

The Challenge

Since the 2008 market crash, cultural producers have struggled to come to terms with the new economic landscape. Artists working within organizations have responded in part by drawing together and sharing knowledge. For example, Dance/USA, APAP, and NPN have all addressed the crisis collectively at their annual meetings. Independent artists have no equivalent infrastructure and therefore face significant challenges.

At the same time, independent artists are experts at making do with limited resources. Precisely because we work outside of institutional structures, we are nimble. We test and implement ideas quickly, risking and experimenting regardless of remuneration. We are rich in non-cash resources: time, ideas, and passion. But we are also isolated from each other, making it difficult to form a community to pool those resources.

Our Answer

OurGoods seeks to capitalize on the strengths of independent artists in order to address the challenges independent artists face. On OurGoods, an artist can find everything they need to complete a project within a community of trust and mutual respect that does not rely on market pricing or money.

A wide range of foundation leaders, technical assistance peers, and other artists see OurGoods as an elegant and essential answer to a longstanding problem. The dominant economy values the outputs of our production (completed artworks) far less than it values than the inputs to our production (rehearsal space, materials, skill, time, energy). OurGoods sidesteps this persistent imbalance by helping cultural producers exchange directly with each other, creating an alternate economy based on shared values.

How It Works

Users post "Needs" - what they need to get their creative projects done - as well as "Haves" - the skills, spaces and objects they have to offer. For example, performing artists can find video documentation, a visual artist can find a specialized tool, a musician can borrow a vehicle, a writer can get graphic design help, and an actor can find rehearsal space. A search engine connects users with matching "Haves" and "Needs." Users work out the details of the barter on the site and then create a contract.

Upon completion of the barter both users leave feedback, creating a trust rating. Users can decide who might make a good barter partner based on trust ratings, tenure on the site, number of completed barters, and their profile, which includes a bio and information on the projects they are working on.

Why it works

Our site works for a very practical reason: we offer workable solutions to concrete problems for under-funded artists. But there are also some bigger-picture factors.

Barter causes people to engage with each other, and with the projects that the barter supports. In this context, artists are able to see their work and the work of other artists more expansively. Because support for projects is based on relationships and common goals, rather than on scarcity or the aesthetics of gatekeepers, work that is difficult to fund traditionally can thrive. Project timelines are freed from the funding

[column 3, lower band]

the growth of social media, and by the economic crisis. Though this trend is growing, it is not yet adequately serving independent artists. Existing barter and recycling sites (e.g. Freecycle, Craigslist, SwapTree, Scoodi) focus on manufactured objects and allow users to operate anonymously, without trust. Existing mutual aid systems like time banking (e.g. TINY, Time|Bank) are not widely used by our peers, in part because our peers do not consider all hours as equal for every task. Most sites ignore skill-sharing entirely, and no sites are built exclusively to connect the creative community in non-cash working relationships.

Our Organization

The five co-founders of OurGoods have formed a powerful R&D team, working towards this site for the past two years. Carl Tashian and Jen Abrams joined the group with years of experience in resource sharing communities, and the other three co-founders (Caroline Woolard, Rich Watts, and Louise Ma) have spent the past two years implementing Trade School, (a project of OurGoods, described in the "Communication" section).

As the senior site engineer for ZipCar's first five years, OurGoods co-founder Carl has helped us understand what it took to shift drivers from seeing themselves as owners to seeing themselves as resource-sharers within a community of trust.

WOW Café Theater is another helpful model. WOW is a theater space that has run on a favor-exchange system for 30 years. Co-founder Jen Abrams has been a member of WOW for 11 years, and is helping us understand the nuances of failure and success there.

Giving an Old Idea New Relevance

We offer an innovative economic model for artists by marrying an old idea - barter - with cutting-edge technology. New technologies, especially social networking models, make barter feasible by expanding the quantity and quality of available connections.

Historically, barter has been challenging because it requires two parties with matching haves and needs. Our online platform achieves sufficient diversity to solve this problem, while offering a search engine so users can find each other. Additionally, we acknowledge that exchange is often motivated socially rather than by self-interest. OurGoods provides a space for connection to a wider community, allowing artists to use barter with one another in order to explore and develop collaborative relationships.

OurGoods shifts the focus from "How can artists get more money?" to the deeper question, "How can artists get more resources?" In doing so, we offer more than cash funding offers. The traditional foundation funding model is a zero-sum game - if you get a grant, I don't get it. With a barter model, the higher the participation, the more resources are available for everyone, and the more value is created.

Re-imagining Value

The scarcity principle that drives the dominant economy does not serve cultural producers. Our greatest strengths are not valued by the cash economy. We need a different model.

When money mediates transactions, the value is finite. When we barter, we get the value of the object/service and we form relationships while engaging with the creative landscape. These relationships connect artists to new professional opportunities, form the basis of friendships that support artists' lives as well as their art, and help us respond to changing conditions within our community. These relationships intertwine to create a network that allows artists to make their work regardless of the economic climate.

[column 3, personnel bios]

Caroline Woolard provides project management leadership, as well as a broad vision for the site. She connects a disparate network of interdisciplinary artists, garnering support and community for OurGoods. In her work, Woolard creates infrastructure for mutualism. Just as she made public seating from 2004-2006, OurGoods makes tangible Woolard's commitment to community. Caroline has organized numerous collaborative, interdisciplinary projects, supported by grants from The MacDowell Colony, iLAND, and Watermill in the past year. Caroline is a founding member of a 30-person, 8-year, 8,000 square foot studio space that runs on mutual respect and financial transparency. OurGoods will expand her network of rigorous, honest, interdisciplinary artists.

Personnel Bio #3

The site is being built by Carl Tashian. He provides leadership in site architecture and prodigious coding experience. Carl was the senior site engineer at Zip Car for five years, bringing the business from a one-city, 50-car network to it's current market dominance. He brings a wealth of knowledge about how to create an online environment that elicits respect for shared resources. He is writing a book on incentives for sharing the virtual and environmental commons. In addition to his personal commitment to enabling resource-sharing, he is interested in OurGoods as a case study for the book. Carl sees OurGoods as Zip Car for the artistic community and has already donated $8,000 in coding time towards the alpha site.

Personnel Bio #4

Louise Ma and Rich Watts design the user-interface and printed matter for OurGoods. Companies like The New York Times Online, The Dart Center, and Grand Opening contract their design firm, The Last Studio on Earth. Louise and Rich took OurGoods on as a personal project because they believe it will revolutionize the way artists and designers work together. So far, they have contributed over $10,000 in design work.

Project Budget

Expenses:

$800 ::	$1,000:	Expense: Administrative Project Expenses: Server Space
$8,000 ::	$8,000:	Expense: Administrative Project Expenses: Office Expenses
$1,000 ::	$1,500:	Expense: Administrative Project Expenses: Supplies
$141,000 ::	$141,000:	Expense: Direct Project Expenses: Personnel Expenses
$1,200 ::	$1,500:	Expense: Direct Project Expenses: Travel

Expense Total Year 1: $152,000
Expense Total Year 2: $152,000

Income:

$3,000 ::	$5,000:	Income / Funding: Anticipated / Pending: Government Grants

Collectively-
Initiated

ORGANIZATIONAL BUDGET
OurGoods proposal to the
Mertz-Gilmore Foundation

	ACTUAL 2011	SECURED 2012	PROJECTED 2012
INCOME			
The Field ERPA regrant	$20,000	$0	$0
Rockefeller Cultural Innovation Fund	$25,000	$50,000	$25,000
Rockefeller Brothers Fund	$0	$35,000	$50,000
Mertz-Gilmore Foundation	$0	$0	$30,000
Lower Manhattan Cultural Council	$0	$875	$2,500
Department of Cultural Affairs	$0	$0	$30,000
National Endowment for the Arts	$0	$5,000	$5,000
Individual Donations	$0	$700	$1,000
Earned Income	$5,900	$7,100	$10,000
TOTAL INCOME	$50,900	$98,675	$153,500
EXPENSE			
Personnel			
Co-Executive Director	$7,163	$23,000	$28,000
Co-Executive Director	$11,075	$23,000	$28,000
Graphic Design and User Experience	$8,863	$12,000	$16,000
Site Engineering	$8,028	$20,000	$40,000
Front End Development	$8,028	$11,000	$16,000
Fringe	$0	$0	$4,200
TOTAL PERSONNEL	$43,157	$89,000	$128,000
OTHER			
Fiscal Sponsor Fees	$3,501	$4,329	$9,975
Bank Fees	$77	$100	$100
Office Expense	$74	$100	$200
Travel and Transportation	$583	$200	$600
Server Fees	$543	$725	$1,000
Marketing	$283	$985	$2,550
Consultants	$585	$600	$3,000
Materials and Supplies	$1,050	$1,000	$1,200
Partner Organizations	$0	$0	$3,000
Misc	$10	$1,000	$3,000
TOTAL OTHER	$6,706	$9,039	$24,625
TOTAL EXPENSE	$49,863	$98,039	$152,625
Surplus/Deficit	$1,037	$636	$875
IN KIND			
Personnel	$76,843	$31,000	$8,000

Budget Notes
Income: All income for FY12 is secured. Income for FY13 is projected, with the exception of the Rockefeller CIF funds, which are secured. The grant from The Field was a limited-time program, and is no longer available. The grant from the NEA in FY12 was a partnership grant for $10k. $5k of that grant came to OurGoods.org, and the other $5k went to our partner organization, Fourth Arts Block.

Personnel: OurGoods.org is ramping up its compensation to a more sustainable level. In FY12, all personnel will work as independent contractors. By FY13 the Co-Executive Directors will become salaried employees. The fringe line reflects taxes for those two positions. The Graphic Design, Site Engineering and Front End Development positions relate directly to the building of the website, and will continue to be contract positions. The FY13 budget shows increased workload based on the activites included in this proposal.

Other: Server fees increase as traffic on the site increases. Marketing increases significantly in FY13 to reflect project activities. Consultants increases in FY13 to reflect the video portion of the proposed project.

In Kind: This line shows the difference between the market value of labor provided to OurGoods.org and the payments to the OurGoods.org team. In order to make OurGoods.org sustainable, we need to significantly reduce the number of hours the team is working for free. This line shows our progress toward sustainable compensation.

From this moment on, Jen and I worked in-person, at her house, around two days a week, and we worked remotely as things came in, throughout the week. We made the following kinds of agreements with Rich, Louise, and Carl:

```
June 12, 2011
Hi all,

Rockefeller expects three major site updates in
the next 12 months. We have $16k for each of you
to make that happen.

1. What we're envisioning is three 10-day
coding caves: one now, one in December and one
next March/April. The $16k covers those three
sessions (plus some travel money). Can you tell
us: Are those three coding cave sessions doable
for you guys? When would you know? Is Louise's
concurrent availability important and if so,
Louise, are you available?

2. If they are doable, when could the first
one happen? What can you envision getting accom-
plished in the first session? In the second?

Looking forward to hearing from you—we're
incredibly excited to suddenly have all
this momentum!

Jen
```

While, in 2011, OurGoods.org had more money that we could have imagined a year earlier, it was not enough funding to keep the best computer engineers around. By the end of 2012, Carl had many offers for web development jobs, and they all paid so much more than OurGoods.org. He eventually took one, and we took years trying to find developers who could work at the same level that he had. We learned that we would have to pay a developer to rewrite much of the code that Carl had written, to update it, which meant that we were spending money to maintain the site. We had not realized that you could spend


```
         NOTE:
We also applied for funding
from the CUE Foundation and
from Creative Capital, among
many other applications, but
those applications did not
advance very far. I began to
understand that there is a
real difference between a
service organization and an
art project, and that
OurGoods.org was a nonprofit
in the eyes of funders.
```

money without adding functionality to the site. We learned a lot about the expectations that developers have about creating the smallest "feature" possible and that we really had to pair down our expectations of the site in order to save money.

By 2014, Rich Watts had started his own company and could not focus on OurGoods.org, and Louise Ma and I were both deeply involved in other work. By 2016, we decided to shut down the software.

> June 17, 2016
> Beloved OurGoods team,
>
> It's time to shut down our software. Caroline sent me this article by Christina Xu called Every Project Deserves a Good Death (2015) a while ago, and I found it to be quite profound. I've been thinking about it ever since.
>
> Caroline and I have had a bunch of conversations, all of which lead to this: It's time to shut down our software. So we wanted you to see the letter we are sending to our members next week before it went out. We also wanted to tell you that we are going to work on some kind of documentation of the project that will live at www.ourgoods.org, so that the project will not just disappear.
>
> I wanted to tell you (and I'm sure Caroline will concur), that the five of us changed my life. OurGoods as a project changed my life, but before OurGoods was OurGoods, it was the five of us, holed up for an uncountable number of hours, hammering out visions and relationships, and what is life if not that. I'll be forever grateful to you all, and you will always be my family, regardless of how much

As individual skills, spaces, and items for barter are aggregated on OurGoods, we will be able to see where we need to build capacity in our community, individually and as a network.

—Caroline Woolard and Jen Abrams, from Rockefeller Foundation's New York City Cultural Innovation Fund Grant Application, 2011

Study

distance and time might grow between any of us
in particular.

Together (and with so much love),
Jen

In December of 2009, Rich, Louise, and I decided to run an experiment "on the side" of our work with OurGoods.org. Jen and Carl did not have time to take on another project. Then, something unusual happened. This "experiment on the side" ended up being far more popular than OurGoods.org, lasting ten years, being replicated in many countries, and involving over 20,000 people—all without any funding.

Rich had been invited to do something in a storefront space, and he opened up the opportunity to Louise and I. We decided to run a learning-space on a barter. We called it "Trade School," with the "trade" being about exchange, but also, about "trades," or, vocational education. The one-to-one barter network OurGoods.org led us to start TradeSchool.coop, a self-organized learning platform that ran on a barter system from 2009–2019: http://tradeschool.coop/story.

This "experiment on the side" ended up being far more popular

It started as a month-long storefront space with classes during nights and weekends, but it ended up being a long-term project. I think it worked because the idea solved three primary issues we were having at OurGoods.org. We felt that one-on-one barters were difficult for artists, designers, and craftspeople because they were: (1) open-ended, online negotiations between two people about what is a "fair" exchange, (2) requiring that both people show up in person, and (3) no clear time or location to meet. At TradeSchool.coop, students agreed to bring whatever the teacher requested, if half of the students did not show up, the teacher would still receive something in exchange, and we hosted a beautiful space where strangers could meet.

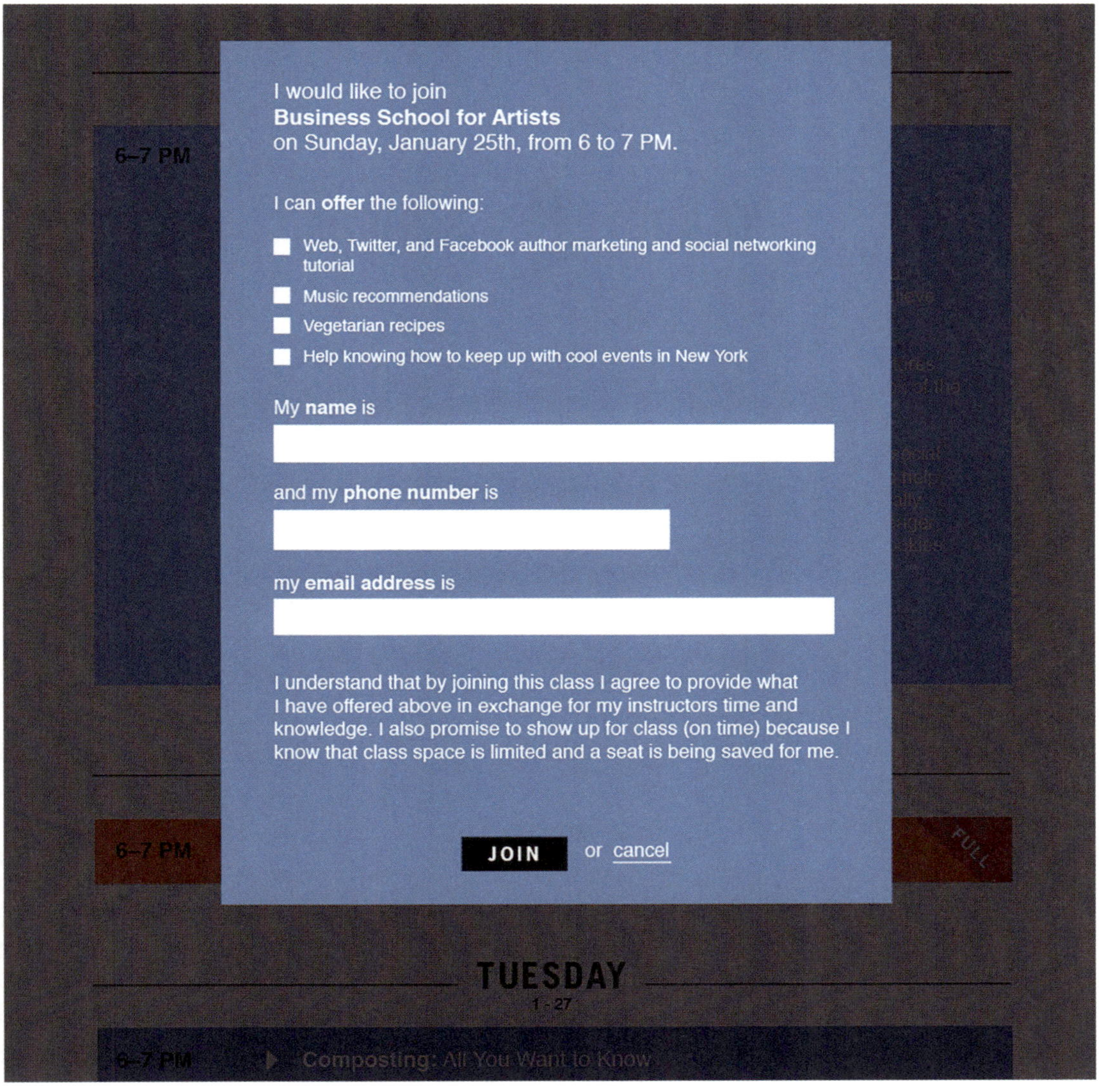

fig. 3-15
TradeSchool.coop user experience.

TRADE SCHOOL

TODAY
1 - 25

6–7 PM ▼ Business School for Artists

Taught by Amy Whitaker

An introduction to finance and economics for artists. Much the same way everyone is an artist, everyone is a business person. This isn't a class in how to do your taxes or market your work but how people believe economics works as a system.

I have both an MBA and an MFA in painting. I used to give these lectures as lunchtime talks to fellow painters at the Slade in London. The book of the lectures is sold at Printed Matter.

To barter, I would like: web, Twitter, Facebook author marketing and social networking tutorial; music recommendations, vegetarian recipes, and help knowing how to keep up with cool events in New York. I am functionally 85 when it comes to understanding new-fangled technology, but an eager student. Or, you can volunteer to bring snacks or drinks to class. Cookies and beer are traditional.

JOIN

MONDAY
1 - 26

6–7 PM ▶ Splinters and Logs: Building Out a Studio Space — FULL

TUESDAY
1 - 27

6–7 PM ▶ Composting: All You Want to Know

6–7 PM ▶ Preserving Function in an Ornamental Wilderness: Foraging and Preserving "Wild" Foods from NYC Streets

WEDNESDAY
2 -1

8–10 PM ▶ Demonstration District

6–7 PM ▶ The nuts and bolts guide to putting together an exhibition

6–7 PM ▶ FORESIGHT IS 2020 — FULL

Collectively-
Initiated

I worked with Cooper Union graduates (Rich Watts and Louise Ma at first, and also, later on, Christhian Diaz and Aimee Lutkin), as well as generous and rigorous artist and computer engineer Or Zubalsky, and the incredible systems-thinker and curator Rachel Vera Steinberg. I have written about this work at length in a book I edited called *TRADE SCHOOL: 2009–2019*.

As majority Cooper graduates, we connected the cost of tuition to the education a student receives. I like to say that there is a "pedagogy of payment" that must be explored in the economies and administrative structures of schools, accredited or not. Through TradeSchool.coop, I learned from great educators and helped groups open similar self-organized schools to understand the open-source software and the principles of self-organization that we were using in New York and adapt it according to their contexts in thirty cities internationally, from Athens to Pietermaritzburg, Glasgow, and Quito. My excitement for education has to do as much with economic justice and self-governance as it has to do with pedagogy; for me, they are inseparable.

While OurGoods.org and TradeSchool.coop ran for many years, we eventually closed both projects due to a lack of market-rate funding for the top-notch computer engineers who are required to keep the software up-to-date. We simply could not raise enough money through grant funding to pay computer engineers, and we did not establish a nonprofit board with people who would regularly give us money to sustain the software and the administrative work required to make the barter network run online and in person.

fig. 3-16
Front end of TradeSchool.coop website, designed by Louise Ma and Rich Watts, 2010.

Here is some writing I did in 2015 (published in the book *TRADE SCHOOL: 2009–2019*) which I hope helps people think through the implications of starting an online platform.

Collectively-
Initiated

SO YOU WANT TO START AN
ONLINE PLATFORM
By Caroline Woolard, 2015

Dear founder,

I'm glad to hear about your idea for
an online platform. Congratulations!
I'm sure we both agree that a diversity of opinions is a good thing, and
that platforms should benefit their
participants, as participation is what
makes an online platform valuable.
What follows are a few questions that
I wish someone had asked me when I
started four multi-year projects.

I am sharing these four questions,
along with bits of advice, because I
hope that you will succeed in contrib-
uting toward the cooperative culture we
want to see. To live in a democratic
society, we all need more experiences
of democracy at work, in school, and
at home. Thank you for helping push
the cooperative movement forward.

You will notice that a lot of what
follows also speaks to founders of
non-profit organizations or social
impact businesses. I am writing this
especially for young, educational-
ly-privileged people who have big
ideas but are newcomers to the neighborhood they live in. This reflects
my own experience as a college graduate, waking up to working class histories in New York City while trying
to build cooperative software and
resource-sharing projects.

It took me a while to learn outside
my immediate group of friends, to
reach beyond the academy and beyond
the Internet to learn.

1. CAN YOU MAKE A PLATFORM FOR AN
EXISTING CO-OP?

In a culture that values ideas over
practices, it might be hard to see
the existing cooperatives around you.
But, I promise you, there are many
systems of mutual aid and cooperation
nearby. These "platforms" are systems
of self-determination and survival
are often created by people who have
been systematically denied resources
through institutionalized racism,
sexism, and classism (read about
redlining if you don't know what that
is). The credit unions, land trusts,
worker-owned businesses, rotating
lending clubs (susus), community
gardens, and freedom schools in your
neighborhood may not have great websites, but they are incredible cooperative platforms that you can learn
from and with.

These initiatives are often not life-
style choices made by educationally
privileged people, and will therefore
not be written up in *The New York
Times*, but they are robust and powerful community networks with organizers
who might be interested in adding an
online platform to their work. Here
is an often-overlooked challenge: try
to join and add to existing cooperative platforms, rather than building your own from scratch. The result

will likely last longer as it will be informed by the deep wisdom of existing cooperative community norms, roles, and rules. Perhaps we need something like the Center for Urban Pedagogy for cooperative software—an organization that matches grassroots groups with developers to build software that is driven by community need.

2. WHO WILL BUILD THE COOPERATIVE PLATFORM?

Let's say that organizers at your local credit union, land trust, cooperative developer, community garden, or freedom school are interested in building an online cooperative platform to add to their ongoing work. Or, they confirm your hunch that the cooperative platform you want to build is necessary. How will you form a team that can make this software come to life?

I have found that innovation occurs most readily in small teams with shared goals but different skill sets. Big groups, on the other hand, are good for education and organizing work, and for refining existing platforms. But to innovate, I like to work in core teams of three to six people, as this allows for deep relationships, shared memory, and relatively fast decision-making, since each person can speak for ten to twenty minutes per hour in meetings. The collective Temporary Services says that every person you add to the group doubles the amount of time it takes to make a decision. So, I say: build a small group of rigorous, generous experts whose past work demonstrates that they are aligned with the cooperative platform you want to make. Ask the larger group to consent to the expertise of your small team, and ensure that your small team will make room for feedback from the big group along the way.

Now, build your team! Find people who are better than you in their area of expertise. At the very least, you will need: 1) a Project Manager to help with scheduling events, facilitating meetings, and tracking budgets; 2) a Communications Pro to craft a clear message and recruit people to try out the platform as it develops; 3) a Designer (or two) to make the front end beautiful, 4) a Developer (or two) to develop the software and annotate it so that other people can add to it in the future; and 5) Advisors—one per area of expertise above, as well as more who have strong connections to the community you aim to work with. Meet with your core team on a weekly, if not daily basis, and with your advisors on a monthly or quarterly basis.

You are likely the Communications Pro or the Project Manager, since you are reading this letter. Find advisors who are retired, or far older than you, and who have seen the field change and are widely respected for their work. Learn about programming languages— which languages (Ruby, Python, etc.) have active development communities, and which languages are most likely to

be interoperable with future cooperative platforms. Find developers who
have worked on social justice projects
in the past. If you are a non-profit
with limited funds, watch out for
developers who want to get paid market
rate, as developers and project managers (like you) should believe in the
project equally and should take an
equal pay cut. Watch out for developers who say they can build the site
quickly in a week or two, during a
public "hackathon" or "sprint,"
because if they do that, the site will
be a sketch, not capable of growing.
The site needs to be built well,
annotated well, and be understandable
to future developers.

3. HOW MUCH TIME AND MONEY DO YOU HAVE?

As you build your team, be honest with
yourself about your existing priorities, and the likelihood that your
life will change in the coming months
or in a year or two. To gauge our
availability to work on TradeSchool.
coop, we did an exercise where each
core member wrote a list of their top
life priorities, including family,
friends, health, volunteer projects,
art, hobbies, and day jobs. This
allowed us to be more honest with
ourselves and each other about the
amount of time we had to work on our
project, which parts of our life were
unknown, and also our reasons for
doing the project.

Plan for turnover by having clear
systems of documentation and open
conversations about how to bring in
people who might join the core team
when someone has to leave. Be sure
that the Developer(s) code in teams,
or that an Advisor looks over the
code, so that it is intelligible to
your other Developers. Be sure that
the Project Manager and Communications
Pro share leadership and responsibility, crafting a clear process for new
people to join the core team, moving
from roles of assistance to core
membership in months. After a year of
organizing TradeSchool.coop, I wrote a
manual to make sure our systems were
clear. Ask yourself: do you want to
get it done, or do you want to get it
done your way? This is the question
that Jen Abrams, a co-founder of
OurGoods.org, brought to us from a
decade at the collectively run performance space WOW Café Theater.

4. WHAT IF YOU RAN EVENTS AND HIRED
A COMMUNITY ORGANIZER INSTEAD OF
BUILDING SOFTWARE?

Last of all, consider the possibility
that you could make a greater impact
on cooperative culture and
resource-sharing in your community by
hosting events rather than building a
new cooperative platform online.
Software does not run itself; it must
be maintained and upgraded by developers who can easily make tons of money
working on non-cooperative platforms.

Remember that people won't take the
time to learn a new app unless they
need it daily. Remember that people

are used to Facebook, Google, Twitter,
and sites that have legions of developers working around the clock.
Remember that hire number three at
Airbnb was a lobbyist. If you are
starting out, build the smallest
feature and do not add to it. It will
be hard enough to maintain and upgrade
that small feature.

Be honest about your ability to put in
long hours and to raise the funds to
sustain the development and constant
upgrading of online networks for
years. Until we have cooperative
investment platforms for cooperative
ventures, you will have to look for
philanthropic support or venture
capital that might alter your mission
and that will rarely sustain the
initiative for years.

If you can't raise $300,000 a year for
a core team of five, don't build a
demo site that barely works or buggy
software that won't last—organize
great events and build community! You
can use existing online platforms that
your members already know. You can use
your funds to pay a community organizer instead. Not only will you
sustain the livelihood of a wonderful
person, but the knowledge built in the
community won't return a 404 Server
Error when someone needs help next year.

In cooperation,
Caroline Woolard

fig. 3-17
The TradeSchool.coop open
source code, which was
written and maintained by
artist, musician, and
developer Or Zubalsky from
2010-2019, enabled the
website to be adapted to local
TradeSchool.coop chapters,
including chapters in thirty
cities internationally.

```python
class Branch(Location):
    """
    A Branch is a chapter of TS in a specific location (usually city/region).
    """


class Venue(Location):
    """
    Venue represent physical locations where Trade School events take place.
    """


class Person(AbstractBaseUser, PermissionsMixin, Base):
    """
    A custom model in place of Django's auth.User model.
    A Person in the Trade School system can be an organizer,
    teacher, and student. Their interaction with the system
    determines their roles:
    When a person registers to a class, they are acknowledged as a student.
    When a person teaches an approved class, they are acknowledged as a teacher
    When a person is given is_staff=True, they are acknowledged as an organizer
    """


class Organizer(Person):
    """
    Organizers are Person objects that have is_staff set to True.
    Conceptually, organizers are the people who use the admin backend
    to run a chapter of Trade School and help others run theirs.
    """


class Teacher(Person):
    """
    Teachers are Person objects that have taught at least one course.
    The distinction is made so organizers can find teacher profiles
    more easily on the admin backend. Teachers can belong to Students
    and Organizers as well.
    """


class Student(Person):
    """
    Students are Person objects that are registered to least one course.
    The distinction is made so organizers can find student profiles
    more easily on the admin backend. Students can belong to Teachers
    and Organizers as well.
    """
```

```python
class BarterItem(Base):
    """
    Barter items are requested by teachers when submitting a course
    and are selected by students registering to a course.
    """


class Course(ScheduledEvent):
    """
    A one time scheduled class that is taught by a teacher in a TS Branch.
    Course is currently the main model that Trade School facilitates:
    A teacher submits a class proposal through the frontend class submission
    form on a branch's website. The proposal includes the attributes of a
    ScheduledEvent model, a list of barter items and the teacher's information.
    The class proposal is either approved or not by the branch's organizers.
    Approved courses appear on the branch's website so students can register
    to them. Students register by agreeing to bring one or more of the items
    that were requested by the teacher.
    A Course also has 7 types of emails that are sent automatically:
        teacherconfirmation: Sent to the teacher to confirm a successful
            course submission. Also includes a link to edit the course.
        teacherclassapproval: Sent to the teacher to notify them the course
            was approved by the organizers.
        studentreminder: Sent to a student to confirm a successful course
            registration.
        studentconfirmation: Sent to all registered students before the course
            is scheduled to start to remind them it's happening and what items
            they said they would bring. It also includes a link to unregister.
        teacherreminder: Sent to the teacher before the course is scheduled
            to start to remind them that it's happening.
        teacherfeedback: Sent to a teacher after the course took place with
            a link to leave feedback.
        studentfeedback: Sent to all registered students after the course took
            place with a link to leave feedback.
    """


class Feedback(Base):
    """
    Feedback is collected after courses take place.
    Emails are sent to both students and teacher after a course has taken place
    with a URL to a form where they can leave feedback on a course.
    Feedback is saved anonymously for students. The only indication is whether
    it was received by the teacher or by one of the students.
    """
```

Mediating

For both OurGoods.org and TradeSchool.coop, collaborators Louise Ma and Rich Watts made exceptionally beautiful print material (business cards, posters, fliers) as well as well-designed websites. Or Zubalsky wrote the code for TradeSchool.coop twice, taking months on end to make sure that the website worked in multiple languages (for text going right to left as well as left to right) around the world.

Rich Watts made sure that we took high quality photographs of every event we held, as well as at many of the classes we organized (when students were open to it). In other collectives, such as BFAMFAPhD [see chapter 5], we have not prioritized documentation of events, exhibitions, or workshops, and I think that the lack of great photographs hurts our grant-writing and exhibitions, and makes presentations more difficult.

... education has to do as much with economic justice and self-governance as it has to do with pedagogy

We were approached by documentary filmmakers Alex Mallis and David Felix Sutcliffe who offered to make videos about our work. Thousands of people learned about our work by watching these videos on our website. From that moment on, I knew that I would commission a video for every multi-year project, as it was one of the best ways to communicate with a wide range of people.

In 2009, when OurGoods.org and TradeSchool.coop were starting, I did not think it was important that we were based in New York City. Looking back, I can see that the press we got was directly related to the people who attended our events from art, design, and technology fields and who lived in New York City and worked in the media. We would not have been written up in *The New York Times*, *The New Yorker*, *The Nation*, *Hyperallergic*, *Fast Company*, or *The Wall Street Journal* if we were not based in a cultural-center with so many media outlets. We continue to be asked to re-open both barter networks, but we do not have the capacity to run them. Before closing TradeSchool.coop, I compiled stories from people around the world to share what we learned in the book *TRADE SCHOOL: 2009–2019*.

Additional thanks to:
Katherine Pradt (Writer), Carl Tashian (Developer), Lauren Voswinkel (Developer), Meerkat Media Cooperative (Video Editor), Ann Chen (Event Facilitator), Saul Melman (Producer, Organizer), Alex Mallis (Videographer), Daniel Dordelly (Event Facilitator), Pritha RaySicar (Event Facilitator).

4

Exchange Café

Exchange Café was an immersive installation and social space created in 2013 by Caroline Woolard at MoMA that was dedicated to exchange-based practices. The café encouraged visitors to question notions of reciprocity, value, and property through shared experiences. Tea from the anarchist Feral Trade Network, milk from prison abolitionists at Milk Not Jails, and honey from BeeSpace—products sourced by Woolard that directly engage the solidarity economy—were available by exchange. Instead of paying with legal tender, Exchange Café patrons were invited to use a currency with fill-in-the-blank sections which prompted visitors to write down their demands and desires. Exchange Café also featured an interactive participatory archive, a matrix of exchange projects, and a library of books and ephemera.

At Exchange Café, visitors were greeted by waitstaff with direct experience working in, with, and for solidarity economies. With the Café as a learning format, education happened in relation to lived experience. Waitstaff included Tychist Baker and Lauren Melodia, organizers for Milk Not Jails; Kenneth Edusei, an organizer for participatory budgeting in Brooklyn; and Carla Aspenberg, Forest Purnell, and Amelia Winger-Bearskin, artists engaged in practices of reciprocity.

What if the café products were as radical in practice as the formal ideas in the artworks themselves?

Exchange Café was a social space dedicated to the power of one-to-one agreement. An emergent archive about one-on-one engagement invited contributions on the wall and the website Woolard created with Amelia Winger-Bearskin, TheExchangeArchive.com, demonstrating that artworks emerge in dialogue between people, not in isolation.

Since money, as the existing and active concept of value, confounds and confuses all things, it is the general confounding and confusing of all things — the world upside-down — the confounding and confusing of all natural and human qualities. He who can buy bravery is brave, though he be a coward. As money is not exchanged for any one specific quality, for any one specific thing, or for any particular human essential power, but for the entire objective world of man and nature, from the standpoint of its possessor it therefore serves to exchange every quality for every other, even contradictory, quality and object: it is the fraternisation of impossibilities. It makes contradictions embrace.

—Karl Marx, Economic and Philosophic Manuscripts, 1844

2012-2013 MoMA
museum as living experiment
Director of MoMA, Glenn Lowry,
    salary of $1.8 million
Occupy Wall Street 2011
2007/2008 Financial Crisis
Banks get bailed out.
They can take our jobs,
    but not our skills.
No money.

elite institution
admission ticket over $20,
    too expensive
museum not open after work
white walling
colonial
barter
swap
local currencies
trade

exchange
mutual aid
gift
associations
1:1
nonlinear time
yawns
two people
eyes
folded paper
clamshell
bilateral symmetry
dyad

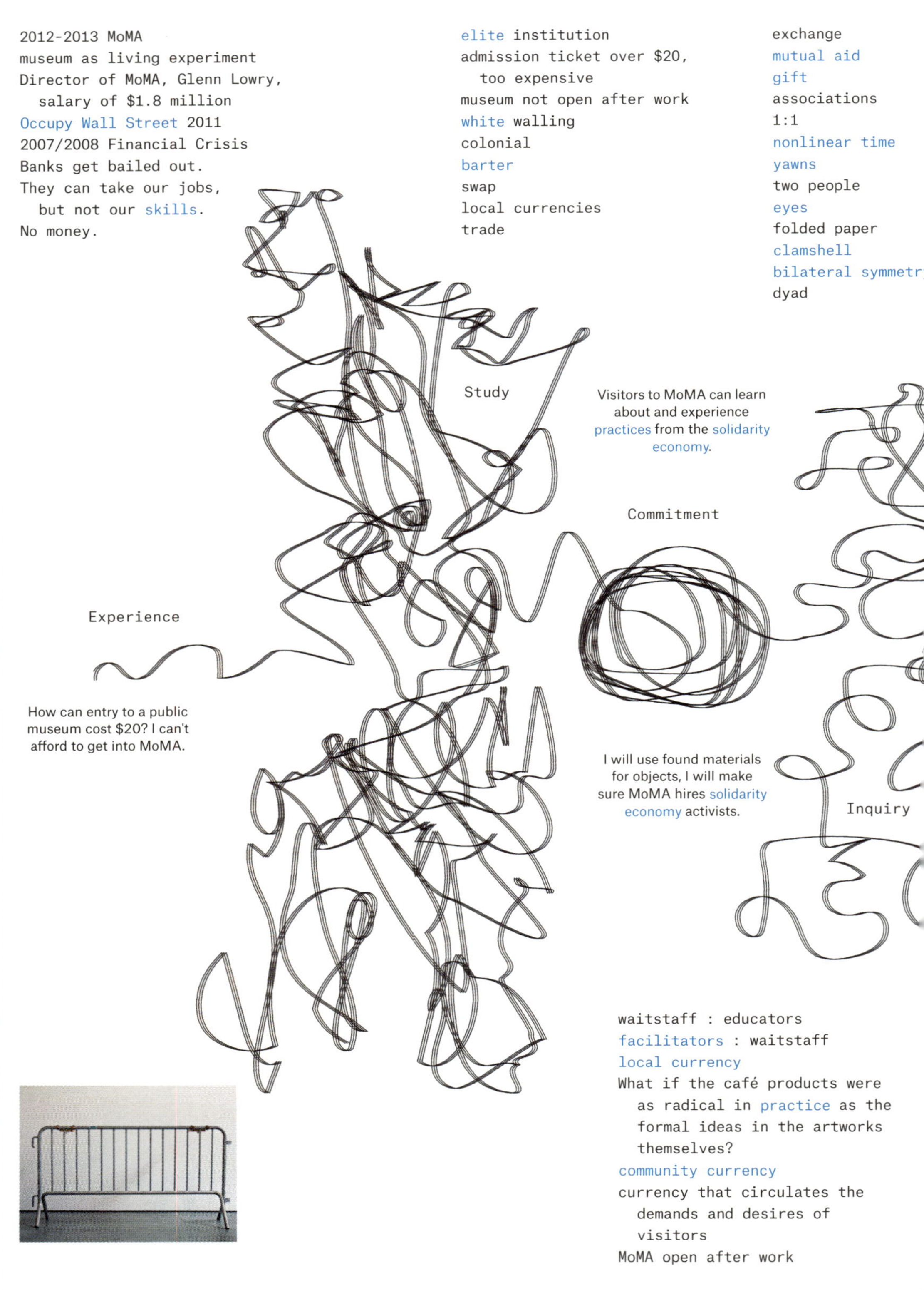

Visitors to MoMA can learn
about and experience
practices from the solidarity
economy.

How can entry to a public
museum cost $20? I can't
afford to get into MoMA.

I will use found materials
for objects, I will make
sure MoMA hires solidarity
economy activists.

waitstaff : educators
facilitators : waitstaff
local currency
What if the café products were
    as radical in practice as the
    formal ideas in the artworks
    themselves?
community currency
currency that circulates the
    demands and desires of
    visitors
MoMA open after work

Institutional
Invitation

life experience of visitors
international
exchange value vs. use value
visitors at MoMA are tired,
  sitting
tourism
visitors in the café are awake
solidarity economy
Eva Zeisel
Feral Trade Network
local honey
Milk Not Jails
Kate Rich
power
Carolina Caycedo
Martha Rosler

Paul Ramirez Jonas
Dave McKenzie
Nina Katchadourian
Adrian Piper
structural violence becomes
  interpersonal
Mierle Laderman Ukeles
police barricades on 5th Ave.
Germaine Koh

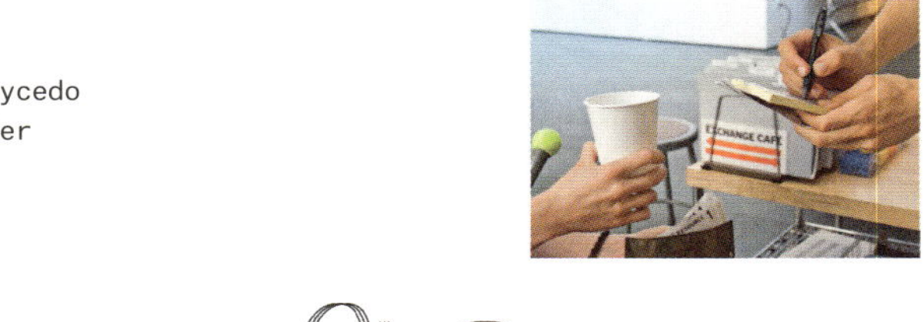

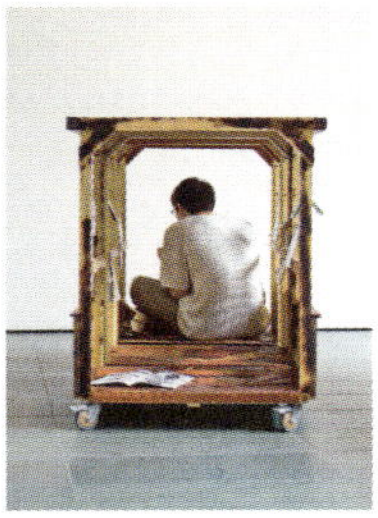

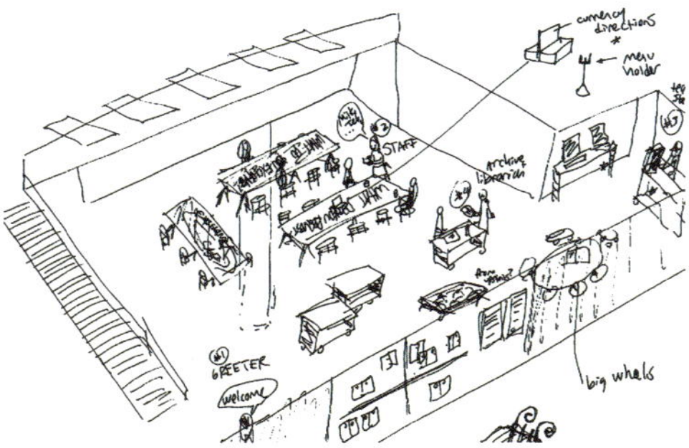

A month-long project, at
the invitation of MoMA.

Timeframe

Currency can circulate
the demands and
desires of visitors.

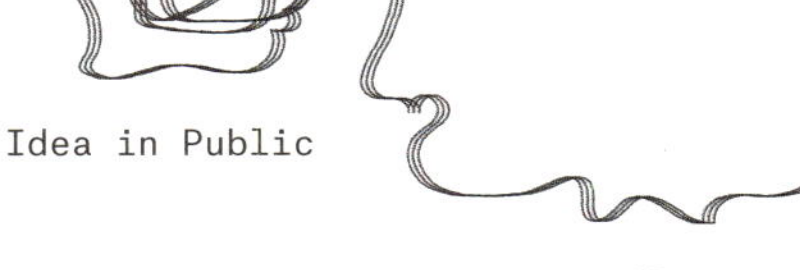

Idea in Public

Reflect

Experiment

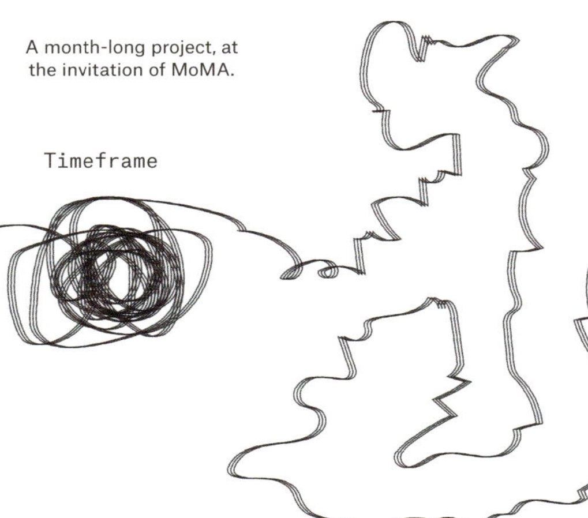

café as format
police barricade as bench
currency
uniforms for waitstaff
hiding furniture
sit inside it
website
events

What, Who, How: Exchange Café

Sheetal Prajapati is an educator, artist, and advisor working across the field of art and public engagement. Sheetal is currently on faculty at School of Visual Arts (New York) in the MFA Fine Arts program and works as an advisor and consultant in the field through her agency Lohar Projects. Previously, Sheetal served as the first Director of Public Engagement at Pioneer Works and the Assistant Director of Learning and Artists Initiatives at The Museum of Modern Art.

Sheetal Prajapati, 2019

a practice
A habitual application of actions or processes with purpose.
an exchange
A mutual offering and reception.
a system
A form of social, economic, or political organization practiced by a group of people.

In 2013, The Museum of Modern Art (MoMA) invited Caroline Woolard to be part of a pilot initiative called Artists Experiment. Artists Experiment took the form of long-term collaborations between contemporary artists and the public programs team to present audiences with experimental, unexpected, and thoughtful experiences with art. Through this collaboration, we made Exchange Café.

What was Exchange Café?
- a social space
- a participatory artwork
- a resource center to consider connected historical and social narratives
- an educational lab to discover and contribute new content
- a collaborative studio to create value together
- a network of people
- a barter system to exchange goods and services
- a free public space for all

Who was Exchange Café?
Exchange Café was a collaboration between and among all organizers, participants, and contributors. Invited project collaborators and workers led workshops, built a digital platform, made and provided goods and services,

Institutional
Invitation

designed currency, contributed research, facilitated action and together welcomed the public to be part of a rhizomatic system— wherein each act of exchange produced multiplying possibilities for expanded forms of engagement and production.

How was Exchange Café?
Exchange Café proposed and welcomed visitors to participate with or activate the space. The crux of these interactions examined the ways we define value. The café served tea, milk, and honey to visitors in exchange for currency created by participants. Each currency note was valued by a set of offerings and needs generated by each visitor. As currency was exchanged for tea, a collection of needs and offerings was created. This collection of currency expressed the ways each participant valued both their skills and their needs—setting up both a personal and communal space for exchange between people, goods, and ideas.

Since this project, I have spent time considering the various modes of exchange that exist in my work with others. The chart below illustrates my own thinking about the experience of the café and my current work.

EXCHANGE AS PRACTICE	PRACTICE OF EXCHANGE	SYSTEMS AS EXCHANGE
practice has intention	exchange produces value	systems are structures
exchange is a form of communication	value is a collective agreement	production is cooperative
develop new forms of currency	practice internal & external negotiation	embed contingencies
repetition is iterative	exchange rates are contextual	structures make discrete spaces
practice communication	employ porous transactions	make space for humanity
exchange between exchanges	a practice of process	a system of possibilities

IMAGINE A GROUP GATHERING

Institutional
Invitation

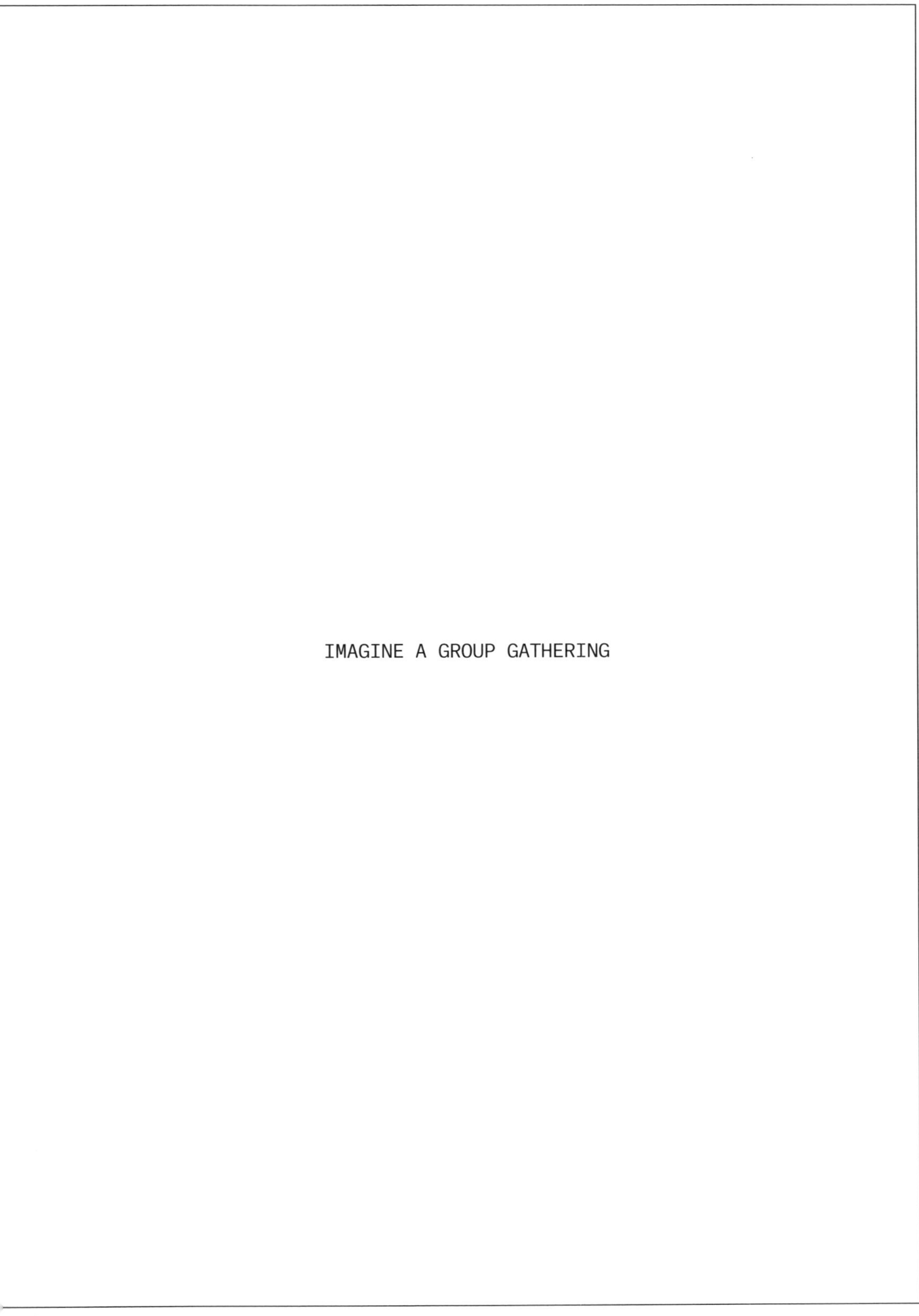

IMAGINE A GROUP GATHERING

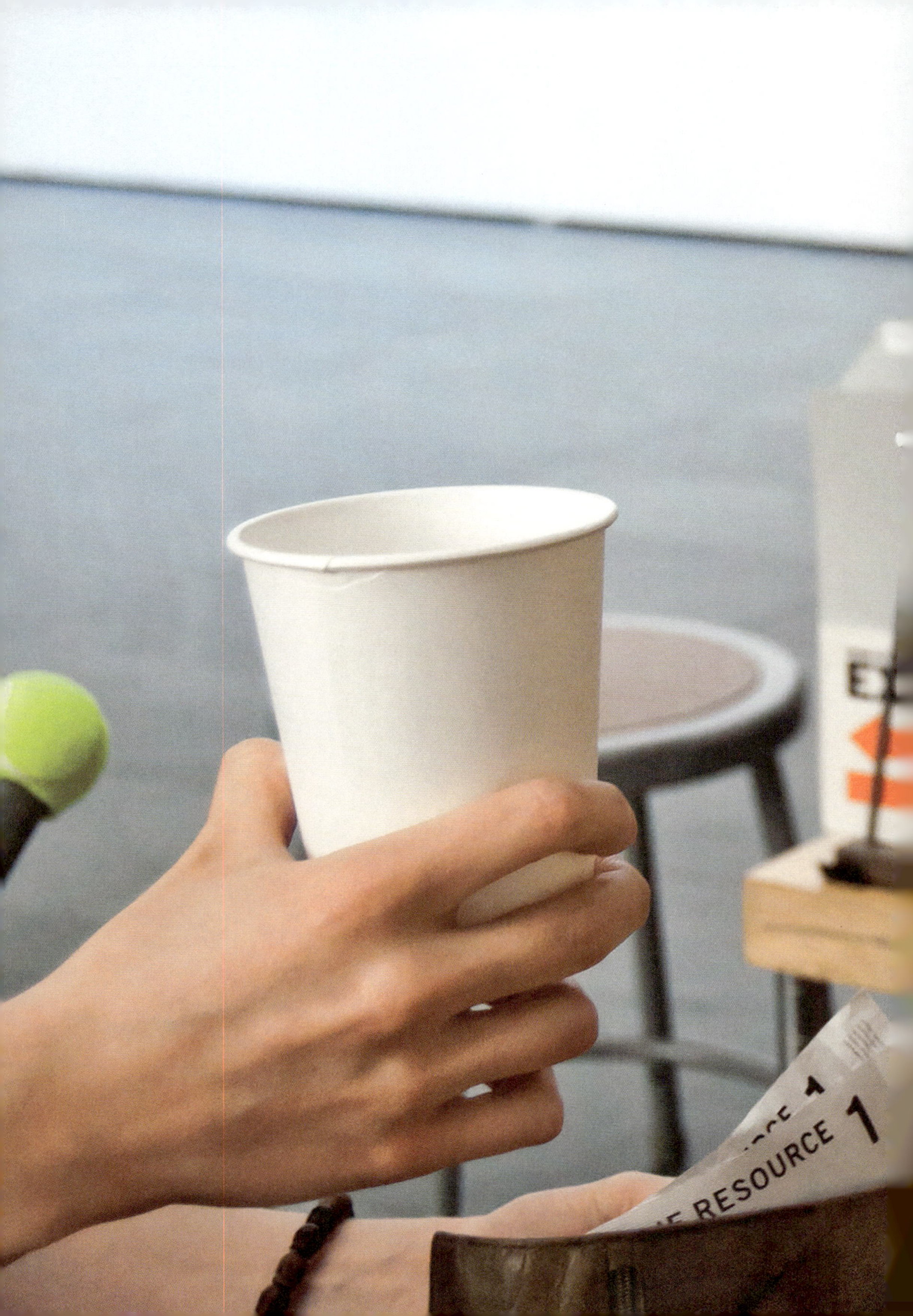
RESOURCE 1

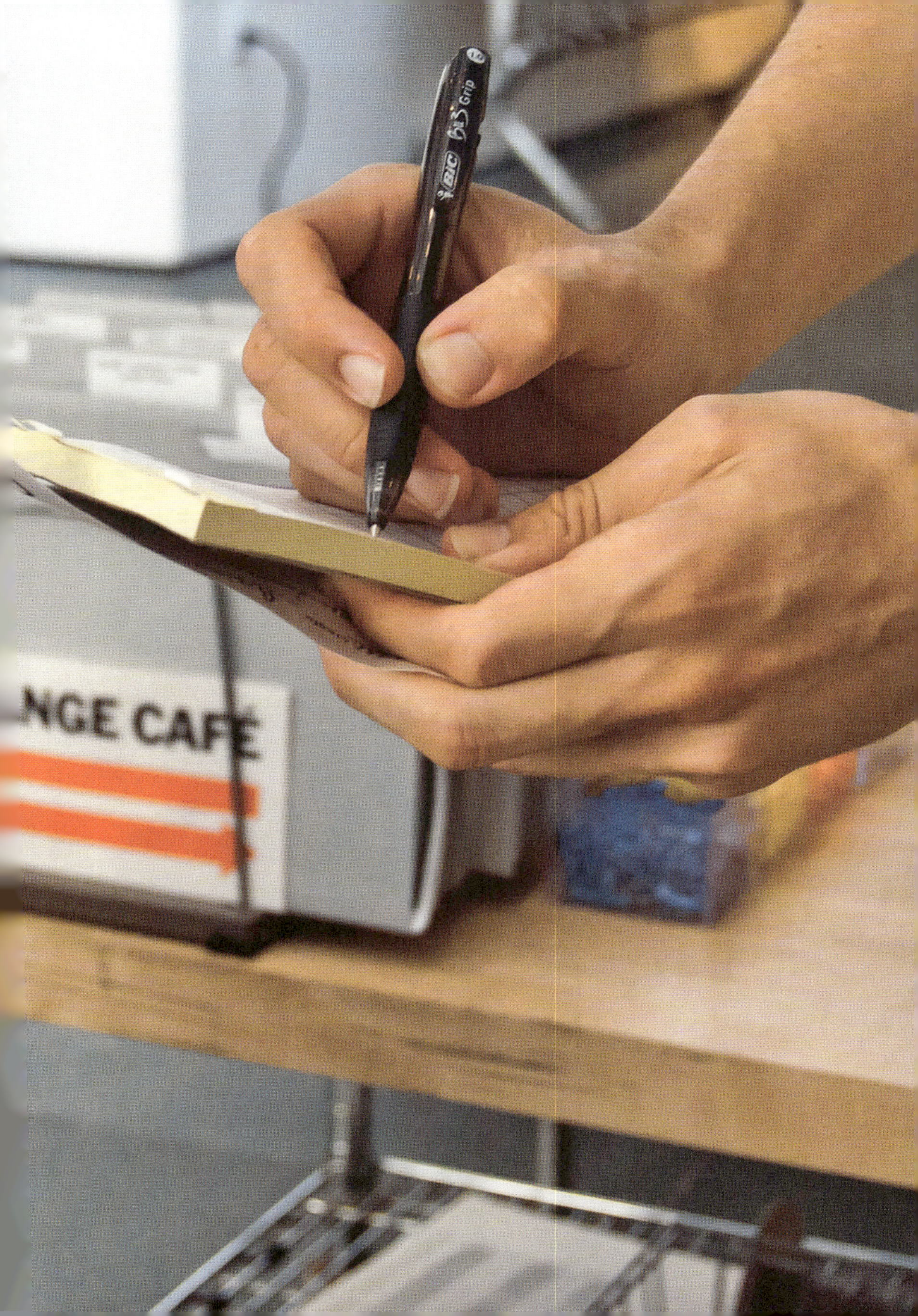
NGE CAFÉ
BIC
Grip

fig. 4-1 (overleaf)
Resources, 2013, tyvek, silk-screen, signature, community currency exchange, performers, 2 $\frac{3}{5}$ × 6 $\frac{1}{10}$ inches. Courtesy of the artist and MoMA: Artists Experiment. Photo by Ryan Tempro.

fig. 4-2
Resources, 2013, tyvek, silkscreen, signature, community currency exchange, performers, 2 $\frac{3}{5}$ × 6 $\frac{1}{10}$ inches. Courtesy of the artist and MoMA: Artists Experiment. Photo by Ryan Tempro.

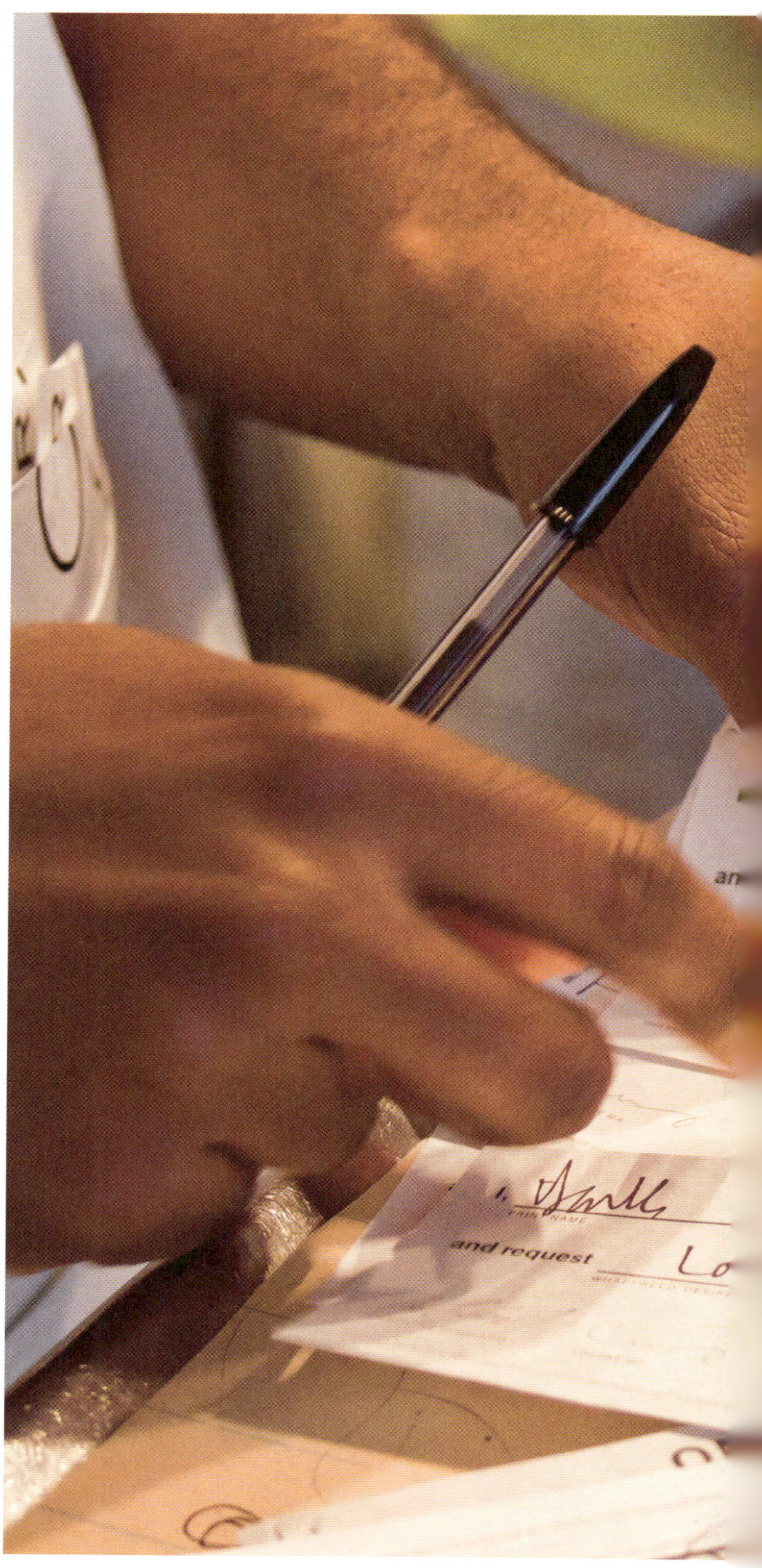

Institutional
Invitation

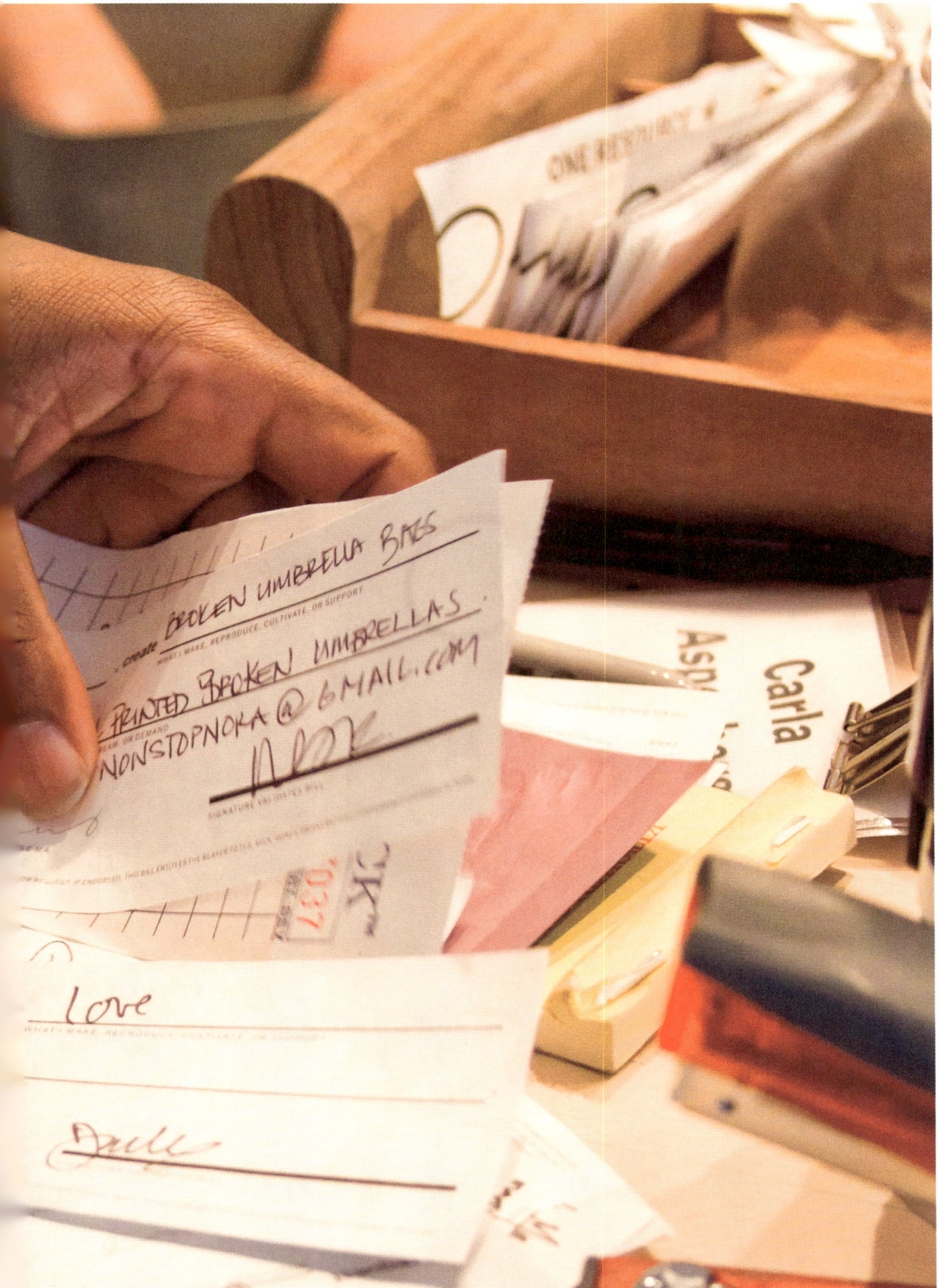

Exchange Café

fig. 4-3
Milk Not Jails—a group that
links farmers to prison
reform in New York—supplied
the milk for Exchange Café.
Photo by Ryan Tempro.

fig. 4-4
Visitors to Exchange Café.
Photo by Ryan Tempro.

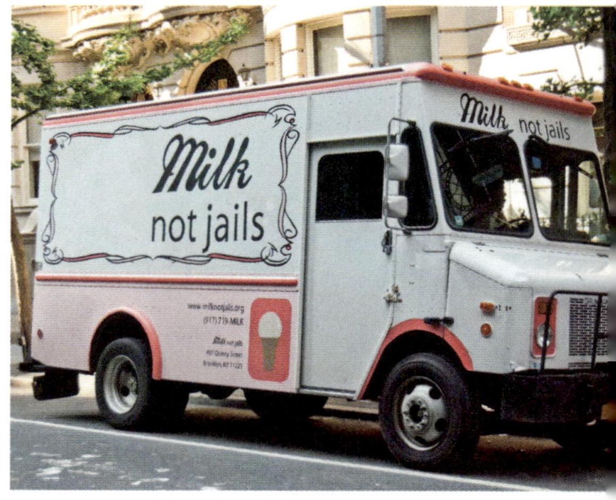

Institutional
Invitation

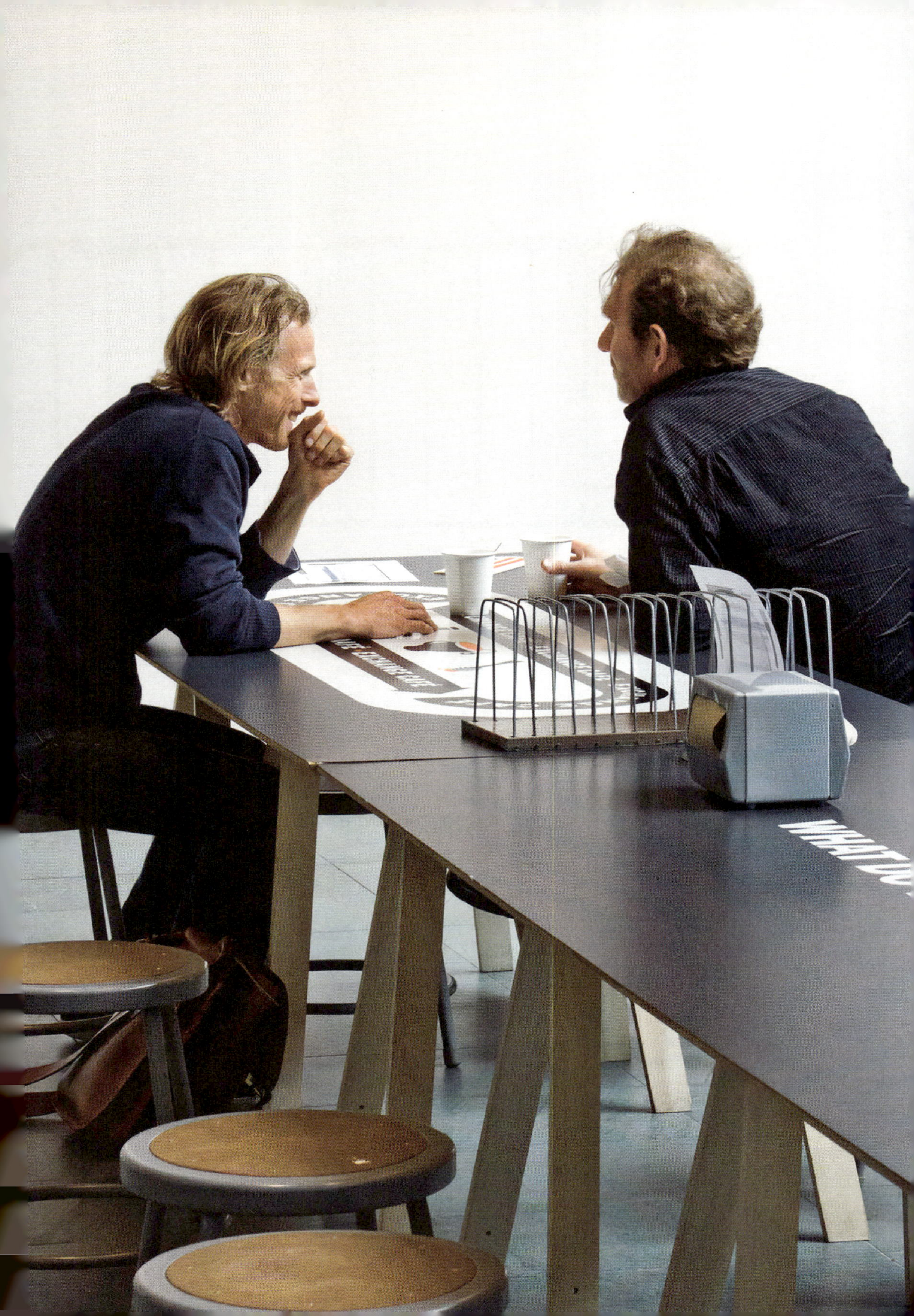

WHAT D

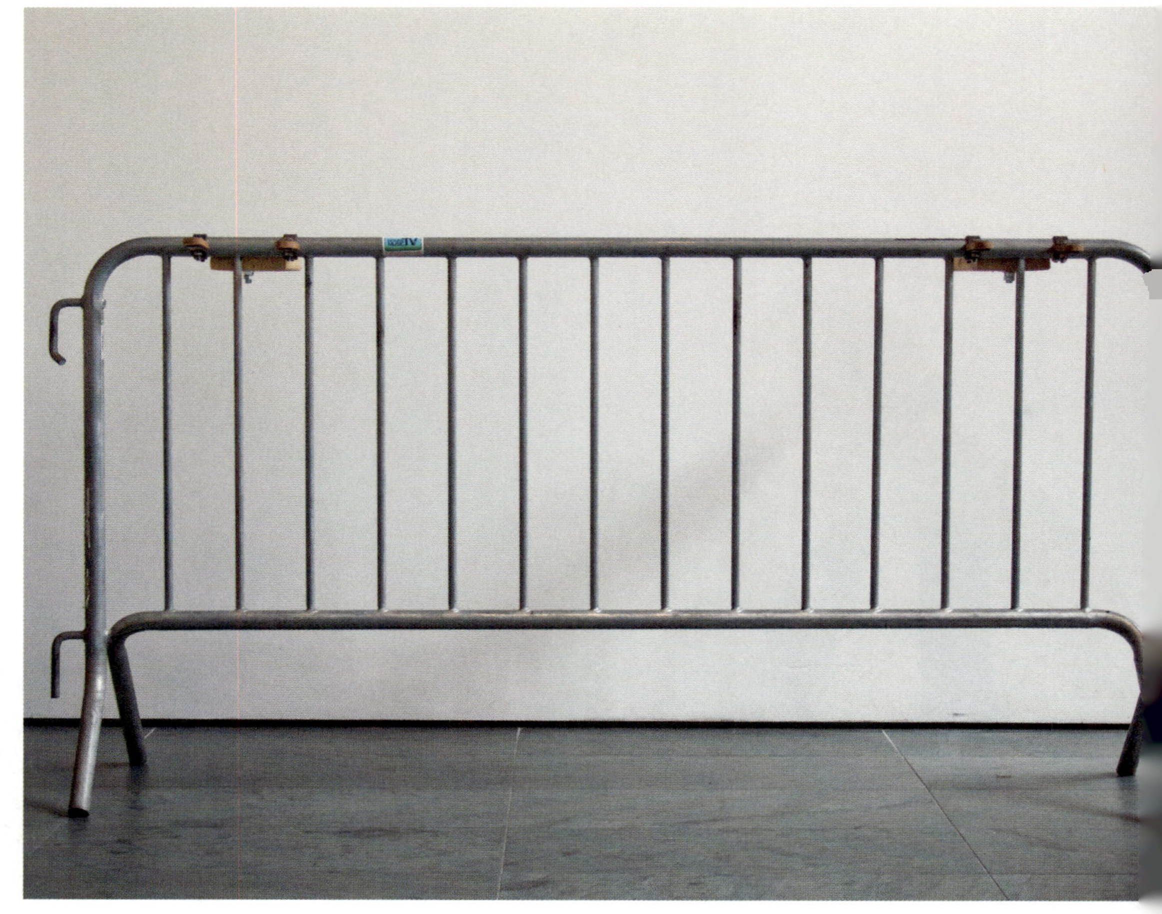

fig. 4-5
Barricade to Bed, 2013, police
barricade, plumbing straps,
hardware, 2 × 6 douglas fir cut
off, maple wood dowel, tennis
balls, foam, fabric, open access
kit, prison abolitionist 'zines,
16 × 43 × 96 inches. Courtesy
of the artist and MoMA: Artists
Experiment. Photo by Ryan Tempro.

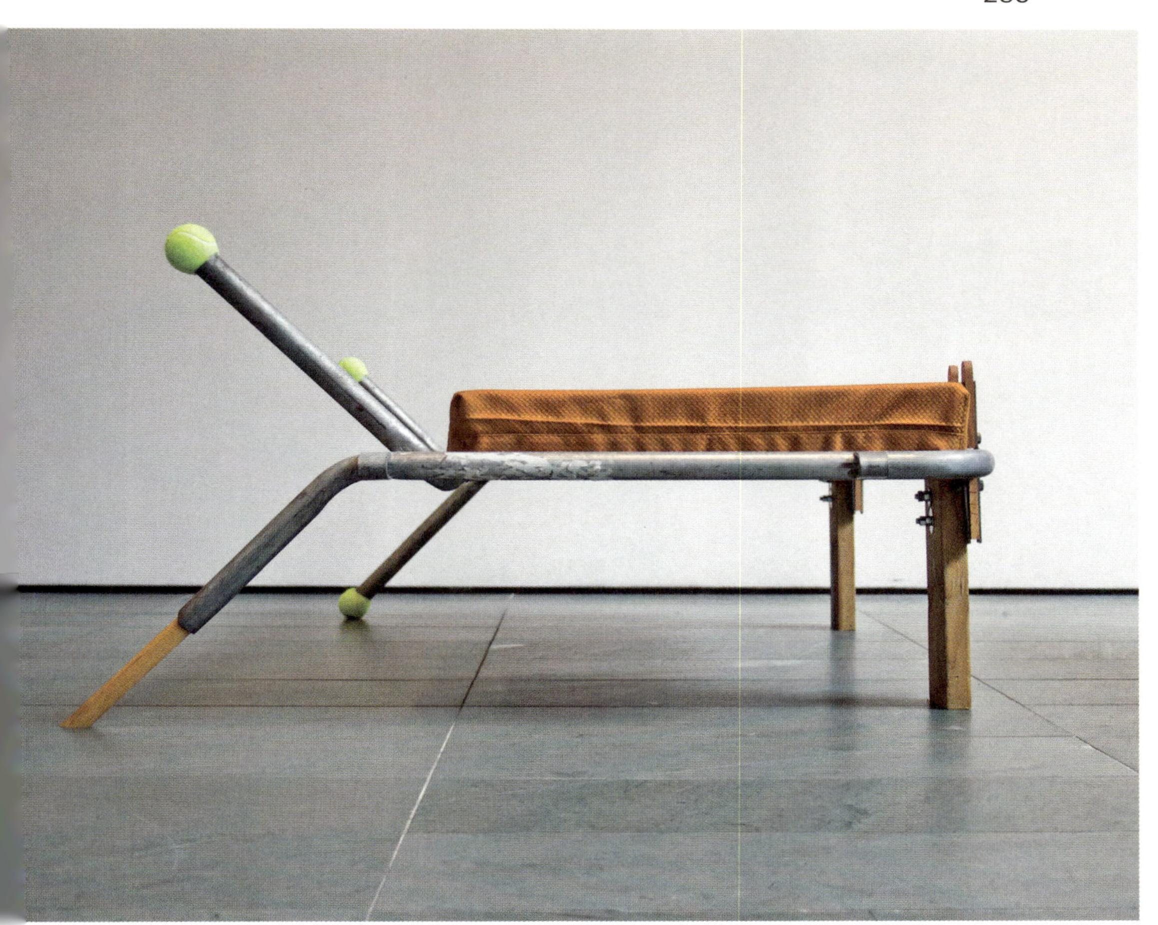

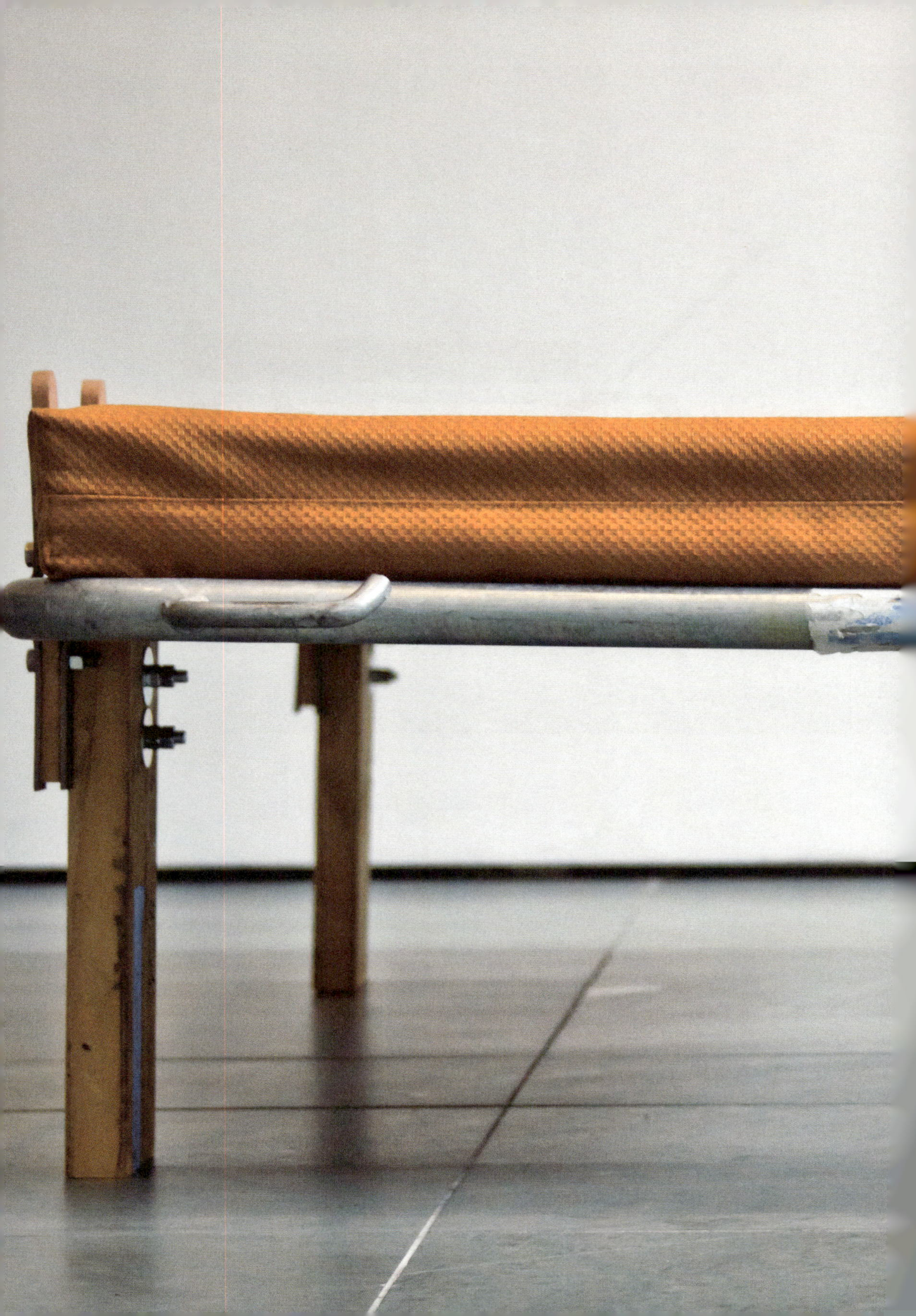

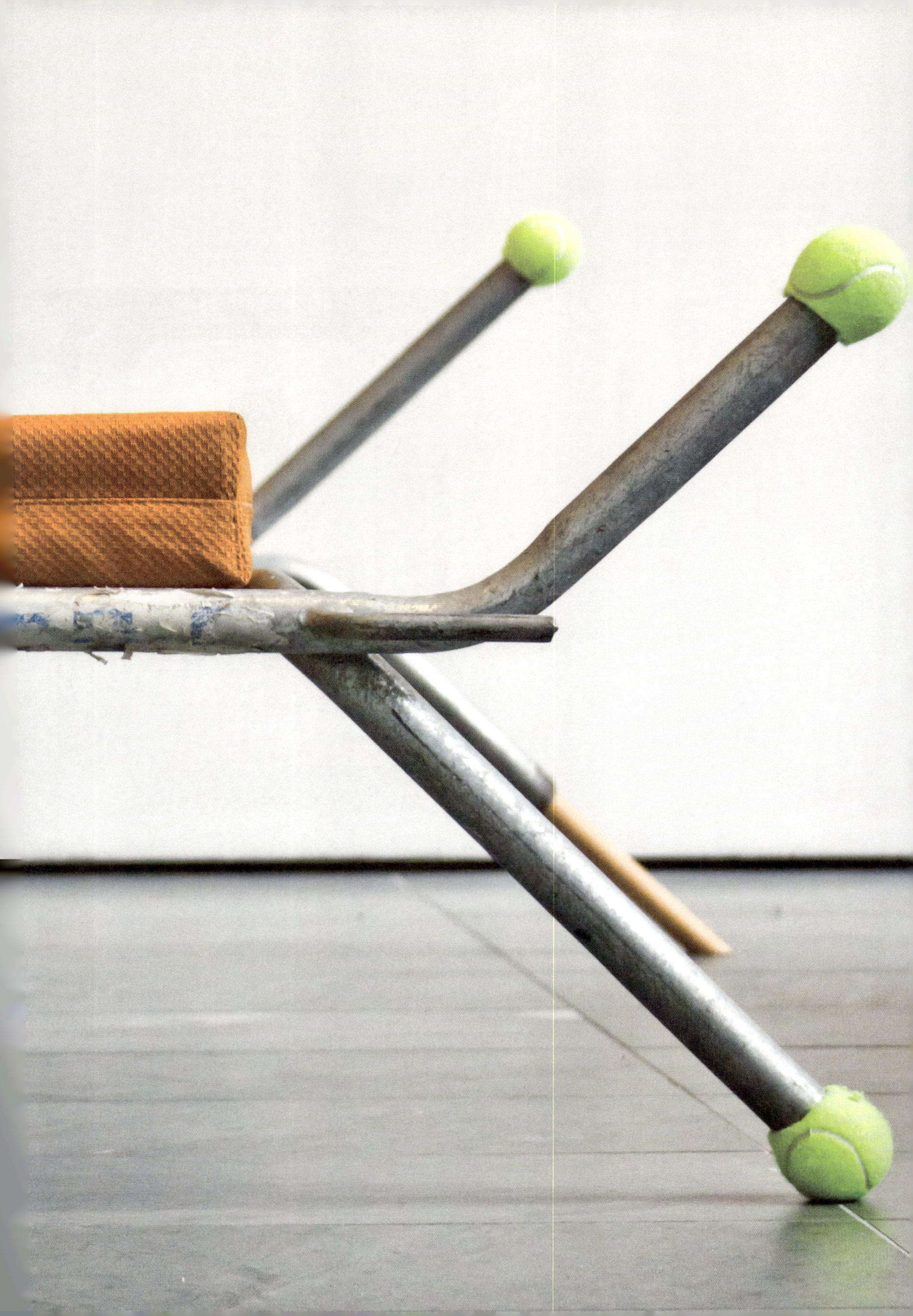

fig. 4-6 (overleaf)
Barricade to Bed, 2013,
police barricade, plumbing
straps, hardware, 2 × 6
douglas fir cut off, maple
wood dowel, tennis balls,
foam, fabric, open access
kit, prison abolitionist
'zines, 16 × 43 × 96 inches.
Courtesy of the artist and
MoMA: Artists Experiment.
Photo by Ryan Tempro.

fig. 4-7
Hiding Tables, 2013, scav-
enged leather, wood, casters,
glass, 34 × 50 × 34 inches.

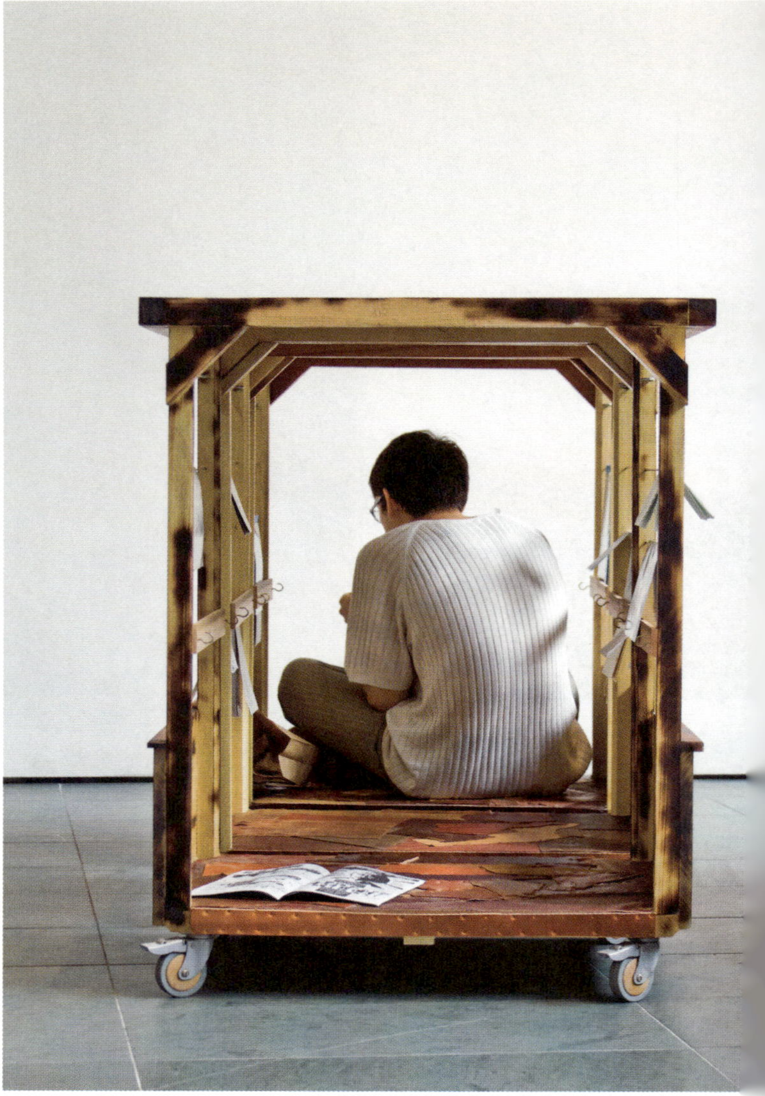

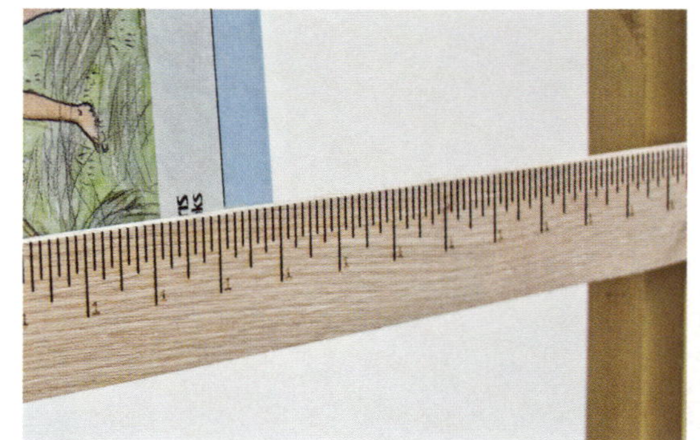

Institutional
Invitation

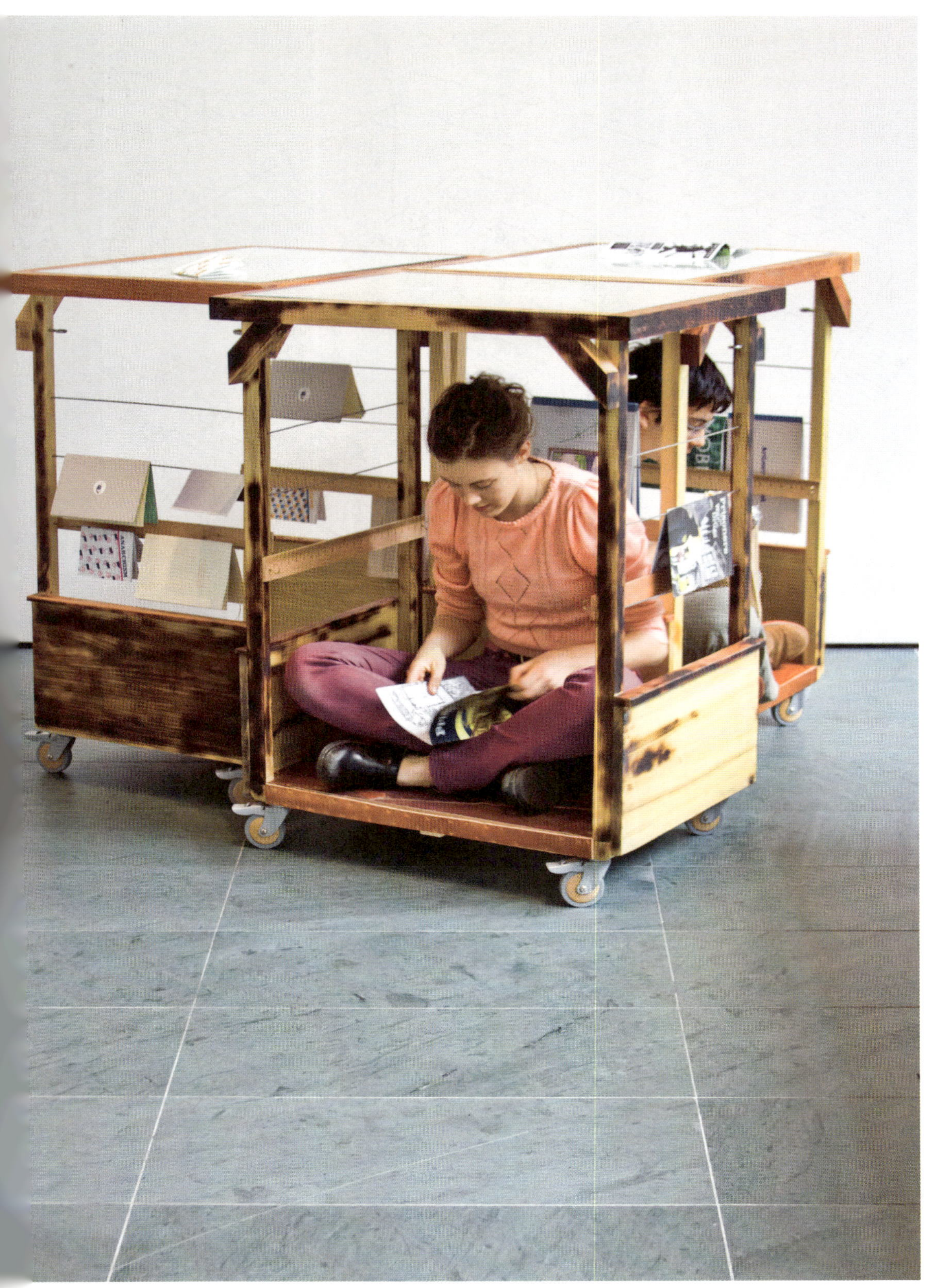

Exchange Café

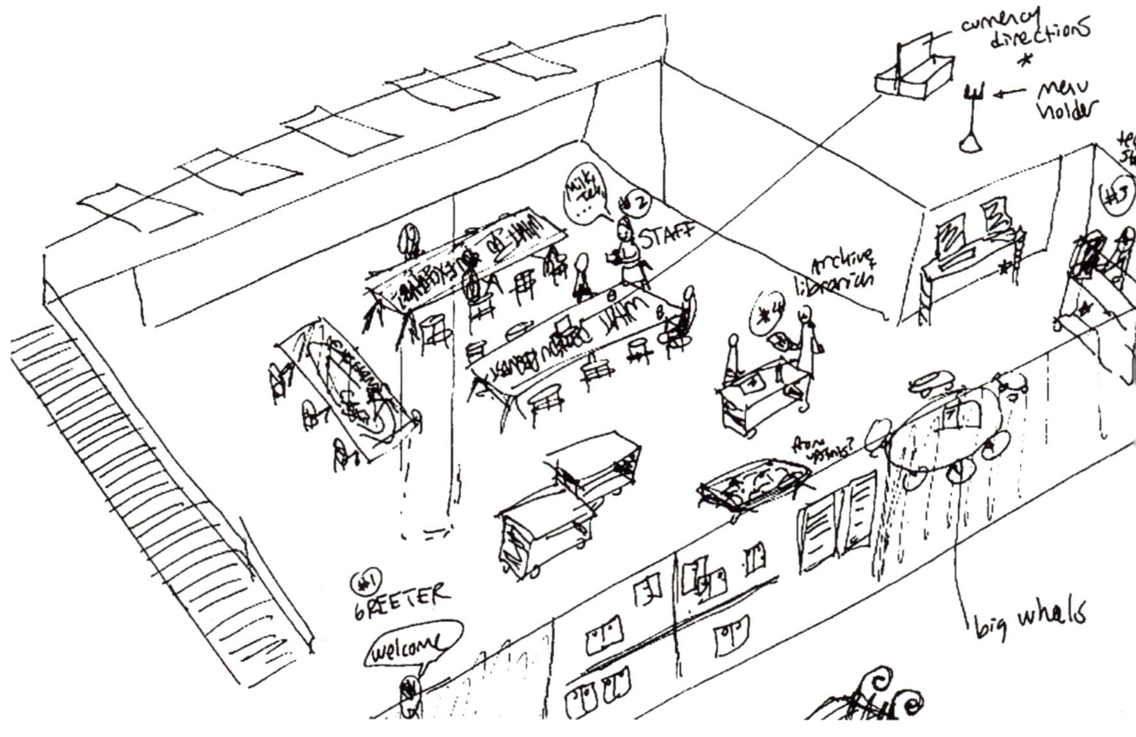

Ephemera

In the following pages, you will find correspondence, budgets, readings, and facilitation guides made in the process of developing Exchange Café. Woolard has selected ephemera that serves as visual reference points for Exchange Café. All materials here are reproduced with the consent of collaborators.

fig. 4-8
Sketch of the installation
plan for Exchange Café.

Study

Institutional
Invitation

Making

I started my research process by visiting the Study Centers at MoMA and spending time going through letters, photographs, and ephemera in the archives. I remember the excitement I felt, being able to read the letters sent between Eva Zeisel and Alfred Bar as they planned the first exhibition dedicated to a woman's oeuvre at MoMA, in the 1940s. Zeisel made sure that her work was available for sale, at an affordable price, to the staff, at the same time that it was on view. I remember touching small photographs of Marcel Duchamp's *Standard Stoppages*, documented resting informally against a fence in a garden. After days and days of research, and many visits to the galleries and spaces adjacent to MoMA, I sent a number of proposals to Pablo Helguera, Sheetal Prajapati, and Sarah Kennedy, the key facilitators of the project. I am sharing this proposal because most artists do not realize how many written proposals they will need to make in order to secure project support.

```
Subject: proposal for Exchange Studio
January 29, 2013
Hey all,

I decided it's easiest for me to get clear
in a PDF … I also have sketches to show you
and there's lots of room for additions and
changes, but I also made a nice PDF for you
all to look over if you have time in advance.

Here's what I'm thinking: The studio is a
café. In the mezzanine, the hardest thing is
to get people in the mood to sit down and do
something unusual. The way to get around this
is to have 1-3 people who greet the public as
they come down the stairs. They will be stand-
ing with tall tables and laptops and be the
"google/algorithm" power of information
people. In addition, the public will be able
to "book" an experience in advance, online or
via phone. This way, the focus is on the power
of the moment, and on our ability as facilita-
tors to connect people to one another. This
```

helps people focus, and will spread the word about the Studio and give us lots of data. The major rule is this: the café will only serve strangers, and they must sit in pairings of 2 or 3. The waitress/waiter is the facilitator, and the menu is milk/tea/honey and a series of actions/encounters/scores with imagery from the collection. This highlights the importance of an encounter, of the stranger. The waitress/waiter is the tour guide and informant.

So, this can be called MoMA Studio:
Reservations about Tea with a Stranger
Yeah?

Until 4 p.m.,
Caroline
—

"Society pays itself in the counterfeit money of its own dreams." — Marcel Mauss

I decided that I wanted to make a café because it seemed that most visitors spent as much time eating as they did looking at art. From here, I began to consider the installation, furniture, and sculptural aspects of the space itself.

Barricades trap and control movement, but could they be used for other means?

When thinking about MoMA, located right off of 5th Avenue, I thought about my experience of the space without cars during protests or parades, from Occupy Wall Street to Pride. Barricades trap and control movement, but could they be used for other means? I wondered if I could "borrow" one and carry it into MoMA, to use it as furniture. The open access toolkit for *Barricade to Bed* demonstrates how to attach wood, a tennis ball, and a dowel to a police barricade to turn an object associated with censorship and state violence into an object of rest and contemplation.

There should be hiding spaces, in the museum, because the museum is so open that it almost feels like you're being watched all the time, so I wanted some hiding spots where people could find solitude and read quietly.

—Caroline Woolard, 2013

Institutional
Invitation

I learned so much about working with institutions to make art, as this was my first time working with a big budget on my own

```
STEP 1: Borrow a public barricade.

STEP 2: Tip it over.

STEP 3: Attach hardware: 4 pcs 1" black plumb-
ing strap (can be found at Decorama Plumbing
Supply in Brooklyn) with 3/4" wood spacers
bolted to 14" tall wooden 2 × 6s or other
legs, plus added safety attachments: 3 tennis
balls on the ends, and a 1.25" diam. × 20"
dowel for the extra leg).

STEP 4: Add a mattress: any "army" sized
narrow and long cot mattresses work, as well
as prison mattresses, or any piece of 29" ×
79" foam from Canal Rubber in Manhattan.

STEP 5: Modify and share revisions.
```

Mediating

In Exchange Café, I knew that the facilitators would get questions from visitors, and that I could shape the visitor experience by creating an "FAQ" that they could refer to. I made sure that MoMA would hire people with experience living and working in the solidarity economy, including Kenneth Edusei, Forest Purnell, Amelia Winger-Bearskin, Carla Aspenberg, Lauren Melodia, and Tychist Baker. I worked with Sarah Kennedy and Sheetal Prajapati to draft a document that we sent to the wait-staff or "studio facilitators."

I made sure that MoMA would hire people with experience living and working in the solidarity economy

Rather than just making a finished work about sustainability, the furniture I produced for the café is made sustainably. I did not want to privilege stories and lore about art projects from the past over lived experience and ongoing practices of mutual aid. I did not want to privilege representation over life.

—Caroline Woolard, 2013

Institutional Invitation

May 20, 2013
MoMA Studio: Exchange Café
Your Role as a Facilitator

FACILITATOR RESPONSIBILITIES
Three facilitators will be at the
Studio each day during open hours.
Together they will be responsible
for overseeing and maintaining the
mezzanine space of MoMA's Education
Building and facilitating visitor
experiences with various components
of the Studio including:
- Overseeing and organizing the
  Studio space including setup, tea
  service, and clean up each day;
- Welcoming visitors to the
  Studio space;
- Facilitating public interactions
  with daily ongoing and weekly
  Studio activities and programs;
- Delivering feedback to
  Education staff;
- Tracking attendance;
- Collecting evaluation data from
  visitors;
- Keeping track of Studio inventory,
  digital equipment, materials and
  activity supplies;
- One mid-Studio meeting.

HOW THE CAFÉ WORKS
The Café layout and facilitation
roles will need to shift, depending
on how many people are in the Café.
There are 3 "modes" we imagine:

MODE 1: Less than 15 people are in
the space = Restaurant Experience
(sit down to be served tea)

FACILITATOR 1 (greeter) greets
people who walk down the stairs
(also be aware of people entering Café from the elevators)
and directs them to have a
seat in the Café, explore the
Exchange Archive, or hang out. If
Facilitator 2 (archivist) is getting busy, Facilitator 1 (greeter)
can help in the Exchange Archive.
Must be really into gauging interest and going from the 1 liner
explanation of what the space is
to a more in-depth welcome. This
is a caller or hostess type job.

FACILITATOR 2 (archivist) helps
people understand the Reference
Works in the Exchange Archive,
helps people submit stories/draw-
ings to the Exchange Archive. If
Facilitator 3 (waiter/tea attendant) is getting busy, Facilitator
2 (archivist) can help at the
tea station. Must be into talking
about contemporary art and helping people connect artworks about
exchange to the project overall, as well as helping people to
submit exchange stories and use
the Archive. This is a meditative
or 1-on-1 job.

FACILITATOR 3 (waiter) greets
people in the Café who are seated
and want to have tea, and gets
them tea at the tea station, handles receipts, and any questions
about the products. Facilitator 3
(waiter) can elect to move into

Mode 2 if s/he is getting too busy. Must be able to take tea orders, give change, and talk about Milk/Tea/Honey products. This is a running around job.

MODE 2: More than 15-20 people = Take-Out Experience (order and get tea in line)

FACILITATOR 1 (greeter) greets people and directs them to get in line for tea. Greeters must be comfortable shouting a bit, getting people in line and explaining that they should fill out currency while waiting for tea. It's like the post office. This is a caller or hostess type job.

FACILITATOR 2 (tea attendant) stands beside the cashier and listens to people's orders, filling tea and giving it to people waiting in line. If necessary, write the name of the person on the cup so they can hear their name to receive their cup when it's ready. This is a quiet, but fast work job.

FACILITATOR 3 (cashier/stationary waiter) stands beside tea attendant and takes orders and explains currency system if they still don't get it. Fills out receipt and gives change. This is a conversational job where the currency must be explained and the system understood well.

MODE 3: Groups come to visit Caroline (abnormal, special case) In this mode, the group that comes to visit Caroline should not be counted as "over 15 people," as Caroline will handle these groups. If a random group wants a tour and has not scheduled it with Caroline or MoMA, please tell them to experience the space as individuals, not as a group, as we will be overwhelmed by that.

When special events involving groups in the studio occur during open hours, facilitators can join these events, but should keep an eye on the space, explaining the project overall and the special event in particular, so that visitors don't think that the project is only about group conversation. Facilitators should provide tea in exchange for currency if the visitors don't want to participate in the event and the exchange of tea for resources does not distract from the event.

…

I then wrote an email with a longer FAQ for the facilitators to think about what questions they might be asked. I went over these questions with them when we were in the space together, for their first "training," to talk about what it meant to be on the waitstaff in Exchange Café.

May 21, 2013
Dear Forest, Amelia, Carla, Kenneth, Lauren, Ryan, and Tychist,

I'm honored to be working with you all. My ambition is for this Exchange Café to change the way museums think about education, art, and activism. If this project goes well, I hope to open a long-term Café using this model, and to turn it into a cooperative business so that member-owners influence the direction and policies of the Café. For now, this is an experiment that I'm taking respon- sibility for, and hiring you with MoMA to see what might be possible in the long run.

We will fine tune it along the way, as we all see what's working and what's not working. This project is far more interactive than most museum-exhibitions, and more one-on-one than most museum education programs; this means we are relying on you to interact with the public!

MoMA Studio: Exchange Café has a lot of moving parts, so I made this PDF in an attempt to clarify all of the aspects of the Café. Please read through this document so that you know how to orient a newcomer to the space, tell them what's going on, and help them if they want help. You each have areas of exper- tise and experience, so if a visitor asks about the following topics, consider directing them to the person on this list (Exchange Café facilitators) who are most excited to share that information:

My ambition is for this Exchange Café to change the way museums think about education, art, and activism.

```
Forest: exchange archive, art, alternative
economies, modernist fashion
Amelia: archive on/offline (Amelia made
TheExchangeArchive.com at Vanderbilt)
Carla: exchange archive, art, printmaking
Kenneth: started in business and moved to
philosophy, prison (in)justice, alternative
money, banking/finance, credit unions, susu,
local currency, democratic processes,
participatory budgeting
Lauren: Milk Not Jails, prison abolition
Tychist: Milk Not Jails, prison abolition
Caroline: the making of the space (the "artist"
MoMA invited, who proposed the Café)
Ryan: the making of the space (Ryan works for
Caroline for space, feedback, mentoring)

Thank you so much!
Caroline
```

In general, visitors to the café did not ask many questions, and the facilitators were often quite busy helping people with the currency and the tea.

TABLE OF CONTENTS

CAFÉ INFORMATION
- EXCHANGE CAFÉ: What's going on?
- SCHEDULE: What's happening when?
- CAFÉ PRODUCTS: What are Milk
  not Jails, Feral Trade Courier,
  and BeeSpace?
- CAFÉ DESIGN: Who made the aprons,
  tables, penny machine, graphics?

INTERACTIVE FACILITATION
- How can I order tea? (see below,
  you must create Resources)
- How do I create RESOURCES? (the
  currency used in Exchange Café)
- How do I contribute to the
  EXCHANGE ARCHIVE? (online and in
  real space)

FAQ
- Did barter come before money?
- What is an alternative currency?
- What is the commons? What do
  you mean by movements to reclaim
  the commons?
- Why are you focusing on 1-to-1
  exchange when the economic crisis
  is structural?
- What do Milk Not Jails, Feral
  Trade, and BeeSpace have to do
  with 1-to-1 exchange?
- What is Artists Experiment?
- How does this relate to Caroline
  Woolard and OurGoods.org and
  TradeSchool.coop?

When visitors ask you about the
following:

THE CAFÉ
Q: What is this space?
A: This is a Café that runs on an
alternative currency. Instead of
using legal tender (national currencies), you can pay for tea with
a currency that circulates in this
space. If you want tea, milk, and
honey, have a seat in the Café and
our waitstaff will tell you how to
validate the Resource currency.
This space also features an Exchange
Archive of works from MoMA's collection that focus on exchange:
dialogue, barter, and reciprocity
systems. You can contribute to the
Exchange Archive with your own stories of exchange if you want, and
our waitstaff can assist you with
this as well. If you just want to
hang out in the library area, go
for it!

Long version (from the website):
Organized in collaboration with
Brooklyn-based artist Caroline
Woolard as part of the Department
of Education's Artists Experiment
initiative, MoMA Studio: Exchange
Café is a social space in the mezzanine of MoMA's Education and
Research building that is dedicated
to exchange-based practices. Taking
the form of a café, the Studio
encourages visitors to question
notions of reciprocity, value, and
property through shared experiences.
Tea, milk, and honey—products that

directly engage the political economy—are available by exchange.
Instead of paying with legal tender,
Exchange Café patrons are invited
to make a resource-based currency.
Exchange Café features an interactive
participatory archive, a matrix
of exchange projects, and a library
of books and ephemera.

SCHEDULE
Q: What's happening today? This
week? Next week?
A: Some events are listed in the
brochure, but all events are listed
in the space (where?) and online at:
http://www.moma.org/visit/calendar/
exhibitions/1364

CAFÉ PRODUCTS
Q: What's Milk Not Jails?
A: Milk Not Jails organizes urban
and rural people in New York State
who are hurt by mass incarceration
to build an economic alternative to
the prison industry. Milk Not Jails
partners with local, small-scale
dairy farmers who oppose prison
expansion. In exchange for the farmers' strategic political support,
Milk Not Jails markets, sells, and
distributes their products to urban
consumers through their nonprofit
social enterprise. Talk to organizers Lauren Melodia and Tychist Baker
if they are working in the Café
right now. For more information,
see *The New Jim Crow* by Michelle
Alexander in the Exchange Library.

Q: What's Feral Trade tea?
A: Operating since 2003, Feral Trade
Courier is a grocery business and
public experiment, trading goods
over social networks and outside
commercial systems. Goods are passed
hand to hand, using existing journeys
as a freight system to transport
groceries worldwide. New products
are chosen for their portability,
shelf life, and sociability. Feral
Trade is organized by Kate Rich.

Q: What's BeeSpace honey?
A: BeeSpace honey is the by-product
of ongoing research on biopolitics.
BeeSpace explores the control of
bee populations, allowing humans
to productively remove honey from
the hive. Honey is cultivated in
hives in Battery Park, collectively
harvested by a working group, and
given away, not sold. We have been
working with Jan Mun, an artist and
co-organizer of BeeSpace. She will
be speaking about BeeSpace at MoMA
Studio: Exchange Café on Saturday,
June 29 at 3:00 p.m.

CAFÉ DESIGN
Q: Who made the aprons?
A: Lika Volkova provided uniforms
for Exchange Café. Making mobile
sculptures for pickpockets, delin-
quents, and communitarians, Volkova
works in the legacy of critical
design and collective production,
sharing patterns freely via SANS,

a multipurpose fashion label. Lika Volkova will be speaking about her work at MoMA Studio: Exchange Café on Saturday, May 25 at 3:00 p.m.

Q: Who made the furniture?
A: Caroline Woolard is interested in designing beautiful spaces that reinforce values of reciprocity and solidarity economies. To that end, the furniture here is not for sale with federal money. It was made with diverse economies, from scavenging the surplus or excess of market systems to non-market exchanges like gift giving and barter. To produce the objects here, she bartered with a glass blower, used free/scrap wood, and worked in a non-profit shop. She made this furniture at Eyebeam, an art and technology center in Chelsea where she is currently a Fellow. The wood comes from her neighborhood in Brooklyn, where she can gather scraps from local cabinet makers, column-makers, and spiral-staircase makers.

Q: Who made the Penny Machine?
A: Richard Knox's *Newtown Creek Oil Spill* is a penny machine that commemorates the largest and most devastating oil spill on US soil. Richard hopes to permanently install *Newtown Creek Oil Spill* on the Pulaski Bridge, overlooking the Creek in Brooklyn. RiverKeeper, a clean-water advocate, writes: "Over the last century, between 17 and 30 million gallons of oil were spilled and leaked from ExxonMobil's historic refinery and storage facilities into the soil and groundwater in Greenpoint, Brooklyn. These petroleum discharges formed an over 50 acre underground petroleum plume that underlies local businesses and a residential section of Greenpoint. The contamination has also been leaching into Newtown Creek for decades."

Q: Who designed the Resource currency?
A: Caroline Woolard and Louise Ma, long term collaborators and co-founders of barter networks OurGoods.org and TradeSchool.coop, worked together in a two-week design sprint where they passed files back and forth. Louise Ma is an illustrator, artist, and designer, creating the illustrations and layout for OurGoods.org and TradeSchool.coop. The currency is printed through Ryan Tempro's friends: PIP Printing in St. Augustine, FL.

Q: Who designed the Exchange Café graphics?
A: As Exchange Café sits in limbo between pop-up shop, art, learning space, and design shop, Caroline Woolard wanted to represent the project with a corporate logo instead of a photograph or other traditional fine-art image. After

sending a style guide and suggestions to MoMA's Graphic Design Department, their team of Sabine Dowek, Ingrid Chou, and Althea Penza developed and created the logo, graphics, brand, and type treatment to design and fabricate the Studio signage, stamps, and brochure. Caroline suggested the R symbol for Resources because Ben Franklin (the innovator, printmaker, and American diplomat) designed local currencies for Philadelphia and many early American colonies, often using the paragraph symbol when printing local currencies from 1720s until his death in 1790.

Each Resource must be validated with a request (something you desire, need, or demand) and a creation (something you make, organize, and support).

INTERACTIVE FACILITATION

CURRENCY: RESOURCES
Q: How can I create currency to pay for tea?
A: Instead of paying with legal tender, you need to pay for tea with the currency that works in the Café, called Resources. Each Resource must be validated with a request (something you desire, need, or demand) and a creation (something you make, organize, and support). When endorsed with your signature, you can use Resources to get tea, milk, and honey. 3 Resource bills entitle you tea, milk, honey, or any mutually determined exchange in trade. See the menu on each table for information as well. Find blank resources on the table or ask the waitstaff for blank resources.

Q: How do I order tea?
A: Have a seat in the Café and look over the menu. We serve a different kind of tea each day, as well as milk and honey. Someone from the waitstaff will be with you shortly. While you wait for them, look over the menu and make currency, 3 Resources for each thing you hope to order: 3 for milk, 3 for tea, and 3 for honey. When you pay with Resources, your waiter will give you Resources in change. You can keep this currency for a return visit to the Café and/or exchange it with other Café patrons for goods and services.

THE EXCHANGE ARCHIVE
Q: What is the Exchange Archive?
A: The Exchange Archive is a visual representation of exchange, demonstrating stories, drawings, and ephemera related to exchange practices. Artist Caroline Woolard has

selected a range of artworks and projects that involve exchange prac-tices. Visitors are invited to con-tribute to the Exchange Archive by writing down personal memories and experiences, local myths, or forgot-ten histories of exchange.

Q: What artworks were selected from the collection and beyond?
A: Look for images pinned up on the wall that do not have text around the edges. You will find works by: Marina Abramović, Billy Apple, Janine Antoni, Andrea Blum, Marcel Broodthaers, Carolina Caycedo, Lygia Clark, Tehching Hsieh, Allan Kaprow, Nina Katchadourian, Ed Kienholz, Ben Kinmont, George Maciunas, Max Liboiron, Alan Michelson, David McKenzie, Linda Mary Montano, George Monteleone, Hương Ngô, Hélio Oiticica, Ahmet Ögüt, Yoko Ono, OurGoods.org, Adrian Piper, Paul Ramírez Jonas, Julianne Swartz, Ray Tomlinson, Mierle Laderman Ukeles, José Antonio Vega Macotela, Franz Erhard Walther, Audra Wolowiec, Carey Young, and Or Zubalsky.

Q: How can I contribute my story to the Exchange Archive wall?
A: Have a seat in the Exchange Archive area, and someone from the waitstaff will help you. To contrib-ute memories, myths, and histories of exchange, please draw or write on the other side of the paper. When the card is complete, pin it up in the Exchange Archive in the section that corresponds to the kind of exchange you referenced: from short encounters to ongoing practices of mutual aid, from transfers of goods and services to informal conversa-tions, exchange involves complex flows of trust and value. If you want to add another layer of mean-ing, use colored push pins to tell viewers what kind of relationship was imagined, created, or rein-forced in the exchange. See the Exchange Archive Submission Form for more information.

Q: What is the Exchange Library?
A: The Library offers a range of visual and written materials for visitors to further explore exchange practices in modern and contempo-rary art. The library offers mate-rials about artists such as Lygia Clark, Allan Kaprow, Ben Kinmont, Mierle Laderman Ukeles, and Franz Erhard Walther along with a range of digital resources and texts about alternative economies. PLEASE DO NOT SWAP BOOKS HERE, they are common resources for all.

Q: How can I contribute my exchange-based art practice online?
A: This aspect of Exchange Café is intended for artists, curators, and lovers of exchange-based work. Our goal is to document the inspira-tions, influences, and support networks that are often invisible when artworks are presented as acts of solitary creation. Go to the

computer station nearby and follow the instructions. Talk to Caroline Woolard or Amelia Winger-Bearskin (who designed it with computer engineers at Vanderbilt University) if she is working today. TheExchangeArchive.com (T.E.A.) visualizes a global network of exchange-based projects. When you add your project you will connect with other artists and organizers with similar influences and goals.

FAQ

Q: Did barter come before money? Isn't barter about self-interest? A: "Anthropologists gradually fanned out into the world and began directly observing how economies where money was not used (or anyway, not used for everyday transactions) actually worked. What they discovered was an at first bewildering variety of arrangements, ranging from competitive gift-giving to communal stockpiling to places where economic relations centered on neighbors trying to guess each other's dreams. What they never found was any place, anywhere, where economic relations between members of community took the form economists predicted: "I'll give you twenty chickens for that cow." Hence in the definitive anthropological work on the subject, Cambridge anthropology professor Caroline

Humphrey concludes, "No example of a barter economy, pure and simple, has ever been described, let alone the emergence from it of money; all available ethnography suggests that there never has been such a thing." From a blog post by David Graeber.

In practice, barter is often not about haggling or getting a deal. It is about voluntary, reciprocal exchange. There is a myth perpetuated in economic textbooks that barter was the precursor to monetary exchange, but in fact gift-giving in community was the precursor to monetary exchange. See David Graeber's book *Debt: the First 5,000 Years* and Caroline Humphrey's book *Barter: Exchange and Value* in the Exchange Library for more information. Barter can help people remember community-reliance and to move our culture towards increased gift-giving and mutual aid.

Q: What is an alternative currency? A: Alternative currencies, also called community currencies or complementary currencies, are used around the world by people who want to meet their needs together without relying only on federal control of the supply of money. When an economy fails, there's less money circulating. However, there's the same amount of skills, spaces, and objects for distribution and disbursement. Edgar Kahn, a major proponent of time-banking, speaks beautifully about this. Alternative currencies help with flows of value when the money supply is short. In addition, alternative currencies help the people who use them think through other ways we might meet our needs together.

Alternative currencies, or "media of exchange," mostly follow the characteristics of federal money, but are controlled and regulated by local governments or non-governmental bodies. These "media of exchange" (or monies) are usually durable (do not rot or go bad), divisible (you can get change), portable (not enormous), uniform (recognizable), and acceptable (you can use them). For example, in Massachusetts, the Berkshares are a local currency. BitCoin is another example. In the United States before 1863, a wide range of local currencies were used. See *Community and Money: Women and Men Making Change* by Mary-Beth Raddon in the Exchange Library for more information about this topic.

Q: Doesn't 1-to-1 exchange just reinforce the myth of individual responsibility for your economic reality, rather than pointing to structural economic inequity?
A: These two things (individual responsibility and structural change) are not in opposition. How can we heal ourselves while trying to resist austerity measures? Caroline Woolard sees her work, and Exchange Café, in relationship to the 'resist, occupy, create' motto of the Argentinean factory workers and Brazil's Landless Rural Workers' Movement MST. She thinks that she must protest and resist the closing of schools and hospitals WHILE finding openings to reclaim space for the creation of plausible futures where mutual aid, democratic structures, and interdependence are central. See the statement Caroline wrote next to the Wall Text for more information.

Q: How do Milk Not Jails, Feral Trade Courier, and BeeSpace relate to 1-to-1 exchange?
A: This learning space is dedicated to works in MoMA's collection and beyond that focus on reciprocity and 1-to-1 exchange works. Rather than providing a social space with anonymous products that do not get biographies, Caroline Woolard wanted to bring in groups with edible projects that honor the relationship between art and alternative and solidarity economies. Caroline Woolard is interested in thinking through the logical extension of the propositions that the artists in the Exchange Archive make in their work,

taking artistic projects to their full activist/functional potential, without losing their principles.

For example, if the Exchange Archive reference work called the *Dream Machine* allows anonymous individuals to exchange dreams, and OurGoods.org allows individuals to barter art skills and objects, how could these networks carry goods internationally? The Feral Trade Courier takes the one-to-one transfer to a global scale, moving goods from hand to hand outside of commercial shipping. With Milk Not Jails, products are distributed only when farmers agree to a radical (as in, getting to the root of the issue) policy agenda: prison abolition. Milk Not Jails can be seen as a logical extension of relationship building between culture workers and underpaid, place-based workers. If Mierle Laderman Ukeles worked to give sanitation workers recognition in *Touch Sanitation*, Milk Not Jails pushes for recognition of dairy farmers that goes beyond visibility, advocating for policy shifts to support their livelihood. Lastly, if Ben Kinmont seeks an ethical exchange between participants and artists in his work *I Need You*, BeeSpace looks to research the (im)possibility of ethical exchange in interspecies collaboration.

"The commons" refers to an understanding of space that is neither private nor public, but is managed collectively by the people who use it.

Q: What are contemporary movements to reclaim the commons? What is the commons?
A: "The commons" refers to an understanding of space that is neither private nor public, but is managed collectively by the people who use it. Ivan Illich said in a 1982 speech delivered in Tokyo and collected in a book of his speeches, *In the Mirror of the Past*:

> Commons is a Middle English word. People called commons that part of the environment which lay beyond their own thresholds and outside of their own possessions, to which, however, they had recognized claims of usage, not to produce commodities but to provide for the subsistence of their households. The law of the commons regulates the right of way, the right to fish and to hunt, and the right to collect wood or medicinal plants in the forest.

The enclosure of the commons inaugurates a new ecological order. Enclosure did not just physically transfer the control over grasslands from the peasants to the lord. It marked a radical change in the attitudes of society toward the environment. Before, most of the environment had been considered as commons from which most people could draw most of their sustenance without needing to take recourse to the market. After enclosure, the environment became primarily a resource at the service of "enterprises" which, by organizing wage labor, transformed nature into the goods and services on which the satisfaction of basic needs by consumers depend.

"tragedy of the commons" should be re-named the "tragedy of the unmanaged commons."

This change of attitudes can be better illustrated if we think about roads rather than about grasslands. What a difference there was between the new and the old parts of Mexico City only twenty years ago. In the old parts of the city, the streets were true commons. Some people sat in the road to sell vegetables and charcoal. Others put their chairs on the road to drink coffee or tequila. Children played in the gutter, and people walking could still use the road to get from one place to another. Such roads were built for people. Like any true commons, the street itself was the result of people living there and making that space livable. In the new sections of Mexico City, streets are now roadways for automobiles, for buses, for taxis, cars, and trucks. People are barely tolerated on the street. The road has been degraded from a commons to a simple resource for the circulation of vehicles. People can circulate no more on their own. Traffic has displaced their mobility.

Enclosure has denied the people the right to that kind of environment on which—throughout all of history—the moral economy of survival depends. Enclosure undermines the local autonomy of a community. People become economic individuals who depend for their survival on commodities that are produced for them."

Elinor Ostrom pointed out (in her Nobel Prize winning work) that the "tragedy of the commons" should be re-named the "tragedy of the unmanaged commons." Ostrom documents the multiple ways that common pool resources (CPRs) are managed. These human-made or naturally occurring resources have characteristics that make them costly, but not impossible, to exclude potential beneficiaries from obtaining benefits from their use. Fishermen in Maine, for example, manage their common fishery through collective agreement far better than government sanction. See Elinor Ostrom's book, *Governing the Commons*, in the Exchange Library for more information.

Q: What is Artists Experiment?
A: Artists Experiment is about finding new ways to engage THE PUBLIC WITH ART AND PRACTICE. It's a new initiative in the Department of Education that brings together contemporary artists in dialogue with MoMA educators to conceptualize ideas for developing innovative and experimental public interactions. Caroline Woolard was one of four artists invited by MoMA for Artists Experiment, and she proposed Exchange Café to be developed in collaboration with Sarah Kennedy, Sheetal Prajapati, and Pablo Helguera from January until now.

Artists Experiments was created to respond to the expanding nature of artistic practice—artists are engaging with a range of disciplines, creating new spaces for exchange that consider audience a critical part of that process. From socially engaged works to digital art, artists are increasingly looking to people and the spaces around them as partners in an ongoing creative collaboration. This initiative aims to foster these types of interactions, situating MoMA as a laboratory for experimentation with public engagement. Programs developed through this initiative place collaboration and dialogue at the center, addressing the Museum, contemporary art practice, and various social impulses.

What will become possible if you call it art? What will become impossible if you call it art?

Q: How does this relate to Caroline Woolard's other work?
A: From 2004-2007, Caroline Woolard made her own public seating and installed and maintained it on the streets of New York. She also

made a bag that transformed into
a swing for the subway in 2006.
Moving from small scale projects in
public space to scalable infrastructure for exchange in 2008, Caroline
Woolard cofounded OurGoods.org and
TradeSchool.coop, two barter networks for art and learning. These
groups give Caroline the long-term
support to work with other groups,
as she has in this project, but
Caroline is dedicated to working
and growing with OurGoods.org and
TradeSchool.coop for the long haul.

MoMA Studio: Exchange Café honors
the power of reciprocity. From
everyday barter practices to artistic exchange systems, Caroline
Woolard makes legible a relationship
between works in MoMA's collection
and contemporary movements to
reclaim the commons. Join Caroline
in conversation with long-term
collaborators Jen Abrams, Louise Ma,
Rich Watts, Christhian Diaz, Rachel
Steinberg, and Aimee Lutkin on June
8th at 3 p.m.

Q: Is this art?
A: Dore Ashton reports that Picasso
said, "art is a lie that tells the
truth." Amy Whitaker says "art is
a thing that changes the world to
allow itself to exist." Caroline
Woolard says, "What will become possible if you call it art? What will
become impossible if you call it
art?" At Exchange Café, we are more
interested in talking about exchange
than in defining whether this is
art, design, activism, or all of
the above.

Exchange Café

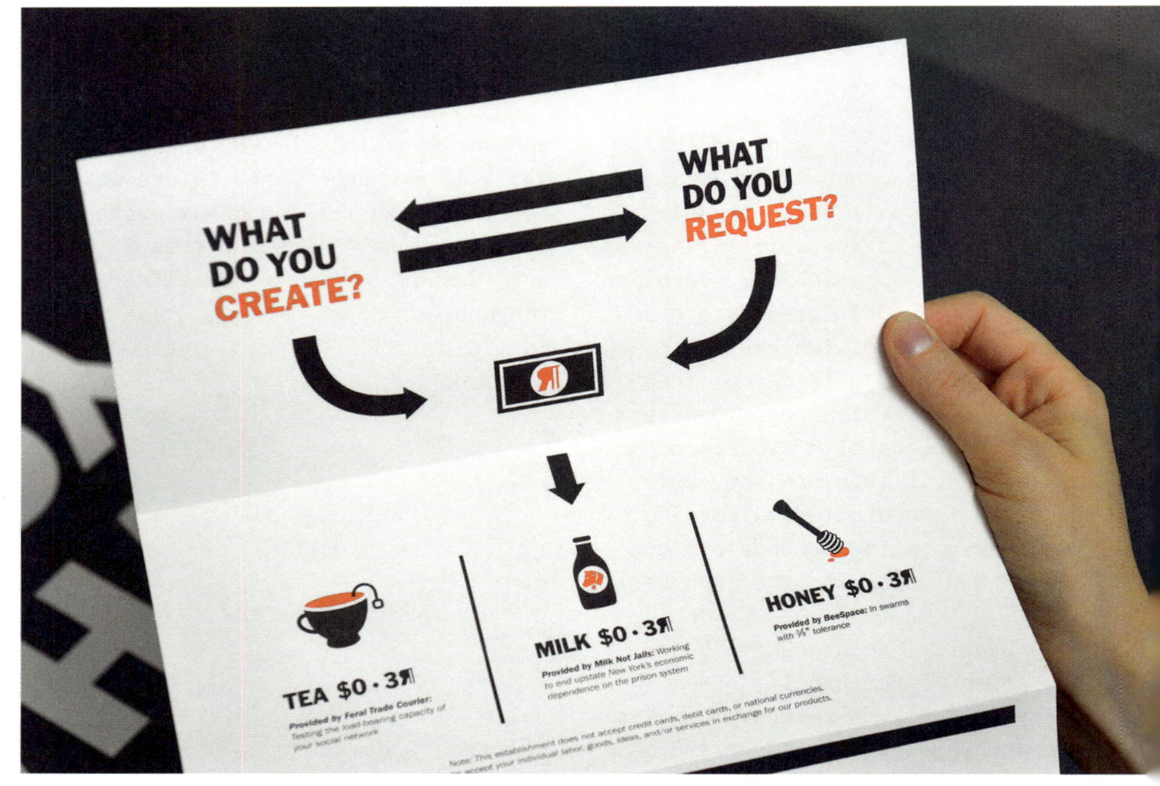

Here is the job description for the facilitators in the café:

    fig. 4-9
Exchange Café identity was
produced in collaboration
with MoMA's Design Department,
with creative direction by
Julia Hoffmann, art direction
by Ingrid Chou, and graphic
design by Sabine Dowek. Photo
by Martin Seck.

Institutional
Invitation

The Museum of Modern Art
Department of Education,
Adult and Academic Programs

TITLE: Facilitator, Museum Education
Interactive Space
Part time, Temporary

DEPARTMENT: Education

DURATION: May 20 to June 30, 2013

DESCRIPTION: The Museum of Modern
Art is seeking facilitators for
MoMA Studio: Exchange Café, a social
space and interactive environment
presented as part of the department
of Education's Artists Experiment
initiative. Taking the form of an
alternative café that will operate
in the mezzanine of MoMA's Education
and Research building from May 24
to June 30, 2013, the Studio offers
a series of programs and activities
that explore alternative notions
of value, exchange, and community
through shared experiences and creative interactions.

Three facilitators will be responsible for overseeing and maintaining the mezzanine space of MoMA's
Education Building and facilitating visitor experiences with various components of the studio space
during open hours.

Responsibilities include:
Gaining a deep understanding of the
studio—including hours, schedule,
content, programs,and activities.

Assisting in the daily management
of an interactive space for the
general public, including but not
limited to: set up and closing up
of space daily including preparation
of project spaces.

Maintenance of the studio space,
including light cleaning, shutting
down tech equipment, and organizing
and stocking materials as needed.

Welcoming visitors to the studio
space with a general introduction to
the Studio and activities.

Facilitating and encouraging public
interactions with ongoing studio
spaces including the Exchange Wall,
Exchange Library, and Exchange
Café spaces.

Maintaining and overseeing the
Exchange Café space in the Studio
including set up, tea service,
and clean up each day.

Facilitating daily ongoing and
weekly Studio programs.

Acting as primary contact with Studio visitors, answering questions about the Museum and other educational programs.

Delivering feedback to Education staff and tracking attendance of visitors to the space.

Collecting evaluation data from visitors. May assist in helping to develop questions and interviewing visitors.

Performing other duties related to the function of the studio as described above.

The ideal candidate is skilled in engaging multi-generational audiences, is personable and professional in their conduct, has experience working in interactive educational spaces, and is well versed in the topic areas explored in the Studio, such as exchange-based practices, modern and contemporary art history, and alternative economies. Flexibility with regard to the flow of activities in the Studio is required as the space is constantly evolving and changing and all activities will be cumulative and reasonably open-ended in response to visitors' engagements. All facilitators are required to attend a mandatory training session prior to the Studio start date.

REQUIREMENTS: Knowledge and Skills: Proficient with computers and digital interfaces. Ability to interact with a variety of museum visitors of diverse ages — children to adults — and engage them in a variety of activities offered at the Studio. Second language helpful.

EDUCATION: B.A. in art history, art / museum education, fine arts, design or equivalent professional experience. Knowledge of modern and contemporary art and artists is important.

EXPERIENCE: Experience as an educator or facilitator in a museum, school, or similar learning environment. Experience engaging the general public in direct ways. Experience with children, teens, and people with different abilities is highly desirable.

QUALITIES: Intuitive, friendly, organized, and punctual. Must have a strong interest in art education. Ability to synthesize complex ideas and concepts for a general and diverse audience.

HOURS: Flexible schedule required. 15-20 hours/week. Shifts are from 12:30 to 5:30 p.m. Thursdays, Saturdays, and Sundays and 12:30 to 8:30 p.m. on Fridays. Studio is open to the public 1 to 5 p.m. Thursday,

Saturday, and Sunday and 1 to 8 p.m. on Fridays. All Facilitators must attend a training session before Studio opens (date TBD) and occasional meetings.

REPORTS TO: ASSOCIATE EDUCATOR, LAB PROGRAMS Interested applicants can submit a resume and cover letter to Sarah_Kennedy@moma.org by Mar 27, 2013. The Museum of Modern Art is an equal opportunity employer and considers all candidates for employment regardless of race, color, sex, age, national origin, creed, disability, marital status, sexual orientation or political affiliation.

Before making Exchange Café, I asked if I could run an educational program that was open to anyone living and working in New York City. The idea was based upon what I learned from TradeSchool.coop, and is related to my ideal graduate school or self-organized learning space, where the students get to select one another. This project happened before the Café opened.

Subject: MoMA Education P2P Proposal
September 3, 2012

Here's a sketch of my idea for classes. Let me know if you need more info or background to go forward … I have many references and readings and reasons for wanting to do this, which I can explain at length. I'm in Amsterdam and doing workshops all day tomorrow, then getting on a plane Wednesday, so I won't be very much in reach except for a small window 12 hours from now.

UNTITLED EDUCATION PROGRAM
(Communities of Practice/P2P/Learning Group)

This program will connect people from various disciplines who have shared interests in a topic or in each other (or both). MoMA will serve as the official container: keeping track of participant commitment (a low, but present sliding scale fee will be required upon acceptance, with institutional pressure to follow through), and providing space, facilitators, specialists (when requested), and the notoriety necessary to draw a wide variety of participants.

Here's how it works:
1. An open call is created for participants interested in joining a Learning Group (formed around specific topics*). If necessary for MoMA, this can be for MoMA members only, but then I want anyone to be able to apply and

include a MoMA membership in the fee they must
pay if they are accepted into the program.
Applicants submit answers to a few short questions,** plus 5-10 images of their work/music/
video/writing/online links, a list of accomplishments (whatever this means to the applicant), information about their heritage/family/
background, how long they've been out of school,
and which Learning Group* they want to be part
of. They must also agree to commit to 1 night a
month to the group.

2. The application process will be anonymous
peer review: every applicant is required to
select 10 other people that s/he would want to
work with in a Learning Group. Based on the
mutual selection of interested participants,
drawn from survey data (from something basic
like survey monkey or more advanced cluster
analysis—we can get help with this from
computer engineers or anyone doing network
analysis)—we will find constellations of mutual
interest. When we have a strong cluster of
interest between people, we will form a Learning
Group. We could potentially have 10 different
learning groups (each with 7 people max), depending on MoMA's resources—facilitators and space.

3. The Learning Group will meet at least one
night (Thursday?) a month (to be determined by
MoMA based on past experience) for a year or
more. The method will be group-directed learning
with a MoMA facilitator, and will have no mandatory specialist/instructor leading the class,
unless the group requests it for a special
reason. Facilitators can provide formats, but
mostly the group will meet to read together,
learn together, and experiment together.

*Possible Learning Groups (up for conversation):

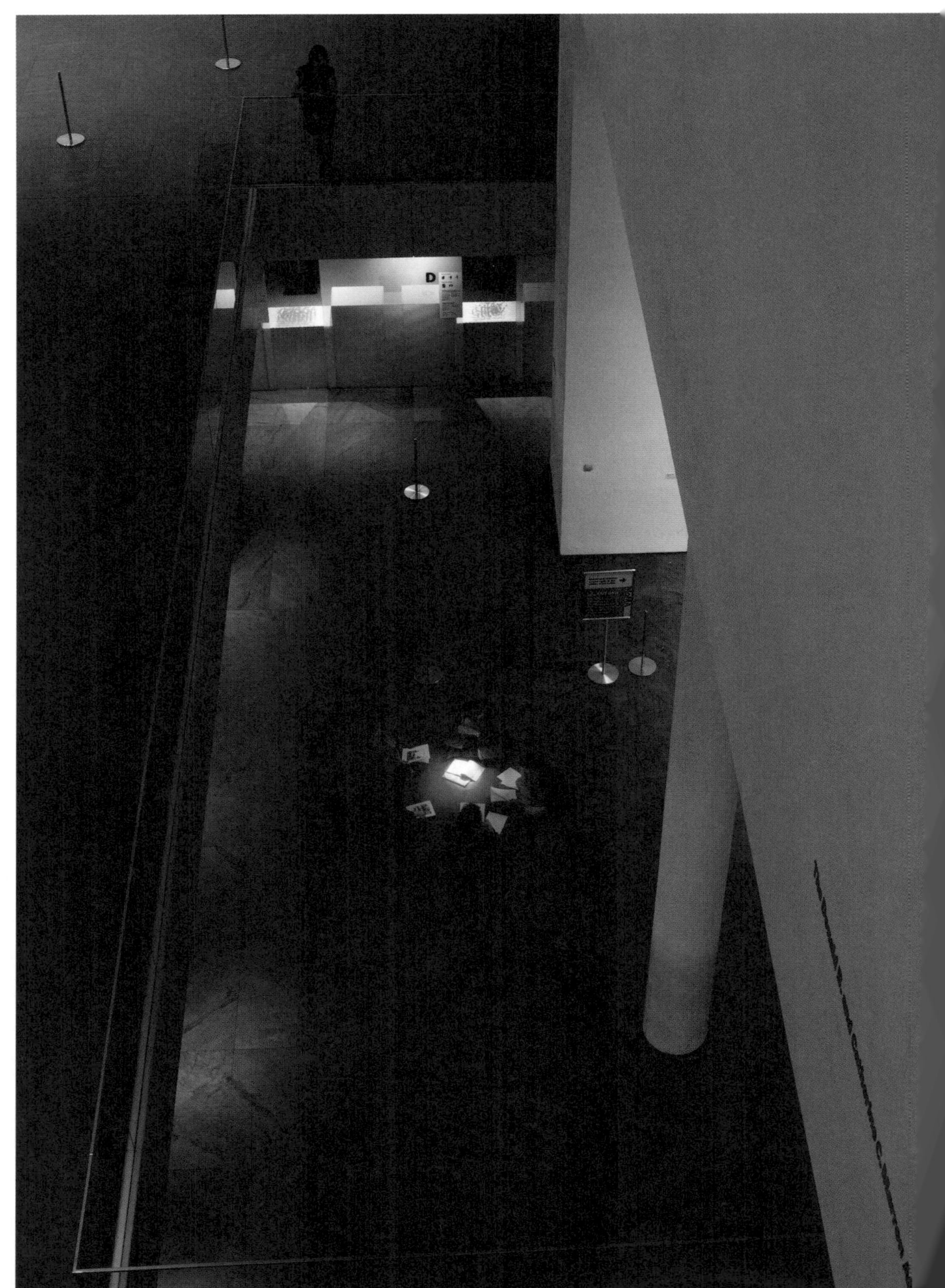

Inquiry

Institutional
Invitation

Design / Art
Economies / Art
Internet / Art
Food / Art
Agriculture / Art
Illegal / Art
Sound / Art
Sociology of Art: language,
  context, relationships
Art / Activism
Spirituality / Mysticism in Art
Science / Art
Performance / Art

** For example (up for conversation):
How does your class background affect your
relationship to learning?
What are you reading right now?
Have you participated in a collective/group
before? Tell us about it.
What kind of schooling have you participated in?

Let me know how it goes!
Caroline

PS: In anticipation of defenses I expect
you'll have to make for this proposal…

Q: Why not just use http://thepublicschool.
org/ or http://tradeschool.coop or any of
these DIY learning platforms?

A: These collect transient groups for single
meetings. This format of commitment, combined
with MoMA's prestige and resources, will
allow real relationships or mutual learning to
occur. The fact that there's a growing landscape of "alternative" education options
shows that there's a high demand for something
besides expensive MFAs and college degrees.
What is missing in most "alternatives" is the

fact that most organizers want to participate, not organize—they eventually lose themselves in the publicity, facility/resource/tech management, and facilitation of the events, which makes for a scattered feel. Here, MoMA can take care of most of this: publicity, facility/resource/tech management, and facilitation.

Q: Why should this be at MoMA?
A: MoMA education should be as experimental as its programming, and has been. To that end, this program will allow participants to fully determine the course of their education. It also sounds quite similar to Barr's classes, where the only reading material was *Vanity Fair*, and students were required to teach major aspects of the course: "Barr referred to all nine students in the class as 'faculty,' making them each responsible for mastering and teaching some of the course content. Although, per its title, the course ostensibly focused on painting, Barr thought a broad understanding of culture was necessary to understand any individual artistic discipline, and accordingly, the class also studied design, architecture, film, sculpture, and photography. There was no required reading aside from *Vanity Fair*, *The New Yorker*, and *The New Masses*, and the numerous class trips were not to typical locations of art-historical interest. For example, on a trip to Cambridge, the class passed over the wealth of Harvard's museums to experience the 'exquisite structural virtuosity,' in Barr's words, of the Necco candy factory."

This resulted in a series that MoMA supported. Once it was approved, I sent individual emails to all the people I knew who ran or participated in self-organized learning spaces. This included Taeyoon Choi, an artist I met at Eyebeam

as a Fellow in 2011–2012, and someone who was part of a
self-organized learning project called The Public School.

> Subject: opportunity at MoMA for Public
> School-types
>
> October 2, 2012
> Hey Taeyoon,
>
> I got to suggest a new learning approach to
> MoMA's Education Department, and I suggested
> the following:
>
> Peer Learning Group (working title) is a
> group-directed learning program, connecting
> individuals to each other and providing access
> to MoMA's diverse resources after museum
> hours. In the winter/spring term 2013, three
> peer-to-peer learning groups will be created,
> organized based on mutual interests and
> expertise. Through an application process,
> individuals will select a topic of focus* and
> provide supplemental information for other
> interested applicants. All submissions will
> be reviewed anonymously by other applicants
> to create clusters of mutual interest.
>
> Based on applicants preferences, MoMA staff
> will create topic-based learning groups. Groups
> will explore the selected topic and collec-
> tively determine group meeting activities over
> 8 sessions: such as readings, guest speakers,
> MoMA screenings, gallery visits, or off-site
> trips. Groups will meet twice a month for four
> months from February-May 2013. Each group
> will have a facilitator who will organize off
> site trips, guest speakers, or events for
> the group. The facilitator will also serve as
> a liaison to MoMA staff to give your group
> access to spaces, resources and facilities.
> This "class" is meant to be self-directed and
> peer driven.

Open House: Thursday, December 6,
6:30-8:30 p.m.:
http://www.moma.org/visit/calendar/events/16878
Application Due: Monday, January 7
Schedule: 8 meetings, every other Tuesday
(Feb 19-May 28) 6:30-8:30 p.m.

Topics* for this term are:
Art and Authorship
Art and Economies
Art and Process

To Apply:
Potential participants must submit an application and agree to review all other applications from individuals interested in the
same topic. Peers will select up to 20 other
participants that they'd like to learn with.
After this, MoMA staff will create four peer
groups based on the strongest clusters of
mutual interest. These groups will receive
access to MoMA and its resources on every
other Tuesday, from February 19-May 28, 2013
from 6:30-8:30 p.m.

MoMA will host a FREE open house about this
new course this Thursday, December 6, from
6:30 to 8:30 p.m. at the Lewis B. and Dorothy
Cullman Education and Research Building at 4
West 54 Street. Learn about this new learning
structure at MoMA, meet other curious learn-
ers, and review the application process:
http://www.moma.org/visit/calendar/
events/16878

Please come Thursday if you're free! I'll send
you the application when it goes live…

Caroline

At Exchange Café, I wanted to honor all of the artists who were working on exchange-based projects, through a sort of footnote system. I thought: if I am a research-based artist, where is the footnote system for my research? I decided to test out a footnote system that all research-based artists could try using, to shift narratives around authorship and citation in the visual arts. To make this a reality, I knew I needed to work with computer engineers. I remembered Amelia Winger-Bearskin, an artist and technologist whom I had met when the artist Stephanie Diamond gathered community-based artists in a project called Community of Community in 2012 at the Queens Museum. Amelia and I stayed in touch, and when I asked her if she was interested in working on a footnote system or network for Exchange Café, she said yes. She then introduced me to three developers that she knew well: Corey Brady, Pratim Sengupta, and Mason Wright. Together, they built an online network to archive the wide range of artists who make exchange-based projects.

if I am a research-based artist, where is the footnote system for my research? I decided to test out a footnote system that all research-based artists could try using, to shift narratives around authorship and citation in the visual arts.

Just as the physical universe is dependent on its dark matter and energy, so too is the art world dependent on its shadow creativity. It needs this shadow activity in much the same way certain developing countries secretly depend on their dark or informal economies.

—Gregory Sholette, 2011

Here is how I described the text and forms that I hoped they could make for the website.

Experiment

EXCHANGE ARCHIVE:
Artists do not create work in
a vacuum.*

All artists work in dialogue with
other people. Why isn't this dialogue visible? In all other fields,
footnotes are the norm. Exchange
Archive hopes to recognize and support artistic dialog and research
by acknowledging the references,
influences, and inspirations that
flow between projects.

All artists work in dialogue with other people. Why isn't this dialogue visible?

Please add your work to the
archive, as well as the projects
that influenced this work. If you
are not an artist, feel free to
suggest possible connections, inspirations, or potential dialogue
between art works.

Thank you!
MultiAgency Collective, Caroline
Woolard, MoMA's Education Department

*Vacuums are for cleaning, not for
divine inspiration. Andy Warhol
traded a print for a vacuum from
Sydney Lewis. Warhol made his work
in a Factory with over 100 artists.

DESCRIPTION OF PROJECT & GOAL OF
VISITOR EXPERIENCE: Exchange Archive
provides tools for flexibly representing and inquiring into two dimensions
of influence between works. In a first
dimension, we see influence as a high-
value form of exchange among artists
that is not always made visible. And
in a second dimension, we see influence
as a impact, linking, and association
in the broader public's experience of
art works.

To get a sense of what this project
will look like, see similar projects
(done for literature and social networks): http://bgriffen.scripts.mit.
edu/www/media/json/thinkers/# and
http://projects.flowingdata.com/tut/
interactive_network_demo/

To bring aspects of the first dimension of influence into the foreground,
we will provide a dynamic visualization of data collected from the distributed community of artists who
thematize exchange in their work.
Descriptive data collected from members of this community will populate
a database that will be used to create
network representations and other
visualizations that can be queried in
real time to identify patterns. This
inquiry into the data is designed to
be illuminating both to the community
of artists themselves and to the
larger public. Café visitors will be
able to click on individual works of

artists and see the influence network of their selected work and artist.

To bring aspects of the second dimension of influence to the fore, we will provide an interface through which visitors to the Exchange Café can choose three artistic projects from the database for temporary display to the Café group, in a form of virtual curation. In building these curations, and as a condition of displaying them, visitors will be asked to articulate their rationale. In this way, they describe a second kind of influence: either a viewer's perspective on inferred influence or affiliation among works of art, or a commonality in the influence (as impact) on them as viewers. [This interaction is explained in more detail in a later section titled "tentative visitor form."] This interpretive network of influence itself becomes a means for the artists themselves and other viewers to tap into an emergent form of knowledge and insight about art works.

These two dimensions of influence interact with one another. The databases for both are constantly changing through contributions that occur both within the Café and on the web. This data and the visualizations that emerge thus form an interactive

bridge between physical and virtual participants, and are the basis for outreach from the Café and a continuation of the conversation unbounded by time and place.

TECH SPECS: The back-end technology required for this project is a webserver feeding into a mysql database which is accessible by our visualization engine. The core software itself can be running on the same computer (server) or remotely. Redundancy on this server is probably not required, though it may be necessary if the external web activity becomes extremely large. Data backup and power backup (i.e., protection from local power outage) is recommended but not absolutely necessary. The hardware for both data and power backup can be provided by MultiAgency Collective. This server will be accessible via the web. It also should be on a local network that connects it with the Café terminals, described below. (Alternative connectivity configurations are possible, but this is our recommendation.) At the front-end, viewers outside of the museum will use a modern web browser (such as Chrome or Firefox) to interact. For interactions within the Café, we recommend two computers be dedicated for visualizing and interacting with the data, and we recommend that secondary displays be attached to these computers to allow other visitors in the café to see visualizations as they emerge. The computers for these terminals can be any model of modern computer and operating system (i.e., Mac, Windows, or Linux, though Mac OSX computers are preferred). Per the above, a network connecting these computers with the server is also required. This network could be wired or wireless.

LIFE OF SOFTWARE AFTER THE PROJECT: The software we are developing is licensed under Creative Commons 3.0 licensing. This means, the software is open source and made available to the public through the Exchange Café website or on Github. We believe that the software, along with the artist questionnaire that is being designed for this project, has the potential to be widely used by artists and scholars of art to map influence networks of artworks and artists. We take responsibility for improving and iterating this software.

TENTATIVE VISITOR INTERPRETIVE INFLUENCE FORM:
The participants (non artists/café visitors/possible online visitors as well) pick 3 art projects from the visualization that are a 'mini-node' or group. The visitor can explain their choices with a few 'buttons.'

I picked these projects to go together because (choose as many as you'd like):
[ ] similar artistic influences
[ ] similar project goals
[ ] they could support one another
[ ] these would make for an interesting contrast
[ ] _______(fill it in yourself)

We think that this way, casual visitors can easily choose a grouping of art projects and within a short period of time describe their curation.

TENTATIVE VISITOR PROJECT INFLUENCE FORM:
To submit a work to the archive, visitors will have to submit the following information:

Project Title:
Project Description: 100 words

This Project is about: EXCHANGE [y n]
It's also about:
[X] and [X] and [X]
It's NOT about:
[X] and [X] and [X] (maybe)

Start Date:
Project Location:
Upload an image:

Your name:
Your collective's name (option):
How to contact you (email):

I am submitting information about
myself and my inspirations: Y N
I am submitting information about
someone else: Y N

Name two artists that may
have inspired this project:

(Can we tell them you were inspired
by them? Email here:)

Name two non-artists that may
have inspired this project:

(Can we tell them you were inspired
by them? Email here:)

Is there another exchange project
you'd recommend for this archive?

Name:
Project:
Email (if known):

I asked MoMA to include a text that I wrote in the wall text for Exchange Café. MoMA has strict regulations about the ways that projects are narrated, and the Education Department wanted to author the wall text. The solution that we agreed upon was to place my writing in italics, so that MoMA would present a wall text that included, "in the words of the artist, Caroline Woolard … " with the following language, from me.

Art making is not separate from the political economy.

Objects are not singular: the labor, materials, production, and distribution are part of the work. Exchange and barter were practiced in the making of the café.

Objects are not singular: the labor, materials, production, and distribution are part of the work. Exchange and barter were practiced in the making of the café.

Moving between Art spaces and non-art spaces allows for multiple meanings, timeframes, and publics.

Meaning is embodied: objects should be touched, used, and/or activated to be understood.

Connecting two people (or more) in a reciprocal encounter or agreement is powerful.

The work is ongoing and should be replicated or modified!

I am not a singular artist. I am a member of society, trying to find hope in a world of fierce inequities. Reciprocity and experiences of mutual support have given me the emotional, financial, and intellectual power to heal and to dream. As a member of many groups (OurGoods.org, TradeSchool.coop[see chapter 3], SolidarityNYC.org, the Pedagogy Group, Splinters and Logs), I am learning to be accountable to my peers, to work cooperatively, and to practice the possibilities of shared livelihood.

My interest in exchange practices comes from living and working for the past decade in New York City. While rent continues to rise and wages stagnate, I am supported by barter, cooperation, and the wisdom of the solidarity economy movement. Rather than going into debt to be further professionalized as an artist, I attend self-organized schools and support movements for educational justice. Rather than looking to sell art to people who may resell it in secondary markets, or throwing away an entire installation at the end of a show, I barter my work, share it as a gift, or live with it for life. Rather than relying on outsourced labor or exploited interns, I refine and enjoy my crafts, exchanging labor for labor when necessary.

I am not a singular artist. I am a member of society, trying to find hope in a world of fierce inequities.

Scavenging in MoMA's archives for the Artists Experiment initiative, I found a small art history of exchange projects from the past forty years: from Franz Erhard Walther's *First Work Set* (1963–69) to Ben Kinmont's *I Need You* (1992). As a supplement, I decided to include exchange projects from outside of the collection, for many of these works offer an expanded notion of embodied exchange. From Jose Antonio *Vega Macotela's Time Divisa* (2006–10) to Carey Young's *Mutual Release* (2008), many like-minded contemporary artists see reciprocal labor, production, and distribution as integral to the meaning of their work.

While rent continues to rise and wages stagnate, I am supported by barter, cooperation, and the wisdom of the solidarity economy movement.

I asked the Education Department if I could work with them to make a printed booklet for the Café, which would be available in the Café, and include well-known works from MoMA's collection, works that I thought should be in the collection, as well as an invitation for Café patrons to contribute their own stories of exchange. They agreed to do this, and I designed the booklet.

Money is not just a medium of exchange, but also, in this case, a means of sharing information between the people who use the currency, who participate in the economy. This seems obvious in a networked information age.

—Caroline Woolard, video about Exchange Café by Alex Mallis, 2013

Study

Institutional Invitation

Yoko Ono
***Shadow Piece* (1963)**

Shadow Piece is one of the scores Yoko Ono published in her 1964 artist's book Grapefruit, which outlines instructions for the reader to enact. By asking individuals to "put your shadows together until they become one," *Shadow Piece* requires an exchange between at least two people in order to be completed. Ono is associated with Fluxus, a network of international avant-garde artists who were primarily active in the 1960s and 1970s. Fluxus artists worked in a wide range of media, exploring politics, culture, and everyday experiences through performance, writings, and instruction-based works.

SHADOW PIECE

Put your shadows together until they become one.

1963

fig. 4-11
Sample of the printed booklet
made for Exchange Café.

Andrea Blum
Lure (1994)

In *Lure*, Blum invites individuals to sit in adjacent booths and rest their arms in an opening between them, resulting in anonymous hand-to-hand contact with strangers. Blum is interested in creating moments of intimacy between two people. The artist has said that her work asks people to choose "between thorough privacy or forced interaction . . . to start going through the decision-making process of 'What do I want to do today? How do I want to be? Alone or with friends, even strangers?'"

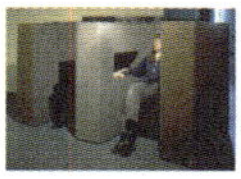

Carolina Caycedo
Day to Day (2002–09)

For her project *Day to Day*, Caroline Caycedo created a seven-year barter practice to meet her needs. This project had two platforms for exchange. Online, she posted her needs on a website, inviting visitors to offer a trade. She also drove a delivery truck, setting up temporary mobile markets in public spaces around the world, allowing her to barter her goods and services. For example, Caycedo traded Spanish lessons for a hot shower. Caycedo says that "art consists in the creation not of objects for passive aesthetic contemplation but of opportunities for cooperation and conversation among a broad array of individuals and communities."

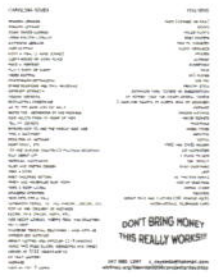

Audra Wolowiec
Freckle Exchange (2008)

For the *Freckle Exchange*, Wolowiec created the following instructions: "Choose a freckle on someone who you love/(Don't let any blemish go unnoticed)/Ask your partner to choose one from your body/Find a willing tattoo artist/Tell your story/Exchange." She intended for these instructions to be followed by any two people. Wolowiec explained, "I wanted to create a simple reminder, through a sentimental gesture, of how we carry each other with us, like imprints. My friend Niels and I each chose a freckle from each other: I chose one on his finger, he chose one on my arm."

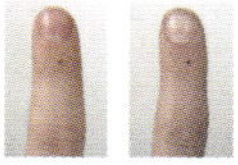

Julianne Swartz
Can You Hear Me? (2004)

Can You Hear Me? was a telephone-like sculpture installed on the exterior of the Sunshine Hotel, one of New York City's last remaining flophouses, or residences that offer cheap housing by providing minimal services. Passersby on the street could call through the tube and be heard in the Sunshine Hotel's lobby. This exchange project provides participants who may never visit the hotel to consider the intimate distance of a phone call with a stranger. As Swartz has written, she selected this site "to explore the complicated social dynamics of the location and to create an opportunity for a person-to-person exchange or connection." The title refers to the one of the first messages transmitted during Alexander Graham Bell's invention of, and early experiments with, the telephone.

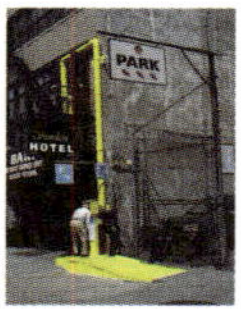

OurGoods.org
2009, ongoing

OurGoods.org is an online network that Caroline Woolard co-founded with Jen Abrams, Louise Ma, Carl Tashian, and Rich Watts. OurGoods.org connects artists, designers, farmers, and activists who want to barter to get independent projects done. The website provides a platform for users to communicate their "needs" and "haves," facilitating the non-monetary exchange of skills, spaces, and objects. At the heart of OurGoods' mission is the belief that "better work can be accomplished through relationships of mutual respect and shared resources. Members of OurGoods build lasting ties in a community of enormous potential by creating a community of resources and trust."

Allan Kaprow
Trading Dirt (1982)

Trading Dirt is one of Allan Kaprow's Happenings, a term he coined in 1957 to describe events "performed according to plan but without rehearsal, audience, or repetition." Beginning in 1982 Kaprow dug up dirt from his garden and traded it for other people's dirt. In one instance, he traded his soil for what he called "heavy-duty Buddhist dirt" from the Zen Center of San Diego, where he was studying. Kaprow believed that "ordinary life performed as art/not art can change the everyday with metaphoric power."

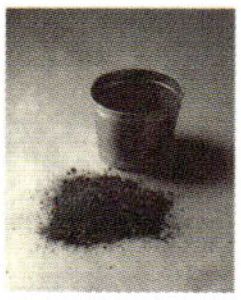

***Ray Tomlinson**
@ Symbol (1971)

In 1971 Ray Tomlinson invented the world's first e-mail system for the United States government's Advanced Research Projects Agency Networks (ARPAnet). The computer programmer appropriated the @ symbol—a character that has existed since at least the sixteenth century as an accounting symbol—as a stand-in for the long and convoluted code indicating a message's destination. Today, more than a billion people around the world type the @ sign every day, transforming the character into a symbol of communication. The sign's function in computer language, as in financial transactions, designates a relationship between two entities, establishing a link between them.

Ben Kinmont
I Need You (1992)

For this project, Kinmont approached fifty-eight strangers on the street in New York, opening conversations with each using the statement, "I need you to help me make a sculpture." Kinmont explained the potential exchange as follows: "In between people there exists a space where communication occurs between the self and another. For many, this space goes undetected even though it forms the basis of cultural differences, personal relationships, and understanding. . . . If you share your ideas with me and provide me with your signature and a means of contacting you, you will be a partial owner of this sculpture in its final form, be notified upon it exhibition, and, if it is sold, receive a portion of the money earned." Sixteen people gave signatures and addresses and were mailed checks one year later.

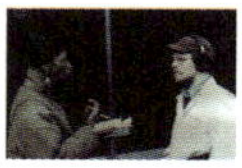

Max Liboiron
Object Ethnography Project (2011)

Each of the objects in this collaborative project was donated with a personal story. The objects were available for exchange on the condition that the new owner submits a narrative about the object, resulting in an online document of an original story, a photograph of the object, and an exchange story. "The Object Ethnography Project aims to show how stories influence the value, meaning and circulation of objects," Liboiron explains. "It is a creative laboratory where participants . . . determine the outcome of the cultural experiment."

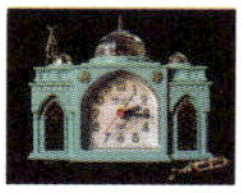

Tor Network
2002, ongoing

Tor is a network of virtual tunnels that allows individuals and groups—artists, programmers, scientists, and others—to improve their privacy and security on the Internet for free. The software maintains users' anonymity by directing Internet traffic through servers that conceal a user's location or usage from anyone conducting network surveillance or traffic analysis. The more populous and diverse the user base, the more secure the system becomes. Because users balance the quantity of files uploaded and downloaded, the system becomes more secure when the user base is more populous and diverse.

Tehching Hsieh and Linda Mary Montano
Art/Life (Rope Piece) (1983–84)

Tehching Hsieh and Linda Mary Montano are dedicated to blurring art and life by engaging in year-long practices that are understood as artworks. In *Art/Life (Rope Piece)*, Hsieh and Montano spent a year within eight feet of one another, never touching. As they wrote in a 1983 statement, "We will stay together for one year and never be alone. We will be in the same room at the same time, when we are inside. We will be tied together at waist with an eight-foot rope. We will never touch each other during the year."

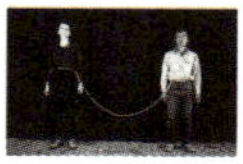

Huong Ngo, George Monteleone and Or Zubalsky
Dream Machine (2005, ongoing)

As the artists explain, *Dream Machine* "will operate forever, archiving our dreams long after we have forgotten them." They ask you to "call the dream machine and leave a voice recording of your dream. It calls you back in about fifteen minutes and plays a random dream from its memory." Impossible to experience without a contribution, this project represents a network of anonymous reciprocity.

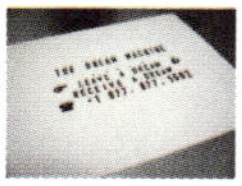

Institutional
Invitation

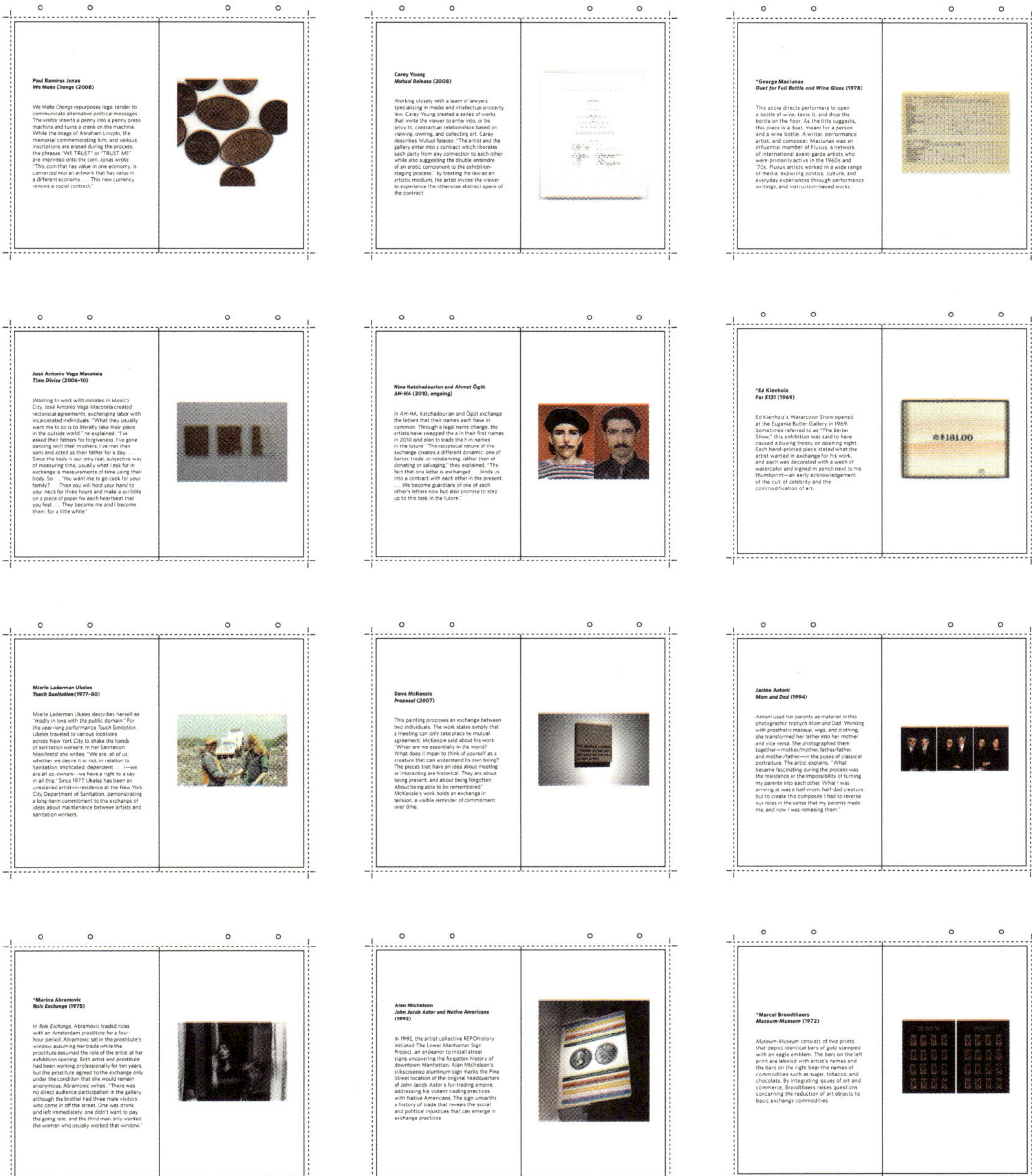

Paul Ramírez Jonas
We Make Change (2008)

We Make Change repurposes legal tender to communicate alternative political messages. The visitor inserts a penny into a penny press machine and turns a crank on the machine. While the image of Abraham Lincoln, the memorial commemorating him, and various inscriptions are erased during the process, the phrases "WE TRUST" or "TRUST ME" are imprinted onto the coin. Jonas wrote, "This coin that has value in one economy, is converted into an artwork that has value in a different economy. . . . This new currency renews a social contract."

Carey Young
Mutual Release (2008)

Working closely with a team of lawyers specializing in media and intellectual property law, Carey Young created a series of works that invite the viewer to enter into, or be privy to, contractual relationships based on viewing, owning, and collecting art. Carey describes *Mutual Release*: "The artist and the gallery enter into a contract which liberates each party from any connection to each other while also suggesting the double entendre of an erotic component to the exhibition-staging process." By treating the law as an artistic medium, the artist invites the viewer to experience the otherwise abstract space of the contract.

***George Maciunas**
Duet for Full Bottle and Wine Glass (1978)

This score directs performers to open a bottle of wine, taste it, and drop the bottle on the floor. As the title suggests, this piece is a duet, meant for a person and a wine bottle. A writer, performance artist, and composer, Maciunas was an influential member of Fluxus, a network of international avant-garde artists who were primarily active in the 1960s and '70s. Fluxus artists worked in a wide range of media, exploring politics, culture, and everyday experiences through performance, writings, and instruction-based works.

José Antonio Vega Macotela
Time Divisa (2006–10)

Wanting to work with inmates in Mexico City, José Antonio Vega Macotela created reciprocal agreements, exchanging labor with incarcerated individuals. "What they usually want me to do is to literally take their place in the outside world," he explained. "I've asked their fathers for forgiveness. I've gone dancing with their mothers. I've met their sons and acted as their father for a day. Since the body is our only real, subjective way of measuring time, usually what I ask for in exchange is measurements of time using their body. So . . . 'You want me to go cook for your family?' . . . Then you will hold your hand to your neck for three hours and make a scribble on a piece of paper for each heartbeat that you feel. . . . They become me and I become them, for a little while."

Nina Katchadourian and Ahmet Öğüt
AH-HA (2010, ongoing)

In *AH-HA*, Katchadourian and Öğüt exchange the letters that their names each have in common. Through a legal name change, the artists have swapped the *a* in their first names in 2010 and plan to trade the *h* in names in the future. "The reciprocal nature of the exchange creates a different dynamic: one of barter, trade, or rebalancing, rather than of donating or salvaging," they explained. "The fact that one letter is exchanged . . . binds us into a contract with each other in the present. . . . We become guardians of one of each other's letters now but also promise to step up to this task in the future."

***Ed Kienholz**
For $131 (1969)

Ed Kienholz's Watercolor Show opened at the Eugenia Butler Gallery in 1969. Sometimes referred to as "The Barter Show," this exhibition was said to have caused a buying frenzy on opening night. Each hand-printed piece stated what the artist wanted in exchange for his work, and each was decorated with a wash of watercolor and signed in pencil next to his thumbprint—an early acknowledgement of the cult of celebrity and the commodification of art.

Mierle Laderman Ukeles
Touch Sanitation (1977–80)

Mierle Laderman Ukeles describes herself as "madly in love with the public domain." For the year-long performance *Touch Sanitation*, Ukeles traveled to various locations across New York City to shake the hands of sanitation workers. In her Sanitation Manifesto! she writes, "We are, all of us, whether we desire it or not, in relation to Sanitation, implicated, dependent. . . . I—we are all co-owners—we have a right to a say in all this." Since 1977, Ukeles has been an unsalaried artist-in-residence at the New York City Department of Sanitation, demonstrating a long-term commitment to the exchange of ideas about maintenance between artists and sanitation workers.

Dave McKenzie
Proposal (2007)

This painting proposes an exchange between two individuals. The work states simply that a meeting can only take place by mutual agreement. McKenzie said about his work: "When are we essentially in the world? What does it mean to think of yourself as a creature that can understand its own being? The pieces that have an idea about meeting or interacting are historical. They are about being present, and about being forgotten. About being able to be remembered." McKenzie's work holds an exchange in tension, a visible reminder of commitment over time.

Janine Antoni
Mom and Dad (1994)

Antoni used her parents as material in this photographic triptych *Mom and Dad*. Working with prosthetic makeup, wigs, and clothing, she transformed her father into her mother and vice versa. She photographed them together—mother/mother, father/father, and mother/father—in the poses of classical portraiture. The artist explains: "What became fascinating during the process was the resistance or the impossibility of turning my parents into each other. What I was arriving at was a half-mom, half-dad creature, but to create this composite I had to reverse our roles in the sense that my parents made me, and now I was remaking them."

***Marina Abramovic**
Role Exchange (1975)

In *Role Exchange*, Abramovic traded roles with an Amsterdam prostitute for a four-hour period. Abramovic sat in the prostitute's window assuming her trade while the prostitute assumed the role of the artist at her exhibition opening. Both artist and prostitute had been working professionally for ten years, but the prostitute agreed to the exchange only under the condition that she would remain anonymous. Abramovic writes, "There was no direct audience participation in the gallery, although the brothel had three male visitors who came in off the street. One was drunk and left immediately, one didn't want to pay the going rate, and the third man only wanted the woman who usually worked that window."

Alan Michelson
John Jacob Astor and Native Americans (1992)

In 1992, the artist collective REPOhistory initiated The Lower Manhattan Sign Project, an endeavor to install street signs uncovering the forgotten history of downtown Manhattan. Alan Michelson's silkscreened aluminum sign marks the Pine Street location of the original headquarters of John Jacob Astor's fur-trading empire, addressing his violent trading practices with Native Americans. The sign unearths a history of trade that reveals the social and political injustices that can emerge in exchange practices.

***Marcel Broodthaers**
Museum-Museum (1972)

Museum-Museum consists of two prints that depict identical bars of gold stamped with an eagle emblem. The bars on the left print are labeled with artist's names and the bars on the right bear the names of commodities such as sugar, tobacco, and chocolate. By integrating issues of art and commerce, Broodthaers raises questions concerning the reduction of art objects to basic exchange commodities.

THIS archive of personal memories, myths, and forgotten histories of exchanges will be collated and made into a book.

Please pin this paper to the wall in the section that makes sense to you. Add your name, email, and phone to the back of this paper if you would like to be:

___ included in the book.

___ NOT included in the booklet.

___ involved in making it.

___ given a share of profits if any are made.

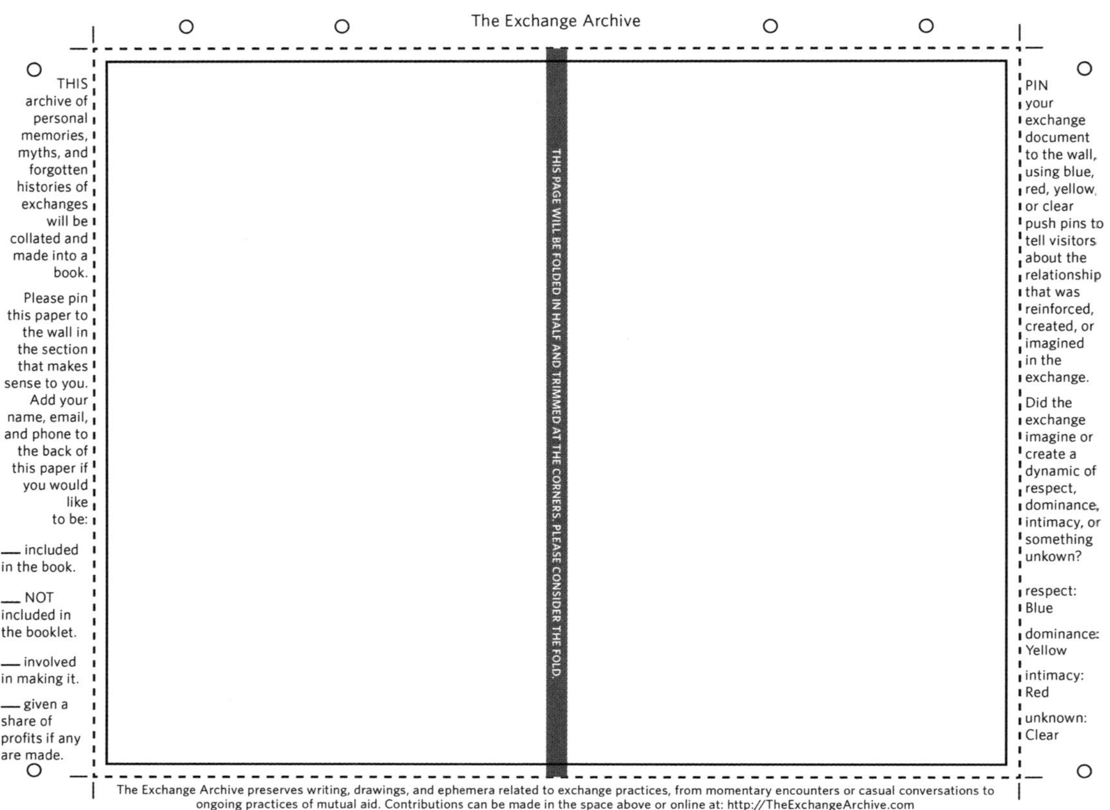

PIN your exchange document to the wall, using blue, red, yellow, or clear push pins to tell visitors about the relationship that was reinforced, created, or imagined in the exchange.

Did the exchange imagine or create a dynamic of respect, dominance, intimacy, or something unkown?

respect: Blue

dominance: Yellow

intimacy: Red

unknown: Clear

The Exchange Archive preserves writing, drawings, and ephemera related to exchange practices, from momentary encounters or casual conversations to ongoing practices of mutual aid. Contributions can be made in the space above or online at: http://TheExchangeArchive.com

Study

Institutional
Invitation

I had to get the image permissions signed from all of the artists, the text edited and approved by MoMA, and the booklet designed so that it could become part of a larger archive, with café patron's additions. Once it was ready, I sent an invitation to participants.

> Subject: MoMA | Image Use & Invitation | Exchange Café | May 24-June 30
> May 26, 2013
>
> Dear Mierle Laderman Ukeles, Carolina Caycedo, Julianne Swartz, Ray Tomlinson, Adrian Piper, Paul Ramirez Jonas, Andrea Blum, Roger Dingledine, Alexandre Allaire, Mike Perry, Billy Apple, Ben Kinmont, Tehching Hsieh, Linda Montano, George Monteleone, Audra Wolowiec, Alan Michelson, David McKenzie, Carey Young, Hương Ngô, Or Zubalsky, Nina Katchadourian, Ahmet Öğüt, Rich Watts, Louise Ma, Carl Tashian, Jen Abrams, Janine Antoni, Jose Antonio Vega Macotela, and Max Liboiron,
>
> From May 24th through June 30th, I hope to share your work with the public at MoMA's Cullman Research Center. Please let me know (1) if you like the image I've selected for your project, (2) if you want to talk to me about your research, and (3) if you can come to the reception on May 30th from 6-8 p.m.
>
> CONTEXT: For an initiative called Artists Experiment, I've been working with the Education Department at MoMA on a learning space dedicated to exchange-based practices. I selected your work to be featured in a social space in the Cullman Education and Research building so that I might make legible a history of exchange in MoMA's collection and beyond. We plan to show a small version of the attached image of your work on an interactive wall in the mezzanine.

I selected your work to be featured in a social space ... so that I might make legible a history of exchange in MoMA's collection and beyond.

IMAGE REQUEST: If you have a high resolution version of the image or project (shown in the attached PDF) that you'd like us to use, I would be grateful if you could send it to us. If not, we'll use what you see in the attached PDF. These image reproductions will be used for educational purposes only.

TEXT SUPPLEMENT: If you've written anything about the work I've selected (or about reciprocity and exchange in general), and want to email a copy for us to read internally with Exchange Café waitstaff/facilitators who will explain your work to the public, please do! If you want us to include it in the Café library for the public to view, we can arrange that as well. Please do not hesitate to contact me (Caroline) to discuss your research or to ask questions about this learning space. I'm reachable by email or cell: 401 935 3071

MORE DETAILS: Exchange Café will be open Thursday-Sunday from May 24th through June 30th. Exchange Café is a social space in the mezzanine of MoMA's Education and Research building that is dedicated to exchange-based practices. The Café encourages visitors to question notions of reciprocity, value, and property through shared experiences. Tea from the Feral Trade Network, milk from Milk Not Jails, and honey from BeeSpace — products that directly engage the political economy — will be available by exchange. Instead of paying

with legal tender, Exchange Café patrons are
invited to make a resource-based currency.
Exchange Café features an interactive participatory archive, a matrix of exchange projects,
and a library of books and ephemera.

SAVE 30 MAY: If you are in New York between
May 24th and June 30th, and wish to visit
MoMA, please join us at MoMA Studio: Exchange
Café. We will have a reception on May 30th
from 6:00-8:00 p.m. and will be open Thursday
through Sunday from 1:00-5:00 p.m., Fridays
from 1:00-8:00 p.m. Please let us know if you
would like to attend the reception on May 30th
from 6:00-8:00 p.m., as space is limited.
There are many events throughout the program,
so if you cannot attend the opening, please
come for Ted Purves and Shane Aslan Selzer's
talk on Critical Exchange, Jon Hendricks on
Fluxus, Milk Not Jails on prison abolition,
or OurGoods.org [see chapter 3] on barter. The schedule
is here: http://www.moma.org/visit/calendar/
exhibitions/1364

Thank you!

Caroline Woolard, Sarah Kennedy, Sheetal
Prajapati, and Pablo Helguera
Artists Experiment / MoMA Studio:
Exchange Café

After Exchange Café had closed, I wanted to publish the
booklet so it would continue to serve as a resource for
people thinking about art and exchange. I asked the MoMA
team if this would be possible.

Subject: publishing that Exchange Archive as
a book

March 10, 2014
Pablo, Sheetal, and Sarah,

I really want to publish that little Exchange
Archive/Exchange Reference Works book. I
remember you (Pablo) saying that MoMA's book
publishing house wouldn't do anything with us,
but that for legal reasons we should make an
offer to them first that they reject. Is
this true?

I'd love to work with you all, and with MoMA's
publishing house, but if that's impossible,
can I make this an independent project, thank-
ing AE and crediting you all, and MoMA, but go
forth and self-publish it? Let me know what is
possible, and what's a sensitive issue.

I know my friends at www.toposgraphics.com
(www.topositu.com) are up for designing it! I
think this book (1:1 exchange, small primary
audiences) could be the dematerialization of
the art object for the 2010s.

Checking in,
Caroline

Pablo Helguera at MoMA got the "green light" from publishing after seven months of dialogue from March through
September of 2014, but in the end, the project fell through.

September 18, 2014
Hi Caroline,

Actually, believe it or not, publications has
finally given you the green light. I do need
to put you in touch with our chief of publications who has been very supportive of your project —
he just needs to sort out a few things with
you. Will send an intro email shortly.

Congratulations!
P

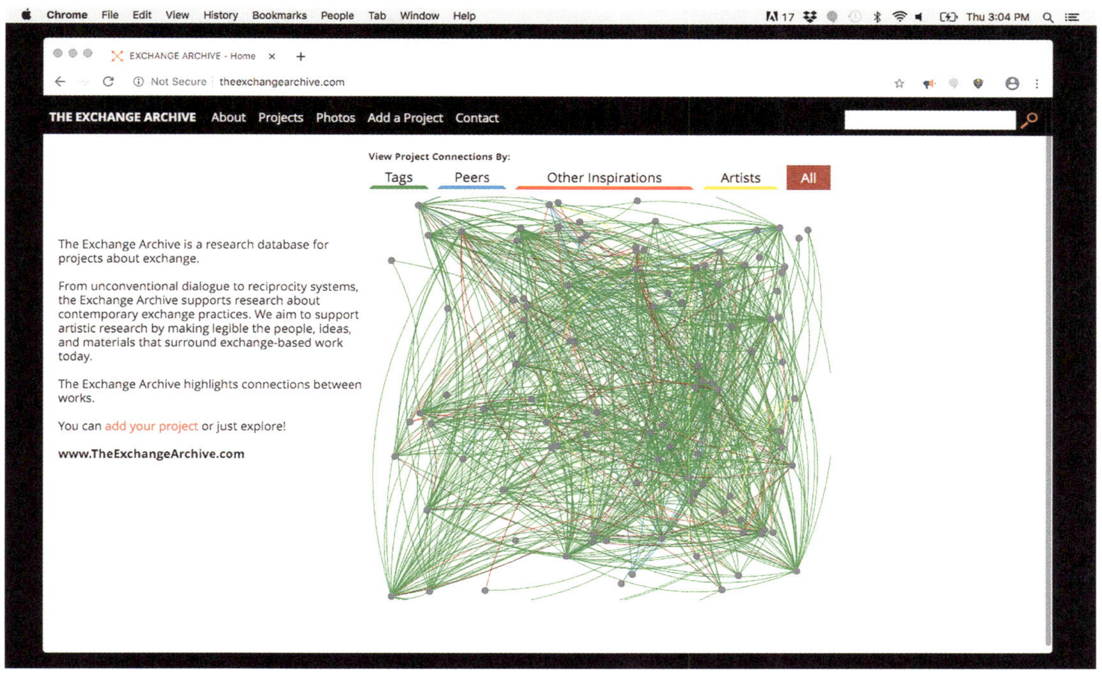

fig. 4-12
The Exchange Archive, 2013,
website, created by Corey Brady,
Pratim Sengupta, Mason Wright,
Amelia Winger-Bearskin and
Caroline Woolard.

I also made a website for Exchange Café, to attempt to make the process visible online and accessible to people who would not be able to visit the Café in person, but was sent a cease-and-desist letter from MoMA's legal team in June of 2013. Sarah called me to explain this, in person, and I cannot share any writing about it in this book.

MoMA did, however, allow me to write two posts about the project, for their website in June of 2013.

FIRST POST
CAFÉ AS LEARNING FORMAT

When asked to propose a new learning format to the Education Department at MoMA, I suggested a café, a place where meaning is made in dialogue, where objects can be touched, and where visceral knowledge is honored. Exchange Café is a social space dedicated to exchange, from unconventional encounters to barter and reciprocal economies. What follows is an explanation of some principles of the café, as well as the ways in which these principles could be extended towards a more engaging visitor experience at MoMA.

1. Waitstaff as Educators

At Exchange Café, you will be greeted by waitstaff with direct experience working in, with, and for solidarity economies. With the café as a learning format, educators are waitstaff with lifelong commitments to the topics at hand—Exchange Café waitstaff Lauren Melodia and Tychist Baker are organizers for Milk Not Jails, Kenneth Edusei is an organizer for participatory budgeting in Brooklyn, and Amelia Winger-Bearskin, Forest Purnell, and Carla Aspenberg are artists engaged in practices of reciprocity. With the café as a learning format, education happens in lived experience, through dialogue that connects artworks to activism and community organizing.

Imagine if every time you walked into MoMA, you could elect to speak to a community organizer about the relationship between real-time organizing and the issues at stake in the artworks on view. Imagine if the interns, fabricators, and artists who made work could be hired as stewards for the work while it was on view, talking to the public about the construction, materials, and dialogue surrounding the work itself.

Imagine if every time you walked into MoMA, you could elect to speak to a community organizer

2. Education through Dialogue

"Because the nature of Dialogue is exploratory, its meaning and its methods continue to unfold. No firm rules can be laid down for conducting a Dialogue because its essence is learning—not as the result of consuming a body of information or doctrine imparted by an authority, nor as a means of examining or criticizing a particular theory or programme, but rather as part of an unfolding process of creative participation between peers."

— David Bohm, Dialogue: A Proposal

Exchange Café takes the social format of a café, taking the embodied roles and rules of a café as a space for learning. Greeted by waitstaff with direct experience in the topics at hand, visitors will be led to consider art works that focus on one-to-one agreements, artists who facilitate engage in short term encounters or long-term relationships of reciprocity.

On the Exchange Café wall, the Exchange Archive acts as an emergent publication about one-on-one engagement, inviting contributions from the public. From artists who facilitate unconventional dialogue to artists who consider the barter of goods and services (the labor of producing a project) as integral to the meaning of the work, the Exchange Archive makes legible a desire for one-on-one interaction in MoMA's collection and beyond. For example, Hương Ngô, Or Zubalsky, and George Monteleone's ongoing project, the *Dream Machine*, asks anyone to "call the dream machine (1-877-877-5602) and leave a voice recording of your dream. It calls you back in about fifteen minutes and plays a random dream from its memory." Impossible to experience without a contribution, this project represents a network of anonymous reciprocity.

Online, TheExchangeArchive.com (made by the MultiAgency Collective and myself) shows connections between projects, artists, and ideas, revealing the ways in which artworks emerge in dialogue between people, not in solitary isolation. As we state: Artists do not create work in a vacuum. Artists work in a dialogue with other people, so the Exchange Archive supports further artistic dialog by showing the inspirations that flow between projects. As a research database for projects about exchange, the online archive serves as a footnote system for research-based artists. What if museums made legible the people, ideas, and materials that surround exchange-based work today, highlighting connections between works as the primary focus, rather than individual artists?

revealing the ways in which artworks emerge in dialogue between people, not in solitary isolation.

NOTE: You can download the Exchange Archive Submission Form and fill out your own submission to the Exchange Archive, or add footnotes for your art projects to TheExchangeArchive.com.

3. Food with an Agenda

At Exchange Café, you will be offered products with political biographies: tea carried across borders, milk distributed by prison abolitionists, and honey gifted by bees. Imagine if museum cafés and food-art projects served products with principles as radical as the propositions in artworks. Rather than providing a social space with anonymous products that do not get biographies (as Martha Rostler did in veiling the staff contributions to Meta Monumental and e-flux did with the farm contributions to Time/Food), I wanted to bring in groups with edible projects that honor the relationship between art and solidarity economies: dairy from Milk not Jails, tea from the Feral Trade Courier, and honey from BeeSpace. Exchange Café celebrates the power of these products; they are logical extension of the propositions that artists in the café's Exchange Archive reveal.

SECOND POST
CAFÉ AS LEARNING FORMAT

When asked to propose a new learning format to the Education Department at MoMA, I suggested a café, a place where meaning is made in dialog, where objects can be touched, and where visceral knowledge is honored.

Exchange Café is a social space dedicated to exchange, from unconventional encounters to barter and reciprocal economies. What follows is an explanation of some principles of the café, as well as the ways in which these principles could be extended towards a more engaging visitor experience at MoMA.

Imagine if museum cafés and food-art projects served products with principles as radical as the propositions in artworks.

1. Exchange means Depth over Breadth

The works in the Exchange Archive, from Yoko Ono to Ben Kinmont, from Max Libioron to Merle Laderman Ukeles, demonstrate a commitment to a primary experience that occurs one-to-one, outside of art institutions.

2. Long-term Experiments

This learning space features an archive with works in MoMA's collection and beyond that focus on reciprocity and one-to-one exchange. For example, if the Exchange Archive reference work called the *Dream*

Machine allows anonymous individuals to exchange dreams, and OurGoods.org allows individuals to barter art skills and objects, how might these networks carry goods internationally? As Kate Rich, Feral Trade grocer asks, "What is the true load bearing capacity of our social networks?" The Feral Trade Courier takes the one-to-one transfer to a global scale, moving goods from hand to hand outside of commercial shipping.

For another example, Milk Not Jails milk products are distributed only when farmers agree to a radical (as in, getting to the root of the issue) policy agenda: opposing prison expansion as an economic driver. If Mierle Laderman Ukeles' worked to give sanitation workers recognition in *Touch Sanitation*, Milk Not Jails pushes for recognition of dairy farmers that goes beyond visibility, advocating for policy shifts to support their livelihood. Lastly, if Ben Kinmont seeks an ethical exchange between participants and artists in his work *I Need You*, BeeSpace looks to research the (im) possibility of ethical exchange in interspecies collaboration.

3. Social Spaces Take Time

Imagine if museums were places to rest, gather, and practice ways of belonging to one another. Exchange

Imagine if museums were places to rest, gather, and practice ways of belonging to one another.

Café is a social space where children and adults climb on furniture without second thought, where books can be touched without gloves, and where fluxus works are understood in re-performance: Forest Purnell and Tychist Baker ask visitors to imagine snow falling and to let shadows touch. With the café as a learning format, education happens when people practice ways of being and belonging. It is my hope that more museums make space for embodied, visceral knowledge. To do this well, the Exchange Café (and other projects of this nature) should be open to the public after work, and should exist as a reliable space for at least six months, if not a year.

Mediating

I wanted to make a reflection document about the experience at MoMA, but MoMA staff (such as Sarah and Pablo) cannot write about MoMA projects, without permission. On my own, I collected the 3000–4000 emails between MoMA and myself, and pasted them all into one, virtual document. I invited a research student who wanted to know more about my process to read them, confidentially, and to notice themes that emerged about the differences between our expectations and process. I hope that one day, this research can be published for other artists to learn from, but I understand that I have different risks and stakes than MoMA staff do. I understand that MoMA employees are required to keep the details of their projects confidential, for example, and cannot share their opinions openly without serious cons. For now, I will not share this document. Sheetal was able to write about this project, in this book, because she does not work at MoMA anymore.

There should be hiding spaces, in the museum, because the museum is so open that it almost feels like you're being watched all the time, so I wanted some hiding spots where people could find solitude and read quietly.

—Caroline Woolard, video about Exchange Cafe by Alex Mallis, 2013

Study

Institutional
Invitation

Managing

I learned so much about working with institutions to make art, as this was my first time working with a big budget on my own, and it was the MoMA Education Department's first time bringing in artists to work with on a project that blurred the lines between an artwork, a public program, and a class. I learned to scale back.

I learned to do much smaller projects, as the institutional lines of communication and policies make moving quickly impossible.

I made many mistakes in my work with MoMA, as I had never made a project based upon an institutional invitation. I learned to do much smaller projects, as the institutional lines of communication and policies make moving quickly impossible. Doing something well, especially if that something requires "unconventional" requests that might seem completely "normal" in a collectively-initiated setting (like sharing a budget, making a website, or changing the hours that a space is open), can take months in a big institution like MoMA.

While I tried to do way too many things, which meant that many of them did not happen or happened in a way that was less finished and well-considered than I would like, I did accomplish a few things that stand out today. Working with MoMA, I was able to:

```
- redistribute money from MoMA to collectives
  and artists of color that I respect;
- change the hours that the café (and therefore
  an area of the museum) was open in order to
  allow working people to visit after regular
  working hours;
- get catering and supplies from local vendors;
- and change the hiring policies so that people
  with "criminal records" could be hired at MoMA.
```

I believe that, whenever possible, commissions from resource-rich institutions should support small businesses, artists who are nonbinary, women, and/or people of color, and that I should use these opportunities to redistribute resources back to social movements. I was able to get funding for many groups and people doing important work in New York City, but I cannot share the budget with you as MoMA has requested that I keep it confidential.

I believe that, whenever possible, commissions from resource-rich institutions should support small businesses, artists who are nonbinary, women, and/or people of color, and that I should use these opportunities to redistribute resources back to social movements.

Experiment

Institutional
Invitation

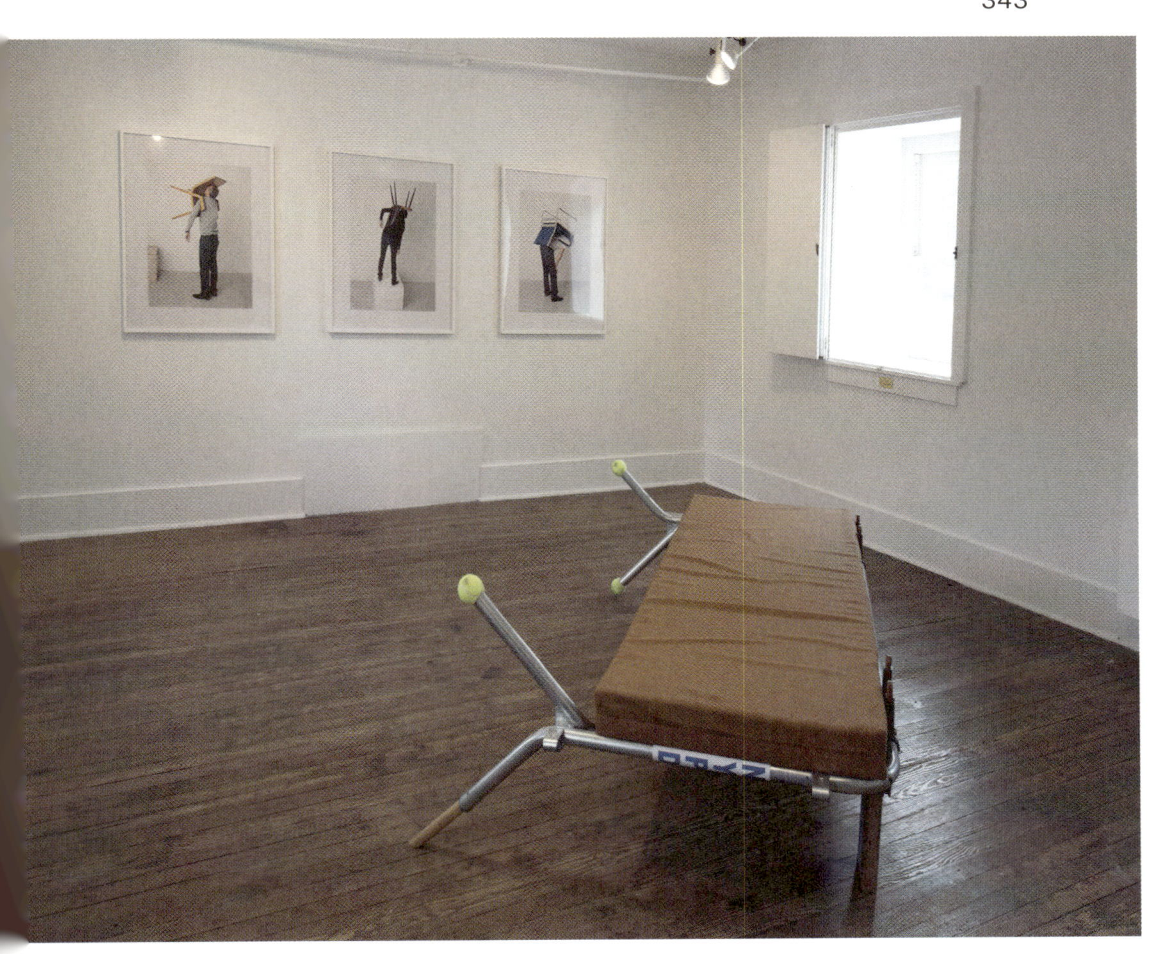

fig. 4-13
Caroline Woolard's *Barricade
to Bed* beside Erwin Wurm's *One
Minute Sculptures* in Discomfort:
Furniture, Function and Form
in Contemporary Sculpture,
curated by Liz Sheehan at the
Hunterdon Museum.

5

BFAMFAPhD

BFAMFAPhD is a collective that makes art, reports, and teaching tools to advocate for cultural equity in the United States. The collective formed in 2012 after a series of open meetings that Caroline Woolard convened. Its name combines all of the degrees that a person could accumulate in undergraduate, graduate, and doctoral programs: a BFA, an MFA, and a PhD. Concerned about the impact of debt, rent, and precarity on the lives of creative people, BFAMFAPhD asks: What is a work of art in the age of $120,000 art degrees? The collective embodies a commitment to bringing people together to analyze and reimagine power relationships in the arts.

BFAMFAPhD core members are: Susan Jahoda, Emilio Martínez Poppe, Agnes Szanyi, Vicky Virgin, and Caroline Woolard. Susan Jahoda is a Professor in Studio Arts at the University of Amherst, MA; Emilio Martínez Poppe is an MFA candidate at the University of Pennsylvania, Agnes Szanyi is a Doctoral Student at The New School for Social Research in New York, NY, Vicky Virgin is a Research Associate with the Mayor's Office for Economic Opportunity in New York, NY, and Caroline Woolard is an Assistant Professor of Sculpture at The University of Hartford, CT. Contributors include: Pasqualina Azzarello, Julian Boilen, Ann Chen, Dia Felix, Art Jones, Ben Lerchin, Alex Mallis, Blair Murphy, Kieran Startup, Mauricio Vargas, Lika Volkova, Jeff Warren, and Zipeng Zhu.

More information is online at: http://bfamfaphd.com

Imagine that this September,
instead of matriculating at
a traditional 4-year school,
prospective freshmen and
first-year MFA students pool
the money they would otherwise
spend on tuition. The class of
2018 (around 100,000 students
paying $25,576 on average)
would have $2,157,600,000 to
work with.

—Caroline Woolard, 2013

2012/2013
Occupy Wall Street 2011
Art & Labor Working Group
Cooper Union threatens to charge
   tuition for the first time in
   154 years
Cooper Union occupied by students 2013
2014 Strike Debt's Rolling
   Jubilee project has abolished
   almost $4 million in private
   student debt for a little over
   $100,000. Rolling Jubilee (a
   Strike Debt project) buys
   student debt for pennies on
   the dollar, but instead of
   collecting it, abolishes it.
Black Lives Matter 2013

hand in
hand in hand in hand
In hand in hand in hand in hand
"education should be as free as
   air and water"
artist as organizer
artist as long term resident
culture : organizing
"Organizing artists is like
   herding cats."

Study

We can learn together,
in public, as a collective, and
embody the participatory
learning that we want to see.

Commitment

Experience

Cooper Union is going to
charge tuition for the first
time in 154 years!

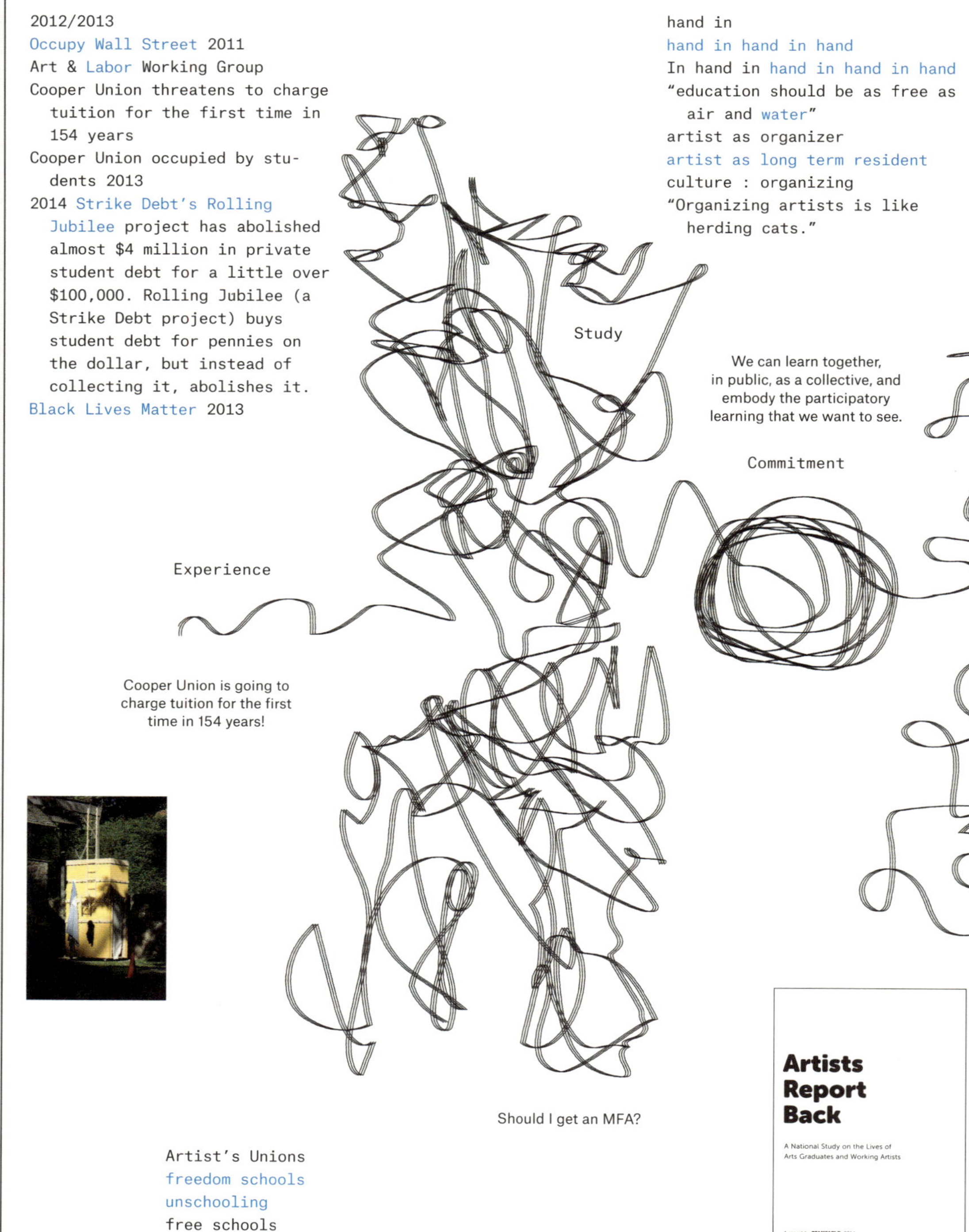

Should I get an MFA?

Artist's Unions
freedom schools
unschooling
free schools
debt

Artists Report Back

A National Study on the Lives of
Arts Graduates and Working Artists

A report by BFAMFAPhD 2014

Collectively-
Initiated

solidarity economies
Howard Singerman
Critical University Studies
Mark McGurl
James Elkins
Every ten years, in the United
  States alone, one million
  students graduate with a BFA,
  MFA, or PhD in visual art.
What might we—1,827,087
  arts graduates since 1987—
  do together?

There are more creative people
  in our nation than doctors,
  lawyers and police officers
  combined—if we organized,
  we'd be larger than the US
  military!

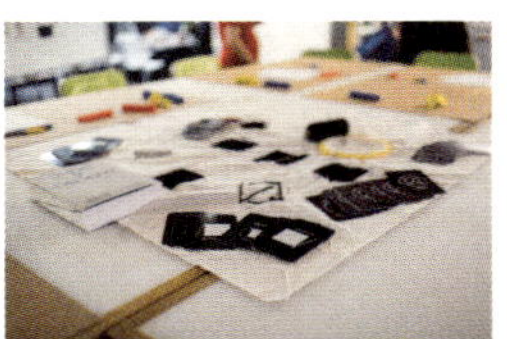

union
advocacy

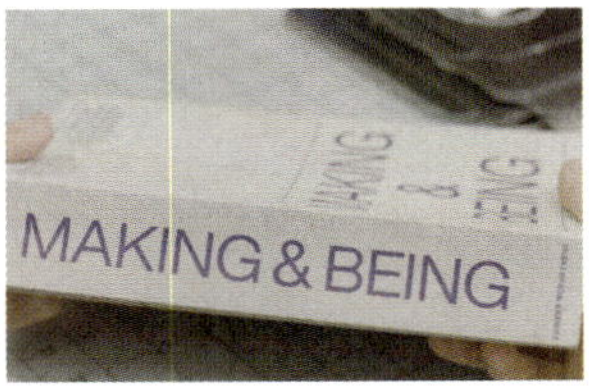

A multi-year platform
because teaching and
advocacy take time

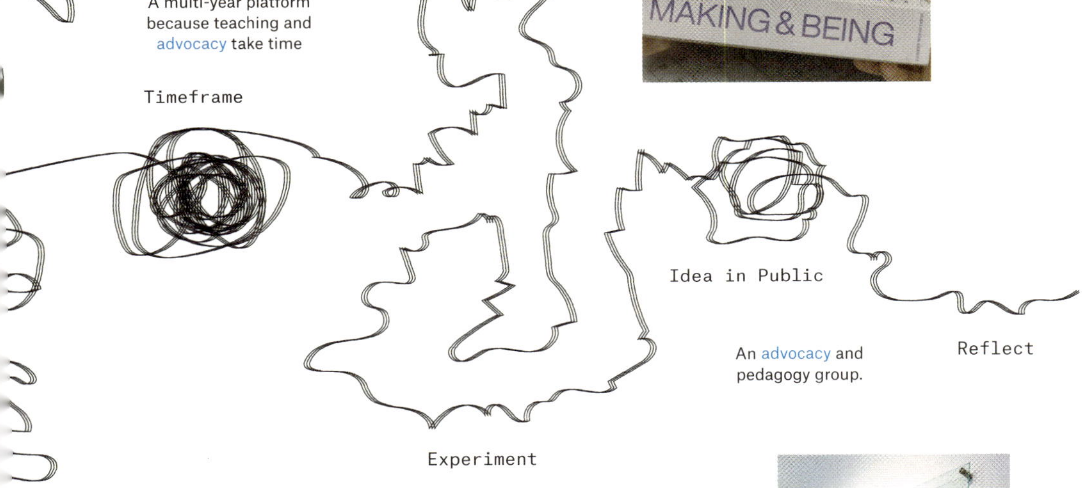

Timeframe

MAKING & BEING

Idea in Public

An advocacy and
pedagogy group.

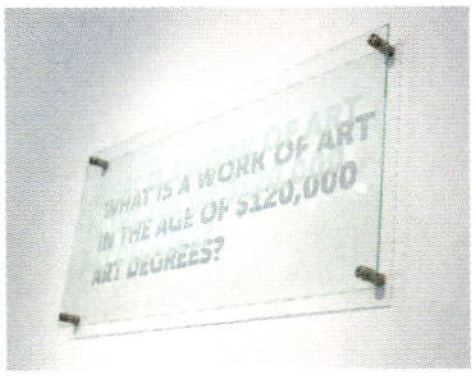

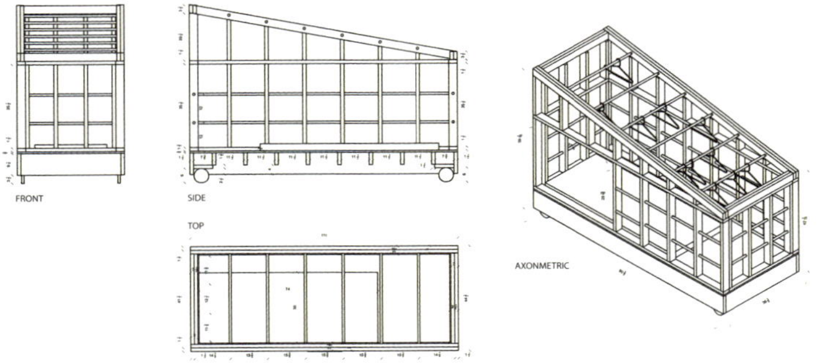

Reflect

Experiment

donor plaque
report
credit card
land trust
art made from disclaimed
  (thrown away) art
events
playing cards

Meta-critical Mobilization

Larissa Harris is a curator at the Queens Museum. Exhibitions at QMA include *Red Lines Housing Crisis Learning Center*, a project on home finance by artist and urban designer Damon Rich; the first U.S. solo presentation of Korean video and performance artist Sung Hwan Kim; *People's United Nations (pUN)* by Pedro Reyes; *13 Most Wanted Men: Andy Warhol at the 1964 World's Fair*; and, with Patti Phillips, *Mierle Laderman Ukeles: Maintenance Art.*

Larissa Harris, Curator, Queens Museum, 2020

Between 2009 and 2013 the Queens Museum expanded, but at a certain point it appeared there wasn't enough money yet to program and staff the doubled building. Our director Tom Finkelpearl had the idea to start a studio program in what would become the old wing. We got funding from a foundation whose guidelines stipulated that it had to include "artist services" and "professional development." Caroline was part of our first cohort, and used this funding stream to hold a series of public conversations under the name BFAMFAPhD, which referred to an emerging collective Woolard hoped would form and solidify.

These events tackled some of the same questions around professionalization or institutionalization of creative work that the funding itself embodied. The series combined community conversations and talking with people who had written about the art-school complex. Against the backdrop of Caroline's own experience in and desire to build para- or counter- institutions whose members could see and control the power and resources they themselves produced, these were open conversations that avoided complete condemnation of "professionalization," and instead debated the possibilities, comprised or not, inherent in the institutions that inevitably shape artists and the arts as a field. As Caroline said at the start of one of these early BFAMFAPhD events, "The question is not the scandal of the individual, necessarily, but how can individuals create institutions that they want to be part of? Where they

Collectively-
Initiated

see the power of the institution as collectively generated, rather than a random chance occurrence they need to participate in." In this case, Caroline used resources at the Queens Museum to imagine and enact collective action outside the institution.

these were open conversations that avoided complete condemnation of "professionalization"

BFAMFAPhD's first major project, *Artist's Report Back*, was produced the summer after this series, amidst the energy of the protests around Cooper Union tuition, Debt Strike, and Rolling Jubilee (now Debt Collective). It revealed data on the interface between higher-education debt and art careers. But the most striking statistic for me was how many more artists without a BA apparently make a career from their art than those with degrees. Debt is obviously one reason for this, but the wide-open definition of art (both in society and in the survey) is probably a bigger one.

The Queens Museum has been a place that sought out and supported working-class creativity. In the immigrant neighborhoods that flank our park, people develop businesses — web design, wedding photography — based on what they have to offer and the needs of their communities. Caroline has also mentioned that this statistic includes a lot of musicians, whose economy has always been broad-based rather than semi-feudal like visual art as conventionally understood. I believe Caroline was the only artist in the studios that year to take advantage of the

funding available for "professional development." Taking her critical mobilization of the concept as a starting point, could "artists services" be a tool to connect the makers of more broadly defined creative work with the people for whom art school *is* a likely proposition (even if it produces debt)? Is this solidarity around cultural work what we will need now, to the extent that it crosses real class and cultural boundaries, and as we face down a world in which at least some patronage may be out of the running?

That year Caroline also built a mobile sleeping unit in her studio, reacting in a practical manner to the realities of life in the "real estate state" (as Sam Stein calls it). Not originally meant for exhibition, but making underlying structural problems visible (and thereby calling up Krzysztof Wodiczko's "interrogative design"), these small refuges (she built a similar structure at another artists residency in 2009) may protect her from the pressure on precious solitude that comes with a commitment to living and thinking together — whether it be your living space or an active life in New York. Caroline extrapolates questions from her own life situations about the structure of society under capitalism, makes and catalyzes tools and communities to address these structures, then ploughs back what she learns into her own life and her commitment to making the process of social change a democratic and inclusive one. Indeed this book itself is an attempt to make this iterative practice visible.

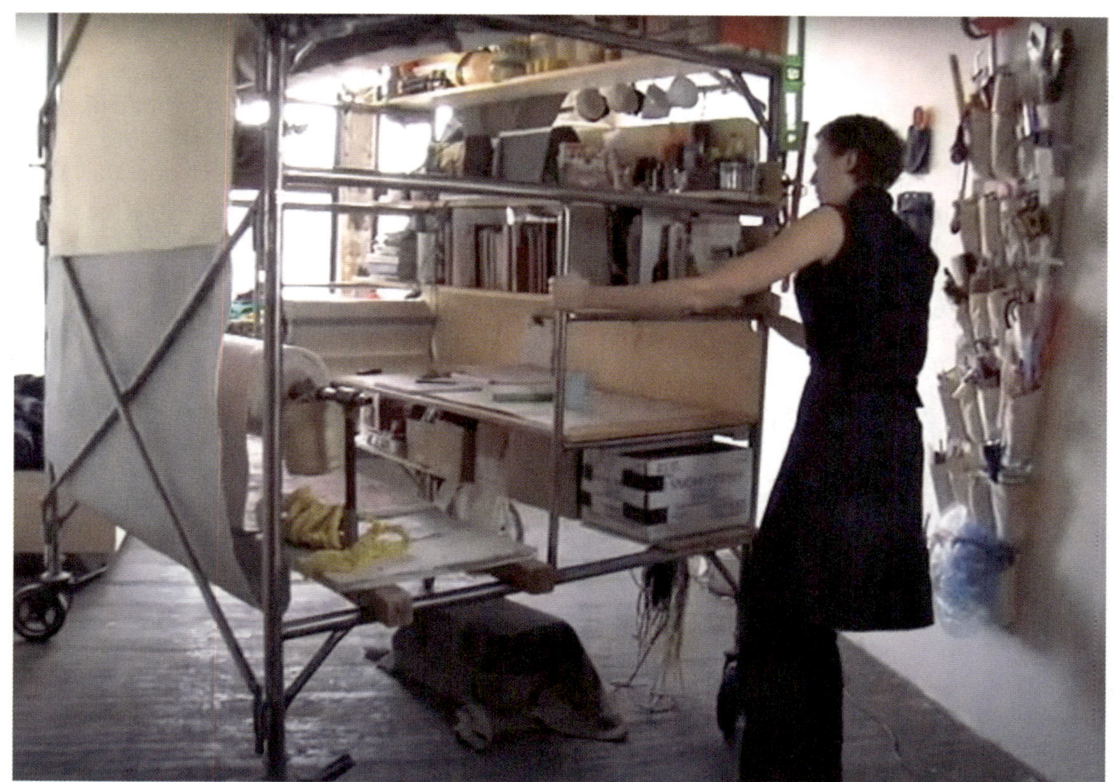

fig. 5-1
Caroline Woolard in her studio
in 2008. Courtesy of the artist.

Caroline extrapolates questions from her own life
situations about the structure of society under capitalism, makes and catalyzes
tools and communities to
address these structures
then ploughs back what she
learns into her own life and
her commitment to making the
process of social change a
democratic and inclusive one.

—Larissa Harris

Art holds the fantasy and
the contradiction of mobility,
of individuality, and of the
desire to resist that, to
imagine cooperative ways of
being. These houses on wheels
at the MacDowell Colony and
at the Queens Museum do that,
too. They might want to move,
but you can't get very far
with those little wheels!
These structures are symbols,
metonyms, for bodies—architecture as an extension of the
body, as supportive spaces
for dreaming, thinking, and
making. They are sculptures
that are functional, that are
places where conversation,
hanging out, and making art
happen. They might imagine
mobility, but in reality, they
are quite fixed.

—Caroline Woolard, interview
with Larissa Harris

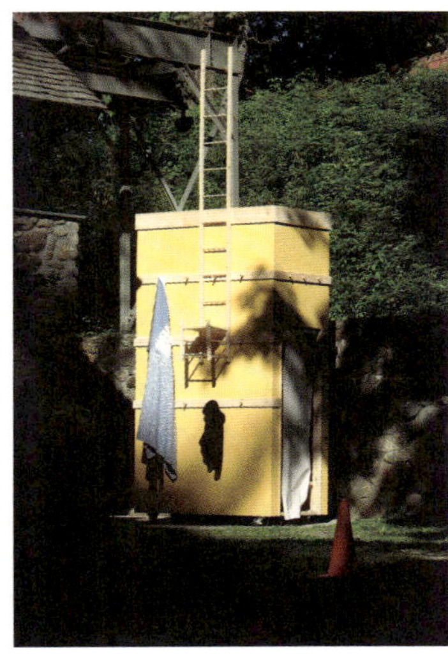

fig. 5-2
Shaker Residence, 2008, birch
wood, sheetrock, paint, per-
formance, 72 × 36 × 144 inches.
Courtesy of the artist and the
MacDowell Colony.

fig. 5-3
Studio/Home, 2014 (reconstructed
2020), framing lumber, hardware,
mattress, fabric, casters, 86 ×
46 × 98 inches. Courtesy of the
artist and the Queens Museum.
Photo by Aaron Strauss.

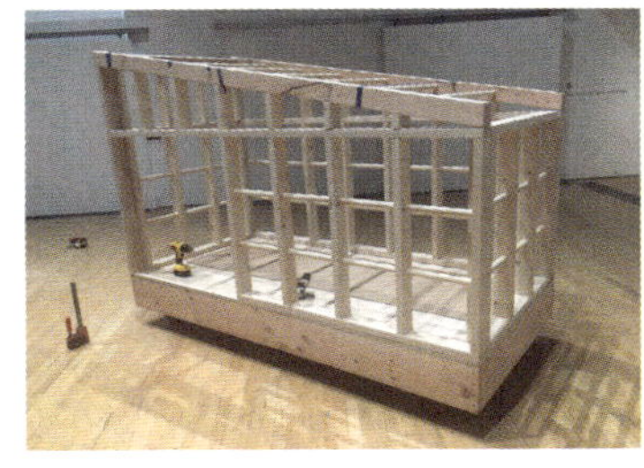

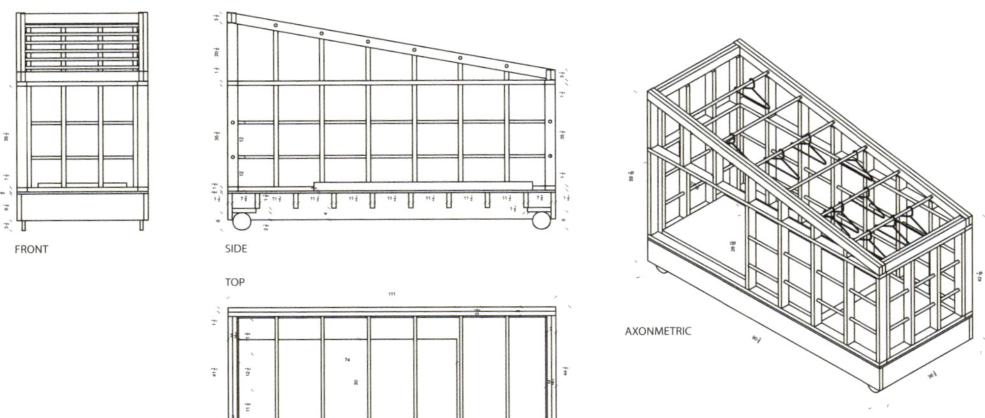

fig. 5-4
Caroline Woolard, *Technical
Drawings for Studio/Home*, dimensions variable, 2019. Courtesy
of the artist.

The Collective Forms of Decommodified Labor

Leigh Claire La Berge, PhD, professes at the intersection of arts, literature, visual culture and political economy. She is the author of *Scandals and Abstraction: Financial Fiction of the Long 1980s* (Oxford University Press) and *Wages Against Artwork: Decommodified Labor and the Claims of Socially Engaged Art* (Duke University Press, 2019). She is Associate Professor of English in the Department of English at BMCC CUNY.

Leigh Claire La Berge, critical theorist, adapted from *Wages Against Artwork: Decommodified Labor and the Claims of Socially Engaged Art*.[27]

"If artists want to survive in a corporate capitalist society, they must organize themselves externally." —Theodor Adorno, *Aesthetic Theory*

In 2014, the artist-run institution BFAMFAPhD—composed of collective members Susan Jahoda, Blair Murphy, Agnes Szanyi, Vicky Virgin, and Caroline Woolard—released the publication *Artists Report Back*. This report was concerned with how artists function as professionals, including how they pay rent, how they pay back loans, how they obtain supplies—in short, how their professional lives as artists are sustainable and how they make due when such a life becomes circumscribed. Perhaps the most relevant of the group's finding for my own study is their claim that while there are over 2 million arts graduates in the United States (there are more artists, the group claims, than there are doctors and lawyers combined), only 8 percent of those artists—some 180,000 people—make a living from their art. How, the group wondered, can one sustain a career as a professional artist if one cannot make a living through the remuneration of one's artistic labor, particularly if one has paid to train as an artist? If the increasing number of conferences, calls, and

27
Leigh Clare La Berge, *Wages Against Artwork: Decommodified Labor and the Claims of Socially Engaged Art* (Duke, 2019).

28
For example, the New Museum recently organized a call for a conference on the theme of "Why Are Artists Starting Institutions?" See also the ambitious convention in Vancouver on "Institutions by Artists" at http://arcpost.ca/conference, accessed March, 2017. Afterall reported on the conference.

See Liz Park, "Pluralising the Institution: On the Conference 'Institutions by Artists,'" Afterall/Online, December 20, 2012, https://www.afterall.org/online/pluralising-the-institution-on-the-conference-institutions-by-artists#.WPDmXtwh5pY/.

Collectively-
Initiated

directed residencies is any indication, one answer seems to lay in the collectivization of artistic labor through artist-run institutions.[28] In my writing, I read the work of BFAMFAPhD as an institution for other artists founded by Woolard in an attempt to redress the decommodification of artistic labor.

Artists Report Back located what are essentially two categories of art graduates. The first group, the majority, have BA and BFA degrees in the arts and often function professionally as artists through a network of nonwaged concessions: artist residencies, museum sponsorships, access to university-based facilities, self-created artistic communities, community centers, and so on. The second group, which is much smaller, comprises those who do in fact make a living through the sale of their artistic labor. This group predominantly includes musicians, photographers, and filmmakers, all of whom probably sell their labor through vocational channels. The striking irony to emerge from *Artists Report Back* is found in the fact that artists trained in art school, artists professionalized qua artists, are probably unable to live off their artistic labor, whereas artists not trained as such were better able to support themselves via their craft. That irony is amplified by the likely art school debt that often comes as a consequence of arts professionalization.[29] Furthermore, the report included demographic analyses of race, class, and gender:

more women and people of color attend art school than are represented in the general population, but less of those groups than represented in the general population will make a living from their art.[30]

BFAMFAPhD's results in *Artists Report Back* empirically amplify the theory that artists often function outside of the wage system in their specific work as artists. The accuracy of this claim increases in the fine arts, and indeed in socially engaged art in particular, which itself has a higher percentage of women artists. Many scholars have made the claim about the wagelessness of art as a generic category, if without the data to support it. John Roberts plainly says: "Artists are not wage laborers." Dave Beech contends that "it is clear that artists are exceptional to the wage structure." Artist and theorist Anton Vidokle's argument in "Art without Market" is rather eponymous. He argues in a slightly different idiom that "art is not a profession."[31] No less an observer than Karl Marx claims that artworks are not included in his study of capitalism for they are "of a special nature." *Wages Against Artwork*, the book from which this text is excerpted, both assumes that "special nature" of art to the wage and asks how and why the relation between the two has been transformed and represented in our economic present. And while critics have long made such claims

29
Artists Report Back, available at bfamfaphd.com (accessed October 27, 2016).

30
Juliana Spahr and Stephanie Young have produced absolutely important demographic findings about similar race, gender, and class disparities in the field of creative writing. See Juliana Spahr and Stephanie Young, "The Program Era and the Mainly White Room," Los Angeles Review of Books, September 20, 2015, https://lareviewofbooks.org/article/the-program-era-and-the-mainly-white-room/ (accessed May 1, 2107).

31
See Anton Vidokle, "Art without Market, Art without Education: Political Economy of Art," *e-flux Journal*, no. 43 (March 2013), http://www.e-flux.com/journal/43/60205/art-without-market-art-without-education-political-economy-of-art.

about art's exceptional status to the wage structure, two features of this contemporary discourse have been updated and deserve attention. First, artists themselves are now making such claims and incorporating those claims into their art. This fact is something that critics, including some of our best on the topic of art and economy—John Roberts and Dave Beech in particular—have not addressed. John Roberts suggests art should be understood to participate in "second economy," that odd space of non-market activity in which a majority of arts production operates; Beech suggests that art is structured by a process he calls "commodification without commodification," in which art is not made as a commodity but sometimes is sold as such.[32] What neither Beech nor Roberts attends to, however, is the manner in which such economic processes are not only the social conditions under which art is often produced; rather, these economic limits become both productive possibilities and heuristic devices in their own right. Art produced without wages must be read, in part, through its wagelessness.

Art has long been positioned as independent of the world of goods and labors, of the world of commodification—a separation that since early Modernity has been understood to constitute "the aesthetic." This separation undergirds art's "autonomy."[33] Yet oppositional independence often belies

a connection, and the institution of art history has been entangled with the wage form.

Capitalism hides the value of labor through the wage, which comes to assume the seeming totality of labor's value. One must begin, not end, with the wage. And once we move past the surface appearance of the wage to the essential relations of wage labor—with all of its compromises, dependencies, and exploitations—the independence of the institution of art is threatened. Conversely, the structures of our capitalist economy make labor power in its commodified form difficult to see and, according to Peter Bürger, provide art as a compensation for that loss of sight. One can't see the economy, but one can see art. Thus the institution of art, oppositional to but entangled with the wage form, is endowed with the possibility of critique.

artists often function outside of the wage system in their specific work as artists

Decommodified labor in art designates a similar if more local struggle over art's potential emancipatory possibilities, the realization of which requires a confrontation with labor's unfreedom. Without a wage to which it is counterposed, it becomes difficult to say what, precisely, art is independent of. Yet those

32

See Dave Beech, *Art and Value* (London: Brill, 2015); John Roberts, *Revolutionary Time and the Avant-Garde* (London: Verso, 2015).

33

See Peter Bürger, *Theory of the Avant-Garde* (Minneapolis: Minnesota University Press, 1984).

34

David Joselit, "Institutional Responsibility: The Short Life of Orchard," *Grey Room*, no. 35 (spring 2009): 108-15, 109.

35

There are many lineages of and requiems for institutional critique—what it wanted, what it succeeded in getting, how it

failed, and how it was institutionalized. The most thorough collection is *Institutional Critique: An Anthology of Artists Writing*, edited by Alexander Alberro and Blake Stimson (Cambridge, MA: mit Press, 2009). In a different register altogether, Gregory Sholette and Blake Stimpson write, in their

changed coordinates of aesthetic disinterest-edness do free art to occupy a place that is not only "interested" but insistent, demanding, organized. It is by now a common enough historical narrative to place socially engaged art after institutional critique, a dating that relies on the assumption that, in David Joselit's words, "Institutional Critique, as we know it, is obsolete."[34] Joselit's is a claim that is both true and incomplete, and what I want to do in this essay is examine how certain artists' historicization of their own and other artists' decommodified artistic labor has organized a particular aspect of the movement from institutional critique to socially engaged art.[35] While the art produced through institutional critique offered critical assessments of the museum, the gallery, their financing, their ties to American imperialism, and the race, gender, and class politics that subtend the foregoing, institutional critique largely did not critique the wage.[36] That is, it did not critique the fact that many artists are not paid for their labor and that we live in a system in which social reproduction is only possible through labor's remuneration.

That omission has begun to change. At the height of the 2008 global credit crisis, the artist group Temporary Services staged a national conversation called "Art Work,"

devoted to art and labor. The organization W.A.G.E. (Working Artists for a Greater Economy) now makes demands for wage rates and work standards for arts. W.A.G.E. states, "W.A.G.E. is made up of practicing artists, but we are not an art collective and our work is not art. We are an activist and advocacy group. Our participation is never in the capacity of being artists."[37]

Woolard has inherited the mantle of institutional critique and enjoined it to her own understanding of the decommodification of artistic labor. And she has done so through the construction of new institutions, a crucial term that, in this essay, will mediate the aesthetic, the historical, and the practical. Caroline Woolard uses the term "institution" to describe many of her collaborative, long-term practices and installations. Tarrying with when and how to move beyond institutional critique, she quite consciously engages in forms of institutional elaboration. She constructs what we might call "institutions as art." Her respective institutions — what she sometimes refers to as "platforms" — have as their foundation the question of how artists might continue to make work outside of the wage form or whether they must organize themselves and fight for inclusion in the wage,

---

wonderful history of artistic "collectivism after modernism," that "Modernist collectivism, as we will have it here, was the first real effort to develop a sustained alternative to commod-ified social life by cultural means, and it was full of the spirited and sometimes foolish ambition of youth." Gregory Sholette and Blake Stimpson, eds., *Collectivism after Modern-ism: The Art of Social Imagi-nation after 1945* (Durham, NC: Duke University Press, 2007), 3.

36

The signal exception here is awc, Art Workers Coalition, and their "Art Strike." See, of course, Julia Bryan-Wilson, *Art Workers* (Berkeley: University of California Press, 2009). As Gregory Sholette writes, "one of the awc's demands was for the establishment of a trust fund that would provide living artists with 'stipends, health insurance, help for artists' dependents and other social ben-efits.'" Gregory Sholette, *Dark Matter* (New York: Pluto Press,

2010), 14. Note in particular his comparison between the awc and the apt (Artist Pension Trust) (116-34). Note also that before the 1960s existed groups including Artists League of America and Artists Equity.

37

See the website, http://www.wageforwork.com/about/6/faqs, accessed June 2015. The group W.A.G.E. and its website is still active, however this spe-cific link no longer functions.

as this chapter's epigraph from Adorno suggests that they must do: "If artists want to survive in a corporate capitalist society, they must organize themselves externally."[38] OurGoods.org and TradeSchool.coop [see chapter 3] respond to decommodification at the level of the individual work, and like these institutions, BFAMFAPhD is another example of a durational institution. Without secure access to a wage, these artists have developed their own institutions to address their own and other artists' precarity. Why, I ask, have artists turned from institutional critique to institutional elaboration?

Without secure access to a wage, these artists have developed their own institutions to address their own and other artists' precarity.

"Something has to come after Institutional Critique," artist Caroline Woolard has said. "And something has to be possible other than ironic institutions," she insists.[39] Such an "afterness" and otherness of artist-run institutions in the wake of institutional critique has been given a variety of names by critics. There is the "counter-institution," so named by Yates McKee; there is "institutional detournement," a term proposed by T. J. Demos; the "anti-institution" is Tom Finkelpearl's term for a similar insistence;[40] David Joselit speaks of a turn toward "institutional responsibility" in his discussion of the artist-run Orchard Gallery; Chris Gilbert notes that Anglo-American collectivism often takes what he calls an "institutional form."[41] In each term we may locate a remainder of the power of both institutional critique and something retrievable from the institution itself. The institution persists, it outlasts any individual, it embodies a historical memory. Perhaps curator Maria Lind best captures the spirit of this kind of work with her term, "constructive institutional critique," itself similar to Claire Doherty's claim of a "new institutionalism" now present in contemporary art.[42]

Indeed, the past ten years have seen a flourishing of actual artistic institutions as well as considerations of them. What both distinguishes Woolard's work and places it on a continuum with institutional critique is that her institutions are centered on the problem of arts production—that's the continuity—but specifically, they isolate the problem of

---

38
Adorno, *Aesthetic Theory*, 33.

39
Personal conversation with the artist, 2014.

40
Tim Finkelpearl, *What We Made: Conversations on Art and Social Cooperation* (Durham, NC: Duke University Press, 2013), 12.

41
Joselit makes the important claim that one of the limits of institutional critique is that "institutions are run by people"; see "Institutional Responsibility," 113. He stops short, then, of looking at labor, what those people produce and exchange to run institutions, and instead introduces a Latourian notion of actors, agency, and networks. A nice response to that tendency is found in Chris Gilbert: "Why is it that most 'institutional critique' has remained satisfied with the easy target of bricks and mortar, while setting aside the more volatile flesh, bones, and brains that are just as much a part of an organization's equipment?" See Chris Gilbert, in Sholette and Stimpson, eds., *Collectivism After Modernism*, Chapter 3, "Art & Language and the Institutional Form in Anglo-American Collectivism," 77.

42
Maria Lind cited in Janet Marstine, *Critical Practice: Collectively-Initiated*

decommodified artistic labor, which is the distinction. Institutions like BFAMFAPhD are durational in that they are ongoing and that they have transpired over a matter of years and continue to do so. These works attempt to reclaim duration as it has been embodied in labor; "what the worker sells is time," reminds Harry Braverman.[43] But these decommodifed workers do not sell their time; rather, they possess time, and it is that resource that will mold and contour the shape of the institutions they construct. The relation of these works to duration echoes Peter Frase's description of the benefits of decommodification. Highlighting the emancipatory sense of the word as Gøsta Epsing-Andersen originally used it, Frase writes, "we can think of the de-commodifying welfare state as giving people a choice about whether or not to commodify their labor. ... The choice that is involved here is not merely about income. It ultimately comes down to how we want to organize our time, and how we want to structure our relations with other people."[44]

If socially engaged art is that which seeks to ameliorate restrictive social conditions, then perhaps the aesthetic reflexivity to be found in the institution-building work of Woolard is best located in how she seeks to change her own working life and the lives of other artists.

Her work asks us to question whether art that remains decommodified may remain recognized as art

In Woolard's work there is no negation, no irony, no moment of "institutional detournment"; rather there is a commitment to endurance. Her work asks us to question whether art that remains decommodified may remain recognized as art. I want to suggest that we think about "institutional reflexivity," the manner in which the institution as a kind of art returns the ability to understand how decommodifed artistic labor frames the work of the art institution itself.

Artists, Museums, Ethics (New York: Routledge, 2017), 21. See also Claire Doherty, "The Institution is Dead, Long Live the Institution! Contemporary Art and the New Institutionalism," Engage, no. 15 (summer 2004): 1-6, 1. Note also Creative Capital's 2013 invitation to fund such bodies: "Over the years, Creative Capital has noticed that an increasing number of grantees have decided to start their own organizations. ... These new institutions have focused on issues of social justice, food, product development and critical thinking skills." Lisa Dent, "The In-between: Artists Build New Frameworks for Institutions," Creative Capital blog, April 11, 2013, http://blog.creative-capital.org/2013/04/artists-build-new-frameworks-for-institutions/ (accessed January 2017).

43
Harry Braverman, *Labor and Monopoly Capital: The Degradation of Work in the Twentieth Century* (New York: Monthly Review Press, 1974).

44
Peter Frase, "De-commodification in Everyday Life," June 7, 2011, http://www.peterfrase.com/2011/06/de-commodification-in-everyday-life.

IMAGINE A GROUP GATHERING

IMAGINE A GROUP GATHERING

fig. 5-5
BFAMFAPhD, *Artists Report Back*, 2014. Courtesy of BFAMFAPhD.

Artists Report Back

A National Study on the Lives of Arts Graduates and Working Artists

A report by **BFAMFAPhD**, 2014

About this report

As artists and art school graduates, we often find ourselves in conversations about the difficulties of continuing our practice as writers, authors, artists, actors, photographers, musicians, singers, producers, directors, performers, choreographers, dancers and entertainers. We struggle to support ourselves with jobs outside of the arts and we struggle to earn a living in the arts. Yet art school administrators and "creative class" reports assure us that arts graduates make a living in the arts.[1] Loan officers insist that art students can afford art school tuition, repaying student loans over time by working in the arts. This is not our experience. We decided that it was time make our own report.

Connecting our lived experiences to national trends, we wanted to know: What is the impact of rent, debt, and precarity on working artists and arts graduates nationally? How many of us are there? If we are not supporting ourselves as working artists, what jobs do we work?

We looked at artists' demographics, occupations, educational attainment, field of degree, and earnings as recorded by the Census Bureau's 2012 American Community Survey (ACS). The ACS is the largest survey that collects data about artists, surveying roughly 1 out of every 100 persons in the nation. With this data in hand, we made this report to reframe conversations about the current conditions and contradictions of arts graduates, and to make informed decisions about the ways we live and work. At the end of the report, please see our recommendations for organizational change and interpersonal action.

Susan Jahoda, Blair Murphy, Vicky Virgin, and Caroline Woolard

BFAMFAPhD

1 Creative Economy Report. Otis College of Art and Design. 2013. Web. <http://www.otis.edu/creative-economy-report>

BFAMFAPhD 1

Contents

BFAMFAPhD 2

Summary

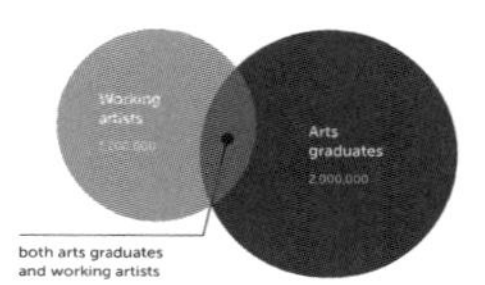

10%
of arts graduates are working artists

16%
of working artists are arts graduates

Most surprising was the lack of overlap between working artists and arts graduates. In the United States, 40 percent of working artists do not have bachelor's degrees in any field. Only 16 percent of working artists have arts-related bachelor's degrees. Though arts graduates may acquire additional opportunities and skills from attending art school, arts graduates are likely to graduate with significant student loan debt, which makes working as an artist difficult, if not impossible. We acknowledge that some arts graduates are satisfied with work in other fields, but the fantasy of arts graduates future earnings in the arts should be discredited. Since 7 of the top 10 most expensive institutions of higher education in the United States (after financial aid is taken into consideration) are art schools, the corresponding proportion of student loans are higher than those for graduates from non-art schools.[2] The majority of arts graduates work in non-arts fields. Out of 2 million arts graduates nationally, only 10 percent, or 200,000 people, make their primary earnings as working artists. Given the discrepancy between working artists and arts graduates, as well as the rising cost of tuition at art schools, we end this report with recommendations for policy makers, administrators, and educators in our field.

> Out of **2 million** arts graduates nationally, only **10 percent**, or **200,000** people, make their primary earnings as working artists.

2 How Does Your School Rank? The Wall Street Journal, February 19, 2013. Web. <http://online.wsj.com/news/interactive/BORROW0216201304216?ref=SB10001424127887324452004578306610055834952 >

BFAMFAPhD 3

Methodology

All statements in this report are based upon data collected by the Census Bureau's 2012 American Community Survey (ACS), unless otherwise noted. This is an annual survey that is designed to sample one percent or about 3 million households in the United States, gathering detailed data that was previously collected in the Decennial Census.

A myriad of issues arise when using data to study artists. For this report we used two variables to identify this population: "primary occupation" (secondary occupation is not collected in this survey) and "field of degree," a relatively new variable directed at those who have a bachelor's degree. We will refer to people who have bachelor's degrees in the arts as "arts graduates" and to people whose primary occupation is writer, author, artist, actor, photographer, musician, singer, producer, director, performer, dancer choreographer, and entertainer as "working artists."

Arts Graduates

We looked at people with bachelors degrees in music, drama and theater arts, film, video and photographic arts, art history and criticism, studio arts, and visual and performing arts, living in the United States in 2012. The ACS does not collect the field of degree for master's degrees, so we define "arts graduates" in this report as people with BAs or BFAs in the arts, who may or may not have an MA or MFAs in the arts. With only 15,929 MAs and MFAs graduating in 2012 compared to 91,222 BAs and BFAs in the arts that year, our focus on undergraduates represents a broad population of artists.[3]

Working Artists

We defined working artists as people whose primary earnings come from working as writers, authors, artists, actors, photographers, musicians, singers, producers, directors, performers, choreographers, dancers, and entertainers. We excluded designers and architects from both the data related to "arts graduates" and from the data based on primary occupation (working artist) because the higher earnings of designers significantly alter the median earnings of our field. We understand that "working artists" are often identified by their level of commitment, and not remuneration,[4] but we cannot track practicing artists who do not make their primary earnings in the arts using the ACS. In fact, no nationally representative data exists for practicing artists. While many artists are missed in our report, we chose to investigate the data we could isolate to learn more about working artists and arts graduates nationally.

3 National Center for Educational Statistics. Integrated Postsecondary Education Data System (IPEDS). 2014. Web. <http://bfamfaphd.com/projects/art-degrees-per-year/>
4 Notice to Applicants Re: Artist Certification. New York City Department of Cultural Affairs. n.d. Web. <http://www.nyc.gov/html/dcla/downloads/pdf/artist_certification.pdf>

BFAMFAPhD 4

Findings

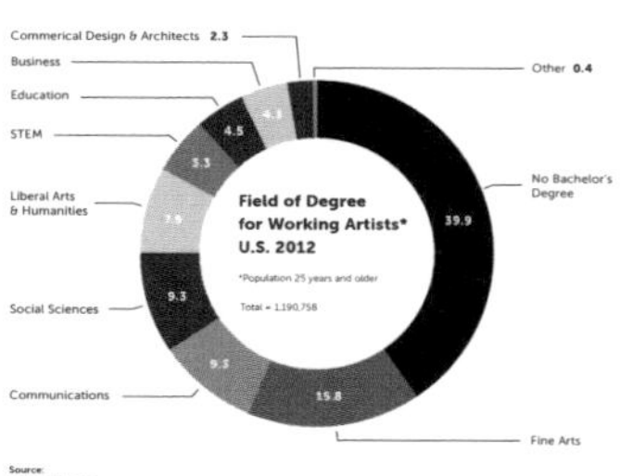

1.4 million Working Artists

ACS data reveals that there are 1.4 million working artists. Of those over the age of 25, or 1.2 million working artists, 476,000 did not get a bachelor's degree. That means that 40 percent of working artists over the age of 25 attended high school or got associate's degrees, but do not have bachelor's degrees in any field. Only 16 percent of working artists have an arts-related bachelor's degree.

> Only **16%** of working artists have an arts-related bachelor's degree.

BFAMFAPhD 5

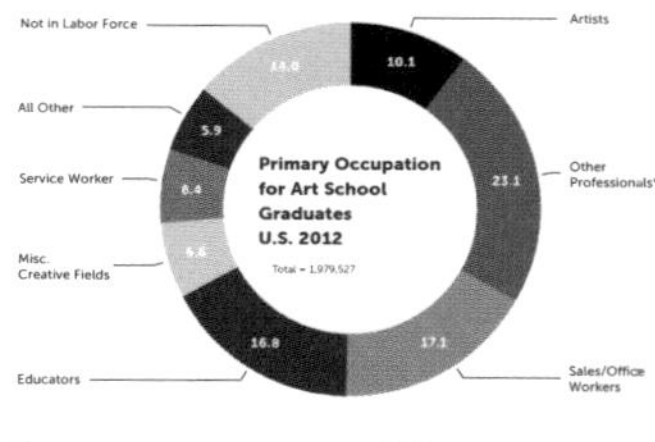

Of the 715,000 working artists who do have bachelor's degrees, only 27 percent have arts-related degrees. The rest studied communication, social sciences, liberal arts and humanities, science, technology, math, engineering, education, business, commercial design and architecture, or another field.

BFAMFAPhD 6

2 Million Arts Graduates

There are 2 million arts graduates with bachelor's degrees in music, drama and theater arts, film, video and photographic arts, art history and criticism, studio arts, and visual or performing arts living in the United States. Fewer than 200,000, just 10 percent, make their primary earnings as working artists. The rest are dispersed across other occupations. 23 percent work in professional and managerial occupations, 17 percent are employed as sales and office workers, and 17 percent work as educators. 14 percent are not in the labor force at all.

> **23%** of arts graduates work in professional and managerial occupations.

BFAMFAPhD

200,000 Working Artists and Art Graduates

Although there are 1.2 million working artists over the age of 25 in this country, there are only 200,000 working artists with arts related bachelors degrees. The majority of working artists have median earnings of $30,621, but the small percentage of working artists with bachelor's degrees have median earnings of $36,105.

Default rates for Arts Graduates

The U.S. Department of Education data show that 7 of the top 10 most expensive schools in this country (after scholarships and aid) are art schools, and arts graduates' debt loads are higher than those of non-arts graduates.[5] The following percentages of students default on their loans.

> **7** of the top **10** most expensive schools in the U.S. (after scholarships and aid) are art schools.

6% of students from **Cleveland Institute of Music** default on their loans.

7% of students from **the New School** default on their loans.

7% of students from **California Institute of the Arts** default on their loans.

8% of students from **the School of Visual Arts** default on their loans.

8% of students from **the Art Center College of Design** default on their loans.

8% of students from **San Francisco Art Institute** default on their loans.

9% of students from **Maine College of Art** default on their loans.

10% of students from **Pratt** default on their loans.

10% of students from **School of the Artist Institute of Chicago** default on their loans.

10% of students from **Minneapolis College of Art and Design** default on their loans.

11% of students from **Berklee College of Music** default on their loans.

13% of students from **Ringling College of Art and Design** default on their loans.

13% of students from **Otis College of Art and Design** default on their loans.

16% of students from **Southwest University of Visual Arts** default on their loans.

5. Simon, Ruth. Loan Defaults Refer to the Three-year Cohort Default Rate on Federal Student Loans. Wall Street Journal, 18 Feb. 2013. Web. <http://online.wsj.com/news/interactive/BORROW021620130216?ref=SB10001424127887324432004578306610055834952>

Predominance of White, Non-Hispanic Arts Graduates and Male Working Artists

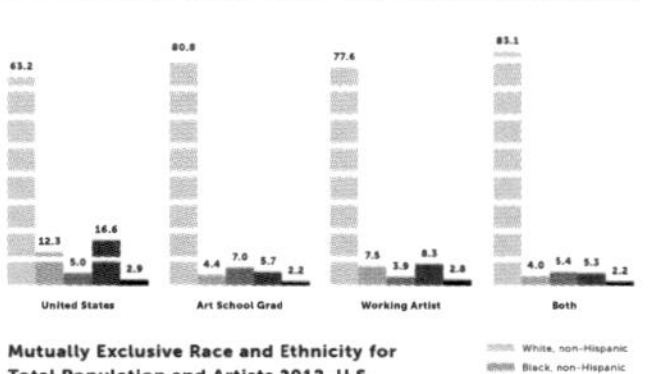

Mutually Exclusive Race and Ethnicity for Total Population and Artists 2012, U.S.

Source:
U.S. Census Bureau
2012 American Community Survey – Public Use Microdata Sample

*Hispanics can be of any race

The population of arts graduates and working artists is not representative of our country. The population of the United States is 63 percent White, non-Hispanic, but 81 percent of arts graduates are White, non-Hispanic. The population of the United States is 12 percent Black, non-Hispanic, but only 4 percent of arts graduates are Black, non-Hispanic and only 8 percent of working artists are Black, non-Hispanic. The population of the United States is 17 percent Hispanic, but only 6 percent of arts graduates are Hispanic and only 8 percent of working artists are Hispanic.

> The population of the U.S. is **17%** Hispanic, but only **6%** of arts graduates are Hispanic.

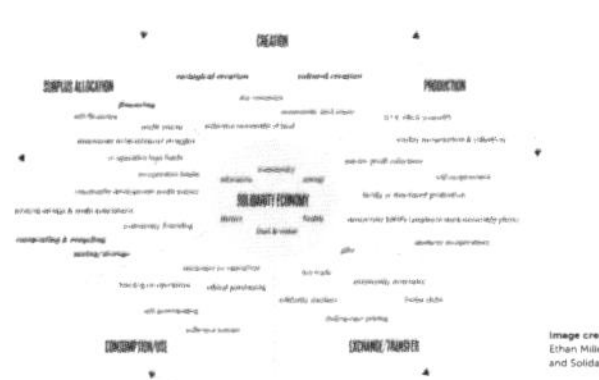

Gender for Total Population and Artists U.S. 2012

Source:
U.S. Census Bureau
2012 American Community Survey – Public Use Microdata Sample

While the United States is split evenly between males and females, males account for only 40 percent of arts graduates but over 54 percent of working artists. Females make up 60 percent of arts graduates but only 46 percent of all working artists. Of the 200,000 working artists over 25 with an art degree, 55 percent are male.

> Females make up **60%** of arts graduates but only **46%** of all working artists.

Recommendations

We have shown that 7 of the top 10 most expensive institutions of higher education in the United States (after financial aid is taken into consideration) are art schools, and that the corresponding proportion of student loans are higher than those for graduates from non-art schools. With more student-loan debt than credit card debt in this country, we are in the midst of an educational and social crisis.[7]

We ask that artists, administrators, and teachers acknowledge the current financial and cultural economies in arts education: those of rising costs and student debt. To begin to imagine and enact economies of equity and cooperation in the arts, we must address the needs and capacities of both working artists and arts graduates. What follows are three recommendations toward the adequate nurturing of creativity in art education, visibility, and workforce development.

> To begin to imagine and enact economies of equity and cooperation in the arts, we must address the needs and capacities of both working artists and arts graduates.

Art School

While this report reveals that an arts degree is not necessary for future earnings as a working artist, as 40 percent of working artists do not have a bachelor's degree in any field, the authors of this report believe that arts degrees remain valuable for critical thinking, skill building, identity formation, and creative innovation that is necessary in the arts and beyond.[8] We acknowledge that some arts graduates are happy to work in other fields, but we hope to show that the fantasy of future earnings in the arts cannot justify the high cost of arts degrees. We know that experience at art schools leave arts graduates with high overhead in the form of student debt, making risk-taking and innovation after graduation more difficult, if not impossible. Still believing in the power of arts education, we point prospective art students toward low-cost and tuition-free arts programs and we defend the liberal arts as integral to higher education nationally.

6. How Does Your School Rank? The Wall Street Journal, February 19, 2013. Web <http://online.wsj.com/news/interactive/BORROW021620130216?ref=SB10001424127887324432004578306610055834952>
7. FinAid, The Smart Student Guide to Financial Aid. FinAid, 2014. Web < http://www.finaid.org/loans/>
8. Whitehead, Frances. What do artists know? The Embedded Artist Project. Artetal. January 2006. Web <http://embeddedartistproject.com/What-do-artists-know.gif>

Visibility

Knowing that 40 percent of working artists do not have bachelors degree's in any field, cultural institutions should honor artists and culture workers who do not have experiences of formal, higher education. Philanthropic and civic institutions should create programs to address the needs of working artists, looking beyond the written application, the lecture hall, the journal, and the museum for emerging talent. While working artists and arts graduates legitimate ideas and find rigorous debate in their spaces and distribution networks, cultural institutions could require that presenters, curators, and publishers look beyond networks of arts graduates. Programs to address the gap between working artists and arts graduates could create informal or formal channels for communication and could establish policies for evaluation and presentation of artists, regardless of educational status.

> Cultural institutions should honor artists and culture workers who do not have experiences of formal, higher education.

Workforce Development

We must close the gap between arts graduates and working artists, understanding that little overlap exists currently, and that both populations have key insights to share with one another. We can provide opportunities for dialogue. Arts graduates have knowledge of elite social norms, shared jargon from lecture halls, shared regard for artists named in journals, and shared contacts at elite institutions. Working artists have an understanding of the market for their work, valuable business networks, and a familiarity with production and management. Both populations could benefit from worker and producer cooperatives, affordable arts institutions, and resource sharing networks.

> Art graduates and working artists could benefit from worker and producer cooperatives, affordable arts institutions, and resource sharing networks.

Image credit:
Ethan Miller, JED Collective and SolidarityNYC.org

This diagram represents a solidarity economy of cooperation and equity that could be adopted more explicitly in the arts, and could be supported intellectually and financially by arts institutions and arts schools nationally.

> "Adequately nurtured, creativity fuels culture, infuses human-centred development and constitutes the key ingredient for job creation, innovation and trade while contributing to social inclusion, cultural diversity and environmental sustainability."
> The United Nations Conference on Trade and Development's Creative Economy Report 2010

How might art education nurture culture? The majority of arts graduates work in non-art occupations to support themselves. Arts education should acknowledge and prepare art students for this eventuality. A disavowal of the connection between expensive tuition and future work and financial independence is no longer realistic or ethical. Preparation for artistic work in other fields, including arts management and administration, as well as training in artist-owned businesses, is essential. Arts graduates can prepare to see themselves as "artists in residence" in sales, education, service, and managerial jobs, while learning how to create an artist-owned business together with other artists, neighbors, and fellow low-income residents. We point prospective art students toward low-cost and free art schools, artist-run spaces, and independent communities of working artists, as we know that the time has come to speak openly about the political economies of art education.

Authors

Concerned about the impact of debt, rent, and precarity on the lives of creative people, BFAMFAPhD makes media and connects viewers to existing organizing work. We are artists, educators, curators, art historians, designers, makers, performers, statisticians, and software developers who want to understand the relationship between our lives and the bigger picture. On our website, visitors can download our datasets, make media with us, and connect that media to lived experience. We aim to underscore that the personal is political.

This report was written by Susan Jahoda, Blair Murphy, and Caroline Woolard, overseen by Vicky Virgin, a demographic analyst, edited by Caron Atlas, Julian Boilen, Adam Forman, Tamara Greenfield, Stephen Korns, and designed by Rich Watts.

Vicky Virgin is a demographic analyst, dancer, and choreographer. In 1987, Virgin moved to NYC to dance, supporting herself with the B.S. she received in economics. Her skills as an analyst were essential to this study, and illustrate the range of expertise that artists develop to support their creative work. In the meantime, she continues to live in NYC, creating art and crunching numbers.

Julian Boilen is a creative technologist and software engineer who is always searching for the intersection of technology, creativity, art, and politics. Currently studying software engineering at the Rochester Institute of Technology, he has also interned at Squarespace, Sitework, and for the Democratic National Committee.

Susan Jahoda is an artist, organizer and teacher who lives in NYC and currently teaches at the University of Massachusetts, Amherst. A member of three collectives, the Pedagogy Group, BFAMFAPhD, and NYCTBD, she is working toward developing equitable methods of teaching and commoning within the context of arts education. Jahoda's upcoming project, in collaboration with her daughter Emma Jahoda-Brown, Documents from the Greenham Common Women's Peace Camp, will open at Interference Archive in December 2014.

Blair Murphy is a cultural worker based in New York City with experience as a curator, writer, and non-profit arts administrator. Before moving to New York, she spent seven years in Washington, DC, working as an administrative jack-of-all-trades for various arts organizations. She holds a BFA from Maryland Institute College of Art

and an MA from Georgetown University. She's currently participating in the Whitney Independent Study Program as a Helena Rubenstein Curatorial Fellow and working a non-art-world day job.

Caroline Woolard, an artist and organizer, moved to NYC in 2002 to attend the only tuition-free art school in the United States (Cooper Union). Since then, her artistic work has been subsidized by day jobs as a graphic designer, teacher, and non-profit administrator, and has been supported by low overhead due to labor-intensive collective living situations. After co-founding and co-organizing resource sharing networks OurGoods.org and TradeSchool.coop for the past five years, Woolard is now a core member of BFAMFAPhD and NYCTBD, focusing on the impact of debt and rent on artists in NYC, and options for affordable space stewardship for all New Yorkers.

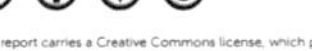

BFAMFAPhD created this report without monetary support.

We welcome donations, reactions, suggestions, and anecdotes from readers of this report at **BFAMFAPhD.com** and **info@BFAMFAPhD.com**

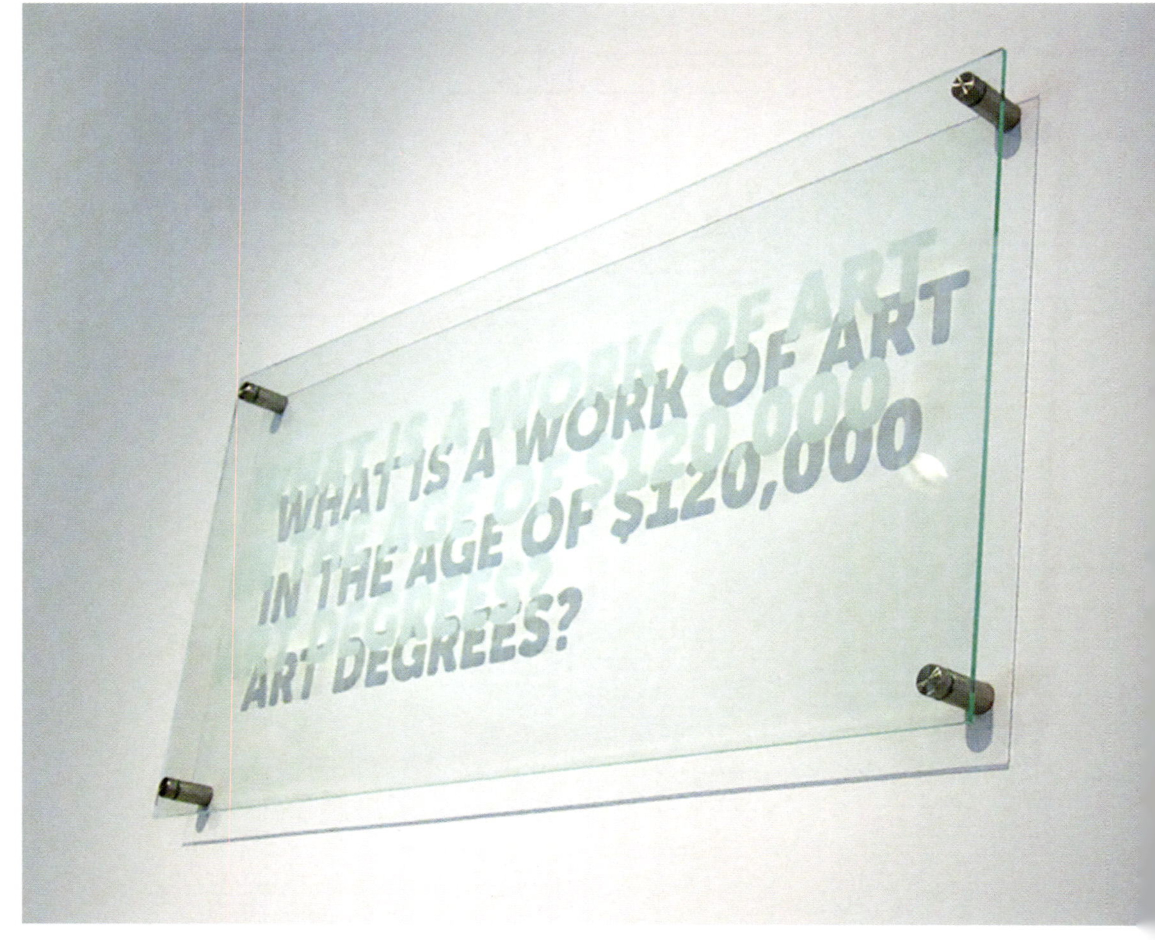

fig. 5-6
Statements, 2013, plexiglass,
hardware, 11 × 23 × 1 inches.
Courtesy of BFAMFAPhD.

fig. 5-7
Artists Report Back: Animated,
2014, single-channel video,
06:40 minutes. Courtesy of
BFAMFAPhD.

Collectively-
Initiated

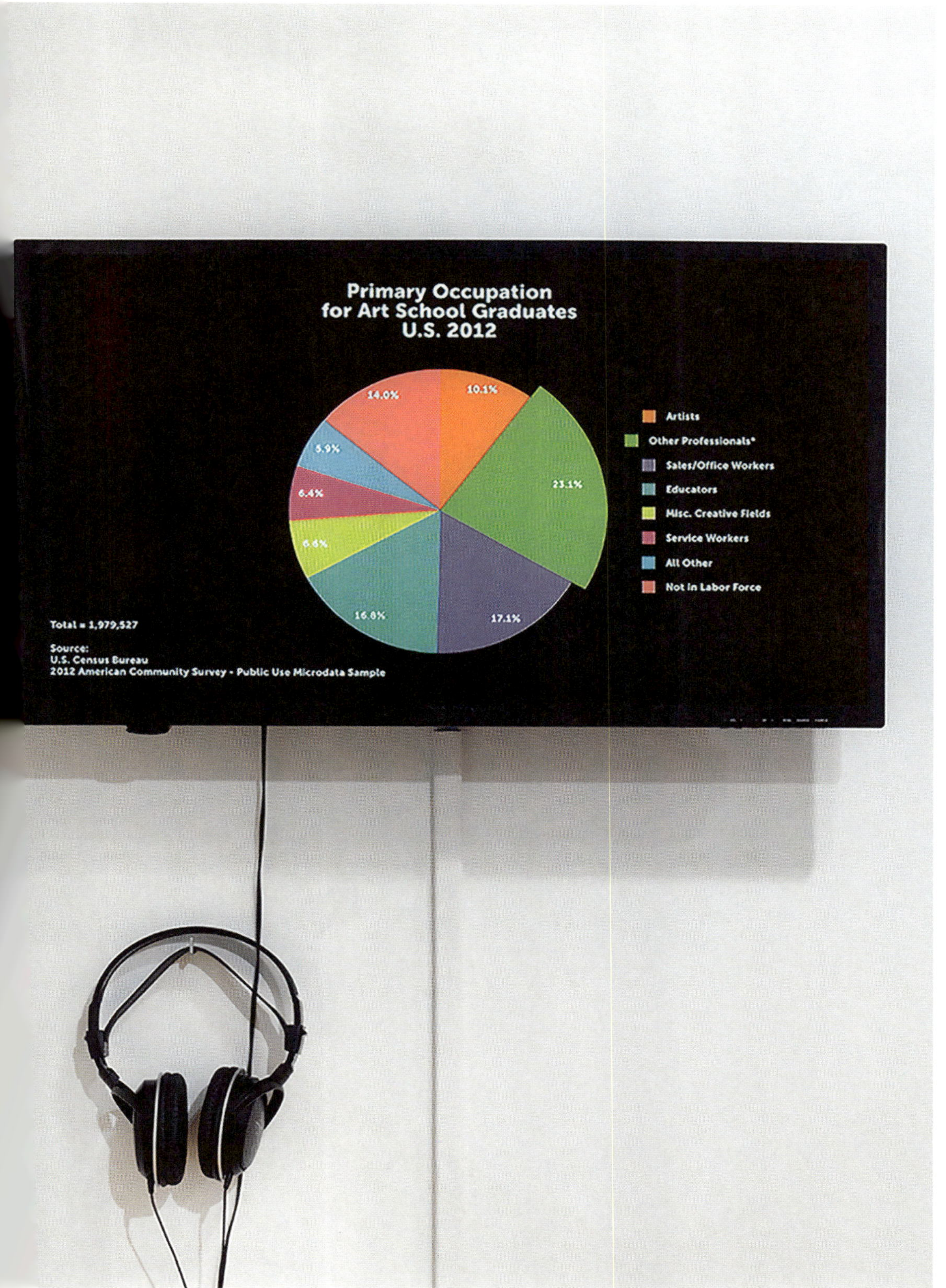

Primary Occupation
for Art School Graduates
U.S. 2012
10.1%
14.0%
5.9%
23.1%
6.4%
6.6%
16.8%
17.1%
Artists
Other Professionals*
Sales/Office Workers
Educators
Misc. Creative Fields
Service Workers
All Other
Not in Labor Force
Total = 1,979,527
Source:
U.S. Census Bureau
2012 American Community Survey - Public Use Microdata Sample

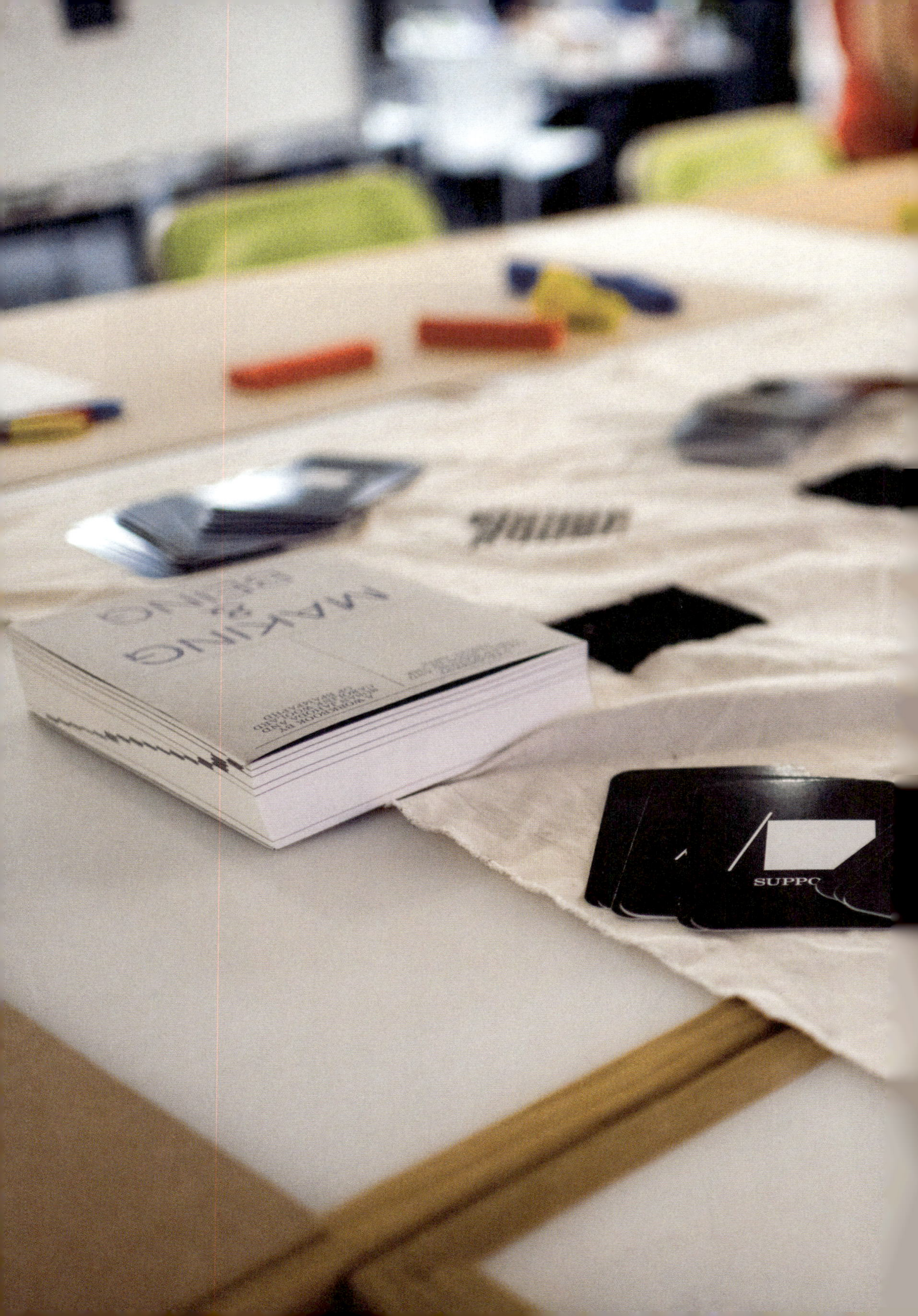

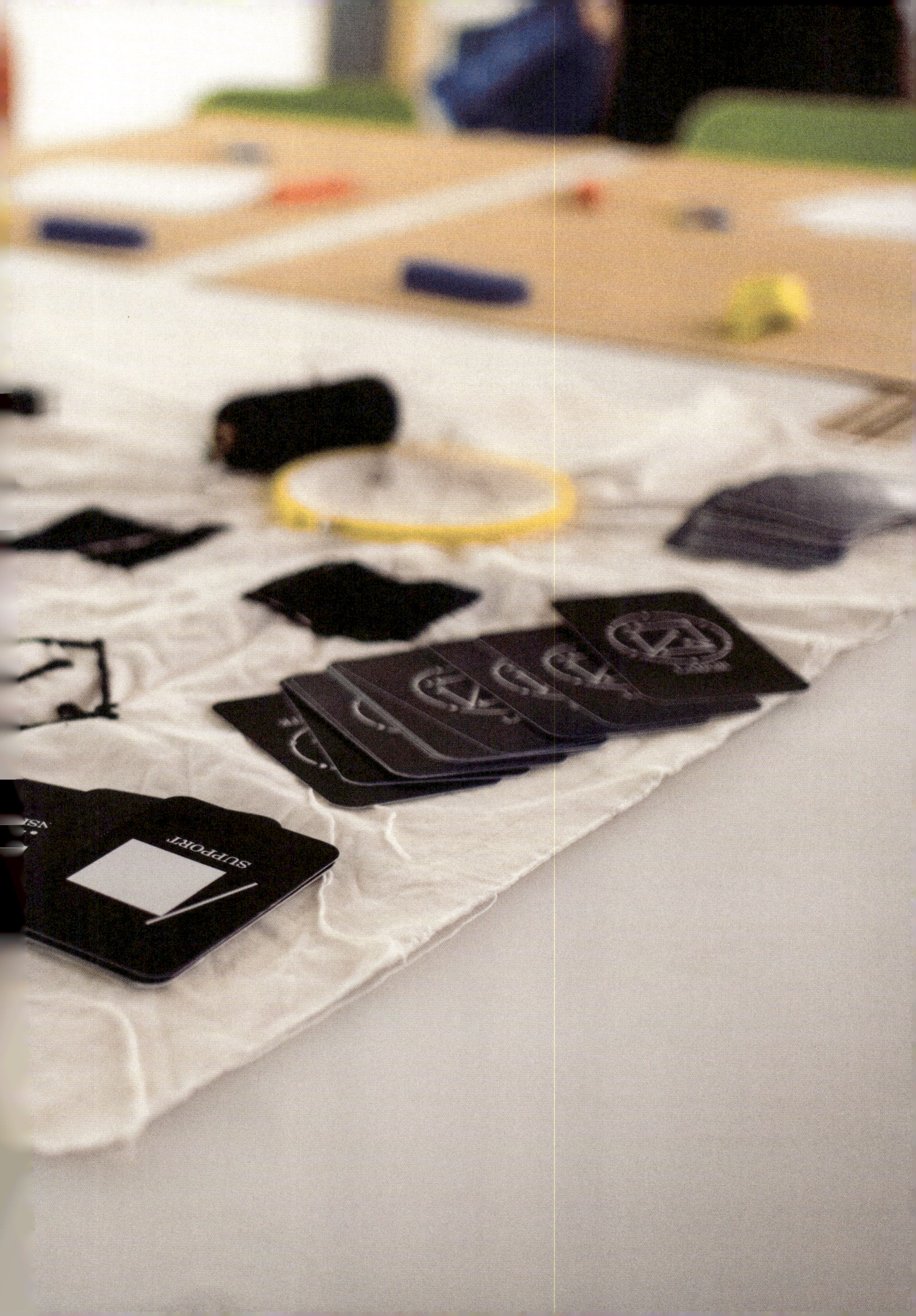

Idea in Public

Ephemera

In the pages that follow, you will see the correspondence, budgets, grants, readings, and writing required to create and run the arts advocacy collective BFAMFAPhD, as well as a printed excerpt from the book, *Making and Being* (Pioneer Works Press / DAP, 2019), co-authored by BFAMFAPhD core members Susan Jahoda and Caroline Woolard with support from BFAMFAPhD core members Emilio Martínez Poppe, Agnes Szanyi, Emily Tareila, and Vicky Virgin.

Woolard has selected ephemera that serves as visual reference points for BFAMFAPhD. All materials here are reproduced with the consent of collaborators.

fig. 5-8 (overleaf)
Making and Being book, card
game, and embroidery pre-
sented in a workshop at Rhode
Island School of Design
facilitated by Susan Jahoda
and Caroline Woolard in 2019.
Photo by Trevor Holden. Courtesy of BFAMFAPhD.

What do we hope, and what
can we hope, that institutions can do for us, as
writers and artists and
intrinsically creative
beings? And how further can
we not be ashamed of and
rather redeem the 'institu-
tionality' of writing and
artmaking in our time? A
utopia where the collectivity we experience in our
institutionalized lives is
redeemed as a precondition
for collective action.

—Mark McGurl, event
organized by BFAMFAPhD at
the Queens Museum, 2014

fig. 5-9
BFAMFAPhD, *Making and Being:
Embodiment, Collaboration, and
Circulation in the Visual Arts*,
Making and Being: Embodiment,
2019. Still from a video by Alex
Mallis. Courtesy of BFAMFAPhD.

Collectively-
Initiated

Making and Being: Embodiment, Collaboration, and Circulation in the Visual Arts is a multi-platform pedagogical project that offers practices of contemplation, collaboration, and circulation in the visual arts. *Making and Being* is for artists and art educators who want to connect art to economy, and for students who want to make artworks that reflect the conditions of their own production. *Making and Being* provides a framework that guides artists to explore both who they are becoming as they make projects and also what their projects are becoming as they take shape and circulate in the world. *Making and Being* is a book, a series of videos, a deck of cards, and an interactive website with freely downloadable content. More information is online at: http://makingandbeing.com

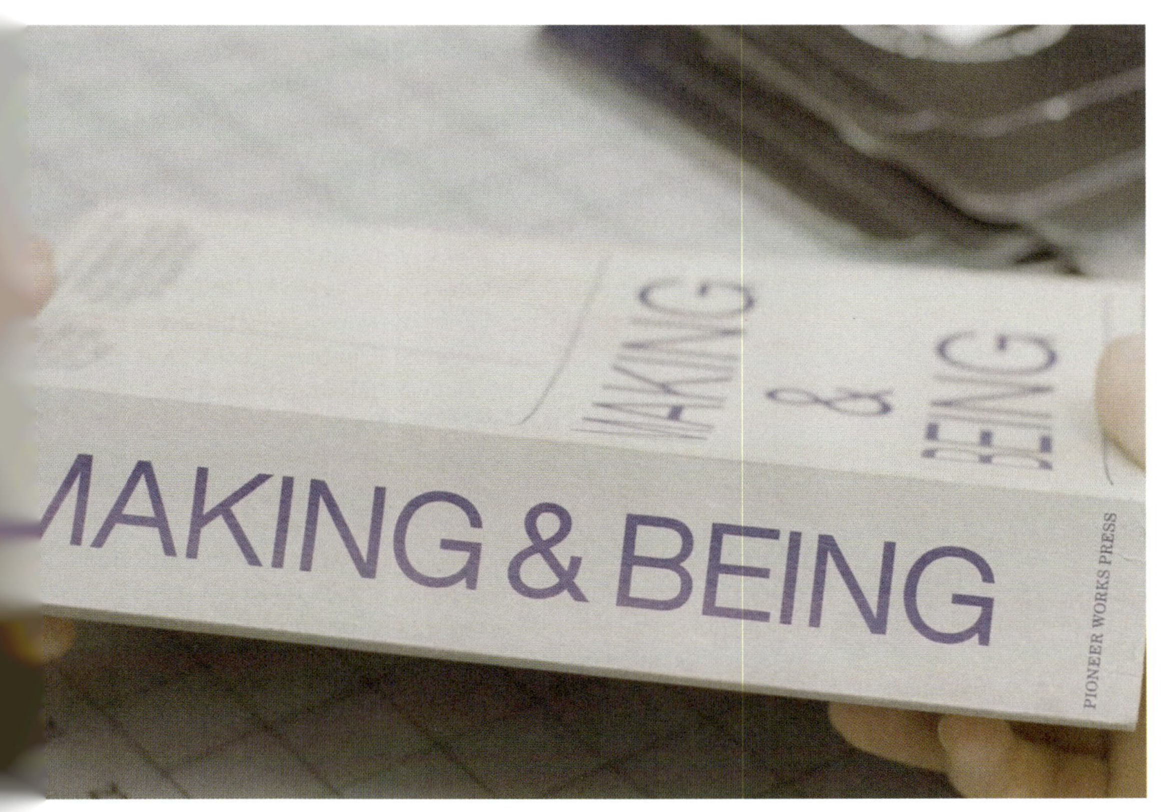

Making

I never considered that the classes I taught at TradeSchool.coop [see chapter 3] would lead to a job in an accredited BFA program, but they did. Teaching at TradeSchool.coop was always an experiment, and I was only 24. I was the primary person who hosted classes during the first run of TradeSchool.coop, helping teachers set up and welcoming students into the space for 35 days in a row. Every now and then, I would teach a class on grant writing (since I had raised over $300,000 with Jen Abrams over the years, for OurGoods.org) and also a class on so-called "alternative" economies (what I would later learn to be solidarity economies). In 2010, TradeSchool.coop was written up in The *New Yorker* and in *The New York Times*, and the classes started getting so full that we had to turn people away. We had a wide range of people in our classes: millenials who thought it was cool, activists who believed in solidarity economies, retirees who wanted to keep teaching, high school students, unemployed artists, well-known artists with art market success, and lots of people who were present for the sake of self-directed learning. Because of this range of students, I thought nothing of the faculty members from The New School who were in my classes.

But in 2010, one of my TradeSchool.coop students, Pascale Gatzen, who was also a faculty member at The New School, and who had met me at an experimental school called Mildred's Lane, invited me to teach a class at The New School. With only a BFA, I never imagined that I would be invited to be an adjunct teacher at the college-level. That summer I got really depressed and felt like all my students would know that I was an imposter. I was so nervous to enter a "real" classroom with BFA students paying over $40,000 a year in tuition. I asked everyone I knew how to teach a fifteen-week BFA course, and a curator named Erin Marie Sickler put me in touch with Susan Jahoda. I was relieved when, a year later, Susan started the New York City-based Pedagogy Group with Maureen Connor, and I could meet with other faculty members, adjunct and tenured, to talk about how to teach.

It was the year of Occupy Wall Street when I started teaching my first class for BFA students at The New School. That fall, the new president at Cooper Union, President Bharucha, also started talking openly about charging tuition at Cooper.

Experience

I never imagined that I would be invited to be an adjunct teacher at the college-level. That summer I got really depressed and felt like all my students would know that I was an imposter. I was so nervous to enter a "real" classroom with BFA students paying over $40,000 a year in tuition.

This would be a radical shift, the first time in the institution's 154-year history when any student would have to pay for their education at Cooper. I knew it was time to move from my work on self-organized learning with TradeSchool. coop and into arts advocacy for cultural equity and for free education. In addition to joining the Art & Labor working group and the Alternative Banking working group at Occupy, and demonstrating against charging tuition at Cooper, I began to shift away from my work with OurGoods.org and TradeSchool.coop. In 2012–2013, I held open meetings throughout New York City with a call to found a collective called BFAMFAPhD which would exist to investigate the relationship between student debt and precarity in the arts, and to advocate for cultural equity and free tuition on a national scale. By 2014, Susan Jahoda was fully involved, and we led *Artists Report Back*, which used rigorous statistical methods and data visualization to advocate for cultural equity in arts education.

So the question is not the scandal of the individual, necessarily, but how can individuals create institutions that they want to be part of? Where they see the power of the institution as collectively generated, rather than a random chance occurrence they need to participate in.

— Caroline Woolard, 2014

To form BFAMFAPhD, I held a series of open meetings in 2012–2013 in New York City where I invited a range of people to a facilitated conversation. At first, I sent emails to people that said things like this:

```
Subject: volunteering on a project about
creative graduates? | BFA MFA PhD

Dear Steve (and Louise?),

I'm coordinating a group of artists, designers,
and sociologists that's doing a project that
attempts to make visible, and organize, creative
graduates in this country. We started with a
quick site: http://bfamfaphd.com and we are
working this December and January to make a more
robust visualization of graduates.

My friend Jeff Warren (of http://publiclab.org/)
is pulling a bunch of data from IPEDS, and I'm
wondering if you can help sort it, compile it,
make sure it's accurate, and even present it
visually to the public. I can explain more on
the phone, if you have time/interest. Here's
where the data is stored right now:
https://github.com/jywarren/bfamfaphd/

Let me know!

Caroline

PS: here's more info …

Summary of the project:

How many artists are in this country, and what
might we do together? Informally called "BFA
MFA PHD," this project visualizes the number of
students graduating with creative degrees, elic-
its proposals for collective work, and generates
dialogue and conversation. A lecture series and
```

exhibition of visualizations will open on
February 2, 2014, in Caroline Woolard and Lika
Volkova's studio at the Queens Museum.

According to the census, there are more artists
than police officers, lawyers, or doctors in
this country. Reporting on the census in 2008,
The New York Times noticed that "if all
artists in America's workforce banded together,
their ranks would be double the size of the
United States Army." In fact, we may be three
times the size of the army, as the census
only tracks people who identify their primary
occupation as "artist." BFA MFA PHD looks at
students graduating with BFAs, MFAs, and PhDs,
noticing that the growth curve is extreme,
and that there are now a million new graduates
in this nation every ten years.

Who's working on the project so far: Jackie
Armstrong: manually pulled data from IPEDs
site/Agnes Szanyi: sociologist, correlated
data for population growth/Jeff Warren: writing code to pull data from IPEDS? we hope!/
Annelie Berner: data viz (we could use more
folks)/Ben Lerchin: website/Christin Ripley:
printmaker, may make prints of data viz/Lika
Volkova and Caroline Woolard: installation

And later on, when more people were working together in
a clear way, I sent emails to remind people of our progress,
like this:

Subject: info and materials for BFAMFAPhD
today: 12-6 p.m. at 63 5th Ave at 13th Street
(6th Floor # 620)

Dear all,

I am so excited to gather together today! If
you can, please bring a laptop, an ID (the

guard needs to see it), and some food/drinks to share with 6-8 people. We will meet at the New School's University Center at 63 5th Ave at 13th Street (6th Floor # 620). It's the new, shiny building on the corner of 13th and 5th Ave.

We will be able to do very focused work today, as there are 6-8 of us fully confirmed, enough to work together and still all be heard. We will get to know each other better, talk through our progress so far, and work together on projects that we care about. These seem to be: Solidarity Research: what groups and organizations should we learn from, support, and work with? and Mapping: based on existing tenants organizations and solidarity economy initiatives, what are ideal neighborhoods for community land trusts and learning together?

Ann, Pasqualina, and I have created an agenda, and will be reviewing it from 11-12, in case you want to arrive early!

Looking forward to it,
Caroline

WORKING GROUPS WE ARE INTERESTED IN:
Mapping: Based on existing tenants organizations and solidarity economy initiatives, what are ideal neighborhoods for community land trusts?

Library and Reading Group (sorting PDFs and links sent, learning together)

Documentation: video and/or audio recordings about WHY we are gathering

All of the above dataviz + exploring financial-social models for community land trusts

Data Visualization/Drawing: race/ethnicity distribution (bring a laptop, if you can)

Collectively-
Initiated

Solidarity Research: What groups and organizations should we learn from, support, and
work with?

Library/reading; mapping; solidarity research;
public calendar; documentation
(I also do not have a laptop)

Solidarity Research: What groups and
organizations should we learn from, support,
and work with?

Library and Reading Group (sorting PDFs and
links sent, learning together)

PS: BFAMFAPHD.com is an interactive website,
an installation, and a community of thinkers
that wonder: How might we mobilize artists in
the United States? According to the census,
there are more artists than police officers,
lawyers, or doctors in the United States.
Reporting on the census in 2008, *The New
York Times* noticed that "if all artists in
America's workforce banded together, their
ranks would be double the size of the United
States Army." How many of us are there, and
what might we do together? BFAMFAPHD.com visualizes the number of students graduating with
creative degrees, generates dialogue about our
collective power, and elicits proposals for
organizing efforts. For example, if just ten
prospective MFA students could agree to pool
$200-2000 a month for four years, they could
generate between $100,000 and $1,000,000.
Rather than going into debt to belong to a 2
year community in a traditional school, this
group could use this money to buy a building, create a community land trust, and secure
space for place-based art, community organizing, internet activism, and community resil-
ience, in perpetuity.

By 2014, we had a clear core group. Susan Jahoda, who became my primary collaborator from 2015–today, proposed this structure, based upon her experiences working in a collective on the journal *Rethinking Marxism*. Susan and I wrote about the structure of BFAMAPhD in our book, *Making and Being*:

> BFAMFAPhD has both a core group and contribu-
> tors. To be a core member you must be aligned
> with BFAMFAPhD's aesthetic and ethical prin-
> ciples. You must be aligned with the solidar-
> ity economy concept that "another world is not
> only possible — it already exists." You must
> be interested in prioritizing the remaking of
> institutions over institutional critique for
> the sake of critique itself. You must be inter-
> ested in looking for strategic opportunities to
> advance cultural equity in the arts and to build
> a community of rigor and care over a cynical,
> ironic, or antagonistic stance that denies our
> capacity to create change in the world.
>
> People become group members by emailing us
> and asking to join the collective or by being
> invited in through existing relationships. The
> core group takes care of all of the adminis-
> trative tasks that keep the collective alive.
> These include maintaining the website and caring
> for the well-being of members through events
> like collective meals, meditation, and movement
> practices. Friendship and emotional labor are
> central to our group agreements, and we privi-
> lege these in order to maintain the collective.
> One benefit of being in a collective is that we
> have five people to draw from. While one of us
> might be sick, two (or four) of us are likely
> rested and awake.
>
> Contributors are people who have created proj-
> ects that the core group has agreed to host.
> Contributors can also potentially become core

members but are not responsible for the maintenance of the group and do not have the right
to approve new contributions or to represent
the group in public. Our book, *Making and
Being*, is one contribution to the collective.
Other core members of BFAMFAPhD are working
on a wide range of projects, including a PhD
dissertation about art and the sociology of
professions by Agnes and a choreographic work
about student debt by Vicky.

From 2013–2014, Susan Jahoda, Vicky Virgin, Agnes Szanyi, Blair Murphy, and I worked together to publish *Artists Report Back*, a fifteen-page report that analyzed data collected by the Census Bureau's 2012 American Community Survey (ACS) to ask questions about race, ethnicity, gender, and inequity in the arts. Vicky knew how to work with data from the the American Community Survey (ACS) because she works by day as a Research Associate with the Mayor's Office for Economic Opportunity in New York City. By night, Vicky is a dancer and choreographer. She knew how to use ACS data, and to ask questions based upon this annual survey that is designed to sample one percent of US households, about 3 million households. This was important because self-reported data (if we had simply emailed our friends) does not account for over-representing or under-representing the population at large. With rigorous methodology and Vicky's experience, our report was taken seriously. We received national attention and we were suddenly in the news, suggesting how established artists and recent arts gradu-ates might advocate for one another, and how cultural equity initiatives might recognize and strengthen coopera-tive and solidarity art economies in the United States. We knew we were on to something, as a collective.

What we realized in 2014, after publishing *Artists Report Back*, is that although we were effective on a national level, in terms of making news headlines and speaking as a kind of think tank for cultural equity, we were still teaching in classrooms and we had not changed our pedagogy, our

In general, therefore, the
fictional institution functions by juxtaposition with
the 'real' institution. The
comparison between the two
opens a question that reaches
the heart of the distinction
between reality and fiction. If
we are led to consider existing institutions as 'natural
facts,' fictional institutions
should reveal the narrative
character of the former,
the fiction that produces
their reality.

—Marco Baravalle, 2020

ways of teaching and learning. We asked ourselves as artists and teachers: How can our production process reflect who we want to be in the world? How can we embody some of the principles that matter to us? How can we bring systems-thinking to traditional studio arts pedagogy? How can our production processes, our projects, our cultural landscapes and ecosystems align? This led us to start trying things out in our classrooms, and to begin writing about our experiences. We did not know that this would become a six-year project that would culminate in a 700-page book, *Making and Being*, published by Pioneer Works Press and distributed by Distributed Art Publishers in 2019.

although we were effective on a national level, in terms of making news headlines and speaking as a kind of think tank for cultural equity, … we had not changed our pedagogy, our ways of teaching and learning.

As I write in our book, *Making and Being*:

June 1, 2019

In 2014, Susan Jahoda and I really found each other as collaborators and friends. There is something amazing about Susan's ability to approach people of any age and status—student, administrator, etc.—with a sense of openness. Susan is able to truly see me as an equal. This is very unusual from someone at her stage in her profession; I rarely feel a sense of mutuality with older faculty members and artists that I have wanted to collaborate with. Other people have "pulled rank" and let me know that we could not grow together or transform one another.

Commitment

There is a comfort between Susan and me in
speaking about everything from our bodies to
research to relationships to careers. We are
curious about one another rather than embar-
rassed to share vulnerable realities. We
think about our differences as generative,
as moments to understand the limits of our
knowledge and to grow together. Collaboration
is pedagogical. I collaborate because I want
my limited perspective to be challenged and
transformed in dialogue with other people.
It allows me to refine my ideas in debate and
in encounters with difference—difference of
experience, of perspective, of values.

Managing

Timeframe

Susan is 66 and I am 36. As Susan and I write in *Making and Being*:

> Working in an intergenerational collective brings together, through lived and embodied experience, a sense of the past, the present, and the future. We bring in readings and references with the specificity of having lived through those debates. We speak about our need for public recognition with an honesty that is possible because we have different needs and goals according to our life stage and financial stability. For example, at the start of writing this book, Susan had job security through her tenured faculty position and supported Caroline in her successful search for a tenure-track job during the writing of this book. Likewise, Caroline and Susan supported Emilio in their search and acceptance into an MFA program. We prioritized Caroline's need for financial stability, and then Emilio's need to focus on making projects and being in a consistent space of learning. Moving through these life stages can bring emotional reactivity to our collective work. We can become emotionally unavailable to one another because we are trying to balance our personal goals with our collective projects.

We created an internal budget for the collective to keep track of the money that we generate from workshops, nearly all of which we put back into projects that we are working on.

From 2015–2019, we channeled most of the money we made from grants, artist fees, and pedagogical workshops toward the expenses related to our book, *Making and Being*.

You can see that here:

Collectively-
Initiated

INCOME

research grant	$1,000.00	UMASS	12/1/2015
workshop	$400.00	Creative Time	12/1/2015
workshop	$400.00	Creative Time	12/1/2015
workshop	$1,500.00	Cornell	8/30/2016
exhibition	$200.00	Chicago G400	9/24/2016
workshop	$100.00	NYPOP	10/14/2016
grant	$700.00	Research Grant	10/14/2016
grant	$300.00	Research Grant	10/14/2016
research grant	$333.15	Leftover Susan $	11/1/2016
exhibition	$600.00	CUE	2/22/2017
exhibition	$200.00	CUE	4/27/2017
workshops	$500.00	Spaceworks	7/14/2017
workshop	$600.00	EFA	7/14/2017
workshop	$500.00	More Art	3/25/2018
website	$2,000.00	UHartford CTEI - dev	6/1/2018
materials for WOB	$500.00	UMASS	6/1/2018
workshop	$150.00	Columbia TC	6/1/2018
Pratt	$1,000.00	Caroline	6/1/2018
Pratt	$1,000.00	Emilio	6/20/2018
residency/materials	$2,000.00	Pratt	6/30/2018
illustrations	$1,200.00	Hauser and Wirth	6/30/2018
writing text	$200.00	Social Practice Queens	9/10/2018
Kickstarter profit (after fee / printing)	$5.00	BFAMFAPhD	9/24/2018
manuscript advance	$3,000.00	Pioneer Works Press	7/18/2019
workshop fee	$600.00	Elizabeth Foundation	4/1/2019
workshop fee	$600.00	Elizabeth Foundation	2/23/2019
workshop fee	$200.00	Art in General / SHIFTER	11/25/2018
project fee	$751.99	University of Toronto	2/1/2019
writing fee	$600.00	College Art Association	1/25/2019
Kickstarter pre-sales	$6,333.42	Kickstarter Backers	9/9/2019
event production	$2,850.00	Hauser & Wirth	2/8/2019
editing support	$2,000.00	Pioneer Works Press	6/29/2019
design support	$5,000.00	Pioneer Works Press (estimate)	6/1/2019
funds for peer review	$750.00	Pioneer Works Press	3/24/2019
Total	$38,073.56		

EXPENSES
Personnel

copyedits	-$50.00	Katherine	12/1/2015
NEW INC residency	-$450.00	NEW INC	8/15/2016
text edits	-$438.75	Sara Bodinson	9/24/2016
retreat	-$63.48	Loomio Workshop	7/1/2017
interview for the book	-$100.00	Oscar	6/1/2018
interview for the book	-$100.00	Stephanie	6/30/2018
kickstarter video	-$500.00	More Art	7/1/2018
interview for the book	-$100.00	Alice	7/24/2018
interview for the book	-$100.00	Edgar	8/15/2018
printing	-$21.60	New School	8/15/2018
overview of art ed	-$500.00	Sakina	8/31/2018
documenting Pratt exhibition	-$500.00	Joao	9/23/2018
documenting Pratt exhibition	-$500.00	Joao	9/23/2018
illustrations	-$1,200.00	Topos Graphics	9/24/2018
book design style guide / brief	-$1,800.00	Topos Graphics	12/20/2018

Timeframe

early edits	-$50.00	Daniel	1/1/2019
early edits	-$350.00	Daniel	1/1/2019
design for newspaper excerpt	-$1,140.00	Angela	1/25/2019
peer reviewer fee	-$750.00	3 Reviewers	3/24/2019
design of book	-$5,000.00	Pioneer Works / Daniel (estimate)	6/1/2019
editing—structural edits pass 1	-$2,000.00	Helen	6/16/2019
feedback	-$500.0	Judit	6/26/2019
editing—structural edits pass 2	-$2,000.00	Helen	6/29/2019
website and card game	-$6,000.00	Or and Ben	8/1/2019
editing—line edits	-$500.00	Helen	8/4/2019
illustrations	-$300.00	Emily	8/4/2019
writing fee	-$700.00	Alta	8/7/2019
editing—line edit of proof	-$500.00	Helen	9/1/2019

Total   -$26,213.83

Materials and Services

window crayons	-$6.08	Blick	8/24/2018
printing newspapers	-$255.85	Linco	1/17/2019
printing deck of cards	-$219.79	University of Toronto	1/17/2019
thank you materials for H&W speakers	-$13.27	Flower Power	2/21/2019
thank you materials for H&W speakers	-$10.78	Paper Presentation	2/22/2019
thank you materials for H&W speakers	-$13.27	Flower Power	4/16/2019
thank you materials for H&W speakers	-$20.14	Paper Source	4/19/2019
thank you cards for H&W speakers	-$40.14	Cards by KT	6/7/2019
font	-$85.35	MyFonts	6/20/2019
thank you materials for H&W speakers	-$16.00	Flower Power	7/7/2019
Kickstarter service fee	-$755.00	Kickstarter	9/1/2019
hard drive (for Kickstarter video)	-$65.31	online	9/6/2019
printing the book for copyedits	-$100.00	copy center	TBA
Kickstarter books	-$2,912.00	Printer Estimate 182 books x $16	TBA

Total   -$4,506.90

Accomodations

workshop	-$65.76	Northstar Restaurant	9/15/2016
workshop	-$42.00	breakfast	9/15/2016
Cornell workshop	-$540.00	bus	9/15/2016
workshop	-$12.00	taxi	9/15/2016
retreat	-$358.62	Food Co-op	5/24/2017
workshop	-$22.68	Barista Panini House	7/14/2017
workshop	-$15.98	Key Food	7/14/2017
workshop	-$10.00	Lyft	7/14/2017
workshop	-$42.06	Lyft	7/14/2017
retreat	-$20.00	greens	6/1/2018
retreat	-$22.00	fish	6/1/2018
retreat	-$17.00	Café and Market	6/1/2018
retreat	-$63.00	Le Gamin	6/1/2018
retreat	-$12.00	coffee	6/1/2018
retreat	-$82.94	Hudson Food Studio	6/1/2018
retreat	-$81.64	Hudson Food Studio	6/1/2018
retreat	-$24.46	Health Market	6/1/2018
retreat	-$46.65	Barista Panini House	6/1/2018
retreat	-$10.53	Tea	6/1/2018

retreat	-$52.09	Pizza	6/1/2018
event space rental	-$70.00	Dzochen Community	2/28/2019
lunch	-$26.50	Court Street	6/26/2019
lunch	-$35.94	Bar Taco	6/20/2019
groceries	-$19.00	Coop	6/20/2019
retreat space	-$295.68	Hartford	6/16/2019
retreat space	-$250.00	Hartford	6/18/2019
drinks	-$10.00	water	2/28/2019
Total	-$1,588.77		

Managing

EXPENSES TOTALS	-$32,309.50
INCOME (FROM ABOVE)	$38,073.56
REMAINING	$5,764.06

BUDGET NOTES:
This budget does not include the salaries of the
staff at Pioneer Works who provided project
management, photography, video, design, marketing,
and sales support for the project. We wish to note
that we were not compensated for the time required
to write the book, but that our salaries provided
income that enabled us the time to do so. We have
relied upon so many gifts. As a collective, we
determined that we would rarely reimburse ourselves for collective meals and transportation.
All money made in workshops has gone back into
collective projects.

It was possible for me to contribute our workshop fees back to the collective, rather than taking that money as income, because I got a tenure-track job in 2017 at the University of Hartford. I had a full-time salary for the first time in my life. When I held open meetings for what became BFAMFAPhD in 2012–2013, I was truly unsure about my relationship to academic institutions. From 2012–2017, the collective had been a place for me to understand how my personal experience connected to the experiences of other students, adjuncts, and administrators within the academic arts institutions in the United States. I now know that this is part of the emergent academic field of "Critical University Studies," and my salary at the University of Hartford supports me, in part, to do this research. In *Making and Being*, I wrote about the balance of day jobs and collective work in the following way:

> In 2014, when BFAMFAPhD's *Artists Report Back* came out, I was four years into teaching as an adjunct at The New School (with a stint at RISD). I turned 30 and began to think about job security with a kind of desperation. I had started to love the dialogue that is possible in the classroom; I also loved being recognized as an academic in the academic art community. The grants that had supported OurGoods.org had dried up, and TradeSchool.coop see chapter 3 had never generated any money; we were opposed to payment in that collective. I was working three part-time jobs at nonprofits while teaching as an adjunct and trying to sustain my organizing work and my artistic practice. I was deeply exhausted. My partner had a tenure-track job, as did Susan, so I knew it was possible, despite all the odds against me; I had no MFA. But teaching in higher education seems to me to be the best job in the United States, despite the contradictions of tuition-driven education. Where else do you get four months off each year, support for experimental art projects, and job security for life?
>
> Mark McGurl has called the university system, employing artists since the 1950s, the "largest patronage system for living artists in history." I was fully aware, from BFAMFAPhD, of

the contradictions held within the neoliberal university, including the fact that
the majority of faculty will be adjuncts. I
started applying for tenure-track jobs while
also trying to find free and fully-funded MFA
programs. I had job interviews at a number
of places, but a few search committee members
told me confidentially that the lack of an
MFA was a real problem. I asked an artist to
put me in touch with someone at SVA, hoping
to get an MFA there. When I asked the Chair
of MFA Fine Arts at SVA if I could get an MFA
for free at SVA, he suggested that I teach in
the program! I went from trying to get an MFA
to teaching in their MFA program, starting in
2016. I kept applying for jobs.

… the university system, employing artists since the 1950s, the "largest patronage system for living artists in history."

After teaching at The New School for seven
years, from 2011-2017, and at SVA from 2016
on, I got a tenure-track job at the University
of Hartford, without an MFA, in 2017. The
summer before I began teaching in Hartford,
I allowed myself to feel the anxiety that
had propelled me from 2011 onward. I had to
confront the difference between the workahol-
ism that was necessary for my survival as a
precarious adjunct and the compulsive worka-
holism that numbs me from the present, numbs
me from feeling, and from being available to
others. The incredible stress of seven years
of adjunct work is starting to wear off, but
the contradictions of inequity between faculty
does not go away. I now have to confront the
inequity of the university from the privileged side of the adjunct-tenure-track

divide. I feel as though I have gotten on a cruise ship, sailing away from my peers, all of whom continue the precarious hussle. With the privilege of a tenure-track job, I am able to devote at least forty more hours per week on my research and organizing.

I had to confront the difference between the workaholism that was necessary for my survival as a precarious adjunct and the compulsive workaholism that numbs me from the present, numbs me from feeling, and from being available to others.

In my first year as a tenure-track faculty member at the University of Hartford, I decided to enroll in a tuition-free MFA program. This year is the first year that Bennington College has offered the Master of Fine Arts in Art and Public Action program, designed "for candidates with significant careers and substantial professional experience in the visual arts, well beyond undergraduate studies." While the University of Hartford and the School of Visual Arts have determined that I have equivalent professional experience to a Master of Fine Arts, and indeed while I have now taught graduate students for over five years, I recognize that for many institutions, it is important that all faculty possess a terminal degree. Bennington requires that I teach undergraduate courses as part of the conditions for the MFA.

So from 2018-2020, I taught three, seven-hour courses per week at the University of Hartford and one, four-hour course per week at Bennington while doing service work and research. My partner is an Associate Professor of English at the

City University of New York, and switched her schedule so that she was teaching on weekends, so that we could commute from New York to Connecticut to Vermont each week. We try to be together, even if we have three different "homes" and beds to sleep in. It is exhausting. My partner has supported me throughout this entire experience. Recently, I was offered a tenure-track job at a Research-1 University, but, after many negotiations, I decided to remain at the University of Hartford. I realized that it was more important for me to stay in place, in community, with my partner and collaborators nearby than to follow some fantasy of an academic career that would leave me in solitude in a totally new context.

Today, Susan and I recognize the importance of being in a "pod" together, in a quarantine of sorts, with another friend and our partners during the COVID-19 pandemic. I just had a baby and Susan is over sixty, so we are both considered vulnerable. I am going to move to Amherst, MA, to be near Susan so we can continue our work together. Our work includes the support that Susan is offering, which means helping me to raise this child. She wrote to me the other day to say, "whatever family is, we are that." This is what I believe chosen family is all about. Collaboration, in its most intentional and holistic form, can produce a deep emotional and intellectual friendship.

Managing

Mediating

It took me a while to realize that I have a skill with meditating, narrating, or "marketing" projects. I think I learned a lot of this from Rich Watts and Louise Ma, with their talent for design and documentation in OurGoods.org and TradeSchool.coop ^{see chapter 3}. First, I knew that *Artists Report Back* should be a video and a written report, as it would spread more easily this way. To get press for our projects, such as Artists Report Back, I emailed over 20 people who were leading cultural organizers, and also over 20 journalists who had written about OurGoods.org or TradeSchool.coop in the past. I wrote emails like this to press contacts:

```
Subject: lead: new national report on art
student debt BFAMFAPhD


Alan,


A friend tells me that you might be interested
in this report a group of volunteers has been
working on for the past year, on student debt
and arts education, and the impact of expensive
art degrees and future work prospects.

BFAMFAPhD is about to release a written
report, animated video, and interactive site
about the lives of working artists and arts
graduates nationally. This coincides with our
work in Crossing Brooklyn, now on view at the
Brooklyn Museum.

If you are interested in our work, please see
the media below, and do not hesitate to contact
us for more information. We ask that you do not
share this media until 2pm this afternoon, when
we are ready for web traffic.

Watch Artists Report Back, Animated:
https://vimeo.com/108889437

Read Artists Report Back, here and attached:
goo.gl/4kLF1x
Interact with national data:
censusreport.bfamfaphd.com
```

WHY DID WE MAKE THIS REPORT?
Loan officers insist that art students can afford art school tuition, repaying student loans over time by working in the arts. This is not our experience. We decided that it was time to make our own report. Connecting our lived experiences to national trends, we wanted to know: What is the impact of rent, debt, and precarity on working artists and arts graduates nationally?

HOW DID WE MAKE THIS REPORT?
Artists Report Back uses data about artists' demographics, occupations, educational attainment, field of degree, and earnings as recorded by The Census Bureau's 2012 American Community Survey (ACS) to make statements about the current conditions and contradictions of working artists and arts graduates.

WHAT DID WE FIND?
In the United States, 40 percent of working artists do not have a bachelor's degree in any field. Only 10 percent of arts graduates are working artists. Though arts graduates may acquire additional opportunities and skills from attending art school, arts graduates are likely to graduate with significant student loan debt, which makes working as an artist difficult, if not impossible. Given the discrepancy between working artists and arts graduates, as well as the rising cost of tuition at art schools, the report ends with recommendations for policy makers, administrators, and educators.

See the written and animated report for more findings, including findings about the occupations that arts graduates work, the degrees that working artists hold (if any), and the predominance of white, non-Hispanic and male working artists.

Please do not hesitate to contact us for more information.

I've also attached the image that goes with our key finding: "Out of 2 million arts graduates nationally, only 10 percent, or 200,000 people, make their primary earnings as working artists."

Caroline, Blair, Susan, Julian, and Vicky
BFAMFAPhD

info@bfamfaphd.com

The story spread quickly. I am good at thinking on my feet, and, in my twenties, I would often prioritize meeting new people in the arts rather than developing and supporting deep friendships. This led to a wide network of contacts, which was helpful for projects, but often made me the primary contact and gave less attention to other collective members. Susan and I began to work on my tendency to jump forward, and to celebrate when it was helpful, in the following way:

> To understand our collaborative dynamics, we engage in the process of "*Threeing*." *Threeing* is a method for group work that was developed by the video-artist Paul Ryan between 1971 and the end of his life, in 2013. *Threeing* is "a voluntary practice in which three people take turns playing three different roles: initiator, respondent, and mediator."[45] By practicing *Threeing* in groups of five, three, or two with members of BFAMFAPhD, we are able to experience the positions of Firstness (the initiator), Secondness (the respondent), and Thirdness (the mediator). We also use the vocabulary from *Threeing* to understand and describe our collaborative dynamic with one another, even when we are working as a group of two. *Threeing* has become such a common part of our vocabulary that we have a spreadsheet that lists every task that has to be accomplished for our group to function, using the roles: firstness, secondness, and thirdness.

45
Paul Ryan, "*Threeing*," Earthscore, 2006, http://www.earthscore.org/New%20Format/Curriculae/*threeing*_curriculum.html.

Collectively-
Initiated

Recently, we were emailed by a person who offered us an exciting opportunity. We knew that if both of us spoke with this person at the same time, the conversation could wander. Caroline is very good at thinking on the spot, and asked Susan if she could take the first calls, to determine the scope of the opportunity, alone. Susan said yes, "be in firstness," and Caroline was able to move the project forward and loop in Susan once the opportunity had been solidified. No big decisions were made without Susan's consent.

formation and maintenance of groups could be a site of investigation in and of itself.

While working on *Artists Report Back* in 2014, I realized that I had been in collectives for over seven years, and that the formation and maintenance of groups could be a site of investigation in and of itself. I felt that I could do this work—learning about how to collaborate—for life, and enjoy it. I also knew that I wanted to keep making objects, and thinking about what objects can do to support group process. With these interests, The Study Center for Group Work [see chapter 2] was born.

6

LISTEN

Cincinnati-based organizations Wave Pool and the Contemporary Arts Center in Cincinnati invited Caroline Woolard to create a socially engaged project in 2017. The artist decided to create a set of "listening objects" for four grassroots organizations—MORTAR, Cincy Stories, the Cincinnati Union Co-op Initiative, and the Welcome Project—each made in direct response to the existing facilitation practices of these organizations. Facilitation, the skillful guiding of the meeting process, is a key part of running these four organizations because they are horizontal organizations that share power and require that members attend meetings in order to make decisions together.

The finished pieces continue to live with these organizations as well as in a common space where the public can interact with them and use them as well as learn more about the project and the four organizations involved. The project debuted at the Cincinnati Neighborhood Summit in March 2018 with a presentation by Woolard, and the works were also exhibited at the Contemporary Arts Center. This project reflects Woolard's current approach to socially engaged art, explained at length in the wall text in the adjacent Wilson Gallery.

The process utilized by Woolard to make *LISTEN* suggests that artists can bring studio-based sculptural techniques to artmaking that emphasizes participation and dialogue. With attention to material, form, and scale, Woolard recognizes daily, ongoing organizing for progressive community-building and political change.

As someone often attempting
to bring artists into
communities for positive
social change, I often find
myself having to navigate
the territory of engaging
visiting artists with
communities that are not
their own. I really appreciated Caroline being upfront
about her schedule as well
as her knowledge and
background that would all
play a role in how she
could best connect with and
understand certain communities within our city as a
visiting artist.

—Cal Cullen, 2017

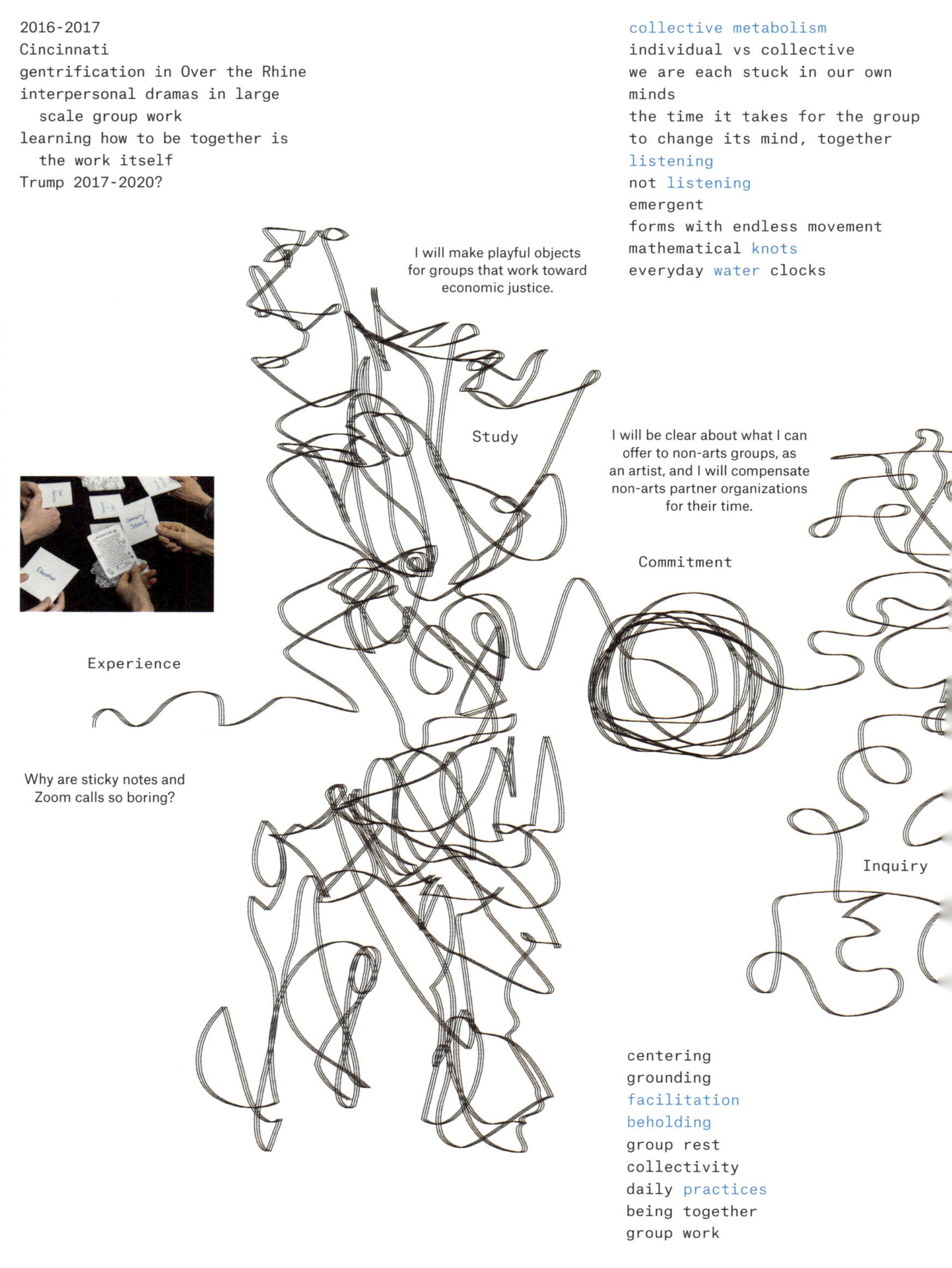

2016-2017
Cincinnati
gentrification in Over the Rhine
interpersonal dramas in large
    scale group work
learning how to be together is
    the work itself
Trump 2017-2020?

collective metabolism
individual vs collective
we are each stuck in our own
minds
the time it takes for the group
to change its mind, together
listening
not listening
emergent
forms with endless movement
mathematical knots
everyday water clocks

I will make playful objects
for groups that work toward
economic justice.

Study

I will be clear about what I can
offer to non-arts groups, as
an artist, and I will compensate
non-arts partner organizations
for their time.

Commitment

Experience

Why are sticky notes and
Zoom calls so boring?

Inquiry

centering
grounding
facilitation
beholding
group rest
collectivity
daily practices
being together
group work

Institutional
Invitation

local groups in Cincinnati
oral histories
MC Reitz
Over the Rhine
CincyStories
CUCI
Heartfelt Tidbits
MORTAR
swing house
can contextual, local collective
  practices be shared?
disability justice
conflict transformation
Generative Somatics
Study Center for Group Work
Judith Leemann and
  Kenneth Bailey
UltraRed
Center for Artistic Activism
Process Work Institute

playing cards
tea
cups
cup : water clock
mathematical knots
card game
events
key

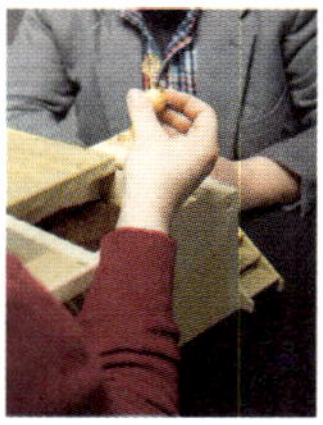

This is a one year project
at the invitation of two
organizations.

Timeframe

Objects for group that live at
  those organizations.

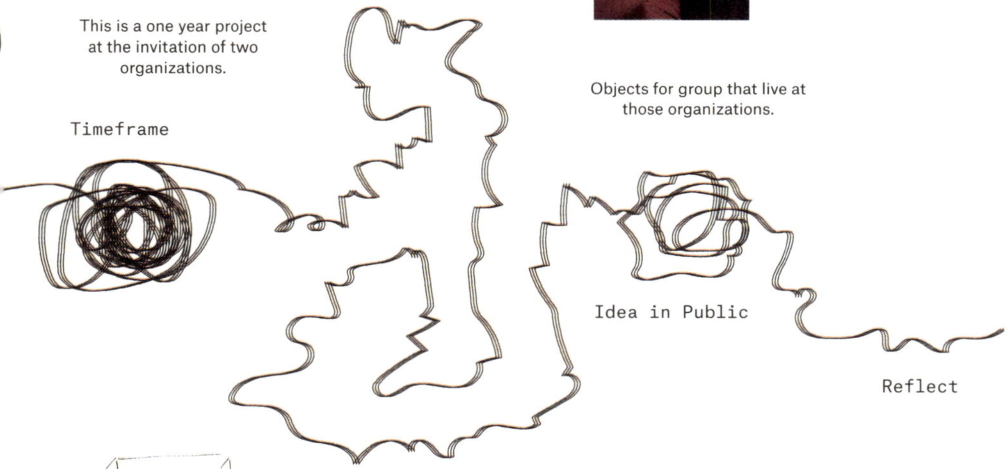

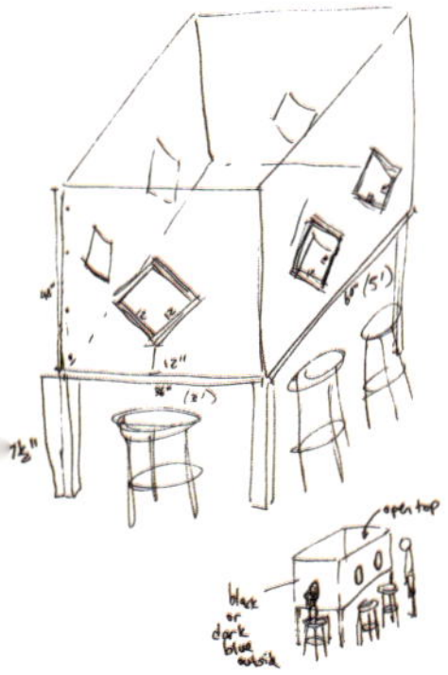

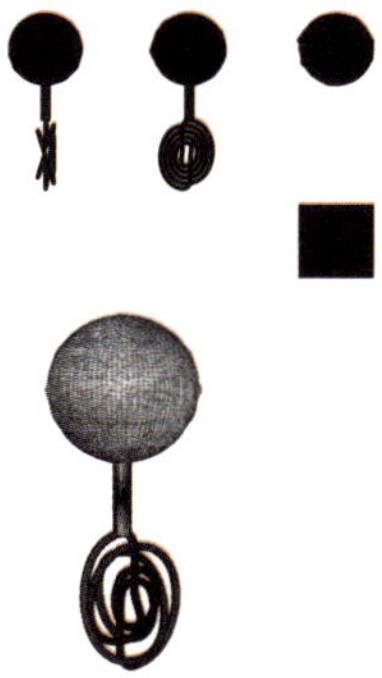

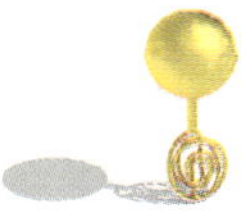

Idea in Public

Reflect

Experiment

objects for meetings a
  vailable at local orgs
hidden objects
stairs
like Clue
ritual
the artist with the candle
  in the ballroom
continuous study
facilitation : sculpture
local facilitators using
  objects I make
booth

Catalyst and Foil

Steven Matijcio, Director and Chief Curator, Blaffer Art Museum, Houston, 2020

Steven Matijcio is the Director and Chief Curator of the Blaffer Art Museum. He won a 2010 Emily Hall Tremaine Exhibition Award for the project "paperless" and in 2012 he was the curator of the fourth Narracje Festival in Gdansk, Poland. Matijcio was also commissioned by the Robert Mapplethorpe Foundation in 2003 to curate one of their first online exhibitions.

LISTEN was as much about an artist listening to local organizations, and those organizations to their constituencies, as it was about arts organizations—Wave Pool and the Contemporary Arts Center in Cincinnati (CAC)—listening to a community, an artist, and ourselves. From the outset, Woolard asked Cal Cullen, Director of Wave Pool, and myself, curator at the CAC at the time: Why do we seek to initiate a social practice project with someone who does not live in Cincinnati? Who benefits and how? What form does compensation take, and what is the legacy of such work? Woolard's artistry is everywhere and nowhere in this process, functioning as both catalyst and foil as she orchestrates situations that prompt each party to recalibrate how they conceive and speak themselves.

Woolard infuses each aspect of her working process with a gentle but pervasive approach to transparency and honest communication, sculpting words, objects, and scenarios that continue to circulate long after their initiation. As a case in point, the artist developed a set of objects that are used as prompts for storytelling, in dialogue with an economic justice organization that wanted to work with her. The organization wanted to move beyond the index cards they were using for storytelling, and Woolard's kit supported an oral history project in the area. After a series of conversations and events, Woolard created objects that come in a *Fluxkit*-like structure, a wooden box with two sets of stairs on either side, miniature objects half-hidden in soil. Participants are asked to select an object, pull it from the soil, and see if it prompts a story.

One participant selected a golden mathematical knot that emerges from a meteoroid-like shape. This knot-object speaks aptly to a cooperative process as a sinuous nexus where authorship is shared and direction is non-linear. The organization that Woolard worked with, MORTAR, provides resources to historically marginalized people to start and run successful local businesses. Woolard 3D-printed each of the golden knots in this project to ensure that they are affordable, accessible, and reproducible. This networked way of producing sculptural objects—in any maker space—feels especially relevant in a time when we must work together, from a distance, during COVID. Like the knots extracted from soil in the respective wooden box, pulled like root vegetables from the earth, the objects of *LISTEN* collectively continue on as enduring icons of actions that are both rooted and mobile, planted without ever being fixed.

sculpting words, objects, and scenarios that continue to circulate long after their initiation

To work with and alongside Caroline Woolard is to inhabit a reflexive arena where one is simultaneously immersed in an interaction with an object and experiencing a project holistically, mindfully analyzing each step and the motivation for every move. In the arts we so often work in shorthand, relying on conventions and upholding what we believe to be enlightened practices—even as the demands of timelines, budgets and the expectations for tangible outcomes erode a priori integrity.

LISTEN opened up the sightlines of that which is obscured in second thoughts, and allowed us to hear, and to heighten.

to inhabit a reflexive arena where one is simultaneously immersed in an interaction with an object and experiencing a project holistically, mindfully analyzing each step and the motivation for every move

IMAGINE A GROUP GATHERING

IMAGINE A GROUP GATHERING

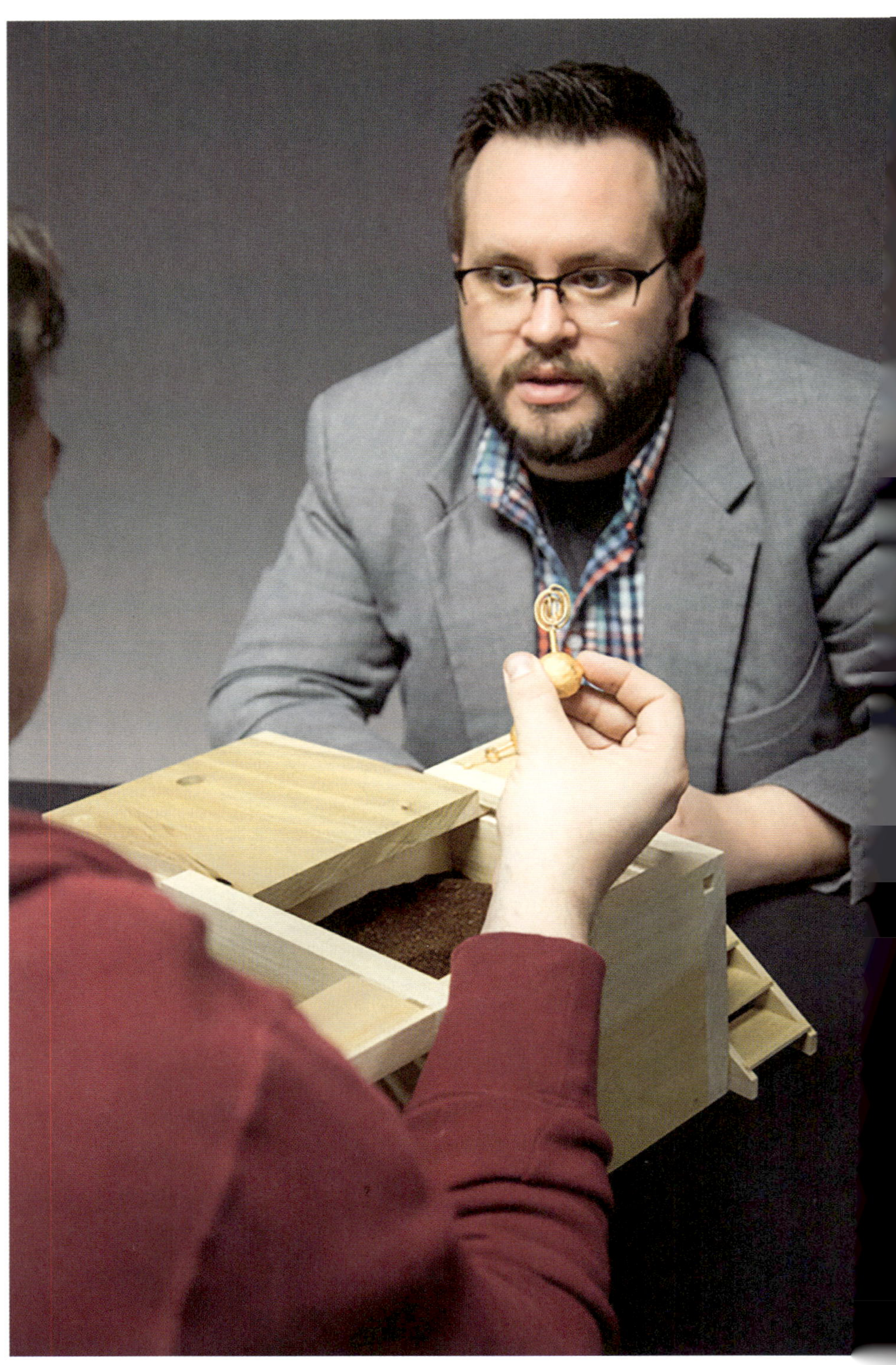

Ephemera

In the pages that follow, you will find ephemera, including correspondence, budgets, readings, and writing made in the process of developing *LISTEN*, as well as excerpts from the reflection document "*LISTEN*: A Case Study in Socially Engaged Art" that the artist asked the partner organizations to contribute to.

Woolard has selected ephemera to serve as visual reference points for *LISTEN*.

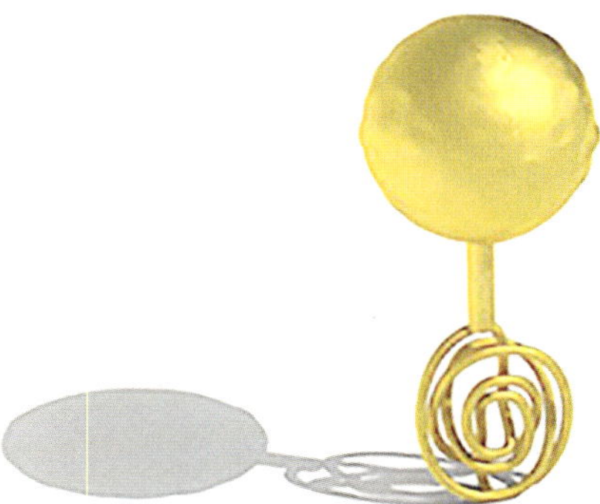

fig. 6-1
Chris Ashwell and Shawn Braley
of CincyStories using the
listening object that Caroline
Woolard created.

Experiment

fig. 6-2
A rendering, technical
drawing, and research imagery
of mathematical knots, used
to inform the creation
of listening objects. Little,
C. N., "Non-Alternate ±
Knots," *Transactions of the
Royal Society of Edinburgh* 39,
no. 3 (1900): 771-78.

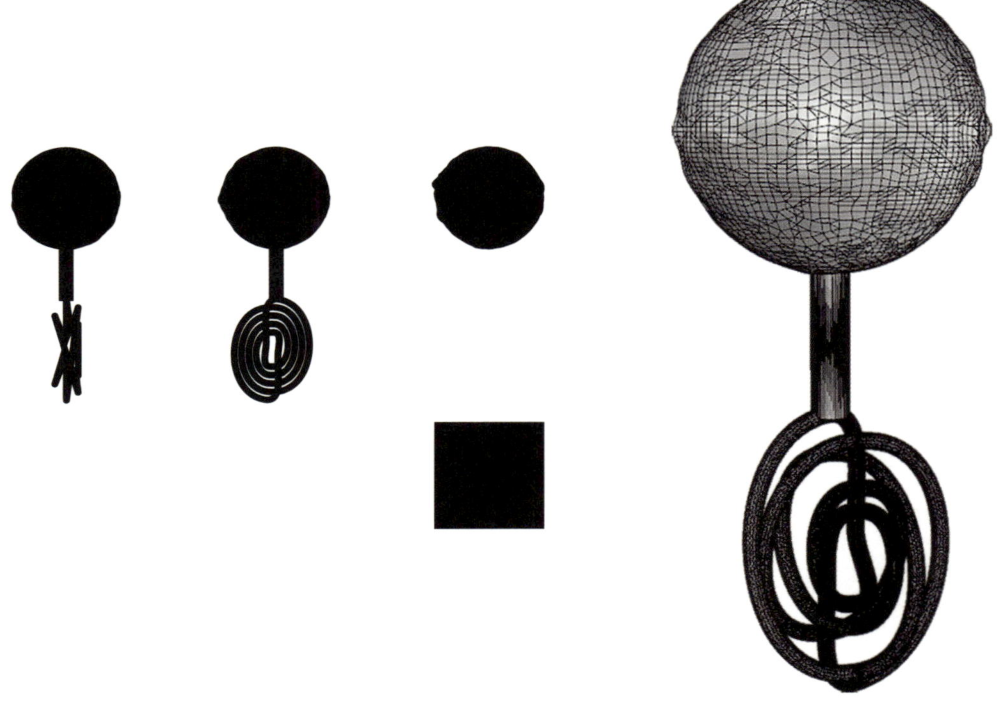

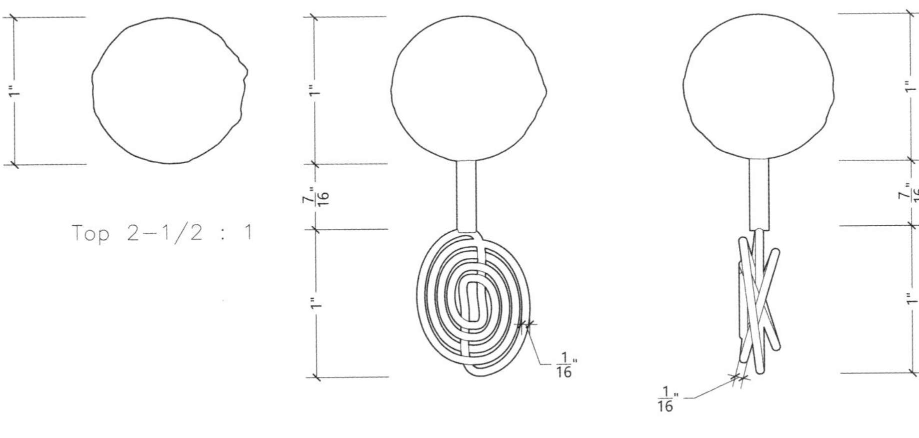
1"
Top 2-1/2 : 1
1"
7/16
1"
1/16"
Front 2-1/2 : 1
1"
7/16
1"
1/16"
Right 2-1/2 : 1
Scale: 1 Inch

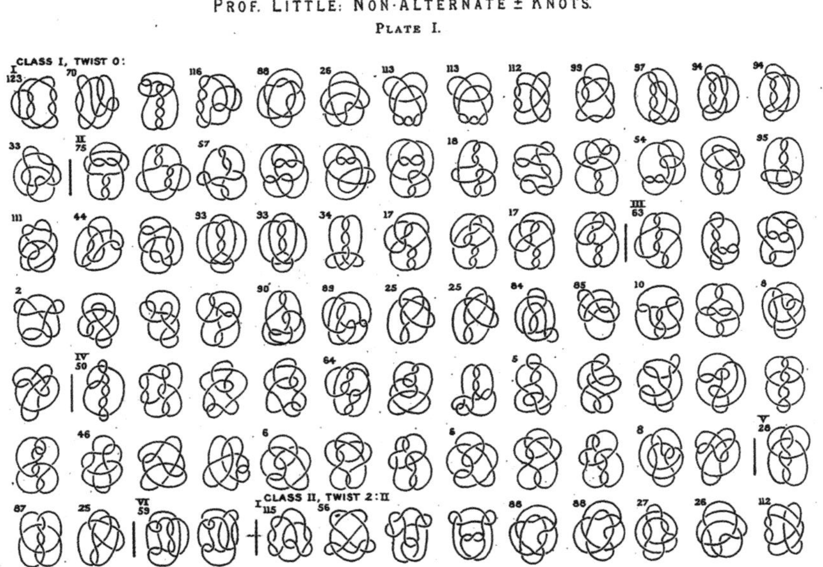
Trans. Roy. Soc. Edin.
Vol. XXXIX.
PROF. LITTLE: NON-ALTERNATE ± KNOTS.
PLATE I.
CLASS I, TWIST 0:
CLASS II, TWIST 2:II

fig. 6-3
A technical drawing and
renderings of the cups created
for *LISTEN.*

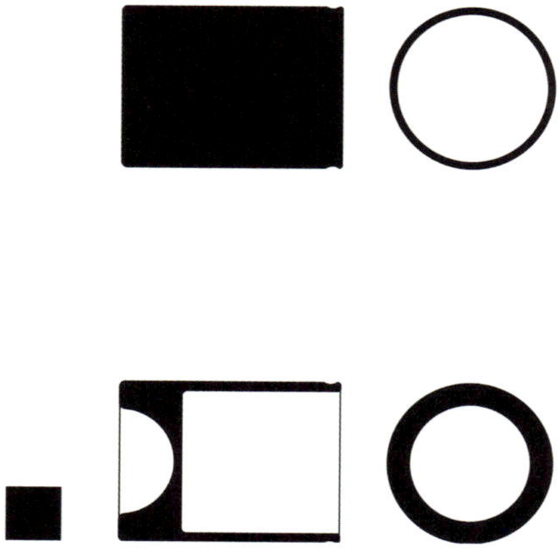

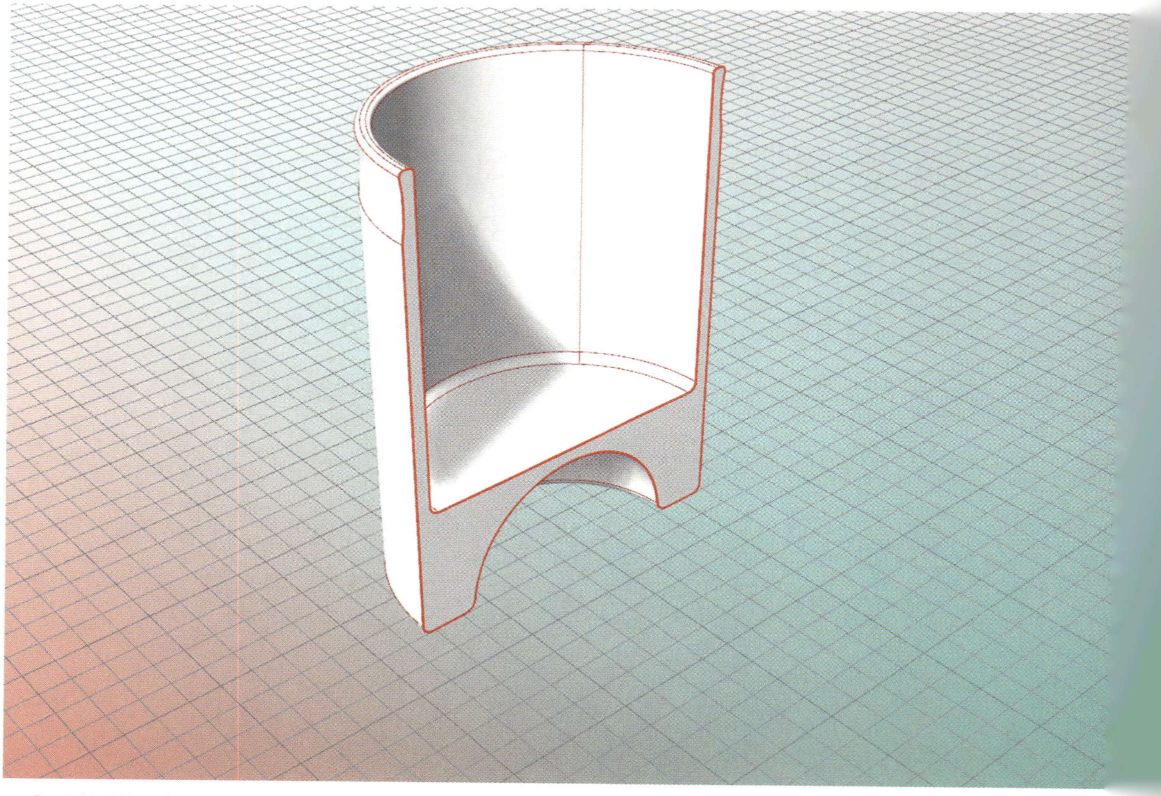

Top 1 : 1

Bottom 1 : 1

Front 1 : 1

Section 1 : 1

Scale: 1 Inch

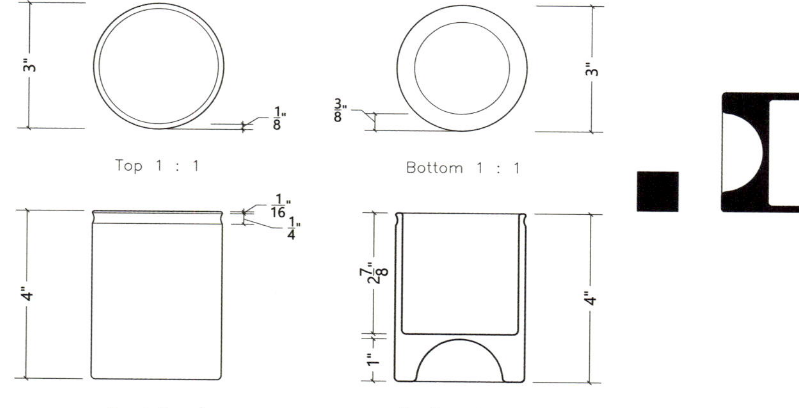

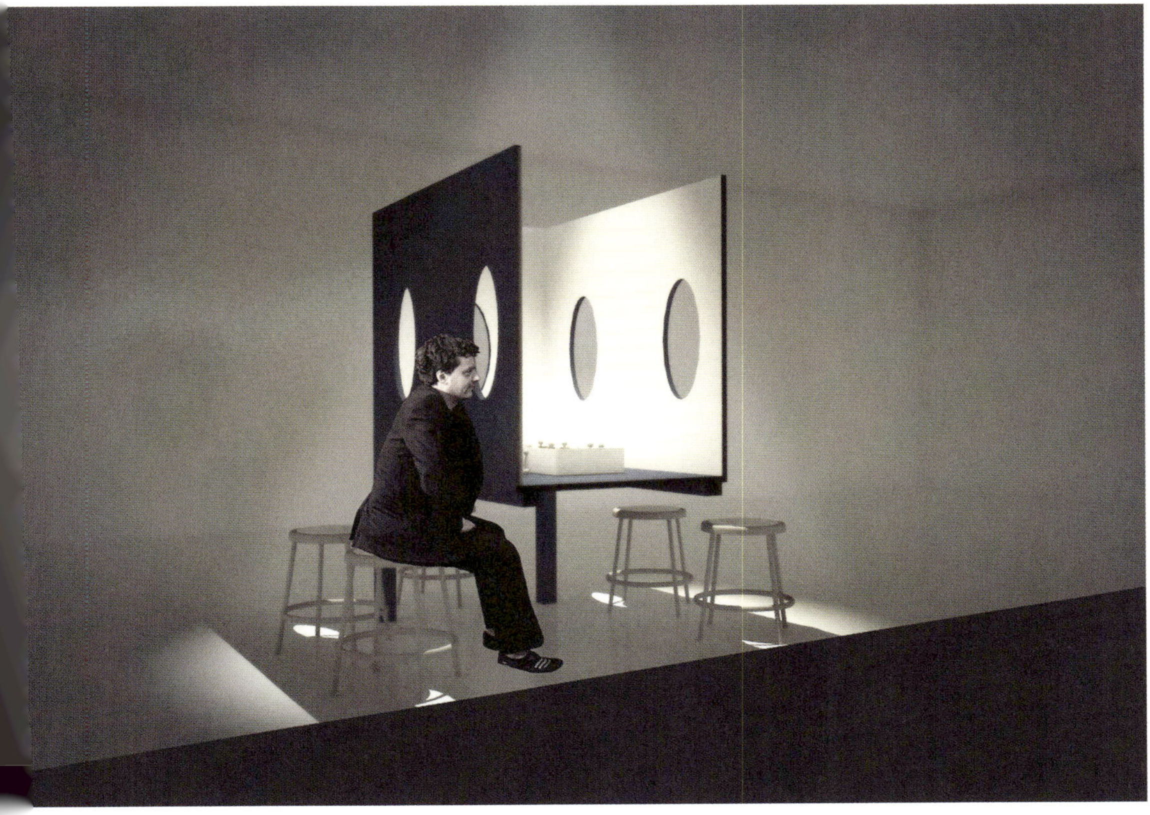

fig. 6-4
A rendering and a sketch
of the viewing station created
for *LISTEN*.

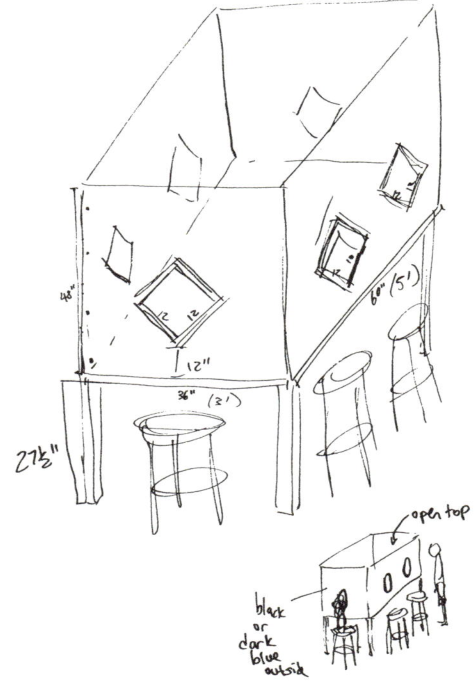

Making

Adapted from *"LISTEN:* A Case Study in Socially Engaged Art"

In January 2017, Cal Cullen from Wave Pool and Steven Matijcio invited me to create a work of socially engaged art in Cincinnati.

```
Dear Caroline Woolard,

The Contemporary Arts Center and Wave Pool Arts
Center are working in partnership to pilot a
new Socially Engaged Arts program this year for
and with the city of Cincinnati, Ohio entitled
'Shouting Distance.' This program will bring a
prominent artist to Cincinnati to respond to
community needs, facilitated in deep partnership
with an organization and a specific neighborhood
or community.

We're very interested in your work and were
wondering if this might be of interest to you?

A few guidelines to note:
- This project can begin at any time but must be
  completed by November 1st, 2018.
- Depending on your proposed project, we will
  work with you to find a compatible community
  partner and assist in building this connection.
- The final project must have a strong
  visual presence.
- We have accommodations at Wave Pool for you
  (or can set up alternative housing if that
  location doesn't make sense), but are willing
  to work with you to figure out how much time
  you would actually be in Cincinnati for
  this project.
- At least one artist talk or public performance
  would be expected.
- We have an honorarium to offer the pilot
  'Shouting Distance' artist as well as funds
  for supplies, travel and hospitality, and
  production/facilitation assistance.
```

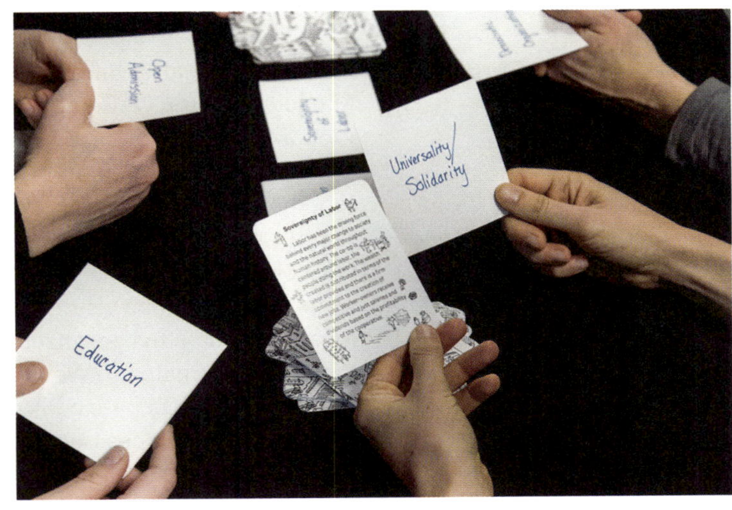

fig. 6-5
Testing the old and new versions of the *Principles of Cooperation Card Game* (one of three listening objects from *LISTEN* by Caroline Woolard) at the Neighborhood Summit in March 2018. Photo by Maureen France.

If you are still reading this and are interested, we'd love to invite you to send us any thoughts or ideas you have. We'd be interested in hearing what concepts you're looking to expand on or if you have something that you'd love to try for which this might be a good fit. By understanding a little bit about the direction you're interested in heading with your work, we'll be able to think more deeply about opportunities, histories, and groups here that might be relevant and worth exploring. We're hoping that we can make this project as constructive and productive for you as it will be for us and the city of Cincinnati.

Thank you so much and we look forward to your reply,

Cal Cullen
Executive Director
Wave Pool: A Contemporary Art
Fulfillment Center
www.wavepoolgallery.org

In March 2017, after three or four phone calls with Steven Matijcio from the CAC and Cal Cullen from Wave Pool, I proposed that the group adapt the Center for Urban Pedagogy's approach to bringing graphic designers and organizations together to support the organization's graphic design needs. Adapting this approach to socially engaged art means asking local organizations what they want, rather than assuming they want to implement a visiting artist's ideas. It took us a few months to come to consensus on this approach, and to shift the budget to match it. We hired MC Reitz, a local artist who was excited to facilitate daily engagement with the groups throughout the process, as I am based in New York City. MC's background in community organizing and ongoing work at a local level gave her the ability to engage with people in ways that would be impossible without her support.

asking local organizations what they want, rather than assuming they want to implement a visiting artist's ideas

In May 2017, I proposed four ideas to local groups aligned with her efforts around economic justice: The Welcome Project, MORTAR, CincyStories, and the Cincinnati Union Co-op Initiative. The Welcome Project's mission is "to engage, integrate, and empower marginalized and at risk refugees and immigrants by providing community connections, employment, education and skills training." MORTAR "exists to ensure that all entrepreneurs and small businesses, regardless of socioeconomic status, gender, race, or background, have an opportunity to participate in the rejuvenation of our city." Cincy Stories exists "to build community through story. We do this by hosting live storytelling events, creating people based documentaries and working in neighborhoods to engage communities using the tools of story." The Cincinnati Union Co-op Initiative (CUCI) is a non-profit that "partners with individuals and organizations to create worker- owned businesses that sustain families and help create an economy that works for all."

I spoke with each group on the phone, first introducing myself and discussing possibilities and requirements for the project, which was commissioned by arts organizations who needed to demonstrate the project's impact to funders through an arts-based framework. A commissioning organization may support an invisible or less visible process, but always needs a public event, and often physical objects, to photograph and document that the funds were well spent. This project would have to fulfill the requirement for a "strong visual presence," even though the medium of social engagement is often about building relationships, a process that is not in itself visually compelling.

I then gave the groups a series of options to choose from, based on projects and platforms I had already developed, including a set of tools for listening, a peer learning space, a sculptural installation based on conceptions of time, and a wild card idea that would be developed together, from scratch, and made sure each group knew that they would be paid for their time. The groups then had time to determine which projects, if any, were of interest to them.[46]

A commissioning organization may support an invisible or less visible process, but always needs a public event, and often physical objects, to photograph and document that the funds were well spent.

Here is the email I wrote to the partner organizations, to let them decide if we could work together, given the context, my skills, the schedule, and the budget.

46
A longer version of this idea is here: http://artmakingchange.
org/voices/the-minute-hand-of-social-engagement/

April 30, 2017
Dear Sheryl, MC, Derrick, Bonnie, Mary, Katy, Lela, and Kristen,

I am so grateful for your time and support in speaking to me over the past few weeks. As you know, I am trying to do something that moves between art and social change in Cincinnati, and I would love to hear your feelings about my ideas in progress, if you have time. If you're too busy, that's ok!

I am very sensitive to the fact that many of you are overworked and under-resourced in a time of urgent social emergency, so I am offering 3 PROPOSALS for you each to weigh in on, over the next month, from now until June 1.

Please let me know what you think by June 1st, so I can begin to incorporate your feedback to make one project that most people here feel is relevant.

I appreciate any and all feedback by email: carolinewoolard@gmail.com or phone by June 1. Before I share 3 proposals with you, I want to reiterate the background, my skills, the schedule, and the budget, below.

If you don't have time, that is totally fine too. I want to hear from you if you have a strong feeling that one of these ideas is best.

Thanks so much!
Caroline

PS: I've pasted the proposals below and also attached this writing as a PDF, for easy printing.

Of course, because social practice art is, well, social, Caroline didn't just come into town and make art on her own. She partnered with four community groups. The challenges brought by the fact that she doesn't live here were mitigated by having me serve as bridge between her and the groups. My deep roots here helped ground Caroline's work. That was key. It didn't have to be me, but it did need to be someone, and hats off to the CAC, Wave Pool, and Caroline for seeing the value in that and putting resources to it.

—MC Reitz, 2017

Study

Institutional
Invitation

BACKGROUND
As you know from our conversations, I have been invited by Wave Pool and the Contemporary Arts Center to do a "socially engaged" art project in Cincinnati. The project should relate to the social issues facing residents today and must have a visual arts component. After I hear from you, I use your feedback to determine which project I feel will be of mutual growth for residents of the area, for each of you, and for the arts organizations. I will try to combine the feedback into one project. That project must be approved by Wave Pool and CAC. The project must also be documented for the funders of this project.

MY SKILLS
I am a facilitator, educator, visual artist, graphic designer, and producer of large-scale, public, participatory art events. As an educator, I've been teaching undergraduate and graduate sculpture and design classes at the School of Visual Arts and the New School in New York City since 2010. As a visual artist, my projects range from a café performance space run at MoMA in New York City (http://carolinewoolard.com/project/exchange-cafe/) to coins I created to circulate as an alternative currency (http://carolinewoolard.com/project/believing-stars/).

In my work as a convener and creative director of solidarity economy and cooperative groups, I have helped to gather groups together in projects like http://SolidarityNYC.org, http://nycreic.com, http://tradeschool.coop, and http://landscapesofprofit.com. I also make sculptures like tables for gathering (http://carolinewoolard.com/project/capitoline-wolves/) and card games for thinking about the commons (http://bfamfaphd.com/cards).

SCHEDULE
I will visit for a week between August 13-21st, to begin work on a project with some of you, based on the proposal I determine is best from your feedback. I will then return for a few days in the fall (anytime Sept 3-Dec 3) to present the project with a public event. The date of my return will ideally be tied to an existing event you are already organizing, or an event that you want attention drawn to.

BUDGET
I have $2000 to pay partner organizations, and imagine that I could pay each group $500-800 (depending on the number of groups involved), or I could pay one group $2000.

PROPOSAL 1:
BARTER-BASED LEARNING SPACE
I facilitate the opening of a learning space that runs on barter,

training the trainers to run the school using open source software and community organizing skills.

TradeSchool.coop is a non-traditional learning community that runs on barter. We celebrate local wisdom, mutual respect, and the social nature of exchange. It works like this:

1) People offer to teach a class about something they know.

2) They decide on a list of barter items they're interested in receiving. Barter items can be in the form of goods or services, both tangible and intangible. For example: jars, music tips, clothes, vegetables, or help with something like finding an apartment.

3) Students sign up for their class by agreeing to bring something from their list.

You can see the online platform I developed at work here, and the sign up system: http://tradeschool.coop/ (we also have a robust back-end system where teachers propose classes and organizers approve them, as well as an email system to remind students).

You can watch a video about it here: https://www.kickstarter.com/projects/OurGoods/trade-school-learning-spaces-that-run-on-barter

PROPOSAL 2: OBJECT FOR COMMUNICATION/LISTENING/GROUP WORK
Through a series of workshops with members, I create a functional and beautiful set of objects that reflect a listening/collaboration process. Maybe it is a kind of rug, a talking stick, a bowl, or another object that members of a group use to set the space for a contemplative practice or a kind of dialogue or group work.

People could learn the skills of listening, attention, and collaboration that are essential to any family, business, school, or team. Whether patrons are working on a new project, an entrepreneurial endeavor, or a community-based initiative, patrons will benefit from practice spaces for approaches to collaboration. Who can build something that they have not yet imagined, drawn, debated, revised, and yet still desired? To communicate dreams—to create discursive spaces for imagination—the arts are essential. Great facilitation tools allow people to communicate across differences of opinion, experience, and expertise.

More information about the Center I have created in New York about this kind of group work: https://vimeo.com/198242353/34f85d904a

PROPOSAL 3:
INSTALLATION FOR REFLECTION
I create a space for reflection
and dialogue about hope for the
future of Cincinnati, working
with members and local residents
to create a large-scale conversation about a shared topic of
interest and an installation of
kinetic / moving objects with water
in a field.

It might feel like this:

On a Saturday afternoon, I found
myself gathering with a large group
of Cincinnati residents in a park
(exact location TBD). Upon entering
the park, I was given a small bowl
with a tiny hole in the bottom. I
walked over to the area where everyone was standing. I saw that they
were gathered around an installation
of many many oval-shaped objects on
the ground.

Resting in the grass everyone was
holding their bowl while looking at one hundred larger bowls,
oval-shaped, like two hands cupped
together, holding water. The still-
ness of the water in the bowls
reflected the clouds in the sky
overhead. After a moment of silence,
we were asked to take the small
bowls we were holding, sit for a
moment with them, and make a wish
for the future of our country. When

we were done with our wish, we were
instructed to walk into the grass
of the installation and to place
our small bowl in one of the oval-
shaped larger bowls that made up the
installation in the grass.

You can see a version of this sculpture in progress here: https://www.
instagram.com/p/BKRRe1sjmrd/?hl=en

PROPOSAL 4:
YOU DECIDE!
What would be most helpful for you?
You tell me.

The groups were most interested in the proposal about communication and listening (in their membership, in their organizations, and between members, organizations, and the public).

This became the actual timeline for our work together.

```
January-May: Designing the Process of
Working Together
- Conversations with all partners and
  proposal creation
- 5 hours of MC's work/20 hours of Caroline's work

May-June: Design Questions
- "Do you want an artist to create an object
  for listening (or contemplation) in your
  organization?"
- To work with: Heartfelt Tidbits (Sheryl), CUCI
  (Kristen), MORTAR (Derrick)
- 5 hours of MC's work/5 hours of Caroline's work

June-July: Interviews—Specific Questions
- When you hit obstacles, what is missing in
  communication? What is your desire
  for communication?
- To work with: Welcome Project/Heartfelt
  Tidbits (Sheryl), CUCI (Kristen),
  MORTAR (Derrick)
- MC emphasizes in-person Aug 13-20 meetings and
  confirms their availability then. $100 per
  group × 3 groups = $300/5 hours of MC's work

July-August: Synthesis of Interviews
- "What is wanted?" Resonant quotation
- 5 hours of MC's work/3 hours of Caroline's work

August-August: Week-long Visit
- "Would this object speak to your desire for,
  or obstacle to, communication?"
- Prototyping/dialogue all week in gatherings
  with partners
- $100 per group × 3 groups = $300
- 5 hours of MC's work/40 hours of Caroline's work
```

```
September-November: First Round of Designs
from Caroline
- 80 hours of Caroline's work

November-December: First round of Feedback
from Partners
- $100 per group × 3 groups = $300
- 5 hours of MC's work/5 hours of Caroline's work

December-March: Production of Final Objects
- 5 hours of MC's work/80 hours of
  Caroline's work
- $100 per group × 3 groups = $300

March: Final Presentation/Celebration
(In Person, with Caroline)
- 40 hours of Caroline's work/10 hours of MC's work
- $100 per group × 3 groups = $300

April: Reflection Document
- 20 hours of Caroline's work/10 hours of Cal,
  Steven, and MC's work
```

MC started by conducting in-person interviews using questions about listening practices that we designed together.

LISTEN —
Interviews for Community-Engaged
Design of Objects for Listening

<u>Your group's experience
with listening</u>
Was there a moment when people in
your group were able to listen to
one another deeply enough to change
their minds?

If so, what allowed that to happen?
Did it have anything to do with a
process or a facilitator?

Was there a moment when your group
was listened to (by the board/out-
side group/important figure) deeply
enough to change their mind? How did
this happen?

If so, what allowed it to happen?
Did it have anything to do with a
process or a facilitator?

<u>Inquiry re: objects as tools for
listening/communication</u>
Artist Caroline Woolard wants to
create, in dialogue with each of you,
objects that facilitate listening.

The object is not going to do more
than the people can. These objects
exist to celebrate and build on the
successes groups and individuals
have had with communication and listening, moments when your mind was
changed AND moments when you changed

the mind of other people. Think of
it as a "trophy" to listening that
you actually use, a tool imbued
with power of what has worked in the
past. A few tools will be made, and
all of them will stay in the area.

What is an object for listening? An
object for listening could be an
object that reminds people how much
they are speaking, it could be a
timekeeping device, it could be an
object for meditation or moments of
silence, or it could be a rug that
encourages people to step on the
area that they are speaking from
(a yellow area if they are proposing a new idea, a red area if they
are responding to an idea, or a blue
area if they are mediating between
a new idea and a response). It could
be a way to make a collective
wish together.

Caroline Woolard will visit in
person from August 14-18 and work
with you from then until late
January to make objects that
reflect the kinds of listening you
want to experience.

Have you ever used a talking piece
or talking stick in your org? If so,
how did it feel?

Have you ever taken a moment of
silence in your group/organization,
or started a meeting or event with a
centering practice or other practice

Inquiry

of being present in your body and mind? See chapter 1

Are there spiritual/religious/ listening/facilitation practices that you bring into your group/organization?

Do you know of any spiritual/reli- gious/contemplative/facilitation practices that members practice at home and might be interested in bringing into the organization?

Do any of your existing practices around a moment of silence or spirit/religion in your group/ organization include objects? If so, what are they?

Have you ever had an experience in which an object or ritual supported or improved communication? If so, was it effective? How did it work?

What do you think about the idea of an object as a tool that cele- brates and builds on prior success in communication?

What possibilities do you see?

What skepticism do you feel?

Do you want Caroline Woolard to work with you to create an object for listening or communication in your group/organization?

Is there someone in your community that Caroline Woolard could work with to create an object together for your group or organization (and be paid), so that the object better reflects local skills and wisdom?

Last thoughts?

Logistics
Are you available to meet with Caroline between Aug 14-18? This is the only time she can be here in person between now and the final presentation, so she really hopes you can meet!

What days/times might be good?

Do any of your members/staff create objects/crafts/art? If so, what skills do they have and what kinds of objects do they create? Do you think they'd want to work with Caroline to create an object?

Do you think any of your members/ staff would be interested in making objects for listening?

Possibilities
Workshops: making things with Caroline from Aug 14-18!

Paid contract work: Caroline working with members/staff to make things from December-February.
Thank you!!!

MC wrote up key anecdotes from the interviews to assist me when I visited for the first time, in-person, in August. After a week-long visit in August, when the groups brainstormed with me and then confirmed what ideas for tools for listening were most interesting to them, I began to prototype sculptural tools, and to refine these objects in dialogue with the partner organizations in the fall and winter.

Each object is a response to an organization's unique way of listening: a storytelling game using small bronze objects for MORTAR and Cincy Stories, sets of ceramic cups for Welcome Editions, and a card game about cooperation for the Cincinnati Union Co-op Initiative. The final objects were presented first at the Contemporary Art Center, at a private, intimate event with the participating organizations and people who teach, fund, or participate in socially engaged art in Cincinnati, and again at the Cincinnati Neighborhood Summit, an annual civic engagement event with 400+ attendees.

Each object is a response to an organization's unique way of listening

The final objects live with the groups, and come with facilitation guides.

PRINCIPLES OF COOPERATION CARD GAME
(draft)

Purpose: This teaching tool helps
people learn about the ten principles of cooperation.

Timing: 30+ minutes, depending on
the group

Participants: 2+

Listening tool: cards

How it works:
(1) The facilitator gathers people
and places all ten cards on the
table, showing the ten principles of
cooperation. Each card has one principle of cooperation on the back of
the card, and the definition of that
principle on the other side.
(2) The facilitator asks a participant to mix up the cards and pick
one.
(3) The participant will read the
card they have picked aloud to the
group, and talk about what that
principle means to them.
(4) The group can talk about how
they sense or don't sense that principle of cooperation in their group,
and how they might emphasize that
principle in their group, even more.
(5) Another participant picks a
card, reads it aloud, and talks
about what it means to them.
(6) Repeat.

Organization:
Cincinnati Union Co-op Initiative
(CUCI) is a non-profit that partners
with individuals and organizations
to create worker-owned businesses
that sustain families and help
create an economy that works for
all. Cincinnatiunioncoop.org

Process:
LISTEN exhibits objects made by
artist Caroline Woolard in dialog
with four Cincinnati-based organizations. Each object is a response to
an organization's unique way of
listening: a storytelling game with
small bronze objects for MORTAR and
Cincy Stories, cups for the Welcome
Project, and a card game about
cooperatives for CUCI.
www.wavepoolgallery.org/
listen-with-caroline-woolard/

Caroline Woolard worked with Kristen
Barker, Olivia Nava Meinerding, and
Maria Dienger to add illustrations
and design to improve CUCI's existing game.

Materials:
Each card is 3.5" × 4.5" and the
test cards are printed by Micah
Hornung. Future iterations of these
cards will be available online as
freely downloadable PDFs and for
purchase through CUCI and Wave Pool.

MORTAR AND CINCYSTORIES

Purpose: This is a game that helps participants get to know one another.

Timing: 30+ minutes, depending on the group

Participants: 2+

How it works:
(1) The facilitator asks the participants to close their eyes as the facilitator buries the objects in the box so that only the spheres are showing.
(2) One participant selects an object and picks it up.
(3) This person tells a story based upon the object they are holding.
(4) Another participant selects an object and tells a story based upon that object.
(5) Repeat.

Organizations:
MORTAR exists to ensure that all entrepreneurs and small businesses, regardless of socioeconomic status, gender, race, or background, have an opportunity to participate in the rejuvenation of our city. wearemortar.com *Cincy Stories* exists to build community through story. We do this by hosting live storytelling events, creating people based documentaries and working in neighborhoods to engage communities using the tools of story. cincystories.org

Process:
LISTEN exhibits objects made by artist Caroline Woolard in dialogue with four Cincinnati-based organizations. Each object is a response to an organization's unique way of listening: a storytelling game with small bronze objects for MORTAR and Cincy Stories, cups for the Welcome Project, and a card game about cooperatives for CUCI.
www.wavepoolgallery.org/listen-with-caroline-woolard/

Caroline Woolard worked with Allen Woods, Derrick Braziel, Chris Ashwell, William Thomas, and Shawn Braley to imagine and implement this game, which is loosely based upon an event that they held together, where friends and neighbors brought in objects that are significant to them. The objects were designed by Caroline Woolard and sit in poplar boxes handmade by Scott Bellissemo.

Materials:
Each object is roughly 1" × 2" × 1" and is cast in stainless steel infused with bronze, with a final composition of approximately 60% steel and 40% bronze. The objects went through an electroplating process that deposits a 0.1 micron layer of gold on the outside of the objects. Due to the electroplating process, the gold may wear off with friction, over time.

WELCOME PROJECT CUPS

How it works:
Drink tea with an open heart. Notice that the cups have two sides. When turned over, the underside of the cup becomes a vessel for a flower, a candle, or a water-clock.

Organization:
The Welcome Project's mission is to engage, integrate, and empower marginalized and at risk refugees and immigrants by providing community connections, employment, education and skills training.

Process:
LISTEN exhibits objects made by artist Caroline Woolard in dialoueg with four Cincinnati-based organizations. Each object is a response to an organization's unique way of listening: a storytelling game with small bronze objects for MORTAR and Cincy Stories, cups for the Welcome Project, and a card game about cooperatives for CUCI.
www.wavepoolgallery.org/
listen-with-caroline-woolard/

This limited edition of ceramic vessels was designed by Caroline Woolard over the course of a year in dialogue with Welcome Project members Zoila Martinez, Lourdes Martinez, NarMaya Rai, Bibi Rai, Binta Rai, Sarmila Rai, Purni Rai, Mariam Al-Zoubi, Fabiola Rodriguez, Krishna Ghimire, and Angele Mputu. These ceramics continue Caroline Woolard's study of functional objects for contemplation and collaboration. The cups were wheel thrown by ceramicist Josephine Heilpern and are sold in sets of four in poplar boxes handmade by Scott Bellissemo. The dividers in the boxes were made by members of the Welcome Project. This is a limited edition of thirty boxes, with four cups per box, for sale at Wave Pool. All profits go to Welcome Editions and feed back into the growth of the Welcome Project, a collaboration between the non-profit organizations Wave Pool and Heartfelt Tidbits.

Materials:
Each vessel is a wheel thrown cup in speckled clay. The interior and exterior is glazed in high gloss green with black speckles. The bottom is a high gloss black with a blue lotus flower. The exterior is decorated with bright blue and green shapes. The size is approximately 4.25 inches tall × 3.25 wide diameter. Each item is handmade and has slight variations in size and finish and color. Food safe and made for everyday use. Hand washing is recommended. Sold in a set of four in a handmade poplar box.

Mediating

I saw at least three major areas of danger for socially engaged projects made by visiting artists like me, who are invited by arts institutions to work in a neighborhood or professional community other than those that the artist is regularly in contact with, and which the arts institutions do not have regular contact with. When anyone claims to "do good" and begins to work with a group or in a neighborhood that they do not intend to return to, it is far more likely that the group or neighborhood is helping that person than the other way around (the visitor helping). I know that the person who spends the most time on the project will be transformed, and that person is likely me.

I asked myself, "How long will I really be involved in this area? Would I be involved if I were not invited to go there? If not, is there a way that I can connect an issue that I am working on locally to a group in the visiting location?"

In this project, I tried to be upfront about the limits of my engagement with partner organizations, to pay them for their time, and to make sure I met their goals for the project as well as my own goals, and the art institutions' goals. For example, with CUCI, I decided to act as a graphic designer of sorts, making an illustration/design project with cards, as that was most appealing to them, and I know we can use it in the co-op movement in NYC.

I initiated a reflection document about *LISTEN* with feedback and commentary from project partners that I published. "*LISTEN*: A Case Study in Socially Engaged Art" compiles a summary of *LISTEN*'s process, a project timeline, notes on the approach, commentary by collaborators, and worksheets developed for *LISTEN*. We hope that it will serve as a case study to think through the possible forms of engagement when a visiting artist is invited by an arts institution to work in a geographic or professional community that the visiting artist does not regularly interact with.

"Caroline did an amazing job of getting this group of women, who struggle to find their voice, to feel comfortable enough to share their thoughts and ideas. What was interesting was the bond that they felt with her in that they were willing to share very honest opinions of prototypes and drawings that she shared … I think it would've been nice to have Caroline on site while she was building some of the prototypes or in person for the discussions because they were so rich. I've given multiple examples related to what worked the best and that was the empowerment it gave to the women who participated. It would've been great to have a bit more time on the end so that Caroline could have shown the women her final product herself. Overall it was a fantastic experience and I know the women really enjoyed their time with her and felt that she respected them and truly wanted and valued their viewpoints. This hasn't been the case with all of the artists they have worked with so I feel it's a very sincere comment from them. Thanks for this and making our world a brighter place through the sharing of your gifts and talents!"
—Sheryl Rajbhandari, Welcome Project

"We were brought in, by MORTAR, to be a part of this. But ultimately, I think it would have been better for us to have been separate. A big reason being us no longer sharing a space—which we didn't expect to happen when we started this project, but also because our organizations likely had different needs for this and the compromises we needed to make to fit both of our needs made the outcome less useful than it could have been with two distinctly separate ideas. This isn't to say that Caroline didn't do a wonderful job of synthesizing the collaborative ideas we had, it is just to say that we could have been free to think directly of the work we do (same for MORTAR) and build from there."
—Shawn Braley, CincyStories

"Sometimes an outsider is exactly what's called for. Caroline Woolard has deep, on-the-ground, hands-on experience with community and artistic engagement in her own home city of New York and beyond, around issues from equitable development, to barter economies, to shared spaces and objects for learning, presence, and listening. Cincinnati has a few active social practice artists, but for most Cincinnatians the idea of "social practice art" is likely to elicit puzzled looks. Most haven't heard of it, don't know what it is. It helps to have a known and respected institution (the Contemporary Arts Center), and a known and respected community-based arts center (Wave Pool) say to Cincinnati, in essence, "Social

Practice Art is a vibrant and valuable genre within fine art. Here's an example of an artist and project in that field being done right here. We think this is important, and could offer something good to our city." It helps to have someone who is cultivating significant experience and mastery in the field to come and show us how it can be done.

Of course, because social practice art is, well, social, Caroline didn't just come into town and make art on her own. She partnered with four community groups. The challenges brought by the fact that she doesn't live here were mitigated by having me serve as bridge between her and the groups. My deep roots here helped ground Caroline's work. That was key. It didn't have to be me, but it did need to be someone, and hats off to the CAC, Wave Pool, and Caroline for seeing the value in that and putting resources to it.

This project brought social practice art to Cincinnati in a bigger more visible way than it has existed to date. So our city benefited, but I gained something important too. I had a lot of quality time with Caroline. Because of who she is and how she works—down to earth, generous, open and transparent, a teacher by nature—I had access to how she was thinking about the project, and at points got to think and talk

through how to solve problems with her. And now I have a relationship with her. This brings value not only to me as a social practice artist, but to Cincinnati; now our city has in me an active social practice artist with a relationship to a leader in our field. All of us who worked with Caroline on *LISTEN* have this. We have what we learned, we have more connected relationships with each other, and we have our friendship with Caroline."
—MC, local artist liaison

"As someone often attempting to bring artists into communities for positive social change, I often find myself having to navigate the territory of engaging visiting artists with communities that are not their own. I really appreciated Caroline being upfront about her schedule as well as her knowledge and background that would all play a role in how she could best connect with and understand certain communities within our city as a visiting artist."
—Cal, Wave Pool

"The CAC formed a Community Engagement Council in the spring of 2017 to help establish a dialogical model when working with various communities on art-inspired projects. Rather than "impose" an artist and/or project upon a community, we aimed to listen to community wants

and needs; determine which of those
an arts organization could realistically address; and connect these
aims with an artist/s who could
engage them through the lens of art.
Caroline was sensitive to these
circumstances and thoughtful about
how best to organize a project that
would not be weighed down with
politics before it began in full."
—Steven, Cincinnati Contemporary
Art Center

I made these worksheets for people to consider, when doing similar projects:

TIME/SCALE/MONEY AGREEMENTS
WORKSHEET 1
(for Visiting Artist, Local Artist,
Inviting Arts Organizations, and
Partner Organizations)

What do you hope to accomplish with this project?

What do you need from the other parties in order to accomplish
this goal?

How will you balance time, scale, and money in order to
accomplish this goal?

LISTEN

Idea in Public

TIME/SCALE/MONEY AGREEMENTS
WORKSHEET 2
(for Visiting Artist, Local Artist,
Inviting Arts Organizations, and
Partner Organizations)

Looking at Worksheet 1 from the Institution and the
Partner Organizations, what overlapping hopes do you see?
What potential conflicts do you see?

How might you alter your goal for this project, in order
to navigate these overlapping hopes and conflicts?

Institutional
Invitation

In the arts we so often work in shorthand, relying on conventions and upholding what we believe to be enlightened practices—even as the demands of timelines, budgets and the expectations for tangible outcomes erode a priori integrity. *LISTEN* opened up the sightlines of that which is obscured in second thoughts, and allowed us to hear, and to heighten.

7

Capitoline Wolves & Queer Rocker

In 2016, curator Stephanie Owens invited Caroline Woolard to do a series of projects at Cornell University for an initiative called *Abject/Object Empathies* which focused on the cultural production of empathy and explored how the objects and images people construct are shaped by interdependent relationships to others. Stephanie Owens asked: What are the ways in which art and design mediate and shape the emotional exchanges between people in tangible form?

In a series of events throughout the semester, Woolard shared her open-access kit for *Queer Rocker* and invited students to make adaptations of the rocking chair. The *Rocker* circulates as an open access toolkit. It was first shown at *The Very First Year*, curated by Laurel Ptak at Eyebeam in 2013, and has been modified for use by students at Cornell University, the State University of New York, Purchase, and at WeMake, a maker space in Milan, using ratchet straps, hardware, and press-fit joints. The kit is available so that anyone with a maker space can modify and produce a *Queer Rocker*.

What are the ways in which art and design mediate and shape the emotional exchanges between people in tangible form?

Capitoline Wolves, commissioned by Owens for the exhibition, was an installation made for conversations about masculine violence and fantasies of "founding brothers." Five tables were placed in a pentagonal formation under the grand dome of Sibley Hall at Cornell University. Each table resembles the she-wolf that raised Romulus and Remus; the cherry-wood table has bent hind legs of steel, distended udders of stoneware, and a hanging mirror for a face. The she-wolves' breasts were filled with water from Ithaca's gorges. Throughout the installation, visitors placed a delicate bowl with a single hole in the water when their conversations began. When the bowl sunk to the bottom, it marked the duration of a topic of conversation at the table.

An object of art creates a public capable of finding pleasure in its beauty. Production, therefore, not only produces an object for the subject, but also a subject for the object.

—Karl Marx

*Capitoline Wolves &
Queer Rocker*

Reflect
Idea in Public
Experiment
Timeframe
Inquiry
Commitment
Study
Experience

2015/2016
Cornell University
interdisciplinary hopes in
   the art school
#metoo 2017
Obama 2009-2017

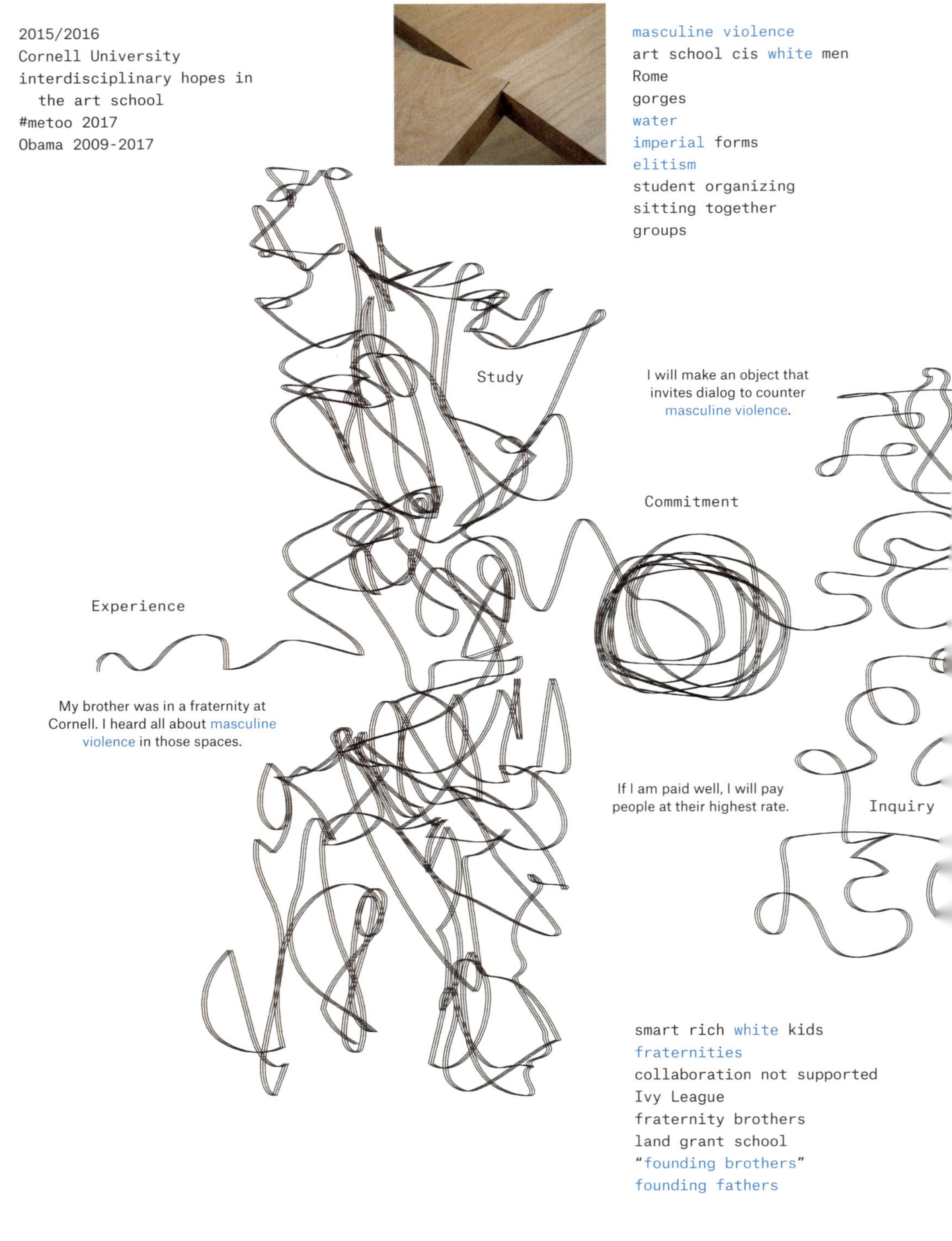

masculine violence
art school cis white men
Rome
gorges
water
imperial forms
elitism
student organizing
sitting together
groups

I will make an object that
invites dialog to counter
masculine violence.

My brother was in a fraternity at
Cornell. I heard all about masculine
violence in those spaces.

If I am paid well, I will pay
people at their highest rate.

smart rich white kids
fraternities
collaboration not supported
Ivy League
fraternity brothers
land grant school
"founding brothers"
founding fathers

Institutional
Invitation

water clocks
capitoline wolf sculpture
corinthian columns
tuscan columns
composite
smugglers carry away marble columns in sections
"Romulus's descendants inherited
  the she-wolf's beastly milk."
breast milk as blood

she wolf
breast as water clock
pack of wolves
udders
tuscan column
mirror as a face

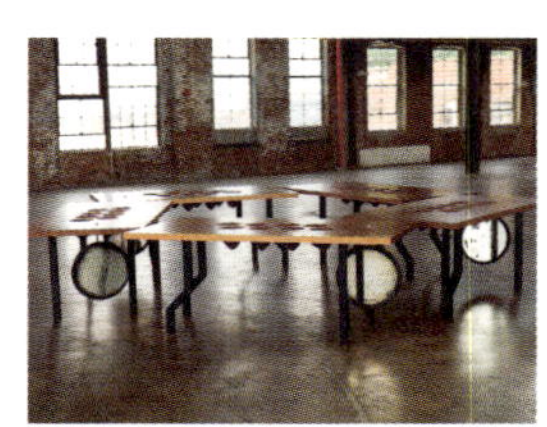

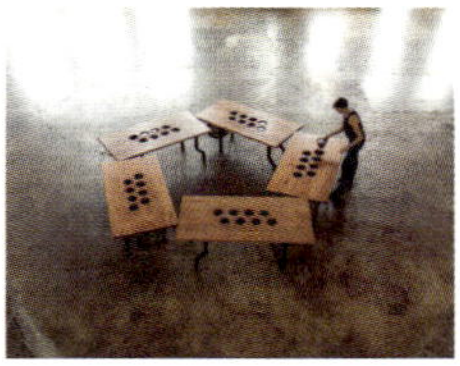

This is a four month, site-specific
project, created at the invitation
of an institution (Cornell).

Timeframe

A series of sculptural
objects that invite gathering
and dialog.

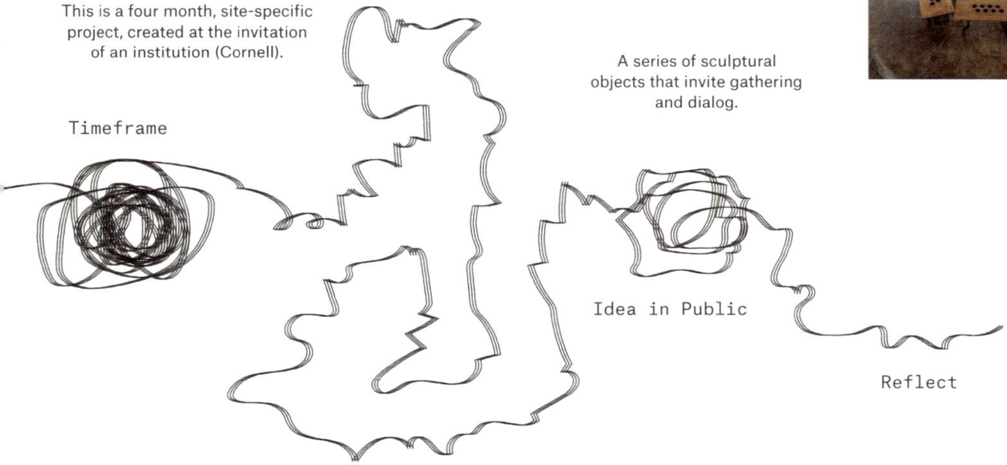

Idea in Public

Reflect

Experiment

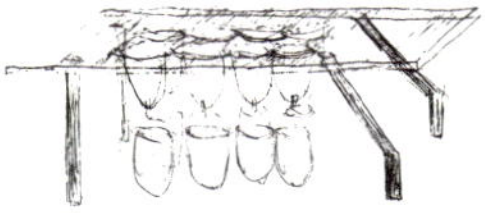

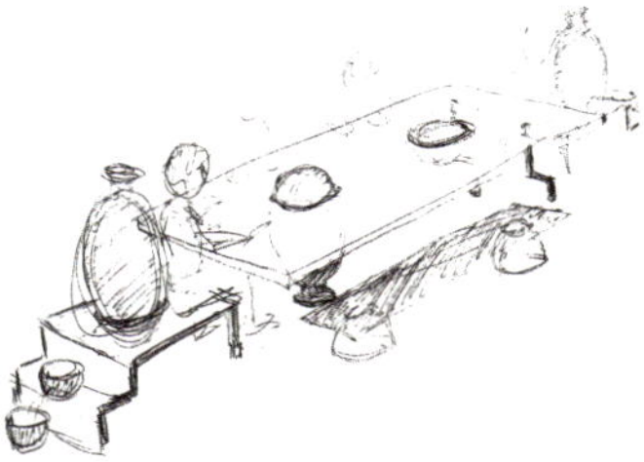

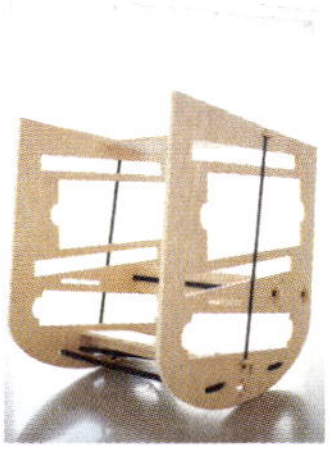

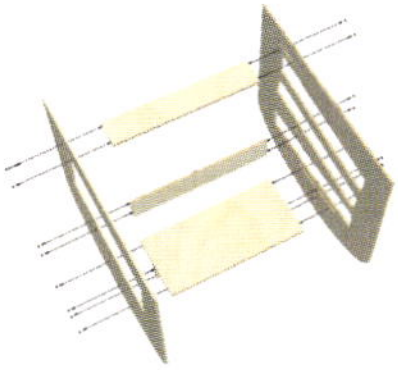

un/stackable column stool
American Wooden Column Corp
CNC column
working with students to
  remake work
open access file
copper hand formed water
  clock
cherry wood
mirrorizing glass
no social practice plywood
  props
lasting objects as gifts
events around wolf tables

*Capitoline Wolves &
Queer Rocker*

An Aesthetics of Interdependence

Stephanie Owens
Head of School, School of Arts + Media,
Plymouth College of Art, UK

Stephanie Owens is the Head of School at Plymouth College of Art and an independent curator. Owens's curatorial projects include *Technologies of Place*, funded by New York Foundation for the Arts, *SELF[n]: Art & Distributed Subjectivity*, *Intimate Cosmologies: The Aesthetics of Scale in an Age of Nanotechnology* (Cornell University), and *Abject/Object Empathies* (Cornell University).

At the time I first saw Caroline Woolard's work, I was immersed in thinking about empathy. As Director of Cornell Council for the Arts in 2016, I had just spent the last month crossing into the art, biology, materials science, architecture, information science, and psychology departments on campus to involve the community of students and scholars in discussions about the origin of the word and its contemporary meaning. Unknown to me before the discussions, empathy has deep historical connections to reception theories in art and aesthetics. Learning that empathy shares common cultural ancestry with early aesthetics gave me inspiration to use the biennial as a platform to explore how notions of beauty, phenomenology, and vitalism might be experienced in the work of contemporary artists in relation to objects. With its deep, cross-cultural and cross-disciplinary foundation in theories of perception, empathy is a concept that merges the making of art with the experience of it, where its primary effect is embodied, connecting artist and audience through the art as mediating object. Seeing Caroline's barricade turned into a bed—literally an object of exclusion transformed into an object of support, it seemed to me that aesthetic empathy had been revitalized in a cogent, purposeful way in her work.

Recently out of her undergraduate studies at The Cooper Union in 2013, Caroline created *Barricade to Bed* [see chapter 4] in the context of the Occupy Wall Street activism and her thinking about economies of solidarity living in NYC. Although I would eventually discover her pedagogical and collaborative practices which questioned the role of the discrete art object in producing $120,000 art degrees, I felt her bed was nonetheless a quiet, insistent proposal that objects can be phenomena of shared experience. Disarmingly simple, her repurposed barrier sculpture inspires immediate associations with Duchamp's *Fountain* and other historical ready-mades.

her sculptures, seem conditional in the most positive sense — an instrument for making economic and affinity networks visible

Yet if transforming a urinal to a fountain by flipping it upside down was a disinterested act of authorship without making, *Barricade to Bed* offers a more radical idea of making as an act of unity and co-creation. With its tool-kit construction plans and material resource list available as part of its display at MoMA, *Barricade to Bed* is an eloquent act of generosity that suggests how reciprocity between people might take shape amid a world that idealizes autonomy and an ethos of self-reliance. The transparency with which she works transforms our complicity with the violence of discrete, isolated objects of art into a curiosity about how cultural form might be symptomatic of the amalgam of thoughts and lives we share with others. Not unlike ritual objects of social incantation, each of her projects, and particularly her sculptures, seem conditional in the most positive sense — an instrument for making economic and affinity networks

visible, and perhaps for making them possible in new ways. Caroline has nearly x-ray vision in perceiving the human and political DNA embedded in objects and the sensitivity to unfold this hidden vernacular into its component parts, like building blocks to reimagine worlds.

Having been struck by this quality of interdependence between artist-object-audience inherent in her proposals, including her socially speculative and pedagogical spaces, I invited Caroline to be an artist-in-residence for *Abject/Object Empathies* for which a number of artists, including Pepon Osorio, Caroline O'Donnell, Alexandr Mergold, and Teresa Diehl were commissioned to make new work in the context of how feeling becomes form. For her first project with the university, Caroline arrived on campus with a whole system of producing art expressed as *Free, Libre, Open Source Systems and Art* (F.L.O.S.S.A), a manifesto for making "free art" which she used to guide students through an understanding of how they might modify her *Queer Rocker* in order to make a version of it, by adapting it, for themselves. In the end, 11 new *Queer Rockers*, made unique in their slight difference of shape, color and texture, were exhibited together like products of an assembly line. Paradoxically, the artist's sharing of the blueprints for her sculpture made the core chair prototype, obviously common to them all when seen in a group, the content of the exhibition rather than the individually modified sculptures. Students embraced this process of making variation as an act of creativity familiar to them in social and platform media and approached Caroline's sculpture as a meme in shape and origin.

Capitoline Wolves &
Queer Rocker

art objects or symbols are not reducible to spaces or contexts of display, but invitations to act and reflect

Part internet of things and part DIY tool-kit, the CNC fabricated *Queer Rocker* is above all a set of rules to engage others in a conversation about ownership of creative process. The openness with which Woolard embraces the whole ecology of making had a profound impact on the college, triggering equal parts gratitude and hostility. Reactions were strong, particularly to the vulnerability of her art objects to the influence of others when met with the artist's invitation to change them. Although there is a rich history of temporal and participatory art that also challenges the notion of permanence and what Woolard refers to, she embraces a very contemporary tension between relinquishing and embracing art in object form. This on-demand production of art, within which both artists and art are made, proved to be a provocative proposal for questioning the material interface between ourselves and others.

Well-known for her pedagogical and economic models of solidarity, Caroline is an artist for whom art objects or symbols are not reducible to spaces or contexts of display, but invitations to act and reflect. The success of her creation of objects as spaces of learning and teaching through *F.L.O.S.S.A./ Queer Rocker* led to my expanding her engagement with the biennial, and we discussed ways that she might

be able to make an object that facilitated public panels and discussions. Embedded in the Doric corridors of innovation and power at a research university, Caroline turned to the story of Romulus and Remus, and the patriarchal myth of the "founding fathers," to centralize the presence of the female she-wolf that nurtured them. Reimagining the she-wolf as having equal power in the birth of Rome/civilization, she detourned the symbol of taking (child) into one of giving (mother), and built an interlocking circle of individual animal-like tables as a prowling interface. The ring of tables, perforated with large fist-sized holes in the wood surface that plunge into ceramic breasts filled with water, suggested that the anonymous she-wolf, like the artist who makes objects which empower others, does not act alone but always acts with and for others. Simultaneously an installation and a stage set, *Capitoline Wolves* is a discursive object that derives its meaning and physicality *a priori*—from its ability to intentionally shape and encourage a shared imagination.

Although she is often aspirational in writing and speaking about her projects in their relationship to economic and societal models of equity, the aspect of her project that is often overlooked is the way Woolard inscribes this social imagination in the most intimate details of the physical realization of her art objects. Easily unnoticed in the complexity of references in *Capitoline Wolves* is the small, exquisitely intimate way one corner of each thick wooden table top fits puzzle-like inside a recessed, perfectly-matched notch in the table adjacent to it. Each she-wolf table is designed to both interrupt and receive in relation to the other, binding them together.

Woolard inscribes this social imagination in the most intimate details of the physical realization of her art objects

From the perspective of neuroscience this is the very definition of empathy in object form. If we imagine mirror neurons (the she-wolf tables have a mirrored face) in an individual brain firing when another's action is experienced as if our own, biologically programming our empathetic understanding, we begin to realize that there are ways of perceiving and knowing that cannot be experienced in isolation. In some real physiological sense, empathy is a structural condition of our interdependence with others which allows us to comprehend and know the world. The *Capitoline* tables—as she-wolves, as objects, and as sculptures—make sensuous argument for art as a form of social cognition. They offer a new aesthetics of interdependence, where they are wholly knowable as individual objects but more meaningfully experienced as an intertwined group, posse, or circle.

empathy is a structural condition of our interdependence with others

IMAGINE A GROUP GATHERING

IMAGINE A GROUP GATHERING

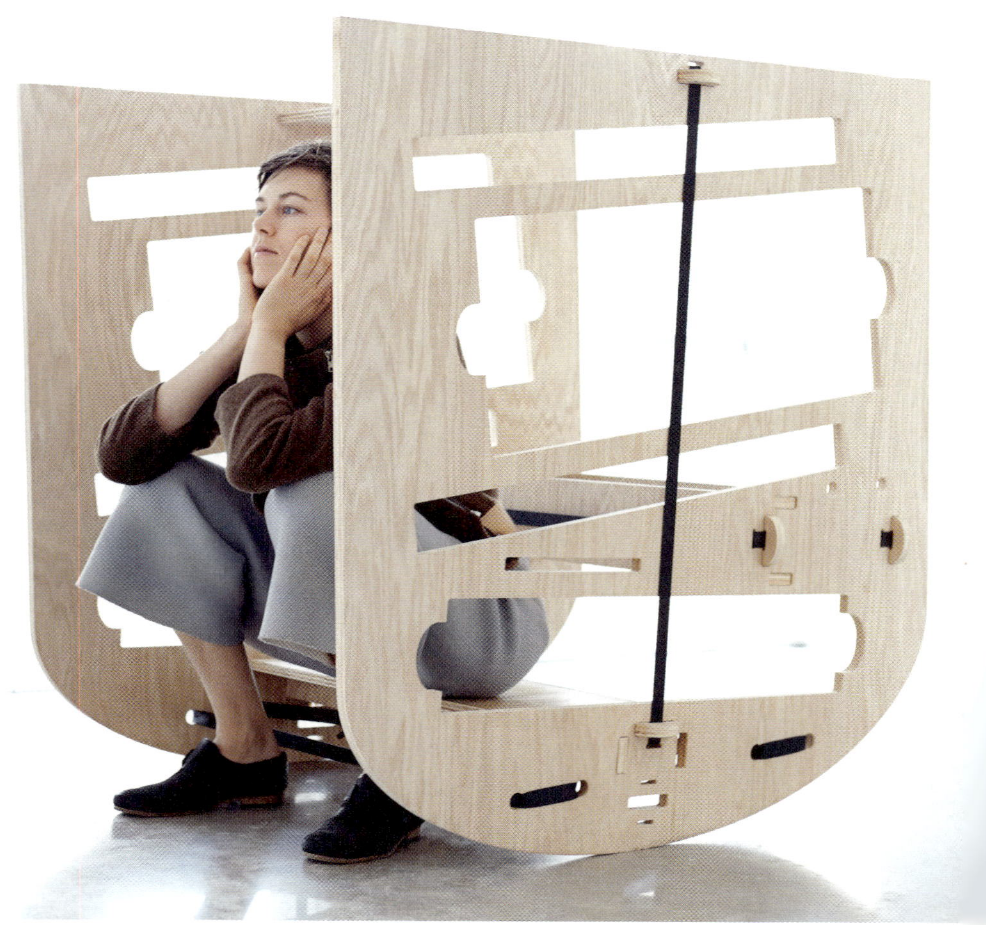

fig. 7-1
Queer Rocker, 2013, CNC prototype
oak plywood, ratchet straps,
newspapers, 48 × 30 × 44 inches.
Courtesy of the artist. Photo
by Ryan Tempro.

fig. 7-2 (overleaf)
Queer Rocker, 2013, CNC prototype oak plywood, ratchet
straps, newspapers, 48 × 30
× 44 inches. Courtesy of the
artist. Photo by Ryan Tempro.

Capitoline Wolves &
Queer Rocker

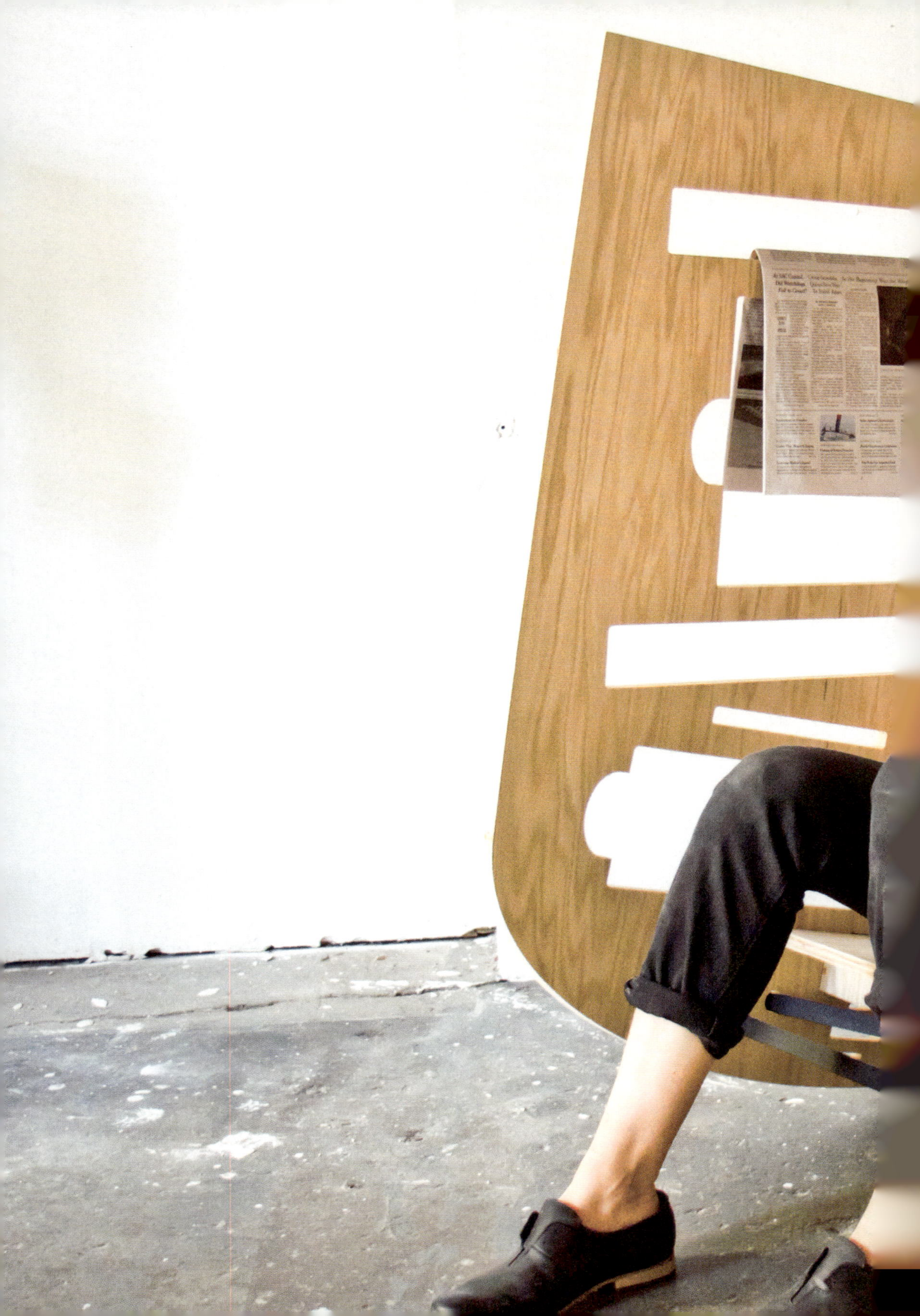

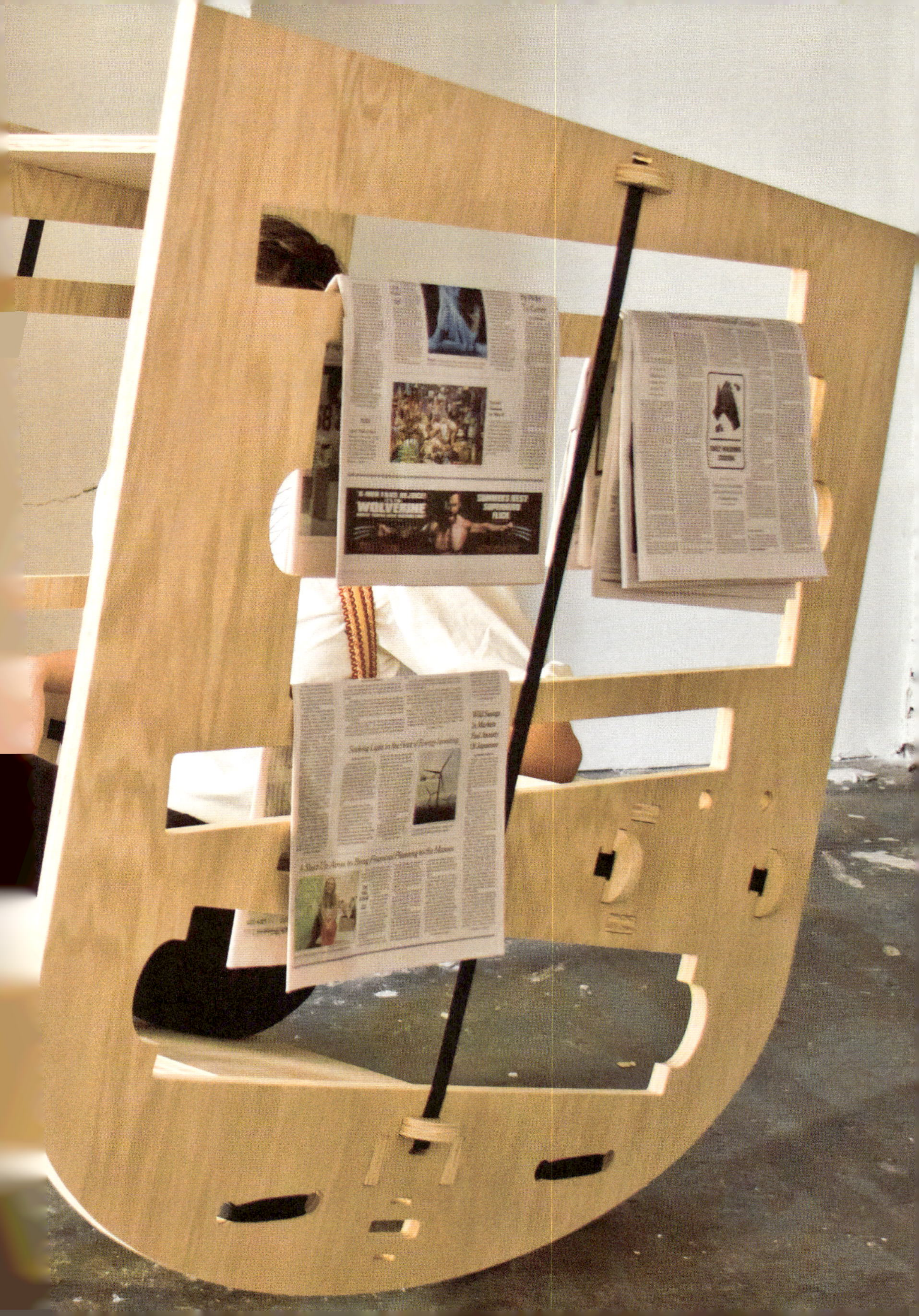

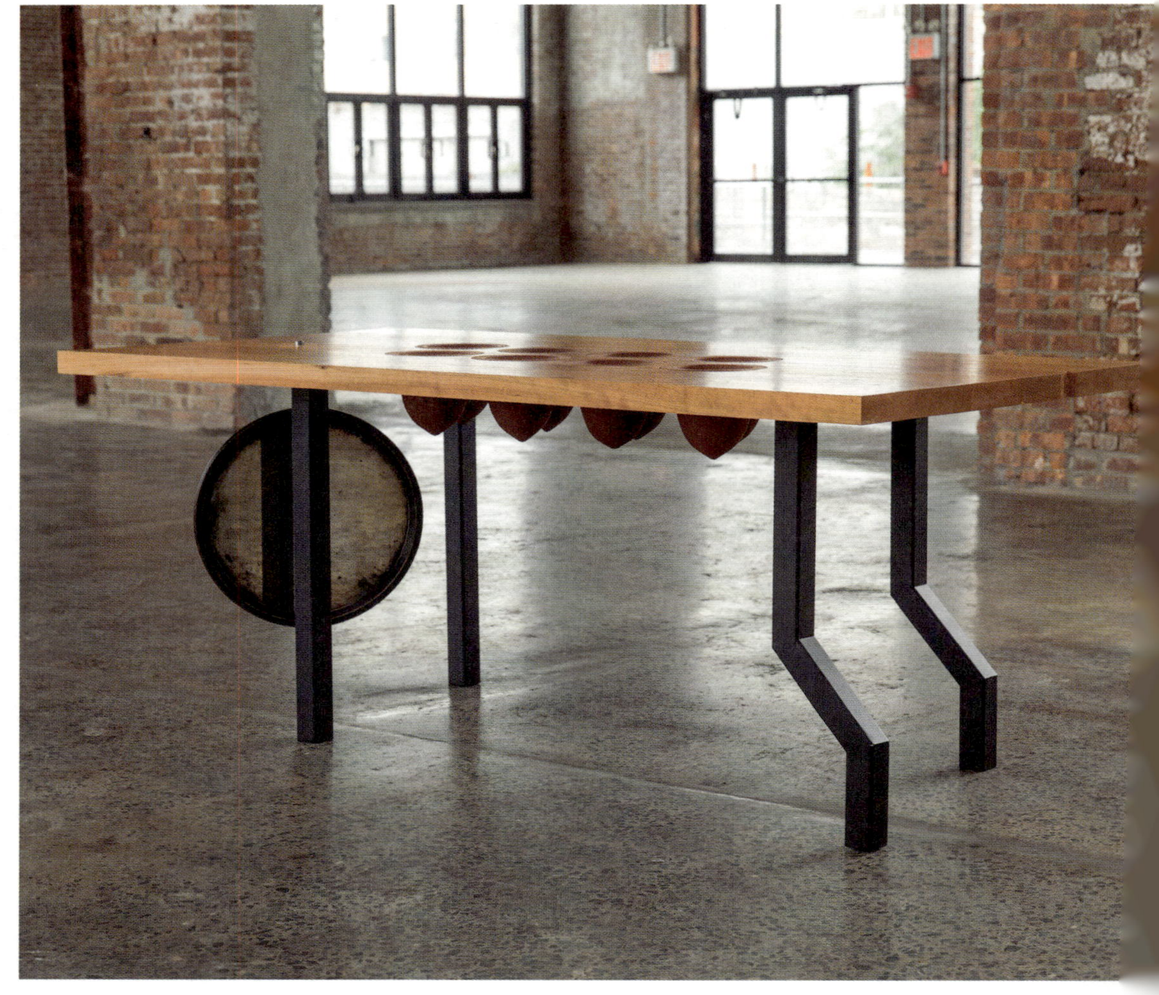

fig. 7-3
Capitoline Wolves, 2016, cherry
wood, powder coated steel, dyed
stoneware, local water, hand
mirrored glass, copper bowls,
performance, 29 × 36 × 72 inches
each, forming a circle that is
15 feet in diameter. Commissioned by Cornell University.
Courtesy of the artist. Photo by
Levi Mandel.

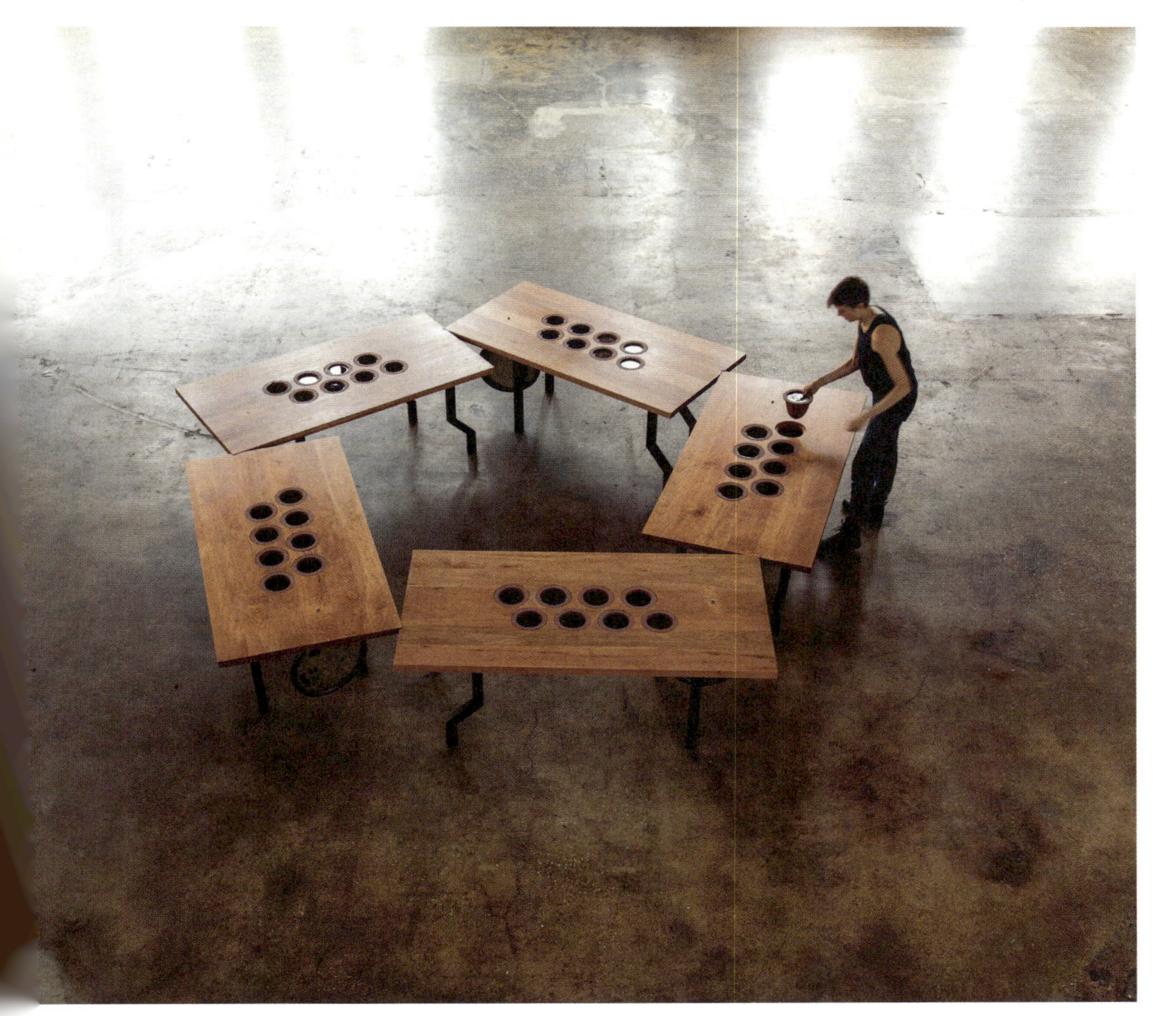

Capitoline Wolves &
Queer Rocker

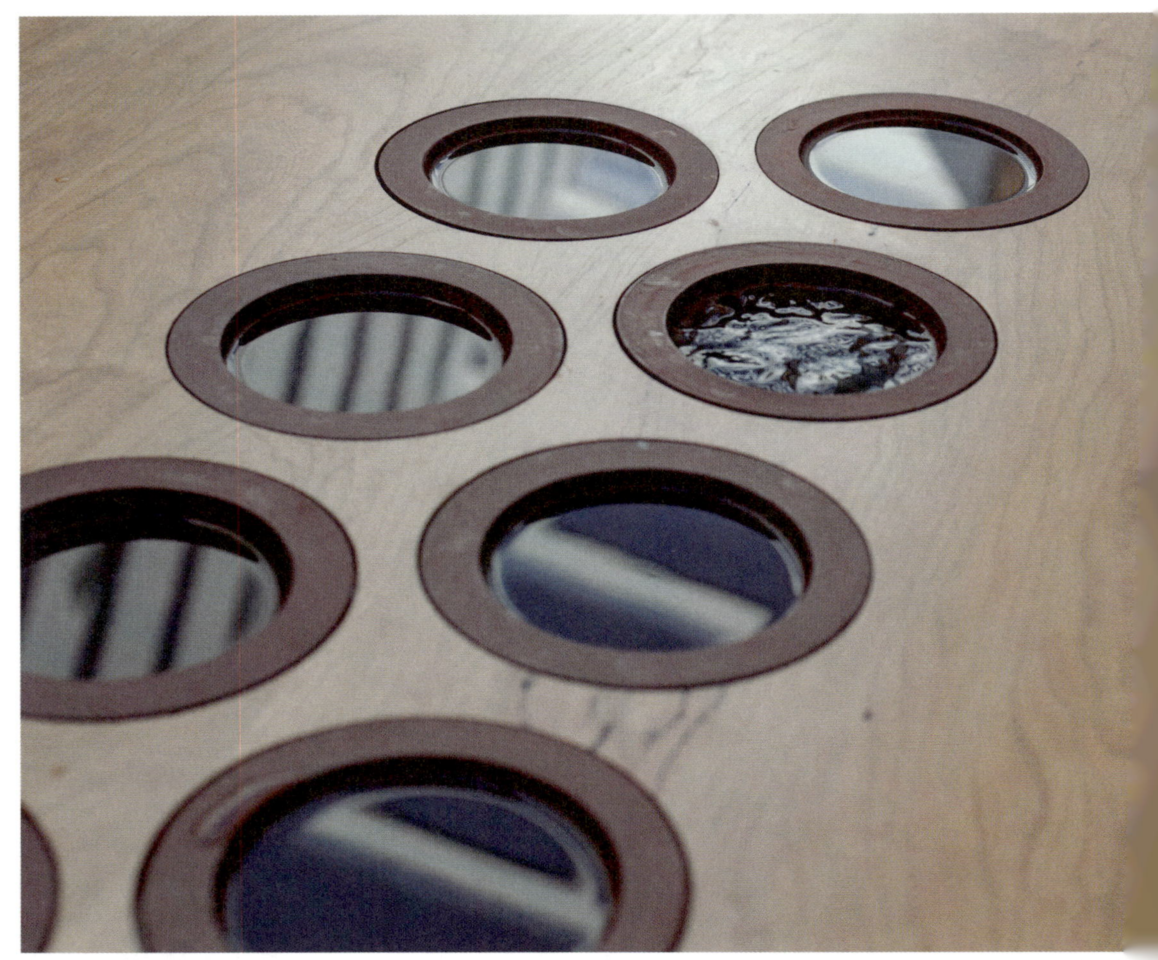

Institutional
Invitation

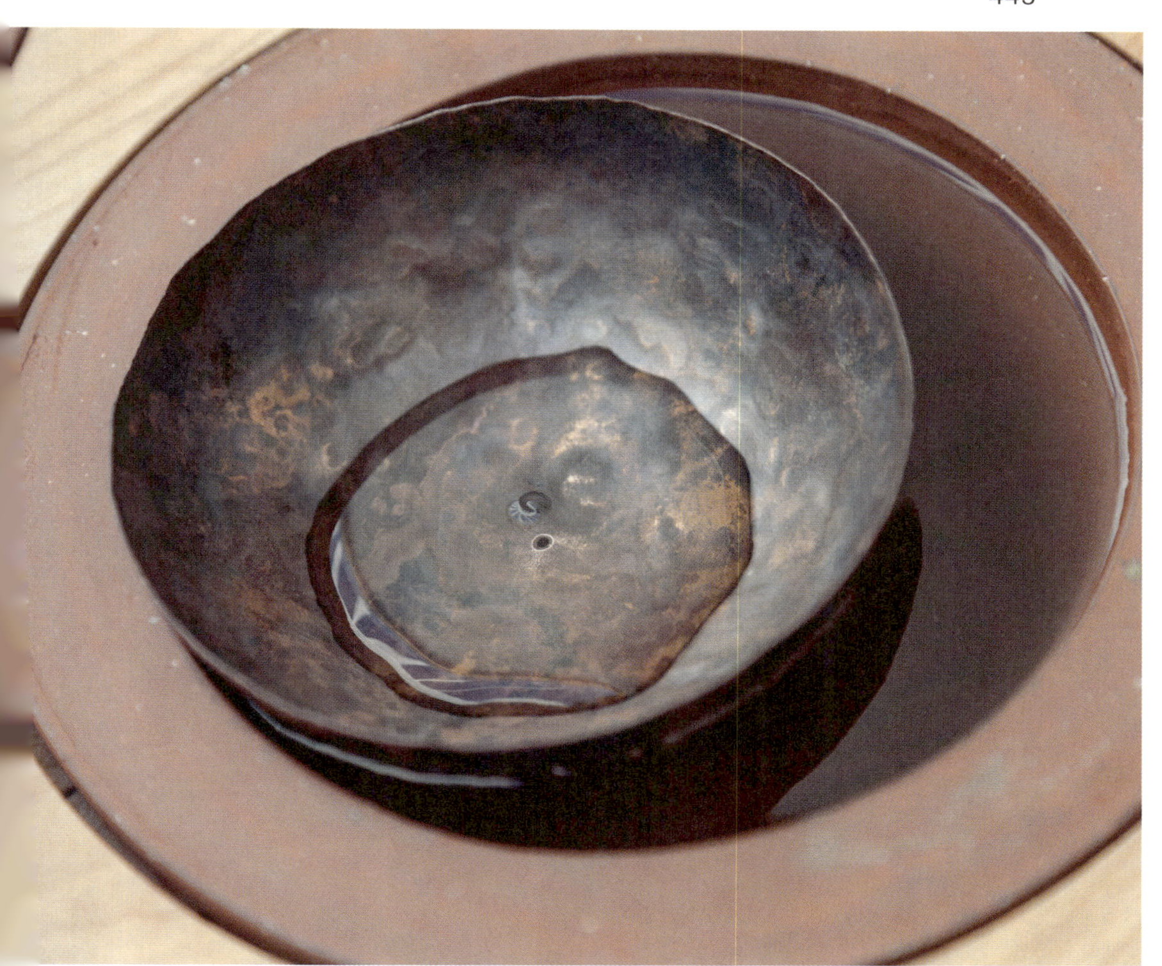

Capitoline Wolves &
Queer Rocker

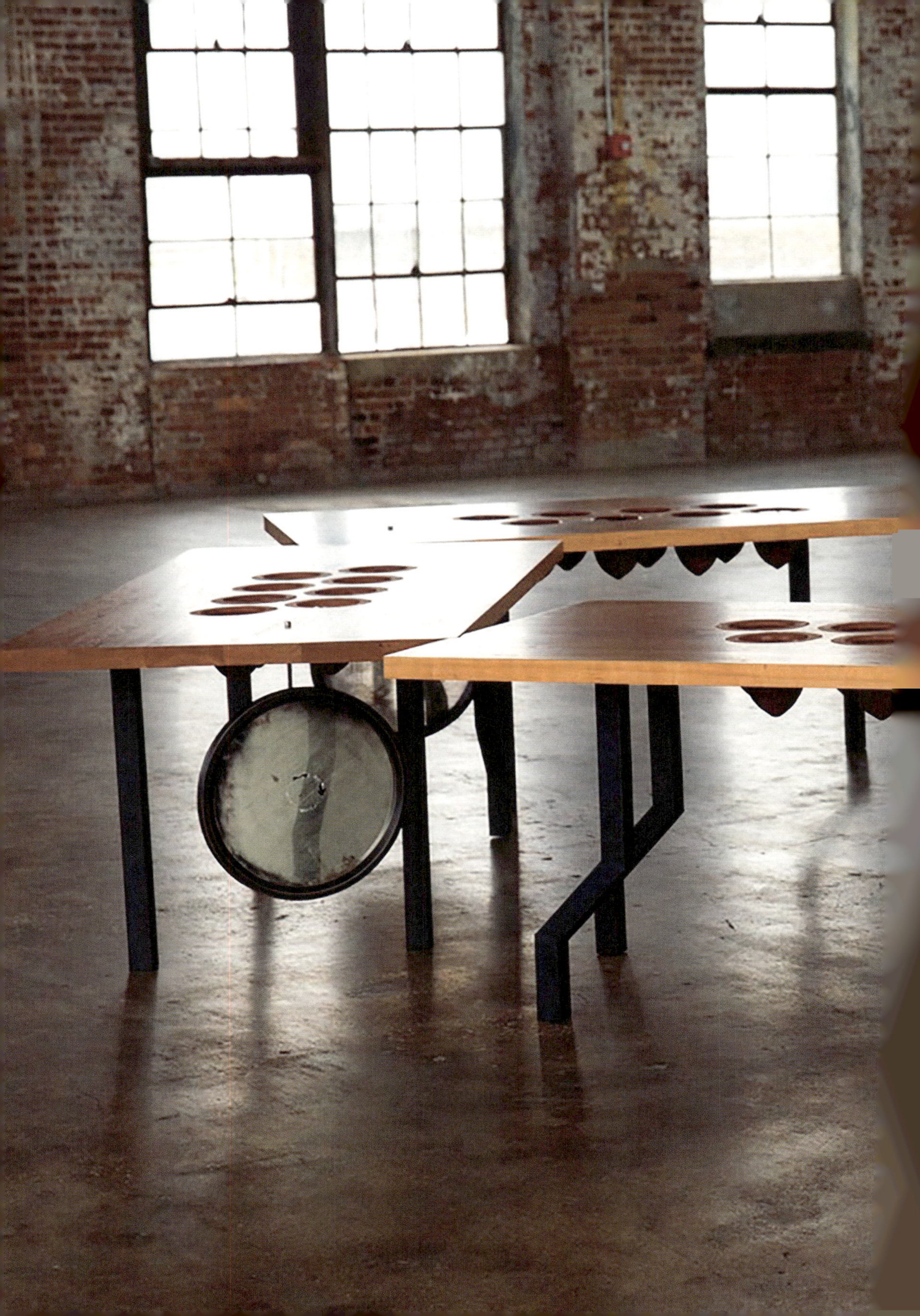

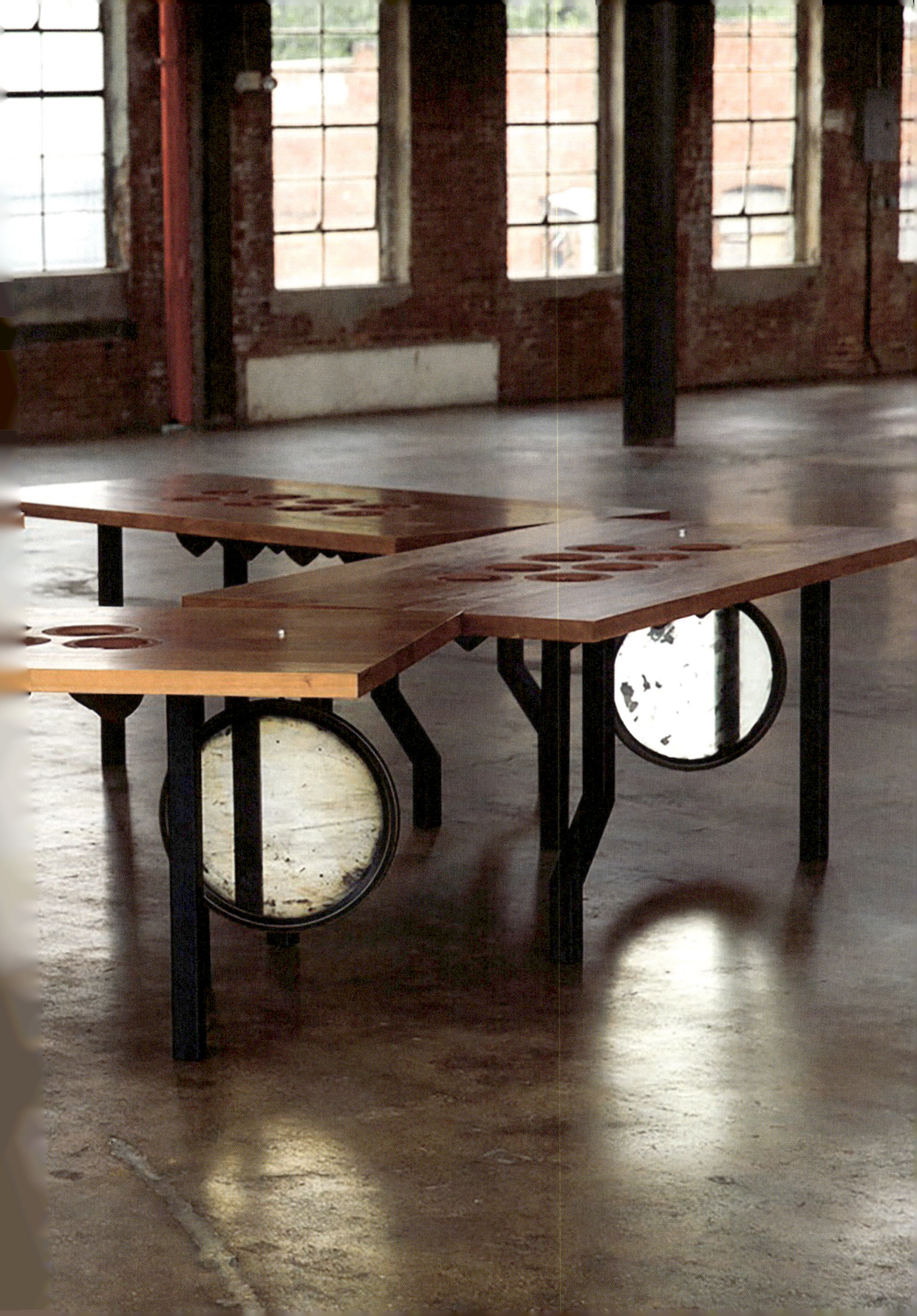

Ephemera

In the pages that follow, you will find correspondence, budgets, readings, renderings, and technical drawings made in the process of developing *Capitoline Wolves* and *Queer Rocker* at the invitation of curator Stephanie Owens. The CNC rocker was made by Caroline Woolard with support from Costantino Bongiorno, Ozden Kose, Francesco Perego, and Zoe Romano at WeMake, a maker space in Milan, and from Isabella Crowley and Melody Stein, students at Cornell University. In *Capitoline Wolves*, the mirrors and copper bowls were made by Caroline Woolard, and her design was fabricated by local craftspeople, with expert woodwork by Mahlon Huston and the American Wooden Column Company, metalwork by Ian McMahon and journeyman ironworker Julia Helen Murray, and ceramic udders by Alex Zablocki.

Woolard has selected ephemera that serves as visual reference points for *Capitoline Wolves* and *Queer Rocker*. All materials here are reproduced with the consent of the people involved.

fig. 7-4 (overleaf)
Capitoline Wolves, 2016, cherry wood, powder coated steel, dyed stoneware, local water, hand mirrored glass, copper bowls, performance, 29 × 36 × 72 inches each, forming a circle that is 15 feet in diameter. Commissioned by Cornell University. Courtesy of the artist. Photo by Levi Mandel.

Institutional
Invitation

Making and Mediating

Queer theorist Sara Ahmed suggests, "queer furnishing is not such a surprising formulation: the word 'furnish' is related to the word 'perform' and thus relates to the very question of how things appear. Queer becomes a matter of how things appear, how they gather, how they perform, to create edges of spaces and worlds." This rocking chair is "queer" because it is simultaneously a dividing wall, a window, a table, and a chair. It is "queer" because its holes become its strength and its structure. It is "queer" because it makes the politics of its own production visible. It is never singular, as it desires adaptation and interdependence. It is "queer" because it rests in organizing spaces that recognize the rights of LGBTQIA+ people, which have been and will continue to be won through grassroots community organizing for economic and social justice.

In 2013, I created a document that described how to make the *Queer Rocker*, so that students in many places could re-make it.

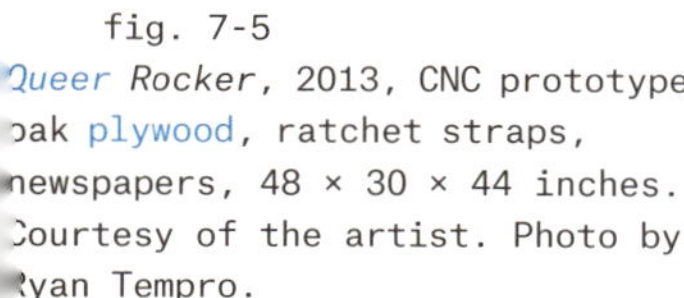

fig. 7-5
Queer Rocker, 2013, CNC prototype oak plywood, ratchet straps, newspapers, 48 × 30 × 44 inches. Courtesy of the artist. Photo by Ryan Tempro.

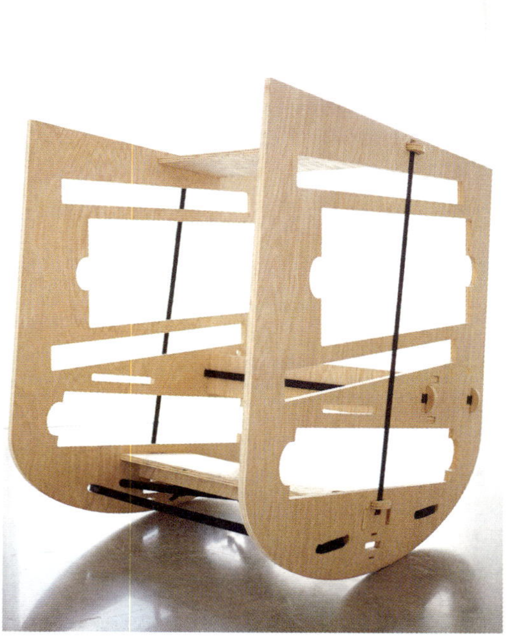

Capitoline Wolves &
Queer Rocker

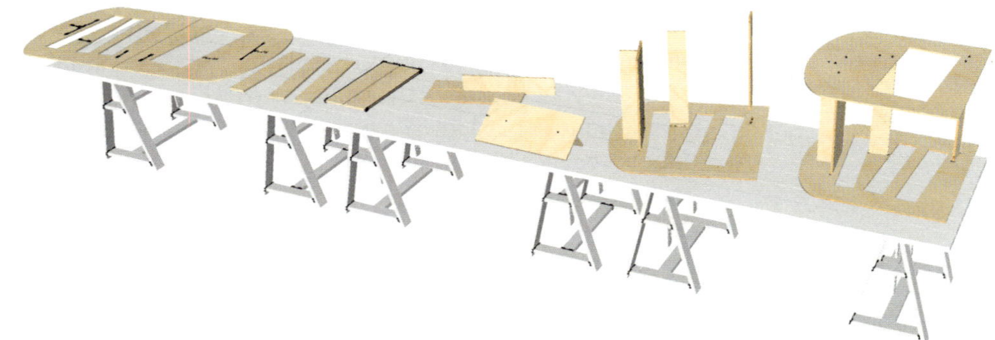

TOOLS AND MATERIALS

DIY/Non-CNC Requirements
(for making it in a woodshop)
 - Illustrator file (printed out
   on a plotter)
 - table saw, router, drill press,
   bandsaw, and jig saw
 - 3/4" birch plywood, 0.71" thick
   (12-15 ply) or found wood
 - email me for woodshop
   directions, or improvise on
   your own!

CNC Requirements
- ShopBot PRS file
- ShopBot PRS Standard 9648 CNC
   Router (adjust the file if you
   have another CNC)
- 1/4" carbide bits (one for a
   downcut and one for an upcut,
   not worn down)
- 3/4" birch plywood, 0.71" thick
   (12-15 ply)

Tools for Finishing the CNC
Queer Rocker
- 1/2" and 1/4" chisels (to carve

out the corners that the CNC
router cannot reach, by hand)
- rubber mallet to hit wood together
   without damaging it. This can
   also be used to hit the chisel.
- power drill to connect pieces
   together with screws below
- corx/star drill bit and
   pre-drill bit
- orbital sander and 240 grit
   (or other fine grit) sandpaper to
   sand the rough edges

Supplies for Finishing the CNC
Queer Rocker
- work table: if you have a work
   table with a surface of at least
   4' × 4', handling the rocker will
   be easier
- screws: 16 pcs per rocker of #8
   construction screw 1-1/4" (3.18
   cm). Boxes of these from grip
   rite are yellow and come with a
   star/corx bit
- optional: finish washers:
   16 pcs per rocker of #8 finish
   washers (if you will use a
   natural finish)

- sandpaper: extra 240 grit (or other
  fine grit) sandpaper for orbital
  sander
- paint, putty, and/or tung oil/wax
  or other finish for the ply
  (you choose)

CNC FILE SETUP

File Assumptions/
Order of Operations when using CNC
1. We will drill holes in the center
   to screw the material down.
2. We will drill the holes for the
   screws after that (pecking),
   and screw the material down in
   the center.
3. We will then cut the channels for
   the wood to slide into, cutting
   inside the lines in the file.
4. We will then cut the slats and
   the big sides of the rocker
   slowly, on the outside of the
   line in the file, cutting halfway
   into the wood as a downcut, and
   then changing the bit so that it
   is an upcut bit and is less rough
   on the edges.

Making your own file/
Ways things can go wrong
1. Software: I have provided an
   Illustrator file and also a CNC
   file that works with the ShopBot
   PRS Standard 9648 CNC Router. If
   you have different software, and
   are using my Illustrator file,
   please read this section

and adjust your new CNC
file accordingly.
2. Plywood Thickness: Adjust the
   Illustrator file based on the
   thickness of your plywood. Be
   sure to measure your 3/4" plywood
   with calipers to get the exact
   thickness of the ply. The
   Illustrator file I've made assumes
   that the ply is 00.71" thick and
   therefore has press-fit channels
   that are 00.735" wide. If you
   need to edit this file, note that
   the slats and channels are at
   5-degree angles and that the T
   channel assumes a 00.30" depth for
   the T. Export a new CNC file. You
   may be able to adjust the ShopBot
   file by adding .025 to the channels all around, rather than
   editing the Illustrator file.
3. Type of Plywood: Make sure your
   plywood has as many ply as possible (12-18 ply) as regular plywood only has 7-8 ply and will
   cut very rough and not look good.
4. CNC File Channel Depth: make sure
   you cut your channels at 00.30"
   depth (everything in purple is
   a channel).
5. Cutting Inside or Outside the
   lines: Always cut inside the lines
   for the channels, but make sure
   all passes for the slats/windows
   and the rocker sides go on the
   outside of the lines in the files,
   otherwise the pieces won't fit!
6. Hole size: make sure you drill

the holes with a 1/4" bit.

7. Many Passes: For all of the lines (the slats/windows and the rocker sides) make sure you make many passes (3-4 passes) with a down cut bit and then many passes (3-4 passes) with the up cut bit to finish it, so that the plywood has a smooth edge on both sides — is not rough and ugly.

ASSEMBLY

1. Chisel the tabs: Dislodge your pieces from the sheet of plywood by chiseling the tabs away from the pieces you want to keep. Be careful not to chip the plywood.
2. Chisel the corners. Every channel has rounded corners due to the nature of round the router bit. Using a 1/4" or 1/2" chisel and a rubber mallet, make the corners of all 6 channels square. Carve it out fully and carefully, or else the slats won't be able to press-fit in. You do not need to elongate the channels.
3. Sand the surfaces and edges. While your pieces are separated, take time to sand the surfaces of all pieces while it is easy. Sand the edges of the long sides of the slats and the entire perimeter of the rocker and the windows of the rocker so that the plywood doesn't chip and is easy to handle. If the plywood is chipped, sand off the chips and remember that you will likely have to putty, sand, and paint the rocker.
4. Put the T seat together. One of the 5-1/2" slats sides into the channel on the large slat, making the seat for the rocker. Carefully

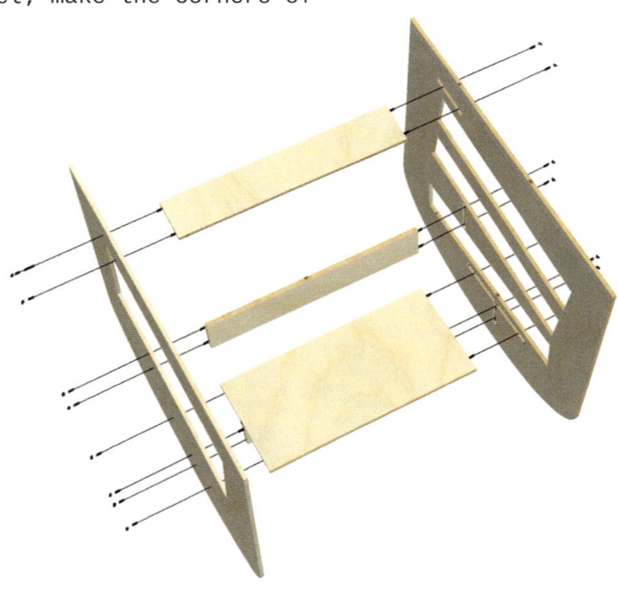

slide the 5-1/2" slat into the channel of the large piece, using the rubber mallet to assist you with this press-fit. Once it's in, pre-drill into the top of the T where you see the 1/4" holes and screw in 1-1/4" #8 corx/star bit construction screws (optional: with #8 brass finish washers if you won't paint it).

5. Put the T, lumbar support, and top slat into one side of the rocker. Place one side of the rocker on your work table, so that you can slide part of it off the work table and get under it to screw it together. You are assembling the rocker on its side. Press fit the T seat, the lumbar support slat, and the top slat into that side. Use the mallet to help you. Get under the rocker and pre-drill holes where you see the 1/4" holes and screw in 1-1/4" #8 corx/star bit construction screws (optional: with #8 brass finish washers if you will not paint it).

6. Place the other side of the rocker on top, carefully aligning all the channels to the slats that you just screwed in place. Use the mallet to help you. Stand on top of the table or use a stool to get above the rocker (still on it's side) and pre-drill holes where you see the 1/4" holes and screw in 1-1/4" #8 corx/star bit

construction screws (optional: with #8 brass finish washers if you won't paint it).

7. Get help lifting the rocker off the table and try it out on the floor! Now, your rocker should be assembled securely, with all 16 screws in all 16 holes. With help, move the rocker from its sideways position on the worktable to the upright position on the floor. Try it out!

8. Finish the piece. You likely see parts of the rocker that need to be sanded, as well as parts that are chipped and that could use putty. Decide whether you would like a natural finish (bowling wax, beeswax, tung oil, etc.) or if you would like to paint it a color. If you are painting it, you can fill the chips/splinters with putty, sand it, and finish it to hide them. Be sure to recess your screws enough so that they are hidden.

Capitoline Wolves &
Queer Rocker

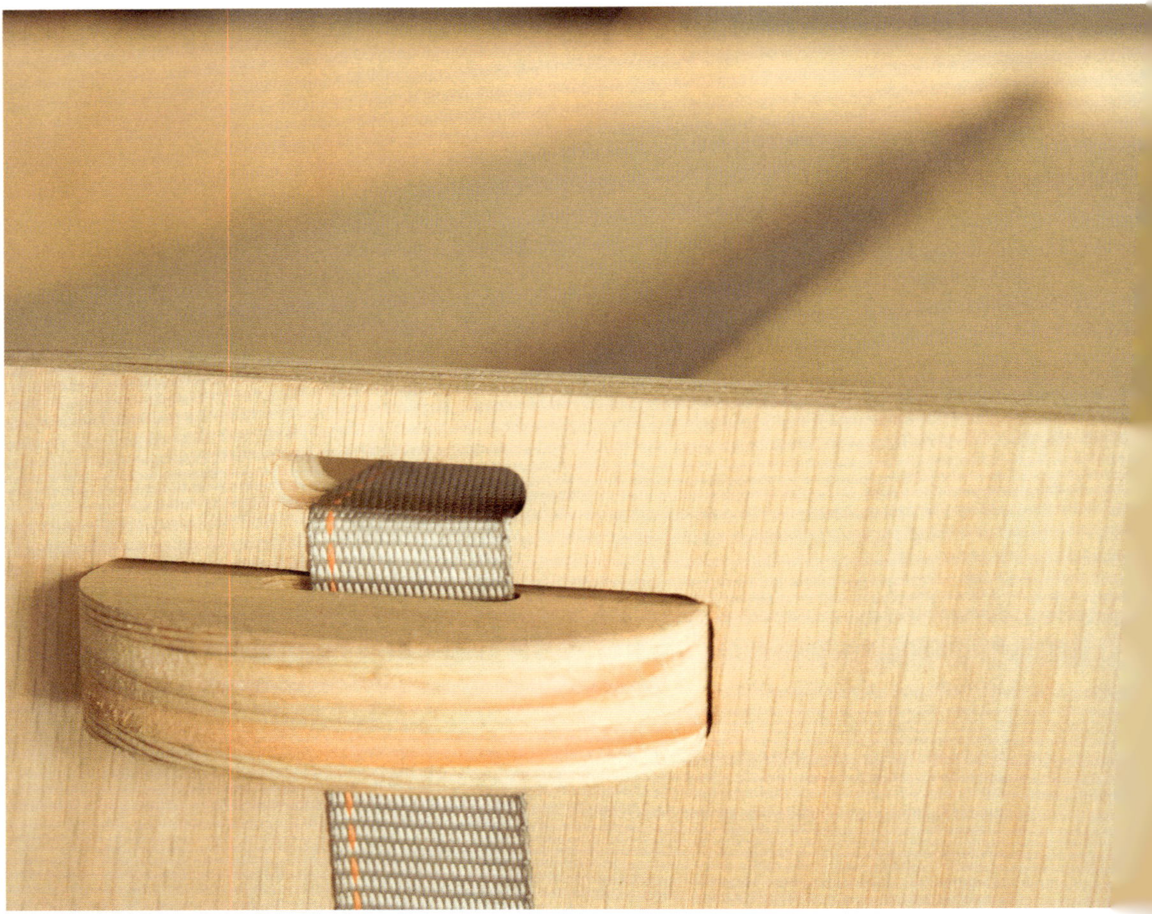

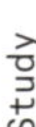

fig. 7-6
Queer Rocker, 2013, CNC prototype oak plywood, ratchet
straps, newspapers, 48 × 30 × 44
inches. Courtesy of the artist.
Photo by Ryan Tempro.

Institutional
Invitation

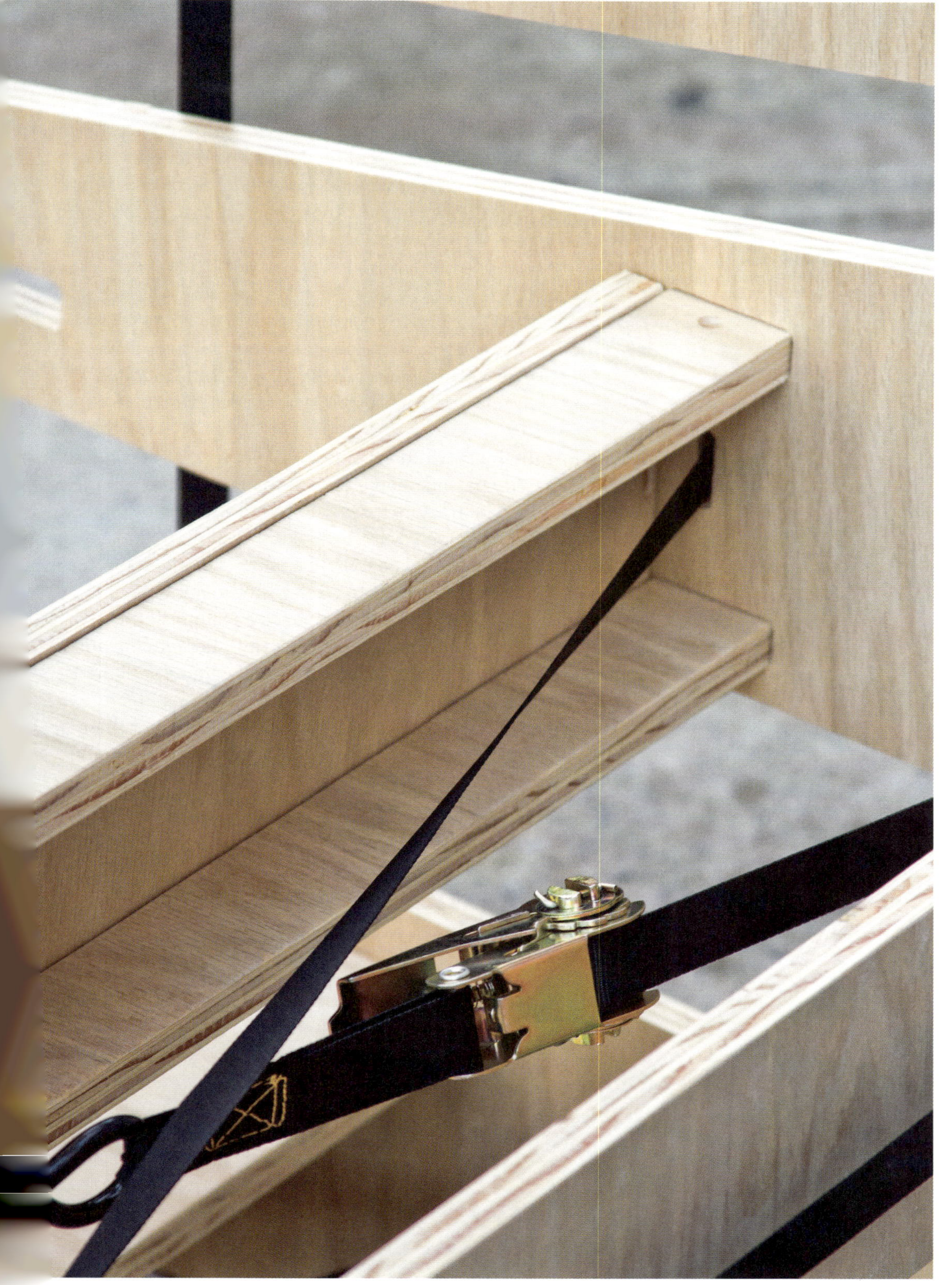

Capitoline Wolves &
Queer Rocker

Making

For the project at MoMA ^{see chapter 4}, I made everything myself, and I felt that it did not go well. The research, meeting, and proposal process at MoMA took more than half of the time allocated for the entire project, so I was left with relatively little time to do material tests to get the forms and materials to a place that I loved. When I worked independently or in groups outside of institutions, projects took over a year to develop and were refined at a high level.

```
An aside: this is why, I realize now, many cura-
tors want to exhibit finished work. They also
don't have to pay to commission it; they can
simply ask for your finished work on loan with-
out paying for the labor to fabricate it.
```

With institutional invitations, and for projects of a certain size, I decided to try paying people to make aspects of the work for me. So, I hired fabricators for the first time with the *Capitoline Wolves* project. I didn't want to make the same mistakes that I made at MoMA. I knew that I could not work on the scale or speed that was necessary to meet the requirements of the commission if I were making it alone. To accomplish this mysterious task—the task of extending my labor into the bodies and hands of other people who are not collaborators —I made hundreds of sketches, and then technical drawings in Illustrator, and then renderings in Rhino, and then sent them to fabricators that friends recommended, to complete the work.

I knew that I could not work on the scale or speed that was necessary to meet the requirements of the commission if I were making it alone.

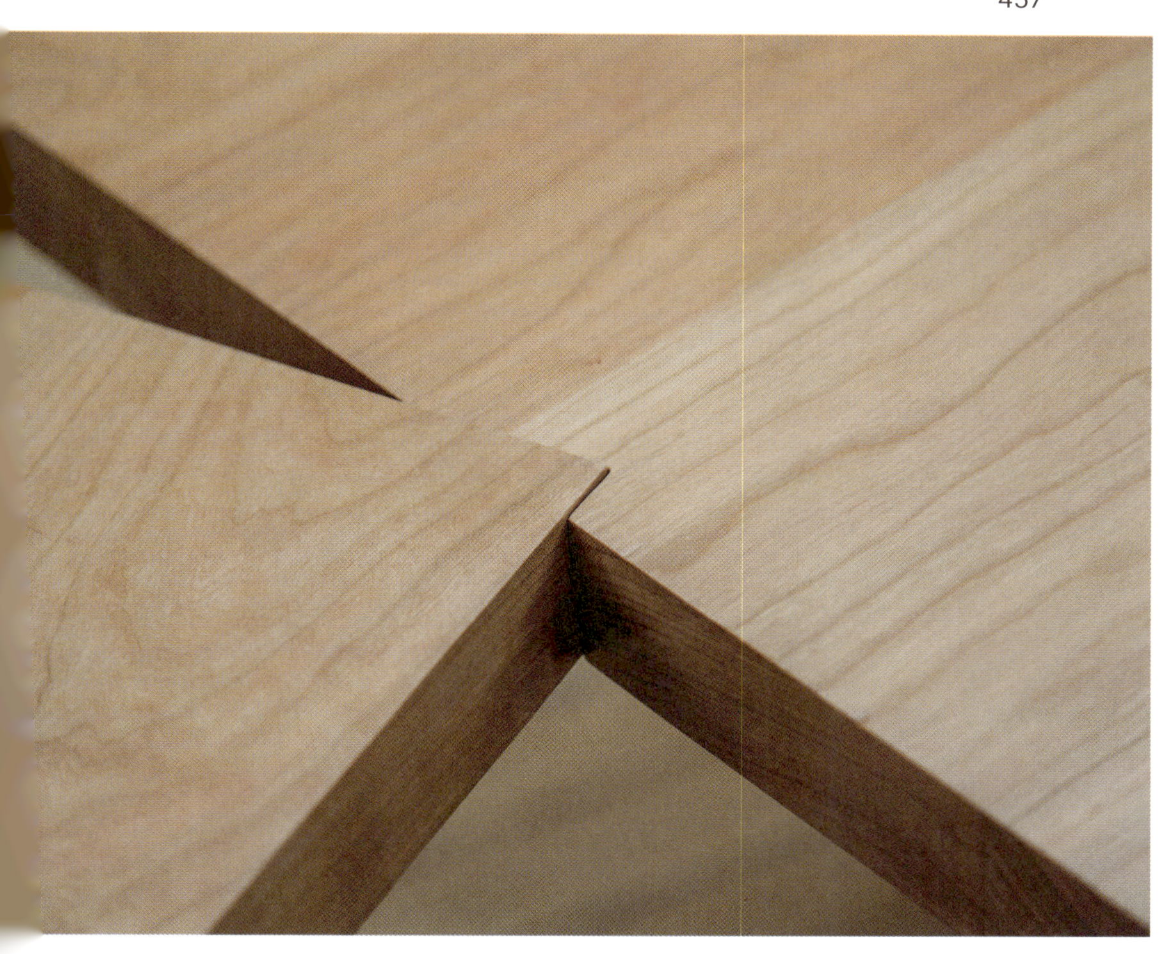

fig. 7-7
Capitoline Wolves, 2016, cherry wood, powder coated steel, dyed stoneware, local water, hand mirrored glass, copper bowls, performance, 29 × 36 × 72 inches each, forming a circle that is 15 feet in diameter. Commissioned by Cornell University. Courtesy of the artist. Photo by Levi Mandel.

Capitoline Wolves & Queer Rocker

It was also important to me, as an artist doing so-called "socially engaged" projects, that the physical objects could stand on their own, as sculptures, regardless of the social engagement. I was upset by the theater-prop approach I often saw in exhibitions, of bright colors and plywood, and tried to convince curator Stephanie Owens that the objects should be made to last.

fig. 7-8
A collage of research imagery that led to the creation of *Capitoline Wolves*, including clocks that use water and smell to mark intervals of time and the Lupa Capitolina, a bronze sculpture depicting a scene from the legend of the founding of Rome.

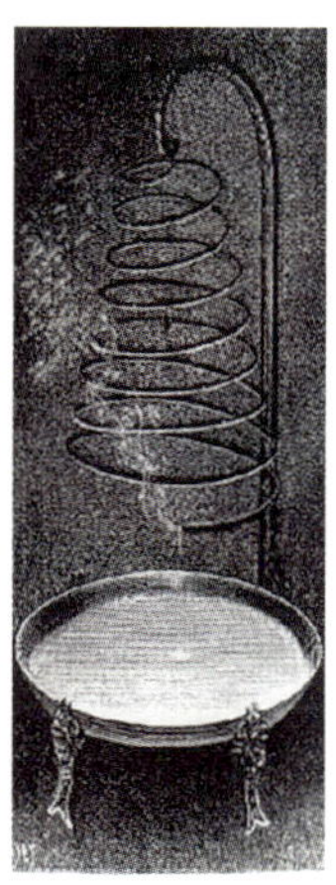

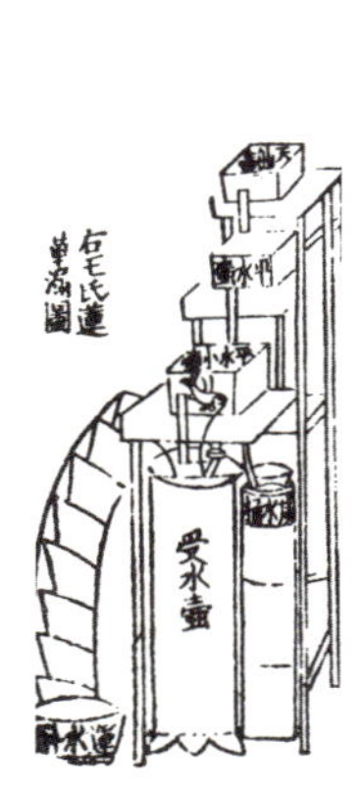

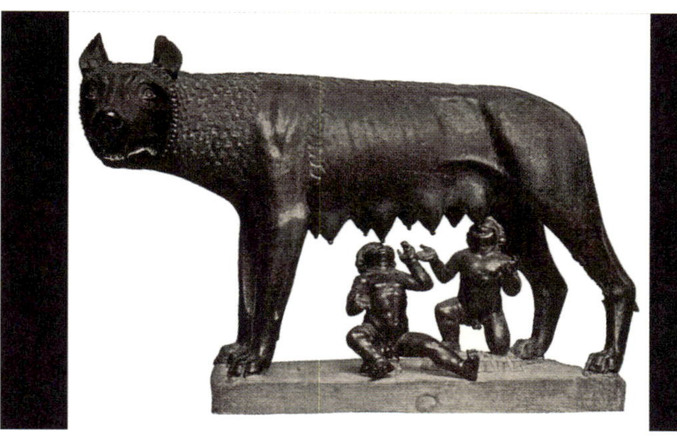

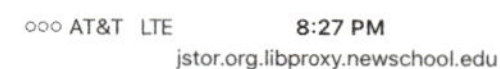

valls of the Leiden model show so...
-MORGAN model of a rectangular i...
Plate 4, top, left; see also the exceller...

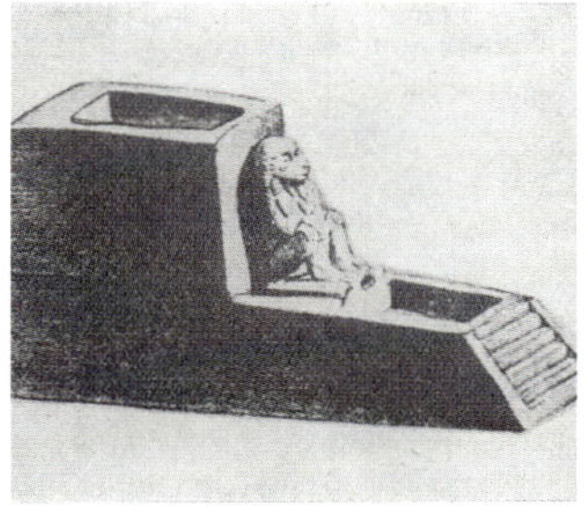

len model of a prismatic inflow clock.
MANS, Monumens égyptiens, P. XIX, no. 47.

gue of the GRÉAU-MORGAN collecti...
the height of this (late dynastic ?) m...
FROEHNER's (22) description, it is a...
devant un cynocéphale accroupi ''; th...

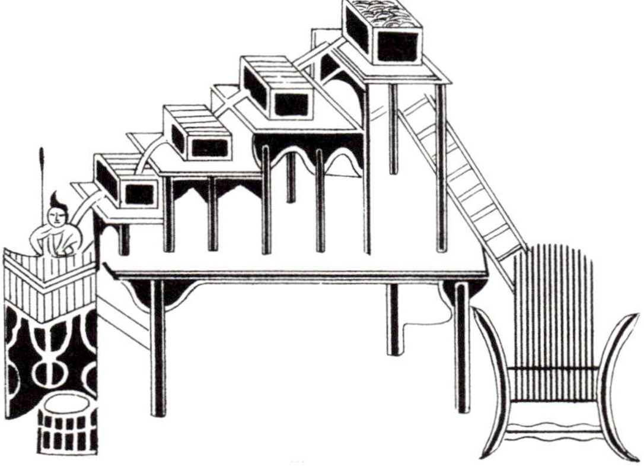

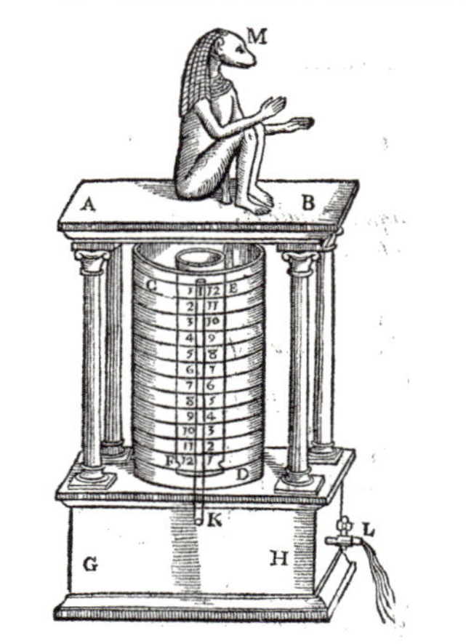

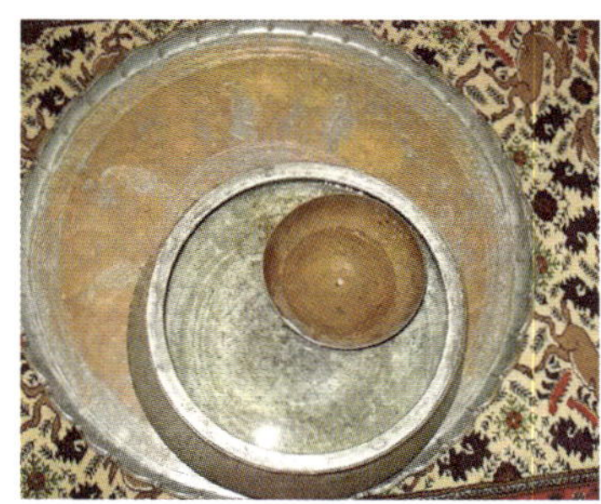

Capitoline Wolves &
Queer Rocker

fig. 7-9
Technical drawings for
Capitoline Wolves.

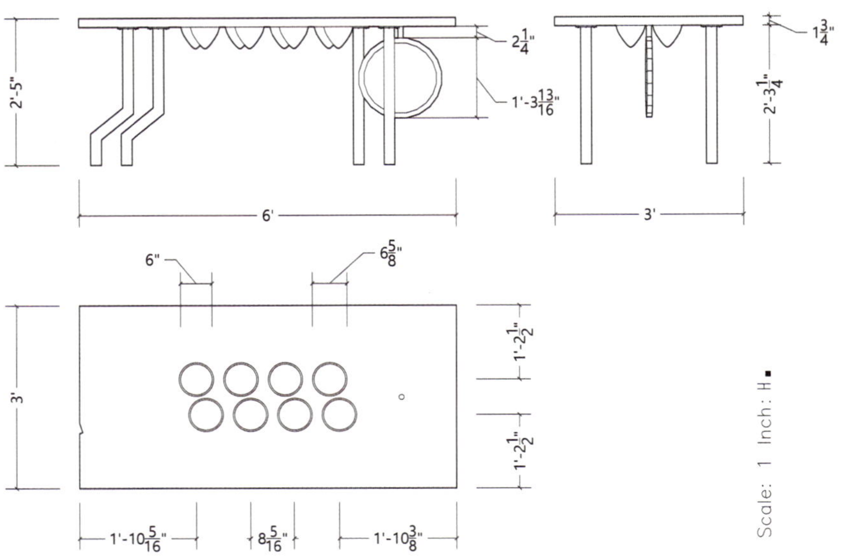

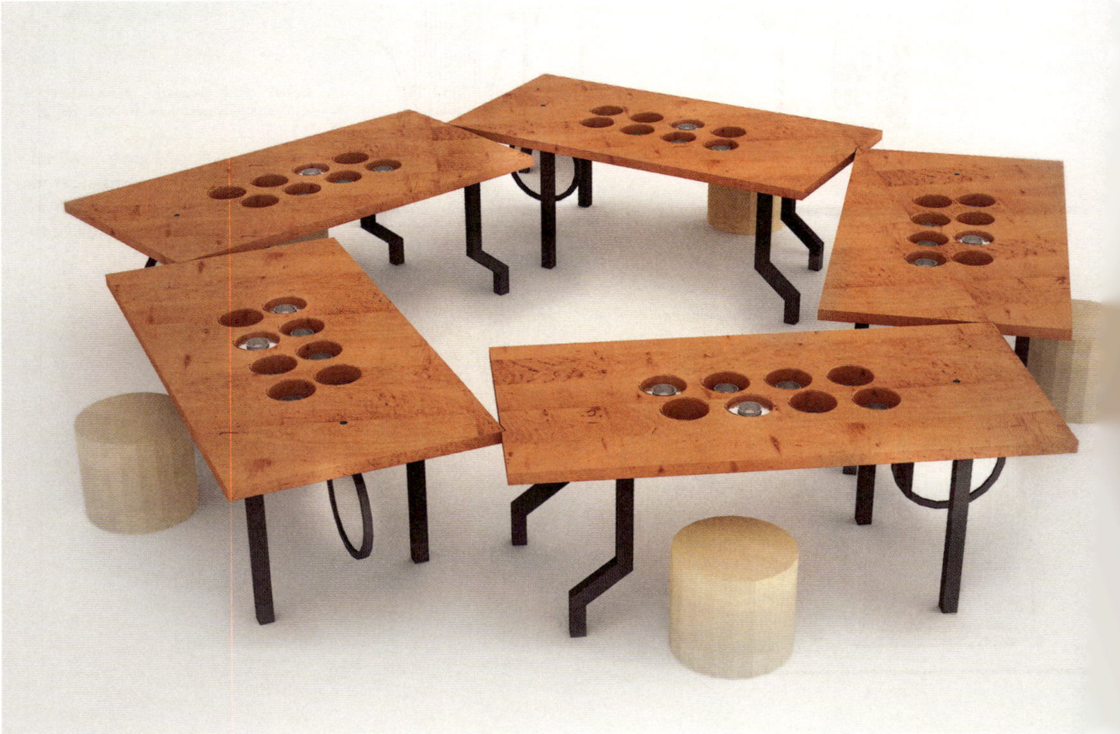

Institutional
Invitation

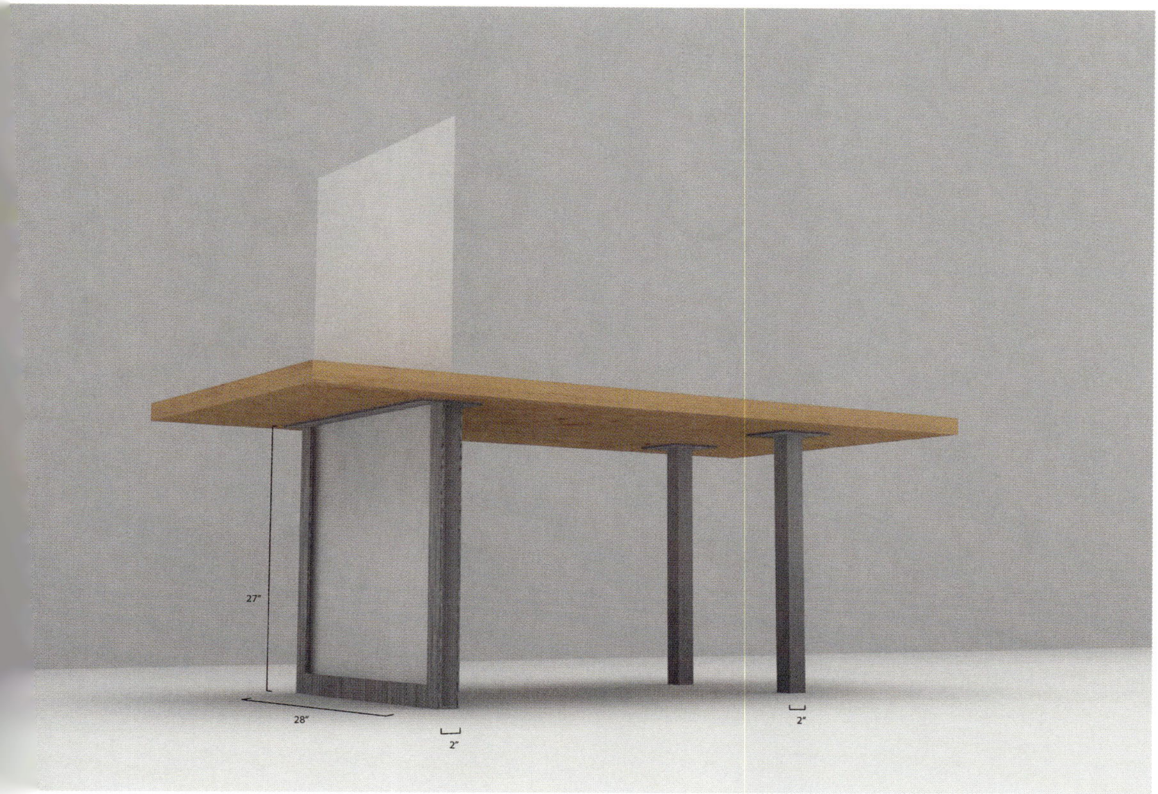

27"
28"
2"
2"

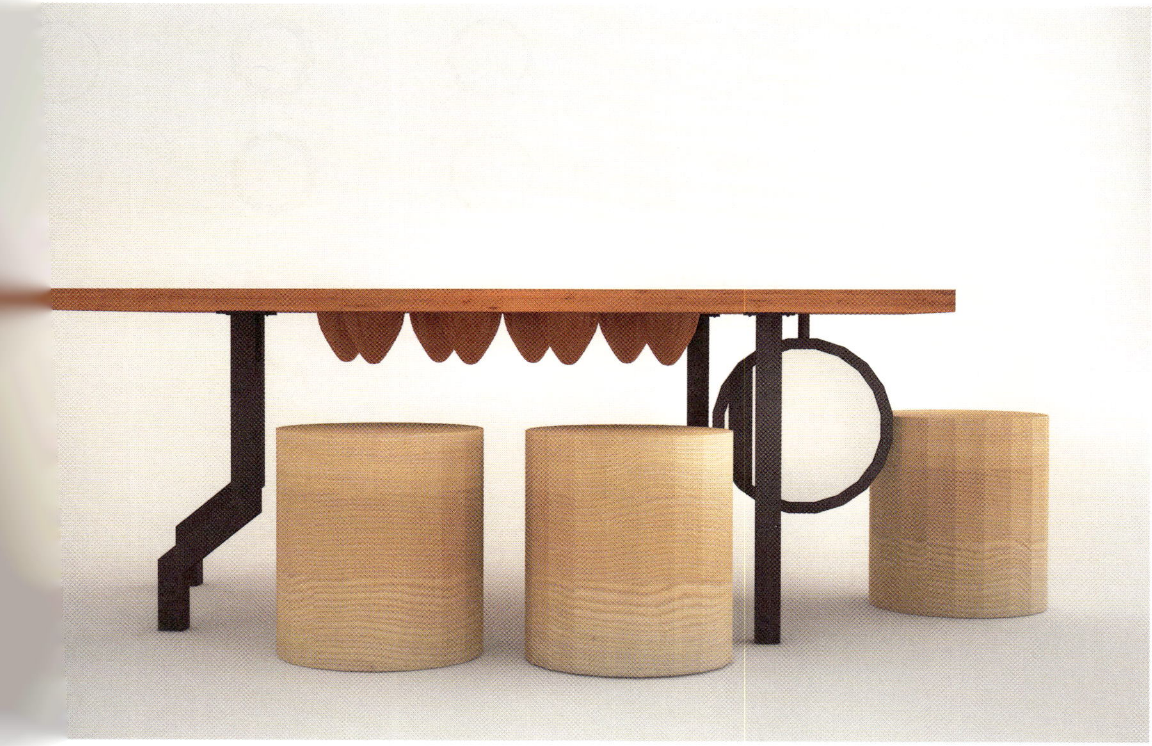

Capitoline Wolves &
Queer Rocker

fig. 7-10
What shape should the table
be, and how will individual
tables fit together to make a
gathering space? To determine
shape of the table, and to
see how tables fit together,
Caroline Woolard created this
geometric study.

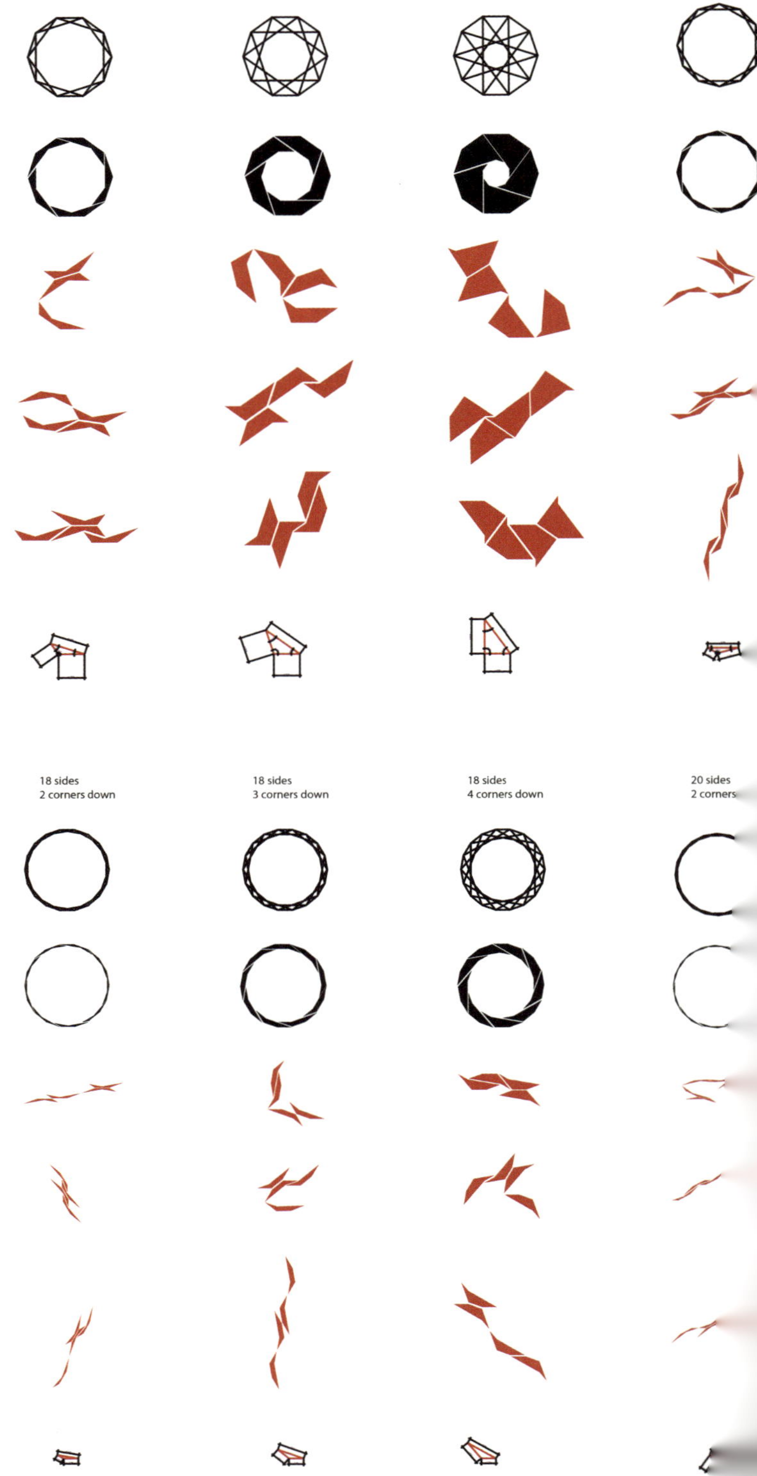

Institutional
Invitation

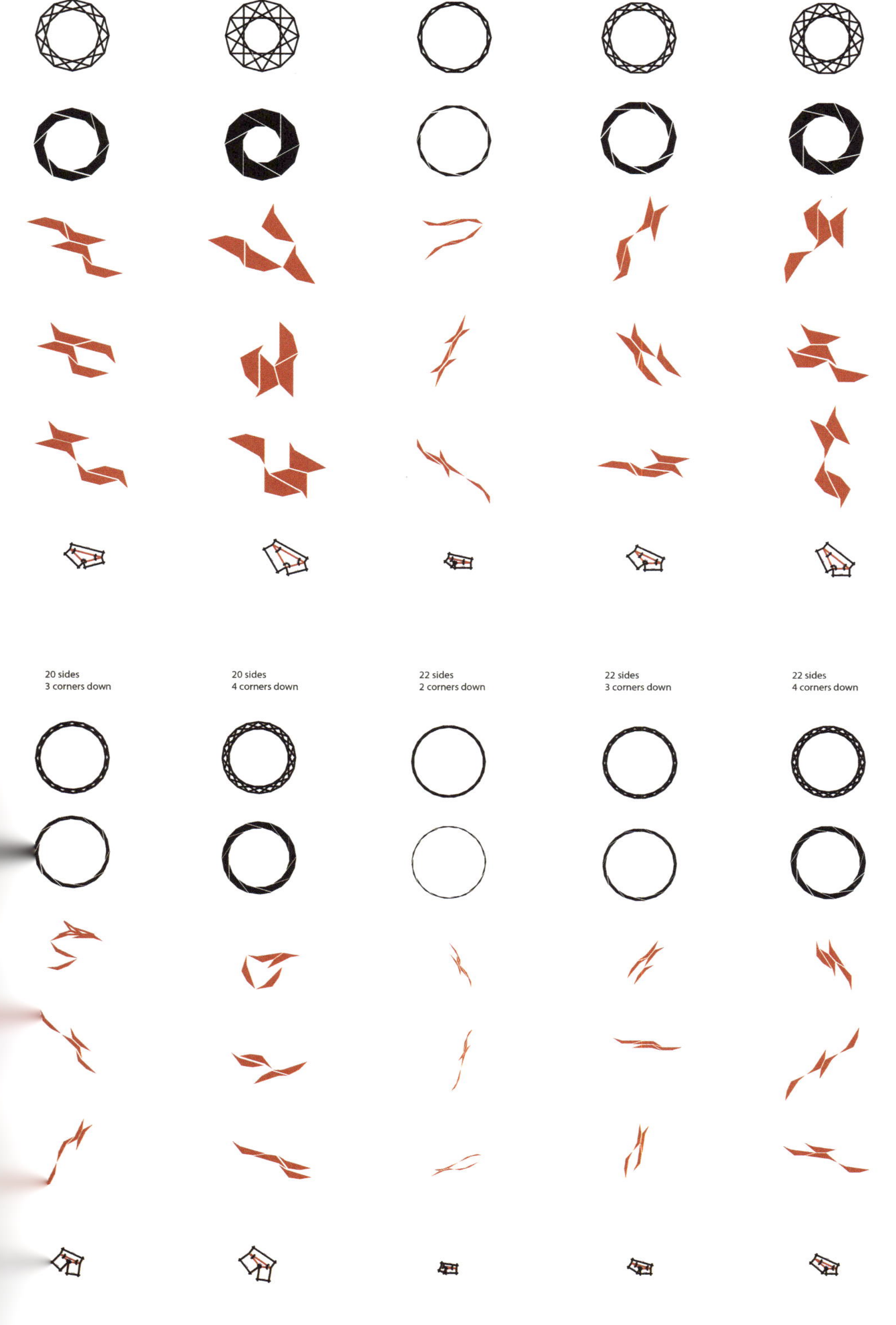

Capitoline Wolves &
Queer Rocker

fig. 7-11
Quick sketches that led to the
creation of *Capitoline Wolves*.

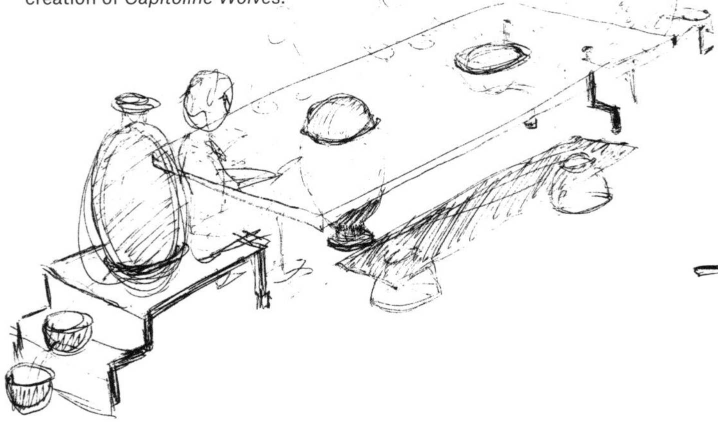

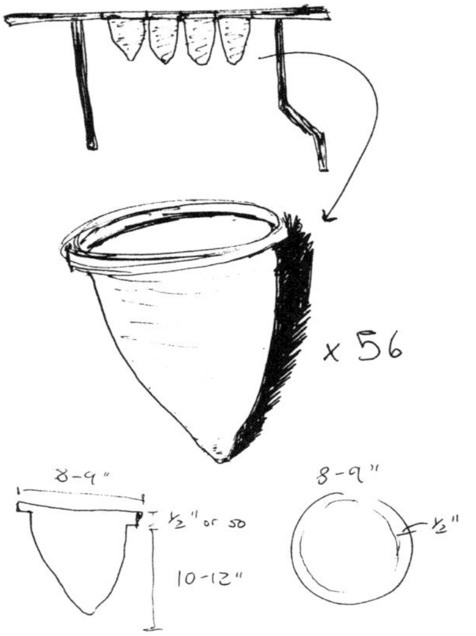

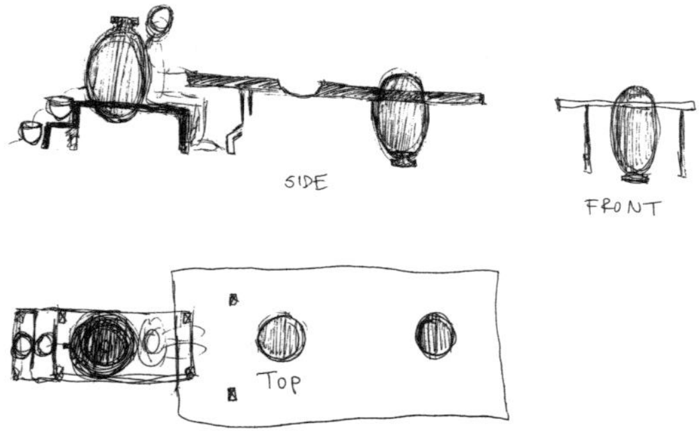

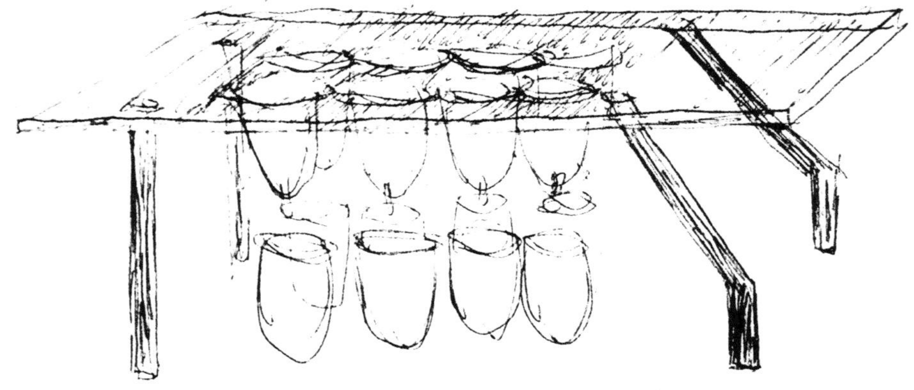

Managing

fig. 7-12
Technical drawings for
Capitoline Wolves.

Since I had a big budget for this commission, I wanted to pay fabricators at a good rate as well. My sense is that artists, designers, and craftspeople should all rise up together in terms of our labor conditions. When one of us is paid well for a job, we should all be paid well. I met one of the fabricators, Ian McMahon when I was a visiting artist at Alfred in 2015. I kept in touch with Ian and his partner, Ashley Lyon, as I was impressed by what they both made, conceptually and technically, and by their ambition and generosity of spirit. I thought: these are incredible people. I want to do more together, one day. Ian connected me to a woodworker, Mahlon Huston, and Ashley connected me to a ceramicist, Alex Zablocki. In the following examples, I want to share some of the correspondence that was required to coordinate with many people so that art students and emerging artists have a sense what is required to find, contact, and work with fabricators in a respectful and clear way. I made the mirrorized glass "face" of the wolves and the copper bowls for time keeping myself, but everything else required coordination.

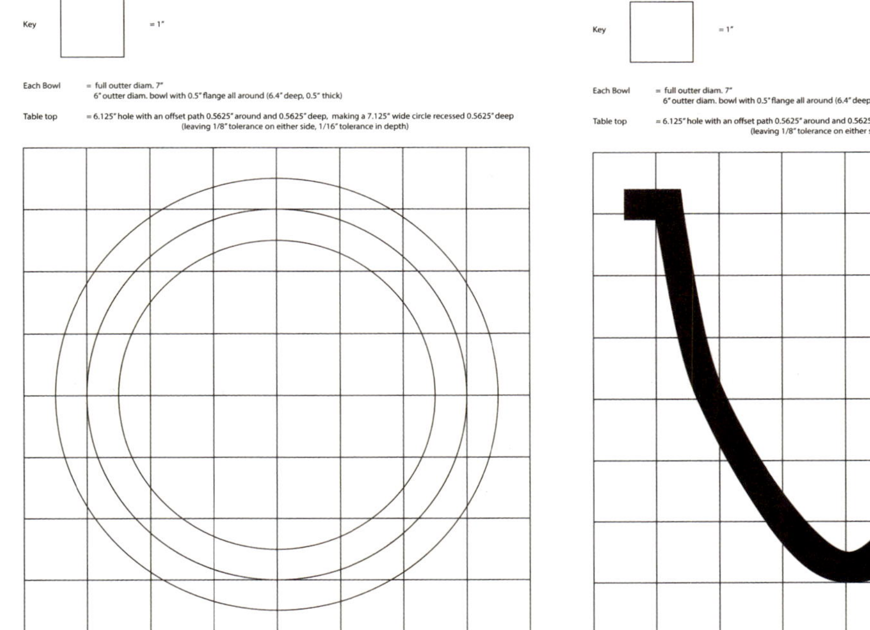

fig. 7-13
Technical drawings for
Capitoline Wolves.

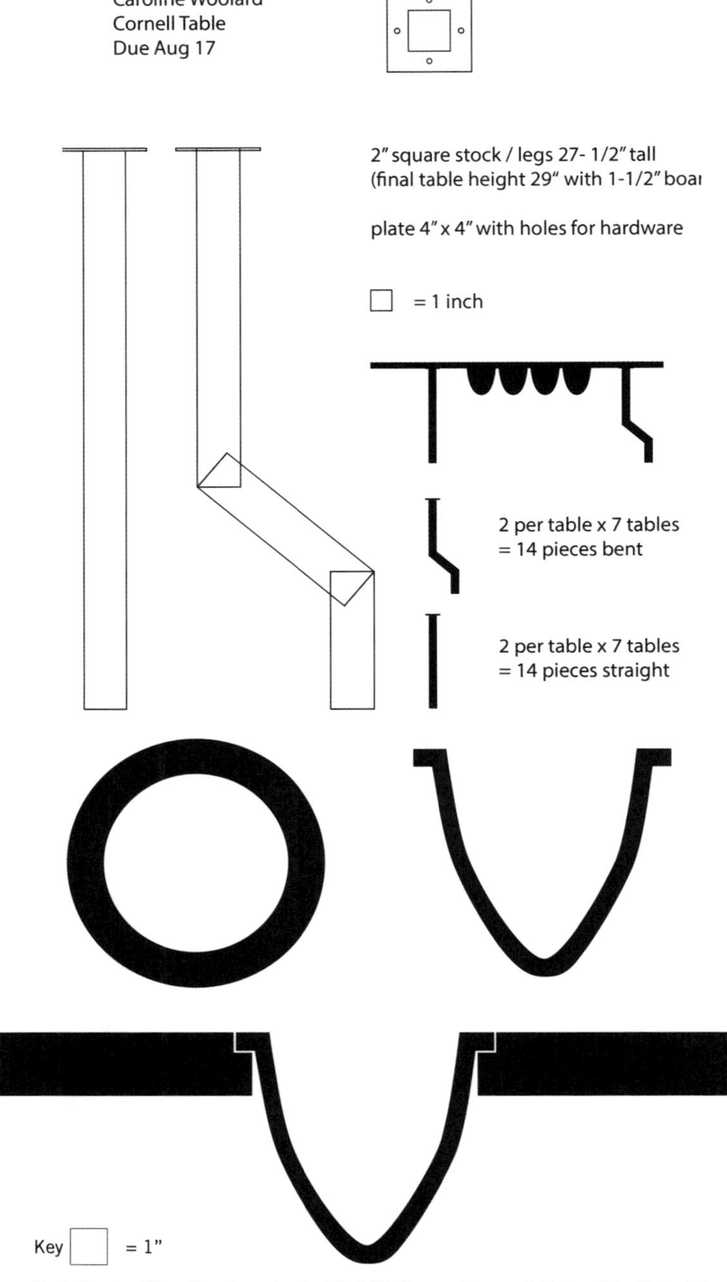

Each Bowl = 6" outter diam. bowl with 0.5" flange all around / full outter diam. 7"
(6.4" deep, 0.5" thick)

Table top = 6.125" hole with an offset path 0.5625" around and 0.5625" deep,
making a 7.125" wide circle recessed 0.5625" deep
(leaving 1/8" tolerance on either side, 1/16" tolerance in depth)

I wrote to Ashley to see if she knew anyone who might be able to fabricate my design in ceramics. I wanted to work with someone who was local, or close to local, and Alfred, New York was a lot closer to Ithaca, New York, than New York City was to Ithaca, New York, where the work would be installed.

> July 6, 2016
> Ashley,
>
> I hope the summer is treating you well! Congrats on your new job and your amazing shows. I've been following your work from FB and am so honored to have a framed print of yours! Whenever I make a print that you want, or another edition, come get it.
>
> I'm writing now because I am looking to find someone to throw a breast-like shaped bowl and then cast 56-60 copies of it, in stoneware, this summer. I can send drawings to give exact measurements, but it's about 8" wide in diameter at the widest and 10" deep, tapering down. Do you know anyone who'd be up for this job? I'd love to talk to them soon, and get a quote.
>
> Ian has connected me to Mahlon, who will be making the table that these shapes fit into, and he's welding the legs, so you may have heard something about it. It's due the first week of Sept at the latest, or Aug 16, ideally, and it will be transported to Ithaca.
>
> Hoping to hear from you,
> Caroline
>
> PS: so you know the whole story, here it is …

I've been commissioned to make a big series of
tables for a performance at Cornell, and I'm
maxing out the budget to make this table I've
always wanted to make that has bowls/breasts in
it, based on the she-wolf that raised Romulus
and Remus. It's made of cherry with steel legs
and the cherry has 8 holes cut out with a
recessed lip for 8 bowls to rest in. Images of
an earlier version are here: https://www.drop-
box.com/s/69j217osjl3hb9w/Caroline%20Woolard%20
Capitoline%20Wolves.pdf?dl=0

Ashley then generously put me in touch with Alex Zablocki, a
ceramicist working at Alfred with her at the time. I wrote to
Alex, to see if I could hire him.

July 18, 2016
Alex,

Please see a near-final design for the breast
bowls, in 3 formats for easy viewing (I hope).
I wanted to share this with you to ask about the
depth the cherry wood should be routed, and how
the connection from the flange to the wood will
work in the design.

To figure this out, I need to know:

- how thick will the bowls be? I want them to be
  sturdy, but not overly-heavy. This will impact
  how deep the cut into the cherry wood is, and
  the design, of course…

- what kind of radius can the ceramic make, as
  it transitions from the flange/lip to the
  breast shape?

See the attached drawings to get a sense of
the clay thickness/curve I am wondering about
… right now I designed it as though the clay
flange would be .875" thick, which is very

unlikely. Once I know the thickness and the
radius it needs (I imagine it can't make a 90
degree angle), I will send the final design.
These are 8" in diameter, going down to 4.5"
and then 1" and the whole thing is 9" deep.
The cherry wood is 1.75" thick, so I will
design it to rest in there snugly.

Thanks,
Caroline

From there, I talked to Alex on the phone, and he asked for
half of the money up front. I had not been paid by Cornell
yet, but I paid him anyway, as I wanted to respect his labor.
I learned later that this was a very bad practice for me, as
I was going into debt in order to be more punctual with
payment than the commissioning organization. More on
that, later.

hey caroline,

here is the break down for the project

hope this all makes sense let me know if you
have any questions

the only thing that might change slightly
is the material cost i really need to start
making them to see if i will need more clay, i
think it should be fine

but we can talk more about that later this is
a great start i think

I usually do $^1/_2$ up front $^1/_2$ upon completion.
Will this work for you? I will keep you
updated throughout the process. Excited to be
a part of this project

thanks
alex

Breast shaped pots for tables project

Making = 30/hrs $1500
Clay Mixing = 4.5/hrs $225
Testing/Maintenance = 5/hrs $250
Materials = $275

Total hrs= 39.5 @ $50/hr = $1,975
                  Materials + $275

                Total Cost = $2,250

Extra info:
Clay needed 550lbs Custom Red Stoneware:
material per pot = $6.25 × 44 pots = $275
(material cost)
Clay= $12.50 per 25lbs roughly 1 bag/2 bags
needed 22 × 25 = 550lbs (this is only for the 44
pots, I know I will need to make at least 60 to
account for cracking, warping, slumping, etc …
or any other mishaps that can happen throughout
the drying and firing process.)

I have decided not to charge for firing since
I will be firing it here at alfred. Though the
project will require two gas firings which will
consist of loading, unloading of work, kiln
clean up/maintenance prior to and after firing
along with making sure the kilns reach temperature (each kiln will take roughly about 8-10
hours to fire to temperature). I would normally
charge around $150-200 dollars for this depend-
ing on the job, but since we are not paying for
gas of course there will be no charge for that
so that's good. I factored in the labor involved
in loading and unloading/maintenance into the
testing and maintenance category above.

Ian did the welding for the project, but asked me to go through
his friend Mahlon, as the primary contact person for the project. Here is what I wrote to him:

July 10, 2016
Mahlon,

I am not completely done with the table top
design, but since you still don't have your
wood, I figured I can take a few extra days!
That said, I finished the leg designs, as I
want Ian to be able to move forward as soon as
possible, as I know he is gone in August.

Please find the designs attached, both to
scale (in illustrator) and letter sized for
easy printing. Feel free to call me anytime
today or tomorrow to discuss.

The legs should be:
- 2" square stock steel
- 14 pieces of straight legs
- 14 pieces of bent "wolf" legs (enough for 7
  tables it might become 5 tables,
  but I'm happy to have 2 extra sets of legs)
- 27-$^1/_2$" tall (to become 29" tall when the
  1-$^1/_2$ boards are on top)

The things you and I need to agree on are:
- the exact size of holes for hardware that
  lines up with the inset hardware or plate
  under the table
- legs welded to 4" plates (or another size
  plate that works for the hardware/plate
  under table)
- flat black/oil finish?

Once we are on the same page, you can hand
this to Ian and supervise his work.

Thanks for all you do,
Caroline

After many conversations over the phone and by text
message, I sent the final design to Mahlon.

July 19, 2016
Mahlon,

Please find the final designs attached. You will see three images, each in three formats. Images of the connection/recessed area for the ceramic bowls, images of the table alone, and images of the tables as they connect to one another. I will have a final rendering by tonight or tomorrow, as well.

You will see that I've removed the curve, going back to a simple table size of 36" × 72," which means you may have extra wood. I'm hoping this means you may have overestimated the amount of wood for the job, so you may have material to give me for my own use since the table is smaller now. You will also notice that I added a small hole near the "head" of the wolf, as I will personally be making a mirror frame that will hang from that area.

We can go over all of these details:
- table top = 36" × 72", 1.75" thick cherry
- holes = 6.125" holes with .5" offset paths around them, routed at .5625" deep, making 8.125" diam. recessed circles routed out around holes (for ceramic bowls)
- steel legs = connect to inset hardware with 4" × 4" plates (or other size, that Ian and Mahlon determine)
- tiny hole = $^3/_8$" hole drilled through cherry with $^1/_2$" routed circle around it, $^1/_8$" deep, making 1.375" diam. recessed circle (for mirror attachment)
- notch = cut into table all the way through to mark pentagonal alignment of 5 tables

We still need to figure out:
- The finish (matte/luster/oil?)
- the bread board (please send me a drawing of this)

- if you think the legs are too far from the
  edge at the "head" side of the table (will
  it tip over?!)
- the metal plate/hardware (how the hardware is
  recessed to bolt/screw the legs on and off)

So thankful for your work, and looking forward
to seeing this realized,

Caroline

Mahlon sent me the final budget estimate, far over the
$8,000 that I had from Cornell for the project. I decided to
go forward with it, anyway.

8-3-16 Updated Estimate Caroline Woolard
PRINCIPAL DESIGNER / CHIEF WORKMAN—MAHLON HUSTON
6270 ICE HOUSE ROAD, HORNELL NY. 14843
419-551-2375
MAHLONHUSTON@GMAIL.COM
PROJECT: Cherry Tables
SERVICES TO: Caroline Woolard
SERVICE TIME DEFINITION
COMPLETE BUILD 120hrs A completed build of
design as agreed by Caroline Woolard and
myself and finished to the highest standard
LABOR HOURLY RATE TOTAL LABOR COST
120 HOURS $40.00 PER HOUR $4,800.00
DELIVERY OF WORK $250
MATERIALS QUANTITY / TYPE / STYLE COST
LUMBER 650 Board ft. of 8/4 Cherry @ $9.50per
board ft. $6,175.00
PLY WOOD 2 Sheets ." Maple @ $60.00 $120.00
STEEL LEGS 28-2" square stock steel legs
$1300.00
ANGLE IRON 38.5' of 1" × 1" × 3/16" @ $1.75
per foot $67.00
TEMPLATE Laser cut template for the routing of
the holes $40.00
TOTAL $7,702.00

Managing

*Capitoline Wolves &
Queer Rocker*

```
TOTAL COST OF MATERIAL AND LABOR
LABOR $4,800.00
DELIVERY $250.00
MATERIAL $7,702.00
TOTAL $12,752.00
PAID $8,175.00
OWED $4,577.00
```

Mahlon, Alex, and Ian were able to work together to make the pieces come together in a beautifully cooperative way. I believe this was possible because they had experience working together in the past, and both knew Ian and Ashley.

```
Mahlon and Alex,

Thanks for your work so far—I'm really glad to
be working with you two.

Here are 3 things that I hope you two sync up on:

1-review the drawings I've sent you (and new
  renderings, attached, nearly done, to give you
  a sense of the way the final design will work
  and look)
2-the color of the clay body/cherry finish (they
  should have similar luster/matte quality)
3-the amount of tolerance between the ceramic
  bowl and the hole/recessed area in the cherry
  (right now I designed the hole and recessed
  area in the wood to have 1/16" extra all around)

Call me if you have a question.

Thanks!
Caroline
```

The project at Cornell came with a total budget of $8,000, but I wanted to pay everyone well, and was committed to my design being done at a large scale. Rather than scaling back the project, after seeing the costs for fabrication, unwisely, I decided to spend more money than I was given. I ended up spending $20,000 more than I should have, which I put on my credit card. I ignored the credit card payments and the

$20,000 ballooned into $40,000 over two years. I learned never to go beyond the budget allocated, to always pay myself for my time, and to negotiate increased budgets with institutions going forward. To make things worse, with this project, I did not make an agreement with the fabricators about giving them a 1099 at the end of the year, so I was not able to deduct the expense I had for the project of paying them. This meant that Cornell paid me, and I paid the fabricators, and then I was taxed on the money that looked like income, but was actually an expense — paying fabricators. I learned to save 20% of any project for 1099 income as I will lose it when I have to pay taxes. I also learned to ask the commissioning organization to pay for materials and fabricators directly, rather than paying me to pay them. This way, it is their tax problem. Also, commissions never pay for your laptop, your software, your studio, your healthcare, your accountant, or your tools, so I try to leave a 10% contingency that allows wiggle room for surprises and these very real costs of overhead.

I learned never to go beyond the budget allocated, to always pay myself for my time, and to negotiate increased budgets with institutions going forward.

Managing

Capitoline Wolves &
Queer Rocker

Mediating

When I presented the project at Cornell, I spoke about all of the labor and artists, designers, and craftspeople involved in making the project. It is important to me to credit people who help with fabrication, and to be in dialogue with them about how to do so in a way that respects their self-presentation. For example, some people do not want their fabrication "day job" to be known about.

Herman Jean-Noel, who I met at a TradeSchool.coop ^{see chapter 3} class, asked me if I would be open to him making a documentary about what I was working on. I was thrilled, and decided to pay him something, to support basic costs.

I wrote to Herman:

> July 21, 2016
> Thank you for your interest in making a film about me. That is SO generous!
>
> One thing: I won't be fabricating the table tops or legs, but I will be making the mirror and the column stools. So there's no welding or wood cutting or ceramic casting here. There will be CNC machine routing and mirrorizing and framing here soon.
>
> I would love the stools and mirrors to be documented, and also the sketching and planning process on paper and computer—yes!
>
> Maybe I could pay you to document the installation at Cornell, and the people involved in the fabrication? We will be installing Aug 17-20 or the first weekend of Sept. Or you can focus on the parts of the project that are happening in NYC this summer?
>
> I'm way over budget and know you're a pro, so didn't ask you. That said, since you're offering, I am thrilled. I'm happy to pay $500 plus

your travel for the documentation. I know
that's not much for your skill, but I want to
pay you something.

Hugs!

Herman wrote back:

July 22, 2016
Good morning Caroline,

All of that sounds good to me.

Thank you for offering a budget!! You are
correct something of this nature can run up
several thousands to say the least. It's very
thoughtful of you to be on the transparency
tip budget wise. I'm happy to accept what you
are offering, since that can cover the cost
of travels, plus audio recorder.

What are your work dates looking like for
your portion of the fabrication process,
also for the casting and welding taking place
at Cornell?

I will need you to debrief me on the scope of
a work timeline.

Gratefully,
Herman

*Capitoline Wolves &
Queer Rocker*

8

Carried on Both Sides

Presented at four locations—The Metropolitan Museum of Art, Lesley Heller, LMAK, and the Knockdown Center in New York City—in 2018, *Carried on Both Sides* aimed to uncover the history of the @ symbol. Featuring carved wooden columns, hand blown glass amphorae, glass murrine, a single-channel video, and soft sculptures made of kevlar, this project questioned how present logics of freedom and exchange carry with them resonances of past imperial lives. This project was the result of three years of collaborative work between Helen Lee, Alexander Rosenberg, Lika Volkova, and Caroline Woolard, and was supported by residencies and fellowships at Pilchuck Glass School and UrbanGlass.

In 2015, Woolard invited Lee and Rosenberg to join her in an application to work together for the Hauberg Fellowship at Pilchuck Glass School. Woolard wrote that she "approached Helen Lee, who 'uses glass to think about language' and Alexander Rosenberg, who concerns himself with systems of display and all things on the edge of breaking, about a collaboration at Pilchuck." When the group received the Fellowship, a three-year research project began that included multiple self-organized residencies and research trips. The resulting work was individually authored in relationship to shared research about the @ symbol, an approach to collaboration that enables deep engagement with shared topics alongside individual expression.

The @ symbol derives from a graphic representation of the amphora, a vessel used in ancient Rome to transport goods like olive oil or grains.

Founded in research and expressed across media, the project explored the visual, political, and material lineage of the @ symbol. The @ symbol derives from a graphic representation of the amphora, a vessel used in ancient Rome to transport goods like olive oil or grains. The project's title references the amphora's original meaning—to "carry on both sides"—referring to the vessel's two carrying handles. The works on view aim to evoke questions about what connections we may find between this ancient mode of transportation and commerce, and today's digital communication. All materials here are reproduced with the consent of the artists. More information is at: http://carriedonbothsides.com

A material-specific approach
to this research endeavor
enabled an expansive way
of thinking about the past,
present, and future of a
symbol and its ability to
change meaning over time and
across cultures.

Helen Lee, 2019

2015-2018
cybersecurity
Ray Romlinson "inventor" of
   email dies 2016
Obama 2009-2017

@
overwhelm
Rome
wired and tired
identity
screens
glowing
glowing books
overstimulated
glass
sleep
cracked

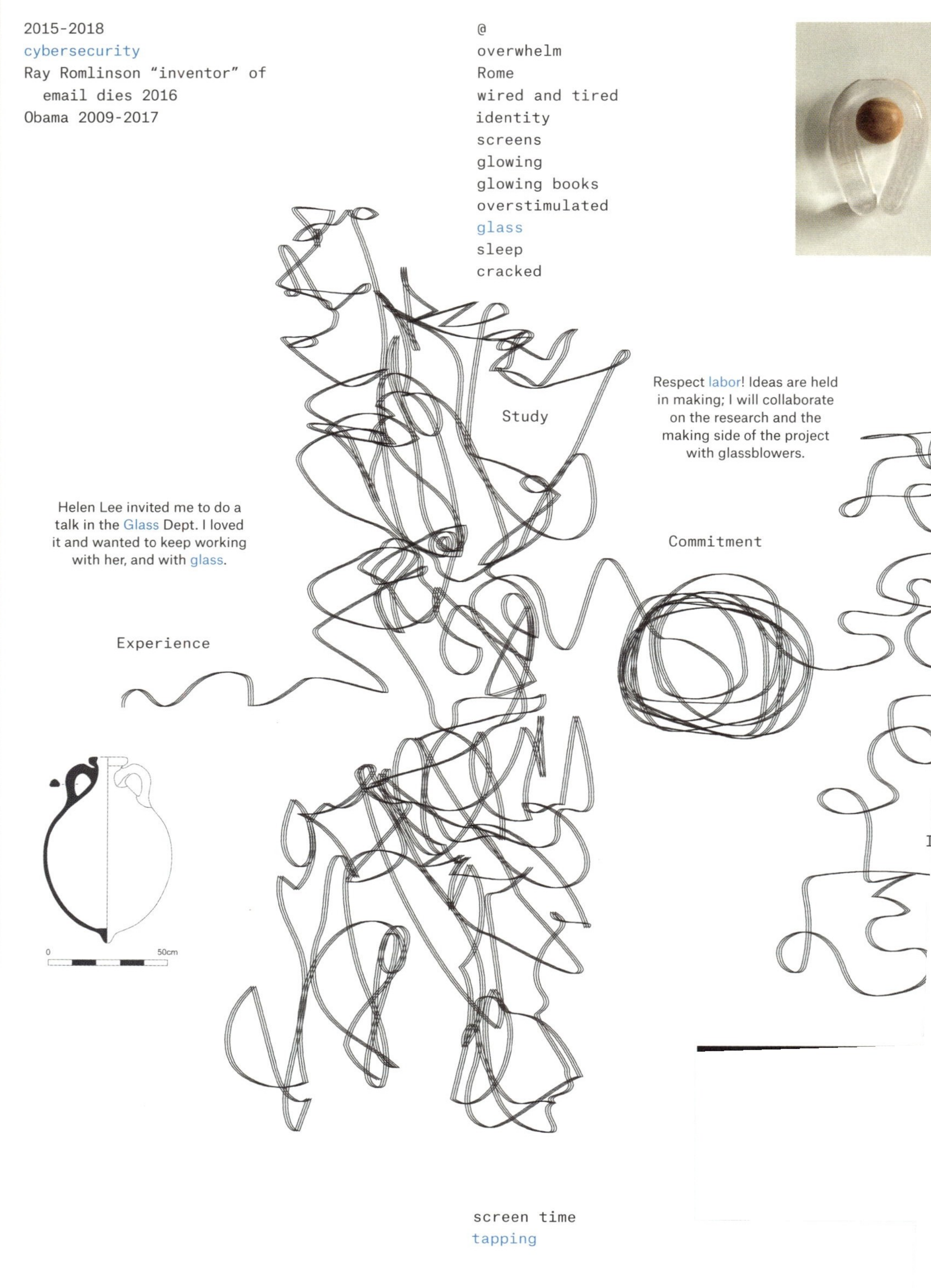

screen time
tapping

Collectively-
Initiated

sound of blowing on a glass
  bottle
glassblowers : smart phones
presentations
  @
something with kevlar
newspaper
columns

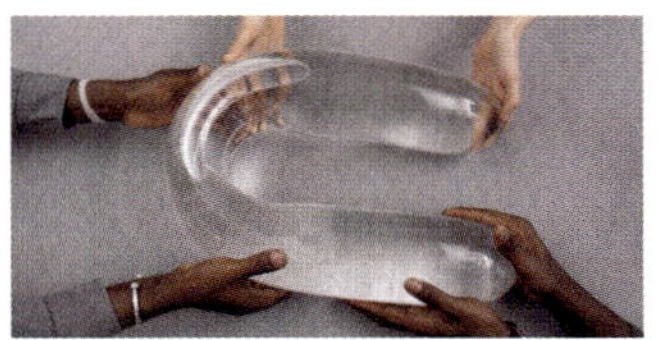

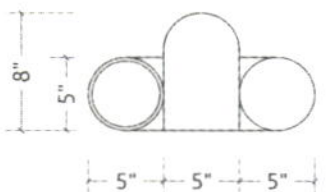

Bottom 1 : 4

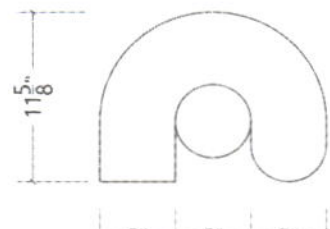

Front 1 : 4

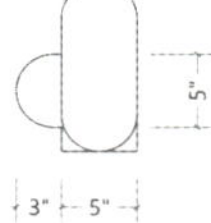

Right 1 : 4

kevlar soft sculpture
kevlar garment
glass level
glass slideshow where glass
  slides are the work itself
slides
@ symbol unfurls to be a wave
coins
blob with plug
open-ended hourglass
sleep video
website only works at night
video of hourglass

This is a short term project
because we want to explore an
idea together but can't commit
to long term collaboration.

Timeframe

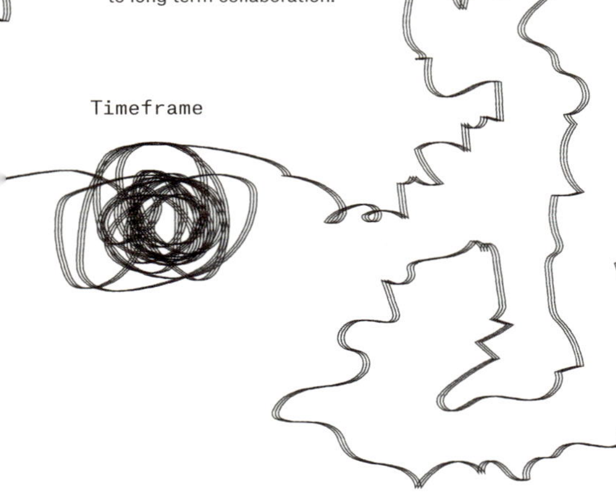

Idea in Public

Reflect

A series of three gallery
exhibitions of sculptures
produced from shared
research.

Experiment

@ for email:Ray Tomlinson,
  engineer
@ at the price of:16th century
  Rome
Giorgio Stabile, historian
[The amphora] is a symbol of
  the wheels of imperial politics in action."
  – David Williams, archeologist
the amphora capitolina" was
  in many ways a notional
  measurement"
vessel 20
amphorae were in essence
  the trade packaging of the
  ancient world."

"Some linguists believe that @
  dates back to the sixth or
  seventh century, a ligature
  meant to fuse the Latin preposition ad—meaning "at", "to,"
  or "toward"—into a unique pen
  stroke. The symbol persisted
  in sixteenth-century Venetian
  trade, where it was used to
  mean amphora, a standard-size
  terracotta vessel employed by
  merchants, which had become a
  unit of measure."
  – Paola Antonelli
sleep

Nancy Rothstein,sleep well-
  ness consultant to Fortune
  500 companies, Director of
  CIRCADIAN® Corporate Sleep
  Programs™
Nicholas Chua, clinical sleep
  research coordinator
Icahn School of Medicine at
  Mount Sinai

Creative Labor Shared by Artists

Cybele Maylone is the Executive Director of The Aldrich Contemporary Art Museum. A non-collecting institution located in Ridgefield, CT, The Aldrich was one of the first contemporary art museums in the country and is today one of the oldest. Prior to leading The Aldrich, Maylone spent five years as the Executive Director of UrbanGlass in Brooklyn, NY.

Cybele Maylone, Executive Director of The Aldrich Contemporary Art Museum, 2020.

In *Carried on Both Sides*, Caroline Woolard, Helen Lee, Alexander Rosenberg, and Lika Volkova explore the amphora, an object that links the past with the present through its use and form. Originally used to store and transport goods like olive oil, the amphora evolved to inform the @ sign, a ubiquitous symbol in contemporary communication. Woolard collaborated with glassblowers to create glass sculptures, a choice of material that connects this Greek and Roman form to 21st century technology.

While primarily made in ceramic, amphorae were in use during an age that was rich for glassmaking: some of the most exquisite examples of early blown glass date to the Greek and Roman empires. In *Carried on Both Sides*, glass serves as a link to both the past and the future. Not only is glass an important record of human creation across the centuries, today it is a defining material of contemporary life; it clads our buildings, supports our telecommunications systems, and mediates our experience with screen-based technologies.

In addition to glass's metaphorical value, the material is perfectly suited for a project exploring physical and intellectual labor. Because of the highly physical—and often incredibly uncomfortable—nature of the glassblowing studio, creating 2,000-degree molten glass necessitates groups of people working together to accomplish a singular piece. An object created in a glassblowing studio is generally overseen by an artist with a specific vision leading a small team. The

teams who work at the bench are the eyes
and hands of the artist behind the project,
serving as fabricators for their vision. For
Carried on Both Sides, Woolard conceived of
a project where the physical and creative
labor would be shared by artists working
together, upending the traditional relationship
in a glass studio.

While Lee and Rosenberg are technically
skilled glassblowers—whose abilities in
the studio would make them highly skilled
fabricators—as artists, they each employ their
technical skills in larger conceptual practices
that engage a variety of media and explore
ideas around language and labor. The natural
collaborative element of the glass studio was
thus pushed even further: Lee, Rosenberg,
and Woolard did not just share the physical
labor of creating amphorae, they shared the
intellectual and creative direction of the project as well, resulting in a work that embodies
the very ideas that it explores.

Lengthening and Twisting 'round Itself

D. Graham Burnett is based in New York City. He trained in the history and philosophy of science, and works at the intersection of historical inquiry and artistic practice. Recent work includes: "Schema for a School" (with Asad Raza and Jeff Dolven) at the Ljubljana Biennial (2015) and The Shed (2018); and "El Halo del Cuidar" (with Lane Stroud and Gabriel Pérez-Barreiro) at the Reina Sofia (2019). Burnett is associated with the research collective ESTAR(SER) and the "Friends of Attention." He teaches at Princeton.

D. Graham Burnett, 2020.

It was at first a dream reported in intimate settings. Because it hardly seemed to merit wider dissemination. Those visited by the vision in the early phase of the outbreak merely shared it with those beside whom they awoke—or if they opened their eyes alone, took up a worn pad by the bed and jotted a few lines. Writing helped. It was good to link the letters in a cursive hand.

I can reproduce my own scribbles here: "It was as if each of the letters of the alphabet, one by one, curled up like a cat, enfolding itself in sovereign disregard. Quite like a cat, in that each letter grew a little tail, which it then wrapped about itself in complacent solipsism. It was the 'a' that did it first, lengthening and twisting 'round itself until it became an @—an 'a' withdrawn defiantly into its shell. The whole alphabet followed: b, c, d, in turn, folding away into cysts of themselves, impervious, inert, durable, solitary."

That was how I tried to describe it. Only gradually did it become clear that the dream was operating along lines of transmission hitherto unknown in the annals of human experience. Was it actually infectious? Did whatever spirit-spore that secreted its principle move between people by touch? By breath?

There were panics, naturally, but they abated—since, for all the mystery, there seemed to be no adverse effects. Indeed, there were hardly even consequences. We sensed, to be sure, that language itself was somehow tiring of us. That those work-horses of our expressive enterprise—the

Study

Collectively-
Initiated

individual letters—were nightly staging an unsettling protest. Even so, we awoke in the mornings and found each character again willing to serve its role, to submit to ligatures, to trip off the tongue, to pulse upon the screen. They were not the pillbugs of our recurrent nightmare.

Now, of course, the dream itself is widely shared, but I think we would all agree that we go about our business much as before. Though it is true that there is something different about the @ these days. Who can see it (on the keyboard, on the screen) and not feel a little nocturnal shiver? It has about it, we sense, an air of rebellion—a certain cloaked recalcitrance.

We use it less, I think. Or maybe more.

Carried on
Both Sides

IMAGINE A GROUP GATHERING

IMAGINE A GROUP GATHERING

Carried on
Both Sides

fig. 8-1, 8-2, 8-3
(pages 490-493)
Untitled (Imperial Forms),
turned cherry wood, poplar,
(not included: glass form and
blow mould), 72 × 12 × 12
inches, dimensions variable.

fig. 8-4, 8-5
(pages 494-497)
Countermeasures: Level, 2018,
glass, mineral oil, turned
cherry wood 18 × 8 × 14 inches. Courtesy of the artist.
Photo by Levi Mandel.

fig. 8-6, 8-7
(pages 496-503)
Countermeasures: Water Clock,
2018, glass, water, turned
cherry wood, 18 × 10 × 10 in
each. Courtesy of the artist.
Photo by Levi Mandel.

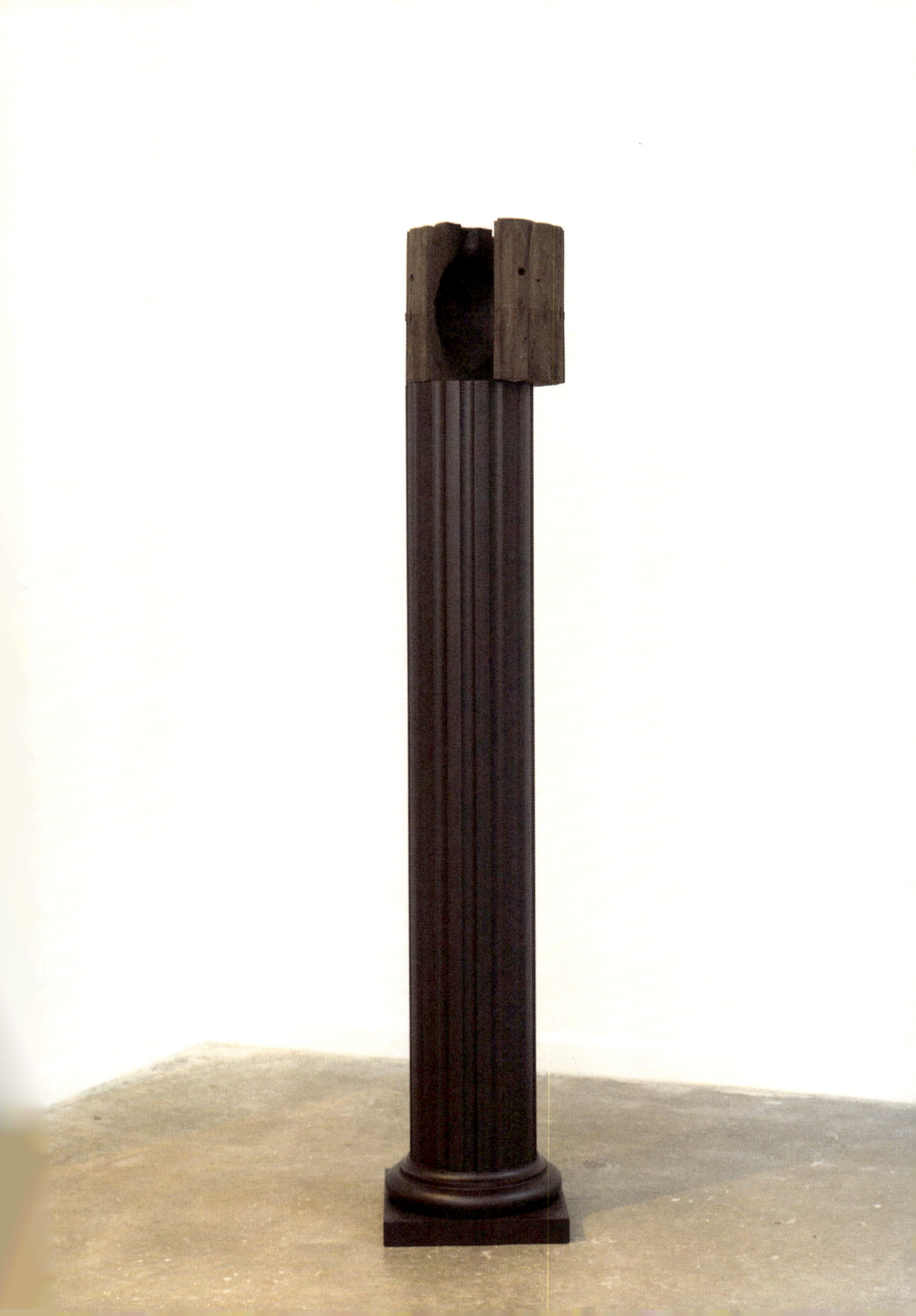

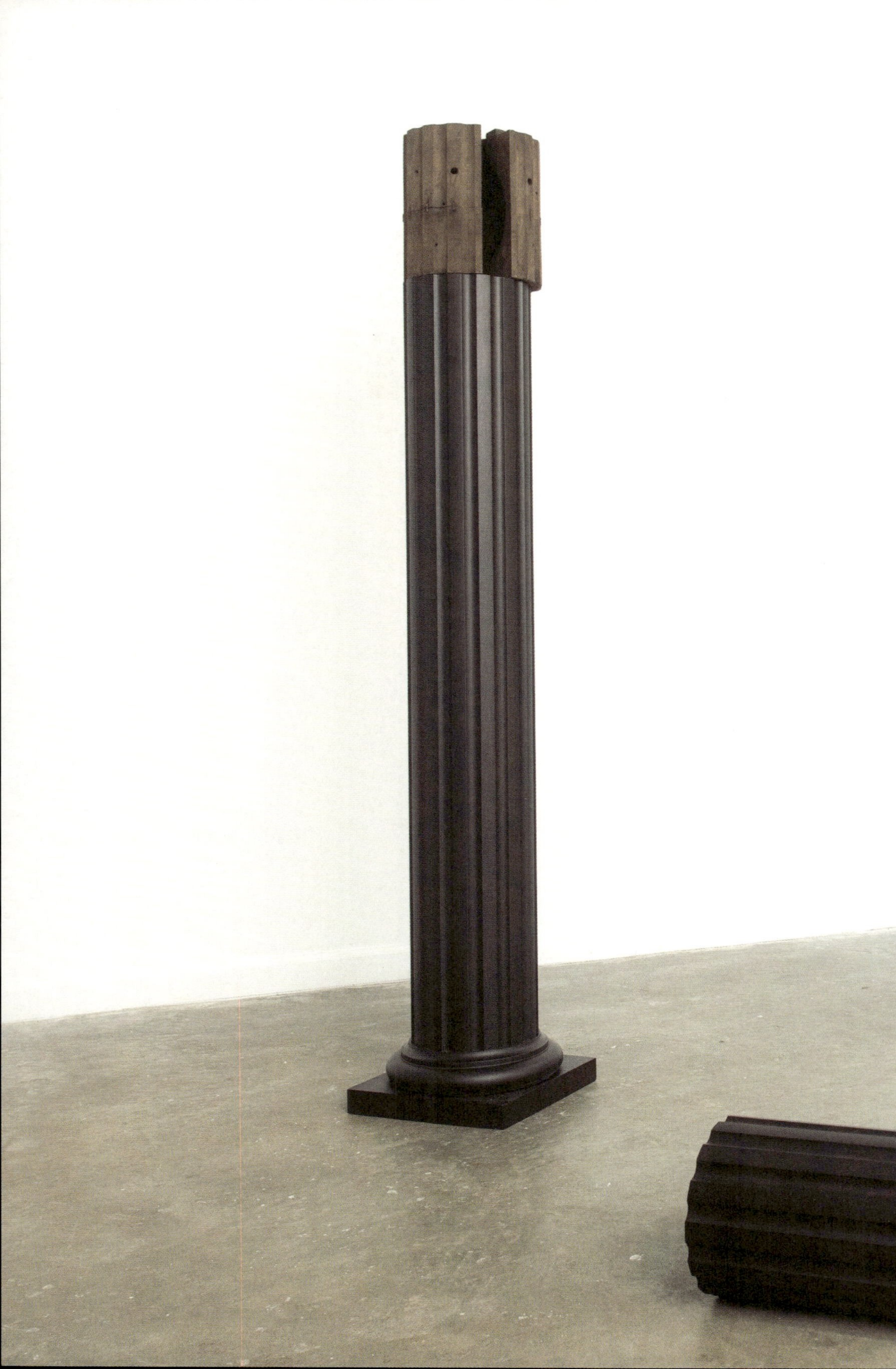

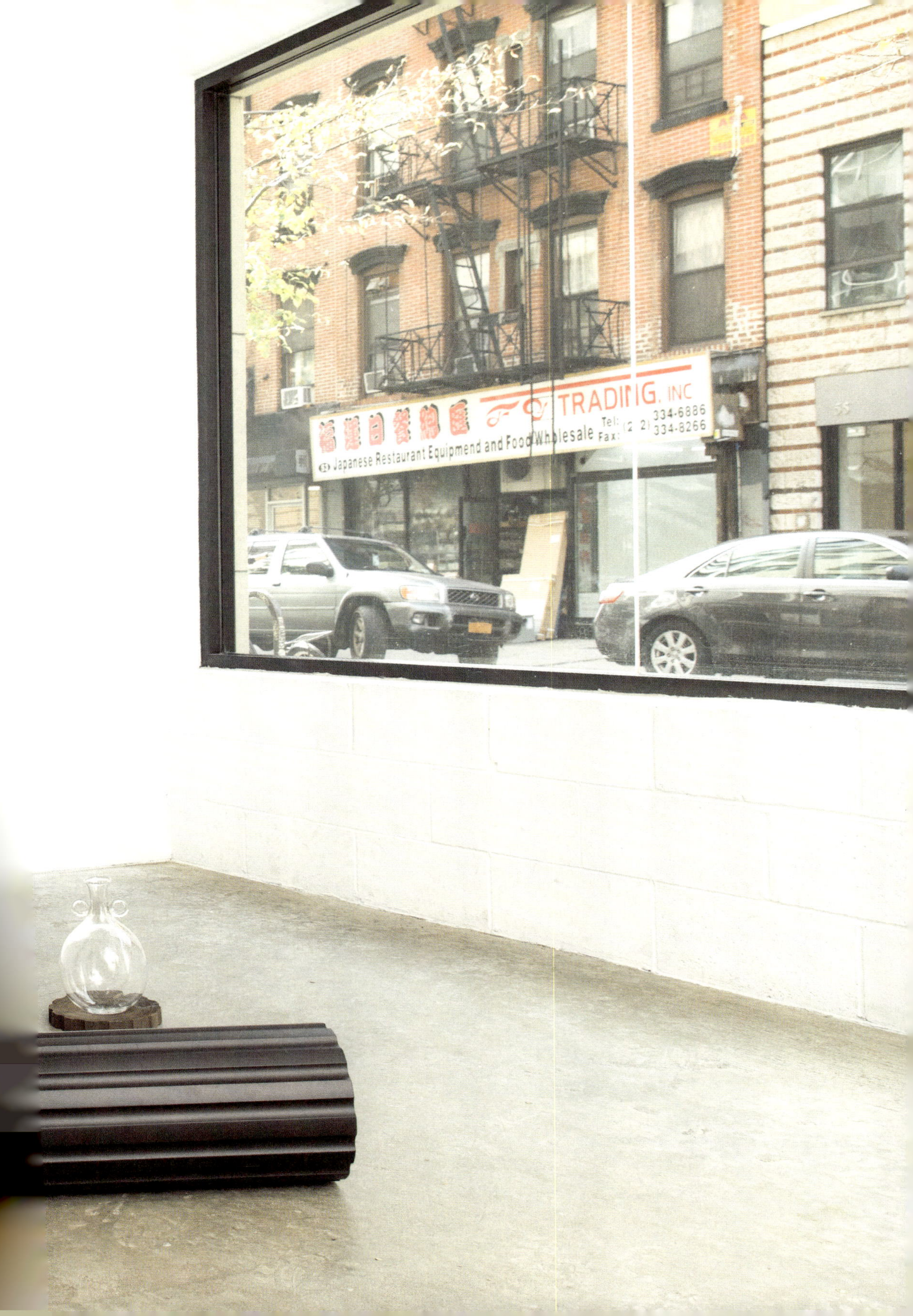
FO TRADING. INC
Tel: (2 2) 334-6886
Fax: (2 2) 334-8266
福運日餐總匯
Japanese Restaurant Equipmend and Food Wholesale

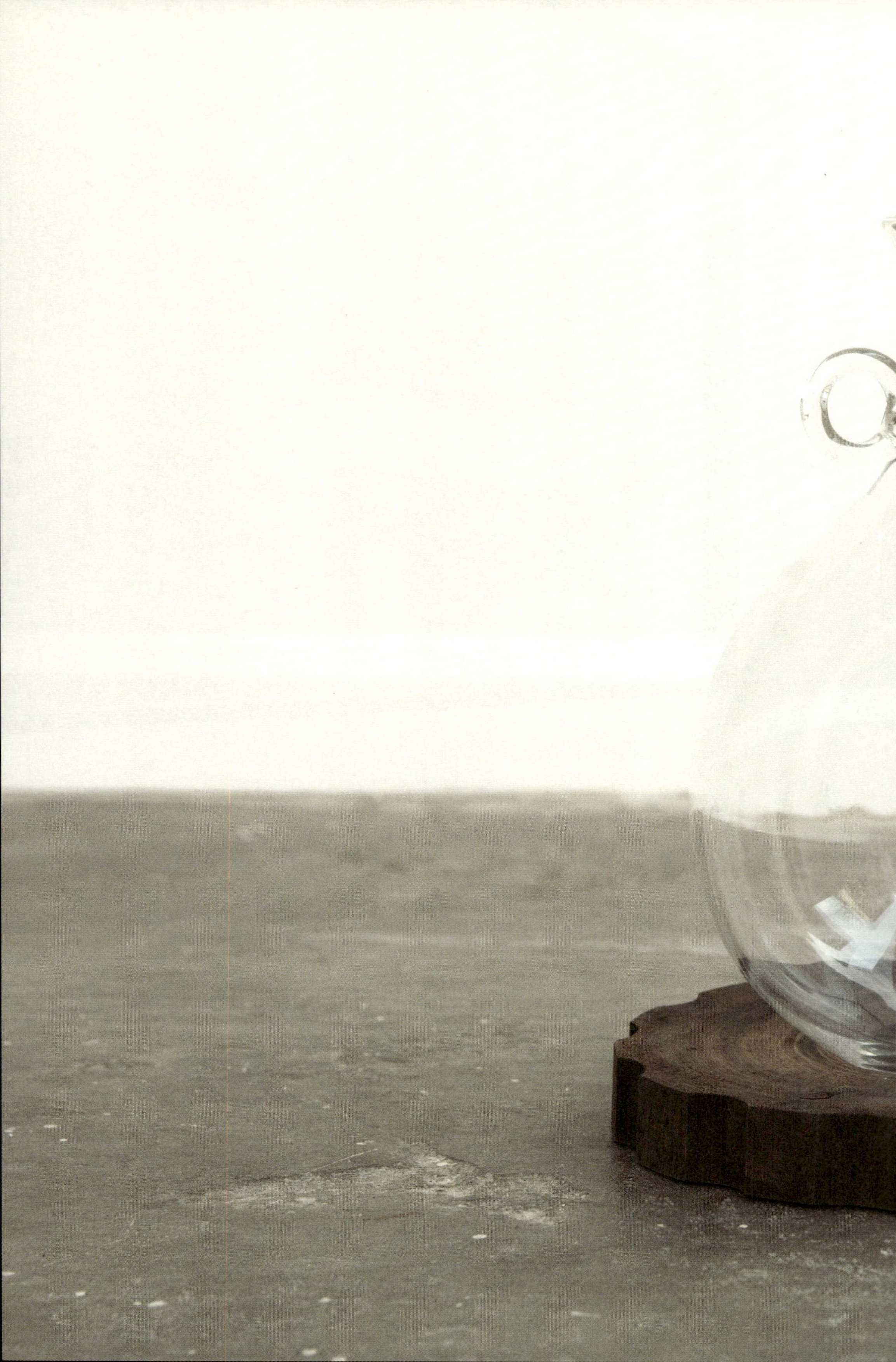

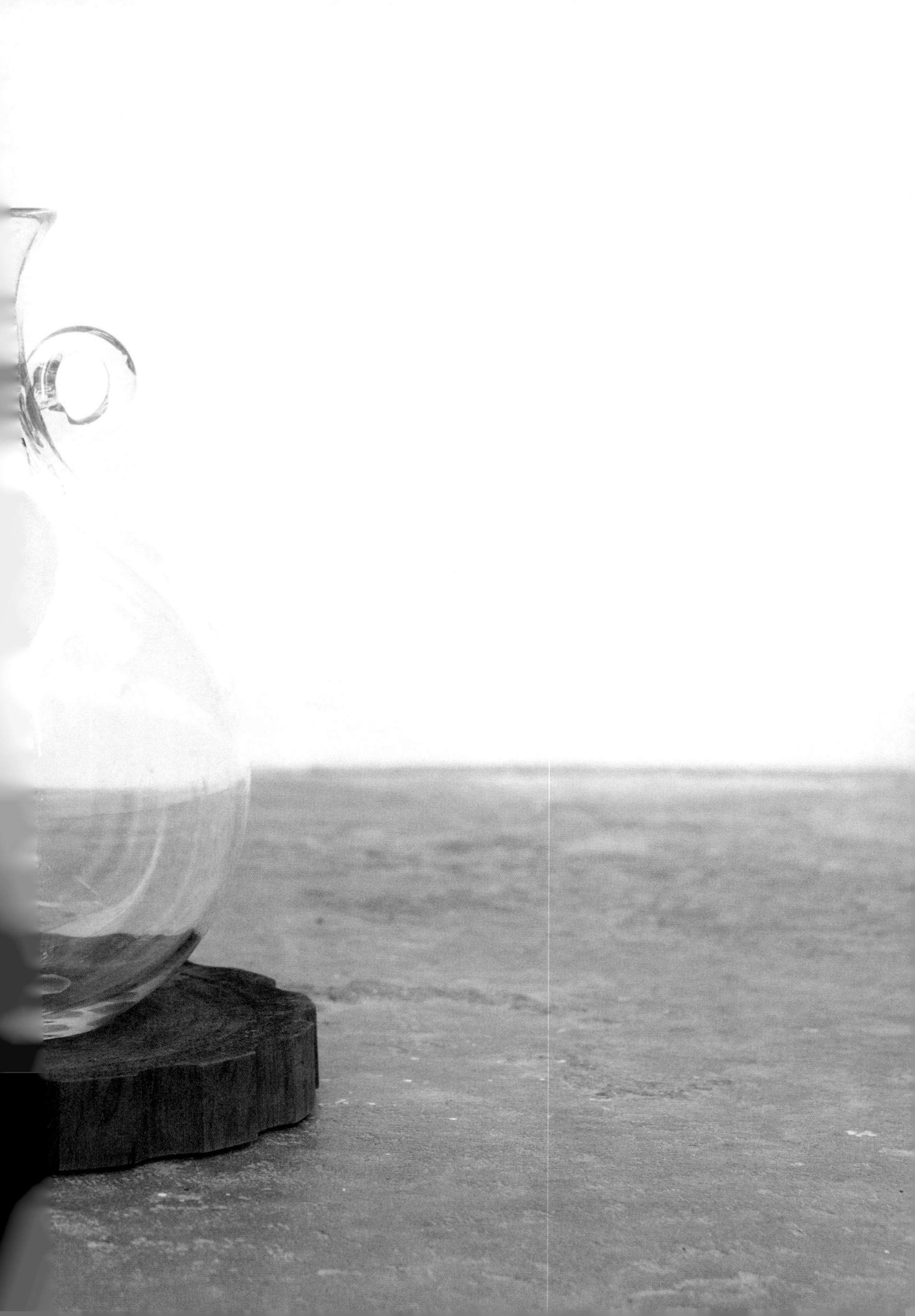

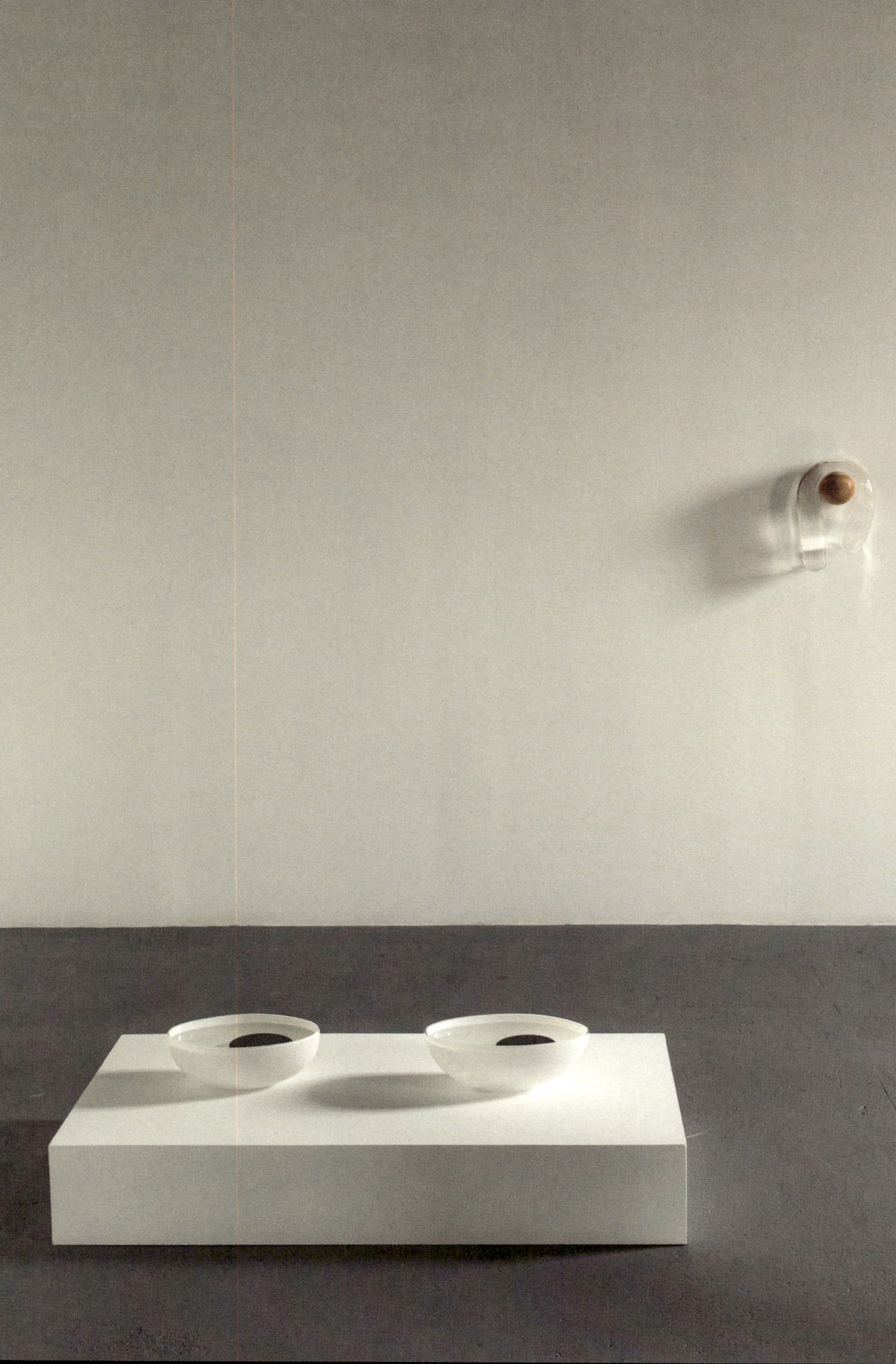

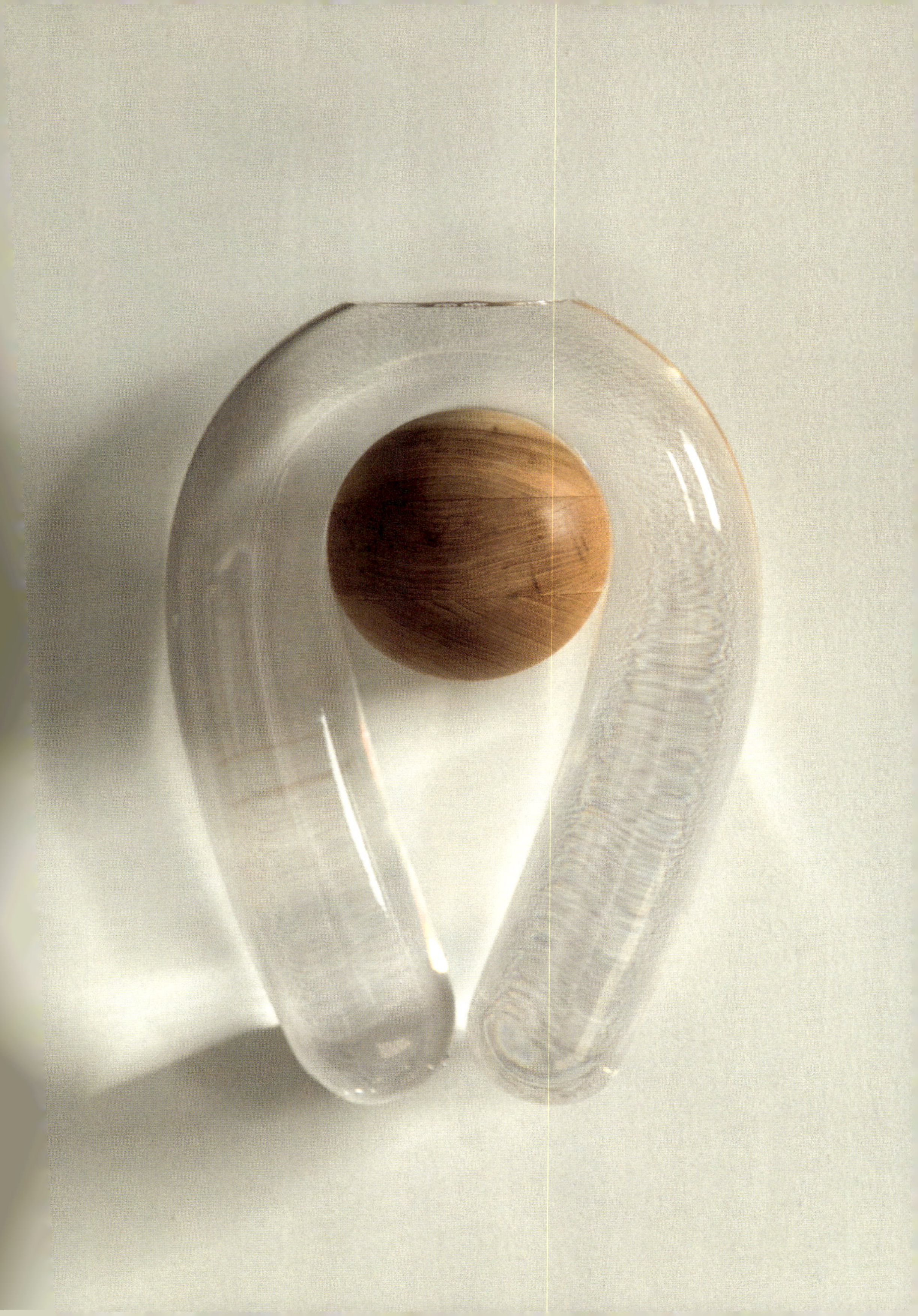

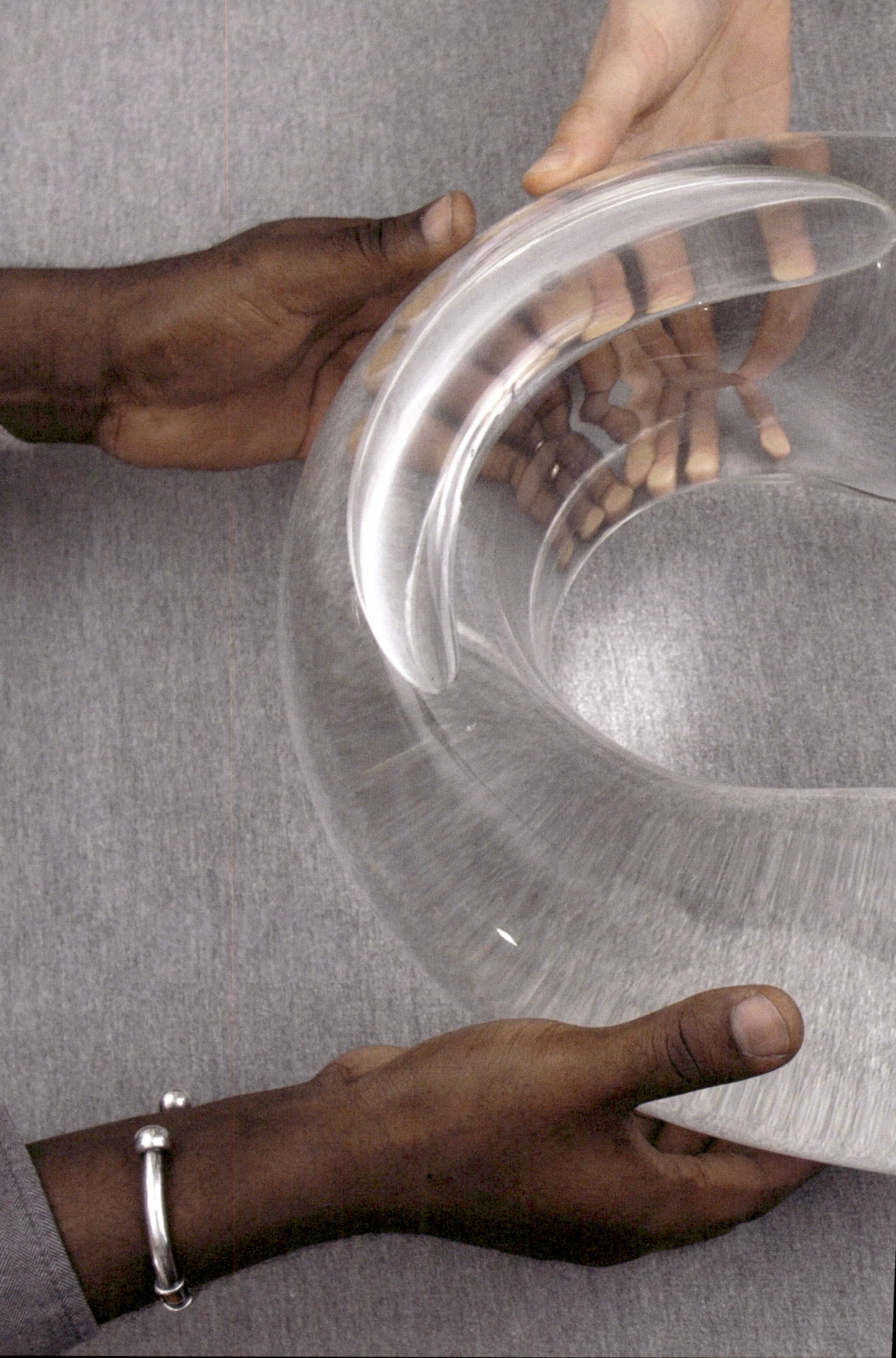

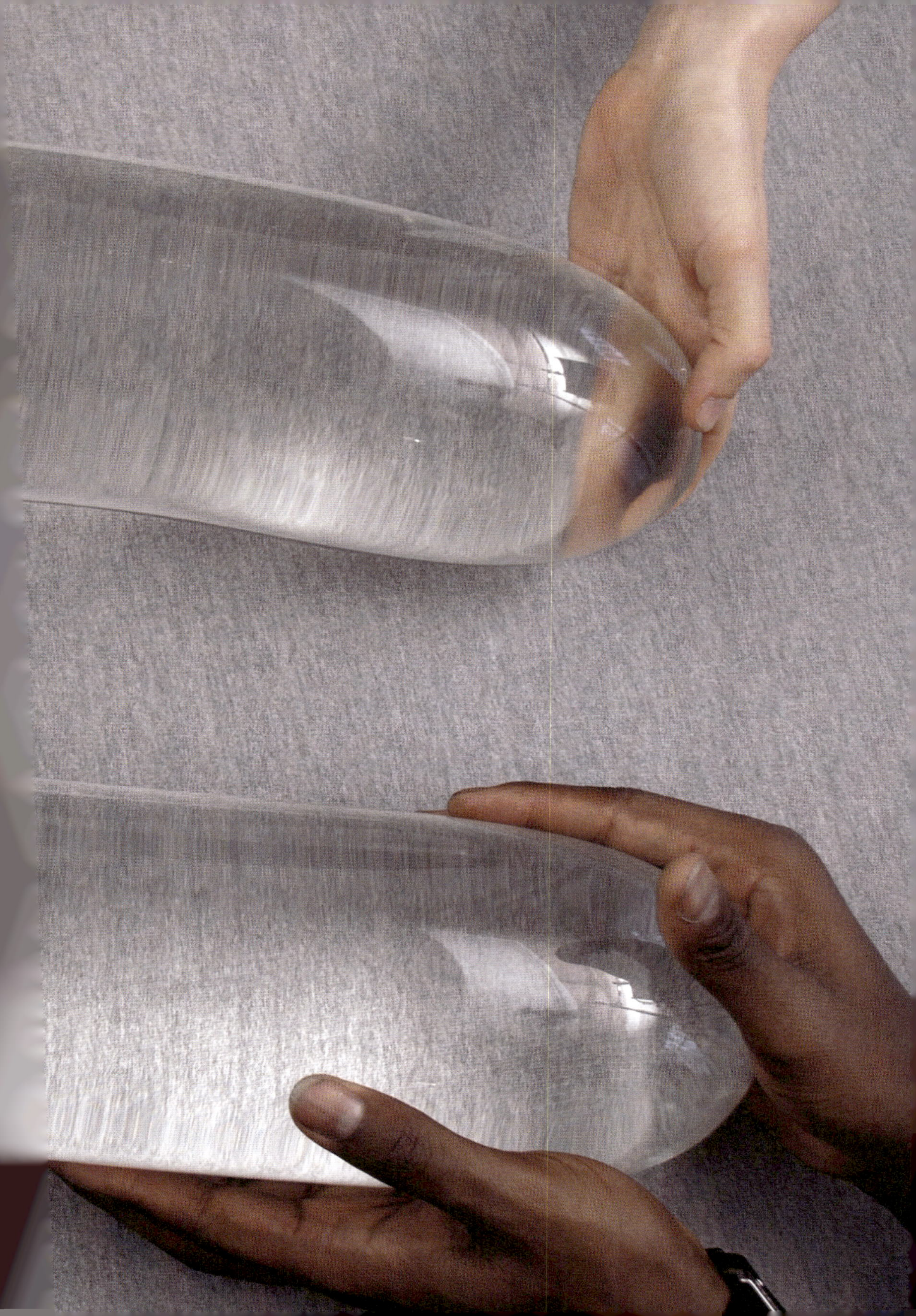

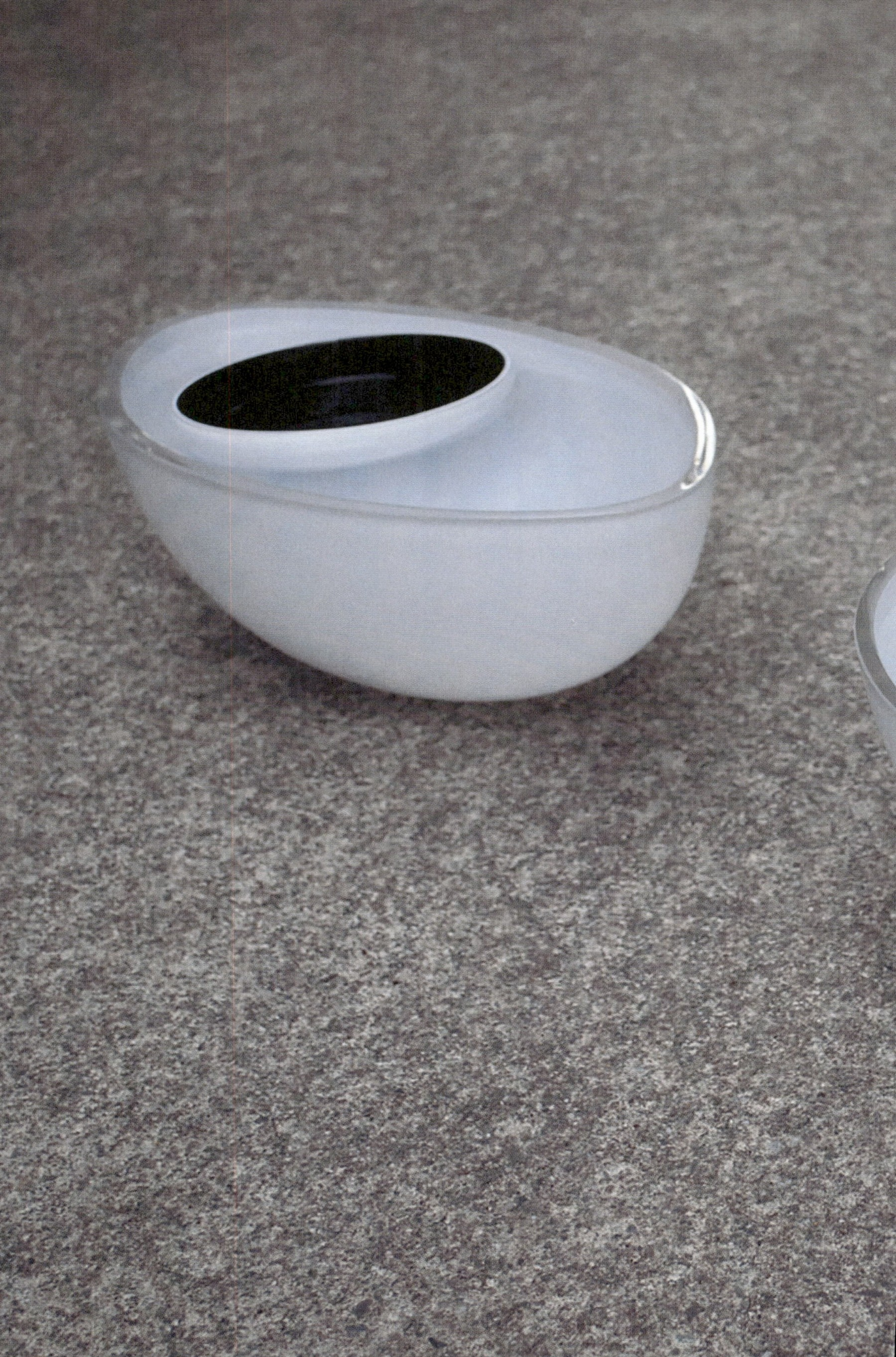

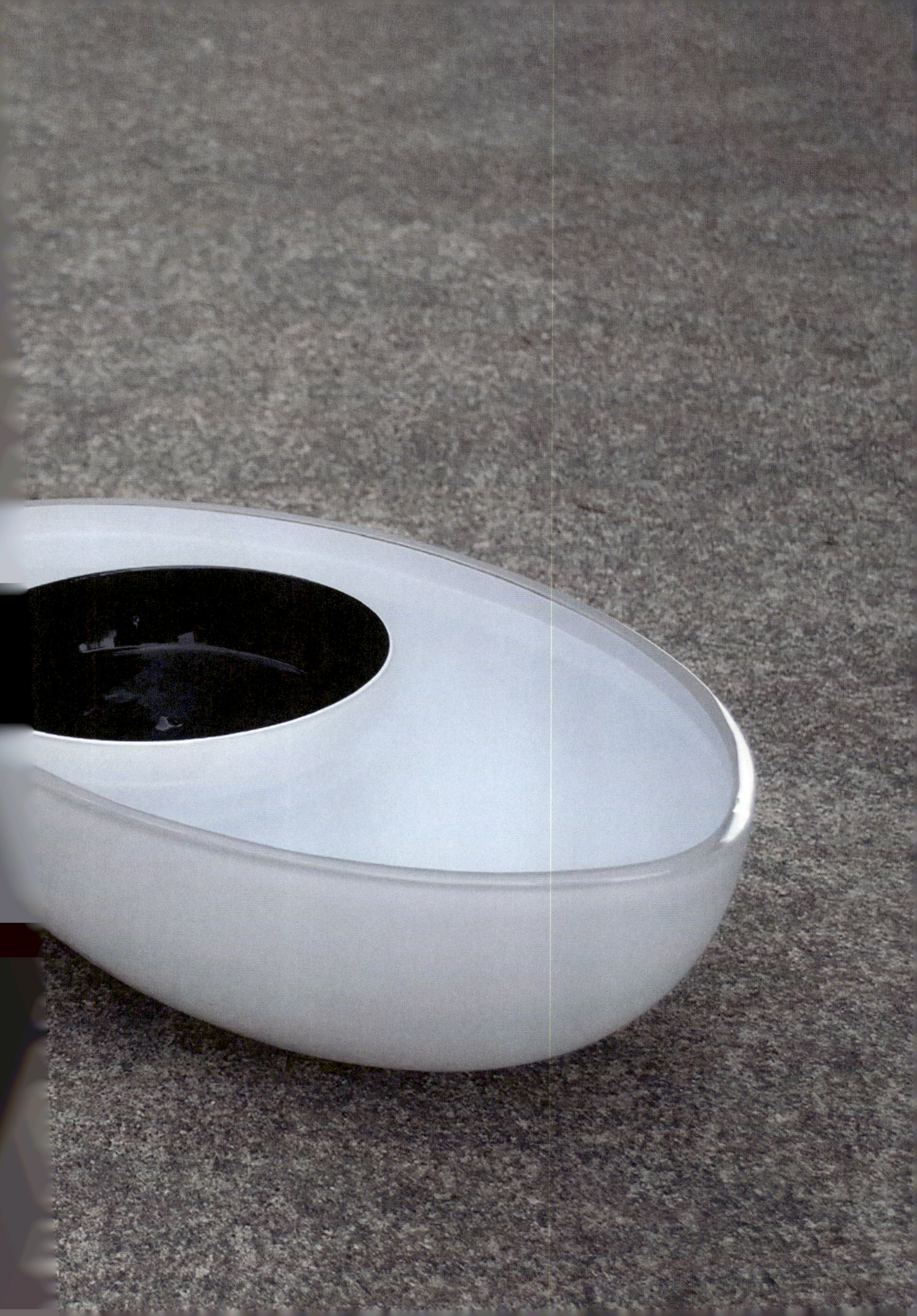

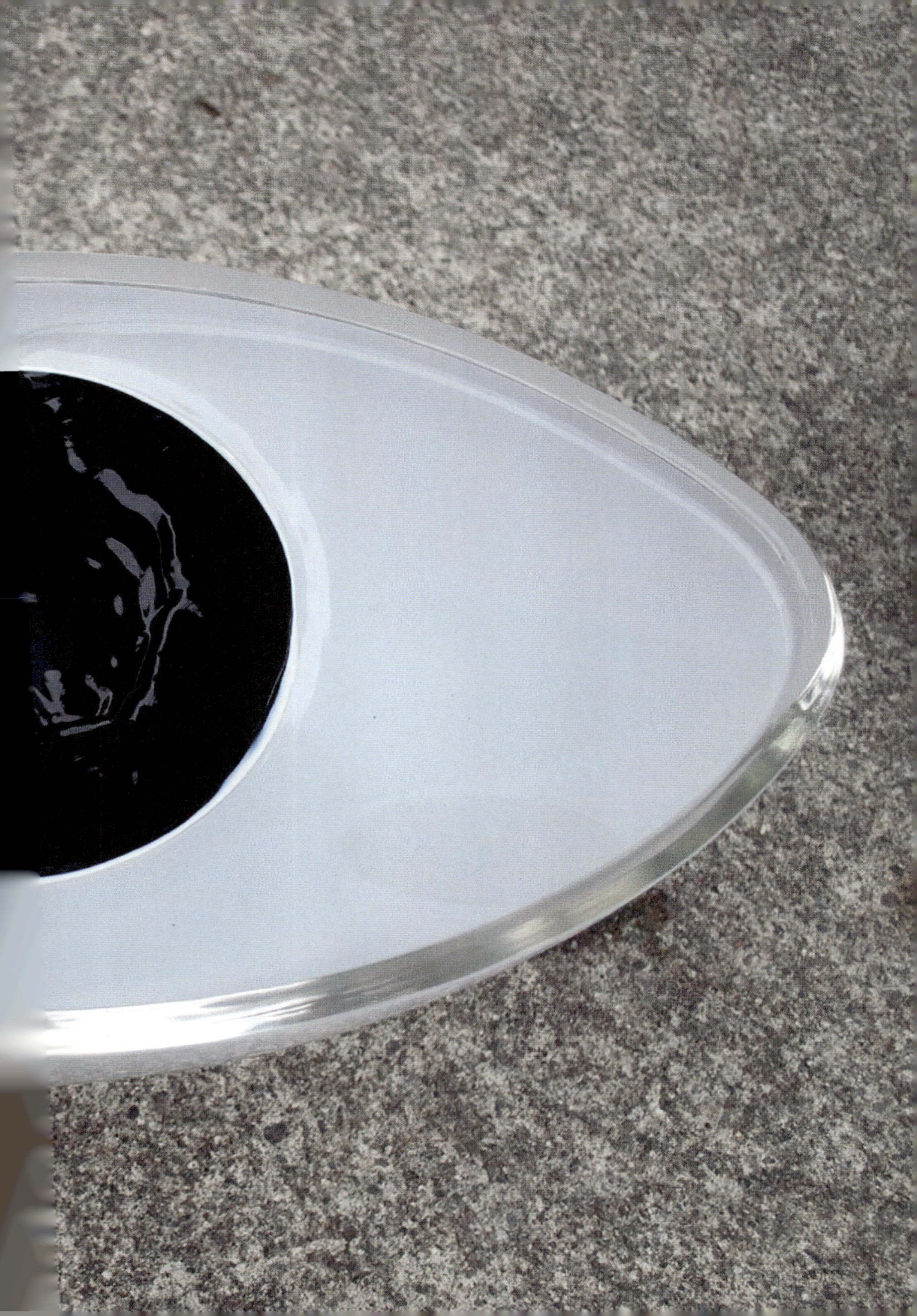

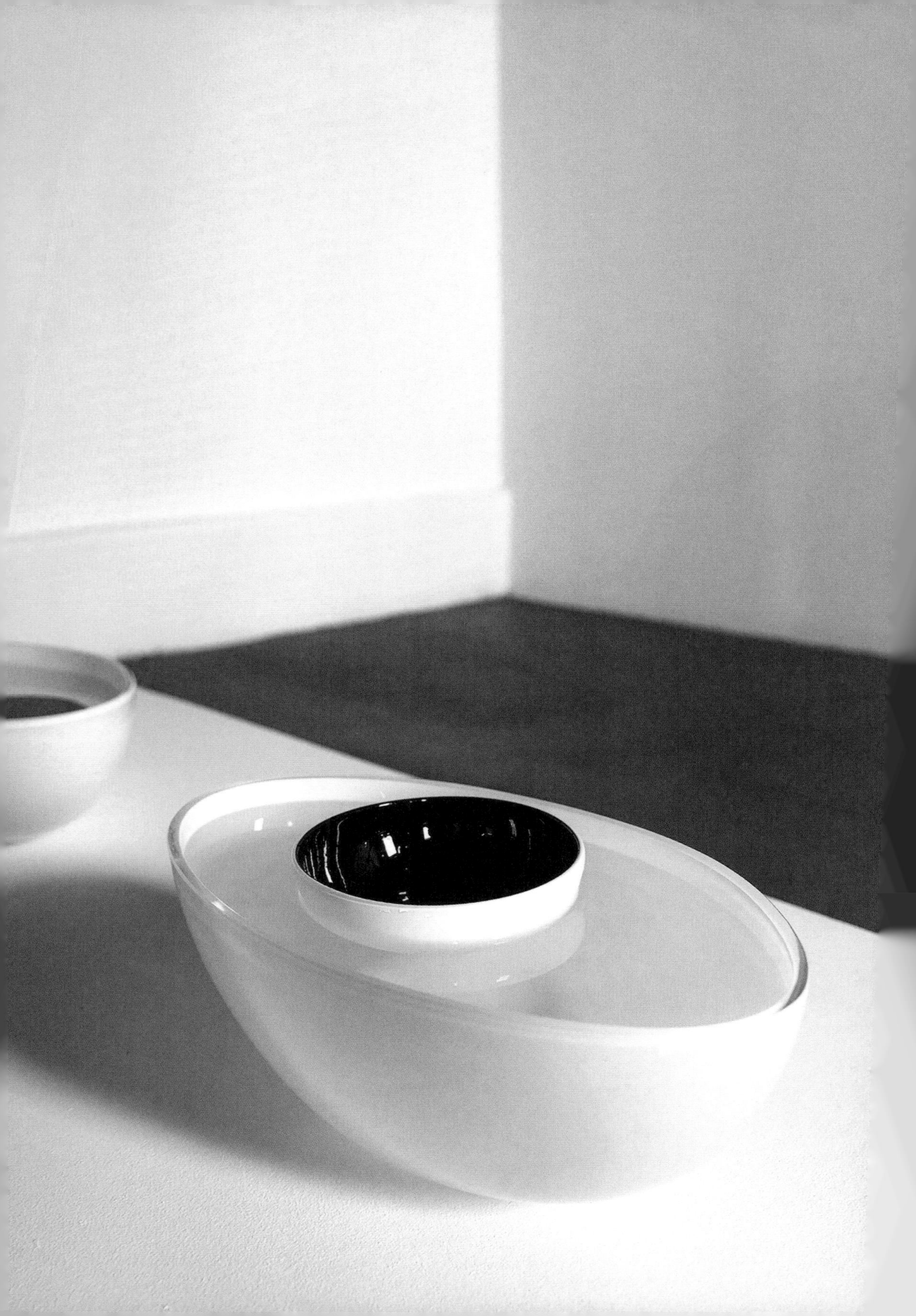

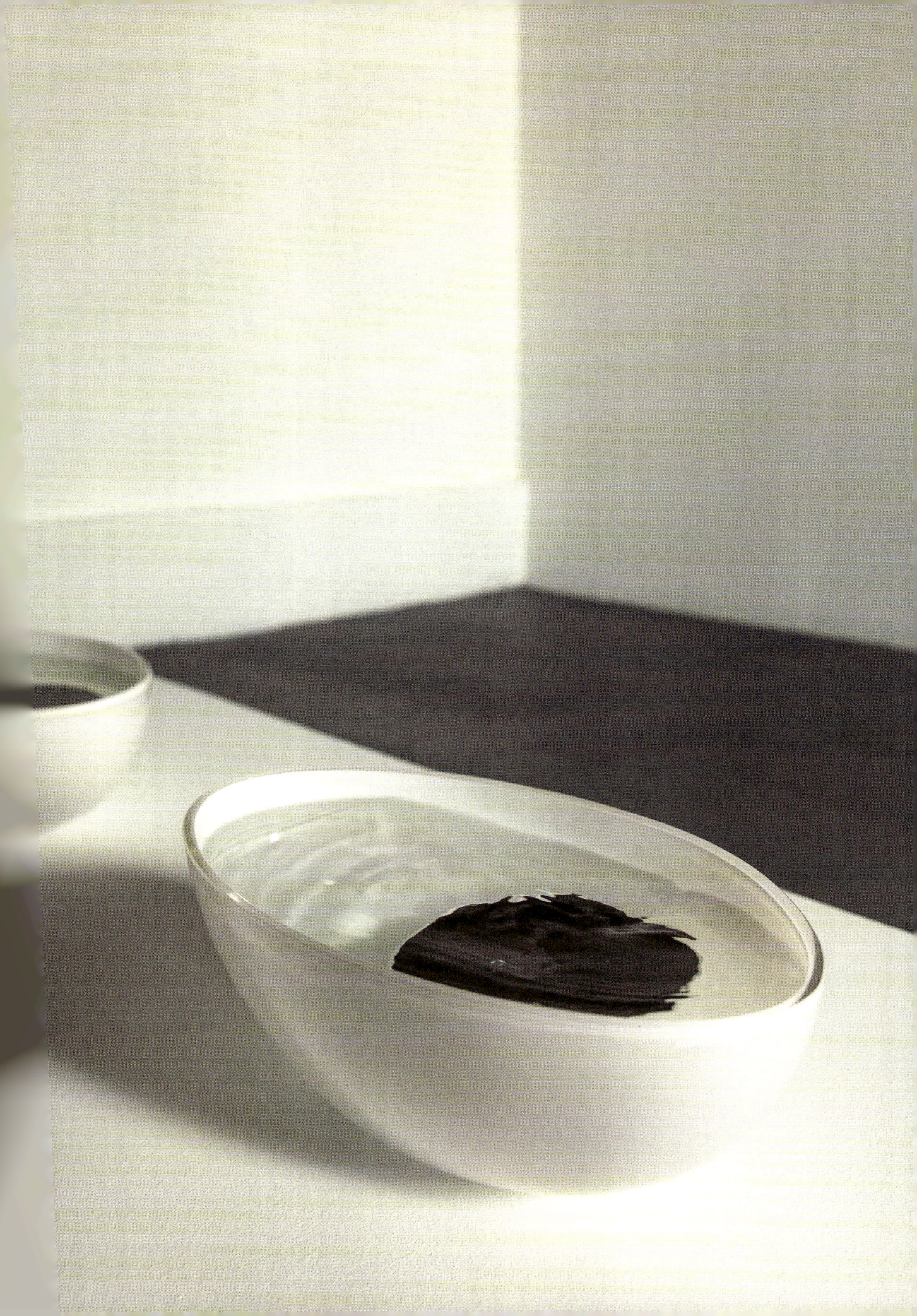

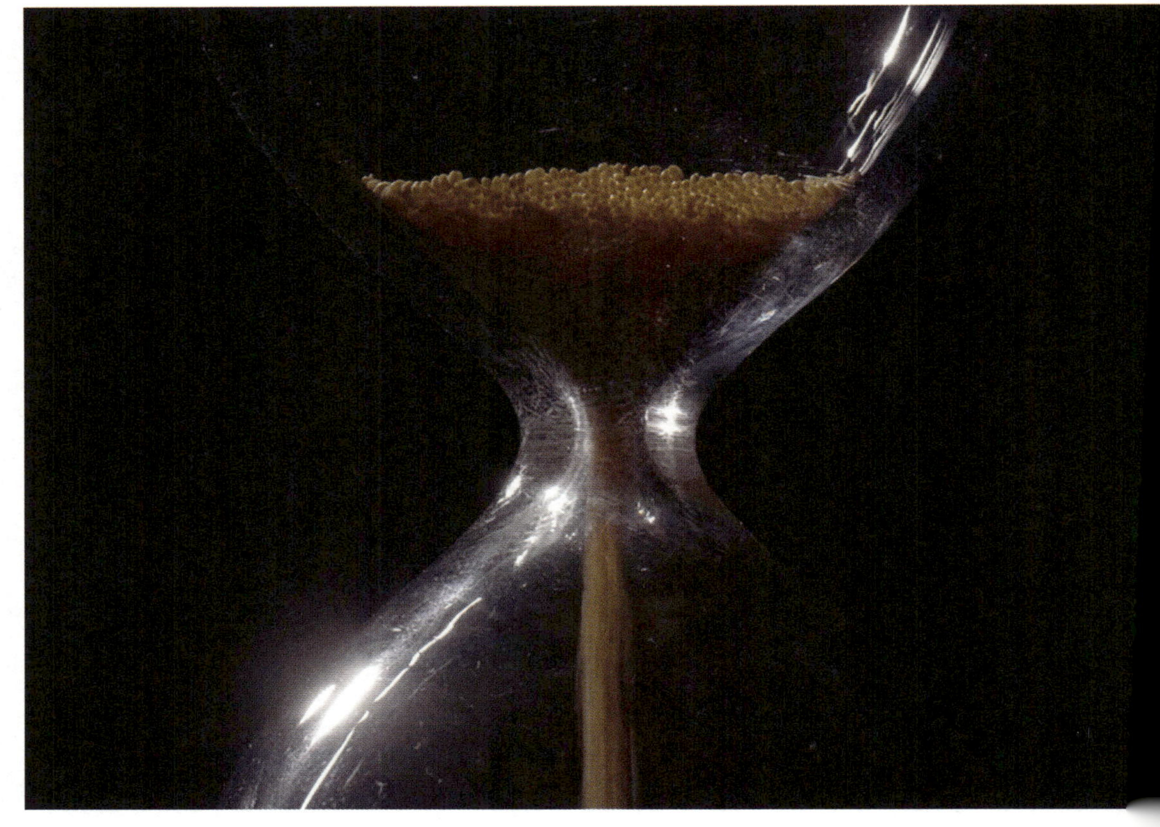

fig. 8-8
Still from *Now*, 2015-2017,
single channel video, 60 minute
loop. Courtesy of the artist and
Leslie Heller Gallery.

Now continues Woolard's interest in time-keeping devices. Rather than understanding time as neatly divisible, linear, and disciplinary—the project of modernization—this artwork begins with the premise that contemplative visual art practices can offer an experience of time which is specifically marked by our social engagement with one another.

The single-channel video was made possible by Jeff Sterrenberg, director of photography and editor, and Meerkat Media. Meerkat is a production company cooperative and arts collective committed to making films through a non-hierarchical collaborative process.

Carried on
Both Sides

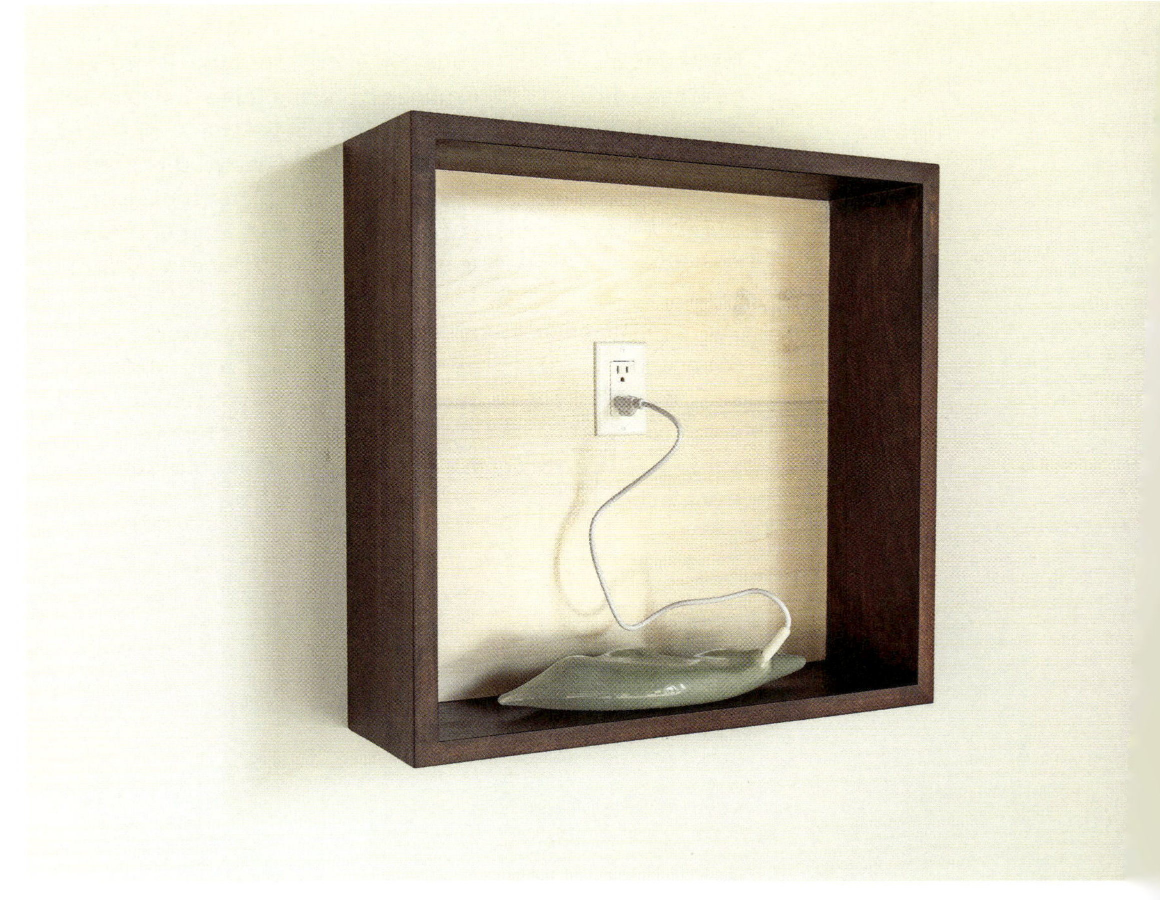

fig. 8-9
TA73060918 (TANTALUS), 2018,
blown glass, outlet, plug, oil
painted poplar, hardware, 24 $^1/_2$
× 24 $^1/_2$ × 7 $^1/_2$ inches each
(set of two).

A glass form sags as it connects to an electrical box in Caroline Woolard's *TA73060918* (2018). The sculpture points at viewers' attachments to devices that must always be charging; Woolard provides outlets which induce desire but which cannot hold a charge. The title, Ta, refers to the periodic table symbol for tantalum. An element distinguished by its exceptional anti-corrosive and conductive capacity, tantalum's presence becomes more common every day; it is crucial in the production of ever-smaller, ever more durable electronic devices, from cell phones to laptops to all varieties of consumer and industrial electronics. Tantalum makes possible our lives of power, portability, and networked sociality. The element's name derives from Tantalus, the Greek mythological figure who is condemned to stand knee-deep in water for eternity, surrounded by succulent fruits that are just beyond reach.

Woolard provides outlets which induce desire but which cannot hold a charge

This project was supported by a residency at Pilchuck Glass School where Woolard had the privilege of working with gaffers Jason Christian and Daryl Smith, and assistants Emily McBride and Phoebe Stubbs.

*Carried on
Both Sides*

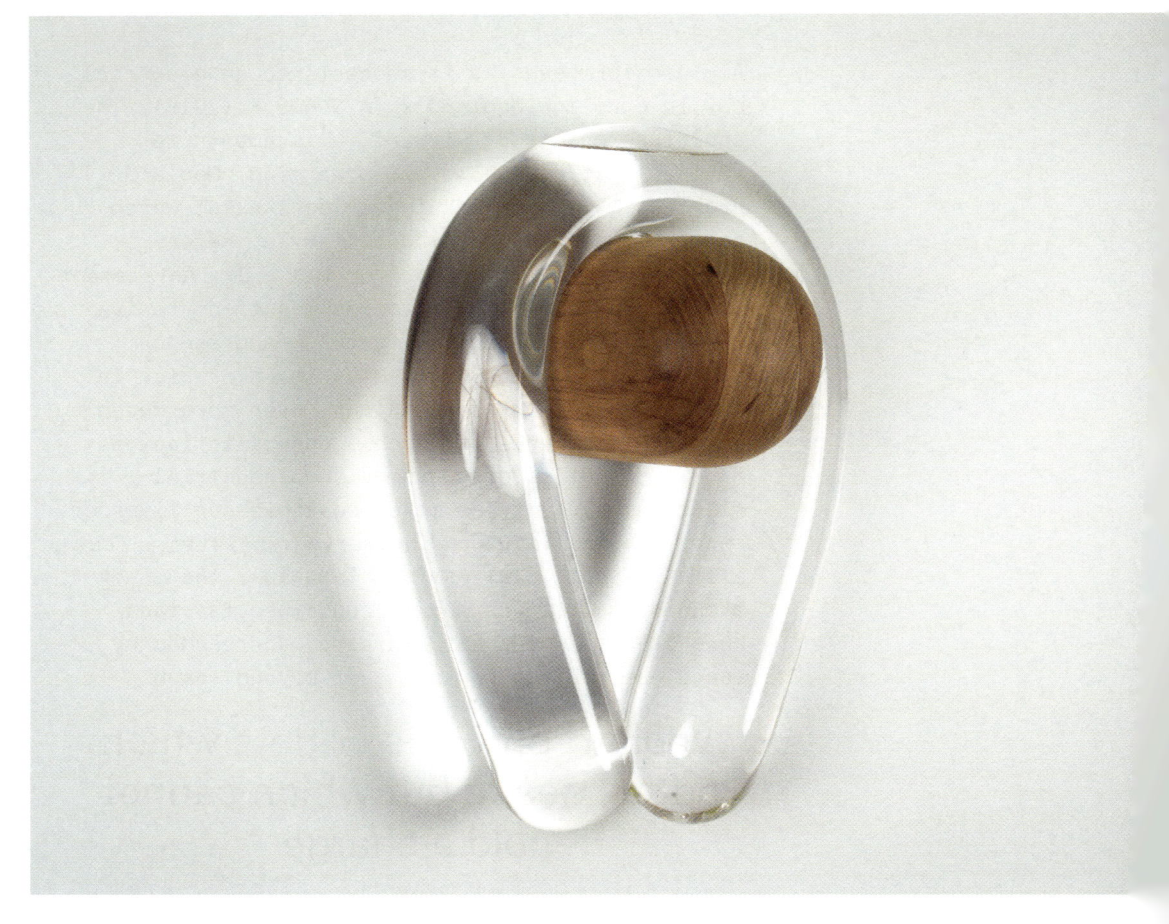

fig. 8-10
Countermeasures: Level, 2018,
blown glass, mineral oil, turned
cherry wood, hardware, 18 × 8 ×
14 inches.

Measures come to us pre-formed and static. This certainty is what allows them to work as measures, of course. But to have a measure then requires that someone is subject to a measure, and in being measured, individuals and groups are denied their own forms of signification. Measurement is always a collective process whose very collectivity is overshadowed by the tool which represents it. These glass objects are countermeasures; they seek to access an immaterial value of the present that originates from nowhere other than the people holding the object. Made of glass and filled with mineral oil, each object may reach a level state through the process of being shared, held, and manipulated. In gatherings facilitated by the artist, visitors are asked to remove these objects from the wall and reach a level with others in the space, whether friends or strangers.

Measurement is always a collective process whose very collectivity is overshadowed by the tool which represents it. These glass objects are counter-measures; they seek to access an immaterial value of the present that originates from nowhere other than the people holding the object.

This project was supported by a residency at Pilchuck Glass School where Woolard had the privilege of working with gaffers Jason Christian and Daryl Smith, assistants Emily McBride and Phoebe Stubbs, and coldworker Celeste Wilson.

*Carried on
Both Sides*

Ephemera

In the pages that follow, you will find the correspondence, budgets, readings, and research documents made in the process of developing *Carried on Both Sides* with Helen Lee, Alexander Rosenberg, and Lika Volkova. Enormous glass levels are pulled by gravity over wooden knobs. A deflated object is plugged into a box the size of a ceiling tile, always charging. An hourglass never runs out of time.

Enormous glass levels are pulled by gravity over wooden knobs. A deflated object is plugged into a box the size of a ceiling tile, always charging. An hourglass never runs out of time.

Water clocks (also called clepsydrae) work like this: one large vessel is made, and filled with water. On the water's surface, a smaller vessel is placed. The smaller vessel is made with a small hole at the bottom that allows the water to flow in. One interval has passed when the bowl sinks to the bottom of the larger bowl. The top of the Column features a "blow mold," a wooden form which is used by glassblowers to replicate forms quickly and are never shown with the final work in glass. Here, the mold has been carved on the outside as well as the inside, becoming a sculpture that reflects its own conditions of production. Alexander Rosenberg and Helen Lee used the mold to create the glass amphora on view in the installation.

The glass edition of *Countermeasures: Water Clock* was made possible by a residency at Pilchuck with gaffers Jason Christian and Daryl Smith and assistants Emily McBride and Phoebe Stubbs, and the *Column* was made in collaboration with Helen Lee and Alexander Rosenberg, with support from John Hallett, who carved the blow mold.

Woolard has selected ephemera that serves as visual reference points for *Carried on Both Sides*. All materials here are reproduced with the consent of collaborators.

fig. 8-11
Technical drawings for
Countermeasures: Water Clock.

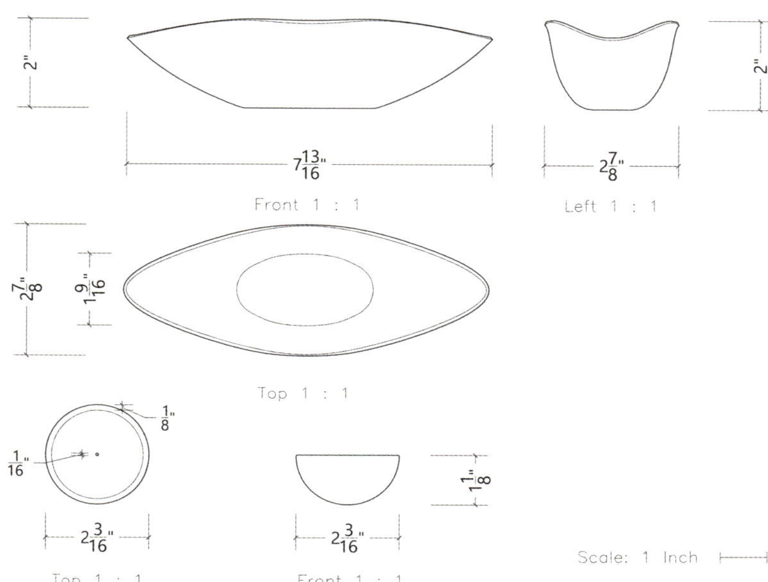

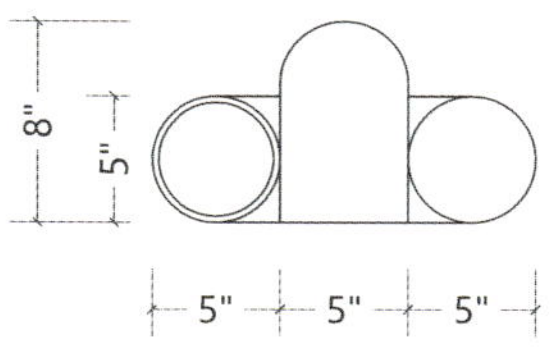

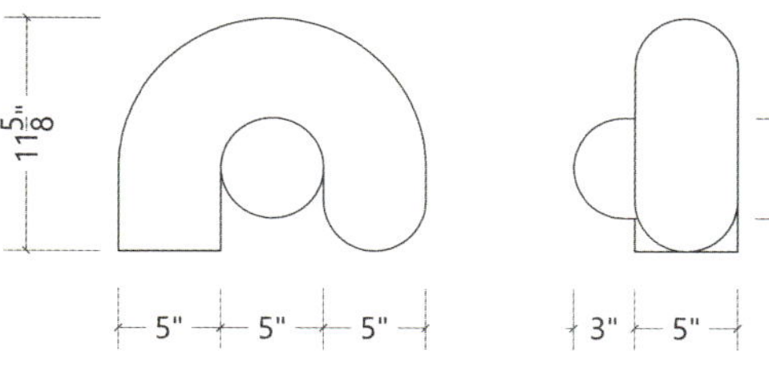

Making

While I loved being able to work with expert craftspeople and artists to fabricate my designs for *Capitoline Wolves* ^{see chapter 7}, I did not like being so distant from the process of making and thinking. While I made rough prototypes with cardboard to scale, and spent hundreds of hours doing small material tests, I missed the making, as the process itself often influences the final project; thinking happens while making. This brings up a real issue with conceptual art that is not based in one material practice. If conceptual, project-based, and research-based artists believe that form and material follow concept, but do not know enough about a given material to understand what forms it might make, how can these artists determine that the material is truly appropriate for any given concept without spending months learning about that material? I wanted to return to a thinking-making practice, and *Carried on Both Sides* allowed this to happen.

If conceptual, project-based, and research-based artists believe that form and material follow concept, but do not know enough about a given material to understand what forms it might make, how can these artists determine that the material is truly appropriate for any given concept without spending months learning about that material?

I made the following rules for myself, when thinking about the form and process in 2015:

Collectively-
Initiated

Where does form come from?
- I go through the following process: I define
  the qualities of the work I want to make. I
  figure out what steps I need to get there,
  and then list which things are supporting me
  and what is blocking me. I then make a list of
  things to do, a schedule, and get started.

Right now the work I want to make:
- is tactile and can be appreciated for its craft
- is well researched/conceptualized
- is the lovechild of Tenorobu Fujimori, Peter
  Ivy, Etienne Boulanger, Bas Jan Ader, and
  Serverine Hubbard
- is something I would want to live with in our
  house (if possible, my partner Leigh Claire La
  Berge likes it)
- is something I could imagine my friends wanting
  as a gift
- is something I could imagine people I know
  using/enjoying in meetings see chapter 1

To get to that place it would be good if I could:
- spend time in the hot shop blowing glass, if
  that is somehow possible
- apprentice with a yakisugi teacher and woodworker
- continue to read about amphorae, reach out to
  amphorae scholars
- look at more work that I love

The things supporting me in the above are:
- a residency in Santa Ana with a storefront at
  Grand Center Arts Center
- time away from work, a new job that supports
  work from afar at CoLab.coop
- relaxation and support from Leigh Claire

The things blocking me from doing the above are:
- my impatience and self-judgement
- finding a method to "just go" or "just start"
- fear of sitting with myself and needing recog-
  nition/immediate feedback from collaborators

*Carried on
Both Sides*

In early 2015, I was invited to be a Visiting Artist at the University of Wisconsin at Madison by Helen Lee, an artist whom I met when I was taking classes at Rhode Island School of Design in 2004 as an exchange student from Cooper Union during my BFA. Helen was now the head of the Glass Lab at UW-Madison, and had been following my work since then. I loved the collaborative, physical, and alchemical properties of glass in 2004, and fell right back in love with the material. I asked Helen Lee, if I apply for a residency to work together, and we get it, will you come? She said yes. Helen is an incredible artist, both conceptually and technically, a generous host, and a clear project manager, so I knew she would be amazing to work with. I also asked Alex Rosenberg, another artist who I met in Glass at RISD in 2004, the same question, and he said yes. I was ready to go.

I wrote the following application in 2015:

Study

When we were students, Caroline and Alexandra Ben-Abba and I were working together in the hot shop. The two of them kept imagining geometries of glass, and I would respond by offering a variety of ways one might approach those geometries on the glassblower's bench. I remember Caroline calling me "a walking Rolodex of glass techniques." It was a dialog between imagination, material, and embodied knowledge that I think still resonates with Caroline's practice. For me, it's very gratifying to see material add value to a given practice, and to play the glass-whisperer role in connecting people's thoughts to glass. Glass occupies a very dominant role in my practice. But in Caroline's practice, it's fulfilling for me to see glass situated within a range of materials that structure spaces and objects — and by extension, the people within those spaces, the people who use those objects, and the systems of exchange that are so pivotal to Caroline's practice.

-Helen Lee, 2019

Collectively-
Initiated

October 28, 2015

PROPOSAL
At Pilchuck, Helen Lee, Alexander Rosenberg, and Caroline Woolard will work together to develop a project tentatively called "@ : Carried on Both Sides." This collaborative group will cast replicas of Roman amphorae and etch a lecture about language and glass on oversized glass slides, to be presented at the Met (where a large collection of amphorae are housed) in New York City, in 2017.

COLLABORATION
I approached Helen Lee, who "uses glass to think about language" and Alexander Rosenberg, who concerns himself with systems of display and all things on the edge of breaking, about a collaboration at Pilchuck. I want to work with them because they are interdisciplinary artists who use the medium of glass with conceptual agility and material poetry. Although I have only worked in glass once, and only for six months (at Pilchuck and RISD with Lee and Rosenberg), I know that my socially engaged, performance-based work will benefit from an exploration of language and display in in the Mold and Kiln shop and Cold Shop.

TECHNICAL ABILITY
We will be using the Mold and Kiln shop and Cold Shop primarily, but would like to access the Print Shop and Wood and Metals Shop as well. Both Lee and Rosenberg are faculty members in Glass Departments (University of Madison at Wisconsin and University of the Arts) who teach students to work with glass on a daily basis. Helen Lee has been blowing class consistently since 1998, is experienced with the Pilchuck printing press, as well as photosensitive sandblast resists. She has basic cold working, mold, kiln, and casting skills. Alexander Rosenberg is an experienced flame worker and mold maker for glass casting. Caroline Woolard has limited experience with flame working and cold working, but will be writing and documenting the process as the collaboration develops.

PROJECT BACKGROUND
I would love a space to work on a project tentatively called "Carried on Both Sides." This year marks the 45th anniversary of the use of the @ symbol online, but at least the 480th anniversary of its use in mercantile accounting, and the 3000th anniversary of the standardization of the shape to which merchants initially referred. I will make an installation and performance that engages this history of transmutation, from shape to accounting to preposition. The installation space will be made with yakisugi wood, optical lenses, and blown glass, using staining and burning

*Carried on
Both Sides*

techniques that I am developing now. The performance will be done using oversized glass slides while wearing kevlar costumes that I am developing with Lika Volkova. Amphorae has been translated to mean "carried on both sides." This two-handled shape connected producers to consumers throughout the Roman Empire; the @ which shares the amphora's philology links correspondents today. *Carried on Both Sides* is both a series of objects and a performance lecture on handmade, oversized glass slides that follows this legacy of exchange at intimate distance.

Before the @ symbol was used for the first email in 1971, the @ found its way to keyboards in the 20th century for accounting purposes. Before that, the @ sign was shorthand, in mercantile script, for "amphora." An amphora was a common, two handled vessel used to transport grain and liquid, both a shape and a measure of mass in the ancient Mediterranean world. Transport amphorae were ubiquitous and thrown away after a single use. As Michael Ezban has written, "at the height of the Empire, an impressive 18,000 metric tons of olive oil, along with 8,000 metric tons of clay amphorae, were imported annually from Hispania to Rome … each year over 280,000 amphorae were smashed and deposited in a series of raised terraces that became Monte Testaccio." This amphorae-only landfill, this hollow hill of terracotta records known as Monte Testaccio, is 115 feet tall today.

We may etch words related to: odometers for email, digital shipwrecks, resting places for @s, repurposed data centers, email auto-responders for digital rest, images visible exclusively at dawn and dusk, or the history of the word talent.

Timeframe

Inquiry

Collectively-
Initiated

Managing

To prepare for Pilchuck, we started coordinating times when we could work together, so that the residency could lead to deeper work together. Alex is based in Philadelphia, Helen in Madison, Wisconsin, and Lika and I in New York City. Here is the schedule that I drafted, and that Helen added to. Alex and Lika were less responsive and I needed to call them to fill out the schedule for them.

```
ROUGH 2015 SCHEDULE
column research/amphora/lens research/
tech drawing by—feb 20

Sat the 13th—Alex in NYC (Sunday is good too)

March 10-13—I'm in Philly

April 27-May 13—Pilchuck

June 2nd-8th—we work together in NYC? 4/5/6/7
8-11, 11-12, 12-3 (end by 5)

late August, early Sept—Madison?(before Sept 9)
```

When we got together in person, we had a huge brainstorm session, to think about how our individual interests, skills, and readings could support our collective research and a group show about one topic. I wrote it down in a shared, digital document.

*Carried on
Both Sides*

WHAT IS THE FUTURE OF THE @ SYMBOL?
The amphora has followed the following transmutation: from quantity
(vessel of terracotta) to accounting
(@mphora in ink script) to identity (@ in vector graphic) ????? to
memory/sleep (in X) ??????

By Viewing format
    Web/Installation/Presentation

By relationship to the @
    Historical/Present
    Speculative/Future

By Collaborator
    Collective US/Alex/Caroline
    Helen/Lika

CW: What should we make next?

AR: A VIDEO of HAND LAPPING showing an
amphora, cut in half, and ground
down to a polish with grit on sheet
glass (a process called hand lapping).

HL: 5x5 GLASS FONT which materializes the experience of reading
vector graphics through pixels on
a screen.

CW: 1. GLASS AMPHORAE at 1:3 scale
of the historic Dressel 20 from the
Roman empire.

2. A BLOW MOLD which is also a sculpture; in this case, the blow mold is
also a section of a Roman column.

3. A VIDEO of HAND LAPPING showing
an amphora, cut in half, and ground
down to a polish with grit on sheet
glass (a process called hand lapping). The grinding process itself
turns the glass opaque, hiding the
amphora until the grit is fine enough
and it comes back to a polish. The
sound of this action becomes the
audio for another video project.

4. A PRINT of HAND LAPPING showing
the image that is created after an
amphora, cut in half, and ground down
to a polish with grit on sheet glass
(a process called hand lapping).

5. COINS with the @ on one side and
an amphora (the Dressel 20 amphora)

Collectively-
Initiated

on the other side. One coin is a circle. One coin is a square shape that functions as a slide for a slide projector.

6. A PRINT of COINS with the @ on one side and an amphora (the Dressel 20 amphora) on the other side, blind embossed into paper.

7. 5×5 GLASS FONT which materializes the experience of reading vector graphics through pixels on a screen.

8. A series of prints that illustrate the words used for the @ symbol in a variety of languages.

9. A sculptural garment for glassblowers, made of kevlar.

10. Clothing for sleep.

11. A clothing hanger which is a level.

12. A video of glass amphorae on the beach at night, with a full moon, and waves gently rolling over them.

13. A neon @ symbol inside an amphora, at the actual size of the Roman vessel used for transport.

14. A blob of glass hangs on a laptop, magnifying the screen.

15. A website is made with a font that is 5 pixels by 5 pixels. Glass

must be used to magnify the screen.

16. The @ symbol unrolls to become a sleeping person like o___ . This mimics the process Helen Lee uses to make the @ handles of the amphorae in hot glass.

17. A sleep app which incorporates all of the objects and proposals here, to lull people to sleep.

18. The amphorae are shown in a glass tank filled with water and sand. One side of the tank can be frosted to display a video projection.

19. A shipping crate which doubles as an exhibition display case. The case holds: glass slides for slide projection during lectures, a blow mold for workshops, and an amphora that results from the blow mold.

20. A newspaper which lists all projects that could have happened. This becomes the folded, wet newspaper used by glassblowers to shape hot glass.

21. A lecture using a slide projector and glass slides. The glass slides move through the spectrum of visible light, as the slides themselves are colored glass or create prisms.

22. A sleep hotline that you can call.

*Carried on
Both Sides*

23. An amphora on a bedside table is a speaker for a recording that lulls you to sleep. Perhaps it is linked to the sleep hotline.

24. A wall text where the periods in each sentence are physical spheres/magnets on the wall. One period is added to the wall to coincide with the sinking of one bowl into another in a large water-clock (clepsydra), like Caroline Woolard's water clocks and Helen Lee's glass periods on the floor and Helen's project *I miss the little ding at the end of the line.*

25. An audio recording of clicks on a computer or phone, similar to Helen Lee's project of finger-prints tapping.

26. The pupil of each person in the portrait is a square. Audio from tapping.

27. A recording of the amount of the distance an email travels, made in collaboration with Jonah Brucker-Cohen.

28. A video of yawns, and a per-formance that encourages yawning. Caroline has always wanted to do this project.

29. The installation when seen in plan view is the @ in the pixel font.

30. The sound in the space is amphoric, made by blowing over the mouth of a glass amphora.

Inquiry

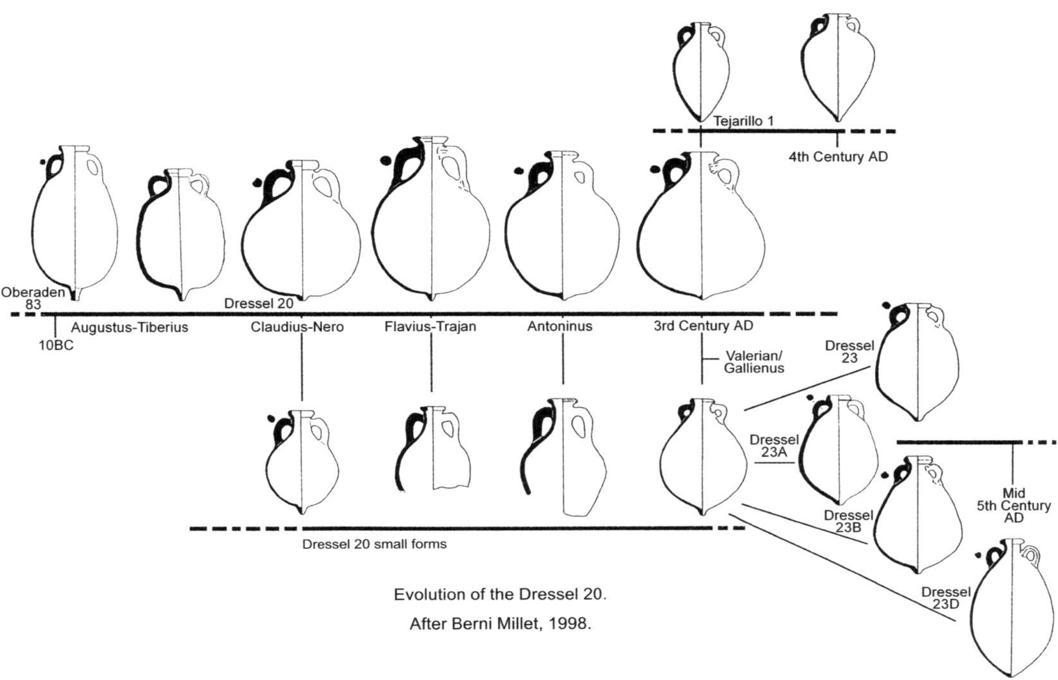

Evolution of the Dressel 20.
After Berni Millet, 1998.

fig. 8-12
Diagram showing the evolution
of the Oberaden 83, Dressel
20 and 23 forms. After Berni
Millet, 1998.

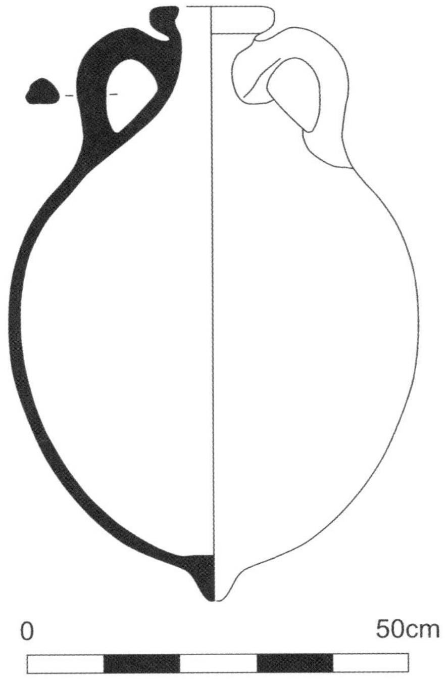

fig. 8-13
Roman Amphorae, Dressel 20 D
rawing at 1:10 scale, after
panella, 1973 Penny Copeland.

Carried on
Both Sides

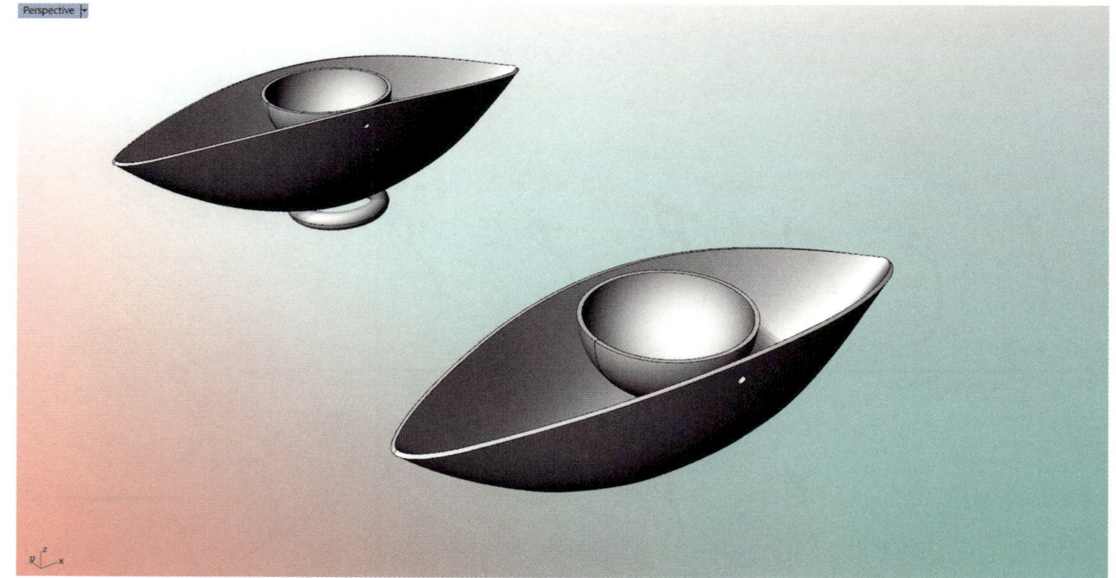

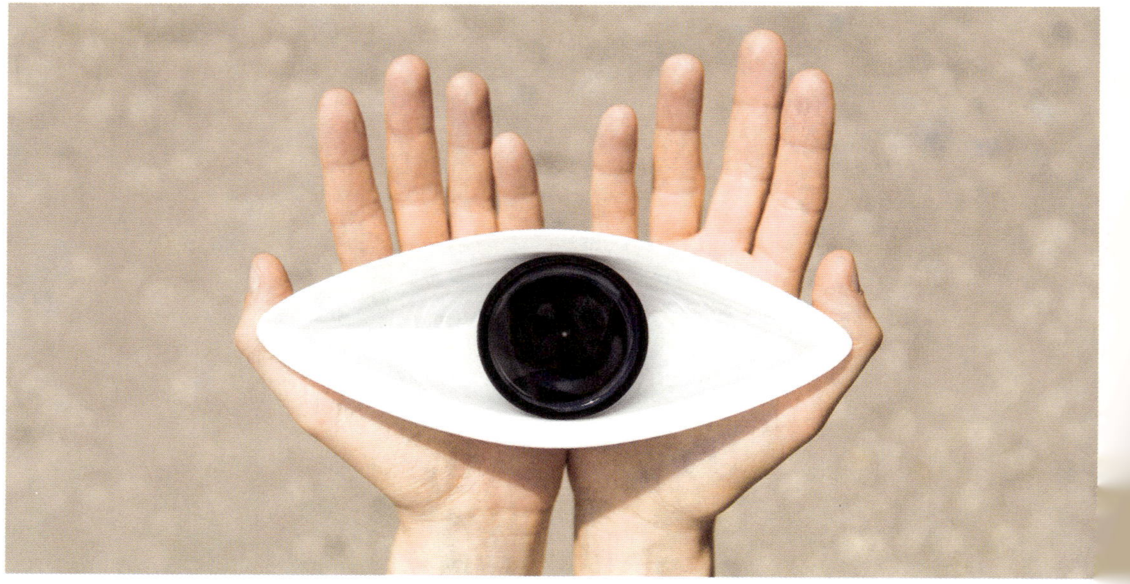

fig. 8-14
Rendering for the smaller,
affordable, 3D printed ceramic
version of *Countermeasures:
Water Clock*, 2018.

fig. 8-15
Countermeasures: Water Clock,
2018, 3D-printed porcelain and
water, 8 × 2 × 2 inches. Photo
by Levi Mandel.

Later on, we talked about the projects we liked the most, and could actually get done, and figured out who was doing what using a spreadsheet.

TITLE	DESCRIPTION	BY VIEWING FORMAT	BY COLLABORATOR	MONTHS TO COMPLETION
GLASS AMPHORA	GLASS AMPHORAE at 1:3 scale of the historic Dressel 20 from the Roman empire.	installation	collective	0
HAND LAPPING PRINT	A PRINT of HAND LAPPING showing the image that is created after an amphora, cut in half, and ground down to a polish with grit on sheet glass (a process called hand lapping).	installation	Alex	0
COINS / CURRENCY PRINT	A PRINT of COINS with the @ on one side and an amphora (the Dressel 20 amphora) on the other side, blind embossed into paper.	installation	Caroline	0
5×5 GLASS FONT	5×5 GLASS FONT which materializes the experience of reading vector graphics through pixels on a screen.	installation	Helen	0
MONKEY TAIL PRINTS	A series of prints that illustrate the words used for the @ symbol in a variety of languages.	installation	Helen	0
BLOW MOLD	A BLOW MOLD which is also a sculpture; in this case, the blow mould is also a section of a Roman column.	installation / presentation	John Hallett	0
CLOTHING FOR GLASS	A sculptural garment for glassblowers, made of kevlar.	installation / web	Lika	0
@ WATER PHOTO				0
HAND LAPPING VIDEO	A VIDEO of HAND LAPPING showing an amphora, cut in half, and ground down to a polish with grit on sheet glass (a process called hand lapping). The grinding process itself turns the glass opaque, hiding the amphora until the grit is fine enough and it comes back to a polish. The sound of this action becomes the audio for another video project.	installation	Alex	1
COINS / CURRENCY	COINS with the @ on one side and an amphora (the Dressel 20 amphora) on the other side. One coin is a circle. One coin is a square shape that functions as a slide for a slide projector.	installation	Collective	1
CLOTHING HANGER	A clothing hanger which is a level.	installation	Alex	1
AMPHORA @ NEON	A neon @ symbol inside an amphora, at the actual size of the Roman vessel used for transport.	installation	Alex	1
AMPHORA ON BEACH VIDEO	A video of glass amphorae on the beach at night, with a full moon, and waves gently rolling over them.	installation / web	Collective / Caroline?	1
EMAIL ODOMETER	A recording of the amount of the distance an email travels, made in collaboration with Jonah Brucker-Cohen.	installation / web	Collective?	1
WEBSITE	A website is made with a font that is 5 pixels by 5 pixels. Glass must be used to magnify the screen.	web	??	1
BLOB	A blob of glass hangs on a laptop, magnifying the screen.	installation	Collective	1.5

Carried on Both Sides

Commitment

AQUARIUM	The amphorae are shown in a glass tank filled with water and sand. One side of the tank can be frosted to display a video projection.	installation	Caroline	2
WALL TEXT	A wall text where the periods in each sentence are physical spheres / magnets on the wall. One period is added to the wall to coincide with the sinking of one bowl into another in a large water-clock (clepsydra), like Caroline Woolard's water clocks and Helen Lee's glass periods on the floor and Helen's project *I miss the little ding at the end of the line.*	installation	Helen?	2
NEWSPAPER	A newspaper which lists all projects that could have happened. This becomes the folded, wet newspaper used by glassblowers to shape hot glass.	installation / presentation	Collective	2
@ ANIMATED TO UNFURL	The @ symbol unrolls to become a sleeping person like o__ . This mimics the process Helen Lee uses to make the @ handles of the amphorae in hot glass.	web	??	2
CLOTHING FOR SLEEP	Clothing for sleep.	installation / web	Lika	2.5
HOTLINE	A sleep hotline that you can call.	installation / web	??	2.5
BEDSIDE AMPHORA	An amphora on a bedside table is a speaker for a recording that lulls you to sleep. Perhaps it is lined to the sleep hotline. (18)	installation / web	??	2.5
YAWNS	A video of yawns, and a performance that encourages. Caroline has always wanted to do this project.	installation / web	Caroline	3
SLEEP APP	A sleep app which incorporates all of the objects and proposals here, to lull people to sleep.	web	??	3
CLICKS	An audio recording of clicks on a computer or phone, similar to Helen Lee's project of fingerprints tapping.	installation	Helen	3.5
PUPILS	The pupil of each person in the portrait is a square. Audio from tapping.	installation	Helen	3.5
SHIPPING CRATE DISPLAY CASE	A shipping crate which doubles as an exhibition display case. The case holds: glass slides for slide projection during lectures, a blow mould for workshops, and an amphora that results from the blow mould.	installation	Alex	4
LECTURE / SLIDES	A lecture using a slide projector and glass slides. The glass slides move through the spectrum of visible light, as the slides themselves are colored glass or create prisms.	installation / presentation	Collective	4

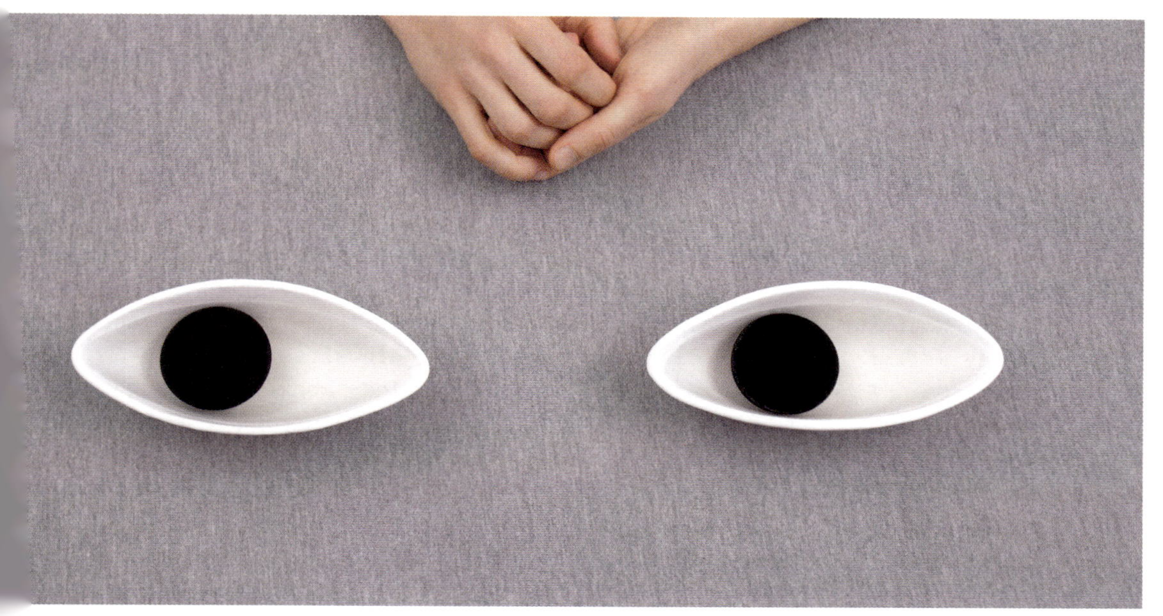

From there, I wrote about our process, to thank Pilchuck for supporting us, and to prepare to create a proposal for exhibitions in New York:

fig. 8-16
he smaller, affordable, 3D
rinted ceramic version of
ountermeasures: *Water* Clock,
018. Image by Herman Jean-Noel.

We, like most research-based artists, believe that artwork tells us more about the time period when it was made than about the author of the artwork. Another way to say this is to ask, "What forms are available to any artist, and where did they come from?" We were interested in the technologies, materials, and cultural conditions that allow individual expression to occur and then be displayed and understood as art. As Marshall McLuhan said, we believe that "the medium is the message." We did this research to understand the histories of the forms, materials, and art contexts that we are drawn to, and to understand how our project will be received by non-artists at this moment in time. The Hauberg Fellowship at Pilchuck allowed us to explore glass as the material through which all digital communication occurs.

We wanted to link everyday experiences with glass screens on smartphones to the history and future of studio glass, so we started looking for connections between the medium and the message, between glass and email. We started reading. I found an article about the history of the @ symbol, made popular in MoMA's acquisition of the mark, and realized that this year marks the 45th anniversary of the use of the @ [at] symbol in email, but at least the 480th anniversary of its use in mercantile accounting, and the 3000th anniversary of the standardization of the shape to which merchants initially referred. Doing more reading about the shape, I read that amphora is translated to mean "carried on both sides." We read that @ is called "monkey tail" and "snail shell" and "ear" and much more descriptive things than the "commercial at" in other languages. We studied the amphorae classification systems used by archaeologists, and made a blow mold of the Dressel 20, a standard shape used to transport olive oil during the Roman Empire. Amphorae were as common as the @ symbol is today, used in such quantity for transporting goods that one landfill in Rome is made entirely of amphorae. We decided to make a blow mold of the Dressel 20, to make murini that mimic the pixels of a computer screen, and to make an object that hangs over a computer screen, among other things. It is our hope that our research will be felt materially, so that people who see our work have a sense that they have seen these forms before (likely in a museum of natural history and on their smartphones), but suddenly we have made these conventional experiences strange enough to notice and question. We are still exploring the final presentation of the project, but we know that *Carried on Both Sides* will reference or take place on sites important to the history of the meaning of the @ symbol: (1) a twitter account, (2) a mercantile script with flourishing a's from 1536, and (3) glass school demonstrations with blow molds of the Dressel 20.

We wanted to link everyday experiences with glass screens on smartphones to the history and future of studio glass, so we started looking for connections between the medium and the message, between glass and email.

Without the Residency at Pilchuck, our project simply would not have happened. We live in different places and are very busy, so we would not have been able to spend the time together that is necessary for a trusting and experimental collaboration. The Residency includes 24/7 access to studios, kilns, a cold shop, and a print shop, all staffed by incredibly generous and skilled technicians. During this time, Helen Lee was able to cut sheet glass and to fuse it to make every letter of the alphabet for murini that will mimic a computer screen, and to print a series of lithographs based on the word for @ in other languages. Alexander Rosenberg was able to make a video that reveals the iconic shape of the amphorae while hand lapping glass, and to cast silver coins that I designed. I was able to make 16 sheets of fused glass which will be used in frames of images from the history of the @ symbol, and to make blind embossed prints of the coins Alex made.

I fell in love with the collaboration, and wanted to find institutional invitations to honor our work. After Pilchuck, I applied to many residencies and exhibitions for us, with the help of Alex and Helen, who sent images, image lists, and edits to my writing. Helen and I went back and forth to refine the writing, and she made floor plans and helped with the administrative work. We were given a short residency at UrbanGlass. This unusual residency came about because our application was not successful, but we got an email back from the Director asking if we would be interested in some kind of short usage of their facilities.

> Subject: UrbanGlass residency
> January 15, 2016
> Hi Helen, Caroline, Alex, and Lika,
>
> Hello from UrbanGlass! Thank you so very much for submitting an application to our recent residency call. A jury comprised of artist Jessica Julius and Shannon Stratton, Chief Curator, Museum of Arts and Design, sat down and evaluated proposals and unfortunately did not select yours for the program.
>
> That said, they felt it was a very strong proposal and suggested that we find out if there is a way that UrbanGlass might support the work in some other way. So I am writing to investigate!
>
> A few questions: do you have a sense of what amount of time in the hot shop would be most helpful? Are you interested in a specific quality of glass (our student furnace uses cullet). And finally, do you have dates in mind?
>
> Thanks again for your interest in this. Looking forward to seeing what might be possible!
>
> All the best,
> Cybele

Cybele Maylone
Executive Director
UrbanGlass
647 Fulton Street
Brooklyn, NY 11217

I did my best to find a gallery for us to show the project. I asked lots of people if they knew of spaces, and I asked my friend Maya Valladares if she would be open to organizing an event with us at the Met, where she worked as an Assistant Educator of Public Programs. Here is what I wrote to her:

Subject: bold question
February 14, 2017
Maya,

I hope this message finds you in a space of revolutionary love. Have you watched https://www.youtube.com/watch?v=LCenwgheIBs&app=desktop? Please do, it's my daily vitamins these days.

I'm writing because I have continued to make the amphora/@ project that I wrote to you about two years ago, and it will be featured in a documentary by PBS/Art21 for New York Close Up this summer. More info is here: http://carolinewoolard.com/project/carried-both-sides/ and a video in progress is here: https://www.youtube.com/watch?v=JQ7m2mXI_60

I would love to do a public workshop/lecture/event at the Met, but I have no idea how or if I could ever propose this to you or someone at the Met. Is there any chance for this? I know this is a bold request, but you have said such nice things about me on FB that I thought I would be bold and ask if you can help me figure out how to approach the Met.

Wondering what the process is,
Caroline

Maya wrote back:

> Caroline you may always ask any question. I
> think the best fit for this may be artists on
> artworks, and I wonder if March might be the
> right month; there are a few possibilities.
> I'll check with a colleague who currently over-
> sees this program and she or I (using the fancy
> met email address) will circle back to you
> asap. Let me know next week if you don't hear
> anything? Thanks for asking!

The event was planned at The Met for July 28th, 2017. After asking friends about how to meet gallerists, a colleague of mine at the School of Visual Arts, Jim Clark, who I taught with in MFA Fine Arts, introduced me to Lesley Heller. This is what I wrote to her, after he introduced us:

> Re: Introduction
> April 30, 2017
> Thanks so much Jim, and hello Lesley,
>
> I would be honored to meet with you in the
> coming weeks, to talk about this project I'm
> working on, and about my hopes for the ways we
> might work together. Please suggest two days/
> times to meet in person or speak on the phone.
>
> The short story is:
>
> Art21 is making a documentary about a project
> I've been developing with two master glass
> blowers for the last two years, but the venue we
> were going to be in fell through last minute.
>
> I would be so grateful to film an interview
> about the project in your gallery around June
> 6th (the date is somewhat flexible) and to
> discuss the possibility of working with you to
> present the project there in 2017 or 2018, if i
> is a good fit and if your schedule allows.

You can see some information about the project here: http://carolinewoolard.com/project/
carried-both-sides/

I will also give a lecture at The Met about
this project on July 28th, and you can see my
other speaking engagements at http://caroline-
woolard.com/#events

Best wishes,
Caroline

After my first meeting with Lesley, in person, she seemed
interested in having a show with us. This was a huge deal
as Lesley Heller is a for-profit gallery, and we were all used
to working in nonprofit exhibition spaces, including artist-
run spaces and museums. Lesley typically sells work from
every show, and told me directly that our work might be a
bit too conceptual for her collectors, but that she was open
to giving it a try. In May of 2017, she confirmed the show.
It opened in November of 2017, and by that time, we had
been accepted (via an open call application) to a show at the
Knockdown, and I had been invited to do a show at LMAK.
Suddenly, we had more exhibitions than we had ever imagined, and we needed to make more work. We decided to call
each exhibition an "encounter" to link the exhibitions, from
one space to the next, over time.

Managing

Carried on
Both Sides

Carried On
Both Sides:
Encounter III

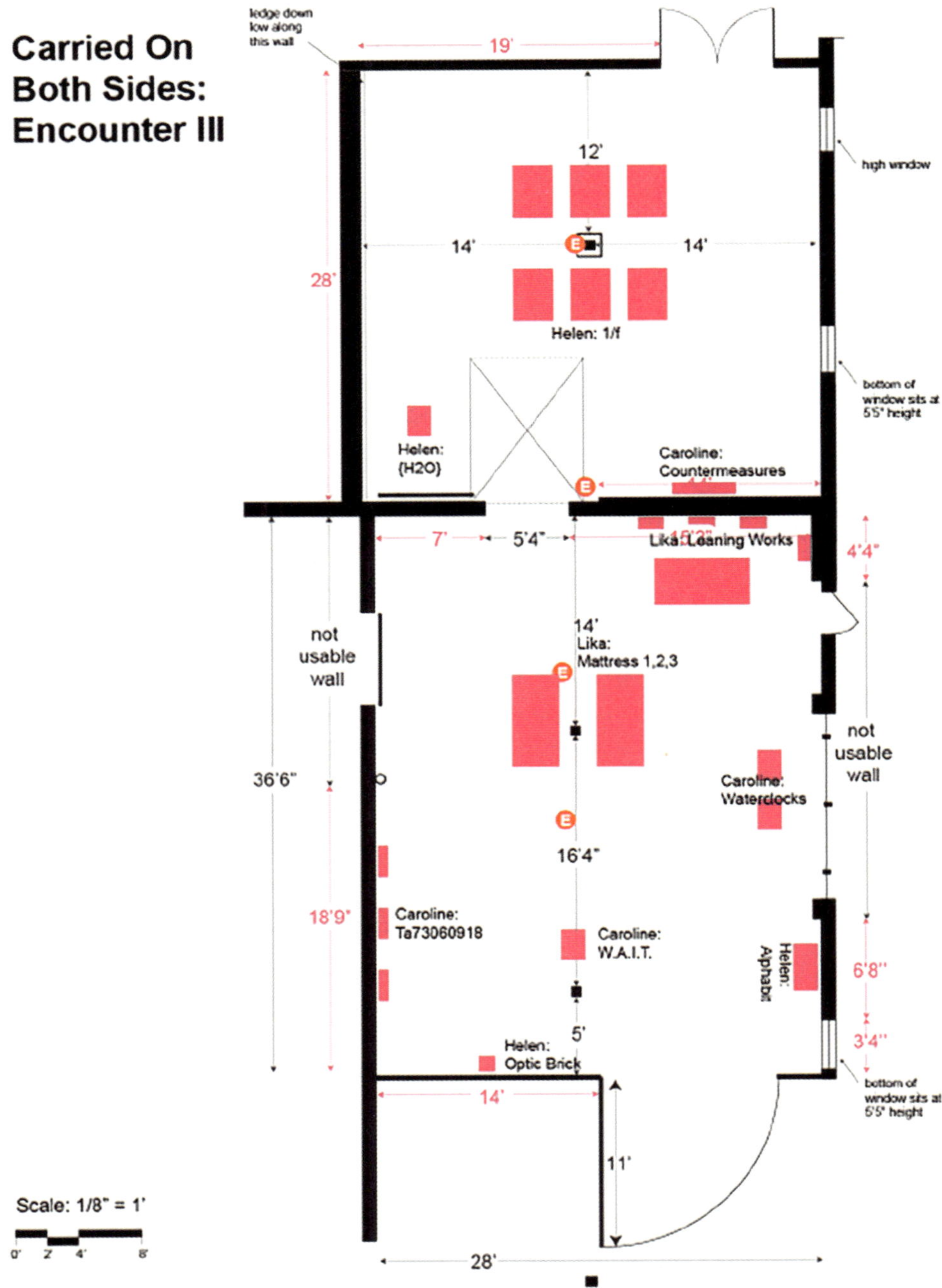

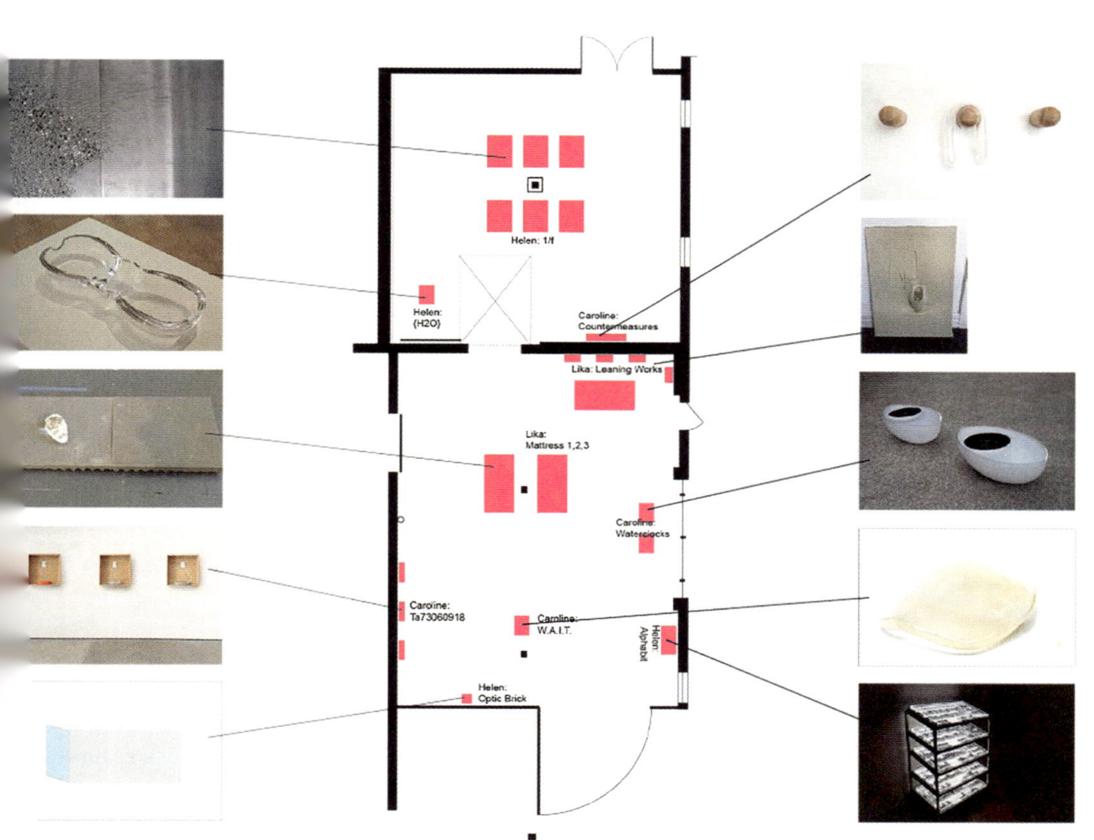

fig. 8-17
Installation floor plan created
by Helen Lee.

*Carried on
Both Sides*

Mediating

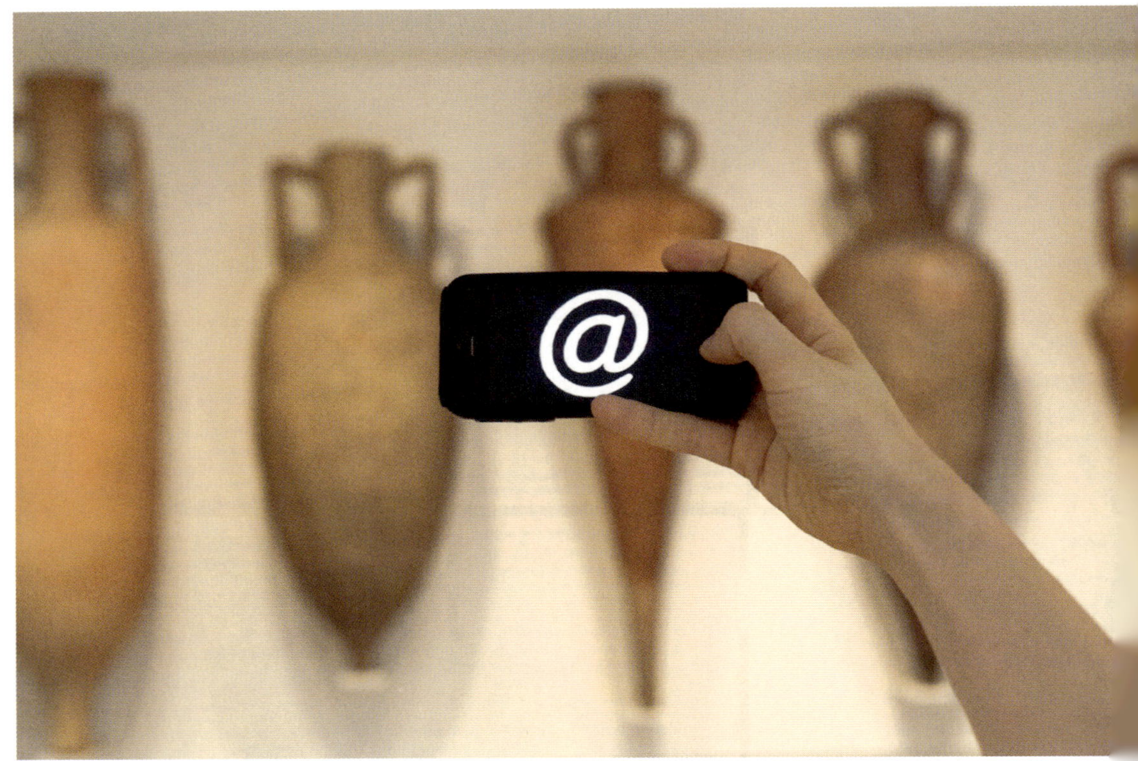

fig. 8-18
Research image for *Carried on Both Sides* created by Caroline Woolard at the Metropolitan Museum of Art for promotional purposes. Photo by Levi Mandel.

I continue to be interested in shaping the way that the public understands projects. Luckily, all of the spaces we worked with were very open to our edits and suggestions for press releases. Here is the version that we all agreed to, and that Helen and I worked on together, with a lot of help from my partner Leigh Claire La Berge, for Lesley Heller:

For Immediate Release:

CARRIED ON BOTH SIDES
Caroline Woolard, Helen Lee,
Alexander Rosenberg, Lika Volkova
November 4-December 16, 2017

Opening Reception:
Saturday, November 4, 6-8 p.m.
Panel Discussion:
Thursday, December 14, 6:30 p.m.

Lesley Heller is pleased to present
Encounter One of *Carried on Both
Sides*, a three-part immersive exhibition and collaboration between
Caroline Woolard, Helen Lee,
Alexander Rosenberg, and Lika
Volkova that uncovers the history
of the @ symbol. The installation
presented at Lesley Heller directs
attention specifically to our contemporary digital world and the
imperial residues that exist in it,
chiefly the ubiquitous @ symbol.

The exhibition stems from an insistence that imperial forms long outlive the empire from which they were
generated. Tributes to this can be
found today on many college campus
and government buildings where the
use of classical columns is abun-
dant. American currency contains
many of these icons; the nation's
symbol—the bald eagle—can likewise
be traced back to the myth of the
founding of Rome. The @ symbol is
derived from what was originally a

graphic representation of a Roman
vessel—the amphora—written with a
flourishing @. Amphorae were primarily used as containers to transport tributes such as olive oil and
grains from the periphery back to
Rome. At the height of Roman power,
so many of these amphorae were sent
to Rome that they were discarded
into a landfill of shards and handles reaching 115 ft high and covering 220,000 sq ft, known today as
Mt. Testaccio.

For *Carried on Both Sides*, the four
artists worked together to collectively investigate the material
history of classical shapes from the
Roman Empire as they have come to
structure our online world and our
current economic environment, which
social theorist Jodi Dean calls
"communicative capitalism." If in
the 19th century, the capitalist
imperative was to "produce," today
it is to "communicate." Online has
now become omnipresent. Using the
legacy of the @ symbol as a provo-
cation, these artists have crafted
new imperial artifacts. The project consists of three exhibitions
over the next year. Each exhibition
will reveal a unique addition to the
project. At Lesley Heller Workspace,
clay amphorae are transmuted into
glass by Alexander Rosenberg; hand
pulled glass murrina by Helen Lee
recall the pixelated imagery of
digital computing; a single-channel

*Carried on
Both Sides*

video by Caroline Woolard records an hourglass which never runs out; kevlar forms by Lika Volkova drape from the walls.

If in the 19th century, the capitalist imperative was to "produce," today it is to "communicate."

Carried on Both Sides is the result of two years of collaborative work between Woolard, Lee, Rosenberg and Volkova and was supported by residencies at Pilchuck Glass School and UrbanGlass.

For more information on this project, see:
http://CarriedOnBothSides.com
Art21 documentary:
https://art21.org/watch/new-york-close-up/caroline-woolards-floating-possibility/

Carried on Both Sides: Encounter One
November 4-December 16, 2017
Lesley Heller Workspace
54 Orchard Street
New York, NY 10002
http://www.lesleyheller.com/exhibitions/20171
104-caroline-woolard-carried-on-both-sides

Carried on Both Sides: Encounter Two
January 19-February 25, 2018
LMAKgallery
298 Grand Street
New York, NY 10002
http://lmakgallery.com/

Carried on Both Sides: Encounter Three
Summer 2018
The Knockdown Center
52-19 Flushing Ave
Maspeth, NY 11378
http://knockdown.center

Collectively-Initiated

Before we heard back about the residency at Pilchuck in 2015, I was already working on mediating the project. I knew that Art21, the PBS documentary film series, was interested in making a second video about my work. I knew that a video of this quality would help us get an exhibition, as galleries like visibility, so I wrote to Art21 to ask about a second documentary, focused on glass, research, and collaboration. Nick Ravich, the Director of Production, who had made the first video with me, wrote back right away.

> Subject: Checking in
> November 8, 2015
> Caroline,
>
> Very nice to hear from you.
>
> Glad to help the cause. Very proud of the work
> we all did on that one. Slowly submitting it
> to festivals now. But I'm guessing your dedi-
> cation and charisma has as much to do with
> protest turnout as the video.
> BM protest is Tues Nov 11 or Wed Nov 12?
>
> And let me know if/when you're up for another
> video. Maybe something not quite as epic as
> the last one, but hopefully effective.
>
> Good luck,
> Nick.
>
> Nick Ravich
> Director of Production, Art21
> 133 West 25th Street, #3E
> New York, NY 10001

My reply:

> November 8, 2015
> Hey!
>
> Wow—festivals? Sounds amazing. Protest is
> Nov 17, but it turns out I have a speaking
> gig that whole day and want the cash, so

```
I'm organizing a bunch but won't be there.
Of course I'm up for another one! I'd love
to do something this winter if possible, or
spring … What's good for you all?

I'm working on a blown glass vessel with
collaborators that I can explain.

Carried on Both Sides
hand blown glass, yakisugi cedar wood
2015 (and ongoing)

Carried on Both Sides is a project about the
ancient Roman shape that a common computer
symbol comes from. What if every tap of the @
symbol conjured an image of an ancient Roman
vessel? Next year marks the 45th anniversary
of the use of the @ symbol in email, but at
least the 480th anniversary of its use in
mercantile accounting, and the 3000th anni-
versary of the standardization of the shape
to which merchants initially referred.
```

Nick from Art21 and I talked about the video, and I told him that I wanted it to be used by art teachers to help students think about research-based art making. I "directed" my own speech to give him audio that would flow in that way because I think videos of this kind should be about the artist herself and also a broader concept that applies to many artists.

When he sent me the rough cut of the video in July of 2017, I sent him detailed edits.

```
FEEDBACK / SUGGESTIONS / QUESTIONS
00:00-00:53 — perfect start / great intro!
[music, waves, to talking about voraciously
curious, perfect]

Then add this: As a research-based artist,
How do I balance conceptual rigor with
material poetry?

I begin with a line of inquiry, a question that
might sustain my attention.
```

```
                Collectively-
                Initiated
```

I then determine the methods and expertise
that I need to follow this line of inquiry,
which often involves bringing in collaborators
in areas of expertise beyond my own.

We open ourselves up to the process itself,
allowing the material to speak, in dialogue
with our research.

We then find conceptually relevant ways for
the project to circulate.

00:54-1:23—great audio, but don't show the
click at 01:06-01:22 as that's the wrong
amphorae and not accurate at all, so use the
dressel 20 I click on or use other images than
Google search, like http://archaeologydata-
service.ac.uk/archives/view/amphora_ahrb_2005/
details.cfm?id=83 or http://museum-of-ar-
tifacts.blogspot.com/2015/11/ancient-roman-
graveyard-ofolive-oil.html or http://www.
shipwreck.net/documents/OMEPapers42.pdf

1:24-1:50—done, great sequence [conjuring an
imperial form]

1:50-1:55—[skype Helen] (maybe this should
come after I talk about her as an artist?)

1:55-2:03—[economy and exchange] (add something about imperial forms long outlive
empires)

2:03-2:15—[Helen showing the murrine] great,
but add talking about process and intro
collaborators (I then determine the methods
and expertise that I need to follow this line
of inquiry, which often involves bringing in
collaborators in areas of expertise beyond
my own./We open ourselves up to the process
itself, allowing the material to speak, in
dialog with our research.)

Carried on
Both Sides

2:15-2:33 – "people who know glass." INTRO Helen
and Alex's work – they are not my fabricators,
please include me talking about them as artists.

2:33-4:40 – [urbanglass] great. Except for 5
seconds of footage. Please cut this footage from
03:56-04:00 – don't show the ugly handles she's
making, show other Helen b-roll (too ugly of an
object to show) Show footage of me looking at
the vessels on the shelf (the hour glass)

4:40-5:28 – [beach] great, but cut the audio here
04:40-4:42 – please don't have me saying "babies,
lots of babies," and cut the footage from 04:56-
05:00 with Alex and I playing in the sand.

5:28-5:58 – [lovely dream waves] great please add
more of this in the beach b-roll throughout,
I love this wave part. More floating in waves
without the beach being seen! Like 07:21-07:30

5:58-6:48 – [saying yes speculative future
sequence] great, but for the b-roll images from
6:08-6:12 add the best work, the *Capitoline
Wolves* table, the roman columns, Helen's newest
tray of murrine, Helen's marble overhead, etc.

6:48-7:38 – [dream state] YES so good, cut audio
6:55-6:58 "to escape everything" so it just says
"it's where I went to … be alone with myself."
Add "imperial forms long outlive empires."

consider adding http://carriedonbothsides.
com/?time=night which will soon have https://
www.dropbox.com/s/zjiivw0nv0i4npu/Hourglass_
v1.mov?dl=0 on it

We went back and forth, as he kept wanting to start with a
romantic image of me and I kept pushing back.

Feedback/Suggestions/Questions
NOTE: my major requests/needs are in bold
I like "floating possibility" a lot!

00:00-00:12—great start visually, not sure about the "I grew up surrounded by the ocean" audio, but fine.

00:17-00:21—you MUST cut the audio that says "where I went to be alone." This is upsetting to me as it is romantic-era language, not 21st century collaborative language, and not at all about my practice. If you must, you can start with "I grew up near the ocean" but PLEASE cut the audio "to be alone." I am finishing a book now on the future of art education with Susan Jahoda that is precisely taking up this image of the solitary artist right now, to be published this December. It would be very hard for me to show this video with confidence to anyone if that "alone" language is included.

00:21-01:20—great (minor weird audio cut from 01:08-01:09)

01:20-1:30—new image for the amphorae rather than showing "getty images logo." you can use this http://www.gillianmcmillan.com/blog/wp-content/uploads/2010/12/PA170520.jpg and perhaps an image of ancient Rome shipment like this: http://archaeologydataservice.ac.uk/archives/view/amphora_ahrb_2005/images/reynolds_map.jpg or this http://3.bp.blogspot.com/-QlPOpRMkeqg/T1oe911HtMI/AAAAAAAACAw/5PrKYadaw6M/s1600/AmphoraMap.jpg or a general map http://orig09.deviantart.net/d4c5/f/2015/295/1/e/the_roman_empire__ad_125_by_undevicesimus-d7j3bm5.png

01:38-01:40—weird audio jump

01:42-01:50— maybe don't show Helen/Alex's emails? I'm fine with it, let me see if they are.

02:02-02:07— maybe cut audio "for me it felt like a clear direction to go in" to give silence/pause.

Carried on
Both Sides

02:16 or 02:29—drop in title card "Helen Lee—
artist" here.

02:39-02:42—cut this, go straight to the glass,
let the glass image lead.

03:57-03:58—weird audio jump

04:11-04:15—cut the shelf shot, give us more
sexy glass studio shots.

04:49—slow cuts before this, to really prepare
viewers for video shift "we decided to go to
the beach."

04:59-05:03—can you replace this b-roll with
another shot that's less childlike?

05:07-7:21—beautiful, work in the audio with
b-roll and it's done!

05:33-05:39—cut audio "the objects have a
life of their own … what the objects want."
Too romantic.

06:09—please add the slide of Helen's tray of
murrine (in HELEN PICS folder)

07:06—great! This can be the last spoken word
"Suspend disbelief and make a work of art that's
for a dream state."

07:21-07:40—cut audio "what if art could be …
a kind of glistening glass object in the middle
of the ocean … that is the encounter, that is
the exhibition." as this makes no sense at all.
Perhaps in this section you can bring in more
audio from me about Helen's work and Alex's
work? Or just bring up the music and the wave
sounds!!!

In the end, Nick and Art21 determined that the video needed
to be focused on me, as they had not done work about collaborative projects before, and I yielded to their interest in the

Collectively-
Initiated

Political interventions, crossing through art, inextricably linked to the institution, must be aware of the clash between recognition and distribution, or else, politics and the economy and how historically constituted artistic labor operates within this class, or conflict, both materially, and as an analytical category.

—Angela Dimitrakaki, 2018

narrative of the singular artist with adjustments to bring in more audio and context about Helen and Alex. This was a difficult compromise to reach. I agreed to an approach to representing the project where Helen Lee was honored as a conceptual artist in her own right.

In other projects and platforms, such as *The Meeting* [see chapter 1] and *The Study Center for Group Work* [see chapter 2], the group determined that we would produce our own media so that we could more accurately represent collaborative practices. My other book-length efforts, including *TRADE SCHOOL: 2009–2019* and *Making and Being: a Guide to Embodiment, Collaboration, and Circulation in the Visual Arts*, are co-authored because they hold a commitment to a practice of collaboration in writing and reflection as well as in making art. And yet, the writing I am doing on this page, for this traveling exhibition and book, has been done alone, with feedback from collaborators.

My work will continue to hold the tension between "autonomy—as the subjective power of the encounter with an artwork—and heteronomy—as the process of erosion of art disciplinary borders into non-art and into the social dimension" because this tension cannot be resolved on the scale of the individual.[47] The shift toward solidarity art worlds and a dominant narrative of collective subjectivity in the arts will be realized over generations, collectively, with policies and funding that support solidarity economy efforts led by Black, Indigenous, and people of color, especially women, nonbinary people, and trans people.

To maintain a livelihood, I place one foot in the elite institution—the art school, the art gallery, and the art non-profit—and one foot in the solidarity economy: barter and mutual aid [see chapter 3], community currencies [see chapter 4], collectives [see chapter 5], worker cooperatives [see chapter 6 and chapter 2], and group communication and collective governance [see chapters 1, 2, 7, 8]. I hope that you feel, with collective strength and experience, that another economy is possible in the arts, and beyond, because it already exists. Just as you have survived, this solidarity economy has survived, and is surviving. We can strengthen it, together. [see pages 31–39]

47
Marco Baravalle, "On the Biennale's Ruins? Inhabiting the Void, Covering the Distance," The Institute of Radical Imagination, May 2, 2020, https://instituteofradicalimagi-nation.org/2020/05/02/on-the-bi-nales-ruins-inhabiting-the-void-covering-the-dis-tance-by-marco-baravalle/.

Carried on
Both Sides

Practical Cartography: Lexicon

Practical Cartography: Collaborators

Timeline of Material Conditions

DATE	2007	2008	2009	2010	2011	2012	2013
Mentors/ Learning Programs	graduated from Cooper Union, Bruce Chao	Jennifer Wright Cook, year-long mentorship through The Field	Mildred's Lane/ Morgan puett, Jennifer Wright Cook year-long mentorship through The Field	Jennifer Wright Cook year-long mentorship through The Field	Public Science Project, Critical PAR week-long intensive	Soul Fire Farm, apprenticeship	Mary Beth-Raddon mutual mentoring, workshop with Akaya Winwood
Primary Collectives/ Group Learning	none	OurGoods.org (OG)	OG, TradeSchool.coop (TS)	OG, TS, Strataspore	OG, TS, Solidarity NYC	TS, Solidarity NYC	BFAMFAPhD
Public Programs/ Events I initiated	none	none	Hosting OG Idea Labs/ TS classes	Hosting OG Idea Labs / TS classes, mushroom walks with Strataspore	Hosting OG Idea Labs/ TS classes	Hosting (Re) Producing Value lecture series at MAD	Hosting Fucking Up in Socially Engage Art series of conversations at Eyebeam
Institutional-invite projects	none	*Work Dress*	Conflux, *Public Seat*	none	*Was that you or the House?*	none	*Exchange Café*
Grants	none	none	The Field $10k (for OG)	iLAND (for Strataspore) The Field $25k (for OG), Rockefeller (for OG)	Rockefeller Foundation $100k (for OG)	Rockefeller Brothers $35k (for OG)	Rockefeller Foundation $1[…] (for OG)
Residencies, Fellowships	none	Ox-Bow	Mac Dowell, Mildred's Lane	Mildred's Lane	Watermill Mildred's Lane	Eyebeam $30k Mildred's Lane	MoMA, Eyebeam $30k, Queens Museum AIR, Mildred's La[…]
Primary Jobs	Graphic design, Natalie Jeremijenko	Night Shift, Natalie Jeremijenko	Laid off, Unemployed (getting benefits)	Laid off, Unemployed (getting benefits)	Teaching, New School	Teaching, New School	Teaching, New School,
Total Income	unknown	$27,012	unknown	$11,651	$26,000	$28,000	$13,500
Rent	$0, living in car	$0, running Splinters and Logs ($25/hr LLC duties taken off rent)	$0, running Splinters and Logs ($25/hr LLC duties taken off rent)	$0, running Splinters and Logs ($25/hr LLC duties taken off rent)	$0, running Splinters and Logs ($25/hr LLC duties taken off rent)	$0, running Splinters and Logs ($25/hr LLC duties taken off rent)	$0, running Splinters a[nd] Logs ($25/h[r] duties take[n] rent)
Primary Collaborators	none	Louise Ma, Rich Watts	Louise Ma, Rich Watts, Jen Abrams, Carl Tashian	Louise Ma, Rich Watts, Jen Abrams, Carl Tashian, Cheyenna Webder, Michael Johnson, Kate Cahill, Chris Kennedy, Athena Kokoronis	Jen Abrams, Aimee Lutkin, Rachel Vera Steinberg, Or Zubalsky, Cheyenna Webder, Michael Johnson	Jen Abrams, Aimee Lutkin, Rachel Vera Steinberg, Or Zubalsky, Cheyenna Weber	Lika Volko[…] Vicky Virg[…] Balir Murp[…] Susan Jaho[…]

2014	2015	2016	2017	2018	2019	2020
Center for Neighborhood Leadership, year long program	Mutual mentoring with Pascale Gatzen, weekly, therapy begins with Panthea	Round Sky Solutions, Cooperative Leadership, therapy continues	Alta Starr, somatic leadership sessions all year, therapy continues	Alta Starr, Robert Ransick, Susan Scorbati for the Bennington MFA in Public Action, therapy continues	Esteban Kelly workshops, Robert Ransick, Susan Scorbati for the Bennington MFA in Public Action, therapy continues	Esteban Kelly workshops, Robert Ransick, Susan Scorbati for the Bennington MFA in Public Action, therapy continues
BFAMFAPhD	Study Center, BFAMFAPhD, NYC Real Estate Investment Coop	Study Center, BFAMFAPhD, NYCREIC	Study Center, BFAMFAPhD	Study Center, BFAMFAPhD	BFAMFAPhD	BFAMFAPhD
Hosting Peer to Peer Learning, a series of workshops at MoMA	Hosting Pathways to Affordable Housing, a series of workshops at MAD	Hosting many NYC REIC educational events	Making & Being workshops throughout NYC	Making & Being workshops at the NYPL	Making & Being series at Hauser and Wirth	Slow Burning Fire Series on Zoom
Queer Rocker	none	Study Center for Group Work, *LISTEN*	*Capitoline Wolves, Carried on Both Sides, LISTEN*	*Carried on Both Sides*	*The Meeting, A Way of Working*	*The Meeting, A Way of Working*
none	RSF Social Finance $1,500 (for NYCREIC)	Grand Central Art Center $5k	NYFA $25k (for Study Center)	none	Ribicoff Junior Faculty Prize ($10k)	Philadelphia Area Creative Collaboratives Program Grant ($10k)
Queens Museum AIR, Mildred's Lane	Triangle (with BFAMFAPhD), Judson Church Mildred's Lane	NEWINC (with BFAMFAPhD) Mildred's Lane (Session leader)	NEWINC (with BFAMFAPhD) Mildred's Lane (Session leader)	Ox-Bow, Pilchuck, Pratt (with BFAMFAPhD) Mildred's Lane (Session leader)	Impact Maker Residency, Perlmutter Residency, Waletas Fellowship $50k, Pioneer Works (with BFAMFAPhD)	Waletas Fellowship, Mildred's Lane (Session leader)
Grant Writing, Laura Flanders	Teaching, New School, SVA, Laura Flanders	Teaching, New School, SVA, Project Management, CoLab.coop	Teaching, University of Hartford, SVA	Teaching: UHart	Teaching: UHart	Teaching: UHart
$43,644	$24,364	$15,908	$57,636	$73,430	Pending: $62,000 salary plus Fellowship and Grants	Pending: $68,000 salary plus Fellowship and Grants
$0, running Splinters and Logs ($25/hr LLC duties taken off rent)	$500, TS Eliot Collective House	$500, TS Eliot Collective House	$2000, mortgage for Low Income Co-op in NYC	$2000, mortgage for Low Income Co-op in NYC	$4000, Hartford rent plus NYC	$4000, Hartford rent plus NYC
Lika Volkova, Paula Segal, Risa Shoup	Adele Eisenstein, David Glick, Todd Arena, Mara Kravitz, Rafael Jose, K Samuels, Sam Gray, Paula Segal, Risa Shoup, Oksana Mironova, Marlisa Wise, Mark Read, Oscar Perry Abello	Susan Jahoda, Emilio Martínez Poppe	Susan Jahoda, Emilio Martínez Poppe, Helen Lee	Suan Jahoda, Emilio Martínez Poppe, Helen Lee	Susan Jahoda, Leigh Claire La Berge, Or Zubalsky	Susan Jahoda

1:1 Scale Images
of Projects

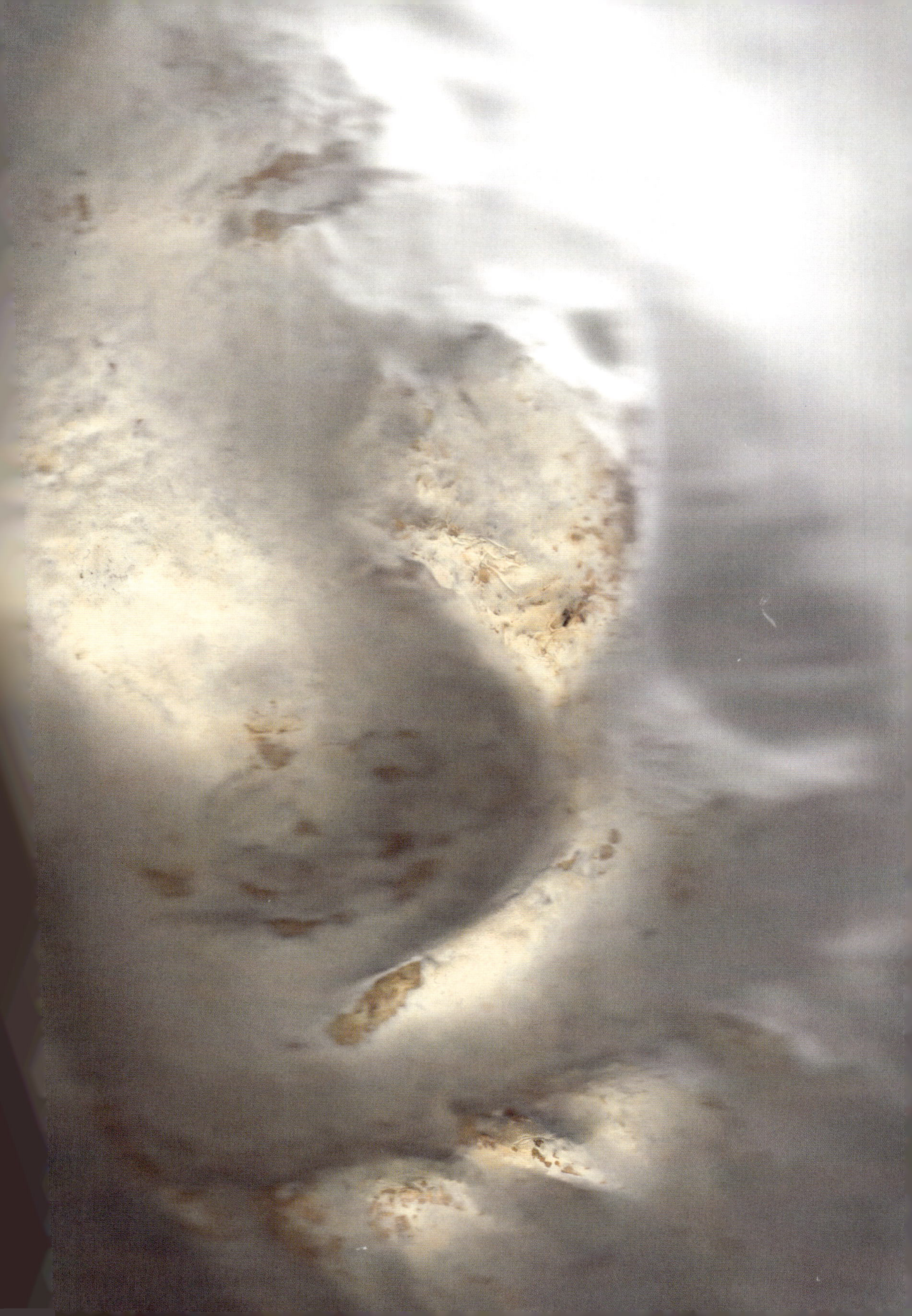

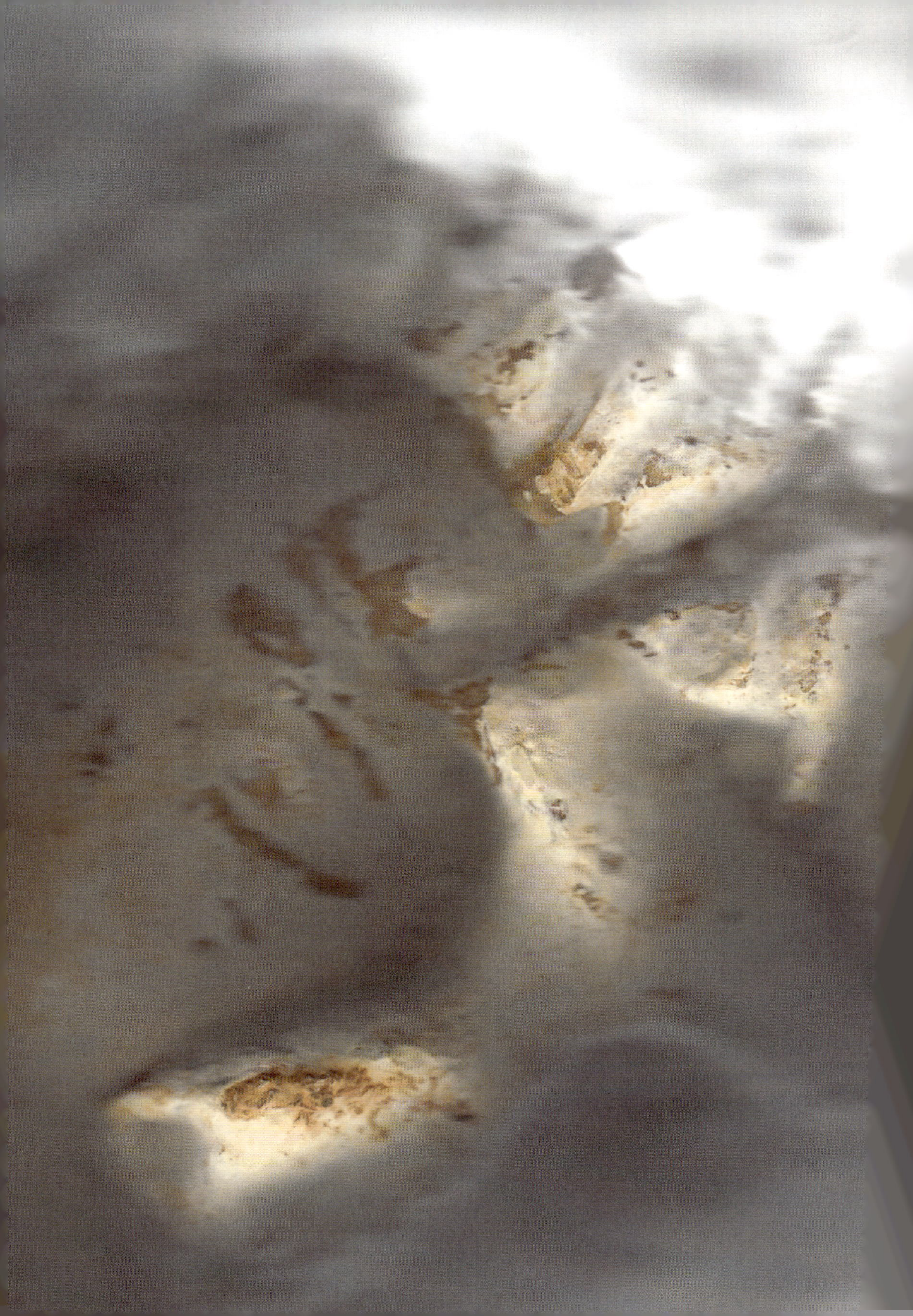

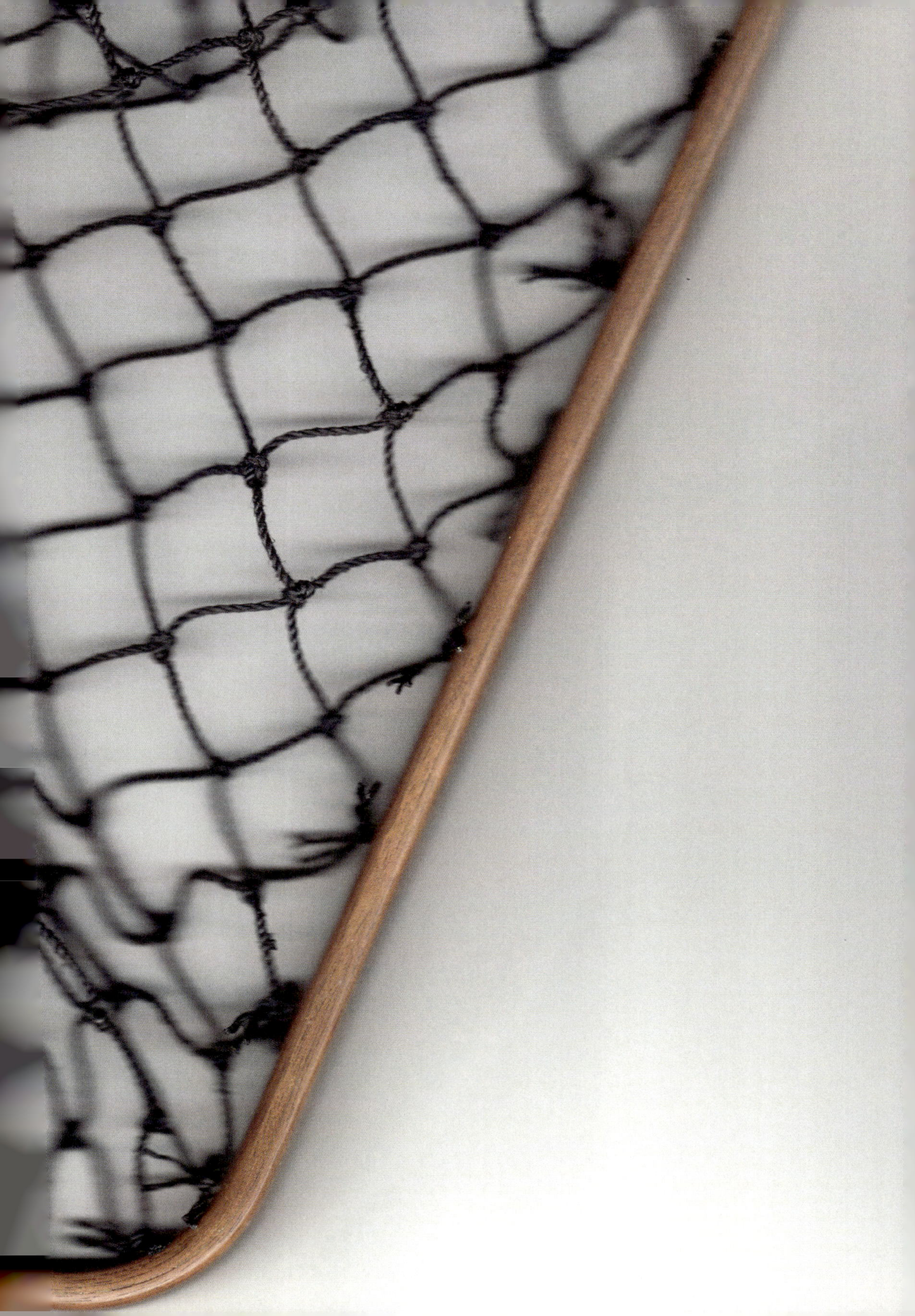

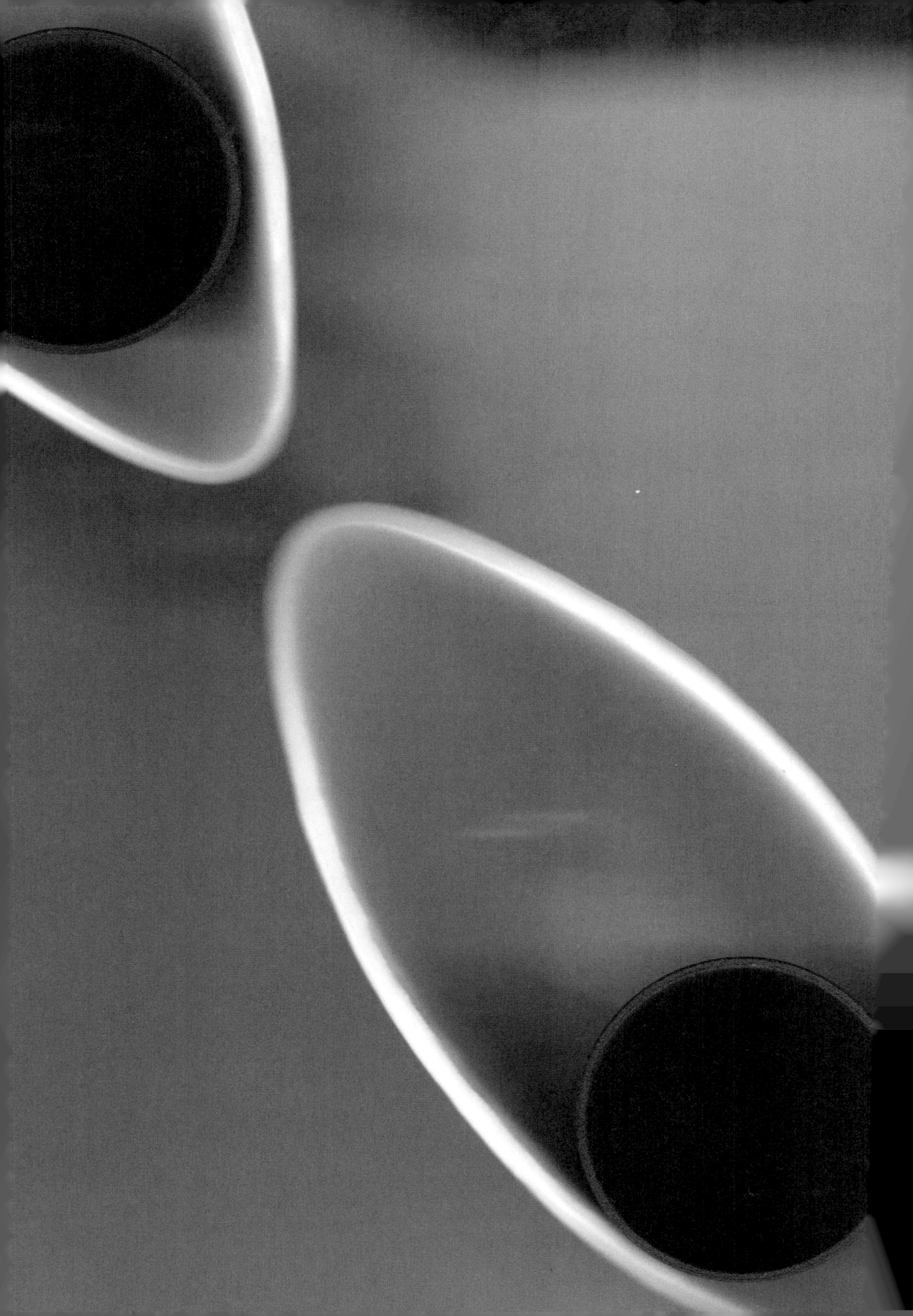

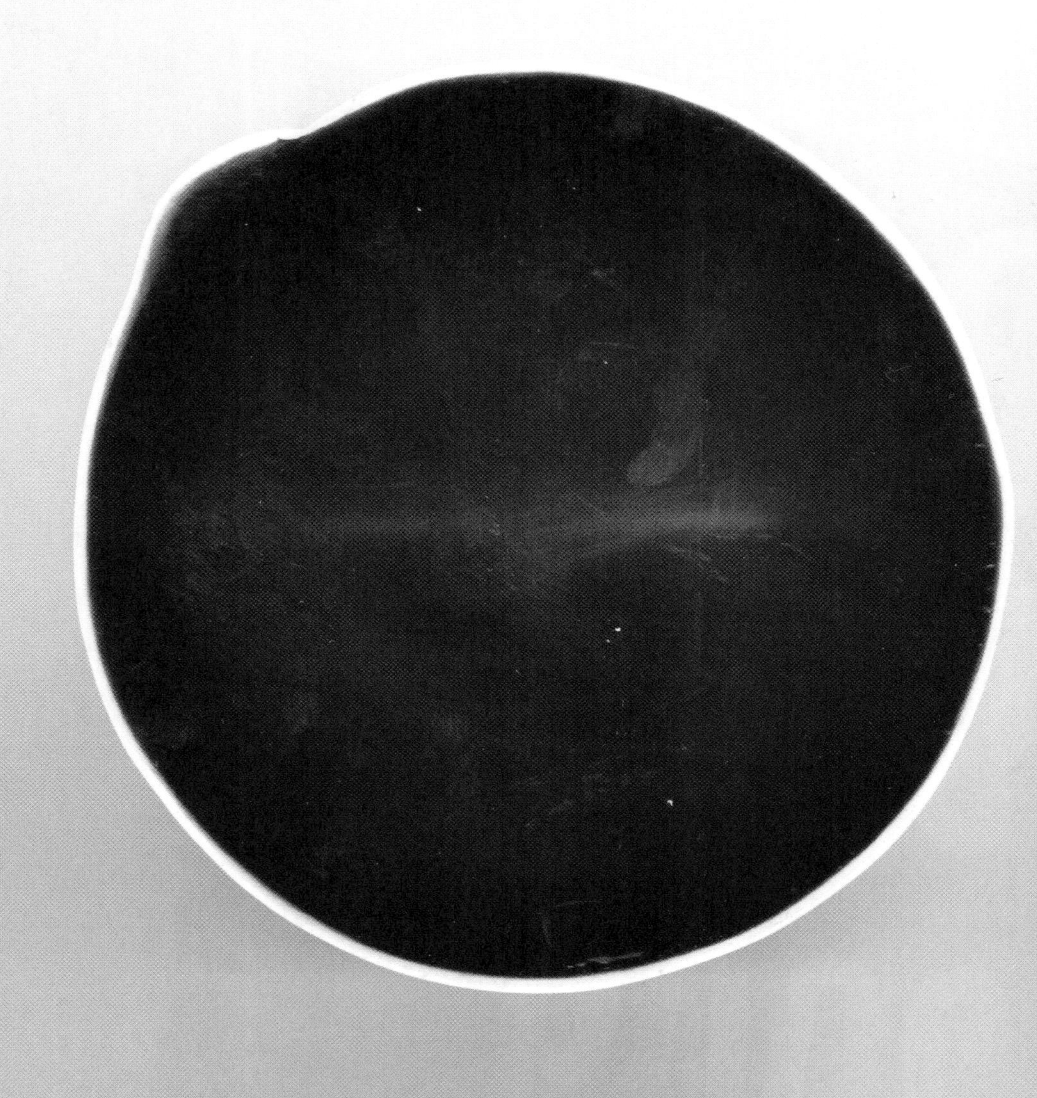

RADE

CHOOL

2009

—

2019

EMBODIMENT,
LABORATION, AND
[?]ATION IN THE
VISUAL ARTS

A WORKBOOK BY
SUSAN JAHODA AND
CAROLINE WOOLARD
OF BFAMFAPHD

MAKING
&
BEING

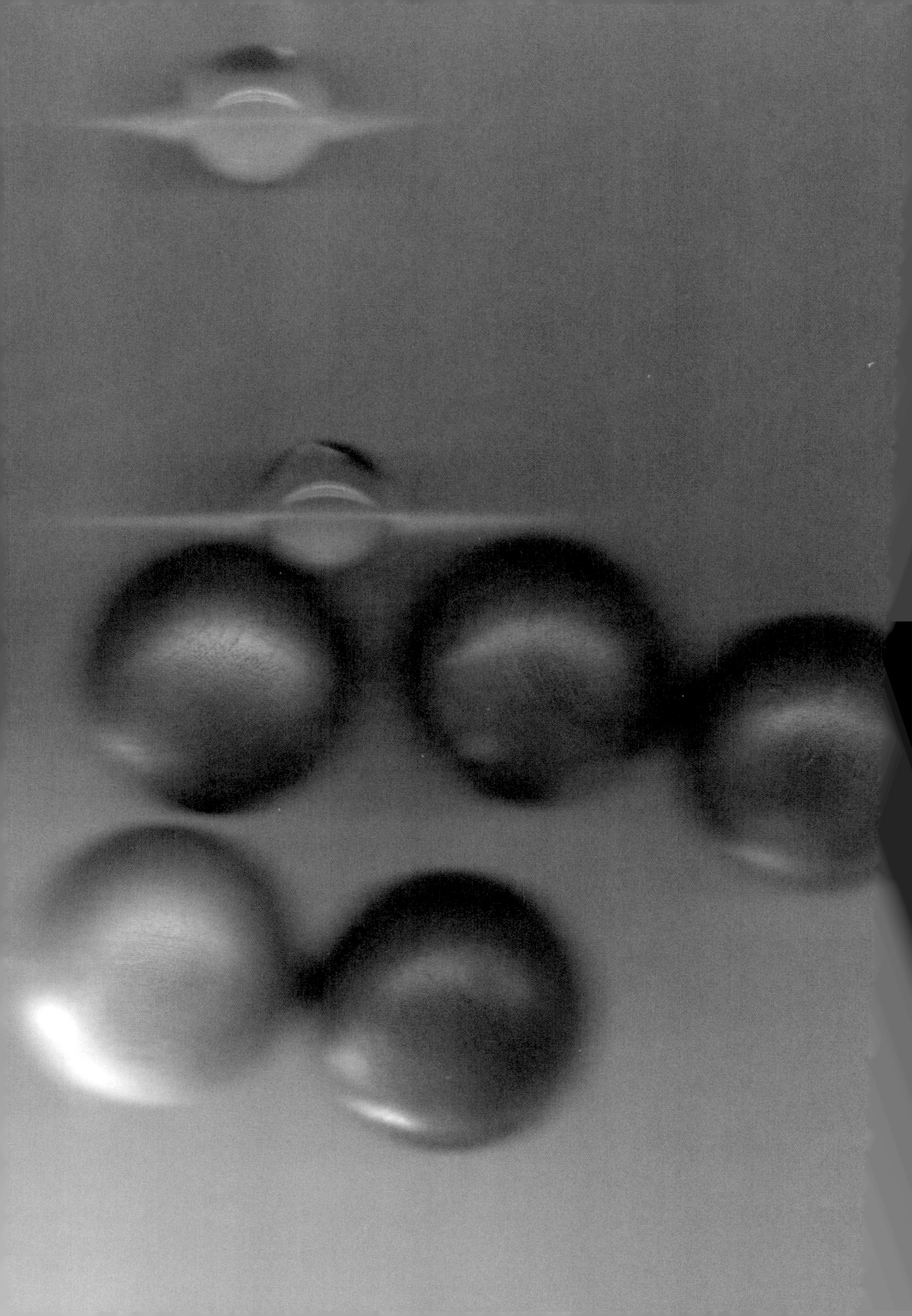

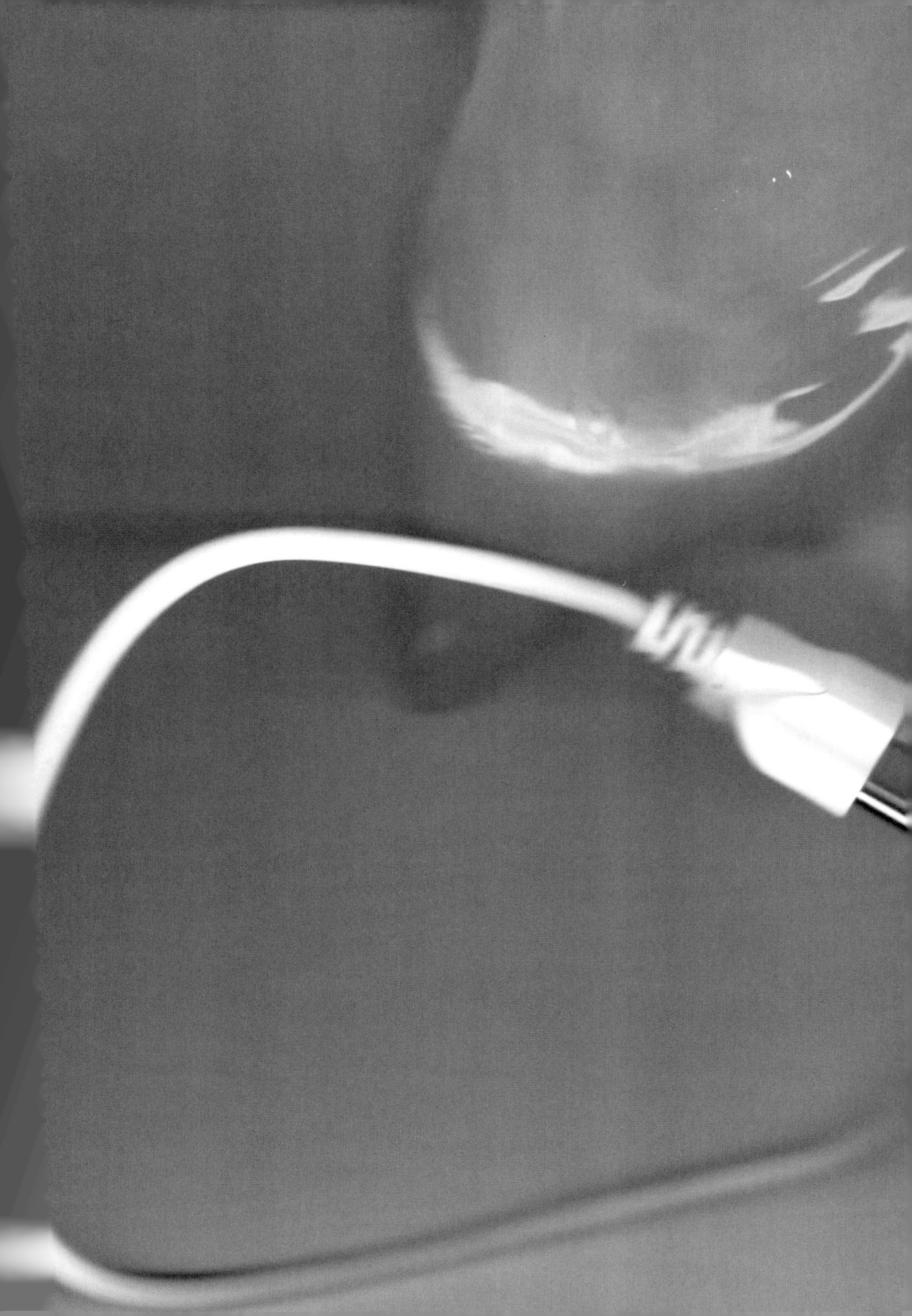

CONTRIBUTORS

D. GRAHAM BURNETT is based in New York City. He trained in the history and philosophy of science, and works at the intersection of historical inquiry and artistic practice. Recent work includes: "Schema for a School" (with Asad Raza and Jeff Dolven) at the Ljubljana Biennial (2015) and The Shed (2018); and "El Halo del Cuidar" (with Lane Stroud and Gabriel Pérez-Barreiro) at the Reina Sofia (2019). Burnett is associated with the research collective ESTAR(SER) and the "Friends of Attention." He teaches at Princeton.

ALISON BURSTEIN is the Curator of Media and Engagement at The Kitchen in New York. As an independent curator, she has curated exhibitions or programs for institutions including Tenthaus (Oslo), Mana Contemporary (Jersey City), The Luminary (St. Louis), Knockdown Center (Queens), Museum of Jurassic Technology (Los Angeles), and NURTUREart (Brooklyn).

STAMATINA GREGORY is the Director of Curatorial Programs at the Leslie-Lohman Museum of Art. She has organized exhibitions for institutions including The Cooper Union, FLAG Art Foundation, Austrian Cultural Forum, the Institute of Contemporary Art, Philadelphia, and the Santa Monica Museum of Art, and was the Deputy Curator of the inaugural pavilion of The Bahamas at the 55th Venice Biennale.

LARISSA HARRIS is a curator at the Queens Museum. Exhibitions at QMA include *Red Lines Housing Crisis Learning Center*, a project on home finance by artist and urban designer Damon Rich; the first US solo presentation of Korean video and performance artist Sung Hwan Kim; *People's United Nations (pUN)* by Pedro Reyes; *13 Most Wanted Men:*

Andy Warhol at the 1964 World's Fair; and, with Patti Phillips, *Mierle Laderman Ukeles: Maintenance Art*.

LEIGH CLAIRE LA BERGE, PhD, professes at the intersection of arts, literature, visual culture and political economy. She is the author of *Scandals and Abstraction: Financial Fiction of the Long 1980s* (Oxford University Press) and *Wages Against Artwork: Decommodified Labor and the Claims of Socially Engaged Art* (Duke University Press, 2019). She is Associate Professor of English in the Department of English at BMCC CUNY.

CYBELE MAYLONE is the Executive Director of The Aldrich Contemporary Art Museum. A non-collecting institution located in Ridgefield, CT, The Aldrich was one of the first contemporary art museums in the country and is today one of the oldest. Prior to leading The Aldrich, Maylone spent five years as the Executive Director of UrbanGlass in Brooklyn, NY.

STEVEN MATIJCIO is the Director and Chief Curator of the Blaffer Art Museum. He won a 2010 Emily Hall Tremaine Exhibition Award for the project "paperless" and in 2012 he was the curator of the fourth Narracje Festival in Gdansk, Poland. Matijcio was also commissioned by the Robert Mapplethorpe Foundation in 2003 to curate one of their first online exhibitions.

STEPHANIE OWENS is the Head of School at Plymouth College of Art and an independent curator. Owens's curatorial projects include Technologies of Place, funded by New York Foundation for the Arts, SELF[n]. Art & Distributed Subjectivity, Intimate Cosmologies: The Aesthetics of Scale in an Age of Nanotechnology (Cornell University), and Abject/Object Empathies (Cornell University).

PATRICIA C. PHILLIPS is Chief Academic Officer at Moore College of Art & Design and an independent writer and curator. Phillips is the author of *City Speculations, It is Difficult: Alfredo Jaar*, and *Ursula von Rydingsvard: Working*. Phillips's curatorial projects include a one-person exhibition on the artist Mierle Laderman Ukeles at the Queens Museum in Flushing, Queens and *Making Sense: Five Artists' Installations on Sensation* at the Katonah Museum of Art, Katonah, New York.

SHEETAL PRAJAPATI is an educator, artist, and advisor working across the field of art and public engagement. Sheetal is currently on faculty at School of Visual Arts (New York) in the MFA Fine Arts program and works as an advisor and consultant in the field through her agency Lohar Projects. Previously, Sheetal served as the first Director of Public Engagement at Pioneer Works and the Assistant Director of Learning and Artists Initiatives at The Museum of Modern Art.

CAITLIN JULIA RUBIN is a curator at the Rose Art Museum at Brandeis University. Since joining the Rose Art Museum, she has organized exhibitions and projects by Mark Dion, Rosalyn Drexler, Jennie C. Jones, and Tuesday Smillie, among others, and collaborated with visiting artists to foster new, site-responsive initiatives, including Caroline Woolard's *INDEX: The Meeting* (2019–20).

ANA RIVERS RYAN, PhD, is a curator, historian, critic, and educator specializing in art since the 1960s. Her work focuses on the roles of new media technologies. She holds five degrees in art history, including a BA from Harvard and PhD from Columbia.

GABRIELLE LAVIN SUZENSKI, Rochelle F. Levy Director of The Galleries at Moore College of Art & Design, began her career in the Fabric Workshop and Museum's post-college apprenticeship program, which led to a full time position working with the founder / artistic director in coordinating the museums's relocation in 2006. She has an MBA in Entrepreneurship & Innovation and a BFA in Sculpture and Printmaking, both from Penn State University.

Since 1977, when MIERLE LADERMAN UKELES became the official, unsalaried Artist-in-Residence at the New York City Department of Sanitation—a position she still holds—she has created art that deals with the endless maintenance and service work that "keeps the city alive," urban waste flows, recycling, ecology, urban sustainability and our power to transform degraded land and water into healthy inhabitable public places.

Editor
HELEN HOFLING is a Baltimore-based writer, editor, and collage-maker. Her work can be found in *Barrow Street, Berkeley Poetry Review, The Columbia Review, Electric Literature, Prelude, Passages North*, and elsewhere. She teaches writing at Loyola University Maryland.

Onomatopee
info @ onomatopee.net

ISBN: 978-94-93148-34-5

DESIGNER
Angela Lorenzo

ARTIST
Caroline Woolard

EDITORIAL ASSISTANT
Paige Landesberg

READERS
Leigh Claire La Berge, Jaclyn Dooner, Paige
Landesberg, Aaron Landsman, Robert Ransick

STUDIO ASSISTANTS
Phoebe van Essche, Jenna Litton,
Ruby Mayer, Sylvia Minehan,
Amalia Petreman, Tess Seaver,
Lydia Thompson, Alexander Terjak Wall,
Rachel Yinger

CONTENT EDITOR
Helen Hofling

PHOTOGRAPHY
Daniel Chou, João Enxuto, Maureen France,
Joseph Hu, Herman Jean-Noel, Levi Mandel,
Nicole Steinberg, Aaron Strauss,
Martyna Szczęsna, Mel Taing, Ryan Tempro,
Filip Wolak

TYPEFACE
Atlas Grotesk and Atlas Typewriter

PAPER
Munken Polar Rough

Printed in Lithuania by BALTO
Print run of 1000
Smythe sewn perfect bound

MADE POSSIBLE BY
Miriam Gallery
Moore College of Art & Design

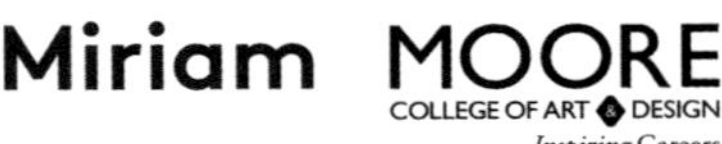

This book has been developed with support
from Moore College of Art & Design's prestigious Jane and David Walentas Endowed
Fellowship. The fellowship, endowed by
Jane Zimmerman Walentas, who graduated
from Moore in 1966, and her husband, David,
underscores Moore's ongoing commitment to
social engagement by offering opportunities
to thoughtful artists who bring their vision for
the future of cultural production to the Moore
community and the larger artistic community
of Philadelphia. Caroline Woolard served as
Moore's inaugural Walentas Fellowship Artist
from 2018–2020.

Please visit CarolineWoolard.com to discover different ways of engaging with the works in this book.

This book would not be possible without Patricia C. Phillips' vision, Angela Lorenzo's design expertise, Freek Lomme's support, Paige Landesberg's encouragement and editorial assistance, and feedback from the following readers: Jen Abrams, Leigh Claire La Berge, Jaclyn Dooner, Phoebe van Essche, Susan Jahoda, Paige Landesberg, Aaron Landsman, Helen Lee, Jenna Litton, Ruby Mayer, Sylvia Minehan, Adelheid Mers, Amalia Petreman, Robert Ransick, Tess Seaver, Lydia Thompson, Alexander Terjak Wall, and Rachel Yinger.

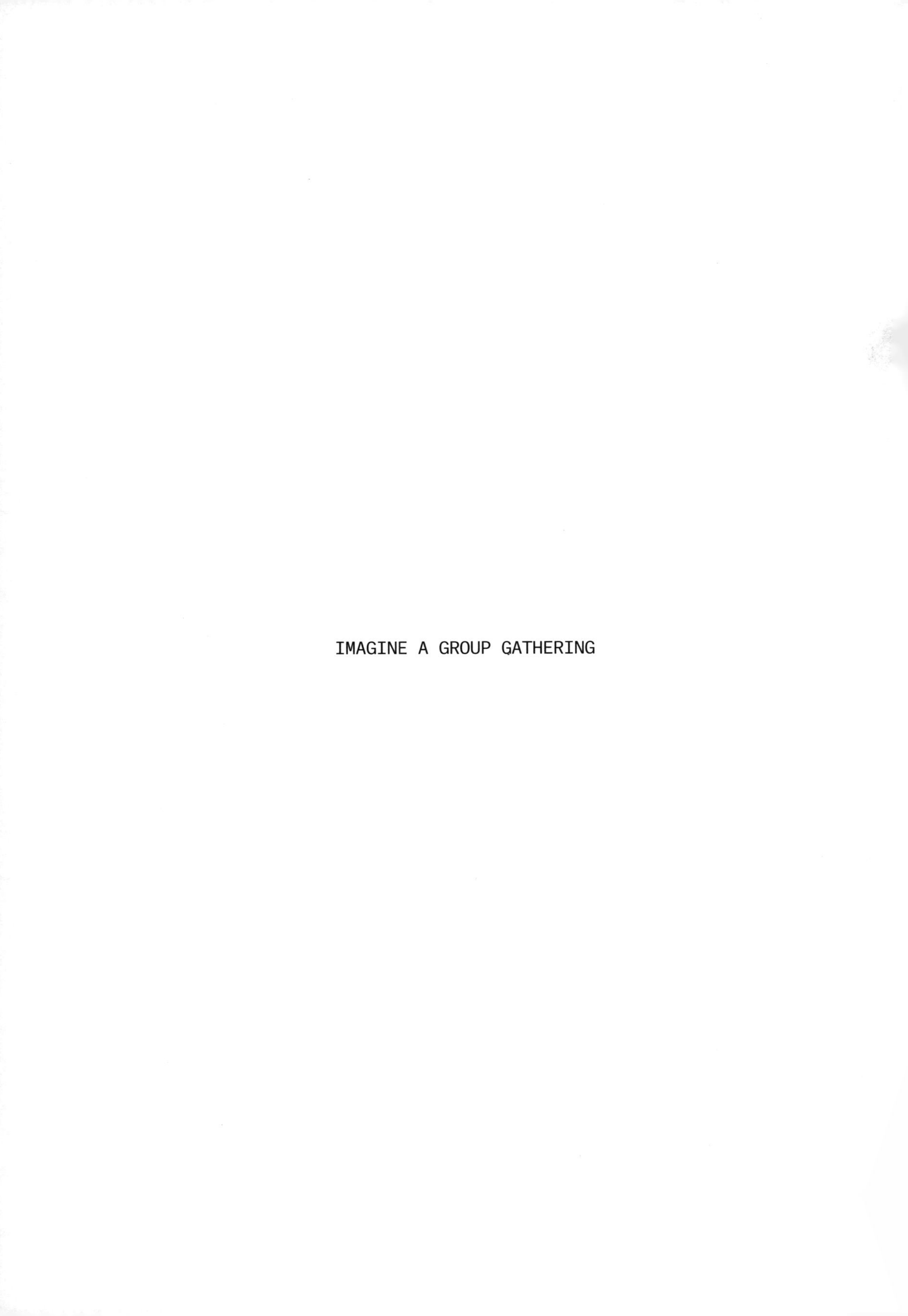

IMAGINE A GROUP GATHERING